Impossible People

Smile a While and Laugh a Little With Words and their Possibilities

by Karina Hayklan

Cartoons by JERI: Marjorie Elizabeth Cochrane

First Published in 2020

ISBN: 978-1-9161589-0-0

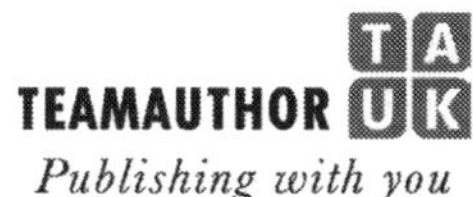

DEDICATION

To my grandchildren

Charlotte, Sophia and Michael the offspring of my charming and successful son, Michael.

and

Laurence and Ralph, the sons of my darling daughter, Alison.

IN MEMORY OF THEIR GREAT GRANDMOTHER

'JERI' OF THE DAILY SKETCH
21.11.1900 - 26.5.1995

INTRODUCTION

When I started to write **IMPOSSIBLE PEOPLE** I meant it to be merely a record of my mother's creative talents and achievements to enable her family and future progeny to 'hold her memory in their hands'.

Shortly after I began to write it my son, Michael, told me he had become a sponsor of a new Cartoon Museum in London. On my first visit I found that, although she was the creator of the first pocket cartoon, not only was her name not among those cartoonists listed on the museum's 'Wall of Fame', the Curator had no knowledge of her. A discovery that persuaded me to make the book of interest to a wider audience.

Thus, over many years, even more toil and a myriad of interruptions it became a mammoth manuscript covering a cornucopia of subjects from the factual to the foolish, the sensible to the silly, the magical to the magnificent, and the historical to the humorous.

Also humorous as 'Boney' gets the odd mention - as do all of the numerous members of my family and wide circle of world-wide friends. This was for two reasons. The first because they all deserve to be remembered and the second to ensure the book would grace many more homes than just my own.

Also those of a few readers of the Daily Mail. A newspaper that, with the inestimable assistance of Nicola Tapsell, compiler of their Peterborough Column, has allowed, with the kind agreement of their authors, for a number of poems and items of interest and amusement that have featured in Peterborough to also feature in Impossible People. Together with a few from their Answers to Readers Questions edited by Charles Legge. Equal thanks go to the Daily Mail's Editor, Paul Dacre for having such an excellent team of columnists.

Where possible all the anecdotes, articles, clippings, cartoons, letters, poems, and jokes are correctly attributed and noted within the text. However, there are a few for which, despite much research, I have been unable to find an attribution or source and therefore, permission. I apologise for these omissions and would be grateful for any information that might lead to their author or origination.

It also includes several anecdotes that, although I believe to be authentic, have, due to the internet, had their verity brought into question. Nevertheless as they are of interest I have left them for my reader to enjoy and, perhaps, to then enjoy researching their authenticity.

My reader may also consider **IMPOSSIBLE PEOPLE** has a 'barren superfluity of words'. A chastisement from Sir Samuel Garth that many writers, including myself, would be wise to adhere to but unfailingly don't. But as **IMPOSSIBLE PEOPLE** is 'all about words' I make no apologies for their 'superfluity'. A superfluity that includes much information that, due to new technology, is now widely known and much that, despite the Internet, is less so.

As the title page suggests it is not a book that requires reading from cover to cover as it allows my reader to piggle into it at random. (Piggle being a word that goes back in the mists of time when my five siblings and I would make up new words and is a meld of 'pick' and 'giggle' and means exactly as it sounds.)

It also includes a number of Grooks by the exceptionally talented Danish author, designer, inventor, scientist, mathematician, town planner and poet, Piet Hein (1905 -1966). His first Grook that was, during the Second World War, written as graffiti over the whole of Denmark was the now oft quoted:

Losing one glove is certainly painful,
But nothing compared with the pain,
Of losing one, throwing away the other,
And finding the first one again.

He wrote it to signify that losing your freedom is better than collaborating with the Nazis and, in so doing, losing your patriotism and self-respect. It would also be a betrayal of your country that would be even more painful when freedom was regained.

Piet Hein's Grooks were first published by Borgens Forlag in Copenhagen, where half a million of his books were sold, and, later, by The General Publishing Co. Ltd. in Ontario, Canada and Doubleday & Company of New York.

In 1970 Hodder and Stoughton published three books of his work; Grooks, More Grooks and Yet More Grooks. In which they maintain that; "Piet Hien is a remarkable man who was often proposed for the Nobel Prize and his Grooks became so popular in America that they formed the basis for a new cult."

There is also a lot of rubbish in **IMPOSSIBLE PEOPLE** including a poem on 'Rubbish'. So should my reader meet within these pages anything they consider to be foolish, facile, fallacious, gauche, inaccurate, incorrect, infantile, offensive, tedious, turgid (a word much used by my Mother), untrue - or just rubbish - I would ask them to enjoy those items they find amusing, entertaining or interesting and forgive the writer for those that they don't.

Fascinated by words, the shelves of my library groan under the weight of books of quotations. I have also, for many years, saved media clippings of clever, pithy, wise or witty jokes and anecdotes that have amused or annoyed me, pleased or provoked me or have made me happy or sad. More recently, via the Internet, I've been bombarded with humorous and interesting oddities destined to end up higgledy-piggledy in the trash baskets of trillions of computers. But, having saved many of those sent to me, I realised they could be the perfect vehicle with which to introduce to a new audience my Mother's Impossible People cartoons before they are lost forever.

One of these, (that confirmed my belief that my Mama is watching over me whilst I write), arrived within days of my putting my Impossible People to bed. A friend, John Sutch, sent me a list of jokes the first of which was; *'A cartoonist was found dead in his home - details are sketchy'.*

Although JERI did die in a 'home' this record of her many years as a marvelous mother, artist, poet, writer - and cartoonist for The Sketch - are, most definitely, not sketchy. As are none of the many dozens of deviations I make and detours I take.

Impossible People also includes a number of poems by poets other than myself and my mother. Most of which are by Daily Mail Peterborough poets, all of whom have given me permission to include their work.

Karina Hayklan

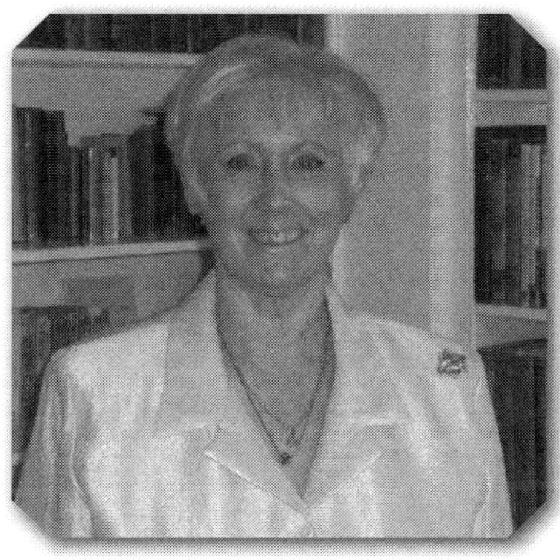

PREFACE

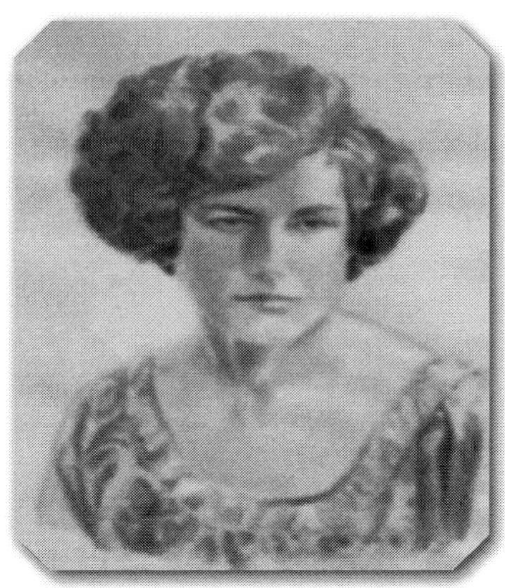

'JERI' of the Daily Sketch
21.11.1900 - 26.5.1995

Marjorie Elizabeth Cochrane was a woman of exceptional gifts and many talents. She possessed the demeanor of a Queen, the wisdom of Solomon, the patience of a saint, the intelligence of an Einstein and the talents of both a Titian and a Tennyson. And - as can be seen from this much treasured sepia likeness that was a gift from my son-in-law, Michael Peter - who copied it from a photograph of my mother when in her twenties – she also had the beauty of a Botticelli.

Apart from her excellent artistic and poetic talents she was a gifted gardener and cook and considered that a house was not a home if it did not have a book or picture in it. A survivor of two world wars, she handled the transition in midlife, from wealth to penury with her usual indomitable spirit and, despite many hardships and setbacks, raised, as a single parent, her six children to be financially independent, aspirational, high achievers.

Under her pen name, JERI, Marjorie Elizabeth Cochrane was the creator of the first 'pocket' cartoon, Impossible People. A cartoon that, for twenty years between 1922 and 1942, were a daily feature of the popular 'sister paper' of the Daily Mail, The Daily Sketch, for which she composed close to six thousand cartoons.

After the war Lord Kelmsley, proprietor of the Sketch, told her that, as some of her pre-war cartoons had lampooned Germany, her name was high on Hitler's

'Hit List' of those people he planned to exterminate once Britain was defeated.

Although it was not Hitler but marriage and children that was the reason her contract was not renewed after 1942. A year in which Hutchinson published two hardback books composed of just cartoons by individual cartoonists - the first of their kind. One with 248 Impossible People cartoons and another of 'Obstinate Artist' cartoons by W.F. Burrows.

The Sketch, that began life in 1909, eventually won 1.3 million readers, On the day it ceased life in 1971, it was, due to a printers strike, only possible to print the front and back page. So, in an inspired move, its proprietors, Harmsworth, enclosed its sister paper, The Daily Mail, within this final cover of the Sketch. A ploy that ensured considerable increase in sales of this, now much read, newspaper.

When, in 1963, JERI's mother, Adelaide, died, among her belongings was a biscuit tin in which were many hundreds of newspaper clippings of her daughter's cartoons, nearly three hundred of which are included in my Impossible People Apart from those in the Hutchinson book, these clippings are possibly the only copies that exist. Although if the British Library really do keep everything ever published, they will have all of them, and, no doubt, in much better condition than those I rescued that had been carelessly clipped from the Daily Sketch and had then spent nearly seventy years of their lives languishing in a tin.

Years that had been nearly as bad for their health as it is for humans, thus some of the captions did not copy well and, in order for my reader to fully enjoy their humour, a few had to be retyped, however most are reproduced exactly as they were when I found them.

My twin, Sonya, and I have, over many years, given many talks on Interior Design in which we always included the mantra, *"It is not necessary to be different to be good, just to be good is different enough."* A cardinal rule that is particularly applicable to art.

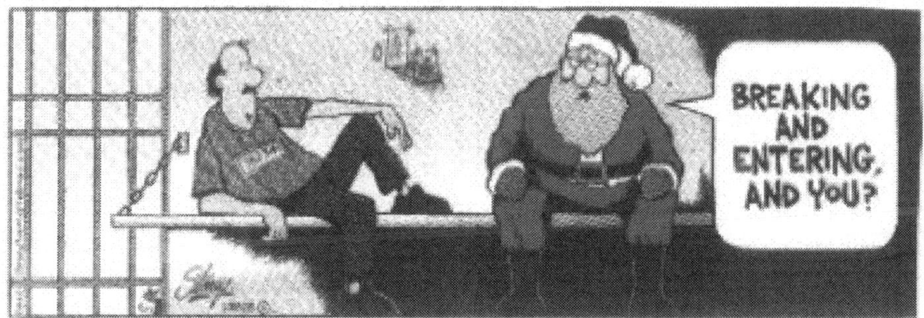

It is also said that; 'Rules are made to be broken', and JERI's Impossible People were not only very good, they were, as the first pocket cartoon, very different. They are also neat biopics of the period between the First and Second World Wars.

From Hogarth to the present day, cartoons have remained one of the finest forms of wit. They also portray, more readily than any other medium, the lunacy in much of life as illustrated in these two inspired Stonytoons 'The Odd Streak' cartoons by Tony Lopes. The first is the epitome of a perfect cartoon as, in just five words, it encapsulates humour at its very best.

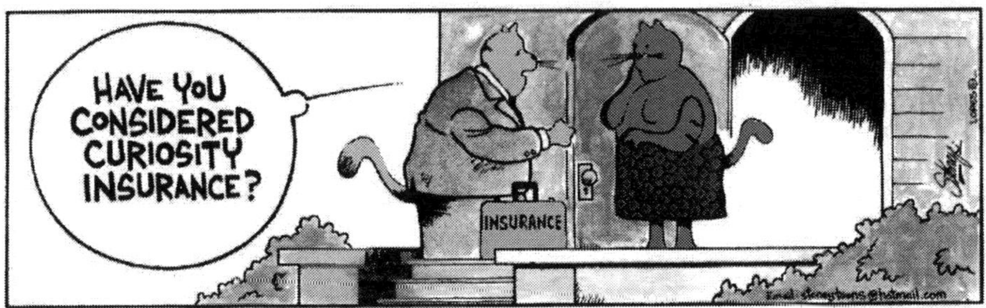

The second, again in just five words, takes a nanosecond for the connection between the caption and the cats to reach the taste buds of the brain. Then, as with good champagne, bubbles of humour explode causing laughter overload.

Early cartoons, such as those featured in Punch, could be considered works of art, but cartoons do not have to be brilliantly illustrated to be brilliant. The instantly recognizable characters - and cats - in 'Garfield' and the masterly cartoons, Chloe & Co. by Gray Jolliffe and 'Up and Running' by Grey & Shack, The Odd Streak by Tony Lopes and 'Peanuts' (a cartoon that also started life in The Sketch in 1959), makes them enduringly dear to their fans.

As will the extremely clever cartoons of Jonathon Pugh, whose genius enables him to compose, for the Daily Mail, a minimum of two or three topical cartoons every day. But, apart from a few notable exceptions such as those by Bernard Jackson, Giles and Mac, it is my view that few contemporary cartoons match the artistic excellence of those by JERI.

Even when following a theme, most cartoonists rely on random captions for their humour, but JERI's followed a strict format and it is difficult to imagine how she was able to devise many thousands of captions worded within a fixed, recognizable pattern.

She told me that it became a way of life and she could develop several at one time. She would also use or adapt ideas sent to her by fans of the cartoon and, occasionally, as many cartoonists do, she would revamp a caption. Which is the case with the cover cartoon in which the caption replicates that of a cartoon I include in a later section of the book, as are a number of other duplicated cartoons within the text.

Also many of her illustrations indicate quite clearly those cartoons she took time over and those she, in her own words; "Just dashed off". While a few are so finely drawn they were, most certainly, destined to adorn more permanent publications than a daily paper.

In later life, and universally known as 'Mama', she had the rare ability to make all and sundry, regardless of age, ability, ethnicity, colour, creed, gender infirmity, status, wealth or penury, feel worthy of, and welcome to, her undivided attention and boundless hospitality.

She also held the firm belief that; 'God looks after the English and gives them what is good for them in spite of themselves.'

This eulogy may seem excessive, but to those who knew her she was all of these and much more. Exceptionally well educated and erudite, she had a plethora of pithy odes that she would recite at opportune moments, one of which was -

As I was going down the stair,
I met a man who wasn't there.
He wasn't there again today,
I wish to God he'd go away.

As we often had to leave our homes in a hurry I thought she might be referring to The Dreaded Bailiff, until, many years later I learnt that it was a plagiarism of this ode by Hugh Mearns's:

As I was letting down my hair,
I met a guy who didn't care.
He didn't care again today -
I love them when they get that way!

Another, with no accreditation but much merit that most definitely doesn't refer to bailiffs, was:

There are tall ships and long ships,
All of which sail the sea,
But the best ships are friendships,
And may they always be

Another of even greater merit so matched her character it could have been written for her if its composer, the Australian poet, politician and jockey, Adam

Lyndsay Gordon, had not died in 1870 at the age 36.

Life is mostly froth and bubble.
Two things stand alone like stone,
Kindness in another's trouble,
Courage in your own.

My mother taught me the wonder of words with words that should be written six feet high in all educational and government establishments. The spoken word is the most transient and the most enduring thing in the world.

From my father, Michael, who, although clever, charismatic and charming, deserves no blessing apart from giving his children life, I learned the following; *"Everyone you meet knows something you don't, so listen and learn, because if you don't know and you don't ask you are a fool forever, but if you don't know and you ask you are only a fool for the time it takes for someone to give you the answer."*

To which my husband Simon, a man of much erudition and great integrity, would say; *"Never ask a question to which the answer might be a burden."* To which his mother-in-law would have said; *"A burden may turn out to be a thing of beauty and great joy - witness of which are my six children and ten grandchildren."*

JERI'S REAL IMPOSSIBLE PEOPLE

Marjorie Elizabeth Cochrane – History

Born in Southampton in 1900, just within the reign of Queen Victoria, Marjorie Elizabeth Cochrane was the only child of Paul Belitza Cochrane, of the Dundonalds of Ayrshire, a Captain with the Royal Mail Steam Packet Company and, later, a Younger Trinity Brother of Trinity House, and his wife Adelaide Slee who, prior to her marriage, was a singer with the renowned Gilbert & Sullivan Light Opera Company.

The following historical details of the family are not exact as many are drawn from early childhood conversations, but where dates are given these have been verified.

Not difficult as the Dundonald family history is well chronicled and it is on record that the name Cochrane originated in the Scottish Highlands from the word 'auchran' meaning 'brave', and the first Cochrane recorded in Scotland was Waldeve de Coveran who, in 1262, witnessed a charter in favour of the 5th Earl of Menteith.

Two centuries later a direct descendent of Waldeve de Coveran, Walter Stewart, who became 6th High Steward of Scotland, courageously distinguished himself with Robert the Bruce at the Battle of Bannockburn. Heroics that won Walter the hand of Robert's only legitimate daughter, Marjorie, who was only child of Robert's first wife, Isabella of Mar.

Walter was granted the title 'Earl of Mar' and part of his bride's dowry was the Barony of Bathgate, which included Bathgate Castle in West Lothian, now the home of Bathgate Golf Club. A site protected by The Historic Scotland Organization.

On the 2nd March 1316, two years after her marriage to Walter and heavily pregnant, Marjorie, while riding near Paisley in an area called 'The Knock', was thrown from her horse. Badly injured, she was taken to Paisley Abbey where she went into premature labour and, although safely delivered of her baby, her injuries were so severe she survived the birth by only a few hours.

Nineteen at the time of her death, as had been her own mother, Isabella, when she also died in childbirth, Marjorie was buried at the Abbey in Paisley at the junction of Renfrew Road and Dundonald Road, where a cairn now marks the spot where she reputedly fell from her horse. In 1371 Marjorie's son, who was then 55, succeeded his childless uncle, David II of Scotland, and became King Robert II.

Thus Marjorie's descendants include the House of Stuart and all of the eventual successors to the throne of Scotland, Great Britain and the United Kingdom and, by marriage, the Earls of Mar, their progeny and all the eventual Cochranes of Dundonald.

One of whom, Sir Robert Cochrane, a master mason and favourite of King James II, was the reputed architect of The Great Hall of Stirling Castle. However, his royal patronage did not prevent him, in 1482, from being hanged at Lauder Bridge by a group of indignant nobles jealous of those favoured by the King.

Fable has it that, owing to his exalted standing with the King, Sir Robert asked his captors if he could be hanged with the silken cords from his tent, a plea that fell on deaf ears.

Following Robert's death the title fell into abeyance until the late sixteen hundreds when a later descendent, William Cochrane, became a favoured architect of Charles II.

During the two hundred years between these two events the family remained strong adherents to the Royal House of Stewart. A loyalty rewarded by the gift of further holdings in Renfrewshire, granted by 'A Charter of Confirmation' from Queen Mary in 1556 and the Tower - or Castle - of Cochrane was built in 1592 by William Cochrane.

Having no male heirs, William's line was continued through a daughter who married Alexander Blair of Blair in Ayrshire who, on the death of his father-in-law, assumed, by Great Seal Charter, the name and arms of Cochrane and, in 1618, acquired the Ayrshire lands of Auchencreoch and, in 1622, those of Cowden.

Alexander had seven sons, all of whom took part in the Civil Wars. Thus continuing the enviable catalogue of military service that earned the Dundonald Cochranes their well earned, highly deserved reputation of honour and valour.

Which begs the question: Did the Cochrane fortitude, talents and strengths stay strong due to a family whose primogeniture was frequently continued via the female line. Which

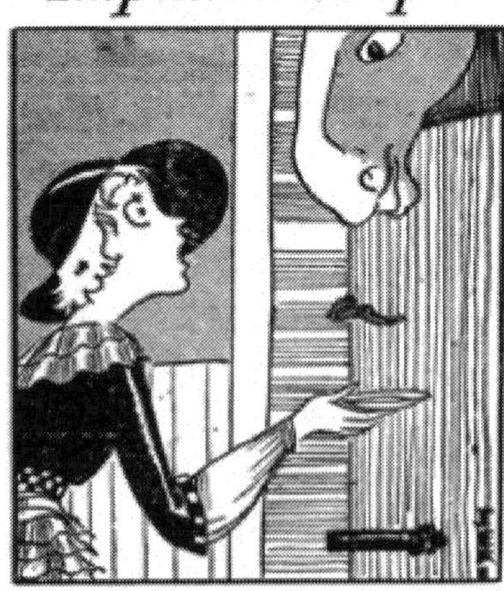

The girl who thought the Royal mews was where they kept the King's cats.

perhaps may also be the reason why few lacked intelligence – but not, it would seem, all of them!

As the family name Mar was still thought of as disreputable, Alexander's second son William chose to take the title 'Dundonald'. Later he was made Lord Cochrane of Dundonald by Charles I and, in 1669, Earl of Dundonald by Charles II.

Our grandfather told us that William's mother was a most feisty lady who worked hard to get her son into Court circles and thus have the Mar Estates returned to the family. I have not been able to verify if there is any truth in this story or whether it was just a family fable as I can find no record of, or reference to, her attendance at the court of Charles II.

A King about whom The Earl of Rochester said; "God bless our good and gracious King, whose promise none relies on; who never said a foolish thing, nor ever did a wise one." Except perhaps, from making one of my predecessors an Earl? And somewhat different from King James the 1st - the driving force behind the most famous book in the world, the King James Bible – a gentleman whom, history tells us, did many a foolish thing but often said a wise one.

Alexander Cochrane, in his informative book, 'The Fighting Cochranes', written with the collaboration of the 14th Earl of Dundonald and published in 1983 writes; *"There is a streak of genius that runs through the Dundonald Cochranes that shows itself in generation after generation."* And: *"It is not often that a great Scottish family has produced a line of fighting men who have served God and country to the degree with which Clan Cochrane can justly claim."*

As a direct descendant of Marjorie Bruce, Robert the Bruce's only legitimate child, our mother was 'gifted' Marjorie, as her first name but, despite its regal ancestry, she disliked it and, in later life, chose to be known by her second name, Elizabeth, a name of even greater regal ancestry.

Her mother, smitten with the idea of possible association with anything to do with Royalty and its subsequent grandeur, nevertheless stopped short of giving her the third name of Victoria.

An odd omission considering our mother was born just within the reign of our second longest reigning monarch. The longest, as I write this, being our much loved, stalwart, Queen Elizabeth II who, on the 10th September 2015 overtook the 63 years, 216 days reign of her Great Grandmother.

However, as a child our mother was universally known by the diminutive 'Gerri', a name gifted to her by a close friend of her fathers, Rudyard Kipling, and from whence she later devised her pen name "JERI'. A name that, due to the daily publication of her cartoons, became nearly as famous as both of her given names.

It also earned a particularly uncomfortable connotation when, in the Second War, we British referred to the Germans as 'Jerries'. Conflict takes us to another of Elizabeth's illustrious ancestors - Lord Admiral Sir Thomas Cochrane, 10th Earl of Dundonald, A seaman and adventurer who fought with Nelson at the Battle of Trafalgar and who, in a career liberally littered with seagoing adventures, was one of the leading 'architects' of the liberation of Peru and Chile from the Spanish.

Activities that, subsequently, led to monuments being erected in his memory in the main squares of both Valparaiso and Culross. Escapades that also led to the publication of his autobiography and a number of biographies that, in later years, did not escape the interest of film producers, as the 2005 film 'Master and Commander' was based on a book by Patrick O'Brian who, in turn, had based his adventure novel on the activities of the 10th Earl.

Among his many other abilities Sir Thomas, as was his father, was also an inventor. His discovery of mustard gas was deemed by the War Office as having little value as it had been invented by 'only an Admiral', and was thus kept under wraps for many years, until, in 1915, at the instigation of the 10th Earl's grandson, Major General Douglas Cochrane, it was passed to the Admiralty

Believing it to be of value, the Admiralty then brought it to the attention of Winston Churchill, who insisted it be unwrapped for use in the First World War when, in doing a great deal of harm, it did a great deal of good. However, as it was an invention that was thought of by his family as evil, and so unlike all the other meritorious activities in which the 10th Earl had been involved, they also kept it under wraps – but, as it is included in a number of the books written about him, I was able to unwrap it for inclusion here.

Not difficult, for, as a man of much interest to biographers, over twenty volumes have been published recording the exploits of this famous seaman, adventurer, erstwhile politician and inventor.

In later life he patented, together with Marc Isambard Brunel, the 'tunneling shield' that Brunel and his son used in building the Thames Tunnel that was completed in 1843. Following which, in 1851, he received a patent for his invention that enabled steamships to be powered by bitumen via a rotary engine and propeller. He also designed a signal light to guide the merchantmen ships which would often, through bad captaincy, lose the main convoy in the night.

The Admiralty had offered a prize of £20 to anyone who could design such a light, but when they learnt the inventor was Cochrane, who had remained a thorn in their side since his foray into politics (see 'Politics, Presidents and Prime Ministers'), they took the idea no further.

Granted The Order of the Bath, he was then stripped of this honour due to a purported Stock Exchange fraud in which, it was alleged by his detractors, he had been embroiled. Then in 1874, having been completely exonerated, his title

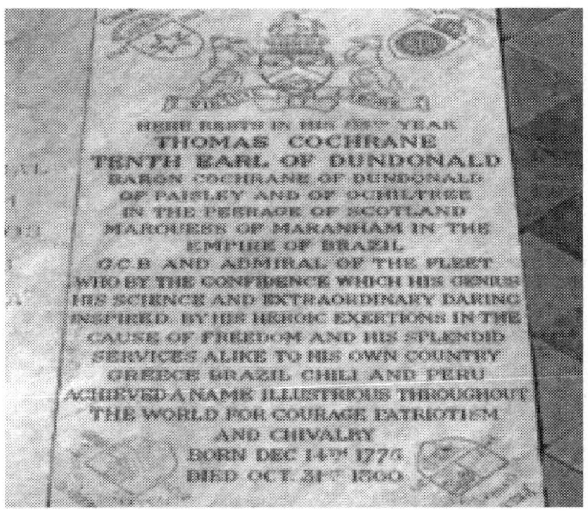

was duly reinstated by direct command of Queen Victoria. However he refused to have his name plaque replaced on the back of his seat in the charming Henry V11 Chapel (or, as it is referred to more prettily, The Lady Chapel), because, he asserted; *"If it was removed once it can be removed again."*
What can never be removed is his tomb, situated in a seriously permanent place, the central nave of the Abbey. It is inscribed with a eulogy written by Sir Lyon Playfair detailing the Earl's illustrious activities and is adorned with his coat of arms, crest and the words 'Virtute et Labore' with, at its four corners, the shields of Chile, Brazil, Peru and Greece.

This photograph of Lord Cochrane's last resting place is the copyright of the Dean and Chapter of Westminster and is reproduced here with their permission Permission obtained via the invaluable assistance of Christine Reynolds, Assistant Keeper of Muniments of the Westminster Abbey Library and from whom I learned that the word 'muniments' is an ancient word for 'archives'. (A neat pun.)

Although Lord Cochrane's Lady Chapel seat no longer has his plaque on it, it

Thomas Cochrane, aka, the 10th Earl of Dundonald, 1775–1860.
British Admiral, ranks among the greatest of British seamen in history and for whom Cochrane street was named. The Admiral reportedly frequented a tavern existing in the early days of Hong Kong near this site marker, spending leisurely afternoons imbibing copious quantities of his beloved "navy" rum. He died in 1860 and is buried in Westminster Abbey.

does have, carved into the back of the seat; "Chili, Cochrane e Libertad Viva" (Long Live Chile, Cochrane and Liberty). Christine tells me it is thought this 'graffiti' was possibly the work of a 19th century tourist. (As it was written in Spanish, presumably it was, Chilean tourist.)

She tells me that the 'graffiti', which had been partly covered by the plaques of more recent claimants to the seat, will, in future, be left clear for visitors to read. However, what is still very clear for visitors to read is a sign that adorns the entry to Cochrane Street in Hong Kong. A photo of which was sent to me by ex-clients, and now valued friends, Barbara and John Leggate, who spotted it when on a visit there.

John and Barbara have homes in London and Cap Ferrat but our friendship is based on their kind hearts not their coronets.

While the Earl's final resting place is where he can have the occasional conversation with such notables as Sir Isaac Newton, he may have preferred to rest in St Paul's Cathedral where he could have the occasional conversation with Nelson, because, as an Abbey warden said when escorting me to The Lady Chapel; *"They say Nelson was our finest seamen but we both know of a finer."* Perhaps, having fought alongside Cochrane at Trafalgar, Nelson may have agreed with my warden's view that, if not better, he was his equal.

A view substantiated by Robert Louis Stevenson when he noted in his 'Virginibus Puerisque' of 1881: 'Their sayings and doings stir English blood like the sound of a trumpet; and if the Indian Empire, the trade of London and all the outward and visible ensigns of our greatness should pass away, we should still leave behind us a durable monument of what we were in these sayings and doings of the English Admirals.'

Thus, as my warden believed, Cochrane stands with Nelson as being among; 'The Great and The Good'. Although, had Stevenson known of Churchill's heroics his eulogy may have included Prime Ministers.

Many of Jeri's illustrious family, including the 9th Earl, Archibald Cochrane, a scientist and inventor of distinction, earned themselves much merit, not only in the field (or rather sea), of combat, but also in the field of the Arts.

These include my mother, her children, grandchildren and great-grandchildren. All of whom have inherited either the artistic talents or entrepreneurial gifts of their forebears and, in many cases, both of these, together with their courage, fortitude and strength of mind.

Notably, Ralph Cochrane, who, during the Second World War, worked closely with King George VI on the planning of the successful Dam Busters raid. A raid that was hugely significant in bringing this ghastly conflict to an end. Which, some may think, bears out the truth of one of my mother's favourite quips: *"All the brightest people come from Scotland and the brighter they are they quicker they come."* Not least of these being her own father, who was one of the last seamen to get his Captain's Ticket under sail and who, on his frequent journeys to China and India, had many passengers whose names are still noteworthy today. Some of whom he remained friends with for many years, one, as I mention earlier, being Rudyard Kipling.

Another was her uncle, Richardson Cochrane, who once worked with the renowned Scottish designer, Charles Rennie Mackintosh. Richardson might have earned the Royal Warrant, as he designed a daisy pattern carpet for Queen Victoria, which, with the quality of Victorian manufacturing and the frugality of the Royal family, may still adorn Balmoral Castle to this day.

Also, during his varied career he was reputed to have imported from the Far East a fabric which, in honour of his most famous female forebear, he named Paisley.

We were told by our mother that he then sold the rights of this now popular, much used design to Liberty's of London, thus depriving his descendants of a comfortable future income in royalties. A fable that may not sit well with the Paisley Museum.

Their penchant for fabric did not end there as Richardson's brother, Thomas, worked with Sam Courtauld on the first of, our now much used, synthetic fabrics. Following a disagreement (when Sam went on to great riches and Thomas went on to great penury), the Cochranes had no connection with the Courtauld family until my twin, Sonya, and her husband Ray bought a delightful home on a large amount of building land that, in an irony lost on them, had once been a brick field, in the tiny Essex village of Colne Engaine, situated within just a few miles of the Courtauld estate.

Sonya maintains she fleetingly redeemed the Cochrane name by winning a village fete contest in which she and Sam's great, great grandson, George, were the finalists.

George's 'Pocket Book of Patriotism', a great little book about a great little country, (from which he said I could filch a couple of quotes), was published by Random House in an illustrated hardback edition with this neat instruction on its cover: 'Makes History Simple'. Equally simple and, for me even more enjoyable, is his anthology of 'England's Best Loved Poems.

So when George treated me to a splendid lunch in a splendid restaurant in order to discuss which bits of his book I wished to include in mine, we also discussed the possibility of our respective ancestors discussing, somewhere in the ether, their descendants discussing their respective books and poems.

But while George's excellent, informative book does much to raise awareness of why Britain is preceded by the word 'Great' mine merely does a great deal of name dropping. Name dropping that includes a few Royals, one being Her Majesty Queen Mary who our mother met when, with her parents, she dined at the Captain's Table on the Titanic for the inaugural lunch held prior to the liner's fateful sailing on the 10th April, 1912.

It is unfortunate that they did not keep their menus from this historic lunch as just over a hundred years later a menu that had been 'saved' by one of the few survivors sold at auction for £45,000, and another, that had been saved by an American First Class passenger, Abraham Lincoln Salomon, was, in 2015, sold in New York for £58,166. But in 1912 no one could have foreseen the continuing fascination and avid interest that still surrounds this particular disaster.

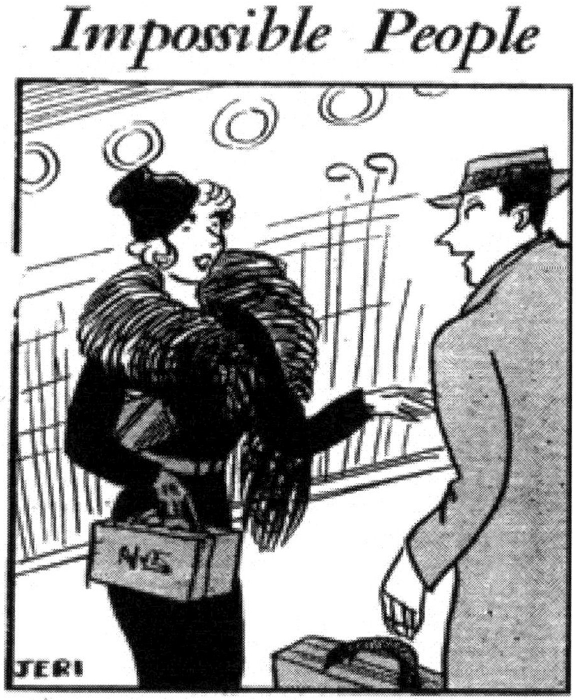

Impossible People

JERI

The woman who said the new liner was so marvellous she would never have known she was at sea if she hadn't been ill the whole time.

Our mother spoke little of this historic day except to tell us that, after a tour of the liner, she told the Captain she thought it very odd that the steerage passengers would be 'kept in cages' and how she thought 'the upper decks were more like a hotel than a ship'. A layout and strict security that ensured the total separation of those passengers travelling First Class from those travelling Second or Third Class or Steerage.

An experience that, had she not died two years before its release, would have made her derisive of the film, Titanic, as, with the layout as our mother remembered it, it would not have been possible for Rose DeWitt Bukater and Jack Dawson to meet, let alone dine at the same table. It would have been equally impossible had they, as indicated by her next Impossible Passenger, been seasick 'the whole time'.

Our mother also told us about the wife of one of the liner's stokers. Following the tragedy each day this poor women would trek several miles from her home to the docks to check the list of survivors. On eventual closure an official had the unpleasant task of telling her that her husband had definitely not been one of the survivors, to which his now widowed wife was deemed to have said; "Thank bleedin' Gawd fer that!" An expression that has been a constant in our family ever since.

It is said: *"Children only want to know about their forebears when there is no one left to ask."* Technology has now overcome this particular problem, but when I and my siblings were young, knowledge of one's early family, unless well chronicled (which our Mother's most certainly is), could only be gleaned either from living relatives or tedious trawls through Government records.

Fortunately we were blessed with inquisitive natures and our mother was more than happy to oblige us with stories about her family. Which is why am now able to relate these next anecdotes.

As mentioned earlier, it was Rudyard Kipling who gifted her with the name 'Gerri' that then gave her the pen name 'JERI'. She maintained that Kipling wrote 'Rolling Down To Rio' for her, as, with her many pleas to he and her father to join them on their many sailings falling on deaf ears, he promised to write a poem for her about the exotic places to which they so often travelled.

She would regale us with stories of her father and Mr. Kipling's association, one of the most amusing being the tale of 'The Parrot'. She said her father would often return from his adventures with attractive pieces of Asian artifacts and, occasionally, the odd animal, one, she maintained, being the first Siamese cat to be brought to England. Or the even odder bird, one of which was a very colourful, extremely friendly parrot.

According to our mother, Mr. Kipling was a gentleman who had a great deal to say and was not backward in saying it. The parrot, as parrots are wont to do, but with somewhat less erudition, also talked a great deal and was thus given the name Rudyard. While housed in a cage at night, during the day Rudyard would rest on an open roost in their large, enclosed entryway and each time our grandfather returned from gallivanting around the globe he would great the parrot and have a chat.

Sometime after the parrot's arrival, our grandmother, taken with all things Asiatic, acquired a Pekinese and the next time Paul returned from his wanderings the dog rushed to greet him, so he bent down to ruffle its fur before greeting Rudyard.

Our mother told us that from that day the parrot would have nothing to do with her father and would screech, *"Rudyard not here"* (or perhaps *"not hear"*) if he attempted to talk to it. Two other of her father's friends were Lloyd George and Charles Shand Kydd, the wallpaper magnate, both of whom our mother knew well.

Her early years were spent in Southampton where, even when tiny, she showed a precocious talent for art and the classics. However, as her father was so often away at sea, she spent the summer holidays in Yorkshire where her mother's family lived.

Impossible People

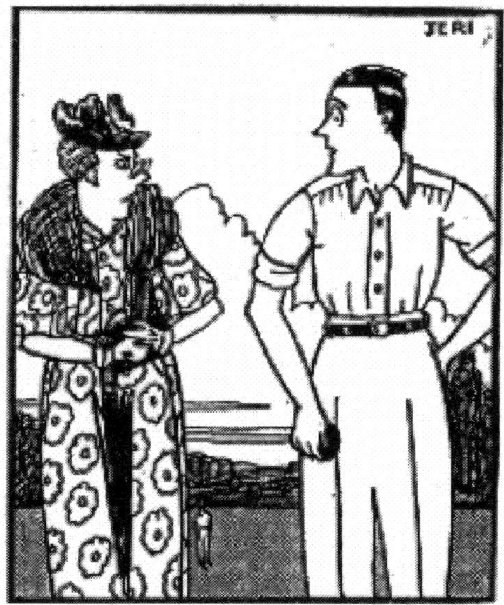

The woman who rebuked a cricketer for bowling a maiden over.

While unheard of today, in the early years of the nineteen hundreds it was not unusual for the well off to 'hire a house and its occupants,' where they would be catered for during the summer season. If the accommodation was comfortable and the service agreeable this arrangement could continue for many years.

Thus our grandmother and mother spent their summers in Flamboro' Head with a couple known as 'The Bayes', who had five children: Ralph, Richard, Bessie, Marjorie and Mary. With all of whom our mother forged a strong friendship that continued into later life.

She told us that, when she was twelve, she had an 'adolescent pash' on The Baye's eldest son, Richard, but their age difference meant it could never develop into anything that could remotely resemble a romance. Many years later, Richard, having returned safely from the battlefields of the First World War, married a local heiress, Ida, and they had one child, a daughter, Barbara.

Being close to Mama's age the three Bayes girls, due to the vast loss of young men during the War and subsequent influenza epidemic, had little opportunity to find suitable suitors and although Mary did eventually marry, none of the sisters had any offspring.

Nor did their older brother, Ralph, who, we were told; 'had died in the Great War'. A demise brought about - fable had it - by being eaten by wolves in the snowy wastes of Russia. A story that, being young, we accepted in equal amounts of doubt, dismay, disgust and disbelief.

Perhaps it was this 'romanticised' Russian tragedy that, years later, precipitated our mother into falling in love with, and eventually marrying, a Romantic Russian herself. Although it took six years for this Romantic Russian to 'bowl his maiden over.'

In the meantime, due to the Second War, the two families lost touch until, in 1959, Marjorie managed to trace our mother. Shortly after this momentous reunion Marjorie introduced us to her only niece, Richards's daughter, Barbara, with the result that our brother, Stefan, FELL IN LOVE.

A coup de foudre that led to Richard and Ida's daughter becoming our mother's daughter-in-law, Marjorie becoming our 'Adopted Aunt' and, eventually, Richard and our Mother becoming mutual grandparents to Barbara and Stefan's two children, Sophie and Guyon.

At the time she 'found' our mother, Marjorie had been elected Executive Secretary of the International Confederation of Midwives. Thus for many years, and at different times, my youngest sister, Sasha and I acted as her Senior Administrative Assistant and, as such, enjoyed early, interesting careers as International Conference and Congress organisers.

Work that was not only extremely interesting but also created many amusing and interesting situations with which I regale my reader in a later section of the book. Marjorie would often say she was not sure whether she was more pleased to have been reunited with our mother or to have found two such able assistants. Although, as we pointed out to her, she could not have had one without the other.

Another pleasing result of this adventure was that Sasha forged a close friendship with another of Marjorie's assistants, Diana Cresswell, and they became life long friends as, having been introduced to our many male friends, Diana married one of them, Dudley' Jack' Hawkins. A marriage that gave them three delightful children, Austen and Alexandra who now have equally delightful children of their own, and James who, fascinatingly, repairs violins – often highly expensive ones.

Throughout her working life and into her retirement, Diana, one of the most pleasing people on the planet, has worked tirelessly for UNICEF, and was the mastermind behind the 'small change charity envelopes' now used by many airlines. Efforts that, in 2011, earned her the honour of being a recipient of the Queen's much treasured gift of Maundy Money – money that, due to its ancient heritage, buys me a route back to the past I've just bypassed.

When, at the start of the First World War, Elizabeth's parents moved to Finchley in North London, she became a pupil at the famous and highly prestigious, North London Collegiate School for Girls where she won numerous prizes in many subjects. Agatha Christie attended the same school but, ten years older, she had left by the time of our mother's enrollment, but she told us that she had, in later years, met Miss Christie at several of the school's social events.

In Elizabeth's own peer group were the future renowned authors Marjorie Allingham and Stella Gibbons. The three women became firm friends, a friendship that continued well into their adult life but which, sadly, was interrupted by the onset of the Second War.

At seventeen Elizabeth gained a degree in the History of Art from Oxford University, and won a place at The Royal Academy of Art. However, on the advice of her father's friend, Charles Shand Kydd, she chose to enroll at the new Regent Street Polytechnic School of Art. A 'school' now known as The University of Westminster.

At the end of her first year at the 'Polly' she won the Industrial Arts Prize for Design. In her second year she became a Gold Medalist in Anatomy and in her final year she won Life Membership of the College. Added to these accolades was admission as a Royal Academician when several of her paintings were chosen to be included in their annual shows. Artworks of such high quality she later, also became a Life Member of the Academy.

In her last year at the Polytechnic, Quinton Hogg, the then Lord Mayor of London, ran a contest in which 'contestants' had to submit designs for two murals that would be used for the main entry of the newly opened Regent Street Polytechnic Cinema.

On winning this, her two vast hand-painted Peter Pan paintings adorned the foyer for over thirty years and were still in situ when I visited the cinema in 1954. A year later they were taken down and replaced by wallpaper with stars - of the twinkly kind, not the famous.

However, as I record in a later anecdote in my section on Entertainment, at that time, many of our mother's friends were of the famous kind. Names that, even though no longer with us, still 'twinkle' today, such as Hermione Gingold and Cicely Courtneidge.

Also, as her family on her father's side were so well connected, prior to her marriage Elizabeth moved in fairly exalted circles. In her twenties, she shared a studio flat in, the rather less exalted, Cock Lane in the East End of London with one of the 'Shand Kydd Girls'. A relative of the extremely wealthy wallpaper magnate, Norman Shand Kydd ,whose son, Peter, later became stepfather to Princess Diana, when, in 1969, he married her mother, Frances Ruth Roche. A family with a somewhat convoluted and complicated background that I have no need to include here as my reader can 'visit;' them via Google or Wikipedia.

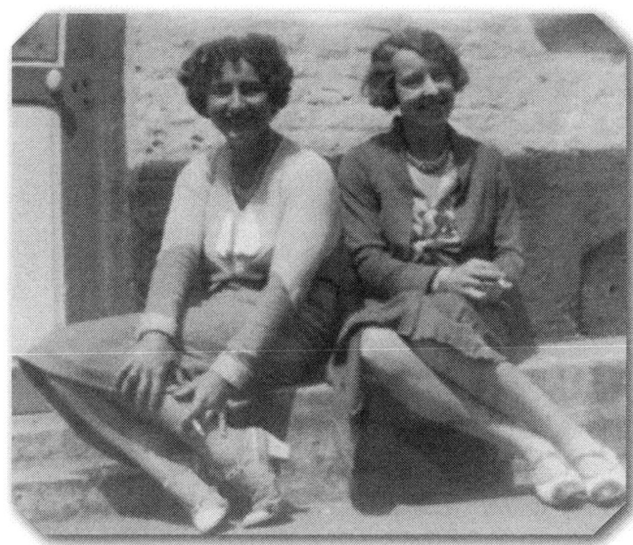

This next photograph is of our Mother with her flat-mate, Squeak. How she came by this moniker we will now never know, although she may have been called Squeak as another of their friends, Phillip Youngman Carter, was known as Pip. So our mother, with her tight curls, may have been known as Bubbles, but, again, this is something we shall now never know.

Following Elizabeth's many educational and artistic successes, her father gave her an open-top Maxwell, and this photograph was taken at the start of one of the many off road events she entered - many of which she won.

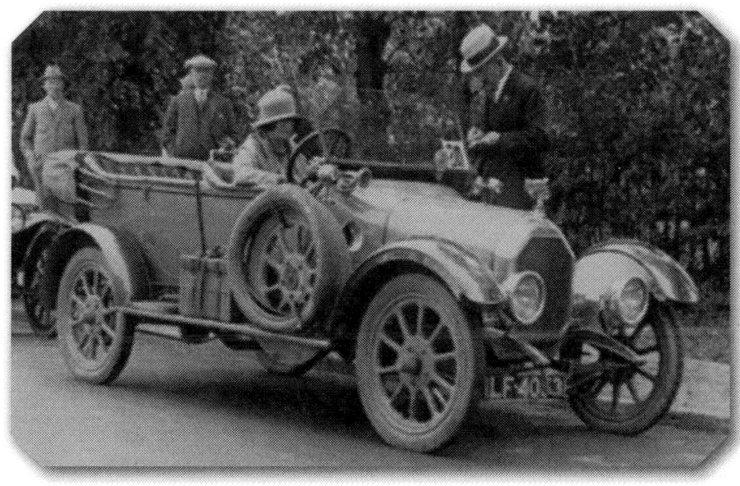

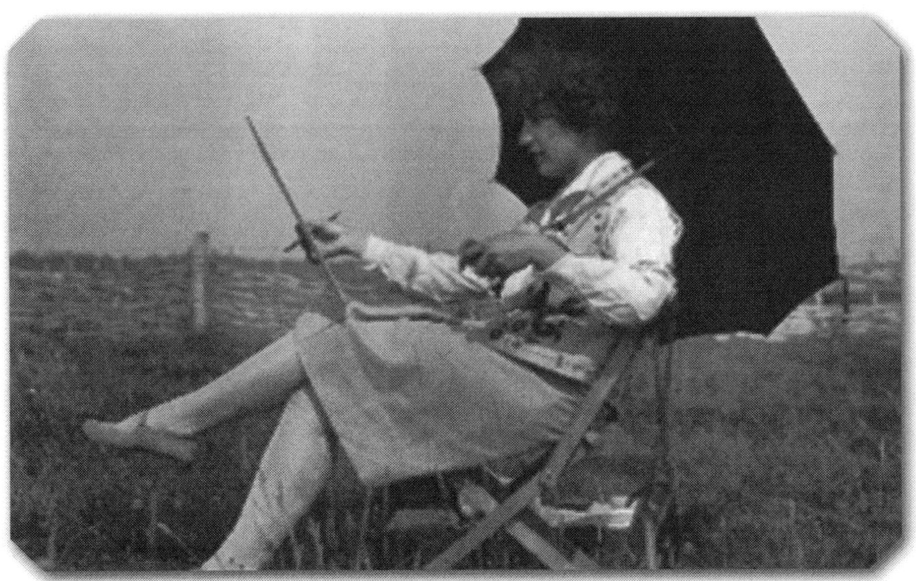

When our mother made her frequent visits to France the only way for a vehicle to 'board a boat' was to be winched from the quay to the deck, and she was always concerned her precious car would not survive this very precarious method of embarkation.

Following this expansive gift, and despite her concerns for its safety, the car enabled her to visit France frequently on painting trips, which is where this photograph was taken.

It is also where she did some of her finest water colours, from which she would make pastel copies and, as I write in 'JERI's Art & Etchings' on page 335, copper etched plates. Plates she later stored in a box that, despite Hitler's best efforts, survived the war.

Many years after I found them still in their newspaper wrappings, I found a magical company with ancient presses on which copies were able to be made. A 'find' I write about in my section on Jeri's Art and Etchings on page 335.

Their expertise then allowed these etchings to adorn the homes of all of her children and not a few of her grandchildren. They now also adorn the homes of several of the clients that Sonya and I worked for during our many years as interior designers.

Our mother was accompanied on these overseas sojourns by many of her artist friends, one of whom was Daisy Freeman, whose brother, Sir Ralph Freeman, carried out the detailed design of the Sydney Harbour Bridge.

Another was the author of the Albert Campion series of thrillers, Phillip Youngman Carter, who, as I mention earlier, was known as Pip to his coterie of female friends. One of whom, Marjorie Allingham, he later married.

During her time at the college, Elizabeth studied with such luminaries as Henry Moore and another friend of her father's, William Russell Flint, who became her mentor.

His work having begun to attract much interest, her father bought her, as a 21st birthday gift, one of his paintings. A much loved picture that in later life, due to her parlous financial situation, she had to sell. But not before she had written this beautiful, emotive poem. A poem that the present owner of this, now valuable, water colour would recognise immediately as having been composed for their picture.

So I must hope that, one day, they may read Impossible People and thus learn of this poem and its connection to their painting.

On A Painting
By Russell Flint

You stand sinking your feet
into the warm wet sand.
The salt will never whiten
on your slim brown hand.
The sunburn never fade
from your shadowed face.
And age will never steal
your strength and grace.

Your parted lips,
with idle wonder, smile.
You will not turn your head,
and all the while the ebbing tide,
will ever suck and swirl,
about the gilded feet
of that fair girl who calls.
And though you hear her call,
You linger still,
and heed her not at all.

If I were you and stood,
as you now stand,
with wet shoes sinking
into the salt-smooth sand,
that small brown crab
would sideways slip away.

The tide would ebb,
beyond the weed strewn bay.

The sun would fall
beyond the ebbing tide.
The day would die
and leave my shoes half dried,
flapping against the sill.
And I, as the last grey gull
answered the gannet's cry,
would sleep,
and eight hours older grow,
and in the bay
the tide would ebb and flow.

But you will always stand,
with your young thoughts,
on the brown ribbed sand

One of her tutors, Sir Augustus John, would organise Art Weekends in the New Forest in Hampshire, an area she remembered with great fondness from her childhood and memories of which gave her the inspiration for her next poem.

A poem she wrote a few years after our father had left for pastures new and she had still not found hers. Or none that could cope with six adolescent children.

Childhood In The New Forest

There is a wood in Hamptonshire
Where a buried treasure lies,
Girded round with flame and fire,
And a great green dragon with sleepy eyes.

Under a pine tree all alone,
Under the drift white sand I drove,
Far from the telegraphs tanging drone,
And buried deep my treasure trove.

My ships that sailed on the dancing sea,
Deep laden, up the Solent came,
Treasure they brought, a wonderful store,
Gold from the sunset, gold from the sea.

Gold from the funnels and masts along shore,
And the legions that marched to battle for me,
Came victorious home again, with tribute,
From the gorse on the common to me.

So long ago I left it there,
All woven round with charm and spell,
And the purple heather and fern so rare,
Guard my gold treasure well

Now I have forgotten where it lies,
Though poor I stand in the heather blaze,
Near time the dragon with sleepy eyes,
And I have forgotten the olden days.

But one of her happiest would have been when, at the age of 21, she won her contract with the Daily Sketch. A contract that changed her life, if not irrevocably, certainly in the amount of leisure time she had previously enjoyed. For not only did she produce a continuous stream of cartoons, she also continued to create numbers of excellent and distinctive paintings in all mediums and styles.

Work that won her many private clients and an equal number of commissions for commercial illustrations for inclusion in numerous journals, magazines and periodicals. Most of which have now disappeared in the mists of time - but not all of them.

Dan, the cousin of my second husband, Chris, worked for the advertising department of BOAC and my mother gave him one of these magazines that included her work. As Dan and his wife Lisa have remained long term friends of the family, on learning I was writing 'Impossible People', Dan kindly gifted this magazine to me.

Our mother was in her late twenties when she met our father. But they didn't marry until several years after their first meeting as his youth (he was eight years younger), and ethnicity (he was born in Paris of Russian parents), created a, thankfully short-lived, rift between Elizabeth and her mother.

Despite this, with few other suitors to dissuade or distract her, she did eventually marry her Romantic Russian. An occasion for which she probably, (and prophetically), composed her next cartoon.

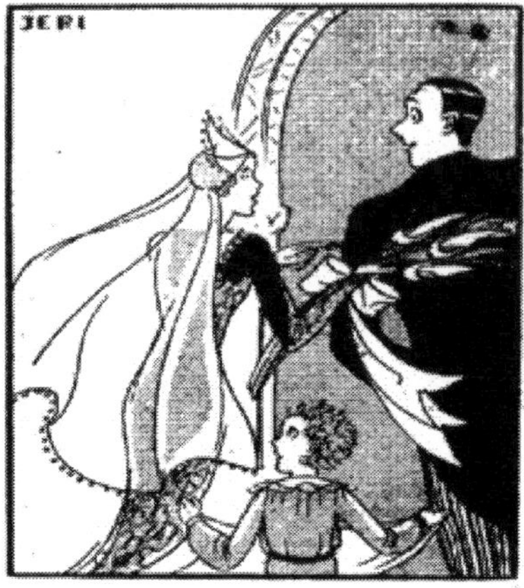

The bride who said she had taken her husband for better or worse, not for good.

Sadly both interpretations of the words 'not for good' applied to our parents marriage, apart, our mother maintained, from her six children, all of whom were born within the six years between April 1934 and January 1941.

This photograph that was taken in 1947 in the department store, Bobby's of Exeter, has Stefan to the right of Boris and in front from the left, Sasha, Sonya, myself and Nicola.

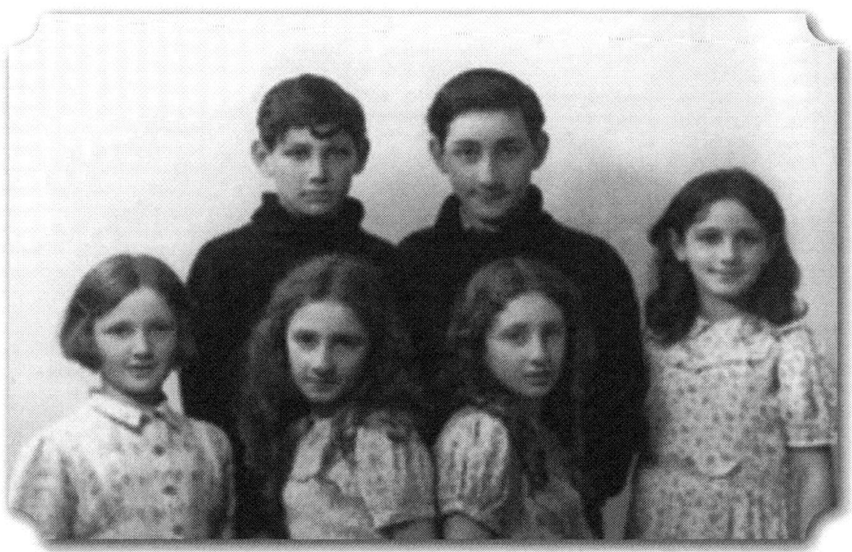

Following the birth of her two sons, JERI was contracted to write children's stories for the Saturday edition of The Daily Sketch. The first, 'Paul & Rory', related the adventures of Stefan and his Alsatian dog, Rory, while the second, 'Bad Baby B', told of the antics and escapades of her much naughtier son, Boris.

In 1942 our mother became pregnant for the seventh time and, although the baby was stillborn, this pregnancy was undoubtedly the inspiration for this next cartoon.

Impossible People

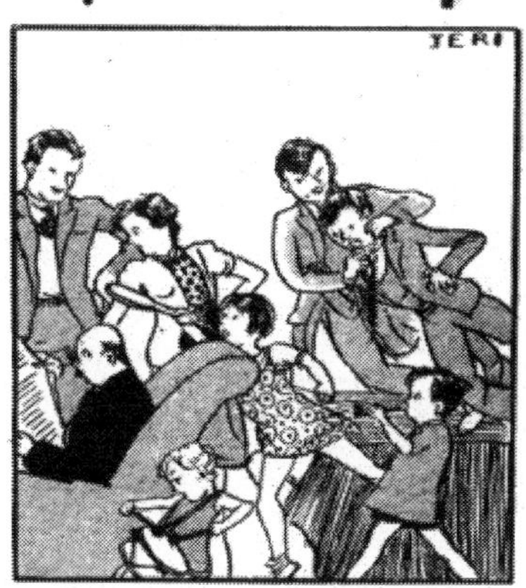

The man who said he had seven children and never raised a hand to one of them except in self defence.

In the same year her contract with the Daily Sketch came to an end and, in 1949 her marriage also came to an end. Thus, with six children to care for and no money with which to buy food, let alone art materials, she put her talents on hold for the next ten years.

During the time our mother was busily having her babies, her father, so we were told, prior to and just into the outbreak of the Second World War, was equally busy acting as a Government Agent for the War Office. An activity that left him with little time for the war going on in his own family.

Perhaps the rift between his wife and daughter might have healed sooner had he not been away from home so frequently.

Years later we learned that our other Grandfather, Boris, who spoke perfect French, would often accompany our Grandfather, Paul, on these supposed espionage sorties, and we wondered how many broken hearts these two very handsome men left behind them in France.

In a most strange coincidence considering its rarity, they had the same second name, Belitza. A name that I have never met with since and is even more strange considering the distance between their countries of birth and their vastly different heritage. A coincidence that neatly takes me to our father's family and how he and our Mother met. A story that starts with yet another coincidence.

Most unusually for the period in which Paul and Boris lived both of these equable, intellectual, gentlemanly Gentlemen, born of the aristocracy, married women whose families were 'In Trade'.

A disparaging and dismissive term of the time that relegated those to whom it was levelled as being beyond 'Acceptable Society'. A society whose boundaries, insofar as single 'upper class' young women were concerned, were similar to that of an open prison.

Thus it is of some irritation that our present popular period dramas set between the eighteen and nineteen hundreds depict behaviour that, due to the mores of that time, would never have been countenanced.

However, our maternal Grandmother, Adelaide, being very beautiful with a voice to match, was pounced upon by the Gilbert and Sullivan light opera company. This allowed her to move up a notch or two in the social hierarchy of the distinct and separate classes of the time and, eventually, entry into the upper echelons of society, where she was pounced upon by our Grandpapa Paul.

She was not a woman who wanted children and, as abstinence was then the only method of birth control, she was happy to marry a man who would be away from home more often than he wasn't.

Thus, our mother's arrival after fourteen years of marriage was not an overly joyous event for Adelaide. So, on the rare occasions he was at home, Elizabeth was spoilt by her father but, in his absence, came under much stricture from her mother.

Our paternal grandmother, Leah, whose father, Joseph Rankoff, was a glass maker, had, in her teens with her four younger siblings, Louis, Sappora (known as Chippa), Katie, Harry and Solomon, run away from two older 'wicked stepsisters' who were unkind to them.

The children 'worked their passage' from Russia's Belarus to France, their mode of transport being by foot or, if they were lucky, carrier's cart. Consequently it took them many months to reach Paris where Leah and her sisters found work with a family of furriers. A trade that eventually brought her to London with not only her husband, Boris, and the first two sons of their eventual fourteen children, also two of her siblings, Katie and Harry.

Many of Leah's other relations, having fled Russia to escape the Pogroms, later died in the excesses of Hitler's megalomaniac desire to rid the world of Jews. One of whom was undoubtedly Solomon. Happily, a few made their way to the safety of America, one of whom was her brother Louis, who changed his name to Cohen and made a very comfortable life for his family in Atlanta.

Leah's younger sisters, Chippa and Katie, were made of equally stern stuff and, after the death of her first husband, Chippa, made her way to England where she met and married a Mr. Zaretsky, a maker of surgical instruments. But our Great Aunt Kate was our favourite. A wonderful woman with a heart of gold who married a furrier called Moses 'Moss' Levy who would give you his last half penny even if you didn't need it.

During the Second World War they moved to live in the West Country, but very soon moved back to Bethnal Green as, despite it being overcrowded and noisy it was, according to to Katie, "The finest place in the world." Although, at that time, due to Hitler's desire to rid the world of Jews and London, most certainly not the safest.

Katie was famously known to say to our mother, who, following the cancellation of her contract with The Daily Sketch, was worried about owing money to local tradespeople; "*Worry! What's to worry, Jeri? You are one small lady with six children to feed, they are all big men. If they are owed money, let them worry.*"

Following the death of Sarala, his second wife, Joseph joined his children in London. Our mother told us he was an extremely handsome, charismatic man, that in later life, led to his third marriage to a lady called Aida M. Bert, about whom little was known apart from her name. But much was known of our Grandfather Boris's mother, Rose, who, we were told, was an indomitable lady, verified by this next, oft told, family fable.

Each week, in order to replenish the household needs and collect the money to pay their workers, Rose would drive from her outlying home to the local town. A journey that took her through a forest and a crossroads that was renowned for being full of footpads. Thus she was always accompanied by a servant.

On one of their return journeys they were approaching the crossroads when she ordered her coachman to stop and return to the town. She then ordered him to take her to the local Politseyskiy where she asked the police to arrest her servant for attempted robbery.

She also asked for a search to be made for his accomplices, who were soon found. When she was asked how she had known she was to be robbed, she said; *"The crossroads have such a terrible reputation that as we approach them my menservants always cross themselves. When this manservant did not do so I knew he must be involved in some nefarious activity."*

Rose's son, Boris, while 'on an adventure' fighting in the Prussian wars, sent his valet back to Russia with a request for 'new horses'. Owing to the increasing unrest in the country, his father sent the valet back to advise his son not to return until things became settled. Which, history now tells us, was to be many years in the making.

Thus, as many might when forced to spend a prolonged absence from home, Boris decided Paris would be the place in which to do it. And as, throughout time, aliens marooned in alien cities have gravitated to areas where others from their own country have settled, this led to the meeting of our paternal grandparents.

Born an aristocrat, Boris, whose extremely wealthy family owned the vast Marina Forest in Georgia would, under normal circumstances, never have met Leah and, even in the unlikely event of their paths crossing, she would have been considered a most unsuitable wife for her future husband.

Nevertheless, within a year they were married and, following the birth, in France, of their first two children, our father, Michael, and his brother Nathaniel, Boris decided that, as it was the business in which his family had made their fortune, he would 'buy a forest'.

On learning that Kent is 'The Garden of England' and must therefore have a few trees, that is where he and his wife headed, where, on finding no forests, (or none that had a 'For Sale' notice attached to them), as had many Jewish people before them, Boris and Leah, with their two young sons made for London where, with Leah's expertise in the fur trade and imported pelts from the Marina Forest, they ran a successful business making fur coats.

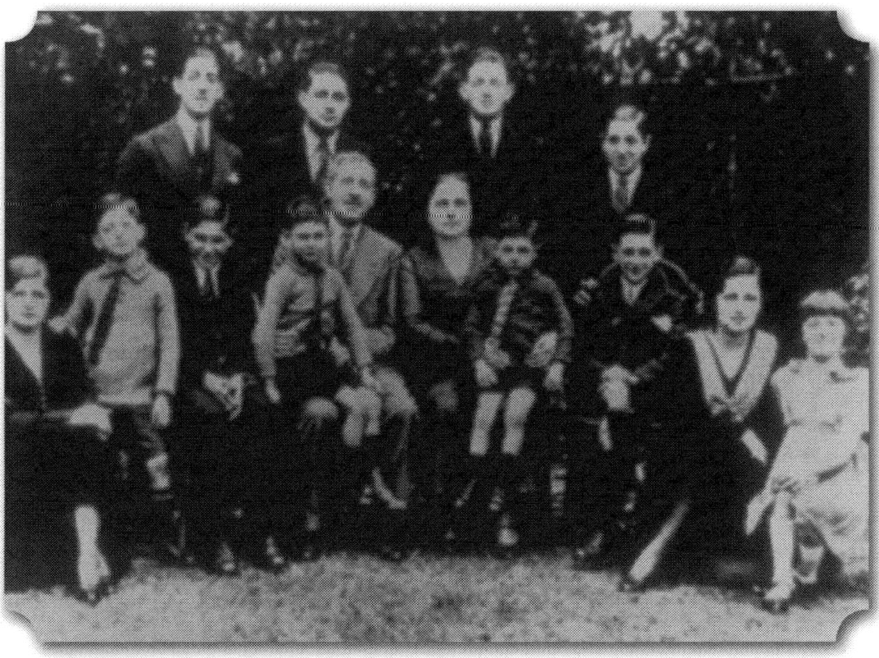

They also ran a successful marriage that produced another ten children. Our father, Michael, who is second on the left at the back, was, unquestionably, their best looking son.

Part of this success may have been because on arriving in England, Boris said to his wife. *"This country has given us sanctuary and a home, so we must now think of ourselves as British and speak only English ."* An ethos he adhered to for the rest of his life.

Some years prior to their eventual meeting, relatives of both our parents lived within a few miles of each other as, during the early part of the 20th century, several of our grandfather Paul's family lived in Acton, West London which, at that time, was a very smart area.

At about the same time, our grandfather Boris, whose family and income were increasing in equal measure, bought a large house in Ealing. An area that was then, and still is, considered one of the more pleasing boroughs of Greater London

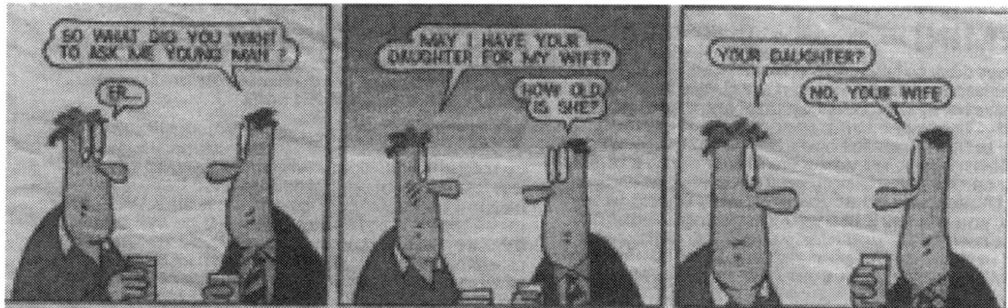

Thus, by the laws of probability and possibility, members of both of our parents families might have met prior to the events I now relate. Events that dramatically changed their lives and created my own and my siblings.

With an ever-expanding family, Boris and Leah needed ever larger houses. A need that led to a viewing, accompanied by their eldest son, of the spacious property in Finchley, North London, that Elizabeth's parents, Paul and Adelaide, hoped to sell. Which is why, where and how, our parents first met.

Shortly after this meeting Michael approached Paul and asked, *"Sir! May I have your permission to take out your daughter?"*. To which Paul said; *"Don't ask me, young man, ask her!"*

It was also a meeting that forged a long and loyal friendship between our two grandfathers who continued to enjoy each other's company for many years - but not so their wives, as Adelaide and Leah disliked each other as much as Paul and Boris liked each other.

They were also more than a match for their upper class spouses in their forceful mental and physical strength, which allowed them to run their respective homes in the same way a General might. Although General's, generally, are not known to be in the habit of changing their names.

When our Russian grandparents first arrived in England with a surname extremely difficult to pronounce in English, they decided to be known by the more comfortable name of 'Bernard'. But a maverick even at eight, our father insisted that, as the eldest son, he would retain the name he'd been born with - a name that, when translated torturously from Russian into English, magically metamorphosed into 'Hayklan'.

Thus our father's eldest brother, Nathaniel and, eventually all their siblings had the surname Bernard. So despite having, on our father's side, nearly a baker's dozen of uncles, all of whom had children, these cousins all had the surname 'Bernard' while my siblings and I had the surname Hayklan.

A name that would appear to be nearly as rare, if not quite as beautiful, as a white peacock. Which, perhaps, is why so many of our Bernard cousins have now 'adopted' as their surname, the double barrelled 'Hayklan Bernard'.

As the names Stefan, Sonya, Nicola and Sasha are now better known and more popular, there may be people outside our family with these Christian names allied to the surname Hayklan. But as the names Boris and Karina are not so often used, the chance of finding another Boris or Karina Hayklan is almost certainly less than the chance of finding hen's teeth - the more polite, French term for 'non-existent'.

Never having to change their names men have far less complicated lives than woman. Having had to change my identity documents four times, when I married my third, (and most durable), husband, Simon, I decided to become 'a celebrity' and thus not have to endure the travails of this tiresome process for a fifth time and chose, as my father did, to remain a Hayklan.

For not only, when allied with Karina, does it give me a pleasingly alliterative name, together they are possibly, or even probably, unique. Also I can be Miss, Mrs. or Ms. as the need arises and, best of all, I have a husband who doesn't mind what name I use as long as I love him.

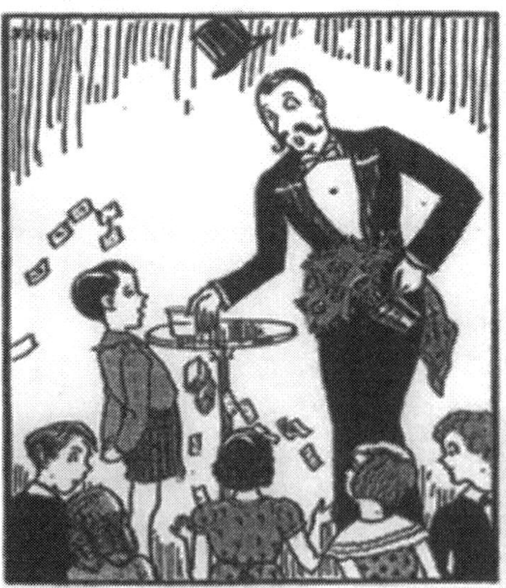

The small boy who said "No, Father" when asked by the conjurer if he knew him.

The French appear to be equally sensible as it seems of little matter whether a woman uses her maiden or married name when dealing with businesses, bureaucrats, or banks. A benefit that is now also gaining ground throughout Europe and America.

Our father's decision to retain the unusual name of Hayklan may, in later life, have

allowed his own father to disown him. A possibility that, with our father's penchant for bending the law, may have been thought of by our grandfather as of considerable benefit.

And while it is unlikely that our

father would ever have wished to disown his father, this is something we will now never know. Or will we?

(A cartoon similar to the iconic line in David's Croft's hilarious television comedy, 'Dad's Army', when, on being asked for their names by a U-boat captain, Mainwaring says; "Don't tell him your name, Pike.")

Not long after the end of the Second World War, our father having, (in the words of our mother), 'done a bunk', and our maternal grandmother having forgiven her daughter for her 'impropriety', much to our delight and not a little of his own, we were able to visit our Grandpapa Paul, who would regale us with his seagoing adventures and other exciting and illustrious activities. A few of which I regale my reader with later.

In her mid-fifties our mother recommenced work as an illustrator, which led to many private commissions for portraits and landscapes in all mediums. In 1965, she was a founder member of the Estuary Group of Water Colour Artists, where she worked with a number of notable artists such as Frank Drake, John Nash and Sydney Vale, who was also a member of the illustrious Royal Society of Water Colour Artists.

Over her career her work was exhibited in many venues, the most noteworthy, as I write earlier, being the Royal Academy. In later years she held exhibitions at the London Albany and Cavendish Galleries, the West of England Galleries in Bath and The Hague. The Beecroft Gallery in Essex and Mandells Gallery in Norwich. Also, together with her Estuary Art Group colleagues, many other venues in Essex, Norfolk and London.

In 1993 her poems were published in two anthologies, one exclusively of her own poems, under the title; 'Reflection' and another jointly with my poems, 'A Family of Verse.' In the same year an anthology of my romantic poem; 'Shades of Love.' was also published. Our mother also wrote three, as yet unpublished, non-fiction books, 'Twenty In The Twenties', Castles and Roses' and 'Hayklan's Luck'.

These and some other examples of her early work, including four of her original submissions for the Polly Cinema, are still held by her family, as are a few of the many water colours and pastels that between the two wars, she composed for book illustrations and advertisements Although, these, with her portraits of the family, are a mere fraction of her total artistic output over seventy five years.

All of her children, despite having little education or, in Stefan's case none, were extremely successful. In particular, Stefan, who, following National Service, established a chain of successful Estate Agencies. Agencies that, very soon made him realise that, due to to the countries dire need for new houses, the business of property development was the business to be in. A business that won him an Architectural Award for his design of six Scandinavian style houses on Vicarage Hill in South Benfleet, Essex. He then became Chairman of Wiggins Construct and, in 1989, Chairman of the London branch of the CBI, in which capacity he also became a member of one of our, then Prime Minister, Margaret Thatcher's advisory boards.

Boris started his working life in the Merchant Navy, which landed him stranded for many months in New Zealand recovering from tuberculosis. On his return to England he thought he would try something a little safer and, with Basildon New Town much more than just a gleam in the Governments eye, he went into Landscape Gardening. A venture that won him an extremely lucrative contract to provide all the green, public areas of this New Town.

He then made even greater profit by constructing a number of golf courses in both England and France. Later, having previously dipped his toes into catering when he and Stefan ran The Lighthouse restaurant in Tarpots near Benfleet in Essex, Boris then became the Licensee of the Horse & Groom public house in Hampstead and the Lillybrooke Hotel in Cheltenham. Following which, and with equal success, he ran a maintenance company for the American Forces personnel based in Norfolk.

As I write earlier, Sasha and I worked, at different times, as Assistants to our surrogate aunt, Marjorie, when not only did we organise a number of overseas conference and congresses, we also arranged extensive, overseas programmes for those midwives who had won bursaries. Work that involved much overseas travel of our own.

Nicola and Sasha then opened a supremely successful ladies wear outlet, and Sonya and I became interior designers, a field in which we remained, with great success and even greater satisfaction for many years in many different countries. Satisfaction and success that did not allow for retirement until our early seventies.

Later I include anecdotes of my several years spent as the Landlady of a large and, during my steerage, extremely successful West London Public House. So successful that the M.P. George Young, (now a Sir), would frequently refer to me as; "Acton's Margaret Thatcher." A title I accepted as the compliment it was meant to be.

As my three sister's husbands were all involved in various aspects of property design, structural engineering and construction, on relocating to Norfolk in the eighties, we four sisters became increasingly involved in the 'business of property and all its ramifications.

To such an extent that, in the mid nineties, The Times published an article about our activities with the headline: "The Four Movers and Shakers of the Norfolk Property World." While Stefan and Boris inherited the entrepreneurial skills of their forebears, and Sonya and Nicola inherited our mother's artistic, culinary and horticulture skills and I was gifted with her gift for poetry, Sasha won the jackpot as she inherited all of the sparkling facets of our Mother's wonderful character. Proof of which is this next delightful ode Mama composed when Sasha was in her early teens.

Our Sasha

On the night that you were born,
The bombs rained down from dusk 'til dawn.
I wondered why I'd brought this child,
Into a world so dangerous, so wild.
But now I know, for your kind face,
Now makes the world a better place.

A truth heartily endorsed by all who, in the ensuing years, have had the pleasure of knowing my youngest sister, whose birth was a miracle in itself as, on the 4th January, 1941, Weston-Super-Mare, where we were living at the time, suffered an horrific air raid.

Early in the evening, our mother, having gone into labour, made a very short, but very scary journey to the local hospital where, on arrival, she could find no one to help her other than a very young, very junior nurse. So, assisted by this young lady, she made her way, very carefully, down to the cellars where, in the very early hours of the 4th January, with no facilities or assistance apart from the very nervous hands of this very frightened young girl, she, very unsafely, gave birth to Sasha. (Making all of the 'verys' in these two paragraphs very, very apt).

When between husbands, Nicola, with her son, Stefan, lived with our mother in homes where they often held art shows. Nicola's aspiration to keep their walls constantly and completely covered with pictures inspired Mama to write this next 'odd ode'.

Our Nicky

Our Nicky, whatever befalls,
Hangs pictures on all of our walls,
"When they pull the walls down."
She remarks with a frown,
"We will hang them on strings in the halls."

Which would all be very fine,
If the paintings weren't mine.
Or she'd at least price them
When anyone calls.

Over time Mama wrote 'odes' for all of her children and I include the one she wrote for Sonya and myself in my section on 'Twins'.

Now all of all the walls in all of her daughter's homes, together with those of her grandchildren, are covered with originals or prints of her water colours, pastels, oils and etchings – none of which, while we live, will ever be 'sold' - whether the walls are pulled down or not.

JERI spent her final years in Norfolk, where she was cared for by her six children and where she was frequently visited by her ten grandchildren. All of whom can be seen in this photograph taken on the paddle steamer, The Old Caledonia, that, before being destroyed by fire, was moored on the Thames Embankment close to Temple Station.

This ancient and interesting boat had, for some years prior to its sad demise, been run as an extremely successful restaurant and bar by close friends of the family, Dan and Liz Flemming who, some years earlier had joined our brothers in their joint venture of the Lighthouse restaurant in Tarpots in Essex.

Following the fire, Dan and Liz then became the Licensees of the popular music venue, the Bulls Head public house at Barnes which they ran very successfully until their retirement in 1913, A music venue that I write of in my item on Entertainment and where we all enjoyed many 'Happy Hours'.

The three girls on the left are Sonya's daughter, Sasha, my daughter, Alisonjane and Boris's daughter, Debbie with, behind them, her brother, Paul. Next to

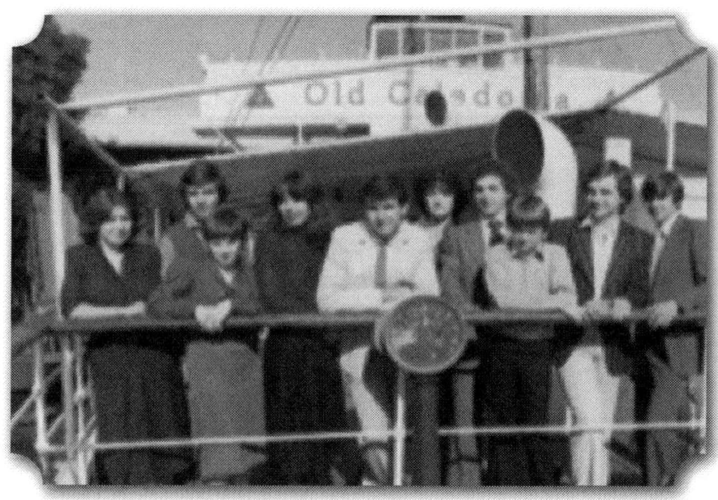

Debbie is Sonya's son, Nicholas beside him is the eldest, my son Michael, and behind them is Stefan's daughter Sophie.

In front of Michael is the youngest, Sasha's son, Giles, and to the far right are Guyon, Stefan's son and Stefan. Nicola's son

Thus, on reading Impossible People, my reader will agree that the Cohrane family motto: Virtute et Labore. (By Valour and by Toil) most certainly applied not only to our Mother but equally to her six children and ten grandchildren.

HOW THE CARTOON WAS BORN

On being frequently asked what had inspired her to create her cartoons she wrote these, hand written, notes recording how they came to life.

In the early Twenties the Daily Herald plastered London with a series of large posters which depicted large pictures of eminent or well-known people. Under each of these was a title, such as; "Ramsey Macdonald writes for the Daily Herald." One of these posters depicted Dean Inge, who was known at that time as 'The Gloomy Dean' because of his many predictions of disaster his gloomy appearance and mournful face.

I was going down Holborn with a friend and we were on an open top bus when she suddenly exclaimed, "What an enormous poster for unsuspected constipation." To which I replied, "My dear, you are an impossible person!"

Back at my Cock Lane studio I roughed out six drawings depicting remarks such as; "The woman who thought Maeterlink was the driver of the Blue Bird car." A famous racing car of the time.

My cousin Tommy worked at the Amalgamated Press. "Don't bother to rush up and down Fleet Street with these drawings." he said, "Your usual magazines such as Passing Show and Everybody's Weekly won't run them long enough. Take them to a newspaper."

"A newspaper?" I asked? "The Daily Sketch." he replied." "The Daily Mirror is going broke." It did not occur to me to make an appointment with anyone at the Daily Sketch. I just took a bus to Grey's Inn Road. At the Daily Sketch building I was met by a large and very formidable porter.

"Who do you want to see?" he asked. "I don't know," I answered, "I've just got some drawings." "Have you got an appointment?" he asked. "No!" I said. "You will want the magazine editor." said the porter.

Was he just a kind hearted man or was it my youth and beauty that made him so helpful? I will never know.

He offered me a chair in his office. He rang the magazine editor. He called a page to take me to the magazine room. Once there I offered my drawings with some trepidation to Mr. Boyle. He studied them for a long time. The magazine room was a whirl of reporters, typewriters and one old gentleman with a long white beard who was making up crossword puzzles.

"Mr. Hayward is having a meeting next week,." said Mr. Boyle, "May I keep these to show him?" "No!" I said firmly, "They are too topical." "Well may I keep them until Monday?" he asked. "Certainly." I said, "I will call for them then. "It was then Thursday.

On Friday afternoon the phone rang at the studio, it was Mr. Boyle. "Can you do us twenty more 'Impossible People' by the end of the week?" he asked. "We want to run them daily." I gasped out, "Yes." and stayed awake all night thinking I couldn't – but I could. As it turned out I managed about 5,760, as they ran for twenty years.

Some years afterwards a woman asked if she could meet me as I was the only person who made her laugh during the war. About the time I became "JERI of the Daily Sketch" Mr. Hayward became Lord Kelmsley. He asked me to do the children's page, which led to my Paul & Rory stories and adventures.

Impossible People

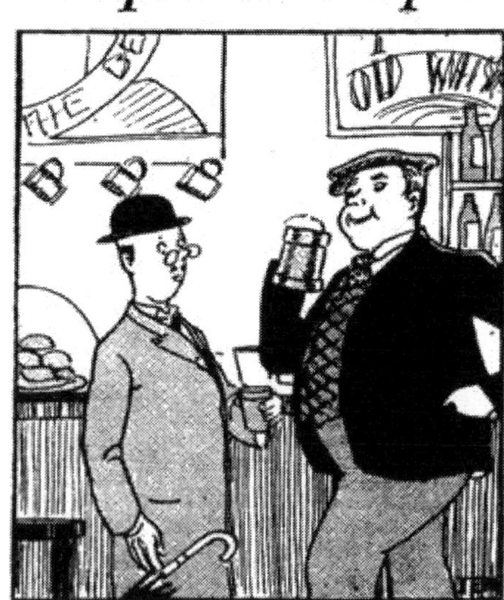

The man who said he would drink their health when his friend told him his wife had just had quinsy.

We had a long and happy association until 1942 when newspapers were only able to publish broadsheets.

Lord Kelmsley said, "Did you know that you are on the Nazi Blacklist? I didn't tell you in case you were scared." "I had no time to be scared,." I said, "What with bringing up six children and doing all that junk for your paper."

He promised to renew my contract after the war, but after the war I had become an Impossible Person myself.

The next Impossible Person was, almost certainly, 'conceived' following the birth of her twins.

By strange irony, twenty nine years after JERI's contract ended, The Daily Sketch, which was founded in 1909, became an 'Impossible paper' itself, when, on the 11th May 1971 it ceased publication.

The final edition was to be a souvenir issue but, on the day it was due to be published, an industrial dispute meant that only the front and back page could be printed. Thus Harmsworth (the owners of both papers who, that month, had changed the Daily Mail from a broadsheet to a tabloid), in a bid to persuade readers of The Sketch to switch their allegiance, enclosed that day's edition of the Daily Mail within their final cover of The Sketch.

Although being a regular reader of the Sketch, at the time of this inspired manoeuvre I was working overseas and therefore could not buy a copy of this final edition, which, if the present popularity of the Daily Mail is anything to go by, was a ruse that worked.

As I mention in my introduction, it is a newspaper whose editorial assistants have gone above and beyond the call of duty to help me obtain the permission of the authors of a number of the anecdotes, poems and odes that have featured in their Peterborough column to feature in a slightly more permanent place, my Impossible People.

JERI'S CREATIONS

It is said that, *"There are people you don't mind being in the rain with and there are people you don't even want to be in the sunshine with."*

What I say is, *"Whether in sunshine, rain, snow or sleet, it is always pleasing to be with 'Impossible People'."*

Apart from being extremely well illustrated, JERI's cartoons have a peerless and timeless wit, making many of them as topical today as when they were first composed.

There are a few that may now be considered as 'not politically correct', but it is essential to bear in mind the unbridgeable divide between that period and the present. For, as L.P. Hartley avers in his oft quoted opening line of his excellent novel, The Go Between; *"The past is a foreign country, they do things differently there."*

So foreign that, prior to the First World War, women rarely married men who were not of their own social standing and we were told by our mother that the tutors at The North London Collegiate advised their senior pupils that, due to the war and the consequent vast loss of eligible young men in their peer group, they would be unlikely to marry.

An assumption based on the fact that our mother and her contemporaries were in their early teens when the war started and were thus nearing marriageable age at its close. As most, 'upper class' young men of a similar age were given commissioned military rankings as Second Lieutenants and, as such, were required to lead from the front, this gave them, while in combat, an average life span of just three weeks.

Therefore any prospective partner of my mother and her peers would be either a great deal older or a great deal younger as there were very few young men of an age and status similar to their own who, having survived, were not either physically maimed or mentally impaired – or both.

Added to which, the few who did return unscathed from the frightful conditions and ghastly deprivations of trench warfare were left with little or no tolerance with which to fight the Spanish Flu. A ghastly pandemic that, between 1918 and 1919 infected an estimated five hundred million people wordwide – at that time about one third of the worlds population.

A pandemic that afflicted people of all ages, over two million in Britain alone and more people worldwide than had died in the war. Facts that take us on another short detour.

While it is common knowledge that the Great Plague of the 17th century spawned the nursery rhyme 'Ring a Ring O'Roses,' it is alittle known fact that, after the First War, children devised a similar rhyme for the Spanish Flu;

I had a little bird,
its name was Enza,
I opened the window,
and in flew Enza.

A much appreciated gift from my stepson, Oliver; 'The Book of General Ignorance' by John Lloyd and John Mitcheson, tells us that the 'Ring O'Roses' rhyme was first recorded in Massachusetts in 1870. This may be so but as, at that time, the population of Massachusetts included many Europeans, it is likely they would have introduced the rhyme to America.

But as the First World War and the ensuing world wide flu epidemic significantly reduced the male population there was little chance for young

Impossible People

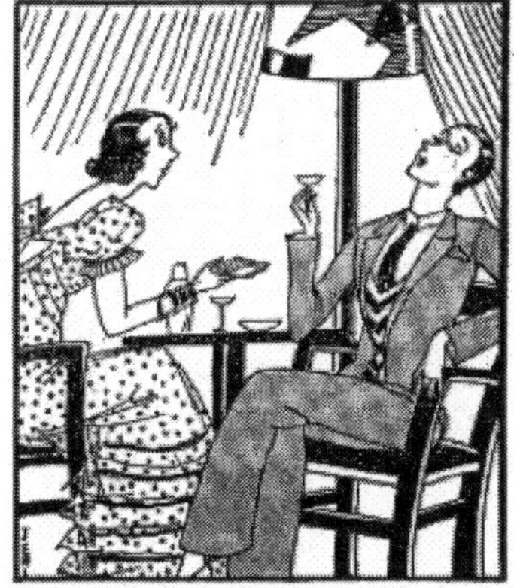

The girl who refused a cigarette as she said it made her look effeminate.

ladies, of any class, of finding a suitable suitor of similar status and age who was not debilitated in some way.

Thus making it necessary for those young ladies who had fought for their country, to fight for their right to enjoy the legal activity of sexual intimacy. Even if this required them to indulge in one that, at that time, was illegal.

Thus the popular 1920's depictions, as in JERI's next cartoon, of girls with cropped hair and wearing trousers may have indicated that they espoused lesbianism from need rather than desire. Although, perhaps a little of that also? Which takes us nicely from one thing that is popular with many women to another that is popular with most women - HATS.

Impossible People

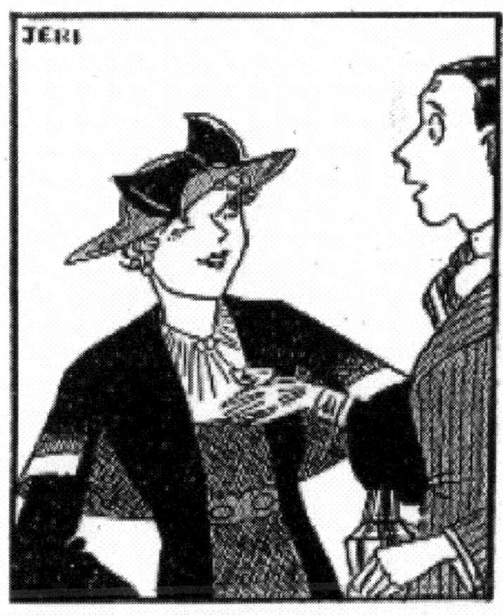

The girl who said cocktails never affected her, but a new hat went straight to her head.

JERI's mother, Adelaide, was a light opera singer, but her three sister were all milliners. A trade that, prior to the mid 19th century, provided work for many thousands of women.

Mama told us that milliner's houses were built with a third floor workroom to allow for more light and, thus, longer working hours. 'Workhouses' that can still be seen today in the many villages of North Essex and, no doubt, many other areas.

The early production of felt, from which most hats were made, included a compound made from poisonous mercury. This could, and often did, drive hatters mad. From which came at least one pleasing thing, Lewis Carroll's even madder creation; 'The Mad Hatter.'

Most of JERI's Impossible People, when depicted out of doors, wear hats as, until the onset of the Second World War, very few people didn't wear a hat of some kind, while women above a certain age and order would not dream of being seen out without one.

When, some years ago, I was in Tenerife with two of my dearest friends, Carol and and Jenny - both of whom were also clients of myself and Sonya - we visited a recently opened boutique of an ebullient, extravagant and extremely large, German lady.

While both Jenny and I are quite well padded, Hoodie (our pet name for Carol whose surname is Hood), is very petite, and, on entering the shop, the owner sized the three of us up and, with no other greeting, said to Jenny and myself; "For you I 'ave zee clothesse." Then turning to Hoodie she said; "For you, only 'ats und 'andbags."

A caption that Keira Knightly might have done well to be mindful of when, as Elizabeth Bennett in Pride and Prejudice, she 'chose' to wander about hatless. Sadly, this prejudiced me against an excellent film as, at the time when Jane Austin was writing her books, it was thought of as most unseemly for a single lady of genteel birth and above marriageable age to go out in public without some form of head covering as, at that time, hats were de rigueur for all woman of any age, income, status, social standing, education - or lack of it.

Early photographs rarely show a man or woman without headwear of some kind and Second World War newsreel pictures depicting crowds of people are a veritable sea of hats.

A photograph in the 2011 book, 'Football: Those Were The Days' by a gentleman called Captain William Featherstone-Dawes, (now there's a name to conjure with), depicts many hundreds of men and boys, all of whom, without exception, are wearing or, in a few cases waving, hats and caps.

Many moons ago, sitting next to me on a flight from New York to London was a young American girl who was busily rejigging the text of one of Jane

Austen's books in order, she said, to make it; "Acceptable to a modern day audience".

I gently and politely remonstrated with her about this and said any 'live' depiction of Austen's work should replicate exactly the speech and attitudes of the period in which they had been written and then asked if she would treat the works of Shakespeare in the same way.

My words fell on deaf ears as the film on which she had been so painstakingly working bore little relevance to the mores of the period in which the author lived. In particular the wearing or, in this case, the not wearing, of hats.

Even the beloved character 'Queenie' in the BBC's enjoyable adaptation of Flora Thompson's 'Lark Rise to Candleford' wanders about capless, when the proprieties and mores of that time would never have allowed such a public show of hair on a mature woman, lowly or otherwise. Regardless of whether she didn't like hats. Or could not afford them.

Impossible People

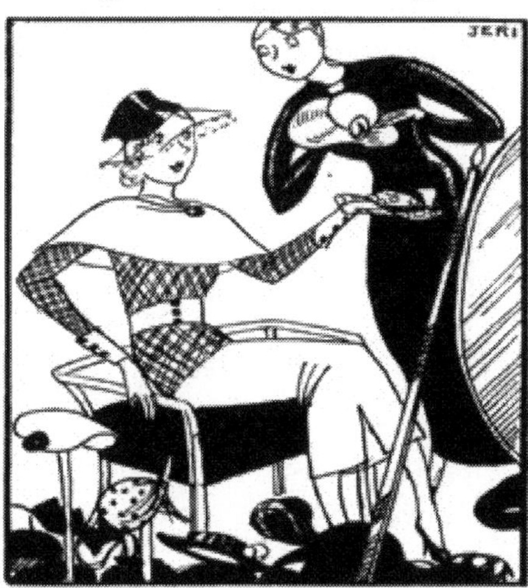

The woman who said there were only two styles of autumn hats— those she didn't like and those she couldn't afford.

Mama said that when she was a child hats were worn by everyone, not just because it was the fashion but in order to hide untidy or, more often, unclean hair. She said that lack of indoor plumbing and adequate hair cleansing products made daily hair care, even for the better off, not just difficult but almost impossible.

She maintained that the film industry was largely responsible for the sudden andpainful death of the millinery business for, much as they do today, people began to copy the celebrities of the Silver Screen.

In the early years of the film business the most used screen was the Silver Lenticular, which led to the metonym 'Silver Screen'. The cinema industry was also the birthplace of many beauty products. One being shampoo, a word that originated in India in 1762 from the Hindu word 'champo' that means to squeeze or massage.

In the 19th century it entered the English language via Saje Dean Mohamed, a Bengali entrepreneur, who introduced the practice of head massages in the London Vapour Baths. A snippet of information I include merely because the proprietor of the first of these steamy, but not unseemly, 'baths' was called Basil Cochrane.

A hair-cleansing product called 'Canthrox,' sold under the name 'Harmony Hair Beautifier' could be bought as early as 1918. However shampoos with adequate cleansing properties did not become readily available until the 1930's, when a product called 'Drene' was marketed.

Thus, over time, clean, tidy hair substantially reduced the need for hats that are now worn exclusively for adornment, protection or, in the case of 'hoodies, concealment and, in the case of men, in order to protect a bald pate. Sadly the likelihood of finding a cure for baldness is still very much in the far future - but not, it would seem, the reason for it.

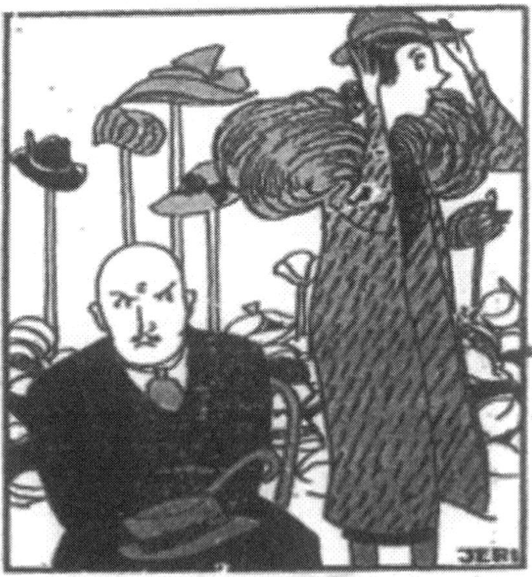

The doctor who said the cause of premature baldness in men was hats.

At a concert in Laval in Northern France Charles Aznavour told his audience, (two of whom were myself and my twin), that his treatment for hair loss was so costly that each new hair was the same price as a first-class trip around the world.

He didn't say whether the vast cost had been worth it, but his concert was most certainly worth every centime of the vast expense of getting to it. There were many other innovations made popular by the film industry. One being the first really effective brassiere, which greatly improved the lives of most women - and not a few men! They were 'devised' in 1893, by a French woman, Madame Marie Tucek, who called her 'invention', 'Breast Supporters'. An 'invention' my husband, Simon, writes about in his extremely amusing book: 'Dear Mr. Archimedes'.

Today's advances in technology will, possibly, do away with many things we now consider essential such as spectacles that, due to laser surgery, will eventually be used merely for protection or adornment.

It has even been said that short-sight can be cured by exercising our eyes in front of a computer programme As computers are now an essential for most people, perhaps there will come a time when all ills will be 'exorcised' with the aid of computer programmes, but not, perhaps, people's addiction to their computers.

JERI's cartoons rarely feature religion. Apart from this, they depict all subjects and situations from the fascinating to the mundane. They also illustrate how life was lived prior to the Second World War, when millions of people were 'In Service' and most of those who weren't, employed at least one maid, and when most of what was bought was bought on credit. "On Account' by the rich and 'On Tic' by the poor.

Impossible People

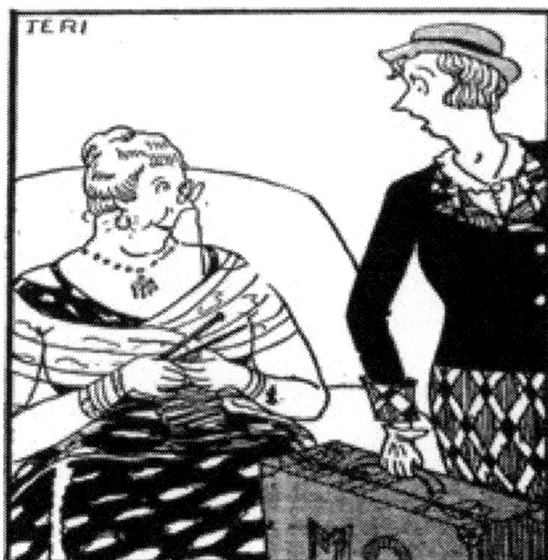

The kind mistress who said she did not really need a fourth maid, but three was an awkward number for bridge.

When my mother was growing up, while nannies and hats proliferated, there were few homes with indoor sanitation and to get hot water you had to light a fire or, if you lived on the right side of the green baize door, your servants or maids did.

Also, despite living in the same house, mistresses, generally, knew little, or nothing about how those on 'the other side' of the green baize door spent their leisure hours - if they had any - for while mistresses had an overabundance, maids had virtually none. Unless, according to JERI's next cartoon, they could play Bridge.

It is also a delightful indicator of the class system that existed then. It would not have occurred to the 'kind mistress' that her maids could not play Bridge or, even if they could, would have the time to do so.

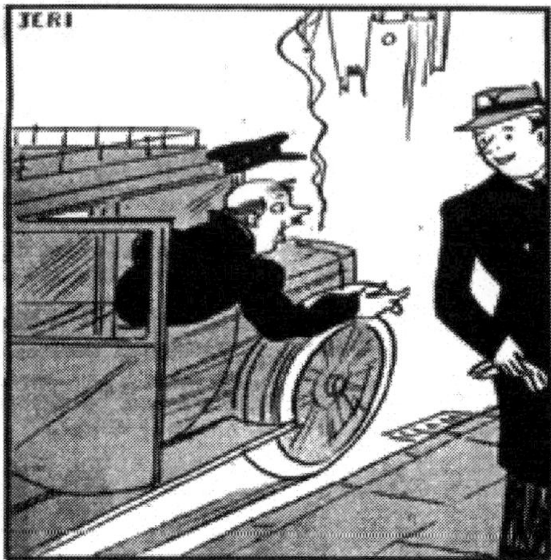

The man who took a taxi to the bankruptcy court and then, instead of paying the fare, asked the driver in as a creditor.

Prior to the birth of the Welfare State that was first proposed by Anaurin Bevan and later instigated following the famous Beveridge Report, it is now hard to imagine why so few well off people knew, or cared, how the less well off lived.

It was an almost universal attitude of the time and meant that working class people to whom no one looked out for - or up to, or after - were left to their own devices which, for many, were parlous. So parlous that even should they have a 'front parlour' in which to play Bridge - or knew how to – few, if any, could afford playing cards

Television programmes such as The Servant, Downton Abbey and The House of Elliot, and even as late as the period in which Call The Midwife is set, admirably illustrate this as they depict employers who are, for the most part, indifferent to the strictures suffered by their staff. Most of whom are forced to work very long hours for meager wages or, even for just ' Bed and Board'.

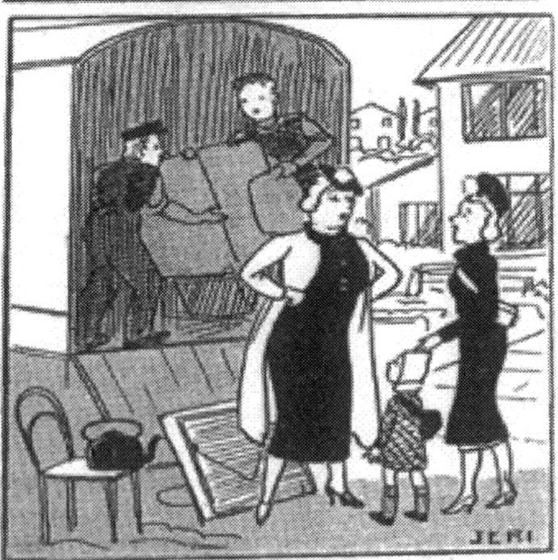

The woman who said they were not being evacuated. They were only moving into a more expensive neighbourhood because the tradespeople had insisted on being paid.

When our mother was composing her cartoons few people owned their own homes, and a 'moonlight-flit' was as unremarkable then as bankruptcy is now. Many tenants, when behind with their rent, would, overnight, leave their homes without a backward glance – or forwarding address – our father often did.

Although, as JERI's cartoon indicates, filing for bankruptcy was not unusual then either.

Nannies also figured hugely, (both in numbers and, apparently, size), in the lives of those on the posh side of the green baize door as many of JERI's cartoons that have children in them, also have a nannie.

In his book 'The Rise and Fall of the British Nanny' Jonathan Gathorne-Hardy avers, (and I'm inclined to agree with him); 'The reason the British were so supremely successful during the nineteenth and, early years, of the twentieth centuries was because Society was based on the tenets of these, in the main, staunch pillars of correctness, courtesy, probity and, above all, discipline.'

Also, in the same way that gentlemen doffed their hats out of 'courtesy', the innate respect that people had for others created the 'courteous queue'. A formality that, despite our present less courteous populace, continues to this day.

Impossible People

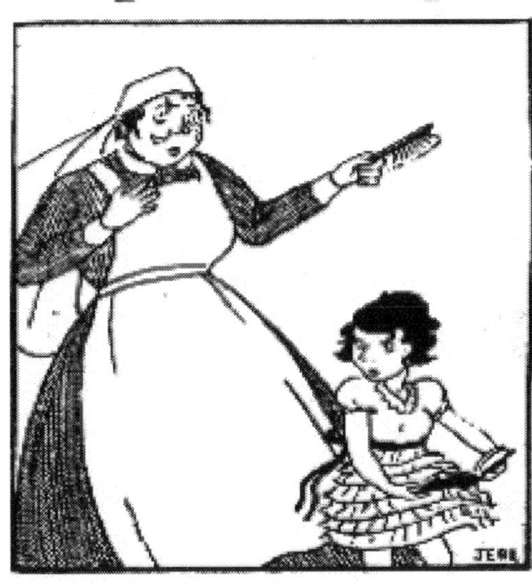

The little girl who said she had always wondered what was meant by a Red Cross nurse.

Due to the high increase of immigrants into Britain a Cabinet Minister suggested that anyone wishing to 'become British' should acquire some of our better national attributes, customs and habits, and cites one in particular, 'queuing'. A custom that can be seen in many early photographs, and is, almost exclusively, British.

An exclusivity it might pay us to legislate for in order to prevent the many tragic deaths that are now caused by the manic, uncontrolled stampedes of shoppers when stores open on the first day of their sales or those who, like lemmings, madly rush to find seats at football stadia.

Following the suggestion that immigrants should be 'taught' this quintessentially, civilised habit and, no doubt, in the hope that it will continue, the exceptionally gifted poet, Martin Newell composed the next, exceptionally clever, poem for the Sunday Express. A paper that, each week, publishes a topical poem by Martin, which makes it even more pleasing to read.

Learning to Queue

There are many pictures from 1932
That illustrate a standard queue.
Quite well.
Implacable in hats and coats,
Dance hall fires or sinking boats,
We won't stampede like sheep or goats.
Pell-mell.

And when we board a train or bus,
We never mill or mob or cuss
For fear of an attendant fuss,
ensuing.

Pushing, we believe, is wrong.
What separates us from the throng,
And has done now, for very long,
is queuing.

It's even said our babes in womb,
If they are twins, as forceps loom,
Come single file into the room,
so doing.

And when the din of life abates.
St Pete, it's thought, appreciates
the British at the Pearly Gates
not carping.

But, quieter than the foreign crowds,
Hands on halos, pinstripe shrouds,
We queue to be assigned our clouds
for harping.

A poem that also confirms that in the earlier years of the last century, most people, whether queuing or not, wore hats.

As Martin's weekly poems are always on topical subjects, many complement the various and varied topics I include in 'Impossible People'. Thus, he kindly agreed I may include any that sit well with a particular subject. A most pleasing gesture, that will make the book even more pleasing to read.

While Martin's poem confirms the natural courtesy of those who travelled by public transport, many of his 1932 travellers would have been 'in service' and would have been attuned to consider the comfort of others rather than themselves.

At that time few people owned their own homes and health care and higher education were something you paid for or didn't have. While anyone born prior to 1940 would have been unlikely to watch T.V. or use a telephone until their teens. But even should they have access to a telephone there were few people to call and as all calls had to be made via an operator and all operators 'listened in' to all calls, everyone, whether they had a phone or not, knew everything about anyone who did have one.

Prior to the mid 1950's, we lived in a world where most men and many women - or those that could afford to - smoked, few women could drive and even fewer people used recreational drugs. Now most women drive, fewer people smoke and many use drugs – all of whom can afford to whether working or on benefits. Neatly illustrated by these anonymous, amusing facts that highlight the vast sea-change in people's lives between the early and latter parts of the twentieth century. I have read it in impermanent settings, but none permanent – until now.

We were born before perspex, plastic, frisbees, videos, xerox. Before radar, split atoms, laser beams and electric typewriters. Before air conditioning, dishwashers, tumble dryers, drip-dry clothes electric blankets, ball point pens, faux fur, fax machines and fitted carpets.

Before mobile phones and texting, computers and e-mails. When instant coffee, pizzas, taramasalata, yoghurt and frozen food was unheard of and 'fast food' was what we did in Lent, crumpet was eaten at teatime, a Big Mac was an over sized raincoat, and 'rock-music' was a lullaby that sent children to sleep.

When a meaningful relationship meant getting along with your cousins and computer dating wasn't even a gleam in anyone's eye, When 'grass' was mown, 'coke' was kept in the coal house, a 'joint' was a piece of meat eaten on Sundays and 'pot' was a cooking utensil.

When 'hardware' meant nuts and bolts and 'software' wasn't even a word and cards were only for playing games with. When Aids meant assistances. A 'gay' person was the life and soul of the party and 'going overseas' was only for the rich or renowned - or those fighting a war.

There were no contact lenses, transplants, artificial hearts, penicillin, polio-shots or the Pill. When 'Cottaging' was a holiday in the country, and neither jogging or dogging existed. When the 'family car' was a rarity and the 'two car family' was almost non-existent.

When smoking was considered 'romantic,' especially when depicted in a film. When 'going all the way' meant staying on a double-decker to the bus terminal. We were before day centers, sheltered homes and disposable nappies. When only sailors wore tattoos and only women wore jewellery. When walking was a necessity, not just part of a health regime.

We had never heard of FM radio, tape decks, CD's, DVD's – Before there were seat belts, air bags or people carriers. When people married first and then lived together. There were no dual carriageways or dual careers. When 'making out' meant how you did in exams.

So while, there is nothing more certain than that nothing is certain', it is certainly certain that nothing is more certain than that times change. For as an eminent sociologist said; "A hundred years ago everyone knew how everything worked but no one could afford anything; now no one knows how anything works but everyone can afford everything."

Thus forecasters, politicians and economists who tell us they are "Planning ahead" would be better advised to plan for today and let those ahead plan for the times in which they will be living. For who can possibly forecast what advances will be made to advance the well-being of citizens a hundred years from now? Nor who will pay for it.

Twenty years ago nine out of ten people would be self-employed or work in the private sector and only one would work in the public sector. Now the number who work in the public sector creeps ever closer to the frightening figure of a third of all employees.

Sarah, my self-employed hairdresser, plays jazz with a group of eight girls and is the only one who is not employed by the Government. Much to her amusement I said to her; *"You don't just play with them you also pay them."*

But however people obtain their money, nearly everyone, to a greater or lesser degree, can afford everything - and there is so much more of everything for everyone to afford. Thus, with so much more to tempt us, we are all seduced with ever more temptation.

For as that supreme maestro of the masterly quip, Oscar Wilde, said in this, oft quoted, quote; "I can resist everything but temptation." Or, as a sticker on my fridge says; "Lead me not into temptation, I can find it myself." Or as JERI's next caption says;

What I say is that the fabric of a book of this nature is cambric and only becomes cashmere with the inclusion of clever words said by clever people

Impossible People

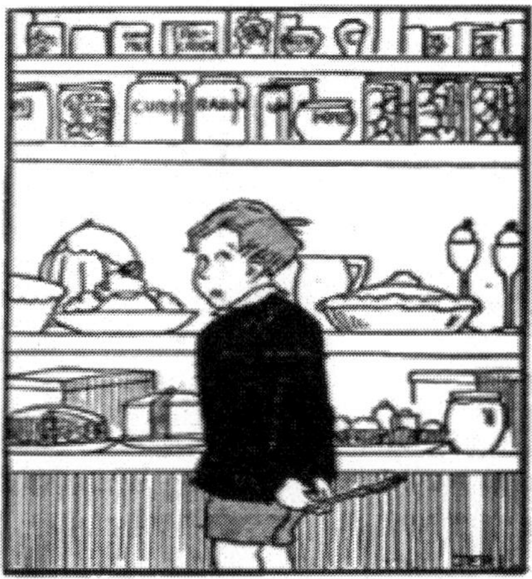

The small boy who, when asked what he was doing in the larder, said he was only resisting temptation.

such as Oscar Wilde, my Mother – and Maurice Silver.

Many years before the birth of my 'Impossible People', a friend gave me a tiny tome of wise and witty words said by the wise and witty, called: 'I Wish I'd Said That.'

Published in 1991 by Robson Books, it was compiled by Maurice A Silver, who notes on the back cover: "It is very difficult to have an original thought. Whatever you have to say on any subject, it's more than likely someone has said it before and have probably said it better." Or, say I, have plagiarised their own work – or captions?

Impossible People

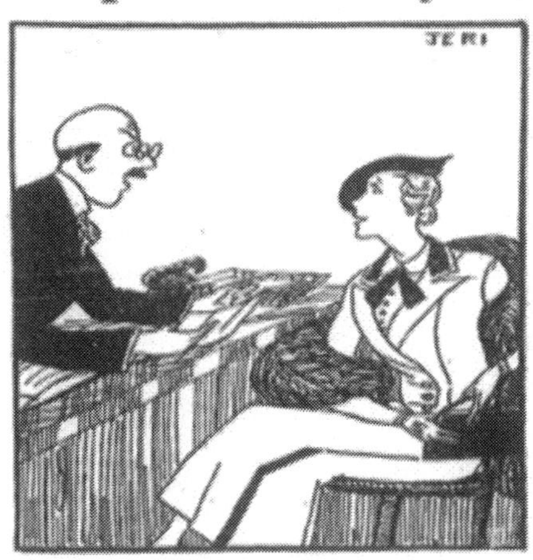

The woman who told the Income Tax Collector she was not as well-off as she tried to make the neighbours think or so hard-up as they tried to make each other think.

Impossible People

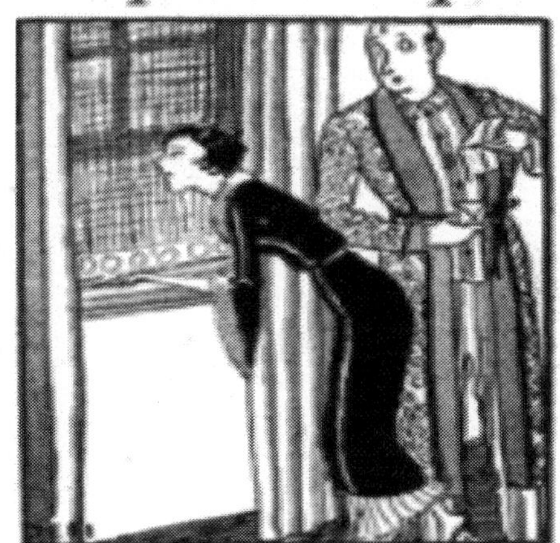

The woman who said she could never save money because the neighbours kept doing things she couldn't afford.

Which fits perfectly with my view that 'Original Thought' is not easy to come by and is even more difficult to prove. So before I include more clever quotes by more clever people I must pay attention to -

The Eleventh Commandment - *Thou Shalt Not Commit* –

PLAGIARISM

Recently I came across this anonymous quotation: 'To steal ideas from one person is plagiarism. To steal from many is research.' As I have 'stolen' many ideas and even more quotations, I must plead that all of these were only for purposes of research.

BUT were JERI's captions always of her own creation or were they, occasionally, plagiarism? As in: 'The man who asked if there was a cure for it when his doctor told him he had hypochondria.'

Impossible People

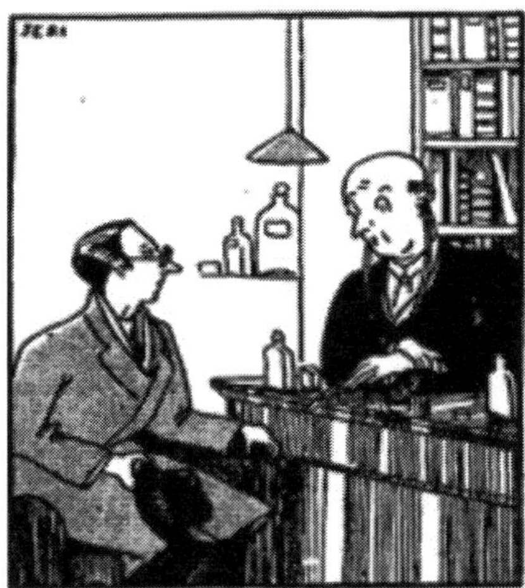

The author who went to his doctor when told he was suffering from plagiarism.

Impossible People

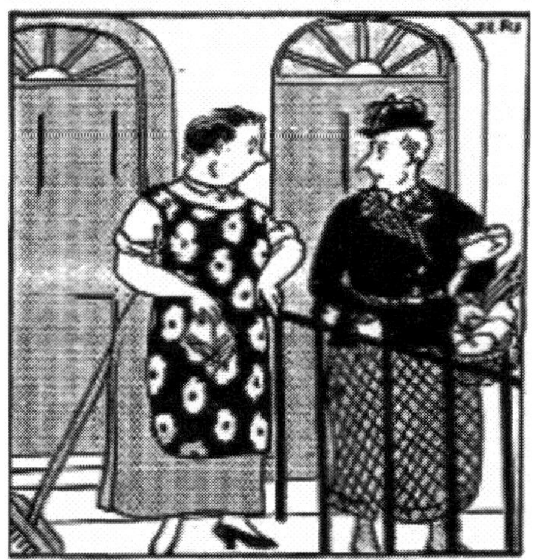

The woman who asked a neighbour suffering from kleptomania if she had taken anything for it.

BUT - Was the joke conceived prior to JERI's creation of these cartoon captions?
AND - Did she plagiarise an existing joke, twice - or even more often?
OR - Did she 'originate' these captions prior to the joke?

Questions to which we will now never know the answers. Nor will we ever know whether my mother was the inspiration behind the now much used saying; 'A pessimist is a person who thinks their glass is half empty and an optimist is a person who thinks their glass is half full.'

As JERI's two previous captions are similar to, but are worded differently, from the the hypochondria joke it suggests she may have known of it prior to composing her cartoons, but as her next caption is now, word-for-word, in common use as a quotation, it is much more than 'just likely' to have been her own inspired creation that is now oft quoted and, equally often, re-invented.

As did Arnold Silcock who includes in his; 'Verse and Worse', an anthology that was not published until 1958, this next four liner that he accredits to himself. The Optimist who always was a fool, Cries; 'Look!' My mug of ale is still half full.'

His brother gives the facts there proper twist – 'My mugs half empty!' sighs the pessimist. While JERI'S next caption was composed and published prior to 1942.

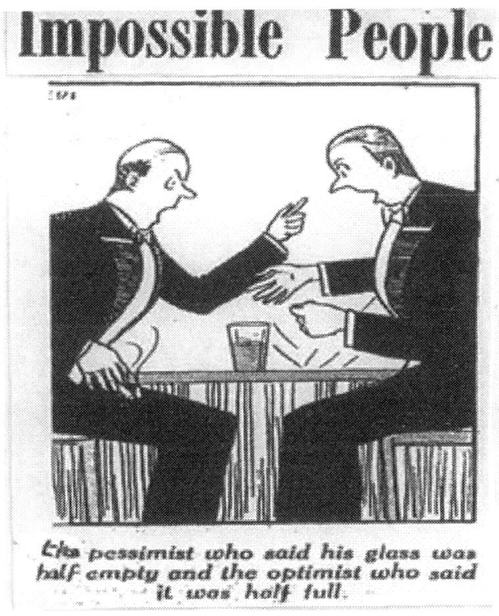

A caption that continues to be used by both cartoonists - and wits.

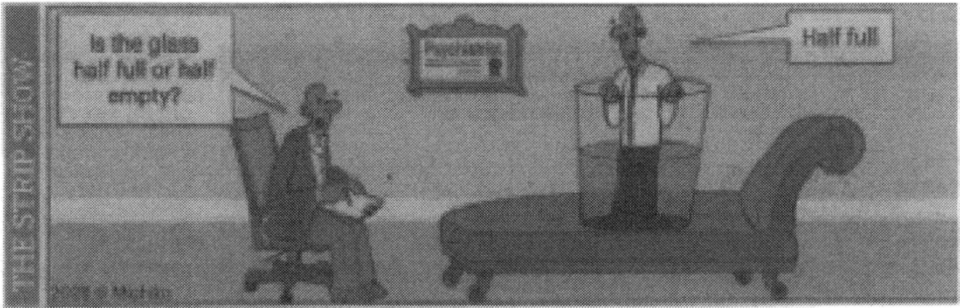

When I told my friend Tina that I believed my mother had created this now oft used, and even more frequently abused, saying, she said she had been told that while the optimist and pessimist were discussing this, an opportunist had nicked the glass and the cynic asked who had drunk the other half.

I have tried to trace the origination of this witticism but apart from the pleasure of delving into the wonders of how words can be manipulated, I am no nearer the truth. Thus, as none of my research takes me any further back than to when my mother was composing her cartoons, I can be reasonably confident it was of her own making and inspiration.

Although if this now well known, oft used, saying was not originated by JERI, it would be pleasing to learn of its true heritage.

Other witticisms that we can be confident were definitely of JERI's own making, and from which she would create duplicate cartoons with minor alterations in their captions and greater changes in their illustrations, are included both in this, and later, topics.

In her nineties our mother's failing eyesight did not allow her to draw, but her mind was as incisive as ever and she could still compose, or recall, gems such as the next two captions.

"The young girl who thought race relations were her uncles the bookmakers." And: "The newly wed couple who said that on their Scottish honeymoon they had missed the views but had viewed the mist."

However, unless the rest of her cartoons come to light, we will now never know if these were new inspirations or plagiarisms of previously used captions. Thus, while it is clear that she reworked a number of her cartoons, apart from an avid or fervent fan, who would remember similar captions that appeared many years apart? Such as:

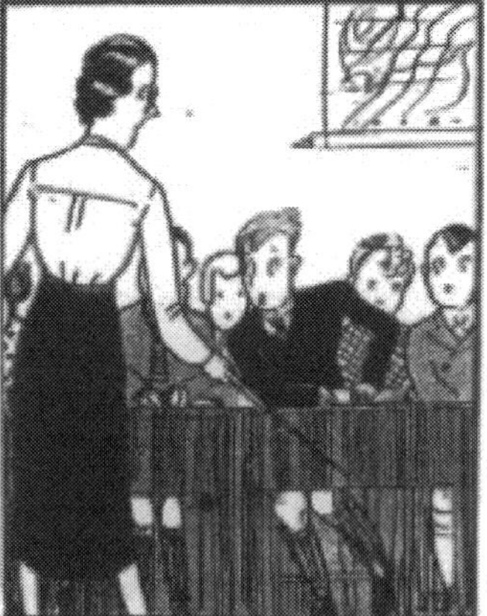

The boy who said "two cuffs and a collar" when asked to name three articles containing starch.

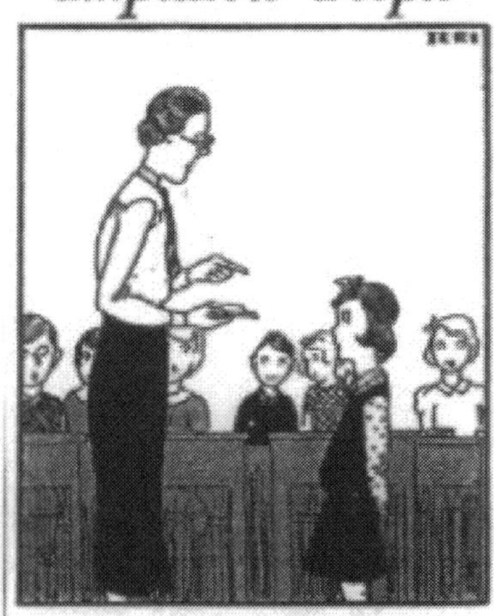

The little girl who said "Five lions and an elephant" when asked to name six African animals.

What is equally fascinating is that it would appear to be the same teacher - or did all teachers look the same in the twenties and thirties?

Or perhaps my mother modelled her on one of her own teachers at the North London Collegiate, who, she told us, was a very thin lady universally known by my mother and her peers as; 'The Sere and Withered Leaf.'

I then came across this in my copy of: 'The Best Test Paper Blunders', compiled, in 2009, by Richard Benson.

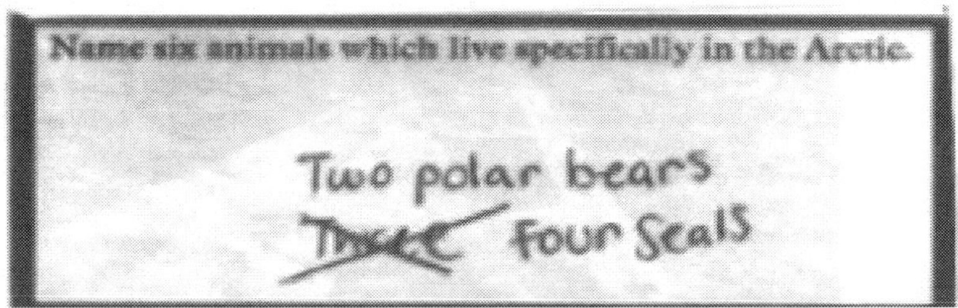

An amusing 'blunder' so similar to both of its allied Impossible People cartoons, it once more vindicates my own and Mr. Silver's views on 'original thought'. As would these next two examples had the caption and the quote not been composed by the same person, albeit many years apart.

For the fortieth birthday of my sister, Nicola's husband, George, a well established, extremely successful property developer, Mama composed a cartoon with the caption: 'The builder who said that not only had he lost interest in the building, he had lost the building in interest.'

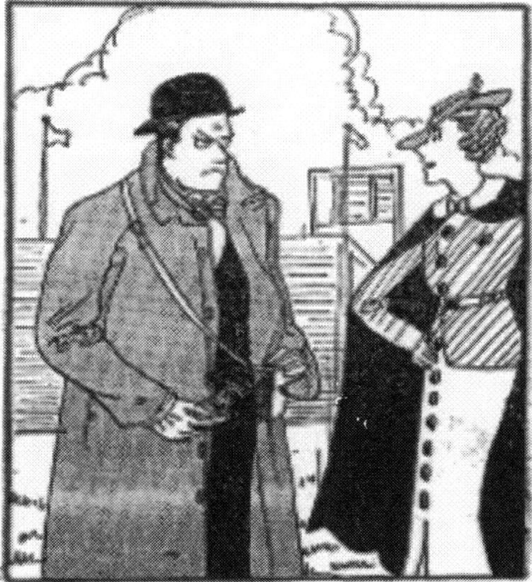

The man who said he had not only lost interest in racing, but capital as well.

So I was delighted when, some years later, I came across this next cartoon that has a similar oxymoron in its caption.

When, in her mid eighties, our mother saw a photograph of Bernie Ecclestone with his, now ex-wife, Slavica, she plagiarised the Mae West quote; “It’s not the men in my life that count, but the life in my men.” into; “The girl who said she would rather marry a rich dwarf than a penniless Adonis, as she was not attracted by the power in men, only to the men in power.”

Had Mama known about them she would not have been remotely concerned about the Thought Police or the Politically Correct Brigade berating her for her use of the word ‘dwarf’ and would have said, in the oft repeated words of her father, “It’s all bunk!”

And it has to be said that if Hitler couldn’t get her, it’s unlikely the P.C.B. or the T.P. would have had much luck either. But unintentional plagiarism works both ways for if, as it is said, everything in the world is cyclical, this applies not just to anecdotes, jokes and quotes but also to cartoons and captions.

Some years ago one of the popular papers ran a section in which they offered to pay £10 for anecdotes and jokes sent in by their reader.

Bill Woodley of Molash, sent: ‘You know what happens to boys who tell lies Tommy?’ ‘Yes Miss, they travel cheaper on the buses.’

While equally likely to have been ‘original thought’, it is possible Mr. Woodley may have read or heard this joke from another source.

Or had even seen the next cartoon.

A caption not dissimilar to a joke (or, perhaps, anecdote) that my brother-in-law, George, regaled me with shortly after I started writing Impossible People.

The man who, when asked why he was travelling on a train with a half- price ticket said; “When I started the journey I was a child.”

Then there are captions that replicate, word for word, those ‘spoken’ by JERI’s Impossible People.

Impossible People

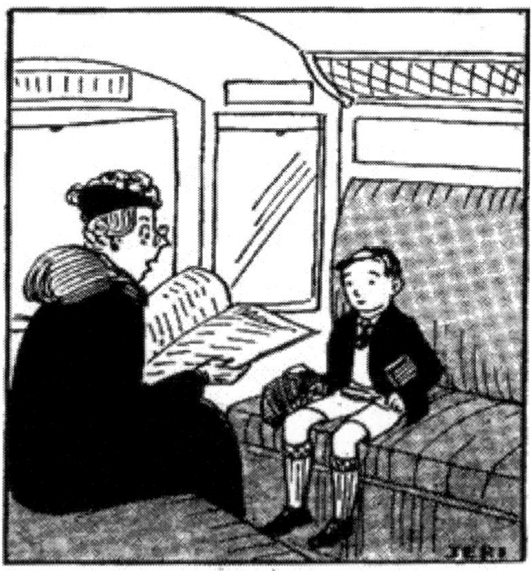

The small boy who said they travelled for half fare when asked what happened to boys who told lies.

Within weeks of starting to write my Impossible People, the Daily Mail included, in their Peterborough column, a Gray & Shack 'Up And Running' cartoon in which the wording was identical to the caption of the next cartoon of our mother's that was published in the Daily Sketch over seventy years earlier.

When having lunch with Gray and his extremely hospitable wife, Nikki, at their equally pleasing 'hideaway' just outside London, Gray kindly said that he would look through his files of cartoons so that I could include it. But with many hundreds to research, I said I would be more than happy if he would allow me to include this reference to it and, as the gentleman he is - in all senses of the word - he said I may.

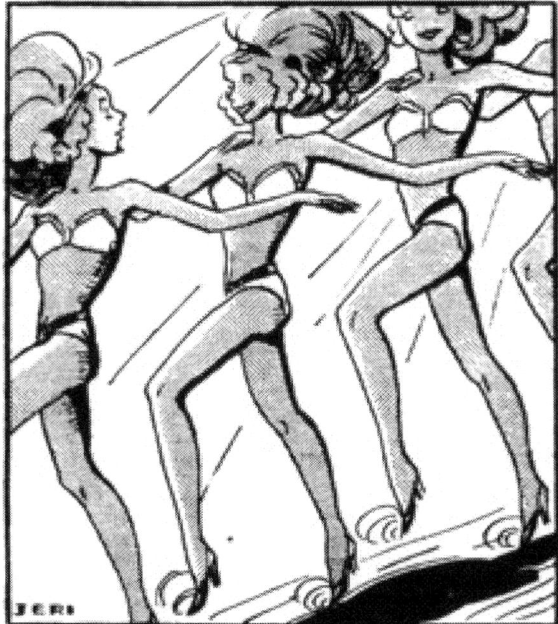

The girl who said she could make a man a millionaire if he was a multi-millionaire when she married him.

He equally kindly said I may use any of his Chloe cartoons that complimented my text or my mother's own Impossible People, two of whom are definitely Chloe and her fat friend.

Over many years and much distance, anecdotes, jokes and captions are often retold or rejigged. As in my Impossible People, where much is gleaned from elsewhere. Thus I have also heard this 'caption' said at various times in varying forms by various comedians.

If these comedians had not seen either JERI or Gray's cartoons, it is yet further affirmation of my own, and Mr. Silver's, views regarding the unconscious replication and/or composition of words that have previously been said or written by others.

A premise confirmed by this next anecdote, with its complimentary poem and allied quote.

Many years ago, when having husband trouble - the sort where he wants to blame you for his desire to explore another woman's underwear - I ran away to stay with my cousin Vivien who, at that time, lived in Brentwood, a district of Los Angeles. A neat coincidence as my twin and I were born in Brentwood in Essex.

Anxious to extricate me from my present man, Vivien would take me to tea at the Bel Air Hotel where we would discuss what virtues I should look for in my next. During one of these excursions into the various merits and demerits of the opposite sex we decided he should be, "Rich and generous, erudite and adventurous, have a good sense of humour and, naturally, be fantastic in bed".

We soon had the interest of several other ladies seated within hearing and my final request, which had them collapsing with laughter over their Earl Grey, was; "These four men should live in different countries, then they wouldn't meet and I would get to travel a lot!"

On my return to England I amused my friends and family with my Bel Air anecdote, but had long forgotten it until Allison Pearson (a gifted writer whom I long to emulate, for her literary style not her fame), replicated it almost word for word in her Daily Mail column in February 2006.

She wrote that she had heard it from an American friend. Her friend may, of course, have heard it from someone who overheard me and my cousin, or perhaps, had even been at the Bel Air, having tea at the same time as Vivien and me! Having found my next four men in one package, I then came across this -

It is important that a man has a job.
It is important that a man helps you around the house.
It is important to have a man who makes you laugh.
It is important to find a man who you can trust.
It is important that a man loves you and spoils you.
It is important that these five men should never, ever meet.

But, as JERI's next cartoon indicates, it isn't always necessary to visit Los Angeles in order to rid yourself of any unwanted men in your life -

Or women? Fascinatingly - perhaps even extraordinarily - in January 2009, Nicola Tapsell included in her Peterborough Column this amusing poem by Norman Myson.

A poem that, apart from the gender, replicates not only the 'It is important' advice, but also my anecdote and that of Allison Pearson's friend.

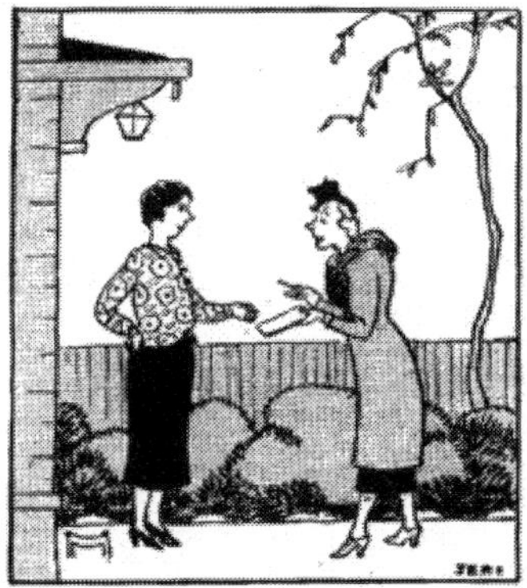

The woman who said they could have her husband when asked to contribute something to the inebriates' home.

Secrets Of A Perfect Relationship

It's important to have a woman
Who keeps a lovely home,
Who cooks and cleans and irons,
And polishes the chrome.

It's important to have a woman,
Who can make you laugh,
Who's adorable to look at
And is good to photograph.

It's important to have a woman,
Who would never, ever lie.
One you'd trust your life with,
And on whom you can rely.

It's important to have a woman,
Who has independent means,
Who is generous with money,
And wears the tightest jeans.

It's important to have a woman,
Who ensures you are well fed.
Then will take you by the hand.
And lead you up to bed

And it is absolutely crucial,
Or the object you'll defeat,
That these five devoted women,
Should never, ever meet.

Nicola kindly put me in touch with Norman, who said he would be much more than just pleased for me to include his poem.

When I asked what had given him the idea, he said most of his poems were inspired either by conversations in pubs or while dining with friends and that, as with many poets, (myself included), a poem will arrive 'unheeded' in his head and the inspiration for this one came from a discussion about how one of his friends could find a new lady.

And there was I thinking that all men ever talked about was sport! Although 'the seeking of a new lady' may be considered as such.

A prolific poet, Norman told me that in 2007 a number of his poems had been published in an anthology entitled 'Poetic Justice'. (How many poets might wish they had thought of that title?). He then kindly sent me a copy that is now a much treasured addition to my library.

So Norman's poem and the title of his anthology confirms, yet again, that where cartoons, jokes and anecdotes are concerned, there is often an indistinguishable line between 'original or 'borrowed' creativity'. For how can we be sure that the things we compose, write and say are not being written or said by someone else, somewhere else, in a different format, style or language?

Despite its unique fluidity and vast range, English cannot be the only language that allows for the use of the wonderful and useful tools, the 'double entendre' and the 'bon mot', both of which, being French, prove my point.

Even so, the fear of unconscious plagiarism, or use of previously written work that has been copyrighted will continue to plague all writers.

Which, if a little unsafely, takes me to a few more –

WRITERS

As I write in 'JERI's Real People', our mother's closest friends at The North London Collegiate were the renowned authors Marjorie Allingham and Stella Gibbons.

Mama would tell us tales about holidays she spent with them, together with a

Impossible People

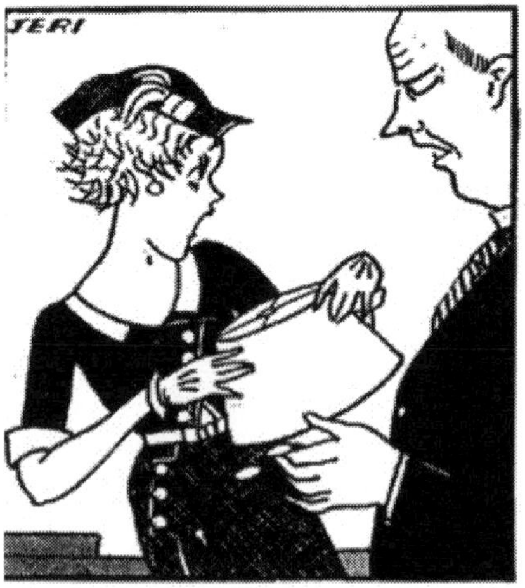

The girl who thought a literary light was a reading lamp.

coterie of other friends, in a dilapidated cottage in the wilds of Essex, (when Essex was still wild), where they would play Raising Ghosts with a Ouija board.

Mama said that on one occasion their ‘Spirit’ talked of smugglers, fights with excise men, secret tunnels and swords left in the thatch of the attic space. It all got rather scary so they went to bed.

In the morning with the sun shining they became braver and thought they would search for the tunnels and swords. They had no luck finding the first, but on clambering into the loft they found two rusty rapiers that had been thrust into the rafters.

Mama maintained that following this experience Marjorie was inspired to write her first novel, and that Stella’s inspiration came from a similar but even more bleak holiday spent on the Devonshire moors.

Despite being a gifted artist and illustrator, Mama always said that she wished she could have written a book as hilarious as Stella’s ‘Cold Comfort Farm’ or as popular as the exploits of Marjorie’s detective, Albert Campion. But as gifted as these two writers were, I believe my mother’s cartoons, paintings and poetry are of equal and long lasting merit.

I am equally confident that Marjorie and Stella were the inspiration for her previous and next two captions. Although my mother may have composed this caption from the oft used remark of her father’s: *“It’s all bunk!”*

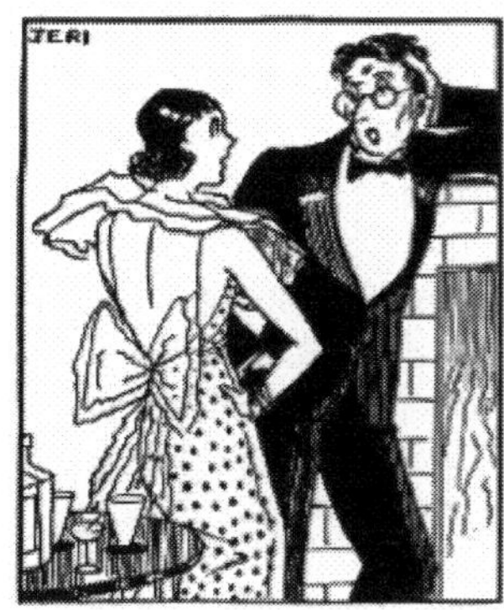

The girl who said, "What about 'Fortnight'?" when her literary friend said he had been looking for the right word for two weeks.

Impossible People

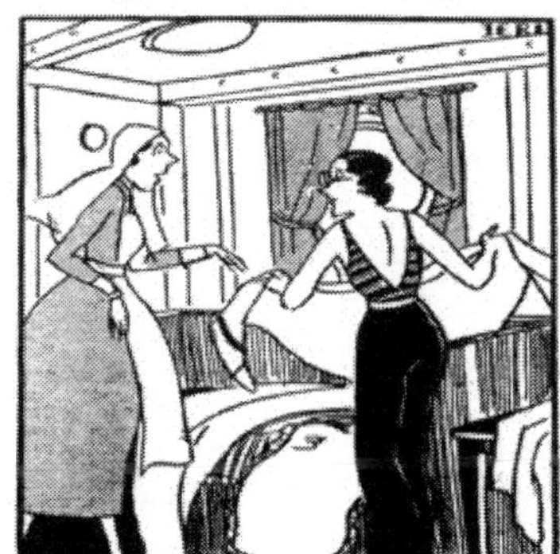

The cruising novelist who said she always made up her own bunk.

IT IS NOT ALL BUNK

Mama told us that the expression 'It's all bunk' was a seafaring term that came about due to the fact that sailors slept in bunks. Whether that was 'all bunk' we will now never know, but what we do know is that none of the following is – well, not all of it!

In the years leading up to the war our parents moved frequently within the West Country and, prior to our move to Exeter, two of our homes, for periods of just months, were farmhouses in Somerset. The first, Rackley Farm, had numbers of rose trees, and the second, Rose Tree Farm, had an even greater numbers of rats.

However, when our mother created her next, very prescient, cartoon she could not have known how 'close to home' it's caption would eventually become. They were not alone.

Within the last half century many things have greatly improved, one of these being the no longer frightening prospect of instant eviction should you fall on hard times that, when we were young, was a fairly common occurrence.

Impossible People

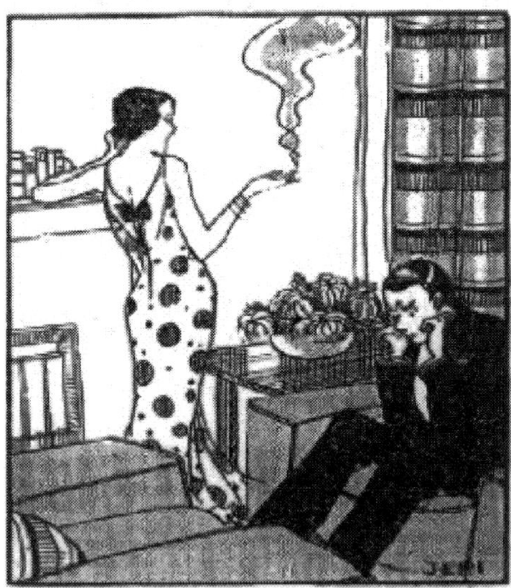

The young couple who said their married life was like the Garden of Eden, because they had nothing to wear and were expecting to be turned out any minute.

Although never before to our mother, who, despite losing her husband to another woman, had not fallen on hard times and, having received no prior warning of this possibility, was not expecting to be summarily and speedily turned out of her own Garden of Eden.

Which takes me with nostalgia, to a place that I and my siblings look back on with great fondness, but was, for our mother, most certainly, the unhappiest period of her life.

Shortly after the end of the war we moved from Exeter to live in Honiton House, a shop in Sidmouth High Street, in which our father had been trading as a furrier. It had substantial living quarters in which he had installed his 'Lady Friend' our Aunt Margaret, and her two daughters, our cousins, Susan and Elaine. Whom, on our arrival, he moved to pastures new – another shop with living quarters in Exmouth.

Left on her own to provide for us, Mama would not, with her considerable talents, have found this difficult had she not, shortly after arriving in Sidmouth, been laid low with severe appendicitis which led to peritonitis which led to her being admitted to the local Cottage Hospital. A hospital where the wonderful doctors and even more wonderful nurses worked tirelessly to save our mother's life while, at the same time, comforting us with hot milk and marmite sandwiches.

But Mama's lengthy stay in hospital meant that, apart from Stefan, we were all eventually 'posted' (with little parcel tags attached to our coats), to stay with various relatives.

Sonya and I were sent to Harrogate to stay with our mother's Aunt Mabel, where, as always, we were teased for having a 'posh' accent, and where I was bitten by a squirrel.

This, and the exceptional kindness of our Great Aunt, is about all I remember of our six months sojourn there. Apart, that is, from the truly scrumptious Yorkshire puddings that preceded our Sunday lunches. Yorkshire puddings that Sonya and I eventually had to forego, but not without great pleasure, for, with God smiling on us, just weeks prior to our mother becoming ill, Penicillin had been released for use in the treatment of such usually fatal conditions and our mother survived.

Following her dice with death, and aided by Stefan's entrepreneurial skills, she then built a thriving business repairing fur coats, taking in clothes for dry cleaning for a company called Bolloms and letting the rear room of the shop to two young ladies who worked on two strange sewing machines repairing laddered nylon stockings.

All of which made sufficient funds to pay the rent, keep the butcher, the baker and the grocer happy, keep us in clean knickers and, so Mama thought, keep the Bailiff from the door. But what she didn't account for was that the Lease on the property was in our father's name not her own.

At that time, and for many years afterwards, unless very wealthy, women were not considered to be financially viable tenants. Thus our landlord, desirous of a rental increase and knowing that our father, the Lessee, did not live with us, planned to evict us.

However the local judiciary, aware that there were six fatherless children involved, and our mother had no debts, found in her favour and refused to grant an Eviction Order. Following this fruitless exercise this gentleman, if one could call him that, took his case to Taunton, many miles from where our mother was known, admired and respected.

He made certain that she would not learn of his machinations and was, therefore, able to secure his desired 'Order of Eviction' and, at seven o'clock on the morning of the 28th July, 1950, (a date engraved in the memories of myself and my twin as it was our twelfth birthday), a Tipstaff arrived at our front door and we were summarily 'Put Out Onto The Street'. A street that was a very public High Street where even one or two of the police who had accompanied the bailiff had tears in their eyes. As, also, did a few of the bystanders.

They would have been even more tearful had they been aware that its surprise and speed did not even allow time for those being evicted to put on their underwear - which meant that I spent the next two days knickerless. Had I been older this might have been of some advantage but, just days into my thirteenth year, for me it was an unendurable ignominy.

An ignominy not shared by Boris, Sonya, Nicola and Sasha, who, having dressed, made a swift exit over the rear roofs into the back lane, while Stefan, with our Alsation, Dusky, barricaded himself into the attic and threatened to set this most docile dog on anyone who tried to remove him before suitable arrangements had been made to pack our belongings.

But of equal ignominy was this swift, public and unseemly end to our exceedingly happy and enjoyable few years sojourn in Sidmouth. The following day we learned that our mother would not be allowed back into the property and, as Boris, Sonya, Sasha and the cat, were on their way to Bristol to stay with our father and his lady love, our aunt Margaret, this left Nicola and myself to do the packing.

But with Nicola, at ten, not considered old enough and Stefan refusing to leave the attic, I was delegated (with or without knickers), to organise the safe removal of all our effects in readiness for storage.

Now, with Mama and Stefan no longer here to ask, we will never know how this hurried decision about the 'division' of her offspring was made. But as, apart from Stefan, we had all frequently been sent away, at various times, to all parts of the country to stay with the various relatives of both our parents, this did not, at the time, seem odd.

Nor did living for months in the cellars beneath a very handsome boarding house in Weston-Super-Mare, owned by another of our father's brothers, Rafael, and his wife, Betty.

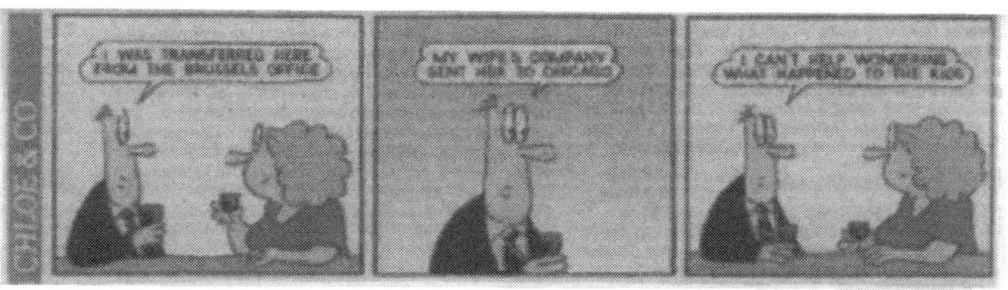

In order to keep us cheerful in this windowless dungeon Mama, with our assistance, painted all of the enormous service pipes with bright blue, green and red powder paints. Sonya, having gone down with a severe case of yellow jaundice, was unable to join us in this venture; however, her yellow pallor made up for the missing primary colour.

At one stage in all of these kerfuffles, our mother was 'threatened' with having her children 'placed in care'. With Stefan now old enough to work, she asked what the cost of care would be for five children until they came of age. On being told a sum of considerable enormity, she said, "Give me half of that and I will be on my feet again in less than a year."

Thankfully the Children's Officer dealing with our case was not a 'More Than My Jobs Worth' individual, so, with great good fortune, sanity prevailed and despite a looming precarious and impecunious future, Mama was able to keep us all together.

A 'together', insofar as her four daughters are concerned that has continued to this day as, more often than not, for most of our adult lives we have lived within a short distance of each other and, with our husbands, have twice lived, albeit in separate areas, in the same, extremely large houses – pictures of which I include later in the book.

After many months and a similar number of moves, which at times made us feel much like 'The Wandering Jews' (which, one could suppose, we were), eventually, our mother, having long ago made peace with her mother, we decamped to Shoeburyness in Essex where, owing to sun, sea and sand, our grandparents had bought a retirement home.

Just days before I reached this page I came across a poem with no attribution other than the letters R.G.K.S. The initials of myself and Sonya, Sonya husband Ray and Nicola's husband George. Then, on reading the poem I was not only amused by its content but was equally surprised to see that it included both of the seaside towns in which we had lived following our enforced and hurried departure from Sidmouth.

Head of the Family
by R.G.K.S

We buried Dad at Weston-super-Mare,
The sand was grey, not gold,
The sea was brown,
He wasn't all that old.

But what with salmon sandwiches and stout,
He lay down on the beach and had a kip,
We buried him but left his noddle out,
And then that donkey caught him such a clip.

I said to Fred and Marge, (there's just us three -
Mum drowned two years ago at Leigh-on-Sea),
I said to Fred and Marge; "It seems a sin
to dig him out." and so we filled him in.

And built a lovely castle on the top -
Just to the right a bit,
Beyond the pier.
Be careful where you sit.

Apart from there being six of us and our mother not having 'drowned' (except in deepest debt), the poem was redolent of our own lives because for us, our father did 'die' in Weston-Super-Mare. Not from death but distance, as we had no contact with him again until many years later when we were living just a few miles from Leigh on Sea.

Being in that part of Essex had many benefits. The first was being re-acquainted with our mother's parents, whom we had not seen for many years. Another was that we were all getting ever nearer to having to find paid employment and as this part of Essex is within easy commuting distance of London, it was an ideal place to do it – and when we did do it, we all did it with great success.

But of most importance our mother became re-acquainted with one of her school friends, Freeman. Despite seeing little of her, Dolly was very fond of our mother and on learning of our plight, gave her £200. A sum that, despite its present low value, enabled Mama to buy a tiny Victorian house in the Doomsday Book village of South Benfleet.

An area where we all continued to live for numbers of years in many numbers of different properties. Many of which we designed and built and most of which were 'posh' enough to be known by 'names' rather than numbers.

However our first, the tiny Victorian terraced house purchased with Dolly's largesse, had no inside toilet and our life there was extremely frugal. So frugal that in the winter we would sneak into the coal yard that was next to the railway station - both of which were our 'nearest neighours' – where we would fashion pieces of coal into 'snowballs' that we would carry home in order to have a fire.

In the house next to our own lived an extremely kind and friendly elderly couple. The husband, a War Veteran, had no fingers on his right hand which he kept sheathed in a heavy leather glove. So we also provided them with copious coal 'snowballs'.

This terrace of five tiny houses with huge numbers, ours was 111, overlooked Canvey Island where, on the night of January 31st, 1953, 307 people were killed or drowned during a violent storm that devastated the Island. An experience I relate on page 321. It also allowed us to attend an excellent, new Comprehensive School where I was fortunate to be tutored in English by the excellent Mr. Ellis about whom I also write later.

Shortly after moving to Benfleet, our mother became friendly with a couple who lived in a large, ancient house, aptly called 'The Old House'. On wishing to downsize, they asked our mother if she would like to buy it.

Our grandfather Paul having died our, by then, very elderly grandmother sold her house which, with the sale of our own much smaller property, allowed for its purchase. As it was only a few hundred yards from our previous home, this move was the least difficult of all those we had endured and we could, at last, enjoy the luxury of living in a large, comfortable house that had an annex for our grandmother, sufficient bedrooms for us four girls to sleep only two to a room and, joy upon joys, adequate internal sanitation.

The Old House, South Benfleet, 1959

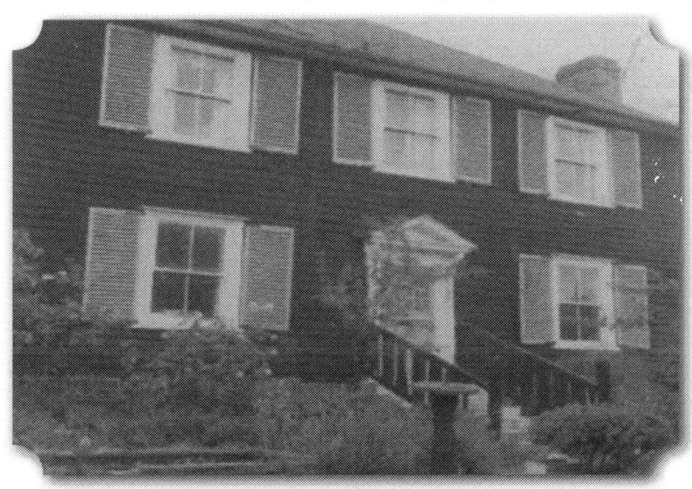

As much as we all loved it and loved living in it, this was by no means the most interesting aspect of this property.

Built near the mouth of the Thames, on the edge of a wide slip creek that separated Benfleet from Canvey Island, the original clap boarded house was reputedly built - but most certainly without its shutters and Georgian front door - by Henry the VIII to allow for his trysts with Anne Boleyn.

Centuries later, so fable has it, Nelson would meet with Lady Hamilton at this same romantic hideaway - which, we can be certain, still had no shutters or fancy front door.

While we will never be able to prove the veracity of it being the meeting place of these 'alleged, illicit liaisons', what we can be confident of is that, had they taken place, the house would not then have been known as 'The Old House'. A name that, as can be seen from this rare photograph, was most apt.

Prior to the Second World War this part of Essex was, relatively sparsely populated but as, at the end of the war, close to sixteen million people were homeless, many areas of England became veritable building sites - one of which was 'our' row of Victorian cottages.

Over several years, Stefan bought all six of these and eventually replaced them with an attractive terrace of five, three story, town houses - all of which had a large first floor, sitting room, kitchen diner, three bedrooms, two bathrooms a cloakroom and a garage.

Which allows me, (for one paragraph), to fast forward to 1978. With both of my children with homes of their own, due to its convenient commuting distance to London, I bought one of these houses as a 'bolt hole' while I worked with the team contracted to set up, organise and run the first Russian Exhibition at Earls Court - a 'venture' and 'adventure' that I write about on page 382.

But back in 1954, a year that, almost overnight, changed our lives from penury to Paradise, Stefan and Boris had begun to be extremely successful in their respective fields of property development and landscape gardening.

Stefan had been granted planning permission to build a number of new houses and, as mentioned in my introduction, Boris had won the contract to provide all the public 'green' areas' for the new town of Basildon which, at that time, was still at the planning stage.

More new properties meant more people commuting to London which created the need for a larger car park near the station. A need that led the Council, via a Compulsory Purchase Order, to buy a large field at the rear of The Old House.

Having built their new car park they then needed pedestrian access to the station, so a further C.P.O. was made on the Old House. Thus this beautiful, interesting historic house not only 'went for a song' but was then demolished.

There were a number of other routes the Council could have taken, but our mother was the easiest, most convenient and certainly less costly, target.

This photograph, with Mama sitting in the Great Hall with her beloved Siamese cat, Sisaket, was taken just prior to the purchase of her beloved home. The only saving grace was that, in this instance, she was given ample time in which to prepare for 'eviction'.

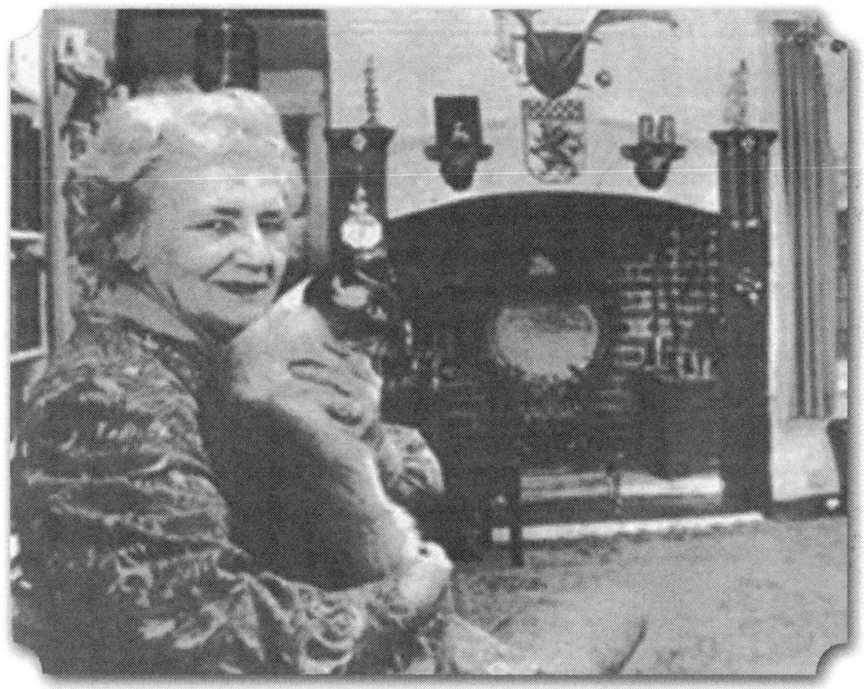

However, with all of her children married, financially stable and with their own homes, it was not the ghastly experience that befell her in Sidmouth and she coped with this loss with her usual fortitude. An indomitable fortitude clearly illustrated by the words of her next poem that she wrote following the demolition of her much loved, historic home.

The Old House - Benfleet

On this sill leaned a dark haired queen,
A sailor looked with blue eyes keen,
Across a marsh with winds so clean,

Here an artist learned to dream,
This was their home.
It was sold for just a song
Under concrete it has gone.
Laughter will not come again,
Nor firelight on the window pane,
Nor children's cries.

We who loved her, gay or sad,
Have other homes to make us glad,
But where will look the dark haired queen?
Where will now the painter dream?
Or go the sailor with eyesight keen?
Or swallows make their nests unseen?
Surely there is something wrong,
When kindly ghosts who lived there long,
Ghosts with names that are well known,
Now have no place to roam, have no home

We know to whom Mama is referring when she 'talks' of a dark haired queen and a sailor, while the artist is Peter Paul Hupner, who was reputed to have lived in the house during the late eighteen and early nineteen hundreds, when he created many beautiful paintings of the area.

The final line of her poem mirrors our own lives as our eviction from Honiton House in Sidmouth led to 'much roaming' that eventually led to the Thames Estuary, that gave us the pleasure of, once again 'Being Beside the Seaside.'

Impossible People

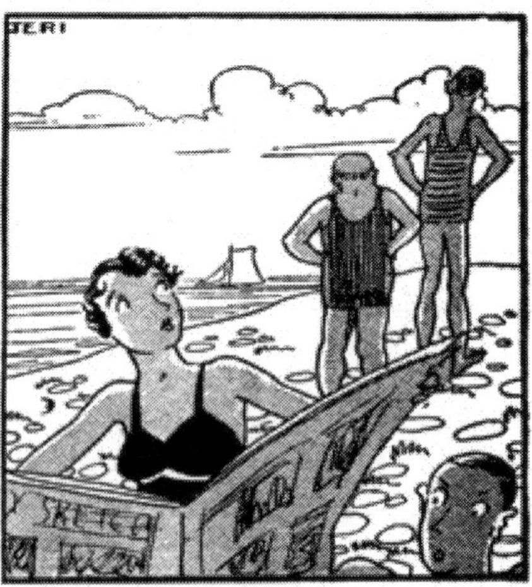

The girl who thought a comic strip was something you see at the seaside.

It also allowed us to pester our Grandfather Paul for tales of -

DARING DEEDS AND DISASTERS

The girl in JERI's previous cartoon and meanwhile's Beryl would no doubt be thought of as 'Posh'. When teased at the numerous schools we attended, the jibes levelled at us always included the rebuke(?) that we were 'Posh'.

This assumption must have had a great deal more to do with our manners and manner of speech than our attire, the latter often being quite threadbare and occasionally a little comical.

In an article in a national newspaper a correspondent wrote that the acronym 'POSH' was not used prior to 1915. But while this next anecdote may only be 'word of mouth', the mouth did belong to someone who had indisputable knowledge of when this word (that can either be taken as an insult or accepted as a compliment), was first used, or implied –

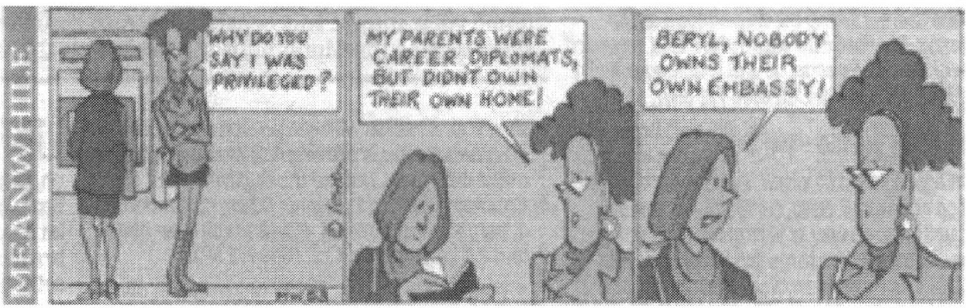

Everyone now knows what the word Posh means, but when young, although we were often referred to as such, we had no idea what it meant. until our Grandfather Paul, told us that on his frequent sailings to and from India only his wealthy passengers could afford the higher cost of the, much cooler and thus more comfortable, cabins that were on the Port side on the outward journey and on the Starboard side on the homeward journey.

He said; *"For ease of allocation, passengers of these more costly cabins were noted on the Purser's lists as: 'Port Out Starboard Home'."* Which, later, was notated as P.O.S.H. Proof that this acronym was used before the 1915 date given in the article.

Two of our Grandfather's seafaring adventures resulted in his deep dislike of both bananas and treacle. The first was due to being becalmed for many weeks in the Azores which led to he and his crew having to exist on their cargo of unripe bananas, augmented by their basic diet of 'weevil' biscuits. So called because if the biscuits were tapped on a table lots of long snouted weevil beetles fell out. *"Which at least gave us some protein!"* said Grandpapa.

The second was due to a Lascar falling into an open hold that held a cargo of molasses. Unable to find his body in the dense, sticky liquid it was decided to wait until they were back in England where, following hours of dredging for his body, all they found were the man's nails, teeth and metal shoe tags.

Despite which the cargo was deemed 'Fit For Human Consumption'. *"But not my consumption!"* said Grandpapa.

Having, for many years, refused both bananas and treacle, on his retirement he also refused a title. He said that if he became a 'Sir' he would be charged more for goods and services. To all his wife's persuasions he would reply with his, oft repeated; *"It's All Bunk."*

Staying with bunks and boats, (which tend to go with one another), when living in Sidmouth we were the proud owners of Rory, a smart sixteen foot clinker dinghy in which we enjoyed many nautical adventures and escapades.

Adventures and escapades that today's children would die for and their parents would die from!

When we left Sidmouth we had no option but to leave Rory, deserted and lonely, on The Ham. A sorely missed boat for which our mother wrote this poem:

The Song of Rory.
For Stefan and Boris

Three quarters of the world is water,
So why should it bother me,
What goes on in the fourth quarter,
Which has nothing to do with the sea?

The moon is a great golden earring,
The wake is like honey for tea,
The seventh long wave is uprearing,
No land is as good as the sea.

The waves make a music like thunder,
The whole wide horizon is free,
I will not dance there again in awed wonder,
No land is as wild as the sea.

I am laid on The Ham's green grasses,

That grow on the shore and the lea,
All I hear is the seagull that passes.
I shall sail no more on the sea.

When my tarred old timbers are burning,
With a hiss like a bow-wave at sea,
Think of the tides that keep turning,
And say a short prayer for me.

When, years later, I came across this next poem, Mama told me she had written it following our eviction. Having no husband, no home, no income and six children to support she could be forgiven for having the odd suicidal thought.

The Ghoul Despair

Once only did I meet the ghoul 'Despair',
On a cliff top where the gulls were screaming free.
Light and colour held him by Medusa's tangled hair,
And tossed him in the peacock-feathered sea.
I pray that if I meet the fiend once more,
It will not be beside a darkened shore.

Fortunately she was made of sterner stuff, but tragically three other 'victims' of the solicitor who evicted us were not so able. After we left Sidmouth our mother learned that he had caused the deaths of an elderly couple who, in a similar eviction to our own, and with nowhere to go, spent the next few nights in the open on Salcombe Hill where, as it was mid winter, they died of hypothermia.

He also accused a junior member of his staff of stealing the petty cash and in her terror at what might befall her, had drunk disinfectant and died a truly terrible death.

A frightful tale told to our mother by one of the Cottage Hospital nurses with whom Mama had stayed in contact and who had, later, also cared for this young lady.

On learning of these tragedies our mother had printed this, edited, tract from the Bible. "Thou shalt not persecute the fatherless, the widowed, the young, the old or the ailing." and each week she would send a copy to the solicitor.

This man whose wife, unsurprisingly, had left him many years earlier, had one son, a handsome young man who excelled in both academia and athletics and who, so we learnt, was the only thing, apart from money, that his father valued.

In June 1954 I was invited by Mama's friend, Mrs. Davies, to spend the summer with she and her daughter, Helen. So a few weeks prior to my sixteenth birthday, in equal amounts of trepidation and pleasure, I went back to Sidmouth.

Sidmouth beach is mostly formed of shingle and has a large man made jetty that was, (and, if the Health & Safety zealots haven't put a stop to it), possibly still is popular with young men, who would gather there each day to try and outsmart each other with their diving prowess.

The day following my arrival, Helen and I went to this jetty where, with a number of other boys showing off their skills, was the son of this solicitor.

He could not possibly have known who I was, or of his father's despicable actions that had so disrupted my life, but with two young girls as an audience, in a great show of manly bravado he made a dive that, short of his intention, landed him on a rocky outlet that landed him in hospital.

Just before I was due to return to Essex, we learned this antic had caused him extreme physical injury and severe brain damage.

To this day I am not sure that God would have wished such unkind retribution on this boy's evil father but, as is so often said; "He tends to work in mysterious ways his mysteries to perform."

On my return, I told my mother of this boy's terrible accident and she said never again would she steer her ire, however justified, where it might be misdirected.

Another of Mama's friends, whom she met when they were students at the Regent Street Polytechnic School of Art, was Beryl Irving (known to us as 'Newie'), whose son is the Holocaust Denier, David Irving. Newie lived just a few miles from us in Brentwood, which allowed she and our mother to re-awaken their friendship.

This meant that we would play with David, or more correctly, being a little older, he would bully us while we, having the strength of greater numbers, would ignore him. Maybe it was our indifference to him coupled with our father's ethnicity that, later, propelled him on the journey that eventually led to his distasteful notoriety and even more distasteful beliefs.

So, towards a more tasteful notoriety, and with ineffable thanks to their creators, here is a collection of anecdotal, amusing, factual, interesting, noteworthy, original, serious, sad and ridiculous bits and pieces, together with some poems, a few limericks, quotes, and jokes, Piet Hein Grooks, and many wise, witty and wacky pearls of wisdom. Much of which can be found via the internet and a lot that cannot.

All of which are enhanced by the inclusion of amusing or interesting items from the Daily Mail, and their daily cartoons of Chloe & Co, Up & Running, The Odd Streak, Meanwhile and Garfield, complimented by -

WORDS AND THEIR WONDERS

Both real and created, with lots of words and a few excursions, diversions and dramas along the way.

ENGLISH AS SHE IS SPOKE AND SPELT

For which Piet Hein may have composed his next extremely clever Grook:

A Grasshopper sat on a flagstone and wept,
with a sorrow that few surpass.
He had painfully mastered his letters and leapt,
to a place where he knew an inscription was kept;
and of course it said: KEEP OFF THE GRASS.

Many of Piet Hein's Grooks (or Grewks), are included in my text. He is a man with exceptional talents in many fields, and is esteemed by his fellow Danes as highly as they prize their Little Mermaid.

During my fragmented schooling I attended, two nursery schools, three primaries, three private schools, two Grammar schools and two Secondary Moderns. Some for just a few months or even weeks and one for just one day.

In my final term of my final year at my final school, my final classmates and I were asked to write a short description of the word we believed was the most important. Now a a teenagers choice might be Money, Fame, Football or even, Sex, but then we lived in a more innocent age and some clever choices by my peers were God, Peace, Wisdom and Love.

Mine was 'Words', the inspiration for which came from my mother who taught me the wonders of both their permanence and impermanence. These words on words earned me one of the few awards I won from any of the twelve schools I attended.

WORDS

Words are the most transient yet the most enduring things in the world. Without words our world would only have sounds, such as the whisper of the wind, the wash of the waves, the song of a bird, the bark of a dog or the clang of a gate. Words all sound different in different languages, dialects, inflections and tongues, but have the same meanings and, often, misunderstandings.

Words bring us into the world and take us out of it. Words can start wars, can bring peace, can placate. They bind us together in a way that even love cannot do. They bring calm, joy, ecstasy, dread, panic, fear and hate.

Words bring us tidings and news, opinions and views. Can incriminate, can exonerate, can be wicked, can be wise. Words give us poetry and prose, limericks and lyrics that rhyme. They help us through the hard times and take the happy ones to highs.

Words, well chosen, give us the gift of laughter and the art of learning. They bring us history and mystery, can urge us to action, can make us cry. Words when spoken, sung, read, or written are free, yet can bring great riches. And some of the best are Voltaire's; *"I may not agree with what you say but will defend to the death your right to say it."*

The Voltaire quotation is often, and variously, misquoted. What he is purported to have said to Helvetius was, *"Think for yourself and let others enjoy the privilege to do the same."* He is also purported to have said to her; *"I detest what you write, but I would give my life to make it possible for you to continue to write."* I know how she must have felt.

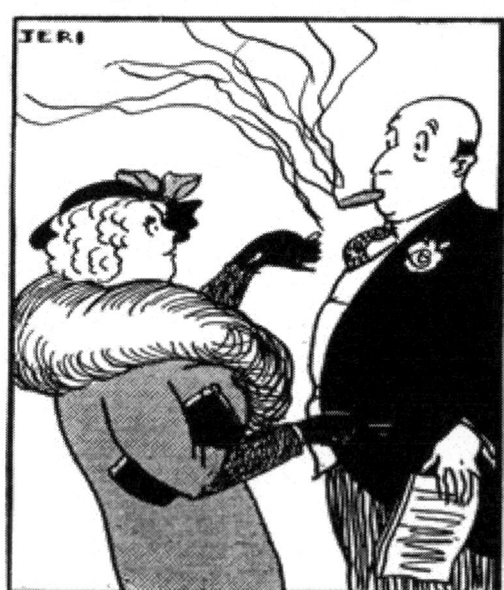

The actress who said tragedy was not her forte; forty was her tragedy.

Words undoubtedly brought great riches to Anna Massey, who said, *"I don't want any dramas in my life; if I'm in a drama I want to be paid for it!"* As, perhaps, did JERI's next Impossible Person.

The first proper, in both senses of the word, school my siblings and I attended was a private academy in Exeter called Edgerton School.

At its helm were two spinsters, the Misses Rylance, who, with a firm hand and equally firm rod, taught Grammar, Punctuation, and Spelling as if they were the Holy Trinity. A torture for which I have been eternally grateful.

They metamorphosed the Three R's into: "Reliability, Responsibility and Respect" to which they added a fourth: "Rewards Have To Be Earned."

It is possible that few teachers know the origination of the Three 'R's, that is now attributed to Sir William Curtis (1752-1829), who made a speech at a Board of Education dinner on 'reading, 'riting and 'rithmatic'. A son of an East London biscuit manufacturer, he eventually became a Member of Parliament for The City of London and, in 1970, an Alderman.

From 1795 to 1796 he was Lord Mayor of the City and, despite being considered ill-educated and a 'pitiably bad speaker', was elevated to the aristocracy via the award of a Baronetcy on the order of his friend, King George V.

In order to keep order, (of a lesser sort), the Misses Rylance relied on a third mantra - The Three C's; Courtesy, Consideration and Common Sense. The first required all pupils to stand when a teacher entered a classroom and for girls to bob a curtsy when addressing one.

If still teaching today they would undoubtedly agree with the suggestion made in a a letter from David Hancock that was published by the Daily Mail, that educators should re-instigate the three 'D's' - Discipline, Deterrent and Detention.

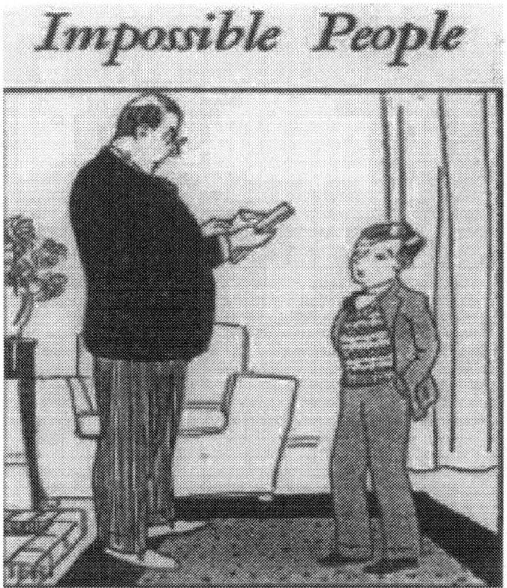

A current view is that parents should leave the learning of the three R's to teachers, but as children are eager to learn at an earlier age than when they start school and the format of the alphabet and numbers are written in stone it is difficult to understand why it is now thought harmful to teach children these basics prior to them starting formal education.

One has to assume that while many parents feel they don't have time, and many more don't care or can't, it can now be safely left to technology to teach young children the three R's. Which, it would seem, has now

Impossible People

The boy who said "The sap always rises" when rebuked for being the dunce of the class.

metamorphosed into: Rough, Rowdy and Rude. To which could be added Rapscallion!

Adhering to the principles of the Misses Rylance, I taught my children to read and count prior to starting school. The counting was not difficult as, when taking them to bed, we would count each step as we walked upstairs. They got so used to this that, when shopping in large stores, they would also count the steps of the shops staircase.

They were tiny when I initiated this habit so it was very amusing to see people's faces when, in public places, we could be heard chanting the numbers of steps as we went up a staircase. Strangely we never counted them when coming down.

My daughter, Alisonjane, being dyslexic, found it very difficult to learn to read but my son, Michael, could read prior to starting school – as could I.

Even so my few months, or often merely weeks, at the many schools I attended did not allow for much education - nor much memory of it. Thus I recall little of Edgerton School apart from my excellent grounding in the art of English, the strict discipline (which, to their early dislike and later benefit, I instilled in my own children), hitching precarious, clandestine trips in the creaking dumb waiter and being frequently caned for my frequent misdemeanours. And, as she didn't like that sort of thing, being caned again for Sonya's. (Caning being the one 'discipline' I eschewed in the bringing up of my own children.)

Being caned for Sonya was not difficult as I would go into the room of the senior Miss Rylance, would be caned and then sent outside to; "Send in the other one." I would go out and then go in again and be caned again because, as they couldn't tell us apart, they did not know which was which, (or who was who), unless they set us a spelling test.

Although being caned twice was fairly fair as I was the chief mischief-maker, after, that is, our brother Boris who would threaten to cut off the ears off any child who teased us. Not the best way to endear oneself to one's peers, but it worked a treat!

Then, any child who complained to their parents that they had been threatened with having their ears cut off would have had their ears clipped for telling lies.

Not only were the Misses Rylance strict disciplinarians, they treated the 'The Nine Parts of Speech' in the same way that most people revere the Bible. Composed in 1886 by John Neale of the Religious Tract Society, it is, in my opinion, regrettable that it is not now still included in the English lessons of primary school children.

The Nine Parts of Speech

Three little words we often see,
Are an ARTICLE - a and an and the,
A NOUN's the name of anything,
Such as school or garden, spade or string.

ADJECTIVES describe the kind of noun
Great, small, pretty, white or brown.
Instead of nouns the PRONOUNS stand,
Her head, his face, my arm, your hand.

VERBS tell of something being done,
Read, write, count, sing, jump or run.
How things are done the ADVERBS tell,
Such as slowly or quickly, ill or well.

PREPOSITIONS stand before a noun,
As in, or through a door, or up to town.
CONJUNCTIONS join the nouns together,
Woman and child, or wind and weather.

The INTERJECTION shows surprise,
As in Oh! How pretty! or Ah! How wise!
The whole are called the 'Nine Parts of Speech'
Which reading and writing and speaking teach.

A neat, instructive verse that led me to question why 'read', 'speak' and 'teach are spelt with 'ea' and 'speech' has two 'e's'? A word that, while it has two meanings, is not also spelt as 'speach'.

Which takes us to the highly acclaimed film: The King's Speech'. As the title could not be replicated in another language, only those viewers whose first language is English, or who know it well, will appreciate the double entendre of the word as used in the title of this film.

Another mantra of the Misses Rylance was the: 'I before E except after C' rule. Thus making words such as, feign, deign veil and vein the bane of my life. Also, height, neighbor, neigh, neither, heir, heiress, heirloom, heist, heinous, weir and the strange word, heinie that means bottom - of a person not a thing. Whilst weirdest of all are the words weirder and weird.

Recently I read that this rule is now considered to be outdated and unnecessary. But those who propound this theory miss the point that this is what makes the English language so interesting and the teaching of these 'finer points' can lead to a fascination for this wonderful and quixotic language.

One of the strangest is why the written word is referred to as; 'It said' not; 'It read'. Less strange but more certain is that children learn more quickly when taught things in verse - but even adults might have trouble reciting the ABC after reading Spike Milligan's version. Strangely, although they make a tiny rhyme on their own, he doesn't include the letters, M,N,P,Q,R,S,T. Perhaps he just ran out of rhymes – or time.

The ABC (or Alphabet)

Twas midnight in the schoolroom and every desk was shut,
When suddenly from the alphabet was heard a loud 'Tut Tut'.
Said A to B; 'I don't like C'. His manners are too lack,
For all I ever see of C is a semicircular back.

'I disagree' said D to A and B, 'I've never found C so,
From where I stand he seems to be an uncompleted O'.
C was vexed, 'I'm much perplexed, You criticize my shape.
I'm made like that to help me spell Cat, Cow and Cool and Cape.'

'He's right' said E. Said F 'Whoopee'. Said G 'Ip 'ip 'ooray!';
'You're dropping me,' roared H to G. 'Don't do it please I pray.'
'Out of my way.' said L to K, 'I'll make poor I look ILL.'
To stop this stunt, J stood in front, and presto! ILL was JILL.

'U know', said V, 'that W is twice the age of me,
For as a Roman V is five, I'm half as young as he.'
X and Y yawned sleepily, 'Look at the time.' they said.
So they all jumped in to beddy byes, and the last one in was Z!

But they would have no trouble with this oft recited verse;

The Days of the Week

Monday's child is fair of face,
Tuesday's child is full of grace,
Wednesday's child is loving and giving,
Thursday's child has far to go,
Friday's child is full of woe,
Saturday's child works hard for their living,
But the child that is born on the Sabbath day
is bonny and blithe and good and gay.

Born on a Sunday, both my sister Sasha and daughter Alisonjane match their day in every way. My sister Nicola, a Wednesday's child, puts no rations on her loving and giving while my son Michael, a Saturday's child, has worked hard in his highly remunerative living.

My handsome husband was born on a Monday and Sonya and I, who were born on a Thursday, have, as Interior Designers,'gone far' when working with clients in America, England, Ireland, France, Scotland, Spain and Tenerife.

While my early working life as a trouble-shooter for my brother, Stefan and then as the Administrative Assistant to the Executive Secretary of The International Confederation of Midwives - sent me to the four corners of the globe – in all weathers.

The Months of the Year
George Ellis (1745 to 1815)

Snowy; Flowy; Blowy;
Showery; Flowery; Bowery;
Hoppy; Croppy; Droppy;
Breezy; Sneezy; Freezy.

Although we can be fairly confident that Mr. Ellis didn't mean that people should jumping into go rivers - however flowing, or fast.

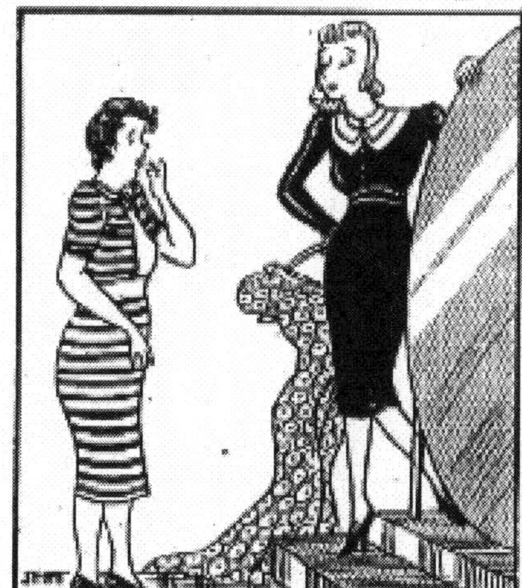

The salesgirl who said, "Why not jump in the river?" when her customer said she thought she would look nice in something flowing

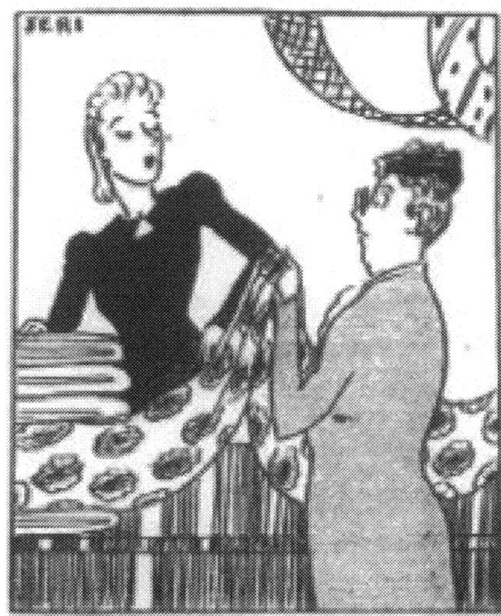

The sales girl who said it depended on the style madam used for her frock when the customer asked if this colour was fast.

Or cheap -

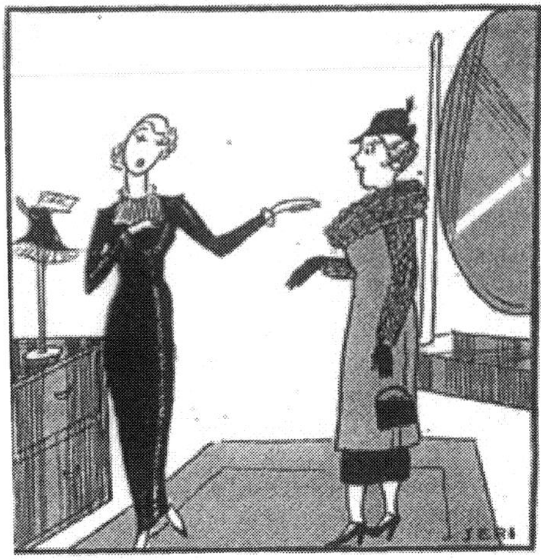

The saleswoman who said the mirror is over there when her customer asked if she could see something cheap in a felt hat.

Or even cheaper -

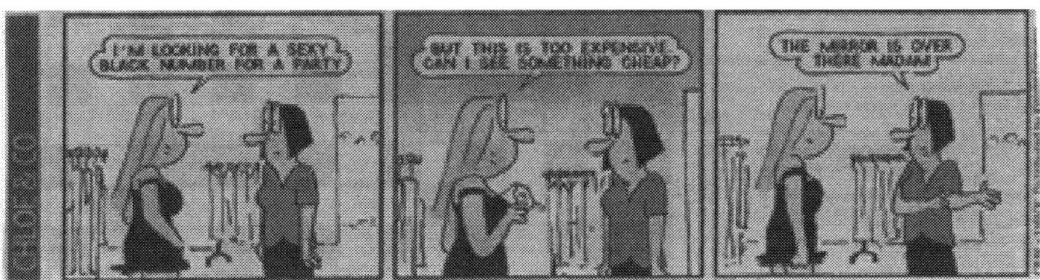

Or deep -

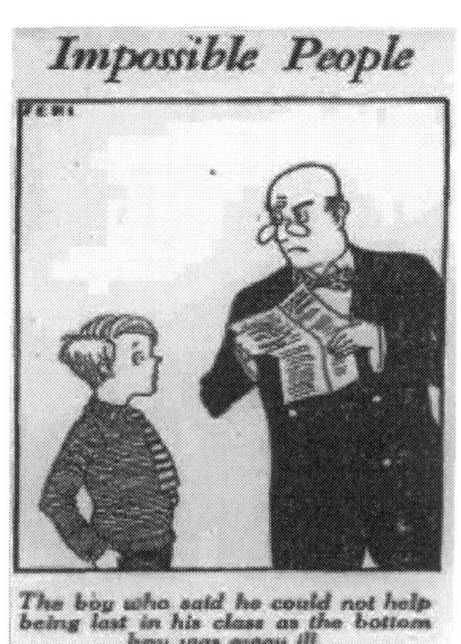

The boy who said he could not help being last in his class as the bottom boy was away ill.

Although I'm given to understand that schools now no longer have 'top and bottom' pupils, only 'middle of the road' ones, and, in place of 'marks', 'commendations' are given out like confetti.

The Misses Rylance would have had little patience with this 'one size fits all' method of awards. You worked hard and obtained high marks or were 'kept in' for longer hours of tuition.

They also taught their pupils to learn things by rote. Far less painful than it sounds.

They had a litany of these, such as; *"In sixteen hundred and forty two Columbus sailed the ocean blue."* And this intrepid explorers trio of ships, *"The Pinta, The Nina and The Santa Maria."* All invaluable in later life for crosswords.

'NEVER split an infinitive' was another 'golden rule' of the Misses Rylance. A rule, that as can be seen from my text, I was never able to master, which made me an Impossible Child, and, in later life, an 'Impossible Secretary'.

Not dissimilar from JERI's next secretary whose knowledge of English, or lack of it - is a neat lead into -

THE QUEEN'S ENGLISH

The National Schools Curriculum has now brought the teaching of The Queen's English to the point where students may now think a split infinitive is 'the crack of doom'.

Even radio and television presenters seem to be in a perpetual contest to see who can split the most - that is if they know of the term at all!

Even some educators appear to find it impossible to master the intricacies of this beautiful language. Although, as Piet Hein says in his next Grook:

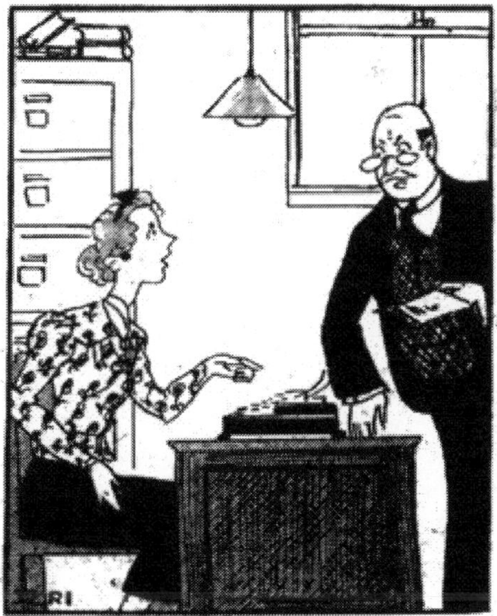

The girl who thought split infinitive meant the crack of doom.

Wanting To Be Able To

Impossibilities 'are good
not to attach that label to;
since, correctly understood,
if we wanted to, we would
be able to be able to.

The following neat rhyme would be another useful addendum to the National Schools Curriculum. Sadly, I have been unable to unearth its source.

Kings & Queens

William, William, Harry, Steve, then Harry,
Richard, John then Harry three
One two three Edwards, then Richard two,
Henry four, five six then who?

Edwards, four and five, Dick the Bad,
Harries twain, and Ned the Lad,
Mary, Bess, then James the vain,
Charles one, two, then James again.

William and Mary, Anna Gloria,
Four Georges, William the 4th, then Victoria,
Edward the seventh and George the fifth,
Edward the eighth, and George the sixth,

And now we have Elizabeth.
And for the future we will have Elizabeth's son,
Charles the III who wishes to be George the Seventh,
Then William the V, with his beautiful wife, Catherine.

And now we have their son George, their number one.
Let's hope the Monarchy's not yet done.

But where is Lady Jane Grey, Queen for nine days until she 'lost her head' in 1555. Or any of Scotland's greats, such as my forebear, Robert The Bruce, about whom James Murden wrote a poem that can be found in his very amusing, equally informative and highly acclaimed anthology; '100 Great Brits – A rhyming history from Bede to Beckham'.

A book from where I have 'stolen' the first and last verses of his poem about an even greater, legendary Briton.

King Arthur c500.
(Reborn C.1138 and Still Going Strong.)

Did Arthur and his Knights exist,
as vested interests insist?
With stone-snatched sword in mailed fist.
did he valiantly resist
that Anglo Saxon lot?
Did Guinevere become his Queen?
Did Gallants joust upon the green,
presenting a resplendent scene - at courtly Camelot.

Le Morte d'Arthur, his famous fable,
Extols the roundness of The Table -
a knightly accolade or label
bestowed upon the supremely able,
(an entertaining lot).
They even set off on the trail
to find the cup, or Holy Grail;
It is an entertaining tale - but history it's not.

Royalty, whether factual or fictional, wave us regally to;

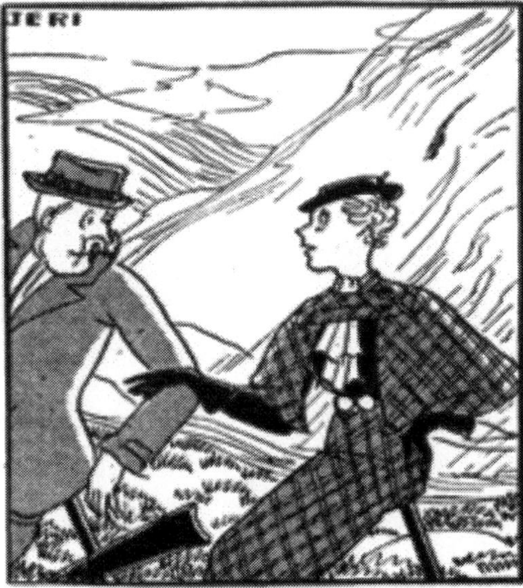

The girl who thought August the Twelfth was one of those Ruritanian kings.

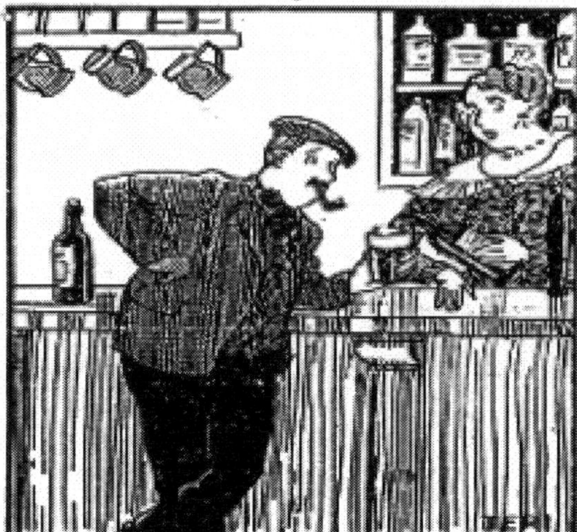

The Communist who said he was having his pint at The King's Head instead of The Red Bull during the Jubilee celebrations.

JUBILANT JUBILEES AND ROYAL EVENTS *(both happy and sad)*

Now that the beheading of kings and queens, even Ruritanian ones, has become less popular, our Royals can sleep more soundly. But not our public houses, which are losing their battle for life at an alarming rate, most notably The Queen's Head and The King's Head –

One of which was the very splendid British Pub, The King's Head on the Champs Elysees in Paris where, in my early thirties, I spent many 'Happy Hours'.

Many years later, the period of my tenure as Landlady of the King's Head Public House in West London, happily coincided with the wedding day of Prince Charles and Princess Diana, which led to a small, very pleasurable, unusual event.

On the evening of the big day, with London at its most jubilant, my pub was packed with happy punters when, on taking a call of nature, I also took a telephone call.

The caller said he was a New Zealand radio presenter and that I was 'live on air'. He then told me that the production unit of his radio station, eager for their listeners to get a feel for the celebrations going on in Britain, had decided to make a call to a pub and mine had been chosen at random from a directory of London Public Houses.

Although it was likely that the words 'King's Head' had led to their choice being not entirely 'random.'

Thinking it was a practical joke I was about to put the phone down when occurred to me that it would not matter if someone had a joke at my expense, but it would matter if I rudely disconnected a genuine call. So, eulogising about the extraordinary atmosphere that had permeated the day and was now pervading the evening, I 'took my presenter' into my bar so that his listeners could experience this.

I said that whilst the same jubilation was most certainly being replicated in every public house in the country, they had chosen well as mine, being one of the larger London pubs, allowed for much louder merriment for his New Zealand listeners to listen to.

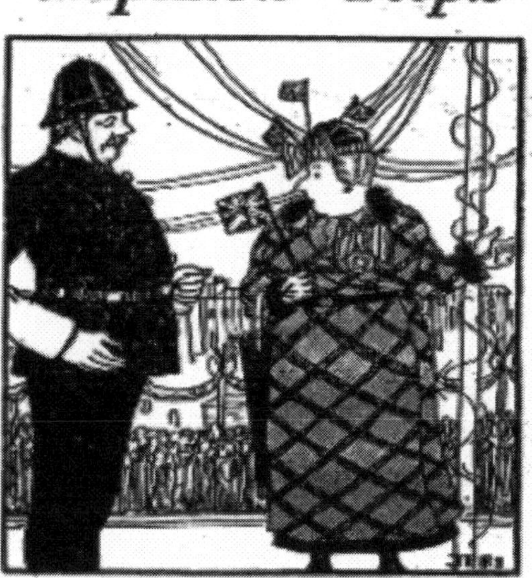

Prior to finishing the call I was able to establish my caller was genuine and was, thus thankful I had accepted it as such. I also felt privileged that it was my public house that had been chosen (if only by chance), to relay (if only by telephone), the wonderful atmosphere of this joy filled day to some of our Antipodean cousins.

But perhaps it was just as well they could only hear us and not see us -

In another strange coincidence Sonya and I had driven through the D'Alma underpass in Paris earlier in the day of the evening of Diana and Dodi's ghastly accident there and, whatever the facts, we can be confident there is no one who would not have wished for Diana to live long enough to enjoy a few Jubilee years.

Particularly as she would have been a participant rather than, as in JERI's cartoon, just a visitor – however decorative.

In yet another equally odd coincidence, some time prior to Princess Diana's tragic, untimely death, I had made an appointment with a Harley Street consultant to record an item that was to feature in a future edition of the Judy Finnigan and Richard Madeley programme, 'Good Morning' on which Sonya and I were due to appear. A date that coincided with the day of Princess Diana's funeral.

My visit to London that day was as extraordinary as had been my call from New Zealand, both of which involved the Princess of Wales. For while the first, that of her wedding to Prince Charles, was filled with crowds of jubilant people, the second, that of her funeral, was a day almost devoid of people in an area where there would normally be many hundreds.

Arriving early in Harley Street, the lack of activity did not appear unusual but when, just after midday, I left my meeting, I was stunned to find myself in virtually deserted streets.

Walking from Harley Street to Portland Place was possibly the most odd experience I will ever encounter for, on streets I know well that constantly teem with activity, I could count the moving vehicles on the fingers of one hand and the pedestrians on the fingers of the other.

There was no sign of the media as they were all elsewhere, recording Diana's funeral, but had just one newscaster filmed that part of London at that time, on that day, it would have been a dramatic demonstration and fitting 'memorial' of the public's love for her.

And while it is not something I would wish to be flippant about, when it comes to 'seeing' people across streets,' on that particular day in the heart of one of London's busiest, most bustling areas, anyone could have seen anyone across any of its deserted streets, but, in that part of London on that particular day there was virtually no one to see except me.

Not even the odd (in both senses of the word) busker –

Impossible People

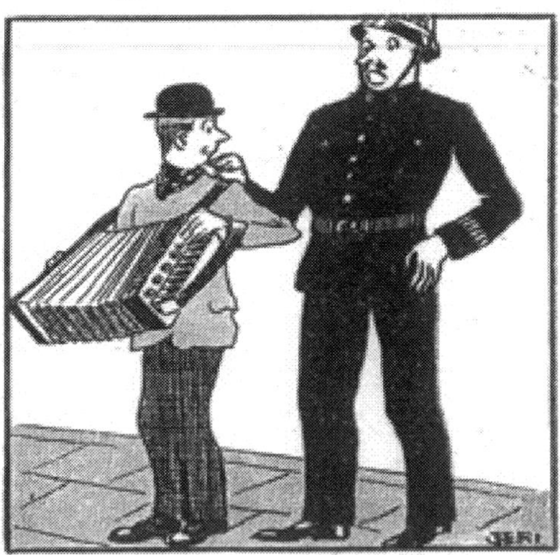

The street musician who asked what he was going to sing when the policeman said he would have to accompany him.

In contrast, the 2011 wedding of Prince William and Katherine, filled London with a multitude of exuberant and joyous people. An exuberance wonderfully illustrated in this lively ditty by Gil Beeton, that was published in the Daily Mail's Peterborough Column, and, with her permission, her Jubilant Verger is now also an Impossible one.

The Jubilant Verger

The wedding was completed
With pomp and circumstance;
The Abbey, undefeated
By undue happenstance.
From the bottom of their hearts,
The Abbey Choir had sung;
The Clergy too had played their part,
The tower bells had rung.
Two thousand people in and out
The verger had to smile,
And then he gave a happy shout -
And cartwheeled down the aisle.

It was one of the most perfect regal occasions and the public's pleasure had much to do with the fact that, Katherine, Duchess of Cambridge, who will one day be our Queen, was not a Royal. But what she brought to the day was inestimable joy to her future subjects, and greater strength to the popularity of our monarchy. A monarchy whose present Monarch is, as the author, Robert Hardman, wrote in his book; 'Our Queen' *"The most famous and, most would say, respected public figure on the planet."*

Among all the merriment many spectators stood out from the crowd, two of whom were carrying banners. One announced in large letters, "Check Mate Kate, You Got The King." The other, held high by a very pretty young girl, proclaimed, "Marry Me Harry." Banners that in previous years would have been considered frightfully louche and plebian, but on that day were 'just right'.

What was equally 'just right' was the expression of goodwill at the birth of their son, George. An occasion that became, for our own family, a personal, very public, media event that requires another short detour.

Our cousin Vivien has two delightful daughters, Jenny and Julie, both of whom, with their families, now live in New York. As does their mother with her second husband, Dr. Richard Tannen, an esteemed Bursary Medical Researcher and Nobel Prize candidate.

In 2003, we four sisters with my daughter Alisonjane, enjoyed the very glamorous, romantic Central Park wedding of Jenny to her charming fiance, Greg who have now given us two handsome, extremely clever great nephews, Matthew and Harrison and an adorable, great niece, Charlotte.

In July 2012 we were guests at the equally romantic wedding of her sister, Julie and her charming, fiancé Jonathan, that was held in the palatial reception rooms of the New York Natural History Museum and who, in 2015, gave us another great-nephew, Benjamin. The Acrostics I composed for their weddings can be found on page 381.

In October 2012 the 'Hurricane Sandy' storm submerged Jenny and Greg's holiday home in four feet of water. So, for their 2013 summer break, they took an apartment in London's Park Lane.

On the evening of the 22nd July, 2013, Jenny and her children were watching the televised coverage of the crowds gathered outside Buckingham Palace in anticipation of the Royal baby's birth

Caught up in the excitement, the children begged their mother to take them down to the Palace, a plea to which, after much persuasion, she agreed. But thinking they would take a quick taxi ride there (and an even quicker one back), she let them stay in their pyjamas.

Their taxi driver dropped them off beside a BBC News crew who were interviewing a Member of Parliament. On seeing the children, the MP suggested to the crew that they include the children in their coverage. Coverage that led to them featuring on the BBC's Running News, an Australian news channel and being featured the The Daily Mail. Which, on seeing the photograph the BBC crew took of them, comes as no surprise.

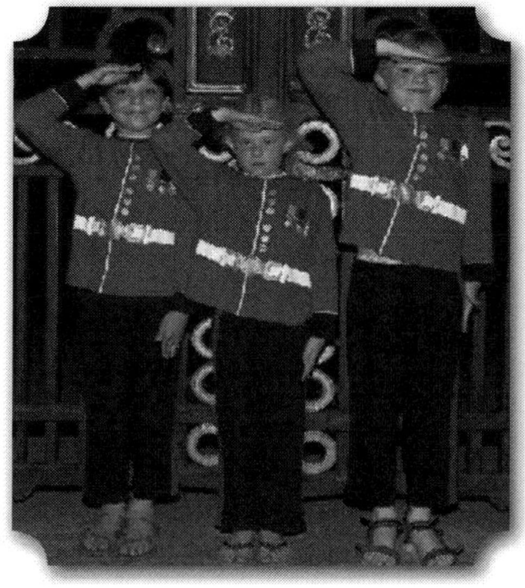

From the DAILY MAIL - 23rd July 2013

Youngsters Harrison, Charlotte and Matthew were among those celebrating at the Palace. They heard the news when getting ready for bed, and rushed down in their pyjamas.

Their renown did not end there. On returning to New York the following day a passenger on the same plane, approached Jenny and said; *"Did you know the photo of your three children is in Hello magazine?"*

We were then astounded to find that the same picture had been published not only in Hello Magazine but also The New York Times and was the lead page of Life Magazine. Discoveries that led to a veritable flurry of these publications winging their way, in both directions, across the Atlantic.

Media interest takes me, yet again, to The Daily Mail, a paper, that much to my pleasure, have deemed a number of my many letters to their Letters Page 'fit for use'. In 2011 I had four published within days of each other. One of which was on primogeniture of the Monarchy.

David Cameron's 'avowed intent' to reform the monarchy so that, regardless of gender, a first born child of a monarch will accede to the throne will have the approval of many of her Majesty's subjects, particularly women.

Without wishing to denigrate any of the meritorious, innovative or valorous deeds of our British Kings (from one of whom, Robert The Bruce, I am directly descended), I have always thought that the three monarchs who have done more for Britain's standing in the world have all been women. Queen Elizabeth the First, Queen Victoria, and our present, worldwide admired, Queen Elizabeth the Second.

And while we have to be thankful that this rule did not apply in the early fifteen hundreds, which would have precluded Elizabeth the First from taking the throne, it indicates that, as far as British Royalty goes, our Queens are better than our Kings, as the reigns of these three royals have, in many different ways, brought to the country greater innovation, stability and status than did the combined reigns of many of our Kings.

At 8.34 a.m. on Saturday the 2nd May 2015, the Duchess of Cambridge gave birth to a daughter who, it was announced a day later, will enjoy the names Charlotte Elizabeth Diana.

A Princess who will not only be, 'Too pretty for words', but, unlike JERI's next Impossible chorus girl, will, in later life, 'have many speaking parts'.

IMPOSSIBLE PEOPLE

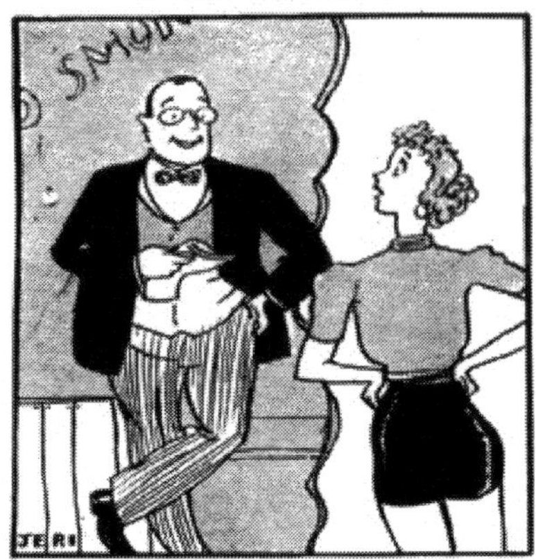

The producer who told the chorus girl he was not giving her a speaking part because she was too pretty for words.

Which wends us back to -

BACK TO WORDS AND THEIR WONDERS

It is fascinating that when JERI composed her previous cartoon, the phrase; "Too pretty for words", was considered a compliment but is now thought of as 'Not Politically Correct.' As, in my view, 'politics' is rarely, if ever, correct, particularly with regard to many 'a word out of place' I will continue to consider my mother's caption a compliment. (Which I can also claim for such a neat alliteration.)

While many children still learn to read from a book and write with a pencil, many more now take their first steps at learning these skills via computerised toys or iPads which has led to the loss of good handwriting.

A loss mourned by many, one of whom is Annette Hennessy of Portishead, who expressed this sentiment in a hand written letter to the Daily Mail. Although Annette would possibly agree that electronic gadgets can give small children an early interest in, and endless opportunities, for creative learning. But not, perhaps, a passion for reading or writing.

Which is tragic for as the thriller writer, Ian Rankin, said; *"I find it miraculous that there are only 26 letters in the alphabet and anyone can sit down and write a sentence that's never been written before."* Or, say I; *"Say a sentence that has never been said before."*

I fell in love with words when, at the age of three, I discovered I could read the large red letters on an advertising hoarding that read, "CRAVEN A". At that time a popular brand of cigarette. Our mother smoked Players and I found I could read that word too.

Perhaps my ability to read these words at such an early age negated any leanings I may have had as a teenager to smoke - which, despite much persuasion from my peers, I managed to avoid.

During the war new toys were a rarity and our birthday and Christmas gifts were last year's dolls dressed in 'new' home-made' outfits, or books, mostly second hand, and I can still recall my delight when, at five, I was given my first 'proper' book: 'Tangletrees' by Lillie la Pla.

It is still among my most treasured books, as are two others that first awoke my passion for poetry; A.A. Milne's: ‘When We Were Very Young’ and ‘Now We Are Six’. My second, which sadly disappeared in the mists of time, was an anthology of twenty six A to Z poems of place names which included the small town near Exeter in Devon that has the very large name of Zeal Monochorum. Although spelt in my book as one word.

To my even greater delight my third was a dictionary. But not able to decipher the book’s guidance on how to pronounce them, words such as ‘catastrophe’, ‘hyperbole’ and ‘parabola’ became ‘cat-as-troff’, ‘hyper-bole’ and ‘para-bowler’.

So when, later, I heard them vocalised correctly, I did not connect them to my own adaptations. Then on learning that understanding the roots of words enables understanding of their correct pronunciation, I became a little more adept. But even now not fully as, despite my much improved articulation and enunciation, there are still many words I mispronounce.

A failing that worried me until I read this next poem that, some may think, is more about persecution than pronunciation.

Personnel at the headquarters of the North Atlantic Treaty Organization near Paris found English to be an easy language - until they tried to pronounce it. So, in order to help them discard an array of accents, this lengthy poem was devised.

Following an attempt to read it, a Frenchman said he would prefer six months hard labour to reading six lines aloud. Michael Peter, who sent it to me, wrote, “As it was an ‘Organisational Enterprise’ it was, no doubt, devised by a number of creative minds rather than just one.” Having read it, I was sure he was right and thus felt at liberty to add a few lines of my own at the end.

But some time before these were written, someone with an equally creative mind, that of Gray Jolliffe, devised the cartoon that sits so aptly with them.

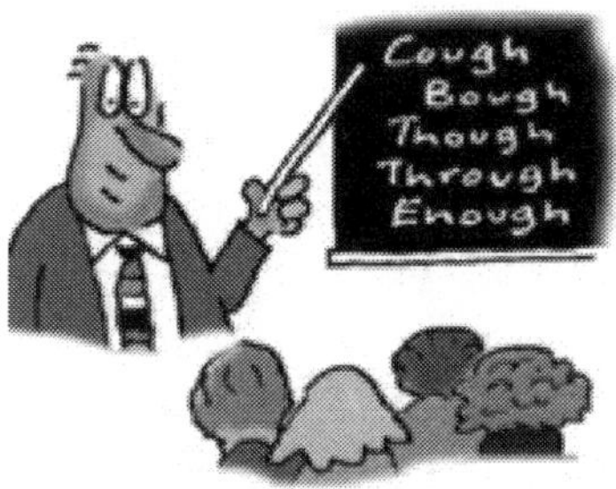

He taught English

English is Tough Stuff

Dearest creature in creation, study the English pronunciation.
I will teach you in my verse sounds like corpse, corps, horse and worse.
I will keep you Susie, busy, make your head with heat grow dizzy.
A tear in your eye, your dress will tear, so shall I, oh hear my prayer!
Just compare heart, beard and heard, dies and diet, lord and word,
Sword and sward, retain and Britain, (Mind the latter how it's written).

Now I surely will not plague you with such words as plague and ague.
But be careful how you speak: Say break and steak, but bleak and streak.
Cloven, oven, how and low, script, receipt, show, poem and toe.
Hear me say - devoid of trickery, daughter, laughter, and Terpsichore,
Typhoid, measles, topsails, aisles, exiles, similes and reviles.
Scholar, vicar, war and far, one, anemone, Balmoral,

Kitchen Lichen, laundry, laurel, Gertrude, German, wind and mind,
Scene, Melpomene, mankind, billet does not rhyme with ballet,
Bouquet, wallet, mallet, chalet. Blood and flood are not like food.
Nor is mould like should and would, viscous, viscount, load and broad.
Toward, to forward, to reward. And your pronunciation's A.O.K. when
You correctly say 'croquet', 'rounded', 'wounded', 'grieve' and 'sieve',

Friend and fiend, alive and live. Ivy, privy. Famous, clamour
And enamour, rhyme with hammer. River, rival, tomb, bomb and comb,
Doll and roll and some and home. Stranger does not rhyme with anger,
Neither does devour with clangour. Souls but foul; Haunt but aunt.
Font, front, won't, ant, grand and grant; Shoes, goes, does. Now say finger,
Then singer, ginger and then linger; mauve, gauze, gouge and gauge;

Marriage, foliage, mirage and age. Query does not rhyme with very,
Nor does fury sound like bury. Host, lost, post and doth, cloth, loth;
Job, knob, bosom, transom, oath. Though the difference seems so little,
Refer does not rhyme with deafer, feoffer does and zephyr and heifer.
We say actual but then say victual, mint, pint, senate and sedate;
Dull, bull and George ate late. Scenic, Arabic, Pacific.

Science, conscience, scientific; liberty, library, heave and heaven;
Rachel, ache, moustache, eleven. Why say hallowed but allowed;
People, leopard, towed but vowed. Mark the differences, moreover,
Between mover, cover, clover; leeches, breeches, wise, precise
Chalice - but police and lice; camel, constable, unstable;
Principle, disciple, label, petal, panel and canal.

Wait, surprise, plait, promise, pal; Worm and storm, chaise, chaos, chair,
Senator, spectator, mayor; tour - but our and succour, four.
Gas, alas, and Arkansas; sea, idea, Korea, area,
Psalm, Maria, but malaria; Youth, south, southern, cleanse and clean.
Doctrine, turpentine, so why marine? Compare alien with Italian,
Dandelion with battalion; Sally with ally, yea with ye,

Eye, I, ay, aye, whey and key. Say aver, but ever or fever.
Neither, leisure, skein, deceiver. Heron, granary, canary,
Crevice and device and eerie. Face but preface, not efface.
Phlegm, phlegmatic, as, glass, bass. Large, but target, gin, give, verging;
Ought, out, joust and scour, scourging. Ear, but earn and wear and tear,
do not rhyme with here but err; but hear rhymes with clear and tear.
and fear and dear but not with swear.

Seven is right, but so is even; Hyphen, roughen, nephew, Stephen.
Monkey, donkey, Turk and jerk; Ask, grasp, wasp and cork and work.
Pronunciation - think of Psyche! Is a paling stout and spiky?
Won't it make you lose your wits, writing groats and saying grits?
It's a dark abyss or tunnel, strewn with stones; towed, solace, gunwale.
Islington and Isle of Wight; Housewife, verdict yet indict.

Finally - which rhymes with enough?
Though, through, plough or dough or cough?
And hiccough has the sound of cup.
So our advice is to just to give it all up

But before we do, I must add a few - such as sew and low - or how.
And used - not in; as it used to be, but in the way it is used now.
And abound, around, cloud, found, hound, loud, proud and wound -
None of which sounds like 'a painful wound'.

And so on and so on, ad infinitum, which, being Latin, is All Greek to me. The next poem, wonderful not only for its skill but its brevity, is by Richard Digance.

Lamp Rhymes with Cramp

Lamp rhymes with cramp,
Tramp rhymes with vamp,
Stamp, camp, damp and ramp,
They're used in rhyme or song.
But it makes you think,
Whoever thought of swamp,
Got it very, very wrong.

And, finally, another three from me;

I never read a red book unless I've read it already.
Are we allowed to speak very loud when we read aloud?
Copyright rightly belongs to writers who write with their right hand.

Then there is the 'TH' sound. A veritable torture for those whose first language is not English as it includes innumerable words, one being teeth, that, uniquely, require the speaker to place their tongue proud of their teeth.

Which leads me to question; "Are the new words 'bruvver, 'bovver' and 'uvver' due to this difficulty?"

As that master of the written word, Richard Littlejohn, so often writes; *"I only ask the question."* Linguistic experts at the British Library aver that Americans have changed the pronunciation of English words to make them their own.

A view confirmed by Highlander Terry Duncan, in a letter to the Daily Mail, who wrote that when he attended the Tain Royal Academy in Inverness (a City whose citizens, my Mama maintained, speak the most 'pure' English), their pronunciation of many words was exactly that now used by Americans – as in: advertizement; monark, garidj, paytriot, skedule and zeebra.

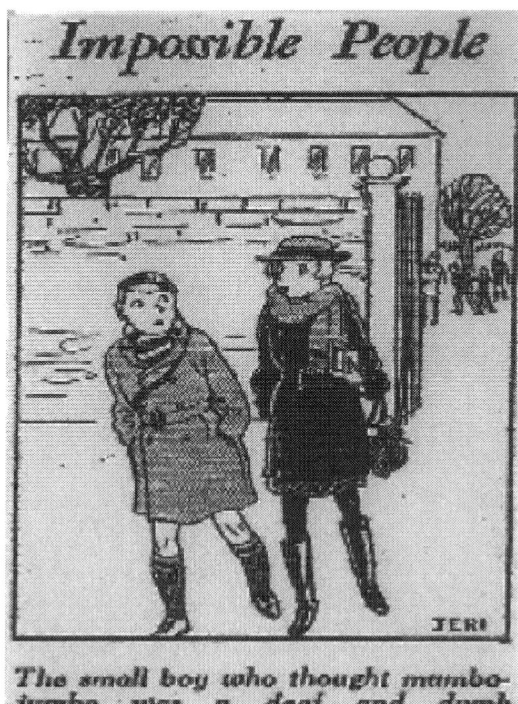

The small boy who thought mumbo-jumbo was a deaf and dumb elephant.

So it would seem that Received English is actually how Americans speak - or is 'American Speak' which, some may think, is Mumbo Jumbo.

Another alteration in the way English is now used is the recent proliferation of words that are juxtaposed. One of which is the word 'less' which applies strictly to 'mass' but is now used for people and things. While this is an irritant to purists and pedants who always use the correct 'few' or 'fewer', should we be critical of those who say 'less people' which, although incorrect, makes sense?

Also the words 'Let' and 'Rent' now seem not to be understood by those who most use them - Estate Agents. Owners 'let' properties, tenants 'rent' them, so it is odd to read, "To Rent' on boards that should display the words "To Let'. But when talking about this with my brother-in-law, George, he told me that To Let is no longer used as graffiti artists have taken to inserting the letter 'I' between the TO and the LET.

Prior to the Second War people were socially categorised by the way they spoke, and those who used correct pronunciation and clarity of speech were thought of as 'upper class', but, as with many things in life, the way we speak changes nearly as frequently as the changes we make in our mode of dress, and those who speak this way are now 'looked down on' as being 'Upper Class' or 'Posh'.

Apart from negotiating the maze of how words should be pronounced and spelt, another pleasing discovery were oxymorons. Those I composed in my youth are now buried deep in the depths of my hippocampus but when I asked Simon if he could think of any, within minutes he had composed eleven:

Accurate estimate; Bitter sweet; Civil war; Dead livestock; Doing nothing; Friendly fire; Hells Angels; House boat; Mutual difference; Never again and Uncrowned King. Within the same time span I could only think of two. 'An impatient patient' and 'Customer helpline.' The latter being a torture that many endure daily.

However, I believe the most amusing is one that can be found when driving through the district of du L'Aube in mid-west France. A sign indicating the villages and locations of this region reads, 'Le Haut Vallee du L'Aube'. Which, for those who don't speak French, is; 'The Top (or high) Valley of the L'Aube'. An oxymoron used frequently by those who live there.

Much in the way that, daily, we use phrases taken from everyday things or people, as in: Bone dry; Brainless; Heartache; Heartless; Heartily agree; Heart sore; Kydney shaped; Legless; Mindful; On your toes;. Put your back into it; Slip of the tongue.

Or birds: Pigeon toed and Bird brained – the last of which has occasionally been applied to me. Or horses; Bit between the teeth; First past the post; Jockey shorts; Jockeying for position; Racing certainty; Reigning in; Strong as a horse; and, At the end of your tether - which, by now, my reader could well be.

So, for those of us who believe the world will not work well without words well worded. Or spelt, pronounced, punctuated or prosed (two neat alliterations), at least we do have seven champions - eight if you include me.

But we do need a few more or very soon correct spelling and pronunciation will be of little relevance, Text Speak will be the norm and the six most used letters of the alphabet, E,N,R,S,T, L, may become the least used, if at all.

To which Sonya would say; "Amen to that!" and, according to his next Grook, Piet Hein agrees with her.

Admonishment to Long-Winded Authors

Long-winded writers I abhor,
and glib, prolific chatters;
give me the ones who tear and gnaw their hair
and pens to tatters;
who find their writing such a chore,
they only write what matters.

It is said; *"If a person speaks three languages they are trilingual; if they speak two languages, they are bilingual; if they speak only one they are British."*

Although now that so many British speak so many different languages, perhaps the 'only one language' applies, more aptly, to Americans who believe that, if they speak loudly enough, everyone will understand them.

In his marvelous and compact reference book of Britain's noble history, The Pocket Book of Patriotism, (which should be required reading in all schools), George Courtauld includes the Cecil Rhodes quote: *"Remember you are an Englishman and have consequently won first prize in the lottery of life."*

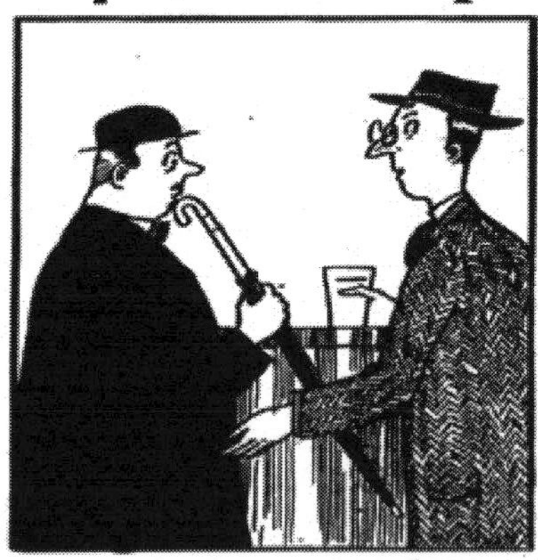

The man who said he hoped his wife would not get to hear about it when he was told a dictionary had been produced containing 5,000 new words.

"A Million Reasons Why The World Loves English" was the headline of an article
published in the Sunday Express on 23 April 2005, in which the journalist and writer, Chris Goodman, admonishes his readers for not treating this particular date, St George's Day, with the respect it deserves.

With Mr. Goodman's permission, below is an extract from his excellent, interesting and informative article:

'Today there really will be something to celebrate this year about the English -

- English itself. The American research company, Global Language Monitor, has counted all the words in the English language and these add up to - 988,968. Close to a cool million. It is estimated by the G.L.M that, with the ten to twenty thousand new words that appear each year, our mother tongue will reach the magical million between November 2006 and April 2007.'

The 'Million Word March' was finally reached - a little late - in 2008. Six years later this mountainous mountain of words had reached 1,025,109.8. A figure that includes many medical, technical and scientific words that are used by few people - or IMPOSSIBLE ones.

This means that, at the time I was writing this book, English had possibly overtaken the country that could previously boast as being the clear winner, China, and dwarfs the number of words in those of the other most used languages; French with about a hundred thousand and Spanish that has between two hundred and fifty thousand to three hundred thousand.

Taki Taki, also known as Sranan has the fewest with just three hundred and forty words. While the Oxford English Dictionary and Global Language Monitor endeavour to find new words, a spate of media articles rejoiced in its increase and that English is now the most spoken.

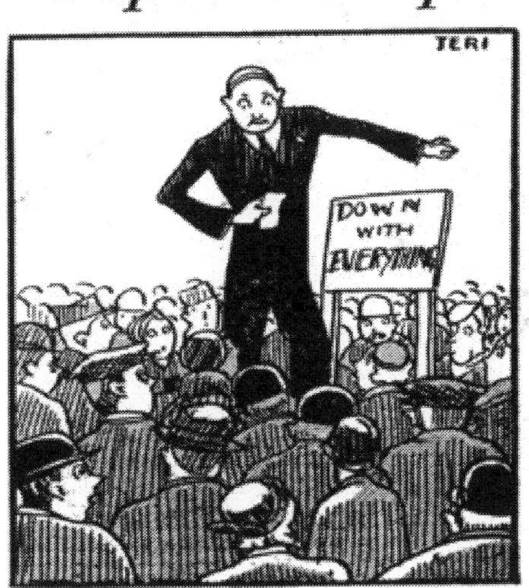

The orator who said he was pleased to see such a dense crowd.

It was also thought that, with the end of the Empire, English would cease to be an important language, but even as early as the nineteen sixties about two hundred and fifty million people world-wide spoke English. A language that when all those who speak it as a second or third language are included, is now the most spoken in the world.

The indications are that China, with the worlds highest population, will soon become the leading world market and, in order to compete, Mandarin will become one of the most essential languages.

Regardless of wvhich we can be confident that for every English person busily trying learn Chinese, there are many hundreds of Chinese busily learning English. And while it is said with a certainty that I believe to be widely (or even wildly), unlikely, that one day everyone will be Muslim, what is certain is, if everyone is Muslim, all Muslims will speak English. But with what accent and how well?

Many media articles now bewail the fact that many British school leavers do not know how to use English correctly or, in a few cases, are hardly able to read or write.

Apart from the sins of poor diction and enunciation there now seems to be little understanding of how words work or where correct syllable emphasis should be.

Even by teachers! On the excellent programme 'Pointless' a contestant who said he taught English to five years olds pronounced the word 'behaving' as behavin' and 'three' as free. Another, now much used, particularly by contestants on this excellent programme is the word 'eymgonago' in place of, 'I'm going to go'. It is not, as yet, listed in the O.E.D. but, no doubt, will soon do so. As will 'eywanago'.

Then there is the British Telecom recorded message, when telling a caller a number is 'out of order' enunciates, very precisely, 'temp-or-air-ill-ee'. Another is the word 'furore' now frequently pronounced as 'fue-roar-ree' rather than the correct; 'fewroar'. Although as it is a French word it's rather uncomfortable pronunciation by the English can be forgiven.

Nevertheless, it is difficult to understand why these words are pronounced so very torturously when it is so much easier to say them correctly. Even more torturous, to the mind if not the tongue, are the two words 'idyllic' and 'privacy', both of which are frequently, now pronounced with a hard, upper-case 'I' not the correct, soft, lower-case 'i'.

As the word idyllic' denotes a blissful, peaceful, pastoral or picturesque place that is perfect or 'ideal', (which gives me another, neat, alliteration), people who pronounce it as 'eyedillic' can possibly be excused, but, unless they intend to pry into peoples private lives, there can be no excuse for saying 'pry-ver-see' instead of the correct 'priv-ah-see'.

There are those who lament the loss of the final 'r' in words such as particularly or similarly. I was taught that the 'r' in these words should be silent, so were my tutors correct, or were theirs?

Perhaps these uncomfortable pronunciations are due to the introduction of phonetics, which is possibly why controversy is now pronounced as contro-verse-ee rather than the correct con-trov-a-sea. But are they right, or am I and, as many people might ask; "Does such controversy matter?"

And, in spelling, does it matter that Americans leave out the 'u' in all the words that we English spell with an ou? Due, I have read and heard it is said, to Donald De Lue, when working on the east plaque of his statue of George Washington in Indianapolis, carved the word ‘honour’ as ‘honor’. An error that sends my spell checker into overdrive.

Although I am confident there would be little disagreement about the lamentable dropping of the double ‘t’ in such words as better, butter, little or matter - the last of which often has the uncomfortable new word, wazza, in front of it.

Then there is the poor little dropped ‘g’ in words such as eatin’ and drinkin’. Mama told us that in the late 19th century lower class people, in the hope that it would make them appear less so started to use the hard ‘g’ they had previously neglected. Thus, within a few years, the ‘upper classes’, in defence of their superiority, began to drop the final ‘g’ on words pertinent to their world, as in; huntin’, shootin’ and fishin’. This may not be so but is as likely an explanation as any other.

Mama’s English was exceptional and thus her captions are neat examples of the way English can be manipulated when used correctly - and cleverly. Another interesting fact they highlight is the subtle change over time in the meaning of or, more correctly, the understanding and ‘usage’ of words and phrases. This constant change in interpretations has led to many words, when used in certain contexts, being understood by only those of advanced years, brilliantly illustrated by JERI’s next Impossible Person.

The huge advances in electronic communication within the last half century that has xgiven us mobile phones and online mail, means that telephone kiosks are now much less used, and there is certainly no requirement for the fine red telephone boxes that, until a few years ago, proudly stood on our streets and country roads. Boxes now highly sought after and bought, at great cost, to be used as greenhouses or to store garden furniture.

Impossible People

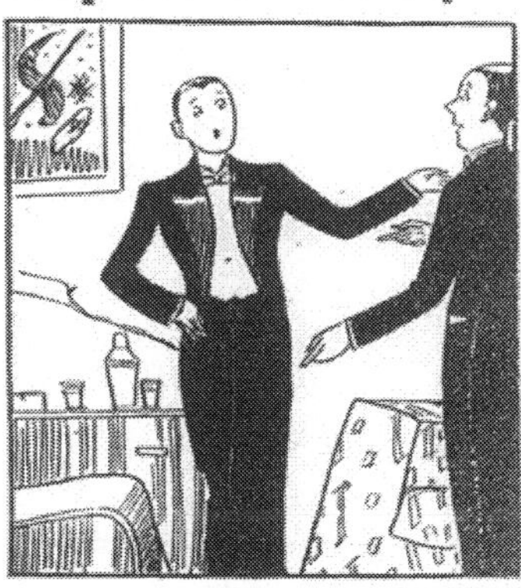

The young man who said his friends thought he was Button B, because they were always pressing him for money.

Very soon all interaction with those at a distance will be by mobile phone or the internet. Or perhaps, with the advances in technology advancing with ever greater speed, merely osmosis?

So although when it was conceived this cartoon of JERI’s would have been thought very amusing, now few people under the age of fifty and none under the age of twenty will have an inkling, (another now little used word), of what the caption means. Similarly, two hundred years ago the phrase, 'to go by post' meant a method of travel but now means the mailing of letters, parcels or packages. Which gives me the opportunity to include another, possibly little known, historical fact.

The first pillar box on the British mainland was erected in 1853 at Botchergate, Carlisle. While a similar box from the same year still stands at Barnes Cross, Bishop's Caundle in Dorset and is the oldest pillar box still in use on the mainland.

Thus, while the words 'box' and 'pillar' were in common usage separately, it was not until 1853 that they were married together in order to describe an everyday item used by everyone, everywhere.

Impossible People

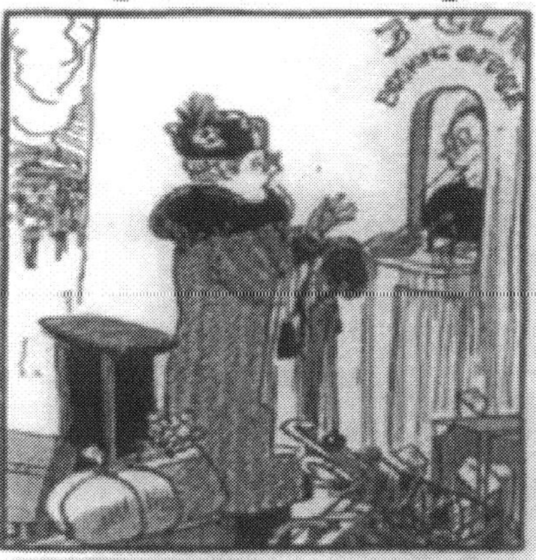

The woman who said she would rather have it now, when the booking clerk said; "Change at Crewe."

This constant change in the usage, and meaning, of words is succinctly illustrated in JERI's next two captions. When she devised these, Crewe was a major terminus and all rail passengers who travelled north out of London had to 'Change at Crewe'. A term that not only became synonymous with train travel but, later, was also frequently used by comedians - and cartoonists.

Impossible People

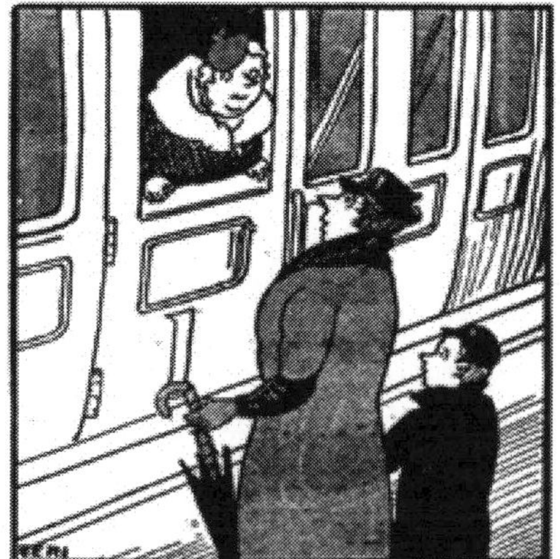

The plump woman who said she always travelled by train now the railways were doing something to reduce their fares.

Another is the word 'fares'. When my mother composed her next cartoon 'fares' also meant those who used public transport not just their payment for doing so. So, yet again, the young of today would neither understand, nor be amused, by my mother's next caption.

During a television programme on home decoration, a presenter, when discussing the merits of a piece of 'decorative' furniture, described it as decorous. Decorous may have a second meaning, but my O.E.D. and Websters only list it as; 'In keeping with good taste, propriety, politeness and restraint.'

Although perhaps this presenters decorative piece had all of these merits because, despite being completely different in both meaning and context, decorous didn't seem out of place when used in this context.

Other frequently mispronounced words are contributed, distributed and comparably, which are often pronounced as; 'contree-byou-ted', distree-byou-ted and 'com-pair-ablee', when, for pedants such as myself, they are; con-trib-u-ted, dis-trib-u-ted and com-pra-blee.

But as these mispronunciations still allow for understanding, does it matter? Particularly as English is now spoken with so many different regional accents, dialects and inflections that - even when understanding is sometimes in doubt - are pleasing to the ear English spoken with a foreign accent is also, always pleasing to the ear, as apparently is ours when we speak another language. On telling some French friends I was determined to improve my French accent, to my surprise and delight they went into shock horror mode and urged me not to.

They said that French spoken with an English accent sounds very romantic. Which is how we hear their accent when they speak English.

They are also amused by our misuse of their language or, more correctly, my misuse of it. A close neighbour and very dear friend, Jeanette, said; "Your French is excellent Simon but Karina's is much more fun." Whether due to my mispronunciation of French words or my misuse of them, she didn't say.

When, in 2005, I attended King's College for the graduation of my 'unofficial' French granddaughter, Aurelie, I met a number of her French and Spanish peers whose spoken English was so superior to that of many of our home grown students it was almost impossible to tell their ethnicity.

Conversation with my late, much missed, aspergic grandson, Ralph, were both torturous and hilarious as his inability to understand or comply with normal interaction made communication a minefield. For while he displayed an impressive ability verging on the Savant when recalling his phenomenal fund of facts and figures, his method of imparting them was studiously pedantic.

My dictionary's definition of the word 'pedantic' is: 'A need to be correct or in displaying technical knowledge.' As I neither 'display technical knowledge', nor can be thought of as 'correct', I do not consider myself guilty of pedantry – even so, my frequent criticism of poorly spoken English has earned me that sobriquet.

The late lamented, Keith Waterhouse, he of the wonderful 'Association for the Abolition of the Aberrant Apostrophe', was a leading proponent of the continuing debate concerning the rights or wrongs of phonetics and its consequent damage to spelling. He pithily wrote; *'You cannot lower your guard for a minute because out of the entomological undergrowth comes John Wells demanding widespread reform in the way we spell our words. Mr. Wells says we should write the way we speak - phonetically.'*

But which we? Cockney? Mancunian? Etonian? Yobs? Yuppies?' Or, say I; "Yankee?"

Thus Mr. Waterhouse, in his inimitable way, raised the wonderful possibility that there may never be a resolution to the argument about how we should spell and, thus, how we should write, and it will be forgotten that the original argument began with how we should speak.

Which will lead to the pleasant possibility that, those of us who take pride in so doing, can continue to speak in the tried and tested manner of 'Received English,' with its myriad of words with the same sound but different spellings and homonymic words that are spelt and sound the same but have different meanings.

While those who use it in a terpsichorean delight of different accents and inflections, together with a cornucopia of eclectic pronunciations, merely add to its wonders.

Impossible People

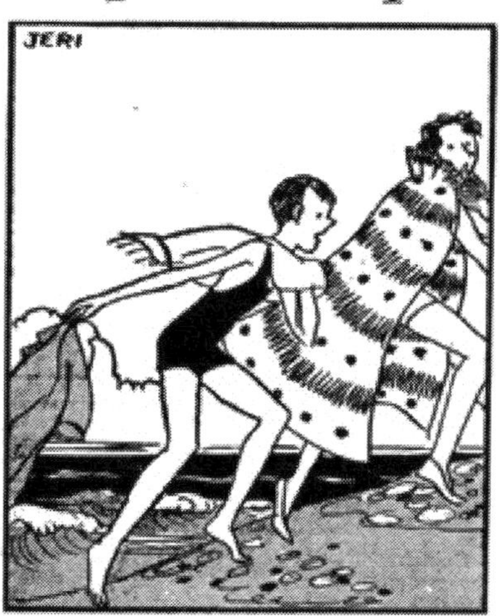

The boy who said his swim had whetted his appetite for lunch.

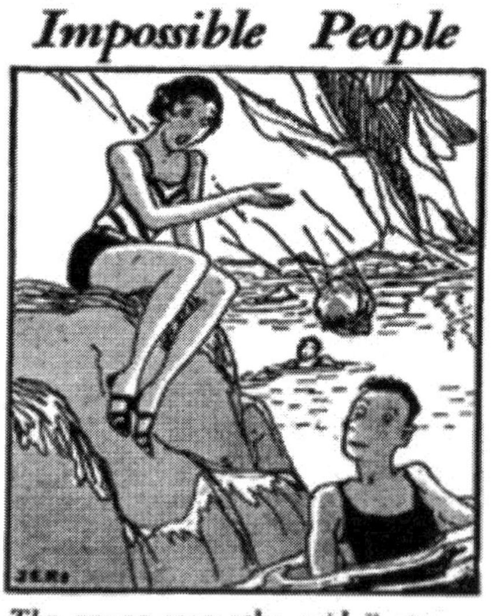

Impossible People

The young man who said it was a wait off his mind when his girl friend said she could not meet him that evening.

All of which are essential tools for those who write comedy or create cartoons - consummately confirmed by all the jokes and cartoons included in my Impossible People and superbly illustrated by JERI's Impossible boy - and her next Impossible young man.

Over time, words, as do languages, change and while the text of the Bible is glorious, it is impossible to imagine its 'way of speech' being used in today's frenetic, frenzied way of life.

When, in the 1380's parts of the Bible were translated into English by the priest and scholar, John Whycliffe, work that was later continued by William Tyndale, it was thought that the language would decline.

The reason for this assumption was that priests, when 'Unfrocked', were, due to their ability to read and write, much sought after by the printing trade. But with the Bible now in English, it was thought there would be far fewer unfrocked priests and the printing trade would need to look further afield for workers who could read who, at that time, were a rare commodity.

Although Michael Schama, in his wonderful programme about the King James Bible, said; *"At that time many more people could read and write than is now supposed"*. Although, prior to the 1870 Elementary Education Act that mandated compulsory education for all children under the age of thirteen, few people could read. Even following a swift increase in the numbers who, due to this mandate, then could, it was to be many years before everyone was able to or, even to this day, understand how, or why words work.

Or, more correctly, the many fluctuations, interpretations and differences in styles of speech that make English the expressive, fluid, lucid, poetic language that it is.

As so succinctly illustrated by JERI's two previous Impossible People - and her next – as it is as imperative to take care of our Grandmas –

Impossible People

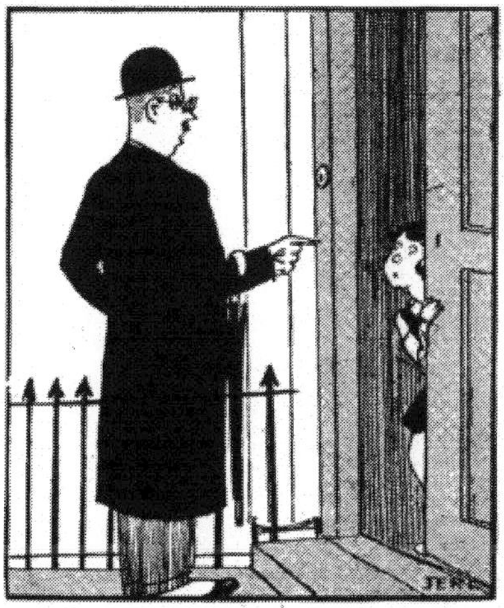

The little girl who said she was having a lay-down when asked where was her grammar.

As it is to take care of our -

GRAMMAR

With great prescience, the First Century Roman Poet, Juvenal, asked, *"Who willstand guard to guard the guards?"* To which the answer is no one, for it would seem that there are now no guards to guard those who should be guarding our grammar.

A necessary evil without which English will eventually become gobbledygook – a wonderful onomatopoeic word that means exactly how it sounds.

And, paradoxically, a sentence that illustrates the lenience that should be allowed in the use of the language. But it is a lenience that should stop at the tiny word 'to' which has become a wood beetle eating away at the foundations of English grammar. It is now used by nearly everyone, including news readers, journalists and even teachers, in both speech and writing

I used to wonder whether this irritating error was due to lack of time, or, in the field of journalism, lack of space, but now know it to be lack of knowledge due to lack of well-educated educators.

Many people who should know better now espouse the use of 'to' in place of the words 'with' or 'from'. These proponents maintain that whichever conjunction is used it is of no relevance to good speech or writing.

However, those wonderful masters of teaching good English, the Misses Rylance, would say to any child who used the lazy 'to', "If you transpose the phrases, 'similar to' and 'different from' into 'similar from' and 'different to', they become meaningless."

So, with my excellent tutors admonishments still ringing in my ears, I composed this for my own two children:

If it makes no sense to say someone is different to his brother,
It is equal nonsense to say something is similar from another,
As can be seen when we compare these two sentences with each other.

This worked until I used it to admonish my grandson Ralph for his frequent misuse of the word 'to'. He said; *"But Grandma if you use the word 'also', which also means to if it has another 'o' on it, it makes it right."* A reasoning to which I had no suitably erudite answer except to tell him that 'too' only means 'also' it doesn't also mean 'to'.

The ongoing media debates about the decline in the standard of education suggest this is the result of the Blair Government's 'catch-all system for all pupils' that created a diminished education for prospective teachers with an inevitable downward momentum in education for their future pupils.

An assumption validated by a 2006 Government publication - referred to by a media wit as; "A guide for skool inspectors", circulated, presumably at great cost, to over eleven hundred school and child care inspectors to 'advise' on correct grammar. A cost that could have been avoided if all these 'inspectors' had been taught correct grammar when at school.

There are many hundreds of fields of employment that do not require grammar to be overly correct. There are also many excellent educators, such as Jim Hourigan who, (as I write), is Headmaster of Penwortham Priory Academy in Lancashire, who should be appointed as arbiters of education, as they consider that curriculums should prioritise those subjects in which particular pupils excel - whether academic, creative or technical.

For as he maintains, and I agree; *"It is isn't necessary to be brilliant at English to be brilliant at mending motor cars."*

The internet and the mobile phone that have given birth to e-mails and 'text speak', may very soon, bring about the death of correct punctuation and spelling and, as efficient and effortless as these eclectic, electric modes of communication are, they may also, very sadly, eventually erase all erudite conversation.

A premise that is not new.

Impossible People

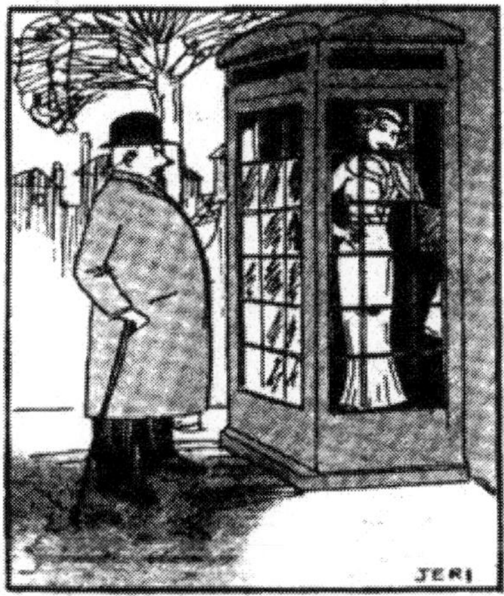

The man who said the art of conversation was dead.

It may have helped both the women making the call and the gentleman waiting to make one, to heed Piet Hein's next Grook –

On Thoughts and Words

If no thought
your mind does visit,
make your speech
not too explicit.

For now, with our present, portable means of contact to whomever, whenever and wherever, no matter the distance, 'the art of conversation' if not yet dead may, (as was first thought when technology gave us the telephone), soon suffer a torturous demise.

Especially as now nearly everyone takes Mr. Hein's advice to keep it short and sweet and not too explicit when writing their e-mails or text messages.

Two means of contact that will, very soon, result in the paradox that everyone will know that words create conversation, but will not understand their relationship to correct phrasing, sentences, spelling and, of particular importance, punctuation and, of even greater importance, pronunciation.

But we must hope that technology will not kill -

THE ART OF CONVERSATION

With its need to be all things to all people, television is another nail in the coffin of this art. A demise hastened by the fact that the only two exclamations now used are 'Wow' and 'Amazing'. Their frequency makes you wonder whether some oligarch has a vested interest in them!

Thus, while the O.E.D. is working hard to provide us with hundreds of new words, these and the derivatives of the vulgar Anglo-Saxon 'F' word seem to be the only adjective, noun, or verb most young people know, and when they do use it they use it incorrectly.

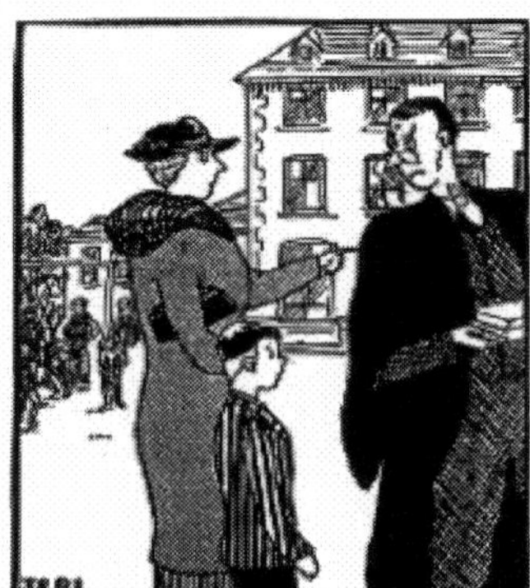

The woman who refused to send her son to the new school when she heard they had a very strong language side.

For as Ben Elton's mother said when admonishing her son; *"The 'F' word should be used as an exclamation, not as a comma."*

This Impossible Person takes my reader to an occasion when, with my mother and my equally much loved but 'very proper', mother-in-law, Muriel, we were walking behind a group of scholars clad in the uniform of the Cathedral School, Norwich, who constantly peppered their conversations with the 'F' word.

Concerned at Muriel's discomfort, my more stoic Mama politely told them the word sounded particularly uncomfortable when said by such well-spoken young men wearing such eminent and distinctive uniforms.

She said if they wished to use an 'F' word, there were many of equal interest, such as Samuel Johnson's 'fopdoodle' or 'fastularian', that would make their conversations more amusing and a great deal more agreeable.

She told them there were many other archaic swear words they may like to research, and although my reader may find this difficult to believe, these young men thought this a splendid idea.

A few weeks later I happened to be walking behind the same group of boys and heard not one 'F' word - not even fopdoodle or fastularian.

Muriel was not alone, Arthur Allen, of South Benfleet in Essex, is also no stranger to the 'effing and blinding' that now passes for conversation. His poem on the subject was published in the Peterborough column of the Daily Mail in October 2009. Once again, via the kind assistance of Nicola Tapsell, I was able to contact Arthur, who said he would be more than pleased to allow for its inclusion in Impossible People - who, one could suppose, are those for whom Arthur composed his poem.

Educated English

Our young people are such clever devils,
Every year they're passing more A-Levels,
With such improvement in education,
We should now be an erudite nation.

Yet when I'm near or passing by schools,
I overhear the speech of foul-mouthed fools,
In public transport, too - trains and buses,
My ears are assaulted by crude cusses.

All these profanities come from the tongue
Of someone 'highly educated' and young.

Sometimes it's hard to follow their English,
But there's one stressed word I can distinguish;

Boldly blared out as loud as a klaxon,
It's their favourite word from Anglo Saxon.
With scholarship so improved, it's absurd.
They use just one 'describing' word.

Having the knowledge to be selective,
Why must they use such a coarse adjective?
When hearing obscenities at the school gate,
It would be foolhardy to remonstrate.

For there's no creature more defiant
Than a liberated teenage giant.
Oblivious to the concept of shame,
He'll rudely give you more of the same

It's prudent then to suppress your outrage,
And calmly accept this is an uncouth age.
Some folk will think I'm a sad old duffer,
In that a few swear words make me suffer.

In these cultured times of free expression,
I'm just a relic of bygone repression.
So though my views may be outdated,
I'm content to remain 'uneducated'.

Arthur speaks for many of us who feel saddened by the constant use of expletives in the public areas of our towns and cities. Towns and cities once renowned for having the most courteous and courtly citizens in the world.

Although it would seem that these offensive words, despite most people's hatred of them, now, unjustly, have justice on their side, as Mr. Justice Bean (a name that could be of much benefit to the pen of Quentin Letts) has decreed the 'F' word can, without fear of punishment, now be used even when directed at the police because, he avers, "Profanity is now so common".

One wonders how, in future, he might treat a 'common' serial thief, paedophile or rapist that, according to media reportage, are also now more common – in both senses of the word.

The many regions of the United Kingdom, as do those of America, Australia and Canada, all have a distinct English of their own, while the vast army of

English speakers from other European countries will, over time, add to the diversity of the way our language is spoken - and written.

A language that assisted in making our country 'Great'. Not just due to our many great writers and orators, but also the numerous pithy, witty quotes said by equally erudite people. An art that can only be achieved by a true understanding of 'how words work'.

George Wigg, a Labour politician from the Sixties said; *"If you don't accept change, you end up like the dinosaur - stuffed."* What is also often said is; *"What is not known is not missed."* Thus in another fifty years correct spelling will be irrelevant and hundreds of words will be pronounced differently from (or even to?), the way they are now.

Nevertheless, the English language will continue its headlong escalation to become the most spoken, with the most voiced, after 'AyemayZing' and 'WoW', being the 'F' word. Which, despite the hundreds of new words that the O.E.D and Websters continue to include in their vast, much valued, volumes of varied and variously worded words, means that even fewer of the million available to us will be used.

Which wins me another alliteration and another opportunity to include another Impossible Person.

Impossible People

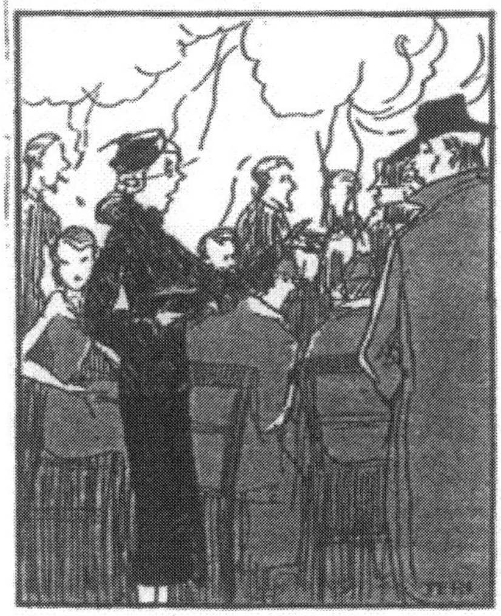

The woman who joined a secret society and was annoyed because she was not told even one.

And another - for the few words we still do use will, no doubt, continue their escalation to be used inappropriately in both speech and writing - particularly in poems – and, equally sadly, in odes -

Impossible People

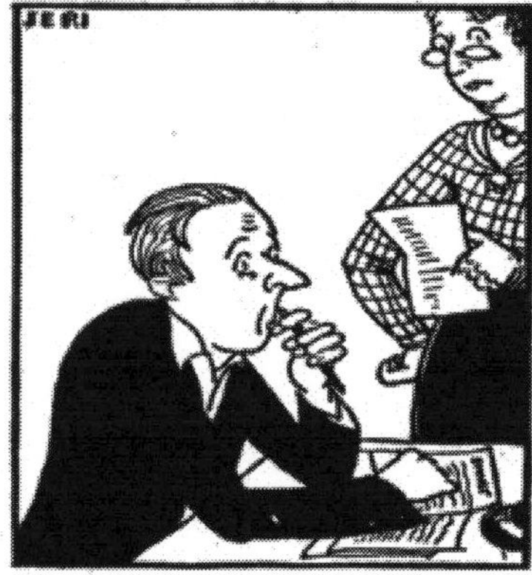

The spring poet who wrote an "Ode to May," but his wife's name was Gertrude.

My love of poetry makes it difficult to have a favourite poet but, after my Mother and Martin Newell, equally high on my list is Arthur Seymour John Tessimond (1902-1962), and JERI's 'spring poet' gives me an excellent excuse to include one of his most emotive poems.

Not Love Perhaps

This is not Love perhaps – Love that lays down its life,
That many waters cannot quench, nor the floods drown –
But something written in lighter ink, said in a lower tone;
Something perhaps especially our own,

A need at times to be together and talk,
And then finding we can walk
More firmly through narrow places,
And meet more easily nightmare faces:

A need to reach out sometimes hand to hand,
And then find Earth less like an alien land.
A need for alliance to defeat
The whisperers at the corner of the street.

A need for inns on roads, islands in seas,
Halts for discoveries to be shared,
Maps checked and notes compared:
A need at times of each for each,
Direct as the need of throat and tongue for speech.

The final line being a natural lead into -

WORDS AND HOW IMPOSSIBLE THEY CAN BE

Many items in Impossible People are from those that 'circulate on the net' making their true heritage almost impossible to trace. Nevertheless I now know the name of the author of this next exceptionally clever poem, which has been sent to me by many people.

Apart from the charming "Thank You, Bill Gates, for bringing all this into our lives." I have found no other eulogy apart from my husband's; "Absolutely Brilliant."

Written by Mr, Ziegler in 1994 it was published by NetGuide Magazine and the Sunday edition of the Seattle Times. Following which it went viral and, at the time I included it here, had earned nearly two million fans.

The Computer Glitch
by Gene Ziegler

If a packet hits a pocket on a socket on a port,
and the bus is interrupted at a very last resort,
and the access of the memory makes your floppy disk abort,
then the socket packet pocket has an error to report.

If your cursor finds a menu item followed by a dash,
and the double-clicking icon puts your window in the trash,
and your data is corrupted, cause the index doesn't hash,
then your situation's hopeless and your system's gonna crash!

If the label on the cable on the table at your house,
says the network is connected to the button on your mouse,
but your packets want to tunnel to another protocol,
that's repeatedly rejected by the printer down the hall.

And your screen is all distorted by the side-effects of gauss,
so your icons in the window are as wavy as a souse;
then you may as well reboot and go out with a bang,
'cuz sure as I'm a poet, the sucker's gonna hang.

When the copy on your floppy's getting sloppy in the disk,
and the macro code instructions is causing unnecessary risk,
then you'll have to flash the memory and you'll want to RAM your ROM,
and then quickly turn off the computer and be sure to tell your Mom!

A final message to those to whom it is sent is; *"Well, that certainly clears things up for me. How about you?"*

But I have no desire to know the author of this next joke (?) that was sent to me at the same time as the 'Computer Glitch' was doing the rounds.

Unable to sort a long term problem with my computer, I eventually asked my neighbour's son - whose bedroom looks like NASA in miniature - if he would give me five minutes to help sort the problem. In less than five seconds he had sorted the glitch and had recovered my lost files. On asking him what the problem was he said, *'Oh, it's nearly always an 'ID ten T' problem; If you write it down you won't forget it.'* So I did and got: IDIOT.'

Many may be of the view that the moniker this young computer wizard attributes to those of us who are decidedly less able at using this addictive, mind-bending, time consuming 'convenience' is most apt.

It also confirms that words can be as idiosyncratic as people. As are these that my twin wrote for a young French girl, Josette, who was staying with her as an exchange student. As Sonya is so severely dyslexic it has remained a mystery to me how she managed to compose it.

A dictionary is of no help to those with this affliction as with no knowledge of how a word is spelt, looking it up is an abortive exercise, so perhaps she asked her children, both of whom can spell well. *"They can also spell most other words well as well."* says Sonya.

Not That You'd Know

Tart as in sharp like taste,
Not as in sharp like a knife
That a Knight carries in a shaft.
Knight in armour, that is.
Not as night and daylight.
Light as in you can see clearly,
Not as in how light it is to carry
Carry as in to lift or to hold.

Not as in to carry forward,
As in sums in a file
Or notes that you write.
Not notes of music
That you listen to with your ear.
Or right as when you keep
To your left or your right.
Not left, as left in a heap.

Alone, with no one near.
Not near as - in here,
Nor here as in - to hea,
Which is not anywhere.
Not anywhere but what you wear,
As in to wear a buttonhole,
Hole where there is nothing there,
Not whole that is something complete.

As in the whole part, not; to part
When two people go their own way,
Not as in weigh to find how heavy.
Heavy as the bough of a tree,
Not as in bow to bend the knee
To your Beau to whom you make a bow,
That ties the knot that is made when Cupid
Fires his bow.

Not that you'd know.

Nor do I know why the word we use for being unable to spell is so difficult for those who can't even spell the word spell.

Which is a natural lead to -

DYSLEXIA

That fine writer Peter Hitchens and the Labour M.P. Graham Stringer, (along with a few people with Doctorates who should know better), maintain that there is no such condition as Dyslexia. So they may like to know that when treating a patient who, with no other mental or physical problems, found it difficult to read or write, the 19th century German doctor, Rudolf Berlin, used this Greek word, that translates literally as 'difficulty with words', to describe his patient's condition.

We may be getting a lot better at mending brains - on Monday 1st September, 2008, surgeons in Nice performed the world's first successful laser surgery on a patient with brain cancer – but we still do not fully understand why such conditions as aspergers, autism and dyslexia occur.

The first two 'afflictions' often lead to those who have them becoming Savants, and, having many relatives who are 'afflicted' with the third, I know they are, more often than not, compensated for their lack of ability to spell by having exceptional artistic or entrepreneurial skills. Many people, among them some teachers, believe it can be 'cured', but those with families liberally littered with people who can't spell, know that, as are autism and aspergers, dyslexia is an incurable condition.

A.A. Gill, a brilliant writer, describes himself as a 'functional illiterate'. In other words, 'A dyslexic'. In a Sunday Times magazine article he says he was asked to give talks to children to assist with a pioneering method of teaching 'word-blind' children to read.

The paper printed Mr. Gill's beautiful and extremely erudite explanation of why our flexible, world-renowned language can be used in any way, whether written, spoken, sung - or spelt, while, at the same time, sharply rapping my knuckles for my intransigence and pedantry regarding this wonderful, fluid, quixotic –and ever changing - language.

"I told them this was their language, this English, this most marvelous and expressive cloak of meaning and imagination. This great, exclamatory, illuminating song, it belonged to anyone who found it in their mouths.

"There was no wrong way to say it, or write it. The language couldn't be compelled or herded, it couldn't be tonsured or pruned, pollarded or plaited, it was as hard as oaths and as subtle as rhyme. It couldn't be forced or bullied or policed by academics; it wasn't owned by those with flat accents; nobody had the right to tell them how to use it or what to say.

"There are no rules and nobody speaks incorrectly, because there is no correctly; no high court of syntax. And while everyone can speak with the language, nobody speaks for the language. Not grammars. Not dictionaries. This English doesn't belong to examiners or teachers. They just run along behind, picking up and discarding usages.

"All of you already own the greatest gift, the highest degree this country can bestow. It is on the tip of your tongue."

Having been asked by Sonya many dozens of times how to spell 'dyslexic', I have begun to wonder why Herr Berlin thought it was a good idea to use this word for people who can't spell. Or why we use the words 'mnemonic' for things we wish to remember and 'lisp' for those who find it difficult to pronounce words that include sibilants.

Or why the word 'abbreviation' is so long, why doctors only 'practice' and, oddest of all, who thought it was a good idea to designate those people with a fear of long words, the thirty four letter word: 'hippopotomonstrosequippedaliphobia'. A word that is fearful even for those of us who can spell! Which spellbindingly takes us to -

SEW TO SPELLING

An article cleverly titled: 'Internet is Blamed for a Bad Spell of English.' cites a number of words where the Oxford English Corpus found such errors as 'just deserts' instead of the correct 'just desserts', 'slight of hand' rather than; 'sleight of hand' and 'fased by' which is; 'phased by'.

However, there is hope for my twin and her fellow dyslexics (among whom are a few more of my nearest and dearest), as for the past hundred years The Spelling Society has been campaigning for the use of the simple phonetic form of spelling.

Their present Chairman, Jack Bovil, maintains that words such as 'argumant', 'thier' 'ignor' and 'speach' are acceptable alternatives to the correct spellings of these words.

Ken Smith, a lecturer from Buckinghamshire University, agrees. He says; "It would not be a world catastrophe to accept commonly used misspelt words, such as embarrassed, millennium or liaison - which 50% of adults spell incorrectly - or definitely, accidentally and separate – spelt incorrectly by more than a quarter of us." (As I so often ask; How do they get these statistics?)

Ken says the top five misspelt words based on a foreign language root are: 'broccoli' (Italian), 'haemorrage' (ancient Greek), and three French ones; 'connoisseur', 'manoeuver' and 'lieutenant' - the 'f' word with no 'f' in it.

Ken maintains that words are often spelt incorrectly due to wrong assumptions as to their source. One of which is 'consensus'. A word, he writes, that is frequently spelt as 'concensus' due to the belief that it stems from 'census', a word derived from the Latin 'censer'('to assess'), when it comes from the Latin 'consentire' ('to agree').

Although my O.E.D. tells me 'censer' is 'a vessel in which incense is burnt. (But as Simon points out, Ken is quoting a Latin word and I am quoting an English one).

Ken writes; *"The other most common words spelt incorrectly, based on similar assumptions are 'supersede' (which apparently, supersedes all others), with 'inoculate', 'liquefy' and 'sacrilegious' as runners up."*

According to yet another study the top ten most commonly misspelt words are;

definitely (definately)
sacrilegious (sacreligious)
indict (indite)

manoeuvre (maneouvre)
bureaucracy (beaurocracy);
broccoli (brocolli)
phlegm (phleghm);
prejudice (predjudice),
unnecessary (unecessary)
and Ken's concensus (consensus).

Mortgage is number eleven, with nine per cent spelling it as 'morgauge'. While, due to their pronunciation, two others are conscience (conshence) and foreign (forren).

I will not insult my reader by pointing out that the misspelt words are those in brackets, but do beg the question - are those of us who believe in the importance of words spelt well, too entrenched in 'dogma' when we criticise those who are careless, or those, such as my twin, who can't?

A point of view that once again allows me to include a lady and a little girl who are two morc Impossiblc Pcoplc who illustrate how our Mother would rejig her captions.

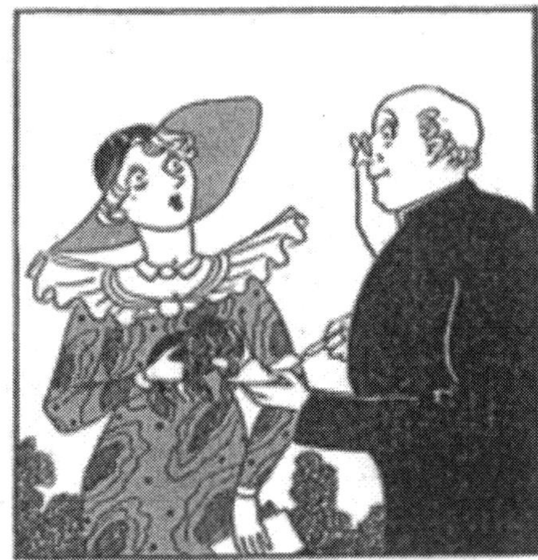

The girl who thought a dogma was the mother of pups.

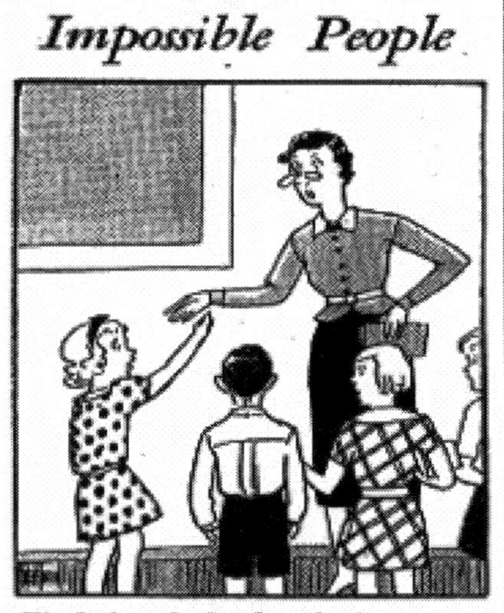

The little girl who thought dogma was a puppy's mother.

Another conundrum, is why the two different meanings of the word 'sentence' (that which we speak or write and that which we are given), have the same spelling, while the word 'sentance', that would create a comfortable delineation between these two very different activities, doesn't exist. In the same way, (as I write earlier), that the word speech, that also has two different meanings, is not delineated by being spelt also as 'speach'.

Yet another combatant in this war is Derek Hines from Suffolk, who says, *"Ken Smith's assertion that spelling should follow speech is ludicrous, his wish to change February to Febuary just because his tongue is too idle is sheer arrogance. I bet he can say brewery."* Which in Scottish, say I, might be, *"I ken, Ken caen say brewery."*

Allison Pearson, whose comments are always worth reading, takes a poke at all this idiocy with, "Don't be stoopid, spelling matters," in which she roundly berates the President of The Spelling Society, Professor Wells, for his view that; "Correct spelling is holding back pupils".

She writes, *"Theres only wun problem if there not gunna teach kids to spell there own language and use the apostrophe no one will have a klew wot there on about, innit? Prufessa Welz and his kind do the younger generation no favours by expecting less and less of them."*

And when he says that; "Spellings used in e-mail and text messaging show the way forward for English," she wants to; *"Skewer him on a sharpened quill."*

Allison continues; *"If Professor Wells was one lone crackpot it really wouldn't matter, but unfortunately he is part of an educational establishment which seems to want to remove all difficulty from schooling in the name of equality. He should try putting forward this theory to a newspaper editor for whom I once worked. Every week would bring a pile of job applications and he had one simple rule for weeding out those applicants who wouldn't get an interview. If there was one spelling error in an application it was binned - accompanied by the words. "Give a job to someone who can't spell?" To which Allison adds the rider; "Uv got 2 b kiddin."*

All of which confirm my belief that correct grammar, pronounciation and spelling are some of the most valuable gifts a child can earn when learning English.

Nevertheless, Professor Wells may have a point as my twin will say and spell the word 'charismatic' as 'carismic' and everyone, even those who are not, understand what she means.

At the time of writing this section I came across a letter in the Daily Mail from Victor Coombes of Bovey Tracey in Devon. A letter, slightly edited by me, in which he says;

People who advocate a reformed spelling system because of the confusion of when a word includes 'ie' or 'ei' would be entering a minefield of linguistic anomalies. Any committees set up to simplify our spelling could start by sorting out the 'ough' in the following sentence: 'A rough, dough-faced ploughman thoughtfully strode, hiccoughing and coughing thoroughly through the thoroughfares of Scarborough.'

It could then move on to the 31 different spellings of the 'oh' sound, as in: oh, no or Oh! No!, toe, low, sew, mote, brooch, soul, depot. Apropos, curacao, de trop, faux pas, through, though, pernod, provost, yeomen. Bordeaux, Courtauld, haut couture, table d'hote, Pharaoh, Renault, Rievauix, Abbey, La Rochefoucauld, Rousseau, Seoul, Stowe, Sherlock Holmes, Van Gogh and Vaud in Switzerland. (Where, by coincidence, I once lived so know it is pronounced as Vo.)

A huge task then to be tackled would be to standardise the numerous homophones we have in the English language, such as cite, site and sight; sighed and side; tail and tale.

It could then move on to the' silent' letters in many words such as gnash, pneumatic and know. Then, if there were any enthusiasts left after months spent changing the thousands of words that don't conform to common sense, the committee would have to tackle how our many regional accents affect the pronunciation and spelling of words.

Yet again, within days of reaching this section, this exceptionally clever, extremely amusing poem by Mike Horgan from Heswall in Wirral was published in the Peterborough column.

So my mother and The Daily Mail - and not necessarily in that order – were, whilst I was writing, definitely 'watching over me'. I am confident that, as are all the other 'Peterborough Poets' whose work now also graces Impossible People, Mike will be equally pleased to see how aptly it fits and how neatly it sits here.

English Spelling

I do not think that I'm obtuse,
But, really, I can't see the use
Of spellings which, like cues and queues,
Are surely written to confuse.
Consider yews and use and ewes,
And juice and deuce and gnus and news,
And brews and bruise and dues and dews,
And choose and chews and also Jews.
And then there's hues and Hughes and hews,
And ruse and rues and mews and muse,
And crews and cruise and shoes and shoos,
And ouse and ooze and lose and loos.

Now tell me, what's the earthly use,
Of making spelling so abstruse?

A brilliant rhyme about words that would sit well with my 'English is Tough Stuff' but, more aptly, takes us to the few words in our language that apparently have no matching rhyming words.

One of my many English teachers, the erudite Mr. Ellis, told me there are four commonly used words that have no matching rhyming word, or words, three of which are colours: orange, purple and silver, the fourth is month.

Conversely, Chambers Rhyming Dictionary lists 84 examples for which there are no rhyming words. I have found matches for a few of them, two of which match within the list, but whether they could be used within a rhyming poem is another matter.

Then there are words that don't - but, with some jiggery-pokery, can be made to – for if one of my favourite poets, and no doubt that of many others, Ogden Nash, were still with us he would find, or invent, rhyming words for all of them, as 'orange' should be no trouble for a man who, while admitting to not being able to find a rhyming word for parsley for his poem, 'Parsley for a Vice-President, then conjures up the word 'gharsley'. A word that, despite its frequent use in many anthologies, I have still to find in any dictionary – or anywhere else.

Mr. Nash also had a magical ability to compose weird words such as the wonderful 'inexpenceslaus', that he married with 'King Wenceslaus', in his poem: 'Remember Yule.'.He trumps even his own previously inspired concoctions when, in 'The Strange Case of Mr. Palliser's Palate', he marries the word 'Bordelaise' with 'disordelaise'. A truly superb 'misorderlaise' that makes him unique among all other poets.

Of equal oddity are the three words: 'overlook', 'oversee' and 'oversight' all three of which, despite 'appearing' to mean the same, have entirely different meanings! And the first has two. As apparently does incognito in JERI's next cartoon;

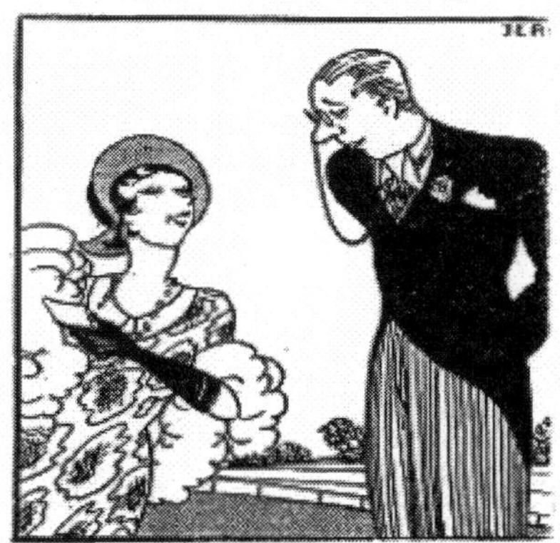

The girl who thought it must be rather difficult to sell when she was told her friend was travelling incognito.

A caption that may not be understood by many as, despite those whose work entails the need to travel in order to make sales, the term 'travelling salesman' is now little used. But not the word 'invoice' that is understood by everyone whether they have a voice or not.

Impossible People

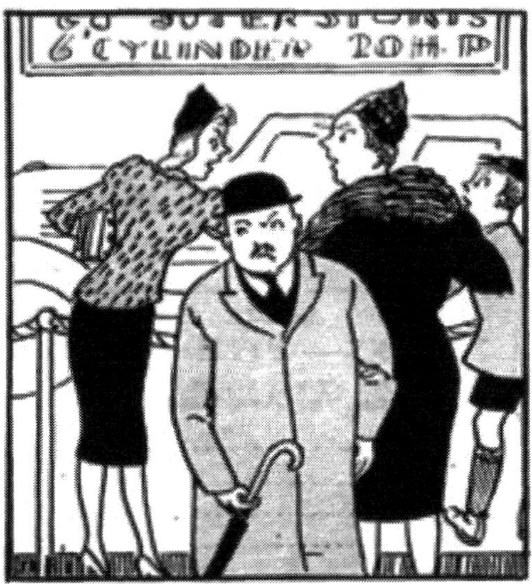

The man who said the only voice he would have in choosing his new car would be the invoice

But - were all of Mr. Nash's inspired creations of 'new' words spelling errors? This next poem, 'The Spell In Checker', written in 1992 by Jerrold H. Zar, of the Graduate School of Northern Illinois University, was first published, in 1994, in the Journal of Irreproducible Results. It was so popular, some years later, the JIR republished it with no accreditation.

Following which it became fodder for circulation on the Internet which, I can be confident, allows for its inclusion here.

The Spell In Checker

I have a spelling checker, it came with my PC.
It plane lee marks four my revue Miss steaks aye can knot sea.
Eye ran this poem threw it, your sure reel glad two no.
Its vary polished in it's weigh, my checker tolled me sew.
A checker is a bless sing, It freeze yew lodes of thyme.
It helps me right awl stiles two reed, and aides me when aye rime.

Each frays come posed up on my screen, eye trussed too bee a joule.
The checker pours o'er every word, to cheque sum spelling rule.
Bee fore a veiling checkers, hour spelling mite decline,
And if we're lacks oar have a laps, we wood bee maid too wine.
Butt now bee cause my spelling is checked with such grate flare,
Their are know faults with in my cite, Of nun eye am a wear.
Now spelling does knot phase me, It does knot bring a tier.
My pay purrs awl due glad den with wrapped words fare as hear.
To rite with care is quite a feet of witch won should bee proud,
And wee mussed dew the best wee can, sew flaws are knot aloud.
Sow ewe can sea why aye dew prays such soft wear four pea seas,
And why eye brake in two averse, buy righting want too pleas.

Simon says; "A bit too confusing to be clever." and many may agree with him. This next anonymous poem appears to be a plagiarism of the previous one. Or is further confirmation of my view on original creativity - a good reason for including it.

The Spell Checker

I have a spell in chequer it came with my pea sea
It plainly marques for my revue Miss Steaks I kin knot see
As soon as a mist ache is maid it nose bee fur two long
And eye can put the error rite, it's rare lea ever wrong.
Eye strike a quay and type a word, and weight four it two say
Weather I am wrong or write, it shows me strait a weigh
Eye have run this poem threw it I'm shore yaw pleased too no,
It's letter perfect awl the weigh, my chequer tolled me sew.

And finally a spell check whoopsie from James Taylor of Rainham in Essex: The Broxhill Centre, Harold Hill - The Brothel Centre, Harlot Hill. Which takes us to another of my published letters in the Daily Mail in which I question whether, with students now using computers for all their written work, they could rely on their spell checkers rather than their brains when checking for spelling errors.

A supposition soundly (or, more correctly 'silently') trounced by Keith Ellel of Rishton in Lancashire, who sent the following inspirational response to my letter.

'Further to the computer spell check debate mine finds no fault with the following; 'Yew no your knot aloud two reed in hear.'

Which in only nine, cleverly worded words, illustrate that automatic computer spell checkers only read 'words', not 'sentences'. (Apple, please take note!)

Impossible People

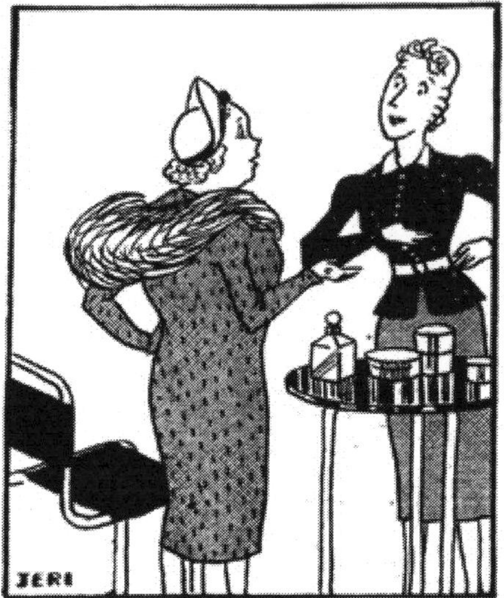

The beauty specialist who said her client would lose pounds if she put herself in her hands.

Which spellbindingly takes us to Phraseology - and chairs. Fascinatingly the chair in JERI's next cartoon, composed some eighty years ago, is identical to a set of six 'modern' chairs that presently grace the kitchen of my sister Nicola and her husband, George.

There may be those who, on reading this caption, will find no humour in it now that beauty specialists' do not reduce people's weight, only their bank accounts, but when JERI composed this cartoon, beauty specialists worked with their clients on all aspects of their regime including weight loss, hence her clever double entendre of the word 'pounds'.

The double entendre is the very breath of brilliant comedy and cartoon captions, which makes it even more fortunate that, despite English having so many words, many have two meanings - one of which is 'pound' - while many others, such as 'drunk', can be a noun or a verb. Which may be difficult to get your head around if, having drunk too much you are too drunk to know the difference.

So with a million words from which to select them, cartoonists such as the masterly PUGH can continue to entertain us with the right word in the wrong place rather than the right word in the right place – or from those they find online - such as -

INTERNET IDIOSYNCRASIES

The World Wide Web is a marvelous innovation when used properly but hilariously idiosyncratic when used improperly, as illustrated by these web addresses that were sourced by that great wit, Stephen Fry - or his equally clever researchers?

whoresearch.com – findsexperts.com - penisland.com - findtherapists.com - and, best of all, from a company that obviously employs people who know nothing about the English language: www.powergenitalia.com

Although, as it is an Italian company, was it intentional?

News Headline Idiosyncrasies

If the Regional Press Awards don't have a category for the most unintentionally amusing headline, they should, as all those journalists trying to win it would lighten our daily read of whichever daily paper we choose to read.
These are ten of the best with another from JERI.

RED TAPE HOLDS UP BRIDGES

LESOTHO WOMEN MAKE GREAT CARPETS

GENETIC ENGINEERING SPLITS SCIENTISTS

NEW HOUSING FOR ELDERLY NOT YET DEAD

CHOPPER SEARCH FOR MAN IN UNDERPANTS

PANDA MATING FAILS - VETERINARIAN TAKES OVER

POLICE BEGIN CAMPAIGN TO RUN DOWN JAYWALKERS

FLAMING TOILET SEAT CAUSES EVACUATION AT SCHOOL

12 ON THEIR WAY TO CRUISE AMONG DEAD IN PLANE CRASH

BODY FOUND IN BOAT SEIZED BY BAILIFFS AND DUE TO BE AUCTIONED

Impossible People

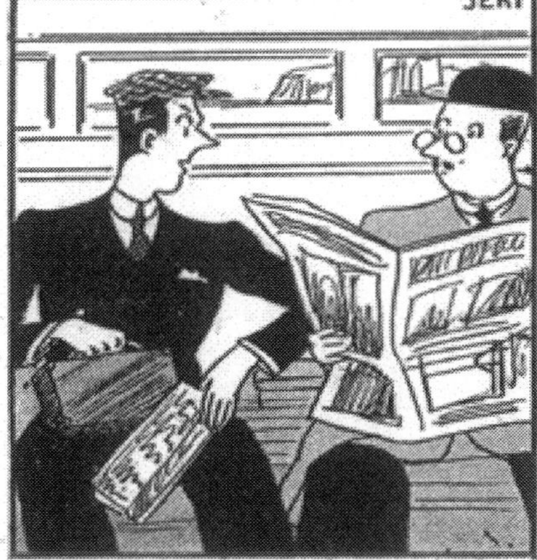

The young man who asked if Arsenal were buying again when told that three millions were going to be spent on defense.

And another - **SOMETHING WENT WRONG IN JET CRASH, EXPERTS SAY** – which flies us to an Impossible Pilot –

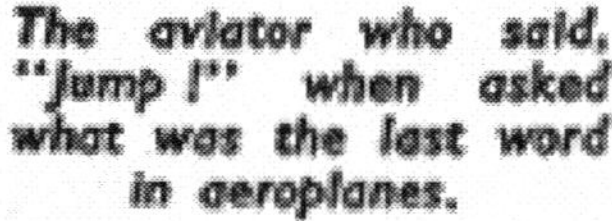
The aviator who said, "Jump !" when asked what was the last word in aeroplanes.

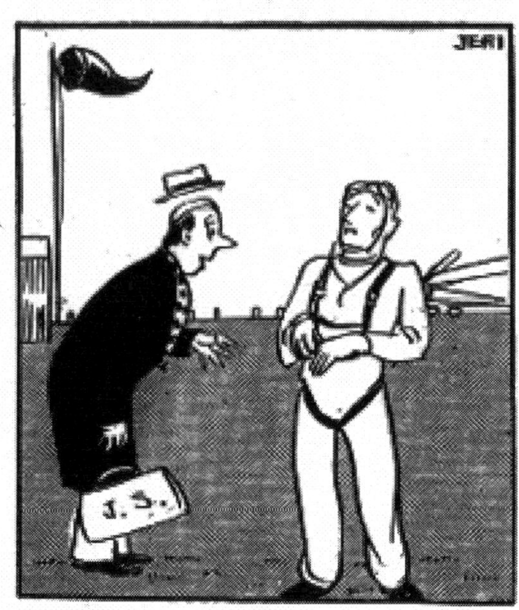

Which may also be the last word in ambulances;

Impossible People

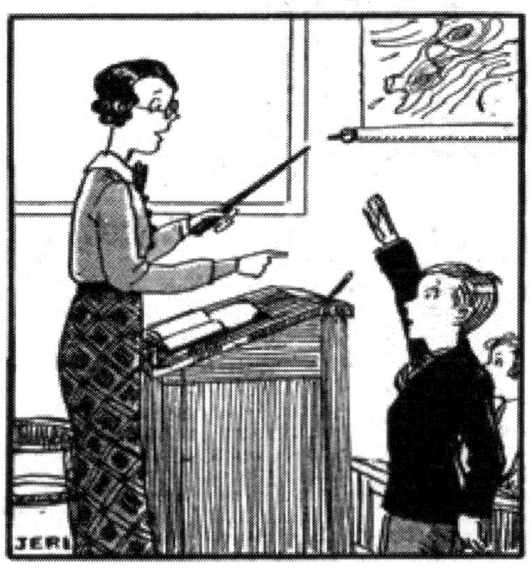

The boy who thought " sic transit " meant riding in an ambulance.

THE HUMOROUS USE OF WORDS

The positive use of the term 'sic transit' in JERI's previous cartoon reminded me of being told by an English teacher that the words 'furl', 'kempt' and 'speakable', are rarely, if ever, used in the positive.

It is possible to 'furl' a sail or an umbrella - but the other two appear unspeakably unkempt when I attempt to use them in the positive.

Does this indicate that English is possibly not only the most interesting but also the most odd language in the world? Which is why it can be used so inspirationally by comedy scriptwriters, comedians and, of course, cartoonists – which allows for yet another short detour.

When, at 27, I suffered three split spinal discs I had to be encased in a plaster cast from the top of my torso to the tip of my tummy. (A tiptop alliteration!) Having to wear this body armour for several months I became the target for every scribbler and scribe in the county. Much as had Michiko's Egyptian lady in his next, very clever cartoon.

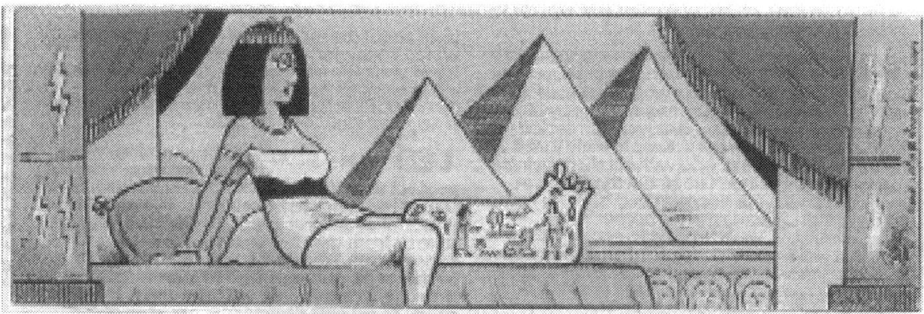

Just days before the cast was to be cast-off. (not such a good pun), I attended a fancy function at which Roy Ullyet was the speaker and in proof that cartoonists are as quick-witted as we believe them to be, within minutes of our meeting, he wrote, on the only available space left, which happened to be at the bottom of the cast; I'M A NAVAL MAN MYSELF. Which gave much amusement to the assembled guests and the medics who, a few days later, relieved me of the cast.

I kemptly kept (which is as close as I'll get to using the word 'kempt' in the positive) this bit of the cast but, as do most things, in the mists of time it eventually turned to dust.

Miss Types, when you meet her, can be equally odd - and amusing. On checking the text of 'Impossible People' I found that where I had intended to type, 'the MP once' I had inadvertently left out the 'M' and thus wrote 'the Ponce'. I apologise to all MPs who, although not my favourite people, I would never presume to insult in such unseemly fashion. (In seemly fashion? See Politics, Presidents and Premiers). Also, it seems, 'seemly' is another word that is now rarely used in the positive (much like MPs.)

Just a few days after finding this strange error I read a letter in the 'Out of the Mouths of Babes' column in the Daily Mail from Dan Peat of London, who wrote:

"When I was five I thought I'd write a book. Within seconds of starting I wanted to use a word I couldn't spell so called to my mother, 'Mum, how do you spell ponce?" Shocked she asked me what I was writing. I said 'I want to start my story with, 'Once a ponce a time."

Another glorious mistype was in an auto response e-mail from the Royal Mint that included the sentence, "We are aware of the incontinence and frustration that this is causing to our customers."

An 'inconvenience' suffered by all customers when attempting to contact all public services, suppliers or organisations on dedicated complaint lines. The frustration caused by the never-ending requests of auto-response voices to press various keys can also, eventually lead to madness, which, in turn, will most certainly lead to incontinence.

Impossible People

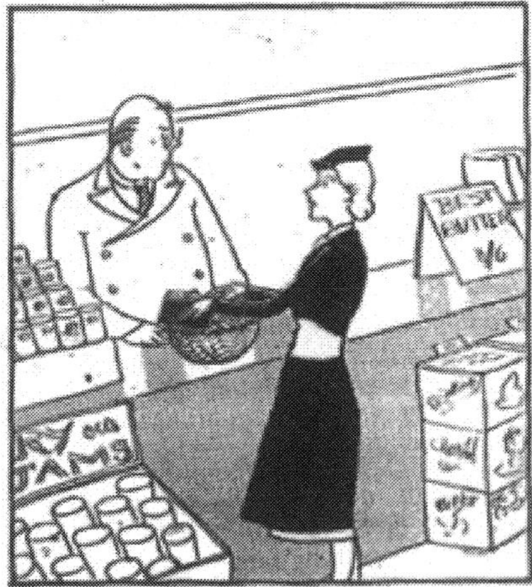

The grocer who said why not buy twenty pounds of rice and boil it when the housewife said she wanted something to show for her money.

If only these auto-responses would include a little humour, we might all feel a lot happier - even if at the end of the call we have little to show for our money!

Copywriters are renowned for their versatility with words. The succinct term for a dying housing market used by the property company, Rightmove was: 'Brickor mortis.' Miss E.D. Punctuation is not quite as amusing - or is she?

An excellent example of why correct punctuation is essential was sent to Allison Pearson by a Daily Mail reader, Christine, who wrote that she first heard it from her father: When a School Inspector once criticised an English teacher for his 'old fashioned' insistence on good punctuation, the teacher said it was vital and wrote on the blackboard; The inspector said the teacher is an idiot.

He then inserted punctuation that made it become; "The inspector", said the teacher, "is an idiot".

Another clever illustration of why punctuation is so important is this next odd ode.

Every lady in the land has twenty nails.	Every lady in the land
Upon each hand five.	has twenty nails upon each hand.
And twenty on hands and feet.	Five and twenty on hands and feet.
And this is true without deceit.	And this is true without deceit.

The misuse of commas (at which my reader will note I am adept), takes us to -

THE ABERRANT APOSTROPHE

Keith Waterhouse, who was one of our most entertaining columnists, inaugurated the marvelous institute, 'The Association for the Annihilation of the Aberrant Apostrophe'.

An inspired concept that advises how the misuse or, more importantly, omission of these punctuation marks can so infuriate those who take pride in our language. Sadly Keith was no longer with us when this extremely amusing poem on the same subject by Pam Cochrea of Newport, was published in Peterborough.

On getting in touch with Pam, a poet of much merit, she said she would be more than just pleased if I did include it because; "Many who still believe in the importance of the correct use of apostrophes will soon be considered to be Impossible People themselves."

Pam, if you ever read this, you will be pleased to know that, having read it, my husband, Simon, said; "Superb."

The Aberrant Apostrophe

Ice-cream's! Cake's or Ripe Strawberry's!
Video's! or Book's! or Cherry's!
On every sign I seem to see,
The Aberrant Apostrophe,

I know that some would say I'm picky,
For punctuation can be quite tricky.
But I was always taught at school,
Apostrophes obey the rule:

'Possessions' - as in Jim's or Molly's;
(Not veggie words like tom's or cauli's),
A missing letter - as in don't.
Or he's, or I'm, or can't, or won't.

To use it in an ordinary word
Is more than daft - it's quite absurd
A sign for 'Pizza's' in a shop,
Makes me nearly blow my top.

A sign that says; 'Buy my flower's'
Make's me fume for several hours
I'll only buy from him when he,
Apostrophises properly.

Not simply throw them in the air,
Then let them fall just anywhere.
"Now calm down, Pam." I hear you say,
"It does no good to fret this way."

But I will always answer, "No!
It isn't right and I just know. So,
I'll scream if one more time I see,
An Aberrant Apostrophe!

Then that erudite gentleman with a capital 'G', Beachcomber of the Daily Express, expressed these amusing, fictitious(?) facts: in his column on the 18th February 2011

'The Government's Target Figures for Punctuational Inflation. The 47 percent figure for misplaced apostrophes includes both apostrophes omitted from words that should contain them and supernumerary apostrophes placed in words such as plurals, where they ought not to be.'

'As always, these figures exclude usage by greengrocers, who have long had a Royal Dispensation to use apostrophes wherever and whenever they choose.'

Which wends us on our way to –

WORDS – AND HOW THEY CAN BE MANIPULATED

The manipulation of words is not new, proof of which is the little known fact that when Julia Caesar was exclaiming to his centurians, “Veni, Vidi, Vici”, Mrs. Caesar was whispering to her hand-maidens, “Vidi, Vici, Veni.” Which has now morphed into, Veni, Vidi, Vino.

A much later, better known, example is the First World War ‘Chinese Whisper’ - or, as the French say, ‘Arab talk’ - ‘Send reinforcements, we’re going to advance.’ Which, on arrival at H.Q. had become; “Send three and fourpence we’re going to a dance.”

These next examples are purported to have been written by schoolchildren during the Second World War. On being asked to compose sentences that included the words; Defeat, Deduct, Defense, Depot, Defender and Delight, two inventively wrote; ‘Depot is under delight beside defender.’ and ‘Defeat of deduct went over defence before detail.’

JERI’s next cartoon also confirms the inventiveness of her more youthful Impossible People.

Impossible People

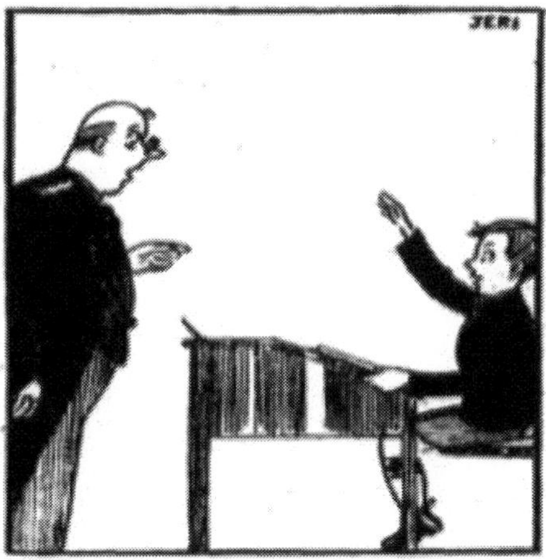

The boy who said “What about Irish Stew?” when told there was no connecting link between animal and vegetable kingdoms.

If the previous anecdote is true, and I have no reason to suppose it isn’t, there were some really bright children around in the forties who grew up to be even brighter adults.

Proven by this much later, and most certainly little known, example of the clever manipulation of words that I met with during the 'Great Winter of Discontent' in 1973.

Every lift in all the multi-story office blocks in the City of London had notices on them exhorting staff not to use them in case of power cuts, to which some wit had added to each one a neat, hand-written, postscript: *"Power cuts and absolute power cuts absolutely."*

An inspired plagiarism of Lord Acton's assertion that; *"Power corrupts and absolute power corrupts absolutely."* Which spurred George Deacon to ask; *"If absolute power corrupts absolutely, where does that leave God?"*

Which is a heavenly lead into –

SPOONERISMS. MALAPROPISMS AND FREUDIAN SLIPS

Spoonerisms (named for the Reverend W.A. Spooner. An English Scholar who frequently and famously transposed words), are now one of the finest tools of cartoonists.

Malapropisms and Spoonerism are also referred to as 'Freudian slips'. Presumably of the brain rather than the tongue. Although I prefer to believe in the latter as most of us have tongues that often have 'a mind of their own'.

A fact that the presenters, James Naughtie, Andrew Marr and Kate Silverston would most definitely agree with. On the 'Today' programme of December 6th 2010, Mr. Naughtie mispronounced the name of the Culture Secretary by replacing the 'H" in Jeremy Hunt with a 'C'. Then later on the same day on the 'Start of the Week' programme, Mr. Marr, while discussing Freudian Slips and Mr. Naughtie's naughty error, inadvertently used the same Spoonerism.

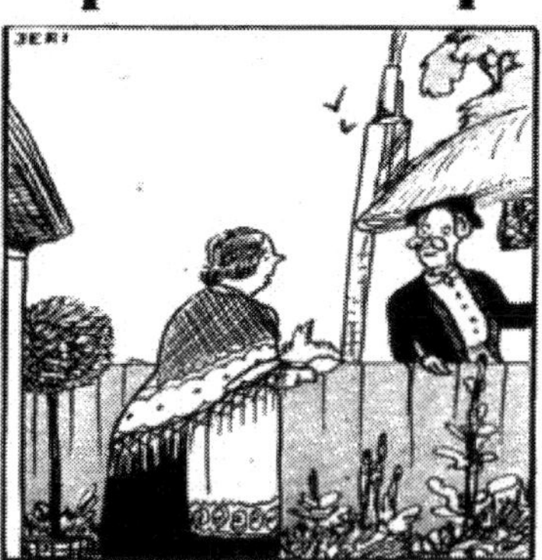

The woman who said she did not look like a septic geranium when her neighbour told her she had reached her seventieth birthday.

Following a spate of both amused and indignant responses from listeners, a BBC spokesman apologised for these crude errors of speech, which were then, on the midday news, compounded by Miss Silverton when she said, "James Hunt's proposals for faster internet service would give us the 'breast' broadband in Europe."

So, as with buses, it would seem that Spoonerisms tend to come along in threes.

Or even fours? A caption not dissimilar to an 'accident of the tongue' made by the mother of my exceptionally bright grandson, Michael.

A prospective client, when enquiring about hiring an au pair, asked from where the girls were mainly recruited. Jacqui told her that most came from Eastern Europe and meaning to say they arrived in the UK in 'fits and starts', Spoonered this into: *"spits and farts."* Needless to say this lady went elsewhere for her au-pair.

Impossible People

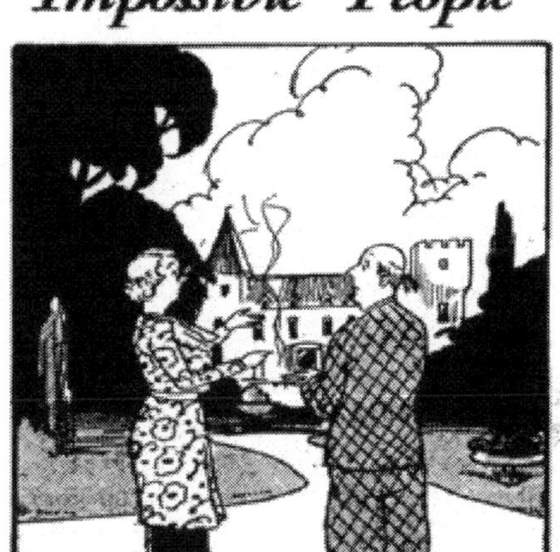

The woman who said she was not quite sure in what style her house was built, but she thought it was reminiscence.

JERI's next two captions include malapropisms that even R. B. Sheridan would have been pleased to attribute to his inspired creation in The Rivals, the marvelous Mrs. Malaprop.

A critique for a television programme was; 'A look at what happens when directors remake Hollywood blockbusters.' They called the programme; 'Shaving Ryan's Privates'. (Which is probably why the newly enlisted private soldier with the surname Parts requested promotion.)

Sonya's severe dyslexia could allow her to have a Malapropism lexicon of her own. One of her best is her use of the word 'breach' when she is 'going to 'broach the subject and, instead of widely, she is often wildly off the mark.

Impossible People

The gas man who told the poet his meter was all wrong.

A few more of my favourites are her frequent use of the words; 'moth' instead of 'myth' - 'regress' instead of 'redress' and 'specific' for the 'Pacific Ocean'. Another is her own word 'parammaters', for 'perimeters'.

As in; "I hate to breach the subject but I have to regress the balance as there is a moth that is wildly held that the Specific Ocean, due to its parammaters, is really a sea."

Impossible People

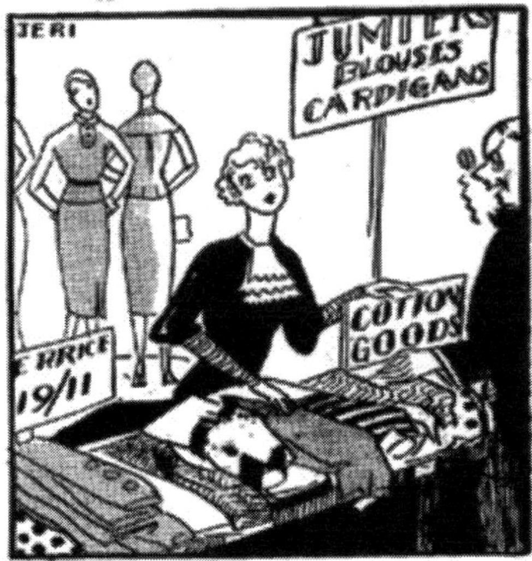

The saleswoman who said she marked the woollen goods "Cotton" to keep the moths away.

As most of Sonya's errors make her conversation amusing I don't always correct her but when hearing her discuss with a mutual friend his recent surgery, I thought it would be unsisterly not to tell her that 'prostrate' is what men become when they have prostate cancer.

As do most dyslexics, Sonya has supreme compensatory skills. She is an excellent artist and exceptional designer.

In conversation she sees pictures while I see words, and she has the rare gift of being able to visualise three dimensionally. Thus for many years we enjoyed a successful partnership in the 'world' of Interior Design, an art that took us to many corners of the globe. (An oxymoron too good to include only once.)

While we both have an equally excellent eye for design, due to Sonya's dyslexia, I acted not only as the 'engineer' but also the 'oily rag'. An 'oily rag' that would often fold up with laughter at Sonya's amusing bon mots – or, as she would spell them – bonmows.

Impossible People

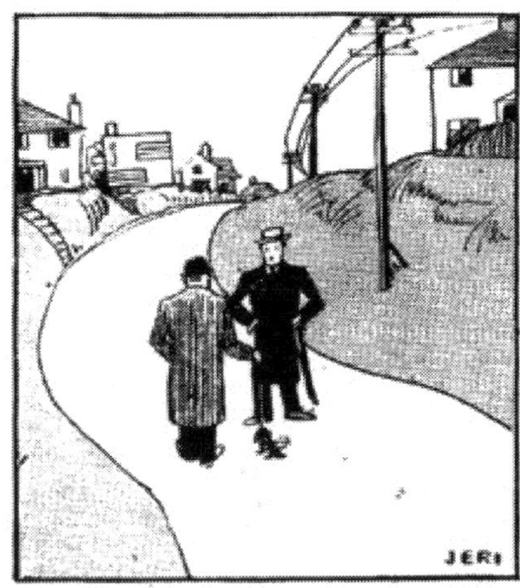

The man who called his wife's dog Restraint because that was what he had to exercise.

One of our suppliers, a marvelous Greek gentleman with an equally marvelous name, Vasily, ran a magical lighting emporium in Acton in West London. When making some purchases for a new client, he asked me for her name for his order book. I said; *"It's Jayne Lambert with a Y."* At which, much to Vasily's amusement, and not a little of my own, Sonya said; *"I didn't know Lambert had a Y in it."*

Our ears can make mistakes that are equally amusing as those made by our brains and tongues. Thus mishearing or mistaking the spoken word can also lead to new words or, as in my next anecdotes, names.

As I write earlier, on leaving Devon, we decamped to our grandparents' house in Essex. As they could not accommodate all seven of us, their very kind next door neighbours, (known to us as 'The Rangers'), who had a young daughter, Claire, and three sons, Dan, Peter and Bernard, kindly agreed to accommodate Stefan and Boris.

A frequent subject when people meet our family is 'Names'. Bernard, who had only heard our grandfather referred to as 'Captain', asked what his first name was. On being told it was Paul, Claire said; *"Well I know Mrs. Cochrane's first name, it's 'Shootapadie"*. A presumption based on the fact that, when in the garden tending to his chickens, our Grandfather could often be heard to mutter in his strong Scottish accent; *"Shut up Adie."*

The years have not diminished our friendship with the Ranger family with whom we still socialise. While this is not due to their cousin, Chris, being my second husband, he is a neat lead to my next anecdote.

When driving to our friends, Diana and Jack, who had just had their first baby, Chris asked; *"What do you think they will call him?"* While, in unison, I said; *"I must send her a card."* To which Chris said; *"What sort of daft name is Amozindereka?"*

Although their new son was given the sane name of Austen, it was some years before we stopped referring to him as 'Amos'.

And then there are Palindromes

This anonymous palindrome is from a picture in the loo of our friend's Vanda and Baz. If my 'Impossible People' is ever published it may end up in a lot of other people's loos too. It asks; 'Is this the longest palindrome in the world?'

To bring him to a doubting maid,
Ned, a bold and dangerous task assayed.
And when he came in triumph home,
Ere half his fervent plea was done,
She answered with a palindrome,
"Now Ned I am a maiden won."

While Andrew Sean Greer's excellent book, 'The Story of Marriage,' includes this inspired four word palindrome composed of only two letters, 'too hot to hoot'.

And Alliterations

The most famous are those said by Professor Henry Higgins in George Barnard Shaw's play Pygmalion; *"In Hertford, Hereford and Hampshire hurricanes hardly ever happen."* Which led Richard Littlejohn, in his inimitable way, to suggest the beleaguered Brummies should ignore the dire warnings from their local council of expected hurricanes because; *"Hurricanes also hardly ever happen in Handsworth, Harborne and Halesowen."*

Of fame equal to Shaw's words are those devised for Mary Anning, known as Susie. Born in 1799 in Lyme Regis, she worked as a seamstress until her death in 1874. Fascinated by the fossilised sea life found in abundance on this Devonshire beach, she took to collecting them to sell to visitors. From whence came; "Sister Susie sits and sew shirts for soldiers while she sells sea shells by the sea shore."

In my last term at school my classmates and I were asked to compose from any of the 26 letters of the alphabet as many alliterations as we could that included countries or towns.

I managed to compose five from just three letters, E, F and T. My sixth was Q and my seventh, K, had a naughty 'and' in it for which I was forgiven. But, on arriving at the letters J, X,Y and Z all attempts of myself and my classmates failed miserably.

Three tired travelling teetotal Tibetans trying to trek timely to Timbuktu.
Four friendly frazzled Finish fishermen frantically fishing for frightened frogs.
Five fantastic French friends feverishly fanning four frail frightened fainting females.
Ten tiny toddling Tansanian tots trying to train their tongues to tunefully trill tunes.
Eleven egotistical educated Englishmen eating eight enormous Ely electric eels.
Queing Qatar quangoe's quietly quoting quirky quips quite quickly.
Kingly Kuwaiti Knights keenly killing Kestrels, Kites, Kingfishers and Kangaroos.

And Anagrams

A 'Weakest Link' contestant told Anne Robinson that she specialised in making anagrams from people's names and had devised 'Iron beans, no!" for hers. But as she was shortly to quit the programme, my own, 'Bin Ann sooner', was slightly more apt.

The Peterborough column of The Daily Mail regularly features anagrams sent in by their readers. Many of which are by Tony Crafter of Sevenoaks in Kent, who crafted, (sorry Tony, I couldn't resist the pun), one that relates to one of today's less happy phenomena; *'An Inner-city's housing estates = Insecure. One stays in at nights.'*

Nicola Tapsell, yet again kindly took the time to put me in touch with Tony who, equally kindly, devised an anagram from the words 'final' and 'demand' as an adjunct to JERI's next Impossible Couple. Who not only won't be able to 'stay in at night' but may, also, not be able to 'stay invduring the day'.

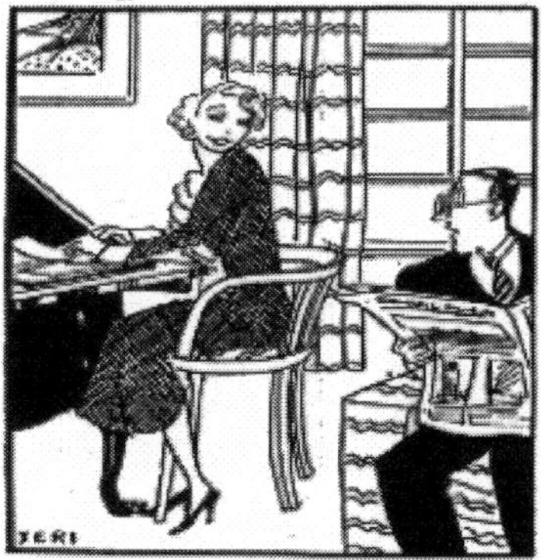

The young housewife who said they need not pay any more rates as a final notice had just arrived, so they were obviously giving up hope.

Despite 'fiddling' about with it, the only one he could find was, 'fiddle an anthem', which includes the additional word 'the' as in: The final demand'.

Which is even better because 'fiddle an anthem' becomes inspired when allied with the brilliant anagram Tony devised from William Blake's anthem, 'Jerusalem'.

A Jam Rule Ends

And did roast beef in olden time
Fill gentle England's inner need?
And was McDonald's just a name
Synonymous with U.S. greed?

And how did burger and French fries
Cause fish 'n' chips to lose appeal?
And what unusual bugs nestle in
Among those dark Satanic meals?

Bring me my honest Yorkshire pud,
Bring me my meat and my two veg,
Bring carrot, turnip, fill me up;
Bring tons of home-made jam on bread.

I will not cease the endless fight,
No, nor will Hell flame-grill my plan,
'Till wholesome fare is once again
Devoured in our ennobled land!

It is a marvelous linguistic contortion that is instantly recognisable as most people will know the words of the anthem from whence it came - and certainly all members of the Woman's Institute. Tony tells me his wife is one which, perhaps, is what gave him the inspiration. It gets even better when his version is sung, as its metre fits the original tune to a 'T'. Or should that be 'tea' as in 'Jam and Jerusalem'.

Tony has a portfolio of over three thousand anagrams. One, on Gordon Brown, is composed from all the letters in the Abba song, 'Take A Chance On Me'. Which, he says, is a 'sonogram' – a word 'composed' by someone at the Daily Mail.

He tells me that composing anagrams is a popular 'sport' and he has restructured the two thousand letters in Kipling's 'Mandalay' (which is just a click away on wordlsmith.org.anagram/mandalay).

Two others by Tony, the first from the haunting poem, 'Alone' and the second from Edgar Allen Poe's even more haunting, 'Do Not Stand at My Grave and Weep' are included at the end of the book.

Tony is a moderator on a website devoted to the creation of anagrams where, each month, enthusiasts compete for awards. He tells me an historic, world-wide record of these can be found on www.anagrammy.com which can bc accessed via: 'Enter The Forum, and then scroll to the bottom to find 'Archives' and click on 'Nominations.'

Emrys Williams of Bedfordshire says; *'Including proper nouns, there are 4,994 four letter words of which 2,204 have no anagrams, 619 can make two anagrams, 6 make three, 102 make four, 36, five, 15, six, while five make seven, and one, ante (an initial stake in poker), makes eight'.*

He doesn't say how many two or three letter words make anagrams, one of which is dog, that, as I write in my section on God is God.' Which, as both God and dogs are so loved by so many of us, is most apt.

And a few even odder oddities -

The day may soon dawn when these magical methods of playing with words will become obsolete as researchers at Cambridge University have come up with the premise that, as long as every word begins and ends with its correct letter, however the other letters are placed the brain will adjust to the text which can then be read as easily as if it was spelt correctly - as in;

Bcuesaeof the phaonmneal pweor of the hmuan mnid, rscheearchres minaitn it deosn't mttaer in what oredr the ltteers in a wrod are, the olny iprmoatnt tihng is taht the frist and lsat ltteer are in the rghit pclae. The rset can be a taotl mses and you can sitll raed it bcuseae the barin does not raed ervey lteter byistlef, but the wrod as a wlohe.

It is also said that words written without vowels are equally easily understood.

Whch s crrct f y knw wht th sbjct s bt, bt wht f y dnt? Fr nstnce cn y ndrstnd ths? r ths? Ys! Bt t ds't t wrk wth wrds f lny tw r trh lttrs.

The first, being easy to read, suggests they are not wrong, but the second suggests that they are. It is also a premise that would eventually prove to be the death of the lyrical use of words for as the inspired Choir Master, Gareth Malone maintains; *"Vowels are absolutely essential when forming the interplay between words when sung."* Or, say I, spoken, read or recited – but not it would seem, when written.

When I wrote my first poems, their crafting was not merely time consuming, it was also very frustrating, so the joy, at sixteen, of being taught how to use a typewriter cannot be overstated. Nevertheless, this still entailed much rewriting as each line of a verse had to be retyped even if the tiniest change in either metre or style was needed.

Which led me to wonder how writers such as Jane Austin, Milton and Shakespeare crafted their hand written works. Works of such erudition, style and beauty that our present technology could not possibly improve them.

How many early parchment manuscripts are original, or are copies of rejected first attempts? Or did their writers all have such superb powers of recall and language skills they could create works that needed no alteration. Or were they all dictated to scribes?

The first book written on a typewriter was Mark Twain's 'Tom Sawyer' and, with the vast selection of both written and typed works now available to read, it is fascinating that Jonathan Swift's 'Gulliver's Travels' first published in 1726, which must have been written by hand, is one of the most read books in the world.

The writer James Chapman listed the most read books based on purchases. These may have changed by the time my reader reads this but, as I write, they are -

27 million: The Diary of Anne Frank;
30 million: Think and Grow Rich;
33 million: Gone With the Wind;
43 million: The Twilight Saga;
57 million: The Da Vinci Code;
65 million: The Alchemist;
103 million: The Lord of The Rings;
140 million: The Little Prince by Antoine de Saint-Exupery *(Whose name plaque adorns a tiny house in the tiny French village of Cabris in France)*

400 million: Harry Potter;
820 million: Quotations from Chairman Mao Tse-Tung;

None of which get remotely close to The Bible that, over the past 50 years alone, outsold all of them with sales of a staggering three thousand nine hundred million. One thousand five hundred of which can be seen in the Bible Museum of St Arnaud, a town in the region of Victoria, Australia.
A
n excellent programme on its heritage taught us that the King James Bible was translated into English from its Hebrew and Greek origins by forty seven of the finest scholars and linguists of Corpus Christi College, Oxford.

Commissioned by James the 1st in 1603, it was eventually completed in 1611 and, excluding Shakespeare, is possibly the finest work in English. It was also believed to be influential in bringing to an end many global injustices, one of the most notable being the Slave Trade.

But I did not need the programme to tell me that the Bible includes (as does the work of many authors and poets), a myriad of maxims that are quoted daily by people who, unless they are devout, regular churchgoers, may not know they are quoting from this ancient and unmatched, uniquely styled, book. Or won't know unless they are, as am I, addicted to poetry, that they may be quoting quotes from this magical 'art' form. Which brings us back to style.

There are many authors whose works, even without attribution, are recognisable to their reader, as a writer's style, unlike art, is almost impossible for another writer to copy. In particular Shakespeare, whose style is unique, and one has to wonder where his plays might sit in the list of most read books if all of the many millions of people who have,over time, viewed his plays, were to be counted as 'readers'.

While artists have always been able to conceal changes to their work quite deftly, this was not an option for writers until the birth of the typewriter and, later, computers. But does the relative ease with which they can now make changes to their text lead to better writers?

Or is technology losing us a few Jane Austens, Miltons and Shakespeares. But not those who compose -

LIMERICKS

With seldom more than thirty words and even more seldom, an attribution, this should allow me the freedom, copyright notwithstanding, to include these very clever verses.

Taken from the pages of my many books of limericks, the first two neatly, (neat being what limericks should be), describe what they are - or what they might become!

The limerick packs laughs anatomical
Into space that is quite economical,
But the good ones I've seen
So seldom are clean,
And the clean ones so seldom are comical.

The limerick is furtive and mean,
And must be kept in close quarantine,
Or she'll sneak to a slum,
And promptly become,
Disorderly, drunk and obscene.

There was a period when the popularity of the limerick became so great the American Government instigated a 'Decree for its Suppression' as confirmed in this next limerick by Professor T.J. Spencer of Washington.

A limerick that is much less well known than those I include later. As are those I include of my own, which were completely unknown - until now.

The limerick, peculiar to English
Is a verse form that's hard to distinguish.
Once, Congress in session,
Decreed its suppression,
But people got round it by writing the last
line without any rhyme or meter. (Or metre?)

As in –

There was a fat lady from Eye,
Who felt she was likely to die;
But for the fear that once dead,
She would not be well fed,
She gulped down a pig, a cow, a sheep,
twelve buns, a seven-layer cake, four cups
of coffee and a green apple pie.

I particularly like the second as, having lived in South Norfolk, the pretty Suffolk town of Eye is well known to me. Whether the town of Limerick is equally pretty I have no idea. What I do know is that it is the spiritual home of Irish Rugby from where, one would think, naughty rhymes would originate.

However it is not the home of these neat, succinct 'odes' of just five lines. Nor, as is also thought, were they the inspiration of the artist, author and poet, Edward Lear who was born in 1812.

Although he undoubtedly re-ignited their popularity, their likely birth was many years earlier as, in response to a Daily Mail readers query about their origin,

Damien Jones of Bath, writes that St Thomas Aquinas who was born in 1225 and died in 1274, was almost certainly the first person to write one which he includes in his letter in both English and Latin.

Let it be for the elimination of my sins	Sit vitiorum meorum evacuatio
For the expulsion of desire and lust	Concupiscentae et libidinis exterminatio
For the increase of charity and patience	Caritatis et patientiae
Humility and obedience	Humilitatis et obedientiae
As well as all the virtues	Omniumque virtutum augmentatio

Monsignor Ronald A Knox, in a review of Langford Reed's 'The Complete Limerick Book' (published in English Life in February 1925), also avers that St Thomas of Aquinas, also known as 'The Universal Doctor' devised, in his Roman Catholic Breviary, the limerick form of verse as early as the 13th century.

I would be even more pleased to learn that Mr. Lear had no prior knowledge of the writings of St Thomas when he composed his limericks for the children of the Earl of Derby, for whom, between 1846 and 1895, he worked as an artist, because if so, it would be further affirmation of my own and Mr. Silver's views.

Although its Latin format fits that of our present day limericks, it did not become a popular form of verse until nine centuries later when, shortly after the end of the First World War, numerous newspapers and periodicals conducted equally numerous, extremely popular contests, which led my mother and many of her friends to compose them.

Following which, in the 1920's, they became a bit naughty - limericks, not my mother or her friends. (Although I believe they also had their moments!)
I only know this because I found, in a copy of W.S. Baring Gould's; 'The Lure of the Limerick', some rather risqué hand-written limericks composed by my mother when sailing with her father on the Arcadia. One of the naughtiest being:

There was a young nun called Maud
Who had an affair with The Lord,
She'd offer up candles alight,
By day and by night,
Which was more than The Lord could afford.

A naughtiness that, no doubt, did not afford to allow for its entry into any of the competitions for which it may have been composed. Or were the twenties, with their Flappers in very high shoes and very short skirts really as 'naughty' as we now suppose them to have been.

I also pray that my reader will not consider it blasphemous, but of those my Mama wrote, this is the least naughty 'offering'. (As naughty as puns that pop up when you least expect them?) Whether my mother and her friends entered any of their efforts in these contests we will now never know, but can be reasonably confident they did.

What we do know is that all competitors were asked to include a sixpenny postal order as an entry fee which, in 1917, led to the purchase of 11,400,000 of these instead of the usual, anticipated, seven to eight hundred thousand.

It is also, very possibly, why we now have so many libraries full of so many books full of so many limericks – and Post Offices that no longer sell postal orders.

I would take an educated (if I were), guess that, as both my mother and I have done, most poets try their hand (or pen or keyboard), at limericks as The Peterborough column of the Daily Mail feature one each weekday.

To my great pleasure one of these was one of mine in which I castigate Tony Blair and Jack Straw for their iniquitous, unkind plan to give Gibraltar to the Spanish. A plan that, to the great relief of the Gibraltans, was soon aborted.

But not, I think, due to my limerick.

If they think they can turn back the clock,
Blair and Straw are in for a shock.
The Gib's anger won't vanish,
They don't want to be Spanish,
And don't want the word Spain in their rock.

Those chosen to grace Peterborough never reach heights as low as the next one that my Mother composed in the twenties when she was in her twenties– but, as far as I know, she was not at Trinity -

There was a young man from Trinity
Who shattered his sister's virginity,
He buggered his brother,
Had twins by his mother,
And then took a first in Divinity.

The next three are my own, much less naughty limericks on British towns and cities that I wrote for use on 'holiday' mementoes such as mugs or tea towels.

Although how a tea-towel can be considered a 'memento' is entirely lost on me.

The streets are paved with gold in London town,
And the high life is so high it can get you down.
But their City is slicker
And makes money quicker,
Than the time it takes to turn half-a-crown.

There's an upmarket 'Uni' in Brighton,
Where the students all use the term 'Right on',
They've lots of pot and beer,
The Lanes and The Pier,
And a grand, but somewhat naughty, Pavilion.

A pastime in Glasgow is to fight,
Which can go on all day and all night,
It's not that they're rough,
Or even very tough,
But it gives their English neighbours a fright.

Writers of limericks are not, it would seem, liable to the laws of libel. This one, from John Letts, 'A Little Treasury of Limericks Fair and Foul', could as easily apply to me as it does to Gert.

I don't like the family Stein,
There is Gert, there is Ep, there is Ein
Gert's writings are punk,
Ep's statues are junk;
And no one can understand Ein.

And this one composed by my mother, definitely applies to me.

A girl by the name of Karina
Dated a boy who had a Morris Marina,
Her mother said dear
Think of your career
Find a boy with a nice Ford Cortina.

I found a boy with a nice Ford Cortina and married him but it didn't help my career. Which naturally strays to:

NICKNAMES AND MONIKERS - a weird word itself

Nicknames and 'Ethnic Slurs' (as Wikipedia calls them), have always been and will, almost certainly, continue to be invented.

Used as insults, some of the most unpleasant and most frequently used are; Chink, Frog, Iti, Limey, Pikey and Spik. Another is Faggot which, until relatively recently, was just a sausage.

As I note in my section on 'Coincidences', there are also surnames that derive from their predecessor's original trades, such as Webber for weaver. Now the present surname of my husband, Simon, who started life with a surname closely allied to 'cowboys', Wyatt.

Another is 'Nob' or 'Nobby', the common and age-old nickname for anyone with the surname Clarke who worked as a clerk in the offices of docks. It goes back to the time when clerical workers were perceived to be a 'bit above' the dockers, and were thus thought of as 'Nobby'. An early term for 'posh' or 'snobby'.
Which takes us to the name given to one of the oldest trades, shoemakers, the earliest of whom were known as 'snobs'. A word that is now, as is 'posh', only used with derision.

The word 'snob' was first used in the English language in the 1780's, as a derivation
of the ancient Norse word 'snub' meaning, 'to cut short'. Thus shoemakers, who 'snubbed'(cut) leather for a living, became known as 'Snobs' which is why, today, snobs are known for 'snubbing' or 'cutting' those they consider louche or plebeian and thus, beneath their notice.

As they would these next two scallywags of JERI's.

Impossible People

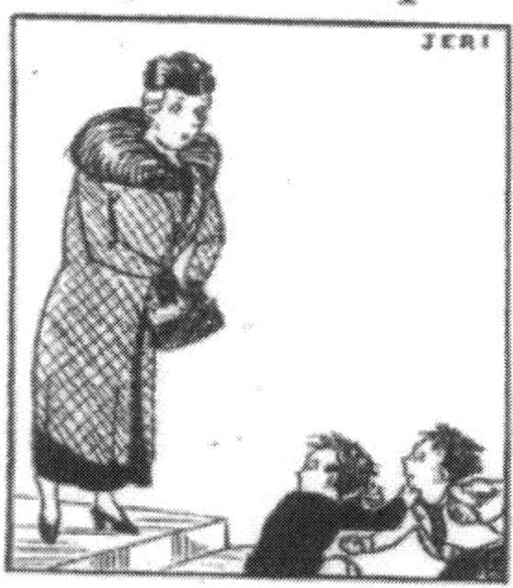

The boy who said "Make it a shilling for the winner." when asked if they would stop fighting if they were given sixpence each.

Many years later the word snob became slang for commoners who behaved in a vulgar or ostentatious way. It then grew in popularity and usage following publication of a book by William Makepeace in which he designates snobs as; *"Those who aspire to be aligned with The Gentry but whose manners are insufficiently refined."* To which he adds; *"Their paucity of social etiquette violates certain society rules which brings ridicule upon them."*

If only ridicule could curb the excesses of those who regularly rampage drunkenly on our city streets today. For while pensioners are asked in supermarkets for proof of age before they can buy a bottle of wine, the 'run-amokers' among us appear to get younger by the day – and night – regardless of whether they are of an age that allows them to buy – or drink - alcohol. But, as the two little 'nignogs' in JERI's previous cartoon indicate, 'run-amokers', of all ages, are not a new phenomenon.

The 18th century French word 'nignog' a term that for obvious reasons is now little used, if at all, also distinguished between those of humble or high birth.

However, when I and my siblings were children the word 'nignog' was frequently levelled at people of all levels and all ages, in particular the very young. Is this, perhaps, why there is a children's playground in Central France called Nigoland?

Again, as so often does the Daily Mail's Richard Littlejohn; "I only ask the question."

During the same period university students used the term Snob when referring to 'townsmen' as opposed to 'gownsmen' which, for some reason, gave rise to the academic myth that the word was an abbreviation of 'sine nobilitate', a Latin term with a similar meaning.

It was originally conceived during the French revolution by the children of French aristocrats exiled in Germany who, it is recorded, married the German word 'nicht' with the French word 'noblesse' to describe those who were: "Not of the nobility".

As children we didn't know we were descended from 'the nobility', albeit that of Scotland, and not knowing the real meaning of 'nignog' thought it had some connection with the word nitwit, a word that is still used to signify stupidity.

Although, with the tendency during the second world war for children to suffer with hair nits, it could have meant that too.

We also assumed it was similar to the now much hated word, 'wog.' A word that, we were reliably informed by our Grandfather, was an abbreviation of the term; 'Worthy Oriental Gentleman' because, in the same way his wealthy P.O.S.H. passengers were notated on the ship's boarding list with these letters, his, mainly male, Indian passengers were notated with the letters W.O.G.

I once read of a dispute between neighbours, one of whom was deeply offended by a gollywog left in full view in a window of the house adjacent to her own. Subsequent reportage of this 'presumed insult' maintained that the word 'gollywog' and it's eventual diminutive, 'wog', originated in Egypt.

The author wrote that, in the early 19th century, British soldiers, on noticing how popular were the ragdolls that Egyptian children played with, took these attractive dolls, that were called 'gollywogs', back to England as gifts for their own children. Gifts that, no doubt, their children enjoyed playing with as much as the Egyptian children did theirs.

The article stated that the word 'Gollywog' was derived from the amalgamation of the Arabic word for workers, 'Ghuls', allied to an abbreviation of the words emblazoned on the armbands worn by the Egyptians that denoted them as: 'Working on Government Service'.

Although, as our grandfather travelled frequently to India many years prior to our British forces being stationed in Egypt, I suspect his version of the origination of the word is possibly, (and probably), more accurate - and is certainly a lot kinder and definitely more courteous. As were all of the Africans, Caribbeans, Egyptians and Indians I had the pleasure of working with when organising overseas conferences and congresses.

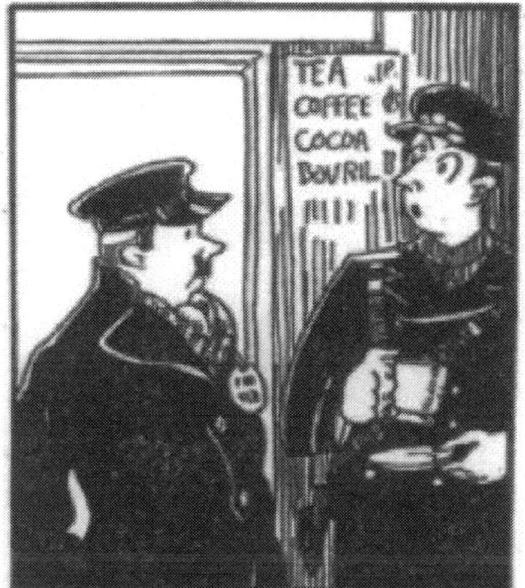

The taxi-driver who said he made his fortune from jams.

My own very glamorous Gollywog is much admired by my much loved, proxy son Hugh, who frequently threatens to nick it. He maintains that, due to his Caribbean ancestry, it would 'feel' more at home in his house than mine. Although if my Grandfather is to be believed, my doll's ancestry is not Caribbean or Egyptian but Indian.

Hugh married his beautiful Slovakian wife, Aneta, in Las Vegas and they have now given me two beautiful 'proxy' grandchildren - twins, Max and Naoli. One day Naoli will own this doll, but for now it sits on a bed reminding me of my first gollywog doll that I so loved as a child. A toy I never thought of as anything other than a beautiful, cuddly doll. I also still have one of the dinky gollywog mascots that were once given to their customers as collectables by Robertsons Jams.

We were also reliably informed by our mother that the word 'nigger' (a word that was often used by the American soldiers who frequented our house during the war), was an impolite term for, as they were referred to then, 'Coloured Americans'.

So we children were very disappointed not to meet any Americans of any other colour than a pale or dark hue. (A pun especially for Hugh). Nor any Red Indians who, we learned later, were not really red, nor really Indian.

Hugh, who frequently works in France and once lived in Spain, told me that the French and Spanish have few inhibitions when voicing annoyance at any perceived slight - such as losing a parking space to another driver - which means he is now inured to having the word Neeagra shouted at him.

He said; *"Their pronunciation makes the word sound so attractive if they really want to insult me they should call me a 'coon', which sounds like an insult in any accent."* How could anyone not love someone who treats such ignominy with such humour? I told him that 'coon' could be considered a compliment as it is a word that not only has an interesting history but is also the name of many varieties of flora and fauna and two of the prettiest things on the planet, cats and butterflies, have species called Coon.

As do dogs. The Blue Tic Coon Hound is bred specifically to track Racoons, and each has its own individual howl that enables its owner to recognise it.

Coon is also the name of a number of places and the surname of even more people. Also an Australian cheese similar to English Cheddar that was given the brand name Coon after the American, Edward William Coon, who patented its unique ripening process.My Australian friend, Wendy, told me this 'down under' Cheddar tastes similar to its English relative, and is just as versatile.

All of which indicate that 'coon' is a word of much merit – as is my, much loved, friend Wendy and my equally loved 'son', Hugh.

The good offices of Wikipedia tell us the word possibly originated in the early nineteenth century, either from the word 'Cajun' or the Portuguese 'barraco' – a building that held slaves for sale. Its racial slant was then 'popularised' by the song, 'Zip Coon' that, in the 1830's, was sung by minstrels at markets where slaves were sold.

It also lists a number of other, less well known, 'ethnic slurs'. A few of which relate to those with white skin, but the majority refer to those of dark skin, the poor or the less intelligent. But these unkind assumptions refer to a time when usage of such words was common.

Conversely, there are numbers of unpleasant words that derive from proper names, such as the frightful word 'crap' that originated from the name of Mr. Thomas Crapper, the highly respected and equally 'proper' gentleman who invented the flushing toilet. A device for which everyone should be eternally (and internally), grateful.

Hopefully, Mr. Crapper was not aware of this derivation of his name while he was still alive. One also wonders whether his progeny continued to feel pride in their surname or have changed it.

Another hated word - of much interest to the media - is 'Paki'. A word not dissimilar from those used for other nationalities such as 'Brits', 'Frogs' and 'Itis', but its frequent use by cretins – a good moniker for the 'brainless' - has led to its unpleasant and distasteful connotation.

Although it is possible it came into use due to the number plate on one of its embassy limousines - PAK 1. Which begs the question: Does displaying this number on their embassy car indicate a necessary sense of humour in those who are more courteous than those who use the word in a malevolent or derogatory way?

Another 'strange' word that refers to people's anatomy not ancestry, is 'fizzog'. A jocular Victorian abbreviation of the word physiognomy which, my O.E.D. tells me; 'Is the 'supposed art or practice of judging human character from facial features' or 'facial features themselves, especially when regarded as revealing character.' Physiognomy is such a tricky word to pronounce it is no wonder they shortened it.

It is also a word that even some teachers may find hard to pronounce, that's if they know of the word at all! But, even if they don't, they will, undoubtedly, know the word 'fizzog'.

We six siblings and two cousins, born within nine years of each other in four different counties devised nicknames that related to three of our places of birth.

Stefan was a Middlesex Moo-Cow, Sasha was a Somerset Sausage and Elaine and Susan, were Devonshire Dumplings. But we could never agree on a name for the four of us born in Essex. A county that, despite its reputation as being of little merit, has a great deal more than many areas of England that are thought of as being superior.

Its unkind reputation was reinforced by publication, in the mid seventies, of 'The Book of Essex Girl Jokes', compiled by Richard Littlejohn and Mitchell Symmons under their inspired pseudonyms, Brent Wood and Ray Leigh.

Place names that allow for another short detour -

Born 'An Essex Girl', and living within its environs for many years, I have a great affection for this county and an even greater affection for the Essex family of my brother-in-law, George. His daughter Fiona and her husband, Chris, have two delightful children, Georgina, a beautiful, intelligent girl who has chosen a career in banking, and Max, an equally clever young man who is pursuing a career in design.

An interesting reversal as not so many years ago it would have been the other way around.

Some years prior to Impossible People being ready to send to a publisher, I needed to transfer the manuscript from my fifteen year old computer to a MacbookAir. A 'journey' that seemed to be beyond the limits of the 'Genius's' employed by Apple, but one that Max achieved in less than thirty minutes.

As do most young girls, not just those born in Essex, Georgina loves to dance, and while she may do so with 'gusto', I doubt she has danced with any young men of that name. Or has she?

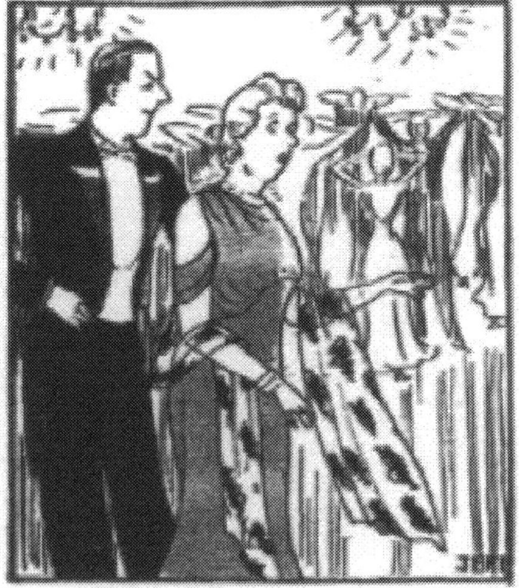

The woman who said she did not know him when told her daughter was dancing with gusto.

A caption that may be obscure to many, or at least those who are not conversant with 1920's English - or Latin - as it is a word that originates from the Latin, 'gustus' meaning 'taste'.

In its archaic form it also meant 'relish or liking' and, strangely, 'style of artistic execution', which fits dancing 'to a T'.

Especially, perhaps, Tea Dances - a fashionable and popular pastime when JERI was in her twenties. It also means 'enjoyment or 'vigour', hence its inspired use in her caption.

In reparation for his earlier misdeed, Richard Littlejohn wrote a book in praise of the girls of Essex. A book for which Martin Newell composed one of his inspirational poems that, as I mention earlier, are a popular feature, (most certainly for myself), of The Sunday Express.

Not only did Martin kindly agree that I may include it in 'Impossible People' he, even more kindly, said I may 'tailor' it to include Georgina's chosen career in banking.

I read Martin's poem to Georgina as she lay sunning herself on the Beau Rivage beach in Nice. It would be pleasing to think that my reader will be reading it in an equally pleasing place, and they could do a lot worse than read it somewhere in Essex. A county, that, regardless of its reputation, is a meld of not only sea and sand, but also many areas of natural beauty and interest.

One of the best being Southend-on-Sea, a much maligned place by the 'posh' that in 2011, was elevated to high status with a depiction of their magnificent Kursaal on postage stamps. Following which a number of media reports asked why this particular landmark had been chosen when there are so many better ones. But those who wrote them patently had not done their homework, as the Kursaal is a fine building with a fine heritage and fascinating history, much like Southend itself – and it's Essex Girls.

The Essex Girl
by Martin Newell (For Georgina.)

An Essex girl - an 'Essex calf',
she'll never mind it if you laugh
or substitute bad jokes for wit.
She's heard them all, she's used to it.
She'll note the things you say and do,
before she stops to yawn at you.

Her sense of style,
her smoke blue eyes,
underlined in pencil black,
were sharpened under endless skies
where linseed flowers and poppies grow,
in summer fields stretched out below.

And if her mode of speech seems plain,
don't underestimate, again,
her power to say what she may think,
once she's matched you drink for drink.
Grabbed her purse and paid the tab.
Mentioned work and called a cab.

As lawyer, lecturer,
Banker, actress, nurse,
An Essex Girl?
You could do worse!

Martin's ability to compose, each week, poems on topical subjects is a gift few poets could lay claim to. Although his agreement to allow me to include a few in Impossible People is definitely a gift to me – and an even greater gift to my reader.

Like all of JERI's grandchildren (whether by lineage or marriage), Georgina and Max are single minded in their commitment to their careers and work very hard at them. Unlike many young people who now believe the taxpayer will pay them to lie in their beds all day. A belief that, according to JERI's next Impossible Boy, is not new -

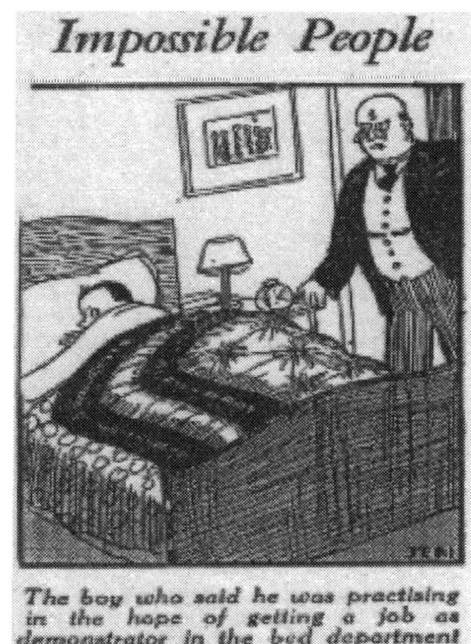

The boy who said he was practising in the hope of getting a job as demonstrator in the bed department of a store.

Apart from those we devised, the only other nicknames I know for 'natives' of other British counties, are the well known 'Tyke' for people born in Yorkshire (which, no doubt, displeased our Grandmother), the Tyneside 'Geordie' and 'Scouse' that denotes the lovely Liverpudlians for whom I wrote this limerick.

In Liverpool music and fame go hand in glove.
While John Lennon's statue looks down from above,
In salute of a tavern
That's called 'The Cavern',
And The Beatles and Cilla and a 'Lorra, lorra love'.

The word 'Beatles' for the group 'The Beatles' was equally inspired. But how many, of us, even hardened music aficionados know the difference between the words 'beet' and 'beat' or 'beetles' and 'Beatles'?

It was said that John Lennon chose the name as a slant on 'The Crickets' and then changed the 'ee' to an 'ea' to give the word a 'double entendre'.

While Paul McCartney and Ringo Star maintain that it came from 'The Wild Ones' in which Lee Marvin says to Brando; *"Jonny we've been looking for you. The beetles have missed you."* ('Beetles' being slang for 'motorcycle girls'.) Of almost equal interest, my dictionary gives three very different meanings for the word 'beetle', eleven different ways that the word 'beat' may be used, but none for the word 'beatle' - now the most famous word of the two. And probably of beetles.

And, as JERI's next cartoon suggests, a lot of microbes?

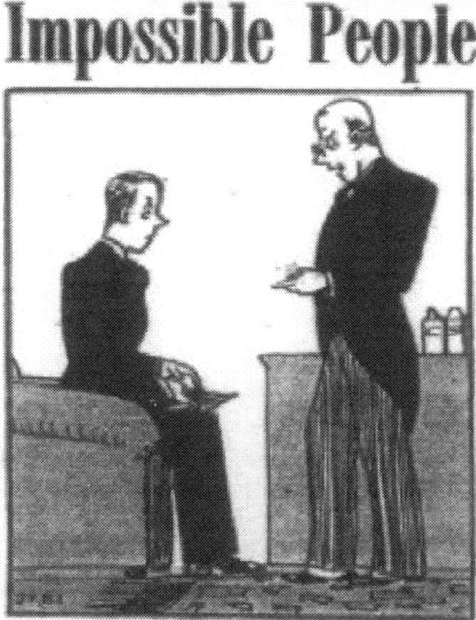

The young man who said that was no way to talk about his baby when the doctor said insomnia was caused by an ugly microbe.

STRANGE NAMES Given strangely to People, Property and Places

One of the regular customers at my West London public house was a gentleman called Harry, (or 'Arry' to his friends), who, to use a neat oxymoron, had a classic East End accent.

Very fond of his wife, he would frequently refer to her as "My Ellen". My manager, Bob, once asked him whether her name was Ellen or Helen. Harry thought for a moment and said; "She's Ellen "wiv' an 'haitch." (The 'Haitch' word that doesn't have an 'H'!)

This mispronunciation of the letter 'H', that has always been associated with the East End, is proliferating to the extent that many television and radio presenters now use it. Although perhaps the BBC has a new policy of only employing presenters who hail from that part of London?

Unthinking parents can saddle their children with unfortunate names. Nancy and Jim Thomas, the eventual parents-in-law of my sister Sasha, having given their son the first name John, then gave him the second name Richard, which, needless to say, he used for business purposes. No doubt to his great relief they didn't add Tom and Harry to this trio. Equally fortunately he was a man of much humour and even greater courtesy, so any allusion to these monikers was always met with much merriment and even greater grace.

An anecdote that brings me neatly, and a lot less naughtily, to the unusual and little used name, Belitza. which, by strange coincidence, was the second name of both our maternal grandfather Paul and our paternal grandfather Boris. A coincidence made more fascinating by the fact that Paul's family hailed from Scotland and Boris's from Russia.

As Mama gave all of her children a superfluity of little-used names, it was odd that she didn't bestow one of her sons with the name Belitza. Perhaps she just didn't like it. I love it and had I known of it before my own son was born he would now be Belitza Bellamy. However, age and a changing world have made me grateful (and my son even more so), that I gave him the sane name of Michael.

If Terry Wogan had kept all the items his listeners sent him they would make a very amusing book. Although it was Terry's inimitable delivery that made them so hilarious. One of the best was from a gentleman who said his three lady friends were called; Marie Kesh, Cassie Blanca and Aggie Dere.

I met Terry at the wedding of his Goddaughter, Samantha whose mother, Anna, and I spent a lot of time together due to our respective husband's spending a lot of time together enjoying their mutual interest in buses. Big, red, double decker ones. Both Chris and Anna's husband, Michael, owned one and after the service all of the wedding guests travelled in these to the reception that was held on a boat on the Thames.

Several years ago I read a letter in a daily paper that asked whether anyone knew of a more amusing name than that of a hotelier whom the writer had met in Vienna called 'Hertz Van Rental'. 'Charity Deeds' was one of the best but the outright winner was Clive Holt who said he'd once spent an unforgettable night of passion with a girl called 'Jenny Tallier.'

At about the same time my daughter, Alisonjane, mailed me this news clip:

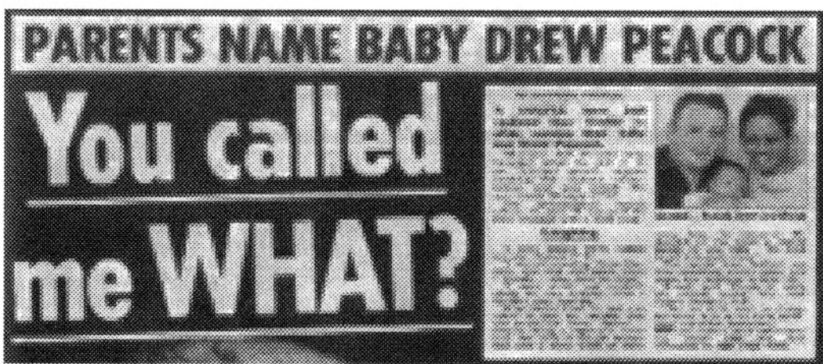
PARENTS NAME BABY DREW PEACOCK

You called me WHAT?

From their photograph and the write-up, this attractive couple appear to have taken reportage of their unwitting, unfortunate choice of name with much humour. Which bodes well for both the future of their marriage and their son - whatever name he may, later, elect to be known by.

Although I have to admit to the insane idea of giving my daughter a name with the delightful alliteration of Lallagay Loveday Minute (Loveday Minute being the name of the little girl in my first 'real book', 'Tangletrees' by Lillie Le Pla. However, common sense prevailed and her name became AlisonJane, which gifted her with the name, Lally.

The years have not lessened my affection for these names - nor my children's gratitude for not bestowing them. But odd surnames are not so easily changed. Or are they?

One of my publishing contacts, Kirsty-Ellen sent me an e-mail in which she wrote; 'Here's a fun fact for you, Karina! The official spelling of our family name is Smellie, but as I was teased at school, in my teens I changed it to Smiley.'

She said that she is still proud of the original as it is a very old, well-established Scottish name and Robert Burns wrote a poem about one of her ancestors, William Smellie, who was one of the first editors of the British Encyclopaedia. So it comes as no surprise that Kirstie-Ellen works within the world of words.

However, all of these names would have been less painful than that which I, as the eldest granddaughter, was nearly made to endure - Grizelda. A Cochrane family name that goes back into the mists of time. Thankfully in this instance the Russians won and I was given the kinder name of that of my paternal grandmother.

My reader will have noticed that my paternal Grandmother's name was Leah, and, despite it being my first given name I am known by my second name, Karina. There is a simple answer to this which I will try to make as complicated as possible.

In some secular Jewish families it is - or probably more correctly, was - tradition for the eldest daughter of the eldest son to be given the name of his mother, but the child could not use this name while her paternal grandmother was alive. Thus, prior to her grandmother's demise, she would be known by her second given name.

Our mother being busy composing cartoons and our father being busy capering about, neither thought to tell me of this, so I only discovered that my first name was Leah when, in my early teens, I needed my birth certificate for something. The shock of finding I was Leah not Karina, made me forget what the 'something' was and, to avoid a crisis of identity, Karina I remained.

Although when dealing with airlines, beaurocrats and clinicians I become LeahKarina.

Thankfully, they kindly gave me a third, the eminently sensible Marion. Which - just as oddly - was the first Christian name of our mother's friend Dolly Freeman. A name I use when wishing, or needing, to become truly English – as no doubt did Dolly.

Added to this panoply of Christian names, having been married to three different men I also have a plethora of surnames, which should make New Scotland Yard grateful that I didn't also inherit my father's unconventional attitude to the law.

Which neatly takes us to a series of 'follow-up' items published in 2015 in the Daily Mail's Peterborough Column when several readers wrote in regarding unusual names or - more correctly - names with unusual connotations.

Mrs. Molly Crimmons (an unusual name in itself), wrote that when, in 1944, she attended Batley Girl's Grammar School the history teacher was Miss Nelson, the biology teacher was Miss Moss, the cookery teacher was a Mrs. Kitchen and art was taught by Mrs. Green. There was also a Miss Bibby who was the Kindergarten teacher while her own form mistress was, unfortunately, Miss Fortune.

This was followed by a letter from David Horchover (yet another unusual name), who wrote that when he served in the RAF among his fellow compatriots were a King, an Earl, a Knight and a Lord.

Then Ann Dyer joined the fray to say that when she and her husband were buying their first home their solicitor was a Mr. Cheetham and their mortgage advisor was a Mr. Crook.

Then B.P. Morris wrote that a friend of hers, when in the film business, worked with the Film Executive for many of the Carry on Films, Norman Hudis, who would answer all telephone calls with "Hudis here – who dat dere." There was then a flurry of similar letters citing similar amusing oddities, all of which would make another, amusing coffee table book. Peterborough please note!

My French hairdresser, Sandrine, has three sons with the delightful names Audrick,
Ellaury and Dorian. Although these are not Saints names, prior to 1993, French babies had to be given a name from a 'list' acceptable to the government and although the list no longer has to be adhered to, a court can still ban names they decide are against a child's best interests.

As a Catholic country, each day has a number of saints names attached to it and, with several saints to each of the 365 days and a few more for leap years, it makes you wonder if it really is so difficult to become one.

Although as, very often, an early death is a prerequisite for this accolade, most might prefer to leave the trials of becoming a Saint to someone else.

As, it would seem, did 'Mrs. Noah', for , much to my joy, the following letter confirming Joan of Arc's marital status was published in Peterborough in 2011.

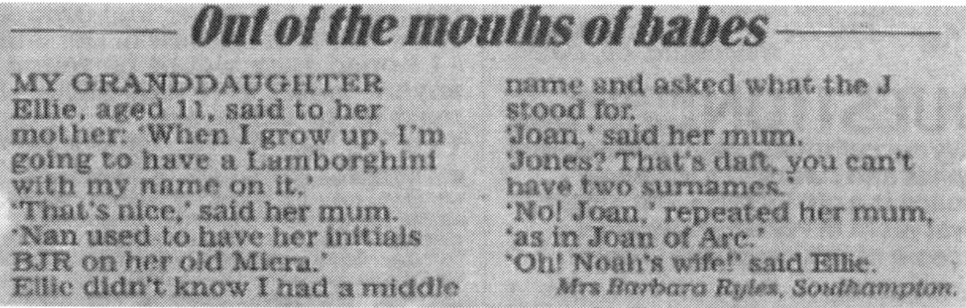

Out of the mouths of babes

MY GRANDDAUGHTER Ellie, aged 11, said to her mother: 'When I grow up, I'm going to have a Lamborghini with my name on it.'
'That's nice,' said her mum. 'Nan used to have her initials BJR on her old Micra.'
Ellie didn't know I had a middle name and asked what the J stood for.
'Joan,' said her mum.
'Jones? That's daft, you can't have two surnames.'
'No! Joan,' repeated her mum, 'as in Joan of Arc.'
'Oh! Noah's wife!' said Ellie.
Mrs Barbara Ryles, Southampton.

A supposition that magically twins with JERI's next caption, conceived some seventy years earlier, and which, yet again, coincides with my own and

Impossible People

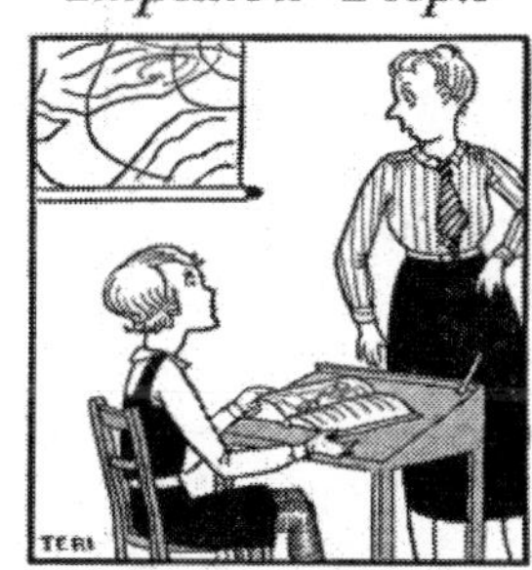

The little girl who thought that Joan of Arc was Noah's wife.

Mr. Silver's view on original thought. While those called William are always being thrown out of the House of Commons.

Impossible People

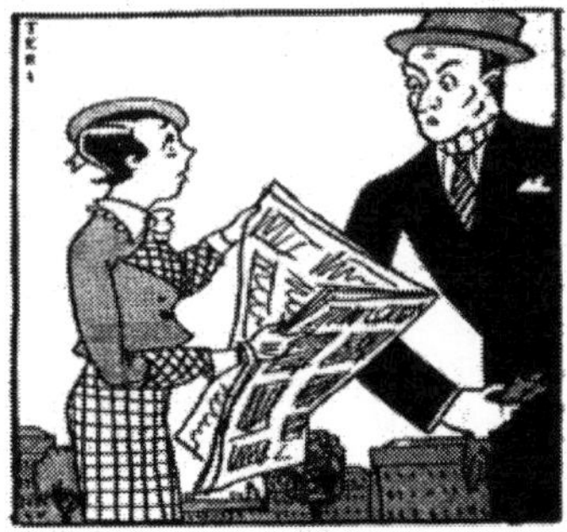

The girl who wanted to know who was this "Bill" they were always throwing out of the House of Commons.

A cartoon that, despite its much earlier heritage, is most apt for the shenanigans that, in 2009, saw the Speaker and politicians, from all parties, leaving the House of Commons in droves. So I have to ask; "Is the House of Commons known as 'The Lower House' due to its occupants un-statesmanlike activities?

While some Saints become literary characters, it would seem that some politicians are thought of as literary characters.

Stephen Glover wrote: *'Gordon Brown, who is built on an heroic scale, compared himself, perhaps unwisely, with the morally ambiguous, untamed, towering figure of Emily Bronte's Heathcliffe in Wuthering Heights, and Jack Straw might serve as a devious cleric in a Trollope novel, but the rest have strayed out of Enid Blyton's Famous Five.'*

Now that Mr. Clinton no longer graces it with his presence, the American Senate may not have a 'Bill' in it either as Americans have no inhibitions when naming their offspring, one of the best being Condoleezza.

Within just days of including her name, I was delighted to hear Richard Digance read this truly inspired, hilarious poem on the programme Countdown. I was even more delighted when he kindly agreed I may include it in 'Impossible People'.

Just a few weeks after my request I met Richard at a party held by my friend Hoodie, where he was the evening's entertainer - and where he entertained her guests brilliantly.

As you can see, Richard, your poem 'fits the bill' admirably -

The Most Powerful Woman In The World

Never mess with Condoleezza Rice
Or you may be in trouble.
Never tell her that her hair's the same
As the wife of Barney Rubble.

Never mess with Condoleezza Rice,
Always do your best to please her,
Unlike the time her parents
Chose to call her Condoleezza.

Now the chances are 'cos of who she is,
She won't be a Countdown fan,
So although Americans can't say too much,
I think we at Countdown can.

What sort of name is Condoleezza?
Eleven letters with two ee's and two zz's.
What were her parents thinking of?
What was going through their heads?
Now Rice is a fairly normal name,
Our friend Sir Tim is one,
Aneka is another,
Her with the lovely bum.

But Condoleezza! Two ee's, two zz's.
The most powerful woman ever?
D'you think they took some Scrabble letters
And slung 'em all together?

No, nor me, on thinking about it,
Scrabble only has one Z.
So, although a masterly theory,
We must think of something else instead.

Or ask a quizmaster? That Master of the quiz, James Black, writes that Condoleezza's parents composed this name from the musical expression 'con dolcezza'.

There are many other odd (or even odder), names of people that are devised from vsimilar sources – as are many place names. As did the Daily Mail reader who asked the same question, I have never been able to fathom out what towns that are 'Without' are without. So I was pleased to read in their 'Answers to Readers Questions' this pithy explanation from Roy Ingleton of Maidstone in

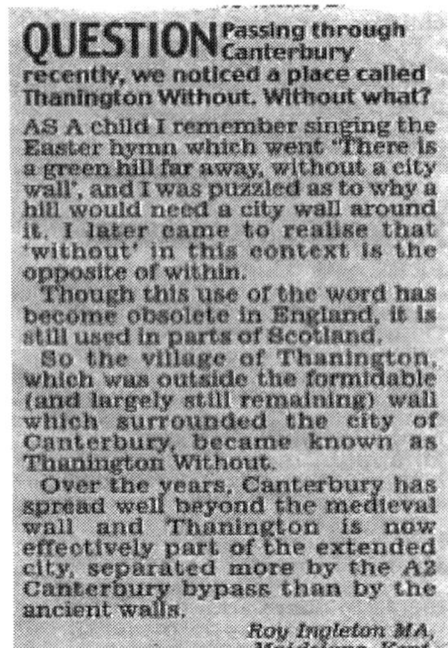

QUESTION Passing through Canterbury recently, we noticed a place called Thanington Without. Without what?

AS A child I remember singing the Easter hymn which went "There is a green hill far away, without a city wall", and I was puzzled as to why a hill would need a city wall around it. I later came to realise that 'without' in this context is the opposite of within.

Though this use of the word has become obsolete in England, it is still used in parts of Scotland.

So the village of Thanington, which was outside the formidable (and largely still remaining) wall which surrounded the city of Canterbury, became known as Thanington Without.

Over the years, Canterbury has spread well beyond the medieval wall and Thanington is now effectively part of the extended city, separated more by the A2 Canterbury bypass than by the ancient walls.

Roy Ingleton MA, Maidstone, Kent.

Kent who writes with such lucidity it is no wonder he is an M.A.

Many people are equally inventive about 'christening' their houses. The Estate Agents for whom my brother, Stefan, worked in the early nineteen sixties were selling a development of new bungalows.

Stefan told us that one of these was bought by an elderly couple who fixed a name plate to their gate with 'Rosie Lee' on it. Shortly after which a young couple, who bought the attached property to the left of the elderly couple, fixed an identical plate to their gate which sported the word 'Cuppa'. One has to wonder whether later owners of these properties rechristened them.

As with 'Rosie' and 'Lee' there are legions of people who cannot resist naming their homes after themselves. Or even other people! In the village of Hempnall in Norfolk is a cottage with the name 'Karina' on its gate.

As it is a relatively rare name perhaps it was used for its anglicised interpretation of the Italian word 'carino' for lovely or pretty. Which may also be the reason why, in my youth, Italian men would tell me my name suits my looks - but then Italian men would say that, wouldn't they?!

However, naming your home 'Cuppa' or 'Rosie Lee' is not nearly as ridiculous as those owners who give their homes names contrived from their own initials.

A one time colleague, Michael, and his wife Pamela, had a daughter Julie and a son Brett, and, in a moment of awe-inspiring madness, named their newly built home PAMJAB.

At about the same time a friend of our family, Jimmy Bates, built a large house on several acres of grounds on which he also built a house for his retired parents. He named his own 'Overdraft' and that of his parents 'Little Overdraft'.

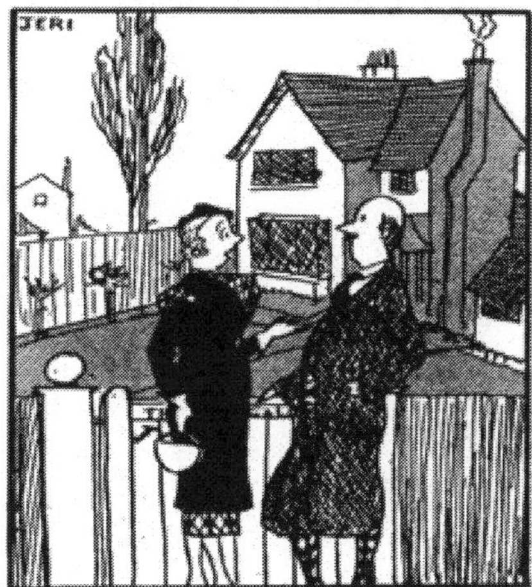

The man who called his house "The Bunglelow," because the builder bungled it and he still owed for it.

These weird names may be very amusing, but a home is more pleasing when it has a name that can be looked up to rather than laughed at, and while I should not admit to it, I always felt slightly superior when giving the names of our titled homes to banks, businesses, or bureaucrats.

Our shop on Sidmouth High Street had the pleasing Honiton House, but our most notable, if not noble, were The Old House in Benfleet, Broome Place in Suffolk and Tasburgh Hall in Norfolk. All of which feature in earlier or later bits of the book.

Nicola and George have lived in homes of equal distinction, Topcroft Hall, Brews Park and The Leys. While Sasha and John lived in a very beautiful Georgian property with the equally beautiful name of Dove House. Sonya and Ray also enjoyed homes that were titled rather than numbered, two of which were; The Croft and Tudor House.

Simon and I had a home in Norfolk with the rather grand name: The Guild House, and, at the same time, owned the house next to it with the somewhat less grand name of: The Well House. But one of our best, in name if not grandeur, was our French holiday home, Le Haut Monestier. I doubt there is a home in England called 'The High Monastery'.

Then there are houses that, despite having no name, have an even greater claim to fame as they are designated by the letters 'ONE' rather than a number. The London business address of my son, Michael was One Hanover Street, and another with this superior mode of address, if not area, is One Churchill Place. The docklands branch of Barclays Bank.

But definitely the most notable is 10 Downing Street. Originally three houses, it became one when, in 1732, it was given by King George II to Sir Robert Walpole.

Now, despite its relatively small footprint, it is, with The Houses of Parliament, a few palaces and titled homes one of the most well known, frequently photographed, viewed and visited English properties. It is also one of the most sought after business addresses.

A business address that leads to -

CLEVER USE OF WORDS

One of my dearest friends, Jenny has a string of employment agencies called, Key Personnel, in which she has, at different times, been ably assisted in this exceptionally successful enterprise by her two daughters, Jacqui, (the mother of my grandson, Michael), and Lisa, both of whom fit well the definition of 'key personnel'.

Often the success of a company is greatly assisted by its name. Robin Hood, the husband of my equally dear friend Carol, has an equally successful, international removal business with the inspired name of 'Arrowpak'.

Anne, the sister of another of our much valued, friends, Vanda, is the widow of the genious who called his company 'Kwik Fit', and Mike Wright, who designed my website has, as his company name; 'The Wright Place'. Which is where he was when I found him.

Despite his excellent workmanship, Peter Elkin, the builder Sonya and I used for our interior design work, always referred to his company, as no doubt do many other jobbing builders, as 'Bodgit & Scarper' or 'Fudgit & Flee'.

Of even greater amusement are the words on the sides of the vans of a company that installs television aerials;' Satisfaction with every erection.' A guarantee few can make.

Equally clever is the signage on the side of an 'Outward Bound Holiday' minibus I once met with on the A12 - 'River Deep & Mountain High'. Although I did wonder what the chances were of finding deep rivers and high mountains in the flat lands of Essex.

Simon, whose field was advertising, maintains that rhymed slogans impede people's ability to remember the name of a company as the slogan will come to mind not the name of the firm. But not, say I, when the slogan is the name of the company, such as the excellent horticultural firm in Essex with the unforgettable name; 'Mown & Grown.'

As I admire the ability to make words rhyme, I will always applaud those who aspire to do so. Even if these are just the name of a horticultural company and even more so when they are as elegant as this elegy to the Rose by Thomas Hood. (1799-1845). An elegy from an anthology that my excellent English master, Mr. Ellis, gave me when I left school.

Flowers

I will not have the mad Clytie,
Whose head is turned by the sun;
The tulip is a courtly queen,
Whom, therefore, I will shun;

The cowslip is a country wench,
The violet is a nun; -
But I will woo the dainty rose,
The queen of everyone.

The pea is but a wanton witch,
In too much haste to wed,
And clasps her rings on every hand.
The wolfsbane I should dread;

Nor will I dreary rosemary
That always mourns the dead.
But I will woo the dainty rose,
With her cheeks of tender red.

The lily is all in white, like a saint,
And so is no mate for me -
The daisies cheek is tipped with blush,
She is of such low degree;

Jasmine is sweet and has many loves
And the broom is betrothed to the bee;
But I will plight with the dainty rose,
For fairest of all is she.

Which leads to Lyrics, Poetry and,

THE ART OF ACROSTICS

I have composed many acrostics but my most clever was for the wedding of my sister Sasha's son, Giles and his fiancé, Kirsten who first met when they were guests at a wedding held on the Great Wall of China.

Impossible People

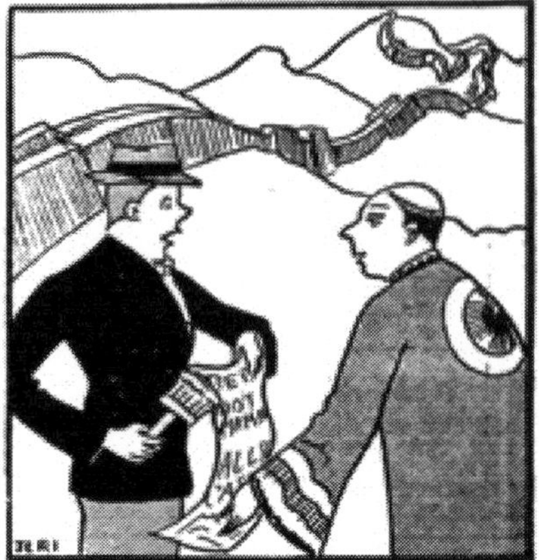

The man who tried to negotiate a bill-posting concession on the Great Wall of China.

Kirsten, as a guest of the bride, had travelled to China from Hong Kong, where, at that time, she was working, and Giles, the Groom's Best Man, had flown to China from London. A journalist with CNN, Kirsten had been looking for work in her home country, Australia, until Giles persuaded her she would be better off searching for it in England.

Relieved to learn that, despite having a daughter with a previous girlfriend, Giles was still a bachelor, within weeks of their first meeting she joined him in England where Kirsty (who might have been forgiven for thinking much the same as the girl in JERI's cartoon), was reassured to find that, although not 'Landed Gentry', her future in-laws occupied a large house situated on reasonable acreage of this, relatively small, Island.

Impossible People

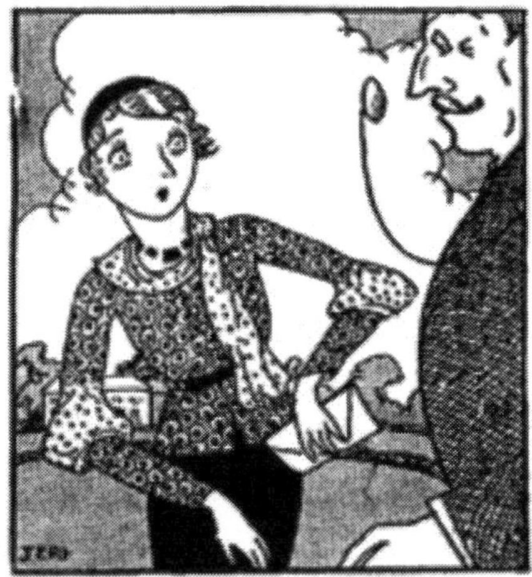

The girl who thought landed gentry were married men.

Georgina, the mother of Giles' eldest daughter, Olivia, and her husband, Martin, are still valued friends of the family, as, of course, are Giles and Kirsty who, prior to their own marriage, gave Olivia two half sisters, Harriet and Freya. As their third daughter, Eliza, was not born until a few years into their marriage, this allowed me to include the Mikado's 'Three Little Girls From School'.

'With A Song In Their Hearts' not only tells the story of Kirsty and Giles romance in rhyme, it is also a conundrum as, apart from their names reading down the side of each of the four verses - which, for those who may not know, is what acrostics are all about. It also has fifty five titles or lines from songs woven within it that are listed on page 465, but can my reader find all of them before looking?

With A Song In Their Hearts for Kirsten Clare and Giles Owen

Kirsten Clare, a girl with flair, golden hair, an Aussie accent and adventurous air,
In meeting Giles said, I'd like to be his lady in red, like to think we'll meet again.
Realizing she'd never want, or care, to wash this man right out of her hair,
She packed up her troubles in an old kit bag and took the last train to London,
Thinking; I would rather be with him in his world than live without him in mine.
Even though, to follow her dream she had far to go, to live in a land she didn't know.
Nevertheless, yesterday was not so far away, for trains and boats and planes.

Could take them here, there and everywhere, to her world or to his, at any time.
Listening to a nightingale sing in Berkeley Square or go waltzing with Matilda in
Australia let them climb the stairway to heaven, discover their own cloud nine.
Roads, the long and winding kind, took them down byways they wanted to be,
Ending their search for that someone to love, that someone to watch over me.

And

Giles said, "Will you be my girl, please, please me, and agree to be my funny valentine?
It has to be you, don't walk on by, stay by my side, stand by me and agree to be my bride.
Love me love my daughter, come fly with me, share my life, have my children, be my wife".
Enchanted, Kirsty said; "Through river deep and mountain high, you'll always be my guy".
So now it's their summertime and the living is easy, they'll not cry, their love will never die.

Olivia, Harriet and Freya, their three little girls from school, are the apple of their eye.
With their world coming up roses they will ne regrette rien, would do it all over again.
Every day in every way, as time goes by, they will never walk alone, will never say goodbye,
Now that love and marriage will keep them together forever - whether walking in sunshine

...or singing in the rain.

As most people have a particular song that takes them to back to a 'magic moment' it would be pleasing to think my reader might find their own 'magic moment' song in my Kirsten and Giles Acrostic.

I wrote the next Acrostic for my sister Nicola as a sixtieth birthday gift. Although my reader may think, and they would be right, she may have preferred a good book.

Nicola was born in nineteen thirty nine, in the season of mists and mellow fruitfulness,
In her mouth not a silver spoon, but a silver trowel, and, in each hand, a book.
Coolly she surveyed a World at War and, finding it not worthy of a second look,
Ordered her life to suit herself, no frills, no fuss, no nonsense, none of which she'd brook.
Least of all when taking care of her family, gardening or deciding what next to cook.
At sixty, misty and mellow she's not, but Sense and Sensibility, she has, in abundance, got

The next was for my brother Boris and his new partner, Kim Regan.

Kim, not one to hesitate, leave a stone unturned or let a good thing pass her by,
In meeting Boris said; "This bloke's no joke, no one's fool and very easy on the eye?"
Much to his surprise and her delight, Cupid chose that moment to let an arrow fly.

And

Boris, as famous for his giving as his girth, and not a man anyone could call shy,
Offered Kim his heart, a fresh start, the contents of his pockets and a piece of apple pie.
Regan thought, "Gosh, not just posh, but kind and funny too, I could really love this guy?"
In no time they had a new home, a new life, a new business whose success became sky high.
So it's fair to say that theirs will be a marriage made in heaven and their love will never die.

Another was for a gentleman who had a heart transplant. He and his wife, Jenny, were close neighbours and very dear friends and Jenny, asked if I would compose an 'ode' for the party she planned to hold in celebration of the tenth anniversary of Ken's 'New Heart'.

Due to the nature of the activity it is usually impossible, and certainly unusual, for a donor and recipient of a heart to meet. However, in a tandem operation, Ken's heart donor, Ron, was given the heart and lungs of a man who, (tragically for him but most fortuitously for Ron), had died in a road accident.

This meant that Ron and Ken were able to meet and remained friends until Ron's demise some years later.

In Celebration of the Tenth Anniversary of Ken's New Heart. 21st Sept 2002

Ken, tonight, with much delight, we make a toast to your new heart, now ten years old,
Even though it first belonged to your dear friend Ron Lippet, it truly is a heart of gold.
Not too many of us get a second chance to stay, but you deserve yours more each day.

Donors also usually don't get a choice, or have much say, when they give their bits away,
Excepting Ron who would be tickled pink if he knew his old ticker was still ticking in you.
When he made your life better he went a long way to make all of our lives much better too.
It won't be a secret, or a lie, when an entry in the Guinness Book of Records states with pride,
Not only has this man refused to die, he has lasted the longest with a new heart inside.
'Going Strong Still', Ken should be your motto, which is why, tonight, we will drink to

...your hearts content until we get blotto.

Ken is a man of much merriment and mirth and a very deserving recipient of his new heart. He is, as is Jenny, so 'big hearted' that most people would find it very hard not to be a friend of his – whether they had given him a heart or not – or, as in the next cartoon, wish to dispose of one.

Impossible People

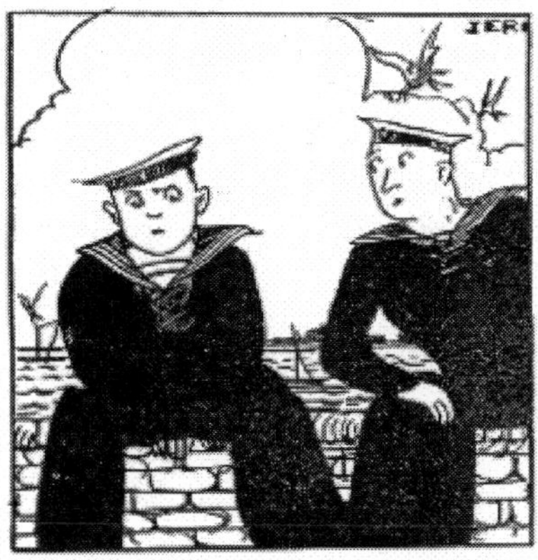

The sailor who said there was one thing he wanted to get off his chest before he married Mary, and that was a tattooed heart with "Sally" on it.

It is also a cartoon with which those who spend a small fortune or, in many cases, a large one, on bedecking their bodies with tattoos may, in later life, have great empathy.

"Life After Near Death" (as Ken refers to his brush with this final fate of us all), gave he and Jenny a strong belief in reincarnation. So, when dining with them one evening, Ken told us that in a previous life he had been a fireman, Sonya and I were quite in awe.

Awe that very soon turned to amusement when he said, "I once said to a young lady, you are the third pregnant women I've rescued today. She said; "But I'm not pregnant." to which I said; "Well that's because I haven't rescued you yet." A similar story at a similar lunch was told to us by our French friend, René, who said that his response to the many assertions from his female patients that they would rather have a baby than visit the dentist, was; "Well make up your mind as I have to adjust the chair."

On the subject of teeth (which my reader may think not the most toothsome), when in conversation with the elderly mother of our client, Jenny Wrightson, we were fascinated to learn that, as a 21st birthday gift, her teeth had been replaced with dentures.

She told us this procedure was popular in the early years of the twentieth century. Not due to the introduction of longer lasting acrylic dentures, nor to the lack of adequate dental hygiene products, but to avoid, in later years, the vast expense of remedial work.

Facts verified by a number of people of similar age who have also told me that many people of their era enjoyed (?) this somewhat bizarre 'gift'. Wikipedia tells us that as late as 1968, 79% of people aged between 65 and 74 had no natural teeth. By 1998 this figure had dropped to 36%.

Which begs the question, should stars of the silver screen and television who enact, as elderly people, scenes set in times prior to the introduction of dentures be depicted with few, if any, teeth.

Impossible People

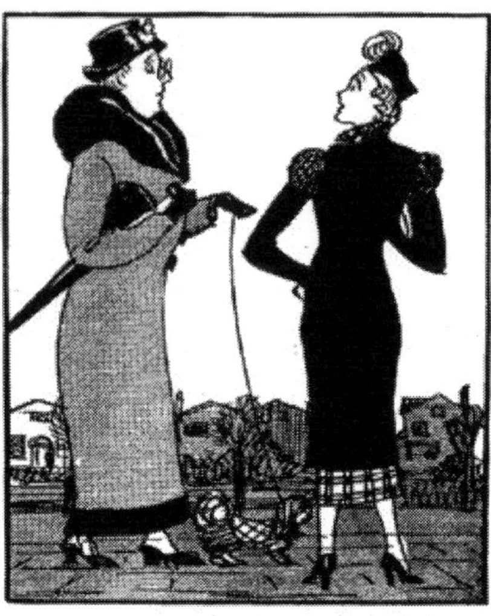

The woman who said she didn't have a local anæsthetic for her tooth; she always went up to town for things like that.

Given the present paucity of practicing NHS dentists even the 1998 figure of 36% is sufficiently high to suppose this practice will possibly regain its popularity Particularly as the popular press now proliferates with publicity placed by people who promise to provide us with pricey, permanent porcelain ivories. (Howszat for two alliterative sentences and a final odd, in both senses of the word, oxymoron?)

Mention of 'going up to town' or anywhere else, reminds me of Churchill's pithy description of one of his parliamentarian colleagues; *"The honourable member reminds me of Columbus. When he set out he didn't know where he was going When he got there he didn't know where he was and when he returned he didn't know where he had been."*

A description that could now be applied to many people who rush frenetically round the globe in the hope of finding something, or somewhere, or someone or even themselves, and, it must be supposed, as far as the latter are concerned, they don't know who they are, or where they are?

My friend Tina will steal clever quotes from clever writers and tailor them to fit a situation, as in; *"If you don't know where you are going, every road will take you there."*

During our teen years many of our friends, on the assumption that; "Thare's gold in them thar hills", rushed like lemmings to Australia and Canada only to find, more often than not that the hills were made of clay. Or water?

"But Papa, I don't want to go to America!" "Shut up Heimie and keep swimming."

A joke that, probably, only those who were born prior to the forties will find

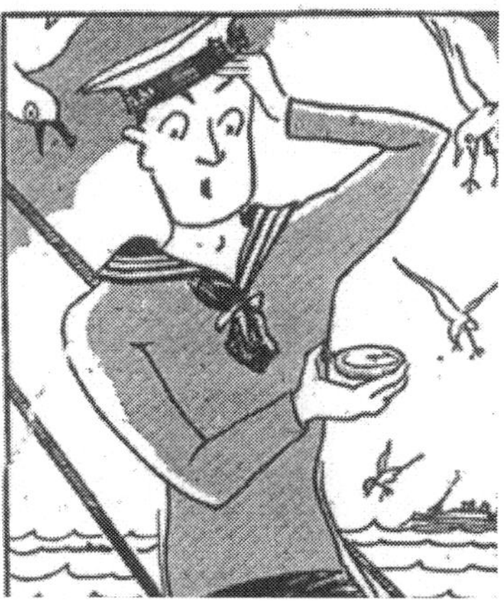

The sailor who boasted that he never slept on his watch.

amusing as, during the decade that followed the Second World War, many Jewish people who had survived the ghastly pogroms and death camps visited upon them by both the Germans and Russians, would do anything to reach America. Even if this meant getting very wet - or going without sleep

Our mother, as did her father and their forebears, had a passion for the sea and would often quote from poems on this subject.

These few lines are by the nineteenth century poet, Paul Laurence Dunbar. The full version can be found, if you are lucky enough to find a copy, in 'Lyrics of the Hearthside'.

Oh for the breath of the briny deep,
And the tug of a bellying sail,
With the sea gull's cry across the sky,
And a passing boatman's hail.
For be she fierce or be she gay,
The sea is a famous friend alway.

Which sails us to -

TRAVEL with a bit of RUBBISH thrown in for good mileage

This next clever play on words - which some may think is rubbish - was sent to me by my dearly loved cousin, come surrogate sister, Susan.

"I have been in many places, but I've never been in Cahoots because you can't

go alone as you have to be in Cahoots with someone. I've also never been in Cognito. Which is just as well as, if you do go, you will not be recognised.

"I would like to go to Conclusions, but to get there you have to jump, and as I have never been much into physical activity I probably wouldn't reach it. I have, however, often been close to In Sane. It doesn't have an airport; so you have to be driven to it and my family and friends frequently threaten to drive me there.

"Flexible is a place I would like to go to more often, particularly when I feel the need to stand firm. A sad place to be, that I try to avoid but often find myself, is in Doubt. And as in old age you need all the stimuli you can get, I now also, often, find myself in Suspense.

"Getting older also allows me to visit in Continent, although when I leave I rarely remember I've been. And now I'm getting even older, I'm sometimes also in Capable and unhappily, seem to go there more often than I would like. Age

Impossible People

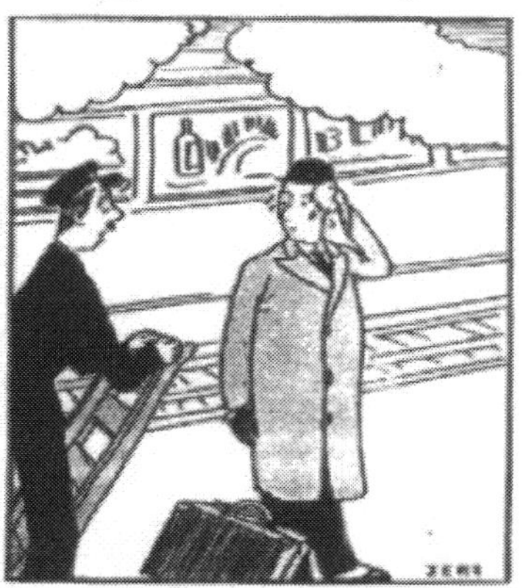

The man who said he had never had time to get really fond of it when the porter asked if he had missed his train.

has also taught me that when I think I'm in Vincible, life generally shows me that I am not! Also, throughout my life, I have also frequently been in Deepshit and the older I get the easier it is to get there."

Unless you miss your train?
Or bus?

I came across this 'Prayer', better known as the Busman's Ditty, in Charles Legge's interesting and informative 'Answers to Correspondents' column in The Daily Mail.

A column in which JERI's Impossible People, with a little help from me and a lot from Charles, have also featured.

Both Dudley Smart of Warwickshire and Dean Taylor of High Wycombe tell us it was first heard during the Second World War and that Ian Drury included it in his 1992 album, 'The Bus Drivers Prayer and Other Stories'. An album that Amazon advises, is still available.

I have read a number of revised alternatives, but much prefer the original.

The Bus Driver's Prayer

Our Farnham who art in Hendon,
Harrow be thy name.
Thy Kingston come,
Thy Wimbledon,
In Erith as it is in Heston.

Give us this day our Leatherhead,
And forgive us our Bypasses
As we forgive them who Bypass against us.

Lead us not into Thames Ditton,
But deliver us from Ewell.
For thine is the Kingston,
The Pinner and the Crawley,
For Esher and Esher.

...Crouch End

Google lists two areas of London that would be a more apt 'Amen' than Crouch End, one in Barnet and the other in Brent both of which are Church End,

My friend Tina says even better would be, Amen Corner in SW17. Although, as I said to her, whoever composed this prayer may have wanted their congregation to 'crouch down' when saying 'Amen'.

But whether they go by train or bus, (or plane), the ease with which people now flit about the world is astonishing when one considers that even as late as the 1970's, you could still meet people born in rural areas who had never travelled further than ten miles from their place of birth. One of whom was my marvelous Norfolk cleaning lady, Vera.

The urge to travel is shared by many species, particularly of the feathered kind. But when combined with a love of adventure it becomes a distinctly human instinct. An instinct that allows for less of us being clumped together sizzling in Africa or freezing in the Arctic. (Which begs the question, if hot is sizzling why isn't cold freezzling?)

Now, with many millions heading, each year, towards the sun, France has many more English visitors than England has French visitors. Nevertheless despite both countries having a similar head count, there are many more French people who speak English than English who speak French.

We would often visit Northern France to stay with our very dear friends, René and Jacqueline - a friendship originally formed between Jacqueline's sister Collette and Sonya, when they met in Sardinia and found they were both one of four sisters, all of similar ages.

In the early days, although we would often visit them, it was difficult to persuade them to visit us until they eventually learned to love England as much as they liked us and their visits became more frequent. In particular those of Rene and Jacqueline whose home, in the Mayenne region of France, had considerable acreage. Acreage that entailed a car journey to put out their poubelle. (Only the French would have such a marvelous word for rubbish).

On leaving for the first of their visits to us, they put their cases in the back of their car together with two bags of rubbish, intending to leave the latter (or rather litter) at their gate. On driving off the Ferry at Portsmouth, they thought someone had stashed a dead body in their car until, on finding the two sacks of rubbish, realised they had forgotten to drop them off. Not wanting to litter our neat countryside with French rubbish nor knowing where should they wish to, they drove to Essex with these smelly bags still in the back of their car.

Impossible People

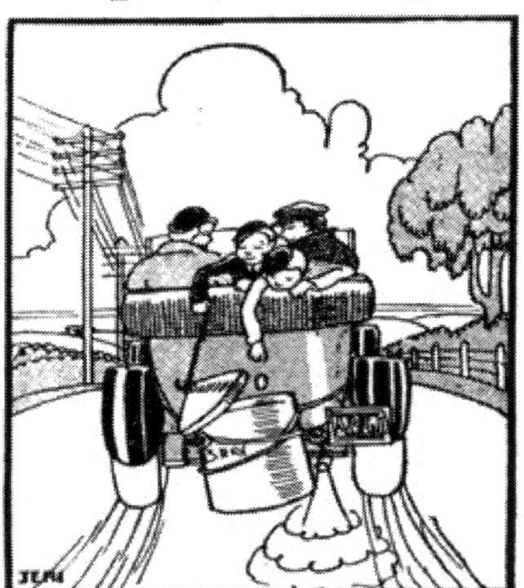

The anti-litter family who took a dustbin when they went on picnics.

Fortunately this bizarre incident did not damage the excellent, long term entente cordiale that our extended families still enjoy. Especially their more frequent visits to England, on one of which they planned to visit Devon before driving up to Essex.

We told them they didn't need to pre-book accommodation as the area had many Bed & Breakfast houses that would have large B&B signs in their windows. As their first visit was early in the year, in the first town they stopped, nearly all of the houses advertised as BnB homes also had 'Vacancies' signs in their windows.

It was quite late in the evening when, very weary, they finally found one with a 'No Vacancies' sign. When the landlady told them they needed to find a house with a Vacancies sign, René said; "Vacance, it mean on 'oliday, n'est pas. Your sign, it say you no on 'oliday. On learning that their word for 'holiday' was

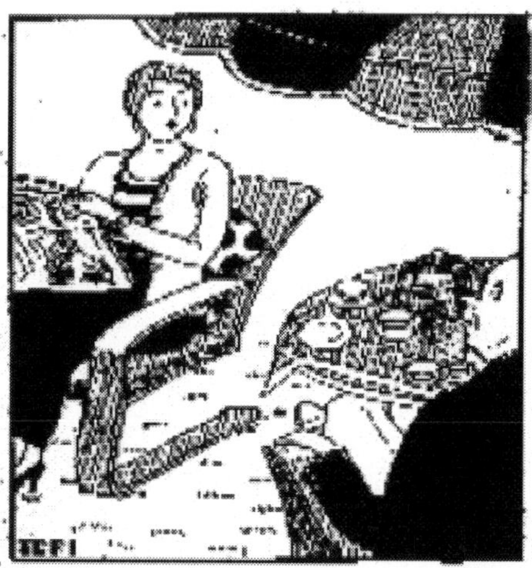

The woman who said these boarding-houses get worse every year when she read that a bed of marbles had been discovered in Sussex.

our word for 'not fully occupied' they eventually found somewhere to stay, but were always a little scathing about our; 'Benighted B&B's with beds like boards and NO duvets".

But it was a long time ago and I'm told B&B's have greatly improved – or have they?

A cartoon that propels us back to the word 'poubelle' and the present problem of its effective disposal. Prior to regular civic waste collection little seems to be known about how people dealt with refuse.

Although there was much talk of how to deal with city slums that had no sanitation apart from their open gutters.

A sight we witnessed when living in Exeter during the Second War, as, unknown to our mother, our daily help, Lizzie, would take us to the home of a young girl who had been 'allocated' to assist her, but who, also unknown to Mama, lived in a typical slum of the time.

These decrepit wooden tenements with external ramshackle stairways and gullies in cobbled yards that ran with stinking sewage, or piled high with filthy debris, have stayed in my memory, (and occasionally my nightmares), to this day.

Many years earlier French was a popular language in many parts of England, and servants, when emptying the previous night's waste into the street from 'po's', (the French word for jug or pot), would shout to the pedestrians below; *"Garder l'eau!" - "Watch out for the water!"* Hence our English slang word for toilet, as in; *'I'm going to the loo do you want to go too?'*

How those living in built-up areas managed before adequate sewage and the disposal of waste became part of everyday life would be impossible to imagine were it not for a most informative television programme that shows the various methods of disposal from close to the dawn of time until now.

What it didn't include was that, prior to plastic, urban householders used metal dustbins that had corrugated lids that children would steal (another cast iron pun), to use as very noisy hoops.

Most country people, having a great deal more space, either burnt or buried their rubbish. When, in the seventies we lived in Broome Place in Norfolk, our children found a refuse pit in the nether regions of its grounds from which they 'excavated' still intact jars and bottles from the Victorian and Edwardian periods that they would clean and sell at the many charitable events we held.

Having had the good fortune to live in three of them, I am aware that charitable events and similar activities are incumbent upon those who reside in large houses. Although many are now owned by celebrities who surround them with high fences, locked gates and guard dogs – safer but not nearly as much fun.

With the present prevailing urgency, and its attendant publicity, to find new ways to dispose of our ever increasing refuse, it's hard to imagine that when JERI created these cartoons, concerns about the disposal of rubbish were similar to those of today, but they must have been for her to compose them.

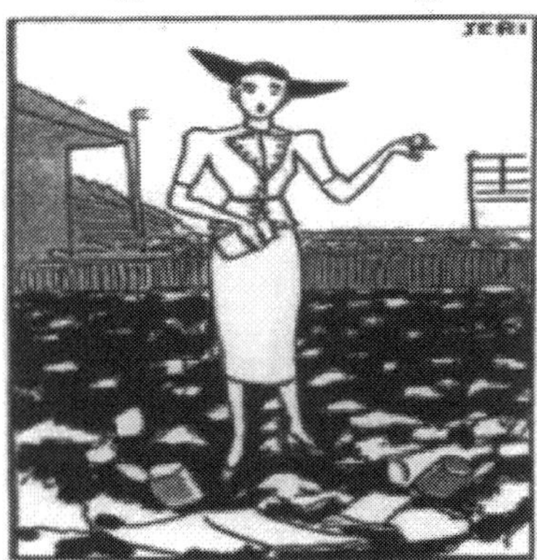

The girl who could not find a litter basket.

Now we are all so paranoid on the subject of the disposal of rubbish and neither burning or burying it - nor throwing it into the streets -

is an option, perhaps everything will become reusable or recyclable - apart, as I suggest in my next poem, from our pee and our poo. A poem that is all about rubbish, or may even be considered by some to be rubbish. As is a lot of the stuff that my twin and I tend to spout – as does Grey's Chloe and her friends.

A cartoon that was published in the Daily Mail just days prior to the seventy third birthday of myself and Sonya - the 28th July, 2011. Thus I like to think of it as an apt birthday gift to me from Grey.

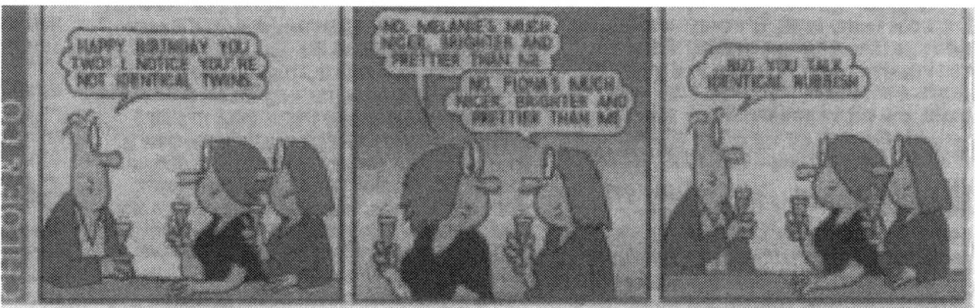

I wrote this poem about rubbish, (or 'rubbish poem'), when, in July 2003, our local council, with the gift of some black and green wheelie bins, lured us into their rubbish recycling revolution. It is no surprise they issued us with these but it is a wonder they didn't have a sign on them saying, 'None of that French rubbish, thank you!'

What Rubbish? or perhaps, Just Rubbish!

Last week the council delivered to our door,
two grey bins and two green ones, and, what's more,
some instructions written bold in several languages,
including Kurdish, demanding we do as we're told
regarding the disposal of our rubbish.

We have to separate the tins from the
peelings and the plastic and the jars,
and then we have to separate the bins,
for on Tuesday the black are sent to Saturn,
and on Thursday the green are sent to Mars

The bottles we must load in crates,
and put them in our cars,
where they noisily clink and clank
and dribble bits of sauce,
and the dregs of the wine we drank,
until we carefully deposit them,
in a different sort of Bank.

It was really rather tough,
but, having got our minds around all
this sort of stuff, and stuffed the stuff
into separate bins and separate crates,
we thought they'd send
another note, in Serb or Croat,
telling us, for all this work,
they would reduce, by half, the rates.

But then the 'Rubbish Commissar'
wrote a note, bizarre in which he states,
that when we sit upon the loo,
we must separate,
not only all the paper,
but also all our pee from all our poo.
But still no word about the rates!

I was going to send a framed copy to the Refuse Department of our local council, but on learning that huge fines were being issued for such minor infringements as leaving a bin lid ajar or popping a bottle in where the paper ought to be, I thought it best not to.

Nowadays refuse collectors and their customers treat each other like dirt. But many of us can remember a time when, each week, our bins were neatly taken from our back yards, driveways or gardens, neatly emptied and then neatly replaced from whence they came.

A service that ensured for all refuse collectors a largesse in Christmas tips that could take them, if not to Venus or Saturn, certainly to a good holiday in Majorca or Tenerife or - for those desirous of doing so - Mars as, according to media reports, there are a few people who wish to go and, it would seem, are now able to do so.

During one of my many 'in-between husbands' periods I was introduced to a young man of the Thomas Cook family and, despite having done a great deal more than my fair share, wonder how much more travelled I would have become had I not spurned his kind offer of marriage.

But, as his lifestyle was not the kind to which I wished to become accustomed, I have no regrets, nor much memory of it.

But it does take us to – or on -

HOLIDAYS

Prior to the Second War, holidays for the less well off were rare and, if taken, were usually spent 'working hard' picking hops in Kent. While middle income families would stay in coastal resorts in boarding houses with 'beds like marbles' and rooms with the odd heavenly view' -

Impossible People

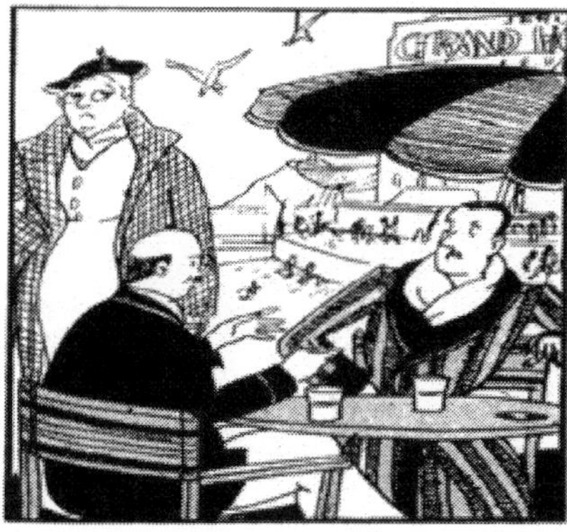

The man who said he had no holiday problems because his boss told him when and his wife told him where.

Impossible People

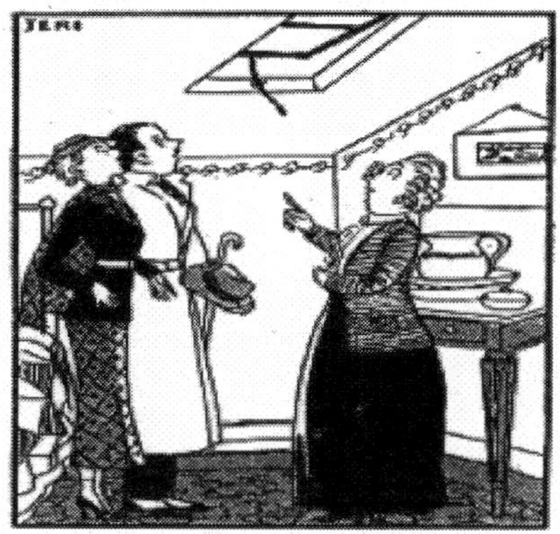

The landlady who said her rooms had a heavenly view.

But as any view, heavenly or otherwise, could be seen only via a skylight was of no matter as most landladies insisted their paying guests stayed out of the house from dawn to dusk. Which, I am reliably informed, is why, having experienced this unkind practice as a child, in 1953, Billy Butlin opened his, initially, somewhat spartan, low priced holiday camps that brought real holidays to those previously denied them.

Holidays are now the Holy Grail as, when asked by Alexander Armstrong on the popular programme Pointless what they would do with their winnings, most contestants say they would take a holiday.

Now virtually everyone, even if they don't win the Pointless jackpot, can afford at least one annual holiday and, as exotic, glamorous or adventure holidays are now an integral part of many peoples lives, most of these are taken overseas or on cruise liners.

But prior to the inauguration in the fifties, of commercial flights, flying could only be enjoyed by pilots, those in the forces, or the rich and eminent.

Thus it was not until 1964 when Thomas Cooke inaugurated package holidays that the world - as the oft repeated remark; 'The world's a small place' suggests - became so.

JERI's next young lady was obviously of the same opinion;

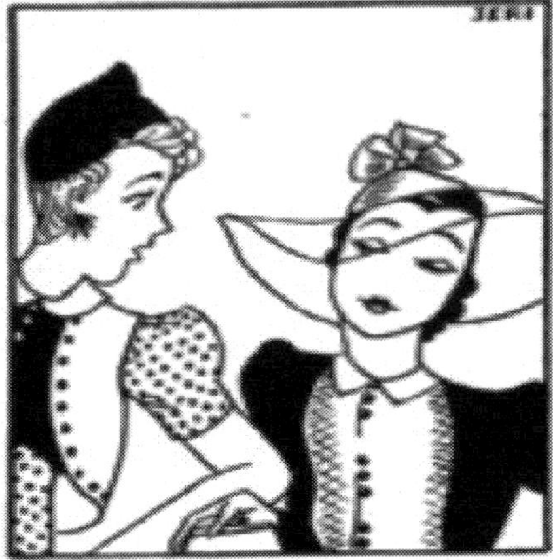

The girl who said her people were thinking of taking a trip round the world for their holidays, but she wanted to go somewhere else.

Many years and even more moons after my mother created this Impossible Person, on Tuesday 12th August 2014, this next joke, from N. Smith of London, was published in the 'Your Jokes' item of the Daily Mail's Peterborough column. *"The other day, on our wedding anniversary, I said to my wife, 'Do you fancy a trip around the world?' She said; 'Can't we go somewhere else?'"*

It is unlikely to have been a plagiarism of my mother's caption - or of any other joke or cartoon on the same theme that has been voiced or composed in the ensuing years. Nor of this next complementary cartoon by Gall that Gordon Irving included in his hilarious book: 'The Wit of the Scots'.

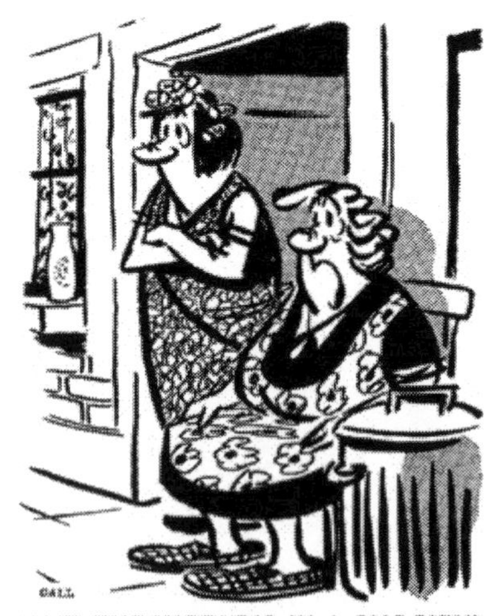

'AYE, THE WORLD'S IN A SHOCKIN' STATE, AN' THE TROUBLE IS THERE'S NAEWHERE ELSE TAE GO!'

Not only do both Mr. Smith's joke and this cartoon re-affirm that plagiarism is not always intentional, Mr. Gall's 'view of life' fits equally well with my diatribe on rubbish. Particularly with regard to the somewhat battered metal dustbin lid that looks as if it may well have been used by these women's children as a 'noisy hoop'.

For as, Piet Hein, that master of the succinct bon mot, wrote:

Nothing is Indispensable

The universe may
be as great as they say.
But it wouldn't be missed,
If it didn't exist.

Then shortly after finding the previous cartoon I came across this amusing quote by the 19th century novelist, Robert Firbank. A quote that, yet again, is excellent affirmation of my own and Mr. Silver's views;

"The World is so dreadfully managed, one hardly knows who to turn to."

Or where to go?

Impossible People

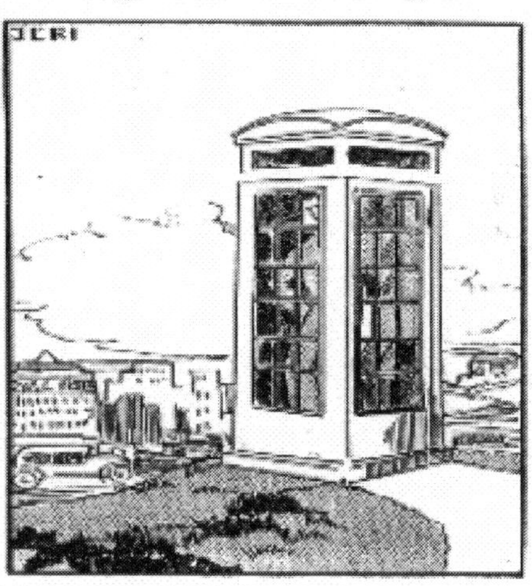

The holiday-maker who went away to be cut off from all the world.

Impossible People

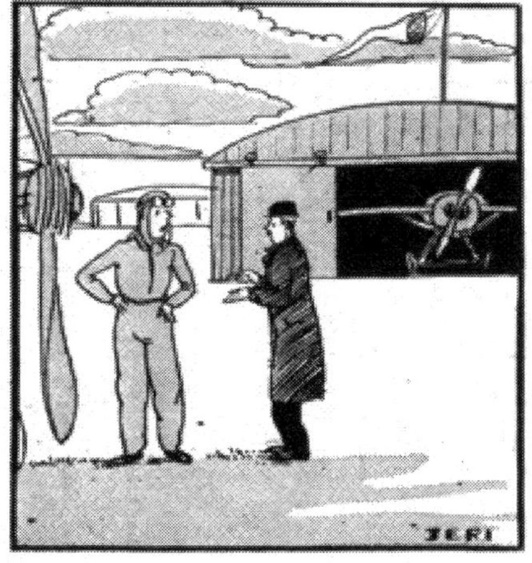

The man who thanked the pilot for the two flights—his first and last.

Presumably planes will continue to be made ever larger in order to accommodate the larger numbers of (possibly larger), people to whom flying, despite its tedium (not to mention dangers), is now essential. Or is it?

While I have enjoyed the luxury of many 'luxury' airliners, I enjoyed even more my many flights on tiny planes, including gliders. Thus 'my first was certainly not my last'.

My first, in 1958, was in an eight seater plane in which I flew from Southend to Paris and despite its discomfort and excruciating noise, I thought it very grand

and, unlike the man in JERI's previous cartoon, really looked forward to my 'second'. The return flight from Paris to Southend.

Many years and even more air miles later, I flew in a very noisy seaplane that, at that time, ferried the wealthy to and from the American Virgin Islands. This unusual and ancient means of aerial transport took me to and from the island of St. Thomas and the private Rothschild Island, where I spent some of the most romantic days of my life.

Romantic as in quality rather than romance – although there was a bit of that too.

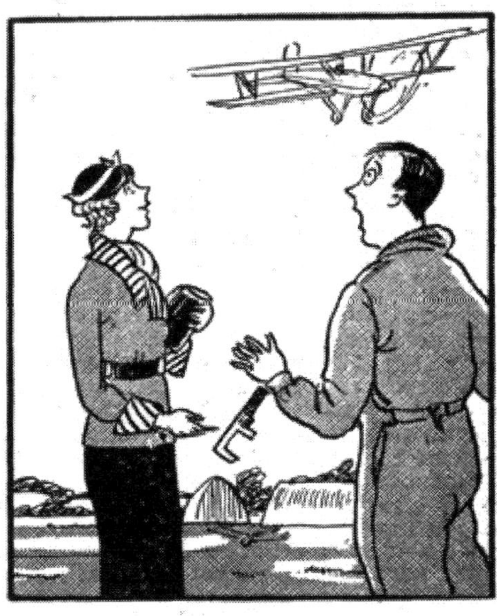

The girl who married an aviator because she wanted a man she could look up to.

But the oddest and, despite the circumstances, certainly most amusing, was a tiny ambulance plane in which, following a road accident in which our brother, Boris, had been severely injured. Sonya and I flew with him from Laval in France to Southend.

When the foam-filled mattress that Boris was strapped to was being manfully hoisted onto the plane at Rennes airport, it became snagged on the metal steps and spewed its filling onto the runway. Filling that, due to the updraft on take off, buried the plane in a sea of white polystyrene bubbles.

René and Jacqueline, who had accompanied us to the airport, later told us that from the ground this tiny aircraft looked as if it was being carried into the sky on a white cloud, which, in view of the severity of Boris's injuries, was most apt.

I have taken several flights since then in rather grander private planes to several corners of the Globe, but none that, on takeoff, were quite so 'Close to Heaven' - or, more correctly, none that had the appearance of being so.

Why do we no longer use that romantic word 'aviator'? Pilot is such a mundane word for these winged keepers of the skies. I remember, during the war, an American aerial acrobat telling us how 'spiffing' it was to fly. (Another now little used word that is an excellent way to say excellent.)

It is wonderful that so many people are now able to travel by plane. It is of equal sadness that they will never experience the pleasure of flying when the big passenger jets first 'arrived'. On arrival at the airport you were relieved of your bags by a porter, and there was no queuing, no crush of people, no security checks and you always had several seats to yourself. And all passengers, even those in economy, were looked after like VIP's and showered with gifts.

As Senior Administrator of the 1968 Third World Congress of the International Confederation of Midwives, I chartered six 747's. The first two to take our contingent of British midwives to Washington, the second two to take them to Miami, and the final two to bring them back to England.

This lured BOAC (now BA), to 'gift' me several free flights for my many necessary trips across The Pond. As at that time so few women flew unaccompanied the crew would often ask me if I was a flight attendant taking a holiday. I did wonder if this was because they needed assistance but as there were so few passengers this was unlikely.

On a few of these flights I was invited to join the pilots in the cockpit. Can anyone imagine this happening today to any passenger flying Economy – or even First Class? A luxury I was also, occasionally, invited to enjoy.

We now have a proliferation of small, low cost, airlines with buzzwords such as Easythis, Easythat, Easycome, Easygo. While a plane I once saw sitting on a runway at Luton Airport sported, on its tail-fin, the word Wizzair. No doubt we will soon see Zzoom and Flywizz, or even Flywhisk - that's if they don't all go out of business before they can get off the ground.

As their names imply, they buzz about the sky like swarms of bees making the world ever smaller - and ever more polluted! And while their pricing endears them to all, their cavalier attitude to the comfort of their passengers and the indignity of their sardine-like seating is almost beyond endurance.

Equally awful is the non-assigned seating that makes boarding a battle. It was reported that an American flight attendant was known to say to her passengers; *"People! We're not picking out furniture here, find a seat and get in it!"*
As Mama was wont to say, *"As things get better so they get worse."* But not, to their great credit, EasyJet, who, in 2013, introduced pre-bookable seating. A snippet of information I include merely as a 'Thank You' to them for making the lives of so many of us so much more bearable when having to endure the travails of air travel.

Sonya and Ray with their children Nicholas and Sasha, together with Sasha and John and their four year old son, Giles, went to Spain on one of the first package holidays. (A misnomer for 'pack 'em in').

The morning after their arrival at their hotel in Majorca, Giles toddled towards a vast plate glass window which, having been opened, was no longer there, and thus fell some twenty feet to what would have been his instant demise had a pile of sun loungers with their cushions piled on top of them, not been suitably placed to break his fall.

Giles, being incredibly small suffered, incredibly, only severe bruising. His parents, being older and less pliable, suffered the heebie jeebies. By sheer happenstance, just days after I had included this 'reportage' of Giles 'Great Escape' I read a media report of a similar incident. Definitely NOT an Impossible Person, the holidaymaker in question, Helen Beard, is justly reported in the Daily Mail of April 23rd 2011 as; 'An Angel'.

When, at the poolside of her holiday hotel in Florida, Helen saw a small girl fall from a third floor balcony, she raced to where the child was about to land and managed to clasp hold of her before she hit the ground, thus saving her from almost certain death or, at the very least, considerable injury. Although this quick-witted, courageous lady wished to make little of her heroic life-saving deed, she was justly awarded a Medal of Merit by Jerry Dennings, the local Sheriff.

These two events could be considered justification to enshrine in law draconian measures that would ensure all holiday hotels are completely child safe. However the cost of implementing such strictures would result in room charges rising to way beyond the reach of most parents.

It would also be a futile exercise because however high the charges might climb, there will never be sufficient money to adequately provide the means of preventing small children from climbing onto things and, regardless of their distance from the ground, falling off them. Nor, regardless of their distance from the ground, preventing adults from jumping off things.

A fine example being Beachy Head, England's renowned and, ironically, safest place from which to commit suicide. (Which gives me another excellent oxymoron.)

It is also a point of view that allows for the inclusion of JERI's next, extremely apt, cartoon -

And my next poem.

Impossible People

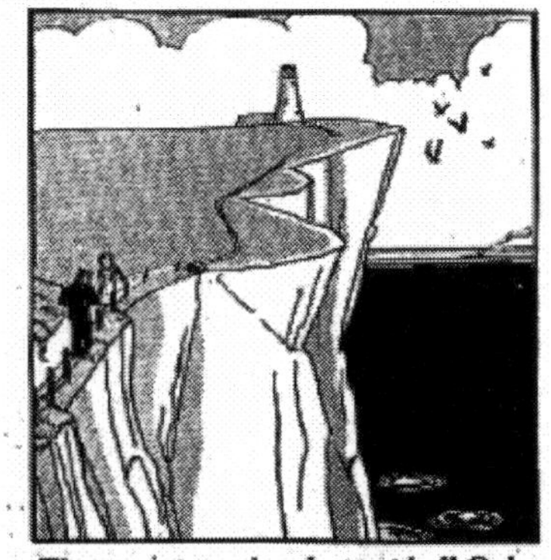

The coastguard who said "Only once" when asked if people often fell over these cliffs.

Many moons ago my nephew Giles' eldest daughter, Olivia, and her class were asked by their English teacher to write about holidays their grandparents might have taken and enjoyed and Sasha asked if I would write a poem about the few we had taken - but had not always 'enjoyed'.

Hayklan Holidays
1945 to 1965

During the war you couldn't travel anywhere,
There were blitzes and bombs and dread and despair.
And children, sent away as evacuees,
Became very homesick for their families.
Once our parents hired a Dawlish Warren chalet,
On the edge of the beach in a little Devon valley,
It was our first 'proper' holiday but we didn't like it much,
For the chalet was too small - like a little rabbit hutch.

The dunes were too tall and the reeds were too thick,
And there were no ice creams or lollies on a stick.
The sand was too hot and the sea too far away.
So we thought it rather dull and didn't want to stay,
But a few years later we moved to Sidmouth, in Devon,
Which, after Dawlish Warren, was like being in heaven.
On the shingle beach we'd dip our toes in the waves,
Or climb the steep cliffs and search for hidden caves.

We'd stay out all day with no shoes on our feet,
And play hide and seek along the Old Fore Street.
We'd throw pebbles in the sea to make them skim,
And, within a few weeks, we'd all learnt to swim.
Our brothers bought a boat, an ancient clinker dinghy,
In which we'd row right out as far as you could see.
Its old and weathered timbers had often been repaired,
But we'd ride the roughest seas and were never, ever scared.

On Good Fridays down to the sea front we'd run,
To collect an Easter egg, an orange and a Hot Cross Bun.
Gifts from the townsfolk wrapped in a brown paper bag.
Our brother, Boris, queued twice, the naughty Scallywag.
In summer we'd stay on The Ham until midnight.
To watch fishermen in their trawlers zaneing by moonlight,
The mackerel rise at night when it's calm and dark and cold.
And we'd carry home as many fish as our fingers could hold.

Sometimes in winter the sea became quite rough,
So to walk along the 'prom' you had to be quite tough.
But we loved the years spent living by a real seaside,
The sort of seaside the poem says it's 'nice to be beside'.
Then we moved back again to live between the sea
And the long flat lands of the Essex Estuary.
We'd bike to the beach to take a swim or sail a boat.
Or picnic in fields that had cows or an old Billy goat.

Even after the war you couldn't travel very far,
But we'd use Grandpa's petrol coupons - and his car.
We'd be three in the front and four in the back,
With our buckets and spades in a great big sack.
We would go on outings to Southend-on-Sea
My mother, my brothers, my sisters and me.
The car was a big one, and easy to steer,
And we'd head for the beach beside the pier.

It was crowded and noisy, cheerful and bright,
With side-shows and carousels all lit up at night.
We would visit a park called the 'Never Never Land',
Which had fairy lights and lanterns and a big brass band.
We'd take cakes and sandwiches - always home-made.
We'd buy cockles and whelks and Corona lemonade,
And candy floss and chips and Rossi's ice cream.
Before heading back home again in Grandpa's limousine.

So as you can see when we were at school,
Holidays were never an annual golden rule.
We made do with whatever there was to be had,
But were never, ever, bored, or lonely - or sad.
(Except at Dawlish Warren.)

Olivia's teacher, Mrs. Webber, (which, by coincidence, is my present husband's surname), said the poem was good enough to win a prize. Little did she know it was one one of the few occasions a teacher had praised any written work of mine quite so highly.

In the poem I use the word 'zaning', which, although not in my dictionary nor listed on Google, means; 'the gathering of huge shoals of fish in huge nets swept along between two huge trawlers'.

I also refer to 'carrying mackerel home at midnight'. It was always dusk by the time the nets full of zillions of squirming, wriggling, glistening mackerel were beached, when we children would stand in line with outstretched hands to have a fish, hitched by its gills, onto each finger. Dozens of children walking home in the dark with eight heavy, shiny fish hanging from their fingers must have been an interesting sight to any holiday makers taking a late night stroll.

As there were six of us we would go home with forty five, enough to feed us for many a day. We had them grilled, poached, pated, steamed, baked, boiled (and burnt!). But it must have been SO good for us.

The Health and Safety zealots will, no doubt, have put a stop to this wonderful childhood experience. That's if they haven't already put a stop to zaning for mackeral from Sidmouth Bay.

Our children had much grander holidays but still maintain their favourite was when, with my second husband, Chris, we took seven of them, with our two Alsatians, Satan and Rusty, on a two week narrow boat trip on the canals. They would talk of this experience in awed wonder at the magical time they had, and said that; "It beat all of our posh holidays abroad into a cocked hat."

They also preferred to spend their days on the beach at Leigh-on-Sea and Chalkwell, much as we had done so many years earlier, where they would spend hours in the water and then return home bedraggled, wet and weary – but with no mackerel.

Living in both Devon and Essex, two very different but equally meritorious counties, gave us a profound love for our country and its history which, sadly, is now being eroded, for with schools no longer teaching it, and pride in one's country left to the Lions at Longleat - who would probably prefer Africa - history will soon be a thing of the past. But Not Geography.

Of the World's 246 capital cities, including Principalities and the Vatican City, the two most used capital letters are 'B' with 27 and 'S' with 26. Four, Islamabad, Ulan Bator Quito and Zagreb, do not share a capital letter with any other, while X' adorns none. Although as a few countries are known to change their names as frequently as the seasons, by the time Impossible People has been put to bed, there may, somewhere, be a country that has a name that does begin with X.

Of nearly equal interest (and a coincidence that would fit better in my section on these odd happenings), I was trawling through my books – and my brain – for something wise or witty on the subject of geography when I recalled, at some time, having read an extremely clever poem in which all of the counties of England were included.

Unable to remember its author or title, I thought I would not be able to find it - but I was wrong!

On starting my search I took down a likely anthology from my large collection of poetry books when the one sitting next to it fell from the shelf to the floor. On retrieving it, I found it had landed face down and open at the page that had the poem I was looking for.

Luck or my Mama? I only ask the question!

Rhymed Mnemonic of the Forty Counties of England
by Donald Monat – A 1959 New Statesman Competition winner

Lying south of sweet Northumber
Lands of Westmor, Rut and Cumber,
Nottingham for forest walks,
Durham, Derby, Lancs and Yorks,
Leicester, Warwick, Wilts ahead,
Fords of Here, Staff and Bed
Shires of Lincoln, Shrop and Ches,
Sexes – Middle, Sus and Es!
Worcester, Gloucester, down the severn
South to Somerset and Devon.
On to Dorset, Kent and Surrey
Passing London in a hurry
Berkshire Thames where Oxford punts
Herts or Bucks for Cambridge Hunts,
Hants and Northants, Norfolk, Suff,
Cornwall, Monmouth – that's enough.

BACK TO HISTORY Before it disappears altogether

Frequently referred to as 'A small place', the World - with its ever changing boundaries (due to wars), increasing knowledge (due to technology), numbers of people (due to advances in medicine), and accessibility (due to ease of travel) - will continue to 'grow' ever smaller, while, in terms of size, its geography will stay static.

And although geography has many mountains, history has many more in the mountains of ever increasing new information each twenty four hours brings - thus making it an 'ever growing' subject.

Perhaps this, and its consequent enormity, is the reason why it has been suggested that history should no longer be included in the National Curriculum for Schools. For how much can children absorb of a subject that, inexorably, grows larger by the day? So, as my mother's next cartoon suggests, it may, one day, not be studied at all.

As JERI's young student smoked, there was possibly not much, future for him whether he studied history or not. A subject that, even if no longer taught in schools, will, it is said and I have read, soon be a requirement for all incoming immigrants to the UK.

If so one of their best routes would be via George Courtauld's 'The Pocket Book of Patriots' and his 'Illustrated Book of Patriotism'. Concise, beautifully illustrated, and easy to read, they are a magical doorway into this ever expanding subject.

Impossible People

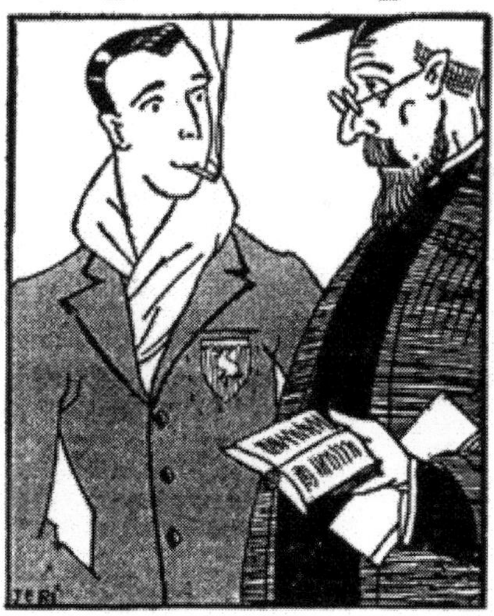

The student who said he would not study history as there was no future in it.

They also include my famous forebears. But not (which, as he is a Dane, comes as no surprise,) Piet Hein, who opined in another of his Grooks –

A Word To The Wise

Let the world pass in its time ridden race;
Never get caught in its snare.
Remember, the only acceptable case
For being in any particular place,
Is having no business there.

Fortunately, I 'did have some business there' when I visited Gray Jolliffe and his charming, extremely hospitable wife, Niki, at their idyllic hideaway just a few miles from London.

A place so tranquil, I stayed rather longer than courtesy allows (deemed to be about four hours), which allows for the inclusion of this next fitting Piet Hein Grook -

The Past

Well it's just like our Great-Aunt Laura.
Who cannot, or will not perceive,
That though she is welcome and though we adore her,
It is now past the time she should leave.

While looking through Gray's incredible collection of work, I came across this next apt and, says Simon, "Brilliant" cartoon, which Gray kindly said I could also use.

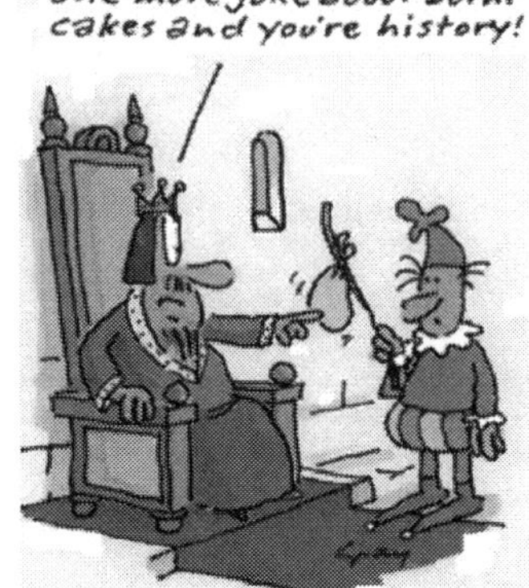

Over a delicious lunch and tea (which didn't include burnt cakes), I was telling Niki and Gray how my mother would occasionally rejig a cartoon years after its first airing. Gray then said that once he also had hoped to get away with a similar ploy.

Due to send in a comic strip to Creative Review, but, being short of time, he sent one he had composed for the same magazine a few years earlier. The editor, Bernard Barnett, then sent Gray a photocopy of a cheque they had sent him in payment for an earlier cartoon he had composed for them. *"Touche."* said Gray.

His cartoon book, 'Christmas Already Again Yet', makes an equally excellent Christmas stocking gift. Having used so many of Gray's inspired cartoons, I should re-title Impossible People to include Chloe as one of them - and King Alfred and his Jester.

Kings (and perhaps Jesters), are patriotic, as are a few of JERI's Impossible People. Particularly cabinet makers and stamp collectors - who, once again, allow for examples of her cartoons in which she plagiarised her own captions.

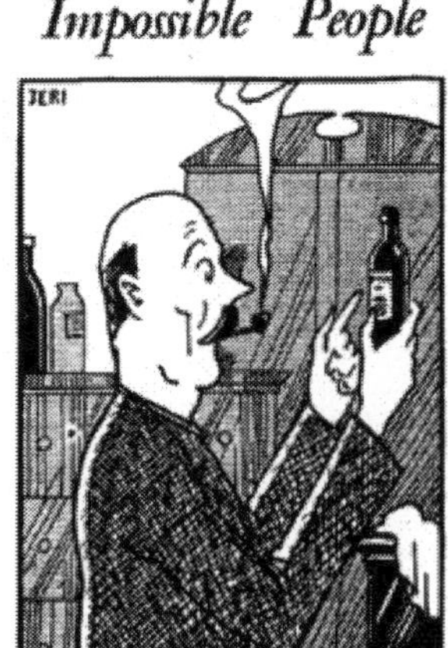

The patriotic cabinet-maker who would not use French polish

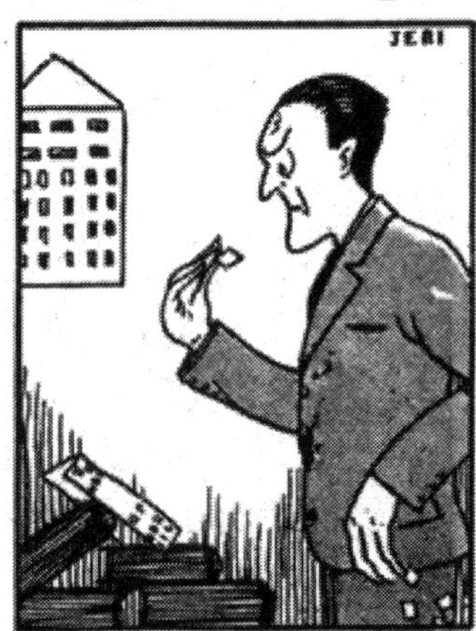

The patriotic philatelist who would not collect foreign stamps.

It is also more than

likely that both these gentlemen were Scottish?

When discussing heritage, many English people will claim a connection, however tenuous, with Scotland. Possibly because generally and perhaps, genetically, the Scots are not only extremely tough, but also exceptionally intelligent. But I would say that, wouldn't I!

It may also be the reason why, in 2014, they held a vote as to whether they should devolve from the United Kingdom. My Scottish heritage led me to hope the 'No' vote would win and I was pleased when it did. But, had it not, I have to wonder whether the Scots would have wished to re-home the Westminster Abbey Tomb of my ancestor that fine Admiral, (in both senses of the word), Lord Cochrane, 10th Earl of Dundonald.

Yet again, as Richard Littlejohn so frequently writes in the Daily Mail - I only ask the question!

It is also a perfect lead into -

PATRIOTISM AND FLYING THE FLAG

The marching Roman legions made the roads across the plains. But the rolling drunken Englishman made the winding English lanes.

It is said; *"The reason the sun never set on the British Empire was because God couldn't trust an Englishman in the dark."* Some might say many of them cannot now be trusted even in daylight!

But, trustworthy or not, it is often said that our unique 'Britishness' is due to the twenty one miles of water that separate us from our more excitable and volatile neighbours. Which should make us all thankful that while water may not be thicker than blood, there is a great deal more of it.

Although most would agree it is due to our seamless constitutional monarchy, established in 1688, together with (until now), our very secure borders. Since 1789 our three nearest blood brothers, France, Germany and Spain have suffered a litany of different monarchies, empires, civil wars, dictatorships and, not least, occupations. We in Britain find a summer drought or winter flood unsettling, so it is not difficult to imagine what all this kerfuffle has done for our more ebullient European partners.

For those interested this is a list of their various upheavals.

France:	5 Republics, 3 Occupations, 2 Empires, 2 Monarchies.
Spain:	3 Monarchies, 2 Republics, 2 Occupations, 1 Dictatorship, 1 Civil War.

Germany: 2 Republics, 2 Occupations, 1 Monarchy, 1 Empire, 1 Dictatorship, 1 Civil War

By contrast, Britain's one Constitutional Monarchy (vaguely disrupted by a Regency and an abdication) was aligned with one Great Empire. An Empire that, despite assertions to the contrary, did a great deal for those countries under its umbrella. Benefits that, in many cases, have continued to this day.

Our Empire was, of course, a direct result of one of our finest monarchs, 'Our Great and Good' Queen Victoria and her husband Albert. Albert was a perfect consort and even better 'mench' – Hebrew for 'A good man'.

An indication of how resoundingly successful our Empire was is that, throughout the world, the most used name for buildings, cities, towns, railway stations, roads, rivers, woods, waterfalls – and whatnots - is the dignified, splendid and proud name: 'Victoria'.

Britain, although a small country has, as I write, a population count that is 22nd out of the 200 countries listed in my search. A population that over millennia has produced a disproportionate number of all the world's inventors, their inventions and their subsequent benefits. A fact that must make most of us, even those such as myself who can only claim to be half of one, 'Proud To Be British'. As was the journalist who, in 2010, wrote an article in which he asked us to 'Consider these figures; We are the world's fifth largest economy. The world's third largest donor of foreign aid. The world's fourth strongest military power. Our armed forces are acknowledged to be the best in the world, and our language is the most spoken".

The most spoken due, no doubt, to the fact that, of the four major world languages, four countries have German as their first language, 21 countries have Spanish, 29 have French and 55 have English. By the time my reader reads this these statistics may not be the same, but, for such a relatively small country, we remain, to many millions of people of other nationalities, of much interest and even greater desire.

Or amusement? After Gordon Brown, when Chancellor of the Exchequer, exhorted the British to; *"Fly the Union Jack in their gardens in order to renew a sense of Britishness."* A Swizz man opined; *"Britishness is about wearing French clothes while driving a German car to an Irish pub to drink Belgian beer, and then buy a takeaway of a Chinese meal, Indian Curry or Turkish kebab, to be eaten in a Scandinavian home, sitting on Swedish furniture while watching an American show on a Japanese television, when the most Britishness thing about the Brits is their deep suspicion of anything foreign."*

Or, depending on your place of birth, also of anyone, or anything English or

Irish or Scottish or Welsh? But while each of the four separate regions that make up Britain have their own decidedly different identities and way of speech, it is only because, secretly, we all like and admire each other that we can all also laugh at each other - as in:

United Kingdom Odd Ode

The Welsh pray on their knees and on their neighbours.
The Irish don't know what they want but are prepared to fight for it.
The Scots keep the Sabbath and anything else they can lay their hands on.
And the English are all self-made men which relieves God of a great responsibility.

Despite my belief that no race can exist without an innate sense of humour, it may be a risk too far to include some of the traits of our more recent 'new' British citizens, so will confine myself, more safely, to a few about our European ones:

European Community Odd Ode

Belgium dreams up the rules,
Germany enforces them,
Britain obeys them,
France bends them,
Spain breaks them,
Italy ignores them,
Ireland pretends there aren't any.
And Greece doesn't even know there are any.

Heaven

The economy is run by the Swiss
The law is made by the English
The cooking is done by the French
The engineering is done by the Germans
The loving is done by the Italians
The holidays are left to the Spanish

Hell

The economy is run by the Italians
The law is made by the French
The cooking is done by the Germans
The engineering is done by the Swiss
The loving is done by the English
The holidays are left to the Spanish

I have changed these slightly to fit my own experience of these six European countries which may lead my reader to think I have been unjustly unkind to the Spanish. However, having experienced both good and ghastly times there, holidays spent in Spain can often be much better than the best but also, occasionally, much worse than thewo rst. A view that many may think, applies equally to all of the other five countries listed.

Apart, in my opinion, Switzerland, as my two year sojourn there working with the World Health Organisation on behalf of the International Confederation of Midwives, left me in no doubt that, unless a matter of life and limb, it was a country to which I would never venture again.

Impossible People

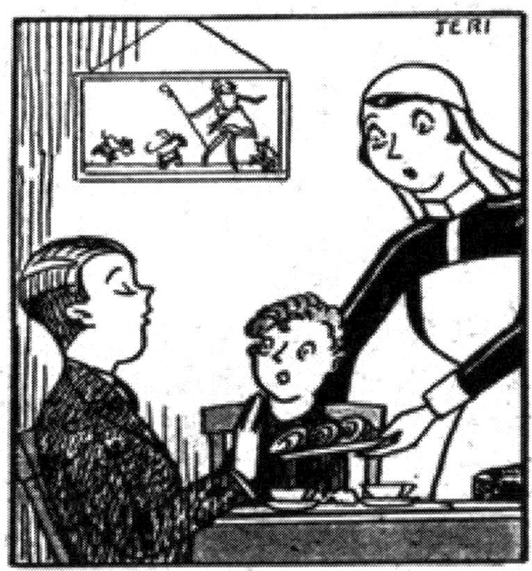

The patriotic small boy who would not have any Swiss roll

A caption of JERI's that takes me back, with some trepidation, to the Geneva based World Health Organisation, that, in conjunction with The United Nations, carried out a worldwide telephone survey. Which, although highlighting the distinct differences between the various areas of the world, was a huge failure.

The only question asked was: *'The organisations of W.H.O. and The United Nations would like you to give your honest opinion about solutions to the food shortage in the rest of the world.'*

In South America they didn't know what 'organisations' meant.
In Russia they didn't know what 'W.H.O.' meant.

In Israel they didn't know what 'United Nations' meant
In Australia they didn't know what 'please' meant
In Eastern Europe they didn't know what 'honest' meant.
In Asia they didn't know what 'opinion' meant.
In the Middle East they didn't know what 'solution' meant.
In Africa they didn't know what 'food' meant.
In Western Europe they didn't know what 'shortage' meant.
In America they didn't know what 'the rest of the world' meant.
And in Canada they hung up because they couldn't understand what the Indian caller was saying.

As many might say; "It is only a joke!" Even so, it is extremely thought provoking. As are paradoxes.

A PAIR OF PARADOXES

Fact: Genetically, all living cheetahs are as close as identical twins.

On the 27th August 2011, Winifred Rippon and Marjorie Woodcock celebrated their hundredth birthday. At the time they were the oldest twins in England and, it was thought, the second eldest in the world.

In 1911 when Winifred and Marjorie were born (and even in 1938 when my twin and I arrived), there was no such thing as scans so twins came into the world not only as a blessing but, often, also as a surprise.

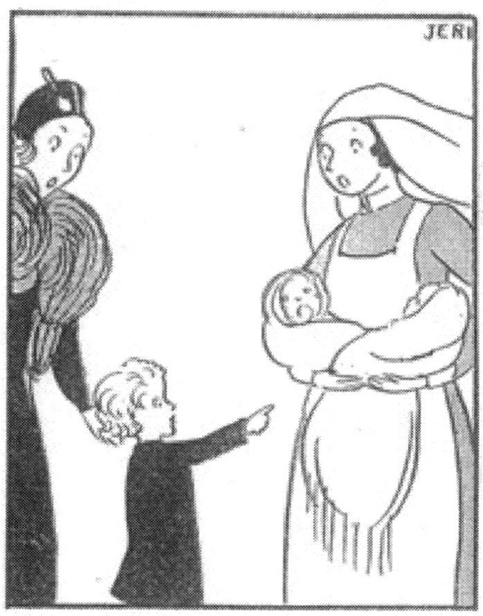

The child who said "I should keep that one" when shown the new twins.

With no history of twins in either her own or our father's family, our mother did not suspect she might be carrying two babies until, assisted by Marjorie Bayes, (her long-standing friend who was a midwife), she was home delivered of her 'third child' me and my twin. (I do not, more correctly, write, 'My twin and I' as, most correctly, I arrived first).

Having catered for one but now needing two of everything, they used a drawer as a cot for Sonya who showed her disapproval of this cavalier attitude to her unexpected arrival by constantly crying. This meant - or so our parents said - they always knew which of us was which. It also wins me an excellent pun as Sonya still refutes the veracity of my eighteen minute headstart that won me the Proper Cot.

She could be right as, now that babies have name tags fixed to them when they pop out, twins can be sure of their place in the hierarchy, but things were different then and we can never be absolutely certain that she is she and I am me. An enigma that, no doubt, inspired our mother to compose the next 'odd ode'.

The Twins Conversation
for Karina and Sonya

How can it be true,
That you are not me,
And I am not you?
Yes, I think so too!

So shall we be
'We', like Royalty?
Although it might be best,
To ignore all the rest
And not make a fuss,
And just be 'us'.

As IVF was then not even a gleam in the eyes of women hoping to become pregnant, when we were born there were far fewer twins and we were seen as a rarity – or even an oddity! This meant that, at an early age, we became inured to people's interest in us. It also had the bonus of teaching us to be extremely confident.

The question most asked of us was, *"What is it like to be a twin?"* A question to which the answer could have been; *"The difference is that our other two sisters are never asked what it is like not to be a twin."*

Which created the paradox that, never having known what it is like not to be a twin, we didn't know, apart from people's interest and there being two of us, how being one differed from not being one or, more correctly 'two'. Although in later life we learned that there is a distinct difference between single and multiple birth children which resolves this conundrum.

Due to the problems associated with establishing the hereditary rights of the first born, all multiple birth infants have not only the date but also their time of birth noted on their birth certificates. (Which is of great assistance if, in later life, astrology becomes of interest.)

Impossible People

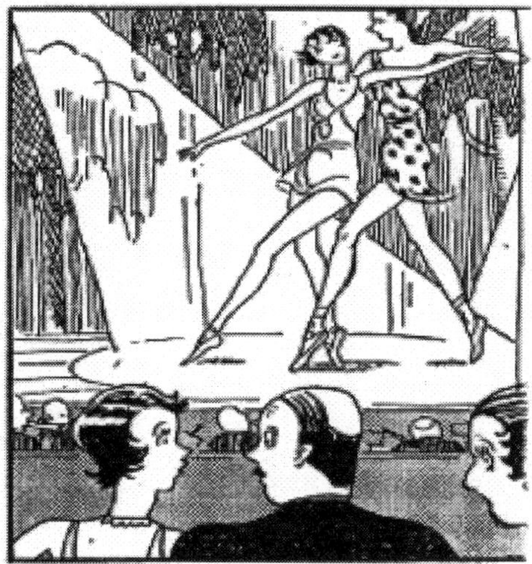

The girl who thought a pas de deux was the father of twins.

When we were very young, other people's interest in us was due, in part, to lack of knowledge about this, then, fairly rare phenomenon - or phenomena? Now, with so many babies conceived via IVF, multiple births are not uncommon.

In 2012, the intake of one infant school's reception class included four sets of identical twin girls. Thus media interest has increased in direct proportion to the increase in these births - and rightly so, as it is a fascinating subject.

It has also led to knowledge being far greater and curiosity far less. Despite which there are still numerous articles that cite examples of the medical or hereditary anomalies of these births.

One is the immediate, mutual bonding that occurs when twins are reunited after a long, or enforced separation. A rapport that remains steadfast even when twins have been raised since birth in different environments and countries. A fact endorsed by two fascinating stories that record cases of twins separated at birth who, on meeting each other many years later, found they had remained emotionally and mentally, 'tied at the hip'.

A BBC programme on the 'Twin Research Register' included the story of Asian twins who, following their separation at birth, had lived oceans apart. Reunited for the programme their immediate attachment was palpable. Fortunately their American and Dutch parents agreed to ensure the two little girls would stay in regular contact.

Ulrike Reichenback and Conny Holzbrecher, Born in 1969 in East Germany, were separated at three months. Ulrike lived in West Berlin where she enjoyed a life of luxury, while Connie stayed in the East where she was raised in deprived circumstances. Reunited in 1989, after the fall of the Berlin wall, the twins found that, in terms of character and events, they had, despite Connie's deprivations, lived parallel lives. Both said they always felt there was 'a part of them missing' and are now inseparable.

Then there are twins who are the same but different – Born in 1997, twins, Lucy and Maria Aylmer are strikingly different as Lucy has the pale skin and straight blond hair of their English father, Vince, and Maria has the dark skin and black curly hair of their half Jamaican mother, Donna.

In 2007 Marcia and Millie Biggs also 'won' this magical combination, as Marcia has the colouring of their English mother, Amanda, and Millie has that of their Jamaican father, Michael.

Then, despite these twins being a one in a million occurrence, in February 2015, Rebbeca Martin gave birth to twin girls; Kendall, who has the colouring of her dark skinned father, Curtis, and Baylee who has the pale skin of her mother.

Three pairs of twins that are the enchanting evidence of the benefits of racial integration and a most fitting foil to the Paul McCartney and Stevie Wonder song, 'Ebony and Ivory'.

Or are different but the same –
As I write earlier, in 2008 my much loved, unofficially adopted, British Jamaican son, Hugh and his beautiful Slovakian wife, Anita, gave me the gift of twins, Max and Naoli, both of whom, in skin and colour of hair, are a glorious meld of both of their parents.

The Timing of Twins:
On the 27th February 2008, a woman gave birth, naturally, to naturally conceived twin sons, Diego and Armani. On 27th February 20ll, at odds of seventeen million to one, she gave birth in the same hospital, to naturally conceived twin daughters, Dolcie and Elicia. With all four children sharing their day and month of birth, their parents, Tracy and Davood Bageban, had more chance of winning the lottery.

A fascinating quadruplets story:
The odds against a women conceiving quadruplets naturally are 64 billion to one. Ellie, Holly, Georgina and Jessica Carles were born from one egg and shared a placenta. They are so alike even their own parents have trouble telling them apart - or, as they grow older, from their beautiful mother, Julie, who has

their curly hair and identical facial features.

A fascinating 'multiple birth' non twin story:
Then there are 'twins' that are not twins. Charlotte Mullineux of Benfleet in Essex (where I once lived), was pregnant with twins when, sadly, one foetus aborted.

However, two weeks later she learned she had, earlier, conceived a baby that was still alive and growing in her womb. While not suggested in the article, it is possible that, having spent nearly nine months together in their mother's womb, and being born just one minute apart, thus giving them the same birth date, these children, despite not being so, will not only believe themselves to be twins, but will also behave like twins.

A fascinating twins born on different days story.
In the 'Answers to Correspondents column of the Daily Mail a writer asked whether twins had ever been born on different days. Of the many replies, the most interesting was from Simon Francis of Eastbourne in Sussex who wrote: In St. Joseph's Hospital in Berlin, Emilyia Dogrusioz gave birth to two healthy boys, Milcem at 11.56 p.m. on the last day of 1999 and Mircan, born at one minute past midnight on the first day of 2000.

Different hour, different day, different month, different year and different century. (But not, say I, different week.)

All of which twins with - The Department of Twin Research:
In the mid-eighties, Professor Tim Spector, a Consultant Rheumatologist at one of London's leading hospitals, St Thomas's, won funding to start a Twin Research programme.

While 'the twin thing' has always aroused people's curiosity there was, then, far less media interest, which meant that initially recruitment was slow.

At its inauguration it was thought that the research would be more effective if the siblings of twins were included. Thus, as the third set of twins to join, I am number 31 and Sonya is 32. Shortly after our registration this system was abandoned, which was just as well as the numbers are now in five digits.

The programme, now known as 'The Twin Research Register', has over ten thousand pairs of twins who happily engage in completing various questionnaires on all aspects of their lives from their fears, fantasies and families to their, eyesight, hearing, height, weight, width, shoe-size, tastes, likes, dislikes and, of most importance, whether they can read each others minds.

Procedures that were initially carried out in the basement, but were later held in the grander areas of St Thomas's where, several times a year, up to a hundred sets of twins would be invited to spend a day in the ornate Governors Hall of the hospital.

An auspicious place in which to be pinched, pricked, prodded, poked and probed in order to establish the mysteries of our inner and outer workings. A small price to pay for being pampered with an excellent lunch. Now most of this research is collected and collated online - less costly but not nearly such fun.

What is certain is that you can take the person away from the twin (even those who are conjoined), but you cannot take the twin away from the person. At the Twin Research sessions, even those twins who rarely meet, either because they live some distance apart or because they don't get on well, will arrive in similar outfits.

Which may not be a true paradox but is certainly an odd conundrum.

Naturally, Sonya and I are very proud that we were, almost, the first twins to agree to this invasion of our lives and it is research that we have thoroughly enjoyed being part of since joining in 1988 - four years prior to the 1992 official Inauguration of the Register.

Annual Twin Parties are held at major venues such as Hyde Park. Parties that are now of much media interest. One of the best being the 2013, 21st Birthday celebration held in the grounds of the hospital where, apart from being well fed, innumerable pairs of twins participated in numerous activities, avidly watched by dozens of spectators standing on Waterloo Bridge.

Lynn Cherkas, Inaugural Researcher of the Register, kindly sent me a detailed listings of the seven different types of twins - and there was I thinking twins only came in two's – but apparently not.

While the explanations for these odd quirks of nature make interesting reading they are rather too 'technical' for what is, supposed to be, an amusing book. So should my reader, whether a twin or not, wish to learn more about these relatively rare sets of relatives, they can do so by accessing the Twin Register site via Google.

Being a twin, I know how fascinating the subject is to those who are not one – or should that be 'not one of two' – so below are the six different categories of Twindom.

Monozygotic - Identical Twins
Dizygotic - Fraternal - Non-identical -Twins
Conjoined Twins
Mirror Image Twins
Polar Body Twins
Semi-Identical Twins

Then there are;
Twins who are not twins:
In April 2015, Niamh Geaney, a T.V. presenter, launched, with two friends, a social media project aimed at finding, within 28 days, their closest 'lookalike'. Their 'Twin Strangers' programme attracted responses from all over the world but, incredibly, Niamh found that she and her own 'doppleganger', Karen Branningan, lived just half and hour from each other and they are even more alike than many 'true' identical twins.

Twins who are twins:
Strangely, considering their ever increasing numbers, Sonya and I had no other twins as friends until late in our career, when, travelling alone to France, I sat next to another pair of twins, Deborah and Phillipa. On telling me that they were non-identical twins. I told them I had an identical twin sister with whom I had run an Interior Design business for many years.

We exchanged numbers and, just days later, Debbie called and asked if we could meet in order discuss the possibility of renovating a property that she and her husband, Roger, had just bought. We said we would be pleased to do so and they were even more pleased with the result. Mutual pleasure that has now forged a strong friendship, as Debbie and Pip, and their husbands Roger and Dean, are four of the most pleasing and hospitable people anyone would meet in ten lifetimes.

As have Sonya and I, Debbie and Pip, have not only stayed emotionally close to one another but, as adults, have always had homes that were within a short drive or walk from one another or, equally often, within the same complex.

When Sonya and I gave our many talks on Interior Design, due to the similarity of our voices and our habit of frequently finishing each other's sentences, our audiences would tell us that they were so fascinated by the way we interacted they often found it difficult to concentrate on what we were saying! But they did listen to the dictum with which we closed our talks;

"There are four things that should be available to anyone who wants them. A weekly massage, cosmetic surgery, interior design and a twin. Thus we would all feel better, look better, have better homes and understand one another better."

The last being a tenet with which most people may agree, for with the increasing media interest in the phenomena of multiple births, nearly everyone, even those who are not, now appear to know what it is like to be a twin. And the parents of twins most certainly do -

Impossible People

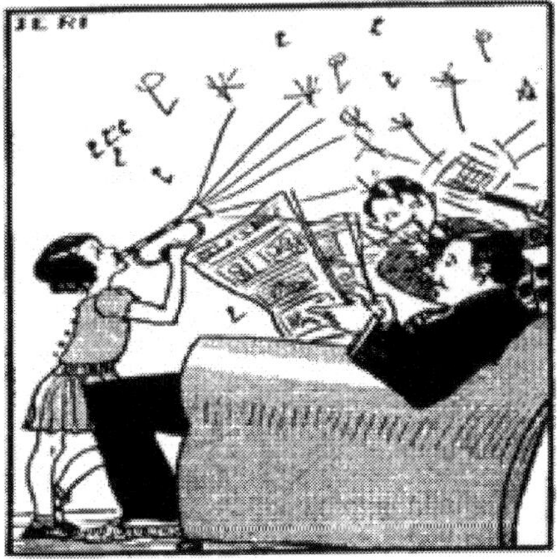

The man who said it was fine to have twins because one made so much noise that you couldn't hear the other.

My O.E.D tells me that 'phenom' means; 'an unusually gifted person.' Which, perhaps, is why Sonya and I are so good at design, and her artworks and my poems win so many prizes?

It may also be why Byron said; *"Happiness is born a twin."* And why Flavia said; *"All who joy would win, must share it."* What I say is, *"They're so right, but could you bear it?"*

While twins are definitely one of nature's most perfect paradoxes, there are many more amusing examples unwittingly conjured up by people in everyday conversation. Which twins well with -

PURE PARADOXES You never get a second chance to make a first impression.

Undoubtedly the perfect paradox. While, in second place, must be the one that I met when in conversation with one of the 'regulars' of my Public House. Henry, an elderly, most gentlemanly, gentleman who, much as he liked ladies, had remained a bachelor.

When I asked why he had never married, he said; *"I have never met a woman I couldn't leave for another."* His response to the suggestion that he could have affairs was; *"It is kinder to break their hearts by leaving them than to break their hearts by being untrue to them."* The logic of which, to this day, is unclear to me.

More clear is this next cartoon of JERI's which, had she known him, could have been composed for my own 'elderly, gentlemanly, gentleman bachelor' -

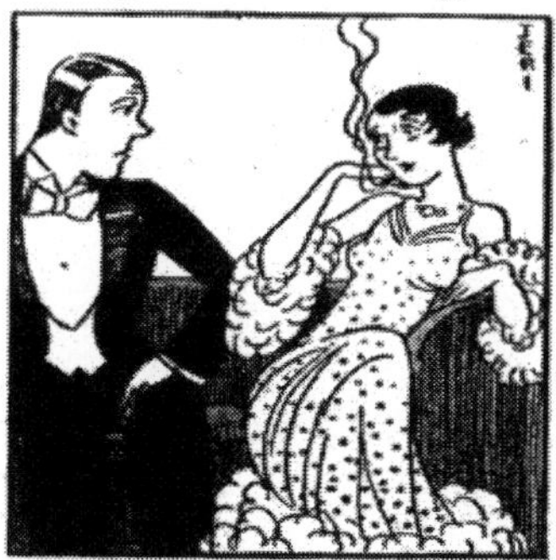

The following are from 'Vicious Circles and Infinity', a fascinating, much treasured book that was a gift from my son, Michael.

How do you cry under water?
In principle I am against principles.
There is nothing permanent except change.
All generalisations are dangerous, even this one.
Is a person who washes frequently very clean or very dirty?
To avoid being swatted a fly is most secure when it alights on the fly swatter.

And my favourite; *'God cannot be omnipotent as he cannot build a wall he cannot jump over.'* Which ties in neatly with A.A. Milne's; *"If God can do anything, can he make a stone he can't lift?"*

While Mark Twain said; *"Only one thing is impossible for God - to find any sense in any copyright law on the planet."* I know how he felt!

The next group were sent to me by Leah, the daughter of my very dear friend, Linda. A friend so dear she named her daughter after me. Although, in another less perfect paradox, in the same way I have only ever been known by the name, Karina, Linda's Leah has only ever been known by the name Tinky.

Which allows me take another short detour. Jo Wood (ex-wife of Ronnie), lived with her parents and siblings in an old Vicarage her father had bought from our brother, Stefan, who then built a house for his own family on the adjacent land between the home of Jo's parents and my own.

Thus the four 'Karslake children', as we knew them, would often join our numerous offspring on their various escapades.

Jo, on learning that my first name was Leah, said - as had Linda - that if she ever had a daughter she would call her Leah and, good as her word, she did. I would like to think the real reason she chose to name her daughter after me was that, in my belief she would make a superb photographic model, I persuaded her, with a lot of help from Sonya and not a little from her parents, Michael and Rachael, to pursue a career that led, eventually, to a little heartache but a lot of wealth.

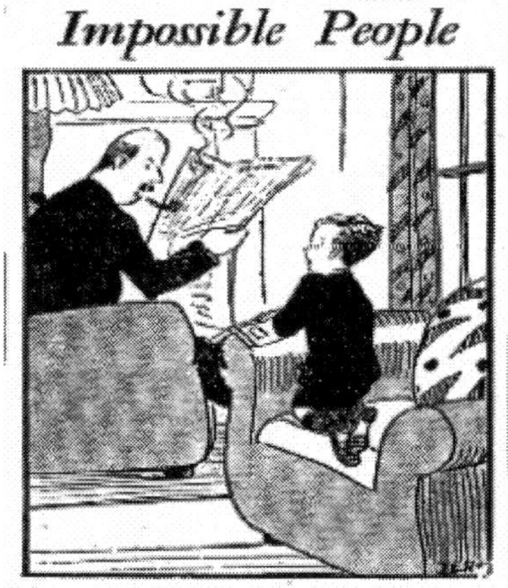

A cartoon that, for the youth of today, will have no humour as they won't know of the silver sixpenny bits (first struck in 1551, in the reign of Edward VI), that were known as a 'tanner'.

Which neatly takes us back to Tinky's questions. The answers to which even us oldies don't know - or are ever likely to:

Why did Kamikaze pilots wear helmets? (Which, according to Simon, they didn't.)
Why doesn't glue stick to the inside of the bottle?
If a deaf person goes to court is it still called a 'hearing'?
If money doesn't grow on trees, why do banks have branches?
Why are sterilised needles used for death by lethal injection?

And from our friend, John Sutch, some more that were, and probably still are, doing the rounds of the Internet -

Why are you IN a film, but ON T.V.?
If people evolved from apes, why are there still apes?
If major retailers are really lowering their prices every day, why is nothing ever free?
Why is it that people say they slept like a baby when babies wake up every two hours?
Why do you undress behind a screen when your doctor is going to see you naked anyway?
Why do people pay to go up tall buildings and then put money in a telescope to look at things on the ground?
How did we manage to put a man on the moon before we figured out it would be a good idea to put wheels on luggage?
How important does someone have to be before they are considered by the media as assassinated not just murdered?

Then, when trawling through some old papers of my mother's, I found this which she possibly used, or planned to use, as a caption because people don't come more impossible than this; *"The gentleman who said he was disappointed to find there was no suggestion box in the club house because he would like to put a suggestion in it about having one."*

And three especially for me:

Why is it always so much easier to get out of bed when you don't have to?
Does a backward poet write inverse?
Where can you buy a poetic licence?

Impossible People

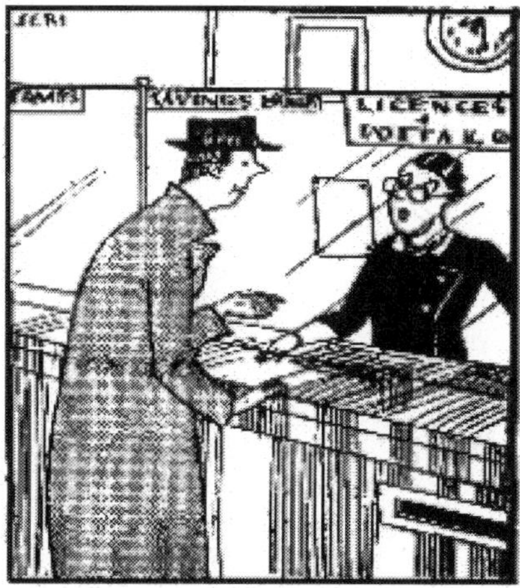

The young man who, wanting to reply to a valentine, went to the post office for a poet's licence.

Although perhaps poets should be licensed, for, as Piet Hein wrote:

If You Know What I Mean

A poet should be of the old-fashioned meaningless brand;
Obscure, esoteric, symbolic, the critics demand it.
So if there's a poem of mine that you do understand
I'll gladly explain what it means 'til you don't understand it.

As with all things, literature has always been determined by the times in which it is written or, more correctly, is written to suit the tastes of the public at the time of writing.

While most tend to think only of Dickens, the late eighteen hundreds absolutely teemed with sorrowful stories about sorrowful lives. 'Who Dunnits' were devoured in the twenties, and Science Fiction was fodder in the sixties and seventies. 'Aga Sagas' were the most read books in the eighties and nineties until 'chic lit' became the preferred read of millions of women - and not a few men.

Now, as I write, the 'life' stories of celebrities, whether or not they have lived lives worthy of being written about, are the new 'must reads'.

Which led that fine writer, Mark Barrowcliffe, to opine in a splendid article in the Daily Mail; "Meanwhile I'm a novelist, a job that requires no brain at all. Easy-peasy. Anyone can do it – and God knows, these days just about anyone who is anyone does."

A light-hearted way of saying it is an insult to literature to suggest that, however talented their acting, beautiful their singing or excellent their sporting prowess, those who have not long passed their driving test, have lived lives of sufficient length or interest to fill a 'Good Book'. Although it does give a lot of employment to a lot of Ghost Writers.

It is frequently said, (as did I in my item on the weather), that most people, whether they have lived a full life or not, will tell you they have a book inside them - but, before the advent of our present electronic gadgets, this is where most of these stayed.

Now, as Mark Barrowcliffe suggests, nearly everyone, with a book inside them or not, writes. In many cases, this is no bad thing - except perhaps for the number of trees that will need to be felled in order to accommodate all this literature. New technology may take care of this, but reading from an electronic gadget will never replace the pleasure of turning the pages of a newly bound book. Although the time may come when few will enjoy this tactile delight?

Unless, of course, we run out of electricity before we run out of paper and thus

- having no reason to make an advance – publishers.

A publisher went off to France,
In search of a tale of romance,
A Parisienne lady,
Told a story so shady,
That the publisher made an advance.

(If only! - say I) A limerick from John Letts compilation; 'Fair and Four Limericks'.

A genre that is never short of advances from both publishers and the public – even the impossible ones. But, impossible or not, obtaining the interest of the public relies on obtaining the interest of a publisher, which depends on the subject of the book, which depends on the prevailing interest of the public. An interest that changes direction as frequently as does the wind. A paradox equal to any of those so far included – which implies there may be a few more.

For many months Simon burnt the midnight oil writing an excellent, much needed, book on how to teach children good manners. Sadly I had to tell him that, despite the W. H. Auden quotation displayed on the bags of the wonderful book store, Waterstones; 'Some books are undeservedly forgotten, none are undeservedly remembered', his book would be one of those undeservedly forgotten as those who would read it don't need it and those who do need it won't read it.

A problem that besets the Government's hugely expensive 'initiative schemes' that produce millions of pieces of printed paper that nobody ever reads.

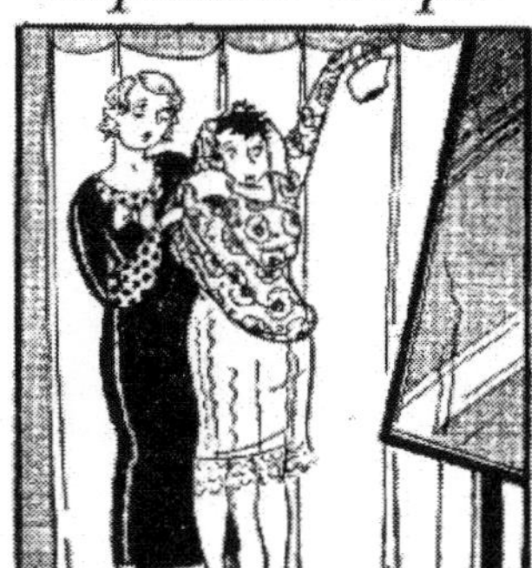
Impossible People

The authoress who said she found it difficult to get into print.

One of the best (or worst?) examples of which is the Brussels excessively wordy spouting (or should that more correctly be 'sprouting'), on cabbages to which I refer in my item on; 'The European Union and the Price of Cabbages'. But borne out rather more succinctly by Piet Hein's next Grook;

That's Why!

Why do bad writers win the fight?
Why do good writers die in need?
Because the writers who can't write,
Are read by people who can't read.

Which, if I don't watch my tongue or, more correctly, my thoughts and fingers, will also apply to me.

A thought that takes us - perhaps a little unkindly - to -

CRITICS AND CRITICISM

My gifted, severely dyslexic friend, Sarah, has a severely dyslexic son, Alexander. She also, as once did my great-niece Hannah, believed that I am the fount of all knowledge.

When she told me she had attended a forum on the trio of the 3D's - Dyslexia, Dyspraxia and Dyscalculia, not having heard of the last, but presuming it meant difficulty with mathematics, I asked her if this was so. She said; *"Yes, in the same way that Dyslexics find it difficult to spell, those with Dyscalculia have difficulty with numbers."*

I said; *"I'm not good at numbers so I must be that."* To which she said; *"At least you are not good at something then!"*

Being one of six children (eight if you count Susan and Elaine who were so often billeted with us they became our surrogate sisters), if you didn't sing your own praises no one else would. Thus I learned to do so when quite young and, despite now knowing of its pitfalls, have continued to do so.

Shortly after this conversation with Sarah, I was eulogising about my abilities to the husband of my friend Jenny, when he asked, somewhat sarcastically; *"Is there anything you are not good at?" "Yes"*, I said, *"Being modest!"*

As both of these conversations took place many moons before the conception of this book, I was delighted, when trawling though Mama's cartoons, to find her next Impossible Person.

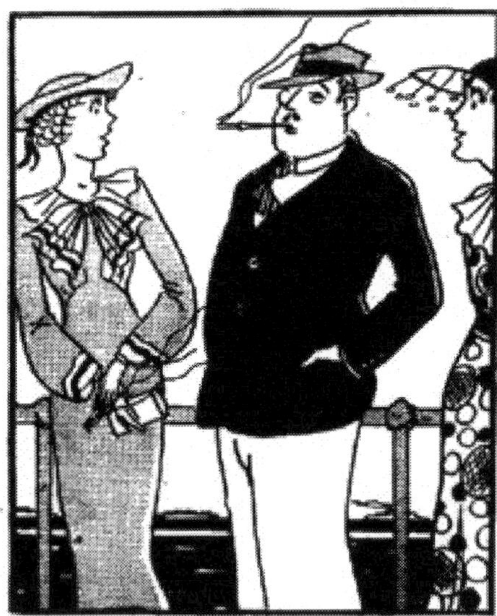

The man who said the only thing he was conceited about was his modesty.

It also ties in neatly with two other, oft quoted, quotes: *"I used to be conceited, but now I'm perfect."* And: *"I used to be indecisive but now I'm not so sure."*

It is said that, if asked what talent they would choose, most people would say; *"To be able to sing well."* Which leaves me as one of a tiny minority, as my gift would be to have the ability to be fluent in every language.

Ask any comedian (but not Woody Allen who doesn't want to be there when it happens – death that is), what they would like inscribed on their gravestones and most will say, *"At least I made them laugh."* Singers do not have an equally appropriate answer, while writers will have a multitude.

But what about all those who write about actors, artists, authors, comedians, singers and cartoonists? How do they become the arbiters of our taste? And why do they presume to suggest that if a piece of art, music or writing is not to their liking, it will not be to ours? Or that we should admire a piece of artwork merely because they do.

Mr. Saatchi, for reasons obscure to most of us, was happy to pay Tracy Emin the staggering sum of £150,000 for her 'unmade bed'. As these are replicated in their thousands in university towns throughout the world I hazard a guess that most of us, and in particular students, would prefer to spend this on having our beds made for us every day with clean linen for the rest of our lives.

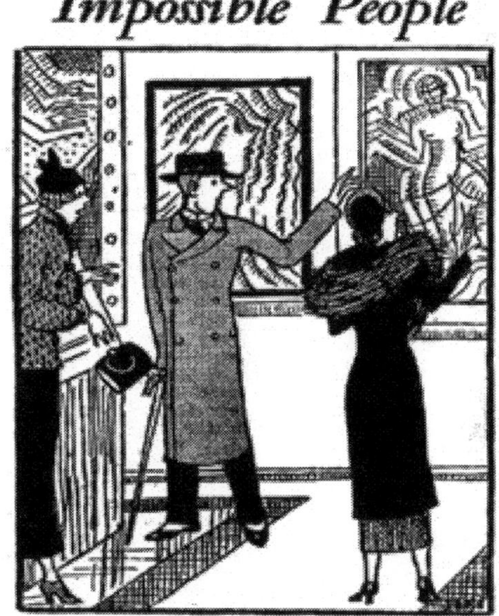

The artist who attributed his success to the fact that he used a model with hiccups.

An expensive desire neatly scotched by the threat of global warming, as washing bed linen - or anything else – may soon be illegal, when what should be made illegal is the present scare mongering about global warming.

Mama could often be heard to say, *"Asking artists what they think of critics is much the same as asking lamp posts what they think of dogs."* and, as critics frequently laud art that to us mere mortals is totally incomprehensible; *"When will some critic snap and be brave enough to say that they and all their colleagues think it's crap?"*

An apt description of much that presently passes for, or poses as, art. Which gives me yet another neat pun – and alliteration.

My mother was not alone in this opinion. I once overheard two visitors to the Tate Modern, agreeing with one another that the show should have been advertised under the heading of: 'The King's New Clothes.'

Mama said that all art in any style or medium is as individual to the creator as their fingertips. therefore, no piece of artwork can be replicated exactly by anyone other than its creator, and often not even by them! Proof of which is that fraudulent copies of the works of great artists, however good, are always discovered. Although Simon asks; *"Would we know if they were not?"* But did he mean 'not replicated' or 'not discovered'?

In 1990, for my mother's 90th birthday I compiled and published an anthology with 90 of her poems and a few of my own. Called a 'A Family of Verse', it includes the next poem that she wrote about the frustrations that artists frequently suffer.

Lament of the Portrait Painter

Think it out, no hesitation,
God be praised, here's inspiration.
Pose the model, make a plan,
Keep her quiet if you can,

Take some photos in the light,
Half of them are not quite right.
Take some more and get them done.
A week's delay is half the fun.

Find a board and size it thin,
It's got flaws, so curses smother,
Get your saw and cut another.
Paint it white and then begin.

Then your basic lines you make,
Pray the charcoal doesn't break.
Put the mouldy thing away,
And try again another day.

Check it up. Don't squint the eyes,
Line it in; Surprise! Surprise!
You've got the child's expression right,
Now lay your palette good and bright.

Paint in the background, gold and sunny.
See the paint is not too runny,
Bash the hair in, set the eyes,
Quickly now before it dries.

Some impasto on the chin,
Not too thick and not too thin.
For Heaven's sake don't over paint.
You really think you're going to faint

Now you've got it running free -
Blast! the kids are in for tea.
It cost ten pounds to have it framed.
So hang it up and don't be shamed.

A fortnight's work and all creation,
Your forehead's wet with perspiration.
You think you have got the 'flu,
And all those bills are overdue.

Will the client come today?
And bring a cheque, and say he'll pay?
Instead your friends come and make merry,
Drinking up your tea and sherry.
Then you hear some bastard scoff;
"Well that one didn't quite come off."

When she wrote this poem our mother was an impecunious artist with six children to feed and could not afford the costly canvasses on which artists usually paint.

So, even when her children could all, eventually, afford to buy canvasses for her she still chose to paint on hardboard. Nevertheless, despite their unconventional backgrounds, the many paintings she did using these are still of much merit.

As can be seen in this portrait of my son Michael that, in his early teens, his grandmother painted from a photograph she had taken the previous year when they were on holiday in Greece.

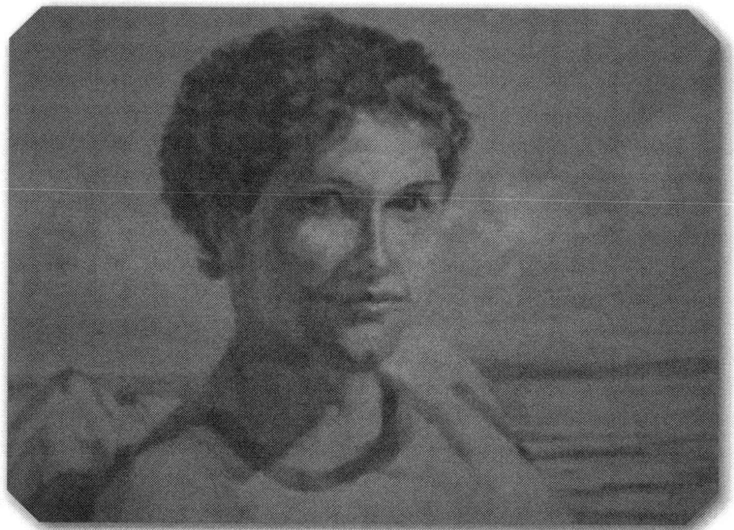

Apparently my son's 'enigmatic smile', captured in this painting, is one of the most difficult things for an artist to portray and that it is her 'enigmatic smile', captured with such consummate skill by Leonardo Da Vinci, that makes the Mona Lisa of such great value.

Confirmed by Piet Hein when he wrote;

The Giaconda Smile

Certainly Leonardo's magical Mona Lisa
may be superbly rendered using a dozen tiles.
Such things are not unusual.
Yet there are those who always feel that there's
something subtle gone from the way she smiles.

We can only hope the many portraits that Mama painted on commission, whether they portray an 'enigmatic smile' or not, are still treasured by their owners as much as are those of our own, for, had she priced them at their real value, she could have bought – if not the Mona Lisa - certainly more than a few crates of canvasses.

Did Piet Hein compose this next Grook due to the 'mystery of the hard to capture smile'? What is a mystery is how I manage to find so many 'twin' things!

Twin Mystery

To many people artists seem undisciplined and lawless,
Such laziness with such great gifts seems little short of crime
One mystery is how they make the things they make so flawless;
Another, what they're doing with their energy and time.

As my mother suggests in her poem, their time and energy is probably spent on feeding people –

FOOD AND DRINK

In the early years of the British Navy, sailors were paid partly in money and partly in food. The food part being three meals a day eaten from a square wooden platter. Hence the expression: 'Three square meals a day.' Every sailor guarded his platter as if it were made of gold for, if lost or broken, they didn't eat.

Impossible People

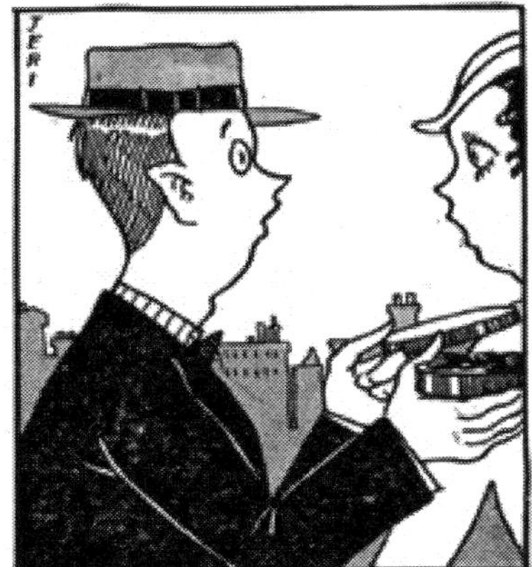

The young man who gave his girl a box of dates.

Unless, one must suppose, they could fish for fish. But not dates or figs; 'The young man who said he didn't give a fig if his girl refused a date.' And –

Much as too much of it is bad for us, salt remains one of our most effective food enhancers. Mama told us that the word 'salary' dates from when Greek workers were paid in salt, which at that time cost a King's ransom. She said its 'high' expense was also the reason why the high born 'sat above the salt' at a banqueting table, while those of lower birth were seated 'below the salt', where they could not partake of this much sought after, costly condiment.

My sister Sasha, one of the kindest people anyone would be likely meet in ten lifetimes, believes that; *'The way to a person's heart is through their stomach'*.

So where most people will say; *"Do come in, please sit down, have you eaten?"* Sasha greets her visitors with; *"Do come in, have you eaten? Please sit down."* Meanwhile, as far as catering is concerned, my own view marries with this next 'Meanwhile' cartoon, that was definitely devised for me –

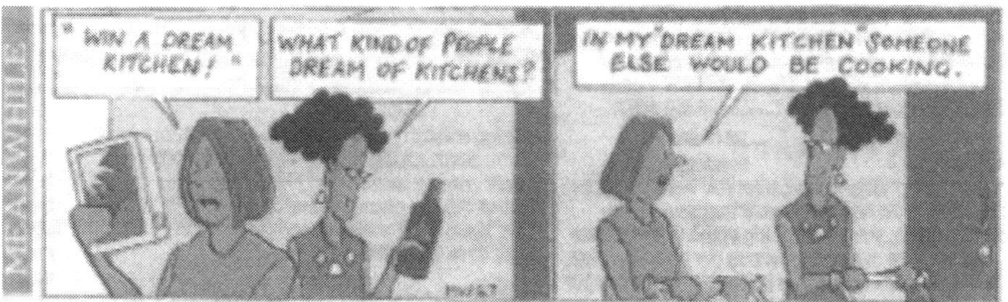

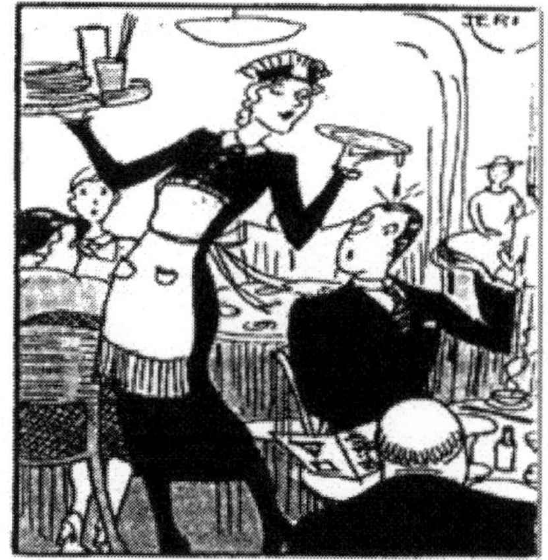

The waitress who said people were always complaining—some if they got hairs in their soup; others if they got soup in their hair.

Sasha's Australian daughter-in-law, Kirsty, told me that when, as a child, she would tell her mother there was a hair in her soup, she was told not to complain as then everyone would want one.

When food is abundant, (regardless of whether there is hair in their soup or not), people will complain about it. True hunger is the only thing that makes all and any food, eagerly and easily edible. Although where taste-buds are concerned, regional preferences remain a constant. Confirmed by Alice May Brock who, kindly leaving out 'gravy and custard make it English', wrote the following:

'Soy sauce and rice make it Chinese; Wine and tarragon make it French; Lemon and cinnamon make it Greek; Curry and rice make it Indian; Tomatoes and oregano make it Italian; Sour cream and beetroot make it Russian; Garlic makes it good.'

She could have said; *"Marmite makes it British."* The only food, and possibly thing, that has no ambivalence in its ability to divide people into two distinct camps – those who love it and those who hate it. I am one of the former and will eat it by the teaspoonful.

As does 'self-proclaimed food hater', John Pearson, who eats only ten things; bread and butter, soft cheese, plain crisps, chips, cereal, Yorkshire pudding, chocolate cake, Marmite and nuts. (Which may bring a few to ask; "Is he nuts?") John says he stays healthy due to Marmite's rich vitamin B, folic acid and niacin, which helps the body fight infection and thus keeps him fit. Fit enough for him to become a Black Belt in Karate.

Another strict dieter in terms of what she will or, (more to the point), will not eat, is Emilie-Lea Hayward who, as reported in the Daily Mail on March 31st 2015, eats nothing but yogurt in only two flavours, raspberry and strawberry, in only one brand Petit Filous.

She eats six for breakfast and another two dozen throughout the day. About eleven thousand pots per year. Doctors say, despite lacking minerals and vitamins, this diet has not affected her health as it gives her adequate protein, calcium and energy.

But one has to wonder what she will eat if Petit Filous stop making strawberry and raspberry yogurts? But many foods, including Marmite –

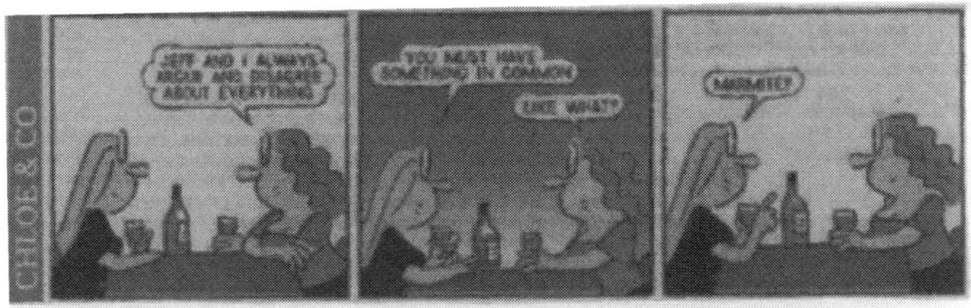

- will one day become a nostalgic memory as our Health Czars exhort us to improve our diets. But as it is unlikely any agreement will ever be reached on what we should or should not eat, Robert Fuoss, late of the Saturday Evening Post, wrote: *'It would be nice if the Food and Drugs Administration stopped issuing warnings about toxic substances and just gave us the names of the one or two things still safe to eat.'*

Although, even if they did, would anyone take notice for food is not now eaten just for sustenance, it has to be either elegant or, as are dates of the less romantic kind, good for you - or both.

Impossible People

The chef who called his soup consomme d'or because it was made of eighteen carrots.

Assumptions our present, prolific food programmes promulgate. Together with frequent exhortations from didactic dietary gurus to either eat less, or more, of the 'good stuff' such as fruit and vegetables.

Or soup -

My supremely sensible but severely dyslexic grandson, Laurence, chose to become a chef and, prior to his tragic demise in 2016, turned his skills into 'consome d'or'.

Among my vast collection of books few are about food, but one that is tells me that in the 16th Century people believed food that grew above the ground or on trees was the Food of the Gods and was thus fit to be eaten by the wealthy, but that which was grown under the ground was fit only for the poor!

As vegetables of all colours, whether root or otherwise, are eaten with red meat, this raises a conundrum. If the first is so good for us, and the second so bad, why do they taste so good when eaten together? Another is; *"Why is food so rarely blue?"*

As Laurence suggested, perhaps this is because it so rarely gives us the blues. And was Laurence such a good chef because his parents chose to use the French spelling of his name? But French food doesn't always taste better, it just sounds better.

One of our fine, but sadly late, friends, Henri Arpurt, published a book of 52 French recipes illustrated by a variety of attractive sepia drawings by Francoise Bargin.

What makes his recipes even more 'tasteful' is that they are written in verse. The first verse for Henri's first recipe has the delightful words:

De Sorges a Bergerac, de Brantome a Nontron,
Il n'est de cuisiniere ignorant ce bouillon,
Puisque'il est une symbole de grande tradition,
Servi depuis toujours dans les bonnes maisons.

And the last equally delightful verse for his last recipe is:

Je vous avais promis un grand moment de fete,
Comme ceux qui vous tranforment un beau soir en poete.
Cela m'est arrive il y a longtemps deja,
On peut changer sa vie avec ces gaufres la!

A promise of delightful meals of delicious food of ample sufficiency with the compliments of Henri. ("If", says Simon, "You speak French!") Simon reprimanded me for my use of the phrase 'ample sufficiency' as he says I should, more correctly, use the term; 'elegant sufficiency'.

However, I remember our mother telling us about the boy who, on hearing his father tell his mother he had had ample sufficiency, asked if he could have some too.

As small boys rarely, if ever, use the term 'elegant', and my Mama would never use poor English, I consider my use of the word 'amply' as 'elegantly sufficient'.

Also as the phraseology of this anecdote follows the same format used by our mother for her cartoons, it is quite likely that, as she frequently did, she was quoting one of her own captions. Sadly, this is something we shall now never know.

What we do know is that when young, my siblings and I would play a game where we would try to outdo each other in our efforts to compose verses that began with the words; 'Dictation, Dictation, Dictation'.

Our numerous variations on various subjects included this limerick based on the nursery rhyme of the 'Three Little Pigs' -

Dictation, dictation, dictation,
Three pigs went to the station,
One got lost.
One got squashed,
And the other was made into bacon.

"When We Were Very (very) Young", my sister Nicola was always being scolded for not eating her rice pudding and to cheer her up, our mother would read her A.A. Milne's 'Rice Pudding' poem.

As allergies were not then thought of, or known about, in the same way they are today, our parents did not realise she had a severe intolerance to milk. An intolerance exacerbated by the daily, and compulsory, half pint of free milk distributed, at that time, to all children at public schools - but not to Public School pupils.

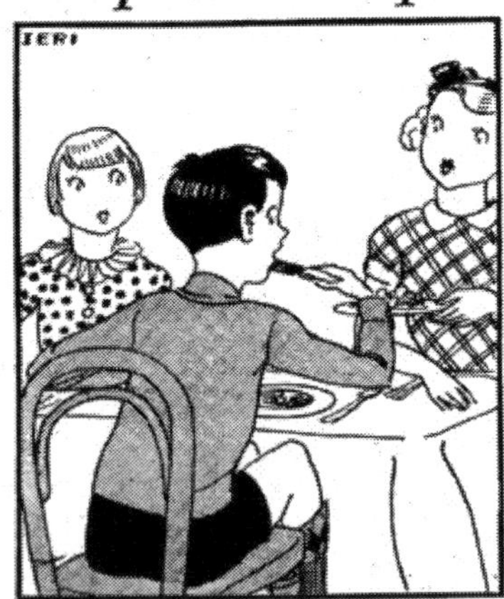

The boy who said his fork leaked when asked why he ate with his knife.

An anachronism my American family and friends find difficult to understand. Not the issuing of free milk, but why parents have to pay for their children to go to a 'Public School'.

Is this, perhaps, because they have no table manners;

Apart from the prevalent and prolific modern allergy to peanuts (which, it is thought, is due to their introduction into Britain by the Americans during the Second World War), some very odd allergies are suffered by people I know.

My daughter, Alisonjane, will die if she eats oranges. My friend Hoodie will die if she eats mustard and Anne, a sister of my second husband, Chris, has such a severe allergy that she will die if she eats anything that has been cut with a knife that has been used to cut cucumber.

Then there are those with an allergy to alcohol, which not only kills people but, even more frequently, makes them not only difficult but, equally often, deadly to live with.

Moving on to something less deadly, children love this next dinky anonymous rhyme and enjoy it even more when, much to the annoyance of their parents, they attempt to eat peas from their knives – with or without honey.

I always eat peas with honey,
I've done it all my life,
It makes them taste quite funny,
But it keeps them on the knife.

Honey, being the only food that never goes off regardless of age - or utensil used – is always safe to eat, with or without peas. Although some might maintain: *"The food of the gods may be all right for some, but it tastes too sweet and it doesn't fill your tum!"*

Equally odd is from whence it comes, for as Jack Prelutsky wrote: *"Every bee that ever was, was partly sting and partly buzz."*

Eating strange things with even stranger things was, it would seem, also of interest to Prince Phillip, who in one of his, (as he refers to them), 'Dontopedalogy' remarks, once famously quoted this description of how the Cantonese refer to the, even odder, eating habits of their near neighbours;

"The Chinese eat everything that flies except aeroplanes, everything with four legs except tables, and everything that swims except submarines."

On telling a friend this, she told me she had recently read about the death, at 69, of a man who, for much of his life, ate particles of metal, plastic and wood taken from old furniture, cars and bicycles - and, perhaps, aeroplanes and submarines.

This was almost certainly an old wives tale, but as these are invariably founded on 'substance', perhaps surviving on a diet of such substances is possible.

(Which gives me another, somewhat less neat, pun.)

There are also a few humans who, when absolutely essential, have eaten each other. One being Dr. Roberto Canessa, who, together with the other sixteen survivors of a plane crash in the Andes, eventually had to eat their dead fellow passengers in order to survive.

A heart wrenching experience that he writes about in his book; 'I Had To Survive.' What makes it even more heart wrenching is that the dead they ate had been their friends.

My brother-in-law, George, has been known, (tarantulas and widow spiders aside), to eat almost any known creepy crawly for a bet, or just a dare. But there are many numbers of beasties and bugs, from the minute gnat to the huge grizzly, that eat, or feast, on humans.

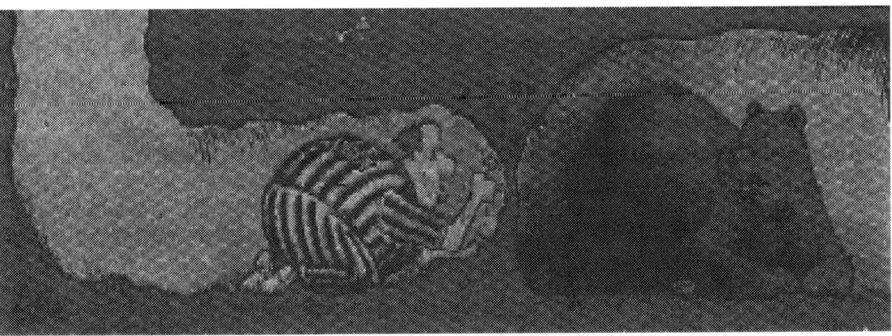

So, with a bear waiting for us in his lair, how many of us would dare to make a break for it? Although if there were, would we know, for as A. E. Houseman wrote:

Infant Innocence

The Grizzly bear is huge and wild;
He has devoured the infant child.
The infant child is not aware
He has been eaten by the bear.

So Houseman's 'infant child' will also never know where strawberries or herrings grow -

The man in the wilderness asked of me,
"How many strawberries grow in the sea?"
I answered him as I thought good,
"As many red herrings as grow in the wood."

Strawberries naturally take us to jam and, along with John Pearson who lives on just ten foods and the little girl who will only eat yoghurt, I once read about a boy who would eat nothing but biscuits and another who only ate jam sandwiches. Media stories that led to a flood of similar tales, one of which was about a teenager who had eaten nothing but chicken nuggets since she was tiny.

Youngsters who, by the time my reader reads this, will now be a great deal older if, that is, their Spartan diets have allowed them to get any older. Which is likely as they are all similar to a lady I met many years ago when staying in a hotel in Bath. Allergic to all food apart from chicken, potatoes, and vegetable compote, her diet, throughout her life had consisted solely of these foods. This cheerful and very healthy lady must give us all hope for when the world starts to run out of food.

That's if we don't first run out of chicken, biscuits, potatoes, jam and yogurts – or metal, plastic or wood. Or fairies -

Impossible People

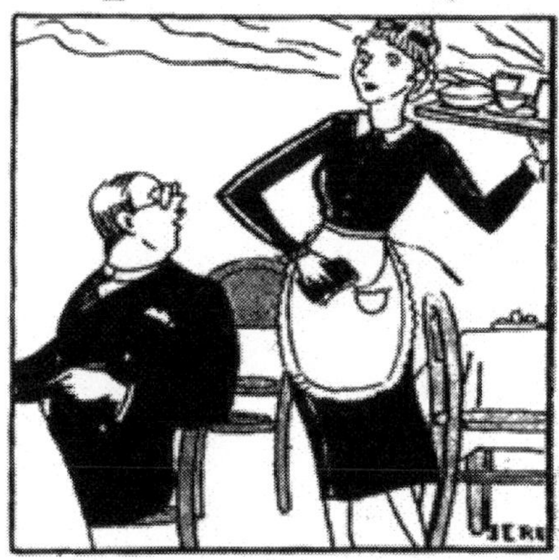

The waitress who retorted that there were no fairies in the fairy cakes when the customer said there was no chicken in the chicken soup.

Impossible People

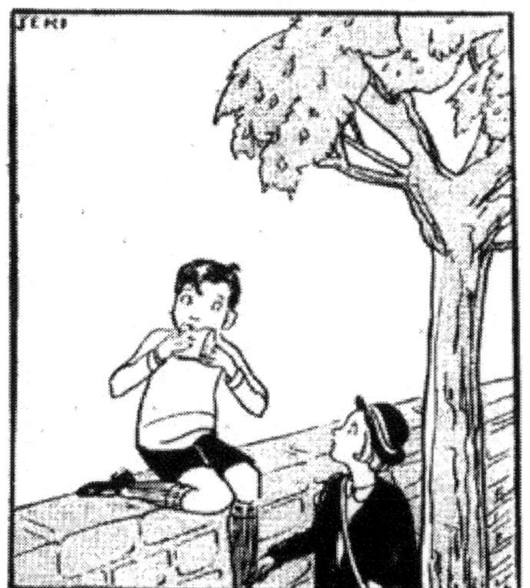

The boy who said his mother only made sponge cake. She sponged the flour from Mrs Brown, the butter from Mrs. Jones and the eggs from Mrs. Robinson.

Which, now that fairy cakes have once again become so popular, we will be eating in vast numbers. With baked beans not far behind? For in his book, 'In Fact', Tom Nuttal includes the extraordinary fact that 97% of the world's baked beans are eaten by the British. In his perspicacious way, Simon asks; "Who eats the other 3%?" Perhaps, say I, they just 'go off. "Or are one of the ingredients of sponge cakes ?"

Mr. Nuttal writes that peanuts are one of the ingredients of dynamite. Which makes them dangerous on four counts, because if they don't give you an anaphylactic shock, choke you to death or blow-you-out, they might 'blow you up'.

Blowing up brings us to burning and a Grook from Piet Hein on how to 'char' for yourself.

Timing Toast

There's an art to knowing when,
Never try to guess,
Toast until it smokes,
And then twenty seconds less.

Dining, while a delightful activity, even if you're only eating toast, (which is so good it has its own song), is less so without wine. As with most things, I have many stories about drink, most of which deserve to be shared - particularly those that include alcohol.

W.C. Fields said: *"I cook with wine, sometimes I even add it to the food."* Which takes us to some -

GOOD WINE

As Michael Caine is wont to say, *"Not a lot of people know this":*

The marching Roman Legions
Made the roads across the plains,
But the rolling drunken Englishman,
Made the rolling, drunken lanes.

Nor this: Apparently, the best wine makes the best vinegar. Nevertheless, as some of the best wine is Champagne, we can be fairly confident it is not one of those wines used to make vinegar. Or is it?

By law only sparkling wine produced in the area south east of Paris, which includes the Aube and Haute-Marne, can be classified as Champagne. All other white and pink fizzy wines are required to be notated as 'Sparkling'. These wines, despite their more humble place of birth are, equally often, as equally pleasant as their more aristocratic cousins.

As are many other wines, proved in this neat ditty by Susan Jarvis of Bexleyheath, Kent. Despite knowing that she now lives in Texas I have not been able to trace Susan, but hope that if she ever reads my book she will be happy to see her poem in a more permanent setting than a national daily. For, as Robert Louis Stevenson so famously said; "Wine is poetry in a bottle." So we should raise our glasses to Susan - even those who, as she affirms in her final two lines, prefer beer - for giving us such an enjoyable, extremely clever poem.

A Glass Of Your Finest

A Margaux or a Bordeaux,
Our tantalising Merlot,
Or a lush refreshing Pino?
Do try our prized Barolo!

A frisky little Muscadet,
A jolly saucy Beaujolais?
Our new voluptuous Vouvray
That boasts a citrusy bouquet.

A bold and brazen Chinon?
A smooth and fruity Mouton?
One quaff of a soft Semillion
Wafts you to heights beyond.

There's a scintillating Chablis,
A mischievous Chianti;
Is a fest of fizzy fun.
Will incite a tastebud party!

Choose Anjou - it's ambitious,
Though Fitou's so delicious,
With a kick that's expeditious.
While Rioja's a tad malicious!

Enjoy a coy Sauvignon,
Or a joyful St Emilion,
A magnum of Dom Perignon:
This frolicsome Frascati,

We have Chateauneuf du Pape,
In an old oak vat - it's on tap!

We've a'helluva Valpolicella;
Save your breath, Old Fella,
Just pull us a pint of Stella.
I'll get one from the cellar.

Somewhat more succinctly, W.B. Yeats writes in the anthology, 'The Green Helmet and Other Poems', this thought-provoking four liner:

It's The Wine Talking

Wine comes in at the mouth
And Love comes in at the eye.
That's all we shall know for truth
Before we grow old and die.

Whether they talk or not, soft drinks such as lemonade are much safer – or are they? My mother wrote this limerick when, in the nineteen twenties these, often naughty, five line rhymes became very popular.

There was a young lady of Lynn,
Who was so exceedingly thin,
That when she essayed,
To drink lemonade,
She slipped through the straw and fell in.

As with most things, our tastes differ wonderfully and widely - and probably more so when it comes to wine. Although the French maintain that we British buy wine based not on its taste but on the design of the label. Or its price?

Wine probably has more books written about it and more discussions debating it than any other liquid imbibed or food ingested. But people's knowledge differs widely and while no one can know everything, some of us have brains stuffed with useless 'bric-a-brac' one of mine being why we clink glasses when making a toast.

When the Greeks were in the habit of regularly poisoning each other, if a host wished to show his guest he was safe from this fate, he would drink from his own glass and then exchange it for that of his, much relieved, guest. So if, after drinking from it, a host did not pass his glass to his guest, his guest, in the belief his own wine might kill him, would not drink it.

Thus the pastime of putting poison in wine declined and, with no fear of an early demise, a guest could safely keep his own wine glass and, equally safely, drink from it.

Impossible People

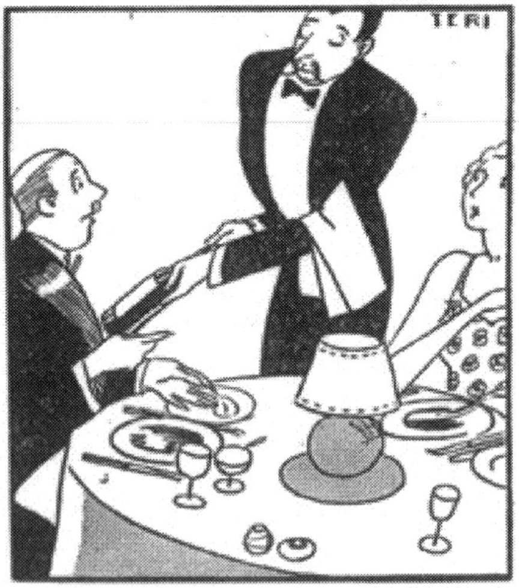

The waiter who said "One shilling" when asked what was the difference between the Burgundy at 5s. 6d. and that at 6s. 6d.

The 'threat of death having died' (a pun I may not be able to better), led to the habit that continues to this day, of 'clinking' glasses together in 'Good Faith' and, of course, 'Good Health'. When toasting one another the French look into eyes of the other drinker, while we English tend to look at the wine. When my French friends ask me about this I tell them we want to make sure we don't spill the wine.

The reason the French look into each other's eyes is not, as some may think, due to their flirtatious nature, but because they are drinking to the health of the person not to that of the glass – or the wine. Although after an 'ample sufficiency' they are just as likely to spill it.

We also learnt from our French friend, Rene, that price doesn't always determine the laying down properties of wine, but the shape of the bottle does. Few people I have discussed this with (apart from my twin who knows a great deal about wine), know which shape of a bottle indicates whether wine can be kept or should be quickly quaffed. Although this is possibly because I don't move in the right circles?

Rene said if the neck of the bottle has 'shoulders', such as those used for Margaux, it is a 'keeping wine' and if they 'slope' as in those used for Beaujolais, it isn't but, as with most things, it is not an 'absolute' rule.

During a dinner party discussion on the subject, it was argued that the shape of the bottle only determines its region, but as different regions produce either drinking or laying down wine, the wine is bottled according to its laying down, or not, properties. (The wine that is, not the imbiber.)

Although while all champagne bottles have sloping shoulders this does not mean that all champagne has a limited cellar-life. Vintage champagne which is made only in good years from 80% of the grapes harvested, have 'dated' labels that denote it can be kept for between five to fifteen years. A relatively short cellar-life when compared with 'laying down' wine such as Margaux, which can be kept for fifty years or more. If you have a cellar to keep it in!

Connoisseurs are often snooty about 'new' wines, but those such as Beaujolais are excellent when drunk early enough - but not enough to make the drinker drunk.

Then there are wines with no cellar-life that, after many years, have been drunk with great pleasure. One being a dessert wine we were privileged to enjoy when in, 1964, we were dining with Jacqueline and Rene at the Laval home of his sister, Pepe, and brother-in-law, Pierre.

Pierre told us that during the early years of the Second War, people hid their wine from the Germans in dugouts, sealed cellars and wine caves and said the wine he was about to serve was the last bottle of their family's redeemed cache. It was also one of the finest wines I have ever tasted, and although there was only enough for each of us to have just one glass, we all made it last as long as courtesy allowed.

Twenty years later, with little knowledge of, or liking for, alcohol, I became, a 'Leading London Landlady'. 'Leading' because, as I write earlier, the MP George Young, always referred to me as "Acton's Margaret Thatcher." A role I 'played' for ten years, during each of which we would ask our regular customers to choose a charity they wished to support, for which we would arrange events and collect donations.

In 1982, knowing we could leave the running of the pub in the capable hands of Bob Stallard, our excellent manager and very good, long term, friend, we decided to do the annual 'Beaujolais Run' and auction the wine for their chosen charity. For added interest we decided to do it by motorbike which persuaded my son-in-law and bar manager, MichaelPeter and my daughter, Alisonjane, to join us.

Two of our staunch regulars volunteered to drive down in a van in order to bring the wine back, which naturally (or even unnaturally), could not be done on motorbikes.

Apart from making a lot of money for that years charity, two things about this sortie will stay in my memory for ever. The first was the cold. I had never before, nor since, experienced such bitter cold, and while I could have travelled in the van, with several bets riding on it I was determined to stay on the bike until the bitter end. (A better pun?)

On our return and arriving in London absolutely freezing, we were met with a most marked and extremely welcome increase in the temperature. Due, not doubt, to the masses of buildings, masses of people and even greater masses of electric lighting, and while being in London is always a delight, I was never more delighted to be in it.

Which is why I wrote the next limerick.

In London there are hundreds of delights to be seen
The Tower, Big Ben, Buck House and, (with luck), The Queen,
It has people of every race,
Who move at such a pace,
You're always keen to leave but always pleased you've been.

The second memorable event occurred just a few days prior to our auction. On dashing out of Fenchurch Street Station to grab a cab I found the cabbie of the cab I had grabbed was Fred Housego who, two years earlier, had won the television show Mastermind.

On telling him of our recent adventure and the reason for it, I asked if he would consider acting as our auctioneer. While he was better at answering difficult questions than conducting an auction, his hilarious efforts ensured a much greater profit than we could otherwise have hoped for.

An increase that was also greatly helped by the fact that it was a particularly good year for Beaujolais. Which takes us from some well travelled good wine that travelled well, to some not so good wine that had done no travelling at all.

When living in London my car's needs, necessities, and occasional bit of T.L.C. were dealt with by a splendid mechanic who ran a splendid garage just off Sloane Square. A garage in which the ceiling was completely covered in a huge vine that, according to it's owner, had been quite small when he first occupied the property.

During one of my visits he told me he had, for the first time, harvested the grapes and made some wine. He gave me a glass and said, *"As you're in the business, you might like to give me your opinion."* While I was sipping it he told me that earlier he had given a glass to another of his customers, a young trendy 'Sloane Ranger' who, on tasting it, had looked up at the vine and then down at the wine in her glass, and said; *"It doesn't travel well does it?"*

It wasn't quite to my taste either but I accepted the bottle he gave me to see whether it would travel well - if only to Acton and some of my hardier drinkers.

'Wine, Wit and Wisdom', compiled, in 2005, by Maggie Rosen, Fiona Jerome and P.J. Harris, is the perfect gift for wine buffs and those who topple over from the odd tipple.

Packed with useful and unusual facts, it includes a list of amusing product names that, the authors say; *"Proves that not all wine producers take themselves too seriously."* Australia has Duck Muck. Spain has Scraping the Barrel, California has Cardinal Zin, Marilyn Merlo, Eye of the Toad and Ptomaine de Blageurs. While the French role out the barrel with: Arrogant Frog Ribet, Dog's Bollocks, Fat Bastard, Ted the Mule, Wild Pig and Utter Bustard.

When my brave husband learnt of these, on his next visit to our local bar in France, he asked for a glass of Utter Bastard. Fortunately the barman understood neither the request nor the words. So did the French use English names in order not to offend their client base?

Although how wines with such names could attract any wine lovers – foreign or otherwise – is difficult to imagine. What is less difficult to understand is why most people of erudition and wit have, at some time, said something worth repeating about this tipple that makes us topple over.

One of the finest were those of Ernest Hemingway who said; *"Wine is one the most civilized things in the world and one of the most natural things of the world that has been brought to the greatest perfection, and offers a greater range for enjoyment and appreciation than possibly, any other purely sensory thing."*

And one of the most amusing from Gray's Chloe.

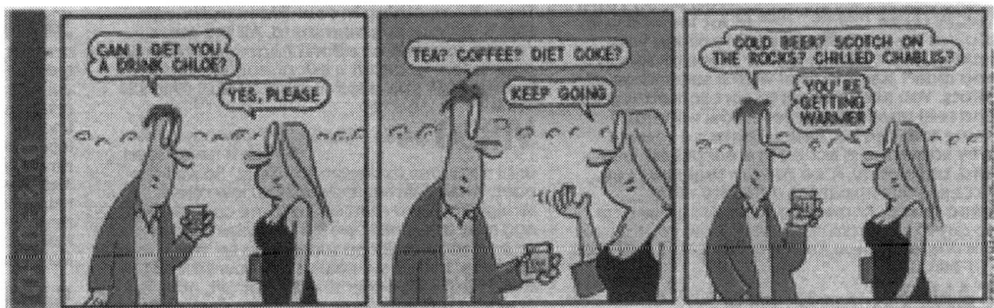

What is possibly not widely known but certainly worth recording, is that during the long wars between France and England many French champagne houses lost their 'masters' and the running of their vineyards was taken over by their widows.

These intrepid women proved, over time, that they could run their vineyards as well, or even better, than their husbands, which is why the French word for widow, 'Veuve', is now used to denote some of the best champagnes.

Madame Cliquot, on learning the English preferred white champagne, perfected the method of leeching out the colour from the pink champagne that was preferred by the French.

Now it takes just a day or two but, at that time, with every bottle angled, cork downwards, in a slotted table and turned daily, it took about twenty eight days. But not that long to drink it!

There may also be many people whose love of champagne may make them wish they could emulate Madame Bollinger who, in one of the most quoted quotes on this drink, said; *"I drink Champagne when I'm happy, and when I'm sad. Sometimes I drink it when I'm alone. When I have company I consider it obligatory. I trifle with it if I'm not hungry and drink it when I am. Otherwise I never touch it – unless I'm thirsty."*

A philosophy voiced a little more succinctly by Noel Coward, who said; *"I'm not a heavy drinker, I can sometimes go for hours without drinking a drop."* And Dorothy Parker's less wordy musing on the subject was; *"Three be the things I shall never attain - envy, content and sufficient champagne."*

Which, no doubt, is why that master of the wise word, Sir Winston Churchill, said to his political colleagues; *"Remember gentleman, it is not just France we are fighting for, it's Champagne!"* And whilst he may have preferred Brandy, Napoleon said; *"In victory you deserve Champagne. In defeat you need it."*

Although should we suffer a shortage we could take heed of Prince Philip, Duke of Edinburgh, who, it is claimed, was of the opinion that; *"Champagne and orange juice is a great drink. The orange juice improves the champagne. The champagne definitely improves the orange juice."* Unless say I, you are, as is my daughter, Alisonjane, allergic to oranges.

In his book; 'All Will Be Well - Good Advice from Winston Churchill', Richard M. Langworth credits this gentleman with the previous quote that I attribute to Napoleon. However as it refers to champagne and not Winnie's favourite tipple, it is more than just likely that, if he did say it, he had 'borrowed' it from Napoleon.

Maybe Mr. Langworth should have heeded Ernest Hemingway's admonishment to all authors; *"Write drunk; edit sober."*

Which does not sit well with Charles Budelaire's belief that; *"One should always be drunk. That's all that matters. But with what? With wine, with poetry, or with virtue, as you choose. But get drunk."* As my reader will have guessed, my choice would be poetry.

I am also in accord with The Vicar of Wakefield author, Oliver Goldsmith who wrote; *"I love everything that is old; old times, old manners, old books, old wines."* While the American drama critic, George Jean Nathan, appears to be less interested in which drink than the reason for drinking it, as he said; *"I drink to make other people more interesting."* What he hadn't considered is that those who drink are likely to become of less interest to other people.

Then there are those who will always be of interest to other people, regardless of how much they drink (or drank), one being Frank Sinatra who said; *"I feel sorry for people who don't drink. When they wake up in the morning, that's as good as they're going to feel all day."*

A point of view with which W.C. Fields agreed when he said; *"I like the odd drink. Three is odd, five is odd, seven is odd."* Which is much the same as James Thurber's view that, *"One martini is all right. Two are too many, and three are not enough."*

Which, perhaps is why Brendan Behan, on seeing a billboard urging people to; 'Drink Canada Dry' said; *"I'll give it a try."* Much as many might do after learning of Ogden Nash's stricture that; *"Candy is dandy, but liquor is quicker."*

Which, perhaps, is why John Doxat maintained; *"The British Empire was created by men who never drew a sober breath after the age of seven."* While W.C. Fields was of the view that; *"Drink is your enemy; Love your enemy."* Although 'loving one's enemy' will not go well with all those who enjoy the odd boozy lunch or evening dram, if, as it is suggested, Muslims eventually convert the world to their beliefs, laws and religion.

So if it is true, as stated in one of Simon's many books on the subject, that many wars have been about wine, these and the last two World Wars will be mere blips by comparison with that which will be fought by those who will fight with all of their might to defend their right to imbibe alcohol.

Or, as Gray suggests; Those who will fight with all of their might to ban all alcohol -

- along with many things we enjoy and that give us the will to live. Which

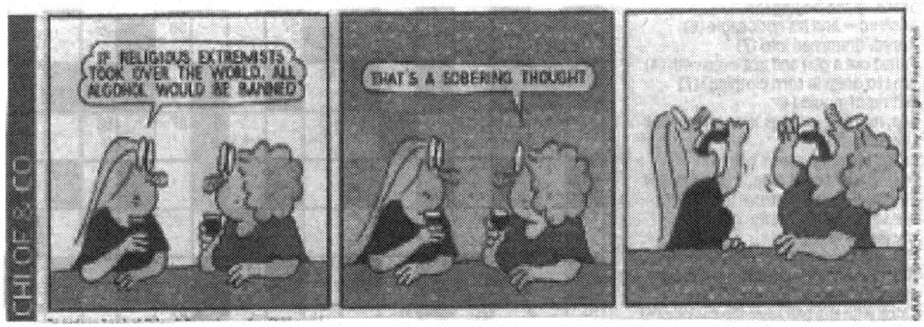

takes us, a little soberly and somewhat warily, to -

WAR

In case they should think themselves all powerful and immortal, Roman generals, when riding in their chariots, would have with them a slave whose sole purpose was, every so often, to whisper in their ear, *"Remember you are mortal."*

It is a great shame that some of our latter day generals of all nationalities, together with our Presidents and Prime Ministers, are not afforded the same admonishment.

But there are some deserving of immortality who had no need of such warnings to remind them they were mortal. They were the many millions who lost their lives during the two worst conflicts the world has ever known but who, had they survived, would gladly have taken a joke aimed at them - such as;

During the First World War, two soldiers were writing letters home when one asked the other; *"Arry, 'ow d'yer spell fought?" "Fought?"* asked 'Arry; *"D'ja mean the fought yer fight or the fought yer fink?"*

An exchange and allied cartoon that might lead many of us to think that,

Impossible People

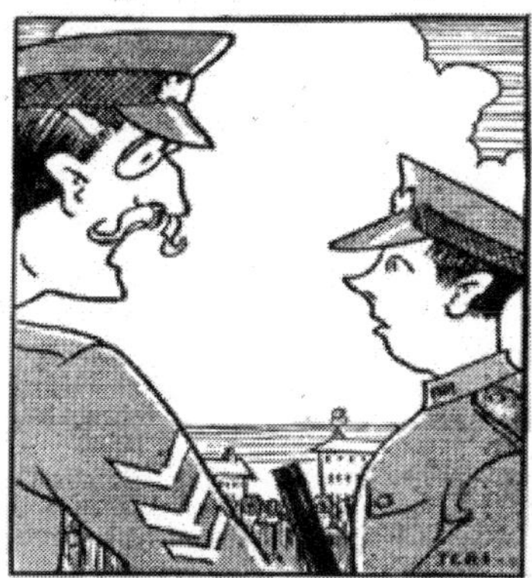

The recruit who thought a fortification was two twentifications.

whenever and wherever there are wars, 'finkin' is not a necessary requirement for recruits allowed to wander about with weapons. *"Or"*, says Simon, *"Wander around yomping."* (A marvellous onomatopoeic word that means exactly how it sounds).

Following two years of National Service, two of Simon's friends, James and Paul, joined the Strategic Reserve while another, Andrew, was in the Royal Artillery.

One evening, with James and Paul wet and weary after a long day marching over the moors, the three young men met up in their local pub where Andrew said; *"Listen, Norton and Lester, you can't just go on yomping about on wet moorlands, you should join the R.A.*

We get to fire at a lot of stuff and then just park our guns in the high street and pop into the nearest pub. The police never move us on as they think we're on special assignment. In life the most important thing is to have a BIG GUN."

Or - if you're in the army - **To Be God.**

The army newspaper, The Union Jack, published the following list of abilities and powers to be found within the hierarchy of military personnel.

A General: Leaps tall buildings with a single bound. More powerful than a steam engine. Faster than a speeding bullet. Gives policy to GOD.
A Colonel: Leaps small buildings with a single bound. More powerful than a shunting engine. Is as fast as a speeding bullet. Walks on water (if the sea is calm). Talks with GOD.
A Lieutenant Colonel: Leaps even shorter buildings with a running start in favourable winds. Is almost as powerful as a speeding bullet. Walks on water in indoor swimming pools. Talks with GOD only when special request is approved.
A Major: Barely clears a Nissan hut. Loses tug-of-war with a steam engine. Can fire a speeding bullet and swims well. Is occasionally addressed by GOD.
A Captain: Makes high marks when trying to leap any building. Can sometimes handle a gun without inflicting self-injury. Dog paddles. Talks to animals. Is run over by trains.
A Lieutenant: Runs into buildings. Is not issued with ammunition. Can't always recognise a train. Can stay afloat if instructed in the use of a lifejacket. Talks to walls.
A 2nd Lieutenant: Falls over doorsteps while trying to enter buildings. Says, "Look at choo choo." Is NEVER issued with a gun or ammunition. Plays in mud puddles. Mumbles to himself.
A Sergeant Major: Lifts tall buildings and walks under them. Kicks steam engines off the track. Catches speeding bullets in his teeth and eats them. Freezes water with a single glance. HE IS GOD.

Mama would say, *"It is their finely tuned sense of humour together with their ability to laugh at themselves that give the British their ability to overcome adversity, however dire,"*

But while we make fun of forces personnel (who, as seen above, will also 'take a rise' out of themselves), they will continue to be essential. As were the millions of young men who laid down their lives, if not willingly, most certainly extremely courageously in the First World War. The centennial commemoration of which in 2014, created considerable controversy.

Many, (one being Michael Morpurgo, author of the magnificent novel, War Horse), maintained that such jingoism should be muted by the wearing of both white and red poppies. Possibly those who promulgate this view do not know why only red poppies are worn, but those who lived through the First War, one of whom was as our mother, would have been derisive of this idea.

She told us that poppy seeds will stay dormant for many years and will only spring into life if the ground in which they lie is disturbed.

The Flanders Fields were not only 'home' to millions of soldiers but to even more millions of poppy seeds which, when disturbed by the digging of deep trenches and artillery explosions, awoke and clothed the entire area in a sea of red poppies.

Proof, if needed, is that road works, with their consequent disturbance of soil often create a similar, if greatly smaller and more muted, rare spectacle. But poppies aside, short memories and even shorter fuses will continue to ensure the necessity of armed forces (whatever their relationship with God), because as scary as the prospect may be, continuing world unrest due to aggression or oppression, will ensure the previous two World Wars will most certainly not be the last. Nor the most dire.

A certainty confirmed by the caption of the next cartoon that my Mother composed just prior to the 1939 'Phony War'. Sadly, it is a sentiment as true today as when she composed it.

Impossible People

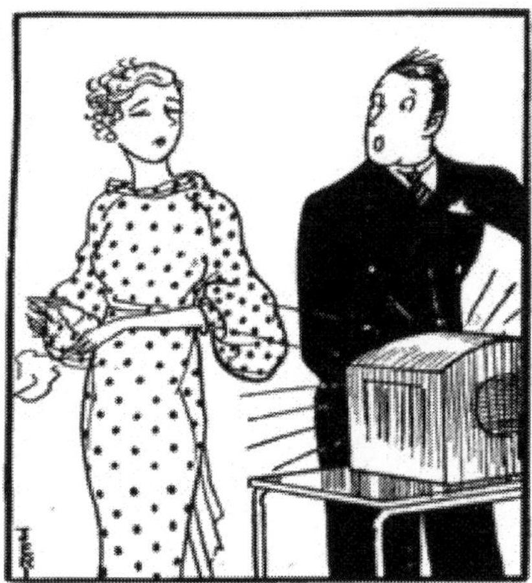

The girl who said these foreigners would have no peace until they had stirred up another war

As are the sentiments in this poem she composed during what was believed, at the time, to be 'The War To End All Wars'.

The Night of the Air Raid
London - 1914-18

Even when a slow star dropped
suddenly through the night,
and a dim buzzing of
mosquito cheers bit my ears,
my cold heart moved me not.

Even the thrumming roar,
the flashing lights, and shuddering
soundful air of blacked out nights,
brought no terrors, or delights,
nor fear, to my soul.

Was I then passionless,
Or merely bored,
that no sorrow made me weep,
No joy soared?

When, through the quivering fog,
the redness glared,
I merely stared,
and looked up geog.

Yet the thin, pitiful strains of a violin
Stretched across a foot of empty air,
can bring my unknown soul,
to laughter, pity or despair.

Young people have always abbreviated words and when our mother was in her teens words such as 'Geog' for 'geography' were very popular. But there can be no abbreviation of 'The Stiff Upper Lip'.

A phrase that is an excellent example of that essential prerequisite for survival in any war and one that is, peculiarly, practiced brilliantly by the British. It is also a trait that is eloquently illustrated in this moving poem by my candidate to be the next Poet Laureate, Martin Newell. His ability to write, each week, topical poems for the Sunday Express makes him an able contender for this exalted post.

The present incumbent may be a good poet but in my opinion, Martin's style and composition are far superior. He wrote the next poem to commemorate the funerals of soldiers who had been killed in Afghanistan. An emotive poem that could apply to all funerals of all the many millions of soldiers killed in all wars. It is also a fitting 'memorial' to the small town of Wootton Bassett that, in 2011, was justly awarded The Royal Warrant.

A Soldier's Funeral

In some small country market town,
Traffic stops, the rain comes down
Under a sympathetic sky.
A black cortege goes slowly by
And, as a shopper bows her head,
The veterans salute the dead.

In dry as parchment voices now
Old women who arranged the flowers,
Whose latter years steal by like hours,
Will hand out hymnbooks from the piles,
And, as the mourners cram the aisles,
Remember other soldiers then.

Husbands, fathers, nephews, sons
Badges, buckles, Number Ones,
In pictures faded in their frames,
Local lads with local names
Destined not to make old bones,
Who'd known these pews and paving stones.

They never questioned. Not one day.
The job was there to do, they'd say,
If you ever asked them why.
Bring them back now - shoulder high.

It also echoes the words of Rudyard Kipling; *"If any question why we died. Tell them, our fathers lied."*

To avoid these sad scenarios it would pay every country to remain neutral, one of which, during the Second War, was Portugal. George said friends of his parents lived in Lisbon and were, therefore, sheltered from the exigencies suffered by their friends and families.

Their letters encapsulated the importance of 'Flying the Flag for England', as in one they wrote that 'they made sure to be seen at the Casino at least once a week' and another included a pithy allusion to the ever dominant lack of essentials with, 'Sugar is short but gin is impossible.'

How they were able to send letters to England at all and by what method they were safely delivered I have yet to discover. Also, how much shorter (or, perhaps, longer?) the war might have been had we then had computers and e-mails - not to mention Google, Twitter and Facebook.

Sugar, which was short everywhere, reminded me of a report I read some years ago in which the writer maintained that those of us who, as children, had a restricted but healthy diet during the war (although it certainly didn't feel healthy at the time), are now, for our age, healthier than those born earlier or later.

So, if it didn't kill you, the war may have done some of us some good. But, as my Mama would say, *"That is NOT a good enough excuse for it."*

Lord Halifax said, *"I often think how much easier the world would have been to manage had Herr Hitler and Signor Mussolini been to Oxford."* While Mama – who was a Gold Medalist in Anatomy and had an Honours Degree in the History of Art, might quote, *"If you study the history and anatomy of war the aggressor can never be victorious as a Victor has only victims to govern."* And: *"The only defence for war is in the defence of your own people and country."*

Had Bush and Blair been sufficiently erudite to know of them, they might have taken heed of these supremely sensible words before waging wars that have resulted in much less defense and much greater danger to their own people and countries.

Or these from our finest wartime premier, Sir Winston Churchill: *"The Statesman who yields to war fever is no longer the master of policy, but the slave of unforeseeable and uncontrollable events."*

Proving that in war: 'It pays to be on the defensive rather than the offensive.' Or, as my sister, Nicola, is so fond of saying, *"Keep your powder dry, you need to win the war, not the battle."*

With Churchill's great leadership we did win, although sometime before his success it was presciently said of him; *"God knows what we should do without him and God knows where we shall go with him."*

For as Douglas Adams said; *"There is a theory which states that if ever anybody discovers exactly what the Universe is for and why it is here, it will instantly disappear and be replaced by something even more bizarre and inexplicable."* To which he added, *"There is another theory which states that this has already happened!"*

Which it has - twice. The First World War not having enough impact, they tried it again in 1939. By the time the effects had worn off (which, some say, never will), the world had, irrevocably, become exactly as Douglas Adams said the universe would.

Despite which, it is still sitting safely within our planetary system, so Nostradamus got it a little wrong when he cited 2012 as the beginning of the end of the world. But did he mean THE END or: 'The End merely as we know it?' All of which makes H.G Wells' 'The War of the Worlds' extraneous, and makes it even more necessary for me to get this book finished before there is no one left to read it!
Or world on which to read it.

I have often wondered, as did Lord Halifax, *"Has anyone ever calculated what the population of the world might now be if all these wars had not killed off vast numbers of people and, in so doing, their prospective progeny?"* Which leads to the questions: How many artists, artisans, architects, designers, sculptors, inventors - and cartoonists –

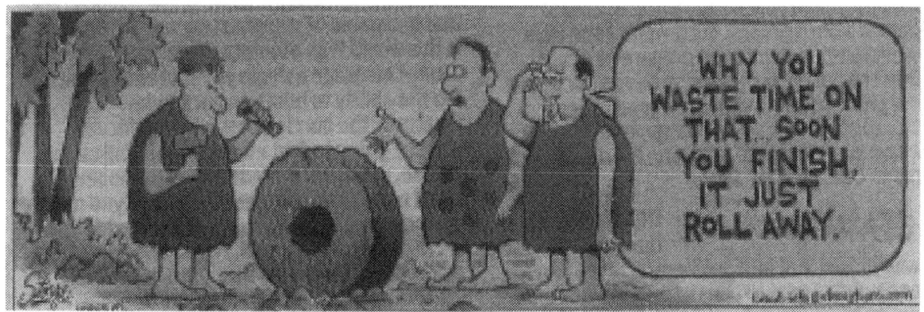

- has the world been deprived of due just to the two World Wars, let alone all those in many other walks of life who, had they had a life, may have made the world a better place?

A premise substantiated by that charismatic president, John F. Kennedy who said; *"Mankind must put an end to war or war will put an end to mankind."* There is now a website dedicated to World Peace which asks people to submit limericks on this subject. The site does not state how this can be achieved merely by writing an odd ode, but as a fan - of limericks not wars - I composed this:

World Peace

World Peace seems an unobtainable dream,
But could be won with this little scheme,
Wherever you go,
And to whomever you know,
Say; "Fight for World Peace" and Win esteem.

Herbert Asquith said; *"The War Office kept three sets of figures, one to mislead the public, another to mislead the Cabinet, and a third to mislead themselves."*

They also misled Hitler, but not soon enough to prevent him causing catastrophic mayhem and murder on an unprecedented scale that changed the life course of many millions of families. Among them ours.

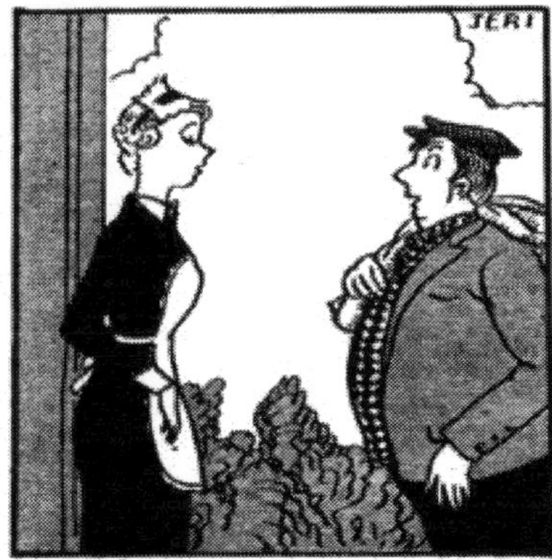

The maid who said, owing to the emergency they were wearing their rags and eating their bones in this house, when the rag and bone merchant called.

Although, despite coming quite close to having to do so, we didn't wear rags or eat bones.

Nevertheless, JERI's previous cartoon is an excellent illustration of the restrictions under which life was lived, both during the war and for many years afterwards, as just about everything went into helping 'The War Effort'.

These included all the extremely attractive railings that adorned the many hundreds of houscs built during the Victorian era and that still adorn many French houses built during the same period. Apparently these mountains of iron railings were never used and, fable has it, are still languishing in a quarry in the wilds of Wales. How true this is we will probably never know.

In a letter published in the Daily Mail, Peter Wilson wrote, "Gangs of children would watch wide-eyed as the iron railings were dismantled to help the war effort. When told they were being taken to stop Hitler, one young lad yelled; *"Stop Hitler! They won't stop him, we can climb over them!"*

It is thought that Hitler planned his air attacks, now known as The Baedeker Raids, on Karl Baedeker's 1937 Great Britain Guide that listed our Cathedral cities as being of great importance. Thus Exeter. where we lived during the war, suffered a first raid on the 7th August, 1940, followed by a further eighteen raids.

As I note towards the end of this section, many cathedrals suffered severe damage, but, in the same way that; 'God looks after the English' he also looks after their cathedrals, and they were all, even those severely damaged, eventually restored to their former glory.

But millions of homes were not. During one raid nearly all of the houses in the road next to our own were completely destroyed. *"Who did that?"* asked Nicola, indignantly. *"The Germans,"* said Mama. *"How DARE they?"* said Nicola, aghast. To which Mama said; *"Well we send our airmen to bomb*

German houses." Mama had no suitable answer for Nicola's riposte of; *"Won't they be horrible when they grow up!"*

Nicola was right; males, whether young or old, can often be 'horrible', and even more so in wars. A gentleman with whom I was once acquainted, Richard Boorman, made the film 'Hope & Glory in which gangs of boys roam among the dust and rubble of London's bombed out houses, many of which had cellars that had become gaping holes in the ground, as they had in all of our blitzed cities – including Exeter.

One day, Boris (as naughty as his dark curly hair and stunning looks made him look angelic), was 'captured' by a similar gang who stuffed him into one of these cellars, which they then covered with a slab of concrete. Fortunately the slab was too heavy for them to drag over the entire opening so, following several hours of parental panic, Boris, having made his escape, arrived home covered in blood from top to toe.

Today there would be a media outcry of gargantuan proportions and the perpetrators would be nabbed and given ASBO's. (Which can be quite useful, for as Linda Smith, that supreme but, sadly, late comic genius once said, *"We shouldn't knock ASBO's as they are probably the only qualifications some of these lads are likely to get."*). But at that time we had more important things to worry us, such as would we survive to the next day?

Mama washed Boris down, made sure he wasn't terminally damaged, scolded him for wandering so far from home on his own, and the matter was soon forgotten. Or was it?

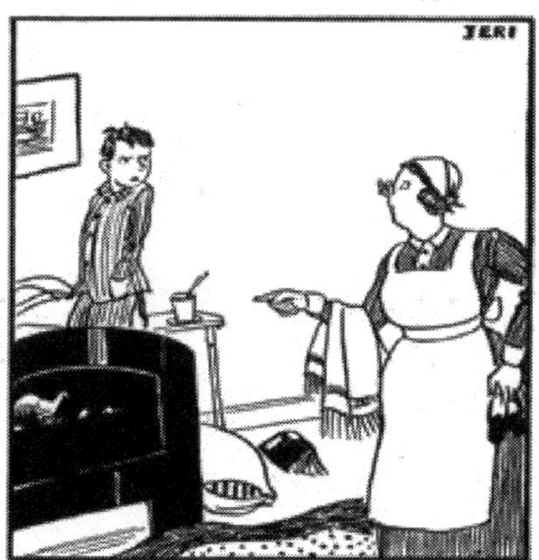

The boy who, when asked why he was always getting into hot water, said he wanted to be hard-boiled.

Regular journalistic debates ask why we need to remember the War and why those who experienced it as children still think of the Germans as 'the enemy' and why we don't now 'forgive and forget'. We have no problem with the forgiving bit, it is the not being able to forget that still gives us nightmares.

In a letter published in the Daily Mail one such protagonist wrote: *"It is racist and dangerous to glorify the war with a pride and smugness that continues to promote hatred and anti-German propaganda."*

One wonders if she is equally eager for any reference to other atrocities, such as the frightful Slave Trade, to cease. With the present propensity to relate all adult woes to childhood ills, it is fairly safe to write how much Hitler's tumultuous and terrifying activities influenced our lives when we were young, and why they loom large in our memories to this day. For unlike children who have placid and structured early years and thus remember little of these, we remember ours vividly.

So, while we don't hate Germany or its people, (or even those Germans who were drawn into believing Hitler was God, many of whom also endured great suffering), we still hate Hitler, his acolytes, among whom were not a few French, and the ghastly horrors they perpetrated.

The following amusing anecdotes are just a few examples of why, despite being tiny at the time, we are not likely to forget or, for far less amusing reasons, ever cease to despise, detest, hate and loathe the Nazi fascist who took us into a Second World War. Even if this was due to the deprivations suffered by the Germans following their defeat in the First. But as they also started that one, they deserve the opprobrium heaped on them by those of us who wear our poppies with pride 'Lest we Forget'.

Even so, for us it did have a lighter side as the Americans, on deciding to join the fray, chose to billet a number of their forces personnel on a base adjacent to our home. A move that gave our father's aspirations to deal in the Black Market a significant boost, as, after a 'hard day's night' of trading he would take a short-cut through their barracks and, to explain away his various nocturnal and nefarious activities, would tell us they had locked him up overnight when he had answered "Foe" to their nightly demands of; "Friend or Foe?"

We believed this ridiculous story and were always saying "Foe!" to the Americans in the hope of suffering the same fate and some chocolate. The possibility of which may also have been the reason why the camp was a favourite haunt of many local 'Ladies of the Night'. Or, as they were then more commonly known, 'Sirens.'

Perhaps these 'Sirens' were the reason why, despite their distance from their loved ones, not one of these young soldiers behaved inappropriately with any of the many children they 'played' with. For with so many to play with, had they done so, it would have come to light – or the ears of their parents.

Our father's shenanigans were considerably assisted by his 'Displaced Person's' passport. A strange anomaly that, as far as I am aware, no longer exists. He also avoided internment, the fate of many aliens resident in Britain. This meant he could continue his somewhat unconventional activities, not just unknown to us but also the authorities.

Authorities who, if the script writers of the brilliant 'Foyle's War' are to be believed, spent as much time seeking out those embroiled in the business of black marketeering and burglary as they did in digging out deserters. An arduous undertaking as, with so many bombed-out buildings, these miscreants (together with any ill-gotten goods), had plenty of places to hide.

Living such a short distance from such large numbers of Americans had a number ofnbenefits not available to those who didn't. For, unlike most people who had to rely on their ration books for confectionery, we relied on 'our' neighbours who, when off duty, would visit us laden with gifts of chocolate and candy.

Many of them, being hardly more than boys themselves, would devise games for us or would regale us with tales of their homeland.

I still have a photograph in which Roy, a young soldier we 'adopted' as a surrogate uncle, is 'adorned' on hip and knee by myself and my three sisters. With no memory of his surname or where in America he lived, despite the ease with which this is now done and much as it would be pleasing to do so, it would not now be possible to trace his family.

Towards the end of the war when England and America were preparing their final push into Northern France, our American neighbours prepared for this with several long and extremely realistic, mock battles.

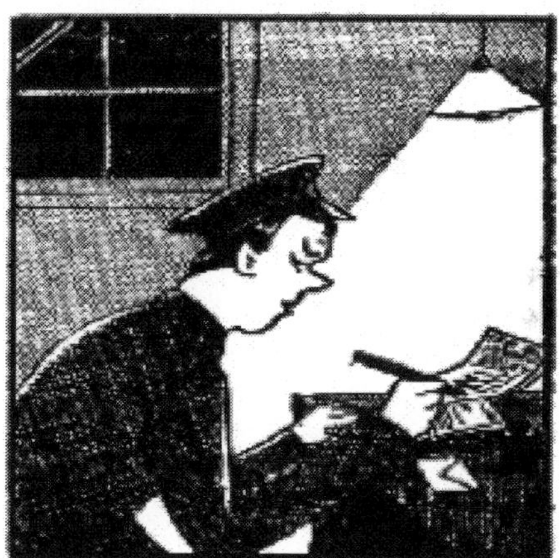

The soldier who claimed on his life insurance because he was a casualty in a mock battle.

At the start of these 'battles' we, together with all the other local children, would climb to the top of the raised perimeter of the adjacent cricket ground which provided an excellent viewing platform from where to watch these scary activities.The last started much the same as had all the others but, as it became more brutal, bloody and violent and the numbers of 'pretend' dead increased, the numbers of watching children decreased. But not all of them!

Following a head count our parents found me missing. On going outside they saw, in the dusk, a lone six year old sitting on the hillock completely engrossed in the mayhem still being enacted by the American forces.

The lack of fear and total acceptance by myself and my siblings, (and, no doubt, many other children of a similar age), of these frightful and savage happenings was because, with 'no memory of peace', the atrocious activities thrown up by Hitler's maelstrom of hatred, horror and destruction were all we knew and were, therefore, to us, 'normal'.

As it was for those children incarcerated in concentration camps that I write about and a truth wonderfully illustrated in this poem by Sheila Webb of Chesham, that was published in the Peterborough column of the Daily Mail in May 2011.

(If only, say I, 'The Road to Peace' were a 'Piece of Cake.')

A Victory Treat On The Read To Peace

There's singing and there's dancing,
At the party in our street,
It's springtime here in London,
And it's such a special treat.

The buntings gently flapping,
Lovely colours in a row.
I'm all dressed up in my Sunday best,
With my hair tied in a bow.

There's lots of yummy jelly,
With orange juice as well,
I've helped myself to seconds,
But I hope that you won't tell.

My mummy's really happy
Over there with Auntie Jen,
I haven't seen her laugh like this,
Since - I can't remember when.

There's food stretched out for miles
With rows and rows of tables,
And everyone from all around
At last have found their smiles.

Mum says the war is over,
And that fears and bombs will go,
It's all a bit confusing,
Cause it's really all I know!

I'm with here with all my friends,
And happy I'm not alone,
But most of all I'm happy,
'Cos my daddy's coming home.

Sheila's poem confirms the universal delight of thousands of children who, after the war, were able to enjoy the party foods they had, for so many years, been denied.

And although she is *'Happy 'cos her daddy's coming home'*, sadly, he may not have been the Daddy she remembered as, on their return, many of our soldiers were not the men they were when they left to 'Go to War'.

It also confirms that children, if they have little or no memory of another, will accept a way of life and environment, however frightful, without complaint. Confirmed during a visit to The Holocaust Museum in Washington where we learned that, after they were liberated, small children who had no memory of life outside the camps, although terribly emaciated and close to death, were not, as would have been expected, traumatised.

They had, when still fit enough to do so, even played games where they would 'pretend' to send each other to the gas chambers. Extraordinary as it may seem, for them, sending people to their deaths was normal adult behaviour.

Dedicated in 1993, the museum should be obligatory viewing for all those who, despite overwhelming evidence to the contrary, vehemently maintain the Holocaust didn't happen.

'Overwhelming evidence' described in all its horror in a letter (a copy of which was given to me by a relation of his), that was written by an American assigned to the Military Intelligence Unit attached to the 82nd Airborne Division. Fluent in German, Daniel was sent, as a Commissioned Captain, to Germany and as such was one of a party of senior service personnel who visited a Concentration Camp the day after being liberated by the Americans.

It is a four and a half page letter that is, possibly, unique, and which is a heart rending indictment of the worlds worst, best recorded, period of man's inhumanity to man.

Written on a portable typewriter late in the evening of the 30th April 1945, Daniel's letter to his parents tells of the ghastly suffering of those held in this horrendous Hell Hole. A Hell Hole that can now be witnessed, but in very much kinder surroundings, by visiting the Holocaust Museum in Washington. A visit that is an overwhelming experience, for, as with much in America, no expense has been spared in order to illustrate the enormity of this horrific and shameful period of our relative recent history.

On entering, as was the case when the interns first entered the camps, the sexes are separated into two queues. While done courteously it is very controlled, which gives an initial taste of the horrors visited on its victims. Each person is then given an Identity Card. Mine, No. 4793, was of a Polish woman, Laura Litwak. Born in June 1900, the second of five, well-educated children, she was fluent in four languages, Polish, German, Russian and Yiddish. She and her fiancé, Daniel, married in 1935 and, in 1937, they had a daughter.

Daniel, had bought them false ID's which, after he was shot in 1941, enabled Laura to obtain work as an interpreter for the German High Command. In order to prove she was a Polish patriot, and at great risk of being shot, she also taught in a Polish underground school. An activity that, when discovered, landed she and her daughter in a Concentration Camp.

Three years after their liberation they came to England where they lived until 1971,when they went to America. So 'I' was one of the fortunate few who survived.

The museums exhibits range from the ghastly cattle trucks used to transport victims, to enormous piles of their effects. Suitcases, clothes, shoes, spectacles and hair (all inmates had their heads shaved), are displayed separately in enormous, fully glazed cabinets. All of which dramatically and horrifically, illustrate, not only the vicious way the inmates were treated, but also that they were thought of as subhuman.

The three floors of the museum are accessed by glazed walkways, with, etched in the glass, the names of the millions of families and many thousands of villages that were wiped out during these ghastly events. A clear indication of the vast manpower and funds expended by Hitler and his Nazi henchmen in their attempt (and degree to which they were almost successful), to rid the world of Jews.

It is an idle wonder, but had not so much effort, time, money and manpower been spent on this evil madness, would the Germans have been better equipped to win the war?

Although it was an 'evil' madness' that began years prior to the start of the War. Confirmed by a series of 'Address Unknown' letters by Katherine Kressmann Taylor that was published, in 'Story 'Magazine' in 1937. The following year they were published in a book of the same name that became a literary sensation and social phenomenon.

This tiny book garnered high praise in America and Europe, but, not unsurprisingly, was banned in Nazi Germany. The foreword and eleven letters, dated between November 1932 and March 1934, that make up 'Address Unknown' take no more than a few minutes to read and I have never known anyone who, on reading it for the first time, has not immediately re-read it.

My first copy was a gift, and I have now bought many as gifts for my family, friends and even, occasionally, the odd stranger. Now a rediscovered classic and international best seller, it has earned much media acclaim:-

Publishers Weekly: *"Address Unknown serves not only as a reminder of Nazi horrors but as a cautionary tale in light of current racial tensions and ethnic and nationalistic intolerance."*

The Star Tribune: *"Akin to the sly plot twists of O.Henry. Believe me, Address Unknown will leave you breathless with admiration."*

And from the illustrious NewYork Book Reviewer: *"This modern story is perfection itself. It is the most effective indictment of Nazism to appear in fiction."*

Naturally, it can be bought at the Holocaust Museum, which, by the time of our visit in 2001, had reached the staggering figure of over forty million visitors. Even so, we were told the sobering fact that it would be some years before duplicate Identity Cards would be needed.

The present day abhorrence for 'numbering people' (done despicably by the Nazi's with tattoos), is understandable. However, at the start of The Second War, everyone of any gender, age, height, weight and hue, was issued with one.

I still have mine - No. DAIF/169/6 - which, in itself, is a good museum exhibit as it has four slips of paper showing the four different addresses to which my parents moved between my second and eighth birthdays.

Although we are no longer issued with Identity Cards, modern technology now numbers each and every one of us from the cradle to the grave, so it has always baffled me why our NHS numbers are not used, with suffix letters, for all of our other necessary I.D's such as driving licence, passport, and pension. Not only would this save a lot of aggravation, it would save a lot of money – and, possibly, fraud.

The subject of things that are more user friendly takes me back to our own American army camp which, towards the end of the War, also housed Italian prisoners of war.

Within days of their arrival, while our parents were busy discussing whether we should be allowed to fraternise with the enemy, we were equally busy making friends with the Italians, who are better at playing with children than they are at playing at war. A point of view that some may think insults these gregarious and romantic people, but, being a woman, I consider it to be a great compliment.

Our parents somehow inveigled day release for some of these prisoners, who would make 'trains and boats and planes' for us out of old pieces of wood. Living in a world where new toys were a rarity, despite their lack of wheels, we thought them magical.

Being so young we had no prior memory of a time when sleeping in shelters at night was not a normal part of everyday life. (Another neat pun?) Many gardens had 'Anderson' shelters, that were built half in and half out of the ground. They had oval roofs made from corrugated iron with steps leading down into them, and could be made quite comfortable. Which was just as well, as once in them you couldn't leave until the 'All Clear' had been sounded.

After the war many Anderson shelters were used as garden sheds. Our grandparents had one that, much later, we made into a playhouse until our grandfather housed his chickens in it at night to stop the foxes eating them. Whether eaten by foxes or not, chickens take us to a little known fact.

Apparently, owing to Britain's far superior naval strength, Hitler, had hoped to negotiate a peace agreement with our Government, and thus 'chickened-out' of early air attacks. So when he did send Zeppelins to bomb Britain, their effect was minimal when compared with the devastation caused in Europe owing to the superior air power England had developed between the wars

I only bore my reader with this 'chicken-out' story, as it allows me to include this English translation of an incredibly prophetic, Latin poem to which my Mother introduced me. An ode that, had it been written in recent times, would not 'open our eyes in awed surprise' but most certainly does when we learn that it was translated from the Latin 'Luna Habitabilis' of Thomas Grey, who was born in 1716 and died in 1771.

The time will come when thou shalt lift thine eyes
To watch a long drawn battle in the skies,
While aged peasants, too amazed for words,
Stare at the flying fleets of wondrous birds.
England, so long mistress of the sea,
Where winds and waves caress her sovereignty,
Her ancient triumphs yet on high shall bear,
And reign the sovereign of the conquered air.

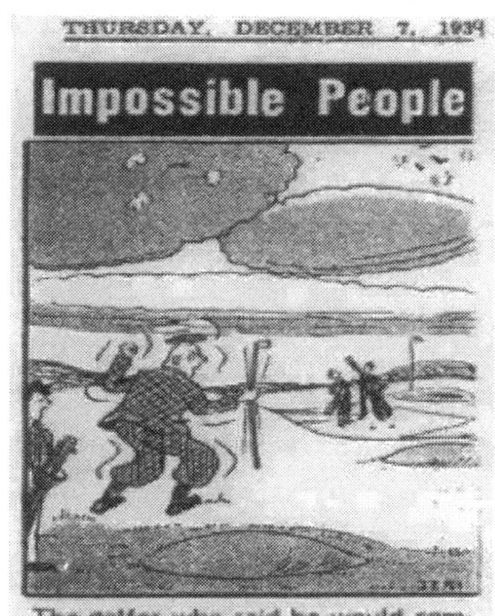

The golfer who said he would complain to the secretary when the twosome in front stopped to watch an air battle.

Apart from those, such as Simon, who have a great interest in the history of the two World Wars, it is possible that few people know that the bombing of England by the Germans began on September 7th 1940 and the bombing of Pearl Harbour took place exactly fifteen months later to the day, on December 7th, 1941.

Even fewer people know that my sister, Nicola, was born on September 6th 1939, three days after Britain declared war on Germany. But it was to be another three years and three months for the Americans, due to the assault on Pearl Harbour, to decide to join the fray.

Ordered to carry out this horrific exercise on a non combatant country, Marshal Admiral and Commander-in-Chief of the Combined Japanese Fleet, Isoroku Yamamoto, on realising his forces had failed to destroy the American aircraft carriers that had all been away from the base on December the seventh, famously said; *"We have awoken a sleeping giant and filled him with a terrible resolve."*

A 'Sleeping Giant and Resolve' without which, Britain would, almost certainly, not have been victorious. Ghastly as this event was, it created a memorial site that, as the many people who have seen it, (four of whom are myself, Simon, Sonya and Ray), would agree is one of the finest of its kind.

While the September 1940 date for the commencement of the 'long drawn battle in the skies' is (possibly), accurate, did our mother's previous and next cartoons, published in the Daily Sketch on the 2nd and 7th December, 1939, suggest that, as was Thomas Gray, she was able to prophesy the start of the bombing - or did the Blitz begin before the recorded date of 1940?

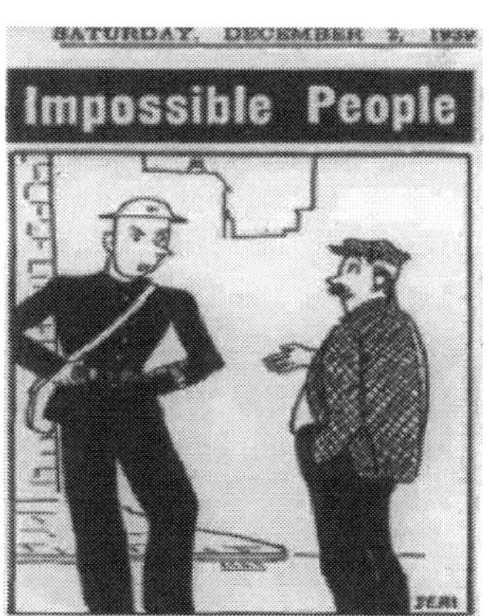

The man who said he was the only person left without a care in the world. He was an out-of-work caretaker.

But on whichever dates the bombing began - or stopped - the number of businesses bombed out of their buildings because of the Blitz, must have left countless caretakers with little to care for - or take care of. (An inspired double alliteration?)

What we do know for certain is that the Blitz continued for 828 nights and, in London alone, nearly 20,000 people were killed. The oldest a lady of 88 and the youngest a baby of three months.

This blanket blitzing, while diminished by the May 1941 Battle of Britain, only ceased when Hitler made his ill-considered, ill-fated decision to invade Russia. Despite the horrific results of this action that afflicted both Russians and Germans alike, not to mention all those in between, I can still hear my mother saying, (as must have many other mothers), *"Thanks Be To God For That!"*

Most people, unless blitzed out of their homes, had great difficulty deciding whether to stay or to go - or, if the latter, to where?

Simon's parents decided that he, his sister Sue and their mother, Muriel, together with her friend, Sheila Higgs and her two children, Richard and Sheila, should go to the country. Soon after settling into their rented cottage in Kent, they learned it was just below the route of the German V1 self-propelled flying bombs known for their distinct, recognizable, 'putt-putt' noise.

Known as 'Doodlebugs' by adults and 'Buzzbombs' by children, these would glide until their fuel was exhausted when they would fall immediately and explode on impact.

However, as Muriel and Sheila knew the V1's were loaded with enough fuel to get them safely (?) to their target this did not worry them. Nor were they concerned on learning that, in an attempt to stop them, Spitfires were sent to shoot them down or, in an exceptionally daring and extremely dangerous manoeuver, their pilots would fly close enough to slip the wings of their planes under the wings of the bombs and tip them over, thus confusing their navigation guidance system and causing them to fall before they reached London.

So it was fortunate they were not being 'observed' by JERI's Observer -

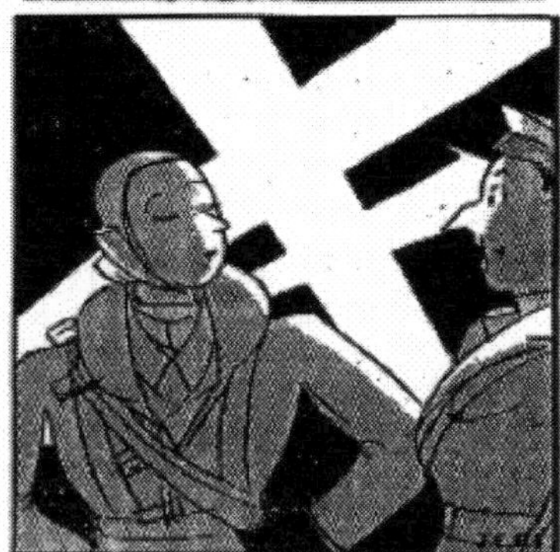

The observer who said he never could get any decent photographs of the positions of the enemy as his pilot got so near that they breathed on his lens.

Muriel and Sheila considered these scary aerial acrobatics an excellent activity by these brave RAF pilots, until, on learning that they frequently took place just above their new home, they hastily packed their belongings and, equally hastily, moved back to London.

A commotion that safely and speedily allows me to return to 'poetry in motion'. Apart from those by such luminaries as Martin Newell and Richard Digance, those poems I have so far included are by unsung or little known poets - such as my mother and myself.

So I was delighted, when editing this section, to find the next poem by another unsung, gifted poet, that was published in the Daily's Mail's Peterborough column at the time of one of the Second World War Remembrance days.

As the accreditation has only initials and surname, I do not know the gender of the poet, but the content and tone of the poem (which, Simon says, *"Is brilliant"*), leads me to conclude he must be a 'he'.

Thus I hope that, along with the one or two other poets whose poems are from the same source and who I have not, as yet, been able to contact, L. H. Day of Llanbradach will, if he ever reads 'Impossible People', be just as pleased to see it here as I was to find it.

GROUND FORCE

Wherever you walk, you will hear people talk,
Of the men who go up in the air,
Of the daredevil way, they go into the fray,
Facing death without turning a hair.

They'll raise a big cheer and buy lots of beer,
For a pilot home on leave;
But don't give a jigger for a flight mech or rigger,
With nothing but 'props' on his sleeve.

They just say "Nice day" and then turn away,
With never a mention of praise,
And the poor bloody 'erk who does all the work,
Just orders his own beer, and pays.

They've never been told of the hours in the cold,
That he spends sealing Germany's fate.
How he works on a kite, 'till all hours of the night.
And then turns up the next morning at eight.

He gets no rake-off for working 'til take off,
Or helping the air crew prepare.
But whenever there's trouble it's; 'Quick at the double."
The man on the ground must be there.

Each flying crew could tell it to you;
They know what this man's really worth.
They know he's a part of the RAF's heart,
Even though he stays close to the earth.

He doesn't want glory, but please tell his story,
Spread a little of his fame around.
He's also is 'one of the few', so give him his due;
Three cheers for the 'men on the ground'.

By September 2015, my Impossible People was almost ready to be put to bed, but for a number of sad, silly and somewhat strange reasons, I hadn't had sufficient time to complete it, or of greater importance, to check it.

So I was even more certain that my mother was looking out for me when, in early October of that year, the following two letters and their allied poems were published in the Daily Mail. In answer to a readers question: *Which British Army regiment likes to boast; 'It is the first in the field and the last to leave?'* Two ex- sappers, Edward Valentine, and John Wall sent in the following letters and pocms.

Mr Valentine wrote: 'A good claimant must be the Royal Engineers. They cleared minefields and booby traps, mended bridges and roads, repaired the airstrips, arranged clean water supplies so other regiments could do their job and, if we had to retreat, the Royal Engineers would be the last regiment out.'

Mr Wall wrote: 'This poem, written by an unknown sapper and variously attributed to Corporal Claude Radley while serving with 18th Field Company RCE in 1942 and also to Sergeant Ken Harrison, South East Asia Command (1944-47), makes a good case for the Royal Engineers.'

A SALUTE TO THE ENGINEERS

Now the Lord of the Realm has glorified the Charge of the Light Brigade,
And the thin red line of the infantry, when will their glory fade?
There are robust rhymes on the Jolly Tar and classics on Musketeers.
But I shall sing, 'til your eardrums ring, of the Muddy Old Engineers.

Now it's all very fair to fly through the air or humour a heavy gun,
Or ride in tanks through the broken ranks of the crushed and shattered Hun.
And it's nice to think when the U-Boats sink of the glory that outlives the years,
But whoever heard an haunting word for the Muddy Old Engineers.

Now you mustn't feel, when you read this spiel, that the sapper is a jealous knave,
That he joined the ranks for a vote of thanks in search of a hero's grave.

No your mechanised cavalry's quite alright and your Tommy has darn'd few peers,
But where in Hell would the lot of them be if it weren't for the Engineers.

Oh they look like tramps but they build your camps and sometimes lead the advance
And they sweat red blood to bridge the flood to give you a fighting chance.
Who stays behind when it's getting hot, to blow up the roads in the rear?
Just tell your wife she owes your life to some Muddy Old Engineer.
Some dusty, crusty, croaking, joking, Muddy Old Engineer.

No fancy crest is pinned to their chest, if you read what their cap badge says,
Why 'Honi Soit Qui Mal Y Pense' is a queersome sort of praise.
But their modest claim to immortal fame has probably reached your ears,
The first to arrive and the last to leave, the Muddy Old Engineers.
The sweating, go-getting, uproarious, glorious, Muddy Old Engineers.

The Royal Air Force, and (with my fingers now soundly rapped, their Engineers and Groundsmen), take us to Rockets.

In April 1942, the, German V2 rocket arrived. Not only did it have vastly greater explosive power, to add to our nightly terrors it was silent. Thus this deadly device, with no warning of its imminent arrival, notched up a further ten thousand casualties.

It also greatly increased the need to 'hide'. Thus if there was no underground station or other authorised shelter close to your home, makeshift sleeping spaces in safer places than bedrooms, became another essential of life.

If you had a garden you could build an Anderson shelter. Half buried in the ground they were made from corrugated iron sheets with steel plates at either end, one of which had steps down to an entryway. They measured six foot six by four foot six by two foot six. But even with earth heaped over them they were much too cold to sleep in during the winter.

In 1941 Ellen Wilkinson was made responsible for air raid shelters and 'chose' the Morrison Shelter, that, between 1941 and 1943, were delivered to three hundred and fifty thousand homes. Named after the Home Secretary, Herbert Morrison, they were made of very heavy steal and could also be used as a table. They arrived in flat-pack form and were then bolted together to form a rigid metal box six feet six inches long, four feet six inches wide and just two feet six inches high.

These 'cages' with wire sides, were extremely claustrophobic and not the most pleasing places in which to spend the long nights waiting to be 'Bombed to Bits'. A fate our brother Stefan would threaten us with if we misbehaved. Although designed to house six, ours, with four little girls in it wearing dresssing gowns made from American army blankets left no room for our brothers, so they slept under the stairs - whatever they were wearing.

It is certain that this contraption with its impenetrable steel plate top and wire mesh sides was why Sonya, became so severely claustrophobic. Which was why it wasn't long before Mama concluded that, air raids or no, we were safer outside it than in it.

But Alan Lock's family were definitely safer inside it than out. In a letter to the Daily Mail, Alan, from Aylesford in Kent, writes that, in early May 1942, their house suffered a direct hit. (As it was Kent, it was probably one of the Doodlebugs 'tipped-over' by our brave RAF pilots.)

He and his eleven-year-old sister and their mother were in their Morrison shelter which was blown across the street onto the roof of a house opposite. He writes, in blitz spirit tones; *"We were seriously injured but survived."* It is hard to imagine anyone today being quite so sanguine about such a terrifying experience.

Before the introduction of the Anderson and Morrison shelters, many people 'hid' in their cellars or under the stairs, which, despite its cramped space, was often safer than a cellar. Proven by the fact that for some years following the end of the war, our towns and cities were littered with vast areas of derelict buildings, with the only reminder that these had once been homes were their still standing internal load bearing walls supporting, still intact, staircases.

Huge numbers of which were in or near The City of London that, many years later, made a fortune for the young entrepreneurs, Donald Gosling and Ronald Hobson, who turned these wastelands into fee paying car parking areas from which the National Car Parking Company, now known as 'NCP', was born.

So while, as a direct result of the war, a lot of people lost a lot of money, many made a lot - and continue to do so to this day, as there are many more documentaries and films on these two world shaking, not to mention world shattering, events than any other subject.

In October 2010, Harper Press published one of the finest books on this period. The extremely well researched 'Terror Of The Blitz' in which Juliet Gardiner gives us many similar examples of the exceptionally stoic and civil character of the British people that created the 'The Blitz Spirit'. A characteristic that saved many people's sanity during the long months of the German air assaults that killed 43,000 of the million Britons who died as a direct result of the war, one in ten of whom were children.

A statistic that, in my teens, led me to write a poem for inclusion in an End of

Year school magazine that was 'killed off' before it was published. Whether this was due to lack of content, lack of funds or my poem, we will never know. Years later I found a scrap of paper in my much thumbed anthology, 'The Land of Poetry' on which I had composed this tiny, untitled, poem.

So, unlike those children who died in the Blitz, it now has a new lease of life – and a title. A title that has been used by other poets but, having searched my dictionary and my brain for a better one, not one of the million words in our language get close to the suitability of this miniscule word -

WHY?

The life that once was ours will now no longer be,
As we've been blown to bits by bombs and debris,
We did not ask to come into this world so cold
But the way we left it caused misery untold.
It was not for us to ask for why or what this war was for,
And now we will never know - for we are now no more.

By 1946, with many millions of homes destroyed or severely damaged, over sixteen thousand people were homeless and up to a thousand people were squatting in empty shells of properties in Kensington High Street alone.

Reading, in my teens, my mother's poem about the more isolated air raids of the First World War, inspired me to attempt one of my own about the much heavier, bombardments in the Second. While it doesn't come close to the value of Mama's, it does describe the dread and despair of those who experienced these raids but nonetheless, stayed stoic.

A stoicism maintained in all the cities that were targets of Hitler's Baedeker Blitz, the first of which, on the four nights of the 23rd to the 26th April 1942, was Exeter where, if not as bad as the devastation suffered by other cities, caused much damage and many fatalities. Among whom were numbers of people who lived in the street next to our own.

The Night of the Air Raid
Exeter 1942

Suddenly without word of warning,
A siren screams its message well,
The world within an instant changes.
Becomes for each a private kind of hell.

A light that from a window beckons,
Within an instant changes to a blacker space
Than the darkness into which it stares,
Draining all expression from a fear filled face.

Cold fear and camaraderie become companions,
Contradictions stretch the senses taut,
Tensing nerves for what is yet to come,
Transcending all emotion and all thought.

Panic hovers, hawk-like, in the air,
A steady drone fills the empty sky.
A prayer, unspoken, fills the empty spaces.
'Please, PLEASE God, let them pass us by.'

Another, due to its vast docklands, was Hull. A city blitzed nearly to oblivion in some of the most prolonged raids. To their lasting credit, succeeding councils have left, intact, the remains of a bombed out cinema as a lasting memorial to this Hell visited upon Hull.

In order to avoid the lowering of general morale, the Government 'hid' from those in the less populated areas of the country the ferocity of these raids and the vast amount of damage or, more correctly, devastation.

Devastation caused not just in London, Exeter and Hull, but also Bath, Canterbury, Coventry, Cowes, Liverpool, Norwich, Plymouth and York. All close contenders in the competition to be the worst hit. But not Vienna - due, perhaps, to their apparent courtesy?

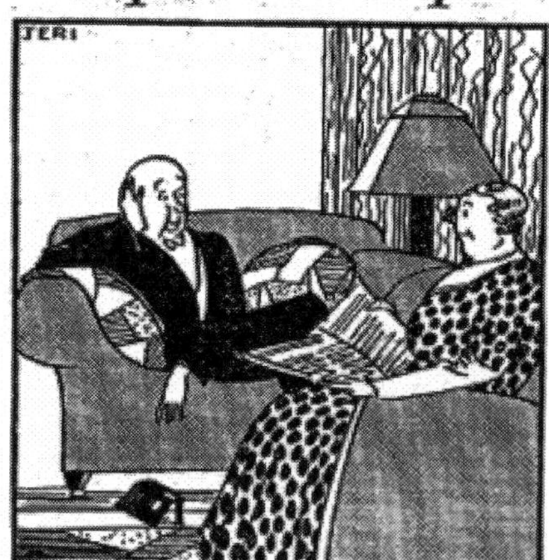

The woman who said she could quite understand about this Civil War in Vienna as she had always found the Austrians most polite.

Aside from these ghastly air raids, another unhappy experience for thousands of children was being evacuated. We did not have to suffer this fate as, not wanting us to be separated and knowing no one would take in six children, Mama refused to allow us to be sent away.

Nevertheless, in one four-day period in 1939, in an operation aptly called Pied Piper, one and a half million children, together with a few parents and teachers, were evacuated from major cities. Followed in the ensuing months, by a further two million.

Some years ago I read the sad story about an evacuee who was never 'reclaimed'.

She lived for the rest of her life with her 'new' family who were farmers and who treated her as an unpaid servant. It is possible her parents died in the Blitz or she just became a 'forgotten child'.

There were many similar instances of children not being returned to, or reclaimed, by their families as, before the dust - both factual and figurative - had settled, many people had disappeared into the great void of the unrecorded dead, displaced or homeless.

But, apart from feeling homesick and a few instances of cruelty, most evacuees were well looked after by their host families and, at the end of the war, safely returned to their parents. Even today there are some who look back on their enforced removal to unknown places and a totally alien environment, as one of the best times of their childhood.

Which, if this next poem is any indication, was certainly so for Pat Rouse from Hornchurch, Essex. Published in the Peterborough Column of the Daily Mail in October 2009, it is a poignant reminder of how many evacuees still remember this uniquely odd, and sometimes heartbreaking, activity that had never happened before and, fortunately, has never been needed since.

I Remember

I remember the parcel all tied up with string,
And my coat with its little brown label,
I remember my mother with tears in her eyes,
Saying "I'll come whenever I'm able."

I remember the station all crowded with kids,
And all I kept asking was "Why?"
I remember my gran holding on for dear life,
Saying; "Come now, big boys don't cry."

I remember my brother and how brave he was,
He was older than me, just eleven,
I remember he'd not let me out of his sight,
Saying; "We're together 'cos he's only seven."

I remember the smell of oil lamps and heather,
In the house where we went to stay,
I remember the lady, Mrs. Green was her name,
Saying; "Hot scones as you've come a long way."

I remember the green fields we saw from our room,
Streams where we fished now and then,
I remember, Mrs. Green's pretty young daughter,
Saying; "I'll change you from boys into men."

I remember the day when we had to go back,
To the place we'd not wanted to leave,
I remember my mother, a new babe in her arms,
Saying; "Come, meet your new brother, Steve

I remember the tears that welled up in my eyes.
Not once in four years had she been.
I remember the way that I looked at my mother,
Saying; "How much I loved Mrs. Green."

I remember as though it was just yesterday,
That wonderful place where I went to stay.

Nevertheless, despite all the many millions of tears that were shed during the war, many of us still have amusing memories of thc ycars just after the war. One, as is often the case, is about food and - by those still around to do so - is talked about to this day.

Our parents would often eulogise about a wonderful fruit called bananas. They said we would love them. We didn't!

To our parents' delight and, on tasting them, our mutual and mute disgust, these odd, yellow things reappeared shortly after the end of the war. But, after their repeated assertions of how much we would like them, we dare not tell them how much we disliked them. A dislike that led to numbers of 'dead' bananas being hidden all over the house and garden.

Mine, foolishly, was 'hidden' on a mantelpiece as, not being able to see above the lower rim, I thought no one else could! To this day I cannot remember when our 'disgust' for this fruit died, but die it did and we now enjoy them as much as we were promised by our parents that we would.

We were all also plagued with the dreaded 'gas mask box' and would try to 'lose' these highly irritating appendages in secret hidey holes where they would be found and returned with strict admonishments about the need to carry them, but never the reason why.

Too young to be told about the perceived ghastliness of possible gas attacks, (which never happened), we couldn't understand why we had to constantly carry them around and were ecstatic when there was no longer any need to do so. Also, conscious of the dire warnings of death if we did so, having never taken them out of their boxes, we had no idea what we might look like if we had worn them.

As didn't JERI's A.R.P. Warden -

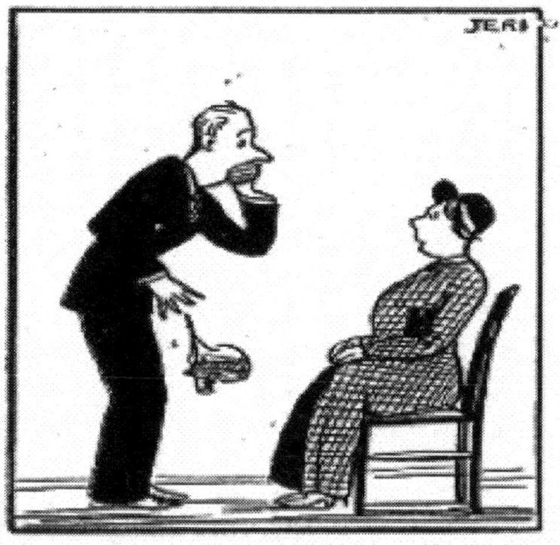

The woman at the A.R.P. rehearsal who said she hadn't one on when told she was wearing her gas mask wrongly.

The Second World War, as did the First, changed most people's attitudes to many things that had, previously, been thought of as being 'set in stone'. One was the new freedom given to women who, during both wars, were required to work in areas that prior to these conflicts, would have been unthinkable.

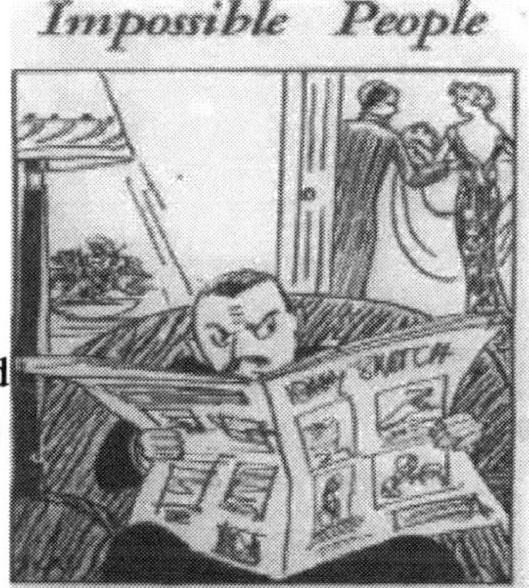

The man who said he did not know whether to worry more about how his son would turn out or what time his daughter would turn in.

A freedom that also allowed them to make their own decisions about what they did, where they went, with whom - and for how long they stayed out -

We children also thought the 'Victory' that was so much talked about would bring an end the constant and boring news announcements that the adults listened to so avidly.

Thus our joy at learning that there was to be NO MORE WAR was as much to do with the fact that there would be NO MORE NEWS.

However it did not take us long to accept the continuation of these horrid bulletins when we realised there would be no more blitz's, blackouts, bombs or gas mask boxes.

To which was added the even happier prospect of being able to enjoy 'proper parties with proper party food'. Delights that had so often been talked about by our parents and so memorably invoked by Sheila Webb's poem.

Towards the end of our own 'End of The War' riotous street party, Stefan and Boris, wearing borrowed Italian Army caps and silhouetted by the dying bonfire, were happily 'Heiling Hitler' while singing the popular war time song:

Hitler has got only one ball,
Goering has two, but they're small,
Himmler's are somewhat similar,
But Goebbels has got no balls at all.

Our neighbours berated Mama for allowing her sons to do this, but at eleven and ten they were just boys doing whatever it is boys do which, at that age, is usually something silly.

I will never forget our mother's response to these irate women as, to this day I can 'feel' their ire deflating when, with hands aloft, she said; *"You should all just be thankful that they can now safely stand out here and do that, and you can all now safely stand out here and complain about it!"*

The words of a wise mother take us, more safely, to -

THINGS THAT ARE NEAT TO KNOW

Despite my best endeavours to avoid them, paradoxes continue to creep into my text willy-nilly.

My Concise Oxford Dictionary gives the differences between a conundrum, a paradox and a tautology as;

Conundrum: Confusing or difficult question - riddle.

Paradox: Seemingly absurd or self-contradictory statement or proposition that may in fact be true, that leads to a logically unacceptable conclusion.

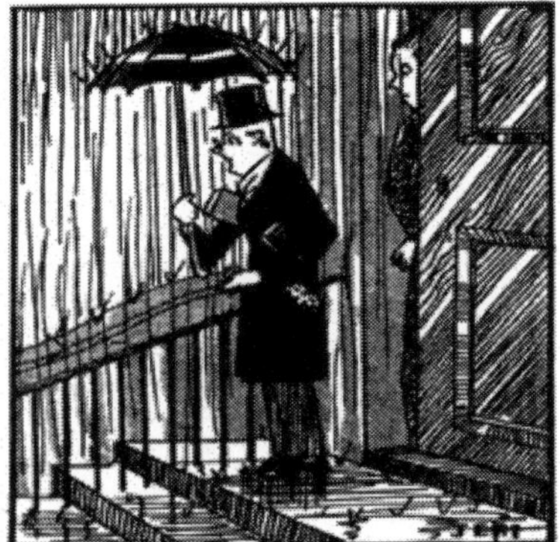

The very precise man who said he was going out William-nilliam.

Tautology: Saying the same thing twice with unnecessary, different words which may alter the meaning of the sentence. As in the now oft used tautology; "I aint got none."

These definitions are relatively easy to understand. But the big the question is: What is the difference between an analogy, a metaphor and a simile? (The definitions are from my O.E.D. the comparisons are mine.)

Analogy: Comparison between one thing and another made for the purpose of explanation or clarification. e.g. Solid as a rock.

Metaphor: A figure of speech in which a phrase or word is applied to something to which it is not literally applicable. e.g. A stick of rock.

Simile: A figure of speech involving the comparison of one thing with another thing of a different kind. e.g. 'Rock Around the Clock'.

Which begs the question - are a conundrum, a paradox and the 'Catch 22' that Yosarian was up against in one of the finest and funniest books ever written, also all the same?

From Joseph Heller's 'Catch 22'

There was only one catch and that was Catch 22, which specified that a concern for one's own safety in the face of dangers that were real and immediate was the process of a rational mind.

Orr was crazy and could be grounded. All he had to do was ask. As soon as he did he would no longer be crazy and would have to fly more missions. Orr would be crazy to fly more missions and sane if he didn't; but if he was sane he had to fly them.

If he flew them then he was crazy and didn't have to; but if he didn't want to he was sane and had to. Yosarian was moved very deeply by the absolute simplicity of this clause of Catch 22. "That's some catch, that Catch 22," he said. "It's the best there is."

Doc Daneeka agreed. From the original and most famous Catch 22 to another, somewhat less famous. In need of a new dishwasher I planned to buy one when I had finished writing this book. But with so much washing up to do, I would never finish it, so would never have a new dishwasher. Which led me to conclude that not having a new dishwasher however much writing I did, or never finishing the book however much washing up I didn't do, meant that neither a conundrum, paradox, nor a Catch 22, will ever lead to any conclusion whatsoever.

But, paradoxically, this one did, as Simon, on reading these 'musings', popped out on the quiet and bought one. BUT - did he buy it in the hope that the washing up would get done, or in the hope the I would finish the book? A paradox to which we would never have known the answer were you, my reader, not now reading 'Impossible People'.

Used as an example of a Catch 22, my 'Dishwasher' anecdote gives me an excuse to include another snippet of coincidental information, as it is an appliance that was invented by a Josephine Cochrane who lived in Illinois. I have not been able to verify if she was a Dundonald Cochrane, but her inventiveness suggests she was.

Factual things that are neat to know -

The Sketch, as do all newspapers, had a letters page, and in the tin in which my grandmother kept my mother's cartoons were also a few cuttings from their 'Letters from the Man in the Street' in which their readers wrote about those cartoons they found the most amusing - and why.

Among them was a letter from Mr. C.J.C. of Surrey that must have been published at the same time our mother was looking for a name for my, unexpected, twin.

This gentleman maintained that; *"The correct pronunciation of Sonia is with the accent on the first syllable. Which, I have been told, is a diminutive of the Greek word Sophronia which means 'of sound mind'."*

It was just as well that he never met Sonya - for whom, having read this, I wrote this:

My twin, whose name is Sonya Rosalia,
Has an 'eye for design' but for words, has no ear,
She will spell as she thinks,
So minks become minx,
Men are mail, see is a sea and hear is always here.

When Ray, asked her why she was always talking to herself, Sonya said; *"Because I'm the only person that listens to me."* A response that our mother would most definitely have woven into a caption, and nearly as good as the one she did weave into this next cartoon.

The next interesting letter was from D. Hood in which he, (or she?), wrote:

My dictionary's definition of the word 'eavesdropper' is: *'In Saxon times owners of private estates were not allowed to cultivate to the extremity of their possessions but were obliged to leave a space for eaves.*

This space was called an 'yfesdrype', thus an eavesdropper is one who places himself in the eavesdrip in order to overhear what is said in the adjacent house or field.'

So perhaps someone is listening to Sonya after all?

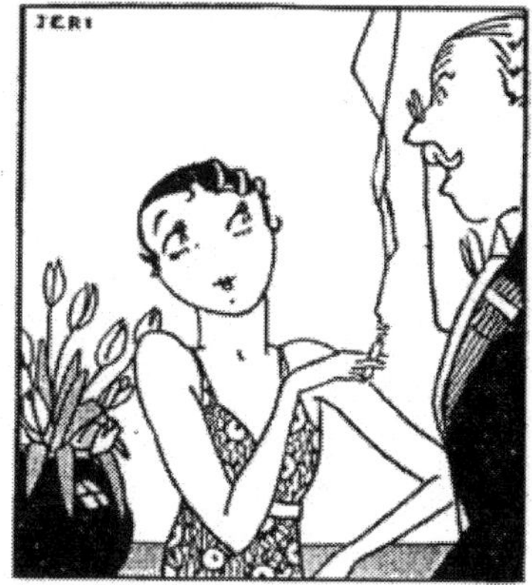

The girl who said she always kept her word because no one would take it.

Why our flag is called the Union Jack. Britain's Union Jack is a flag of such distinction that, as with the national flag of America, no one, regardless of nationality or language, does not recognise it immediately.

The big question is; Had Scotland won devolution in 2014, would they have wished us to remove their St Andrew contribution which, with its blue cross, donates our 'unity with the blue waters of the various seas and channels that surround us?

The pedantic English master who always referred to the "Union John."

When King James VI of Scotland became James I of England, he amalgamated the three saints of England, Ireland and Scotland (Wales was already incorporated), within one standard.

On completion of the necessary legislation on 12th April 1606 , the King made a proclamation ordering all British sailors to fly the new 'union' flag and signed it with the French version of his name, 'Jacques'. A spelling used by his mother, Mary Queen of Scots, who had, previously, been Queen of France. Hence the 'Union Jack'.

Which allows for another cartoon that has a caption my Mother 'plagiarised' from a caption she had, some years earlier, attributed to another Impossible Person.

There is a school of thought that the word 'Jack' may have been used because the flags were hoisted on the mast or 'jack' of a ship, but as the flags were also flown on land from flag poles not called 'jacks' the first version is almost certainly correct.

Or maybe not! George Courtauld tells us, in his delightful and instructive: The Pocket Book of Patriotism' -

Why Flags are hung at half-mast.

Flags flown at 'half mast' (or, as the Americans say; 'Half Staff') would symbolise that, despite being the 'victor', a leader of a conflict had died. Thus the upper, vacant space on a mast is an 'invisible flag' flying above that of the visable flag.

This 'non visable' flag represents the person being mourned. As would have been the case after the death of Nelson at the battle of Trafalgar and is now, as a mark of respect, a courtesy that has been extended to all those of merit or fame - whether seamen or not and regardless of how they died.

This is because, prior to the amalgamation of the three National Saints after James ascended to the throne of England, in order to demonstrate the Union, all ships were obliged to fly both the English and Scottish flags. When the Union Jack became obligatory, tradition decreed that two flags on the same mast of a fighting ship meant a military engagement had taken place, with the victor's flag flying above that of the vanquished.

To make it even more clear (or perhaps not), these two lines are from the poem 'Useful And Interesting Facts' by Richard Digance,

To call our flag the Union Jack is a slip,
It's the Union Flag, unless flown on a ship.

And some general world-wide stuff that, until it was posted on the Internet was, possibly, not widely known.

- Intelligent people have more zinc and copper in their hair.
- It is impossible to lick your elbow (75% of people, when told this, try to do so).
- Numbers, when spelt, have no letter 'A' until the number one thousand is reached.
- Men can read smaller print than women can, but women have better hearing than men.
- Bullet-proof vests, fire escapes, windshield wipers, laser printers – and, say I, dishwashers - were all invented by women.
- More 'collect-calls' are made on Father's Day than any other day of the year.

Which leads to the conclusion that fewer Fathers Day cards are sent than any other. Which, in turn, leads us to -

Why we send Valentine cards -

While there are, possibly, not many people who know the origin of why we now 'love' to send Valentine cards, there are a few who most definitely do. They are the residents of the tiny village of Topcroft in Norfolk and anyone erudite enough to have read 'The Paston Papers'. A lengthy tome of letters and papers that is a valuable record of life in medieval England.

The wealthy Paston family lived in North Norfolk and the Brews family lived in Brews Park in Topcroft, in South Norfolk where, on a visit to the Brews, the young John Paston fell in love with their daughter, Marjorie Brew.

Extremely well-to-do, the Pastons considered that any young lady worthy of their son should have a dowry sufficiently large to merit their union, but, less well off and having set aside dowries of equal value for each of his four daughters, Marjorie's father could not raise hers to the level asked of by the Pastons.

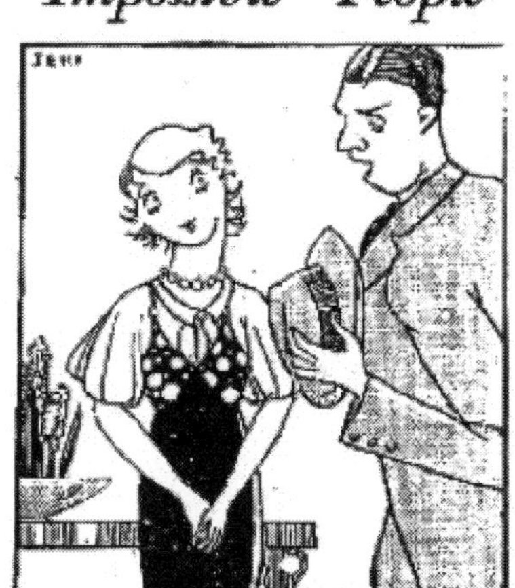

The girl who thought she had been proposed to when her boy friend said he would give her a ring in the morning.

Despite which these two young people stayed in contact and The Paston Papers include a letter from Marjorie, written on this important date in folklore, which includes a St Valentine's promise to John that her love for him remains steadfast.

She wrote her 'avowal of undying love' on this particular date because, at that time, country folk believed the 14th February was the last day for wildlife to find a mate. Although not a fairy story, it did end happily as, realising the depth of feeling her son had for Marjorie, John's mother travelled from her home in Yarmouth to Topcroft to meet the Brew family. At that time a hazardous journey.

Arriving during a period of heavy flooding she then had to stay with them for some weeks, a sojourn during which she came to like and admire the Brews to the extent that she agreed to provide Marjorie with a dowry that would allow for the marriage of the two young lovers. A marriage recorded in The Paston Papers as being 'Ideal'.

Situated ten miles south of Norwich, Topcroft has a village sign depicting Marjorie Brew writing her historical 'St Valentine's Letter' to John Paston. A letter that, in the ensuing years, has made millions of pounds for the makers of greeting cards which have cost their customers a similar amount in postage stamps.

The residents of Topcroft will not thank me for relating this story as they believe that, aside from their postman, few people know of this tiny, idyllic village and they wish to keep it that way.

I only know of it because my sister Nicola and her husband, George once owned Brews Park, (a house situated on land where the original Brews Park House once stood), where we spent many delightful days, a number of which were on February 14th. However, as the village is buried deep in the Norfolk countryside, has no shops or public house nor, apart from their sign, anything of interest to tourists, their idyll will remain undiscovered by the masses for the next millennium at least.

Or at least the many people who haven't read the Paston Papers, and the even greater number of people who won't read my book.

Greeting Cards are a natural lead to Playing Cards -

At a supper party with our friends, Muriel, who is French and speaks excellent English, and her husband Joe, (who being Scottish, speaks English nearly as well as his wife), he told us that a pack of cards is like a relationship with a man as you need -

A heart to love him with.
A diamond to marry him with.
A club to hit him with.
A spade to bury him with.

Created in the Middle Ages, these highly versatile, hugely entertaining, 'magical' cards depict four of the greatest rulers of history.

Hearts - Charlemagne. Wears white ermine that depicts his riches.
Diamonds - Julius Caesar. Has a Roman axe and his hand raised in the Roman salute.
Clubs - Alexander The Great. Holds a Globe, symbolic of the known world he conquered.
Spades - David. Has a sword taken from Goliath after hitting him with a stone from a sling.

Four famous men who take us, magically, to someone equally famous - And even more magical - Jane Austen

It has been said that the reason Miss Austen's novels never include conversations between men is because she believed that, as women are never present in exclusively male company, they cannot know what men talk about when there are no females present.

Therefore, she averred, it was not possible to write of something about which she could have no knowledge.

An interesting paradox as neat as any I have so far included, and while technology has now solved this particular conundrum, will women ever really know what men talk of in exclusively male company, or men know what women talk about when not in the company of men.

Thus the novels of Jane Austin, and the 13th century Paston Papers, tell us a great deal more about the time in which these works were written than any history book.

And to somewhere that is Magic – The Los Angeles Magic Castle

Situated on a hill far from traffic noise, this grand dwelling of a man fascinated by sleight of hand was, in 1968, gifted by him to The Magic Circle for use as a meeting house for magicians. It's magnificent front door leads into a reception area in which all the walls are covered by shelves full of books with no apparent access to the rest of the house.

After signing in at reception a section slides back silently to reveal a bar, behind which is a small salon housing a Baby Grand. This piano, with no pianist, magically plays the tunes of voiced requests or, in our case, complimentary to our accents, God Save The Queen. We later learned from our friend, Leonore, that the couple who devised this illusion were long standing friends of she and her husband, Russell.

At this piano bar Sonya and I were asked by a magician to select and sign a card from a pack he was holding. He then asked us to tear our signed cards into tiny pieces that he then put in his pocket and asked us to select another card at random from the same pack and, on withdrawing these, we found, wonder of wonders, that they were the cards we had signed - and still have.

The house also houses two small theatres where visitors can watch an assortment of many wondrous acts. While in several smaller rooms, magicians work similar trickery within inches of the eyes of their audience. Pleasures that culminate in a superb meal in their 'magical' restaurant.

Few people outside The Magic Circle know of its existence and Sonya and I have always felt very privileged that we were invited to be guests and, in the years since, have met magicians at functions in England who are always pleased to learn that we have been entertained at their magical Los Angeles Magic Castle.

And finally, something even I don't know -

The pages of 'Impossible People' include some zany words that, although often used when I was a child, are now rarely heard, such as 'flimflam', 'heebie-jeebies' and, best of all, 'kerfuffle'. We know what they mean but from where did they originate?

Another is 'gobbledegook', which in his splendid book, the New Fowlers Modern English Usage, R.W. Burchfield maintains was first recorded in America in 1944 to describe the: 'Foolish jargon of officialdom'. If only officials knew how foolish they sound when they use jargon – another wonderful, but now little used, word.

'The Real McCoy' by Georgia Hale, a gift from my stepson Oliver, gives the origins for such sayings and 'A Word in Your Shell Like' by Nigel Rees is another, similar, book that has 6,000 explanations for the weird ways words can be used or manipulated.

As in -

Conundrums, Mnemonics and Numbers - all useful for quizzes.

Last Things First

Solutions to problems are easy to find; the problem's a great contribution.
What is truly an art is to wring from your mind is a problem that fits a solution.

In yet another letter published in the Daily Mail, David Derbyshire wrote that when 30,000 people were asked what number between one and ten was their favourite, most said seven.

Due perhaps, say I, to the; seven seas; seven continents; seven days of the week; seven colours of the rainbow and the seven notes on a musical scale.

Shakespeare wrote of The Seven Ages of Man and Ian Flemming chose 007 for

James Bond. Snow White lived with seven dwarves, there were Seven Brides for Seven Brothers and Sinbad the Sailor had seven voyages.

Twelve is nearly as interesting with months of the year, hours to both day and night, inches to a foot, and, once upon a time, pennies to a shilling.

Then there is the number one; The year 2011 had four notable dates: 1/1/11, 11/1/11, 1/11/11 and 11/11/11, and if everyone adds their age in 2011 to the last two digits of the year they were born these will always total 111 - or, if under the age of 12 - 11.

Equally odd was the date 9/11/13, as with three odd numbers it is a once in 98 year occurrence. Even odder was October 2011 as, with five Saturdays, Sundays and Mondays was a once in 823 year occurrence.

Another magical number is; 111,111,111 which, when multiplied by 111,111,111 gives a total of - 12,345,678,987,654,321.

Then there are mnemonics – a word as difficult to pronounce as to spell.

Oceans: Indian, Arctic, Atlantic, Pacific *' I Am A Person'*
The Rainbow: Red, Orange, Yellow, Green, Blue, Indigo, Violet.
'Richard Of York Gave Battle in Vain.'
Planets: Mercury, Venus, Earth, Mars, Jupiter, Saturn, Uranus, Neptune, Pluto.
'My Very Easy Method, Just Set Up Nine Planets'
Royal Families: Norman, Plantagenet, Lancaster, Yorkist, Tudor, Stuart, Hanover, Windsor. *'No Plan Like Yours to Study History Wisely'*

And now for a final conundrum that sits within this slightly unusual paragraph. Can you find it quickly and work out what it is? It looks so plain you would, in fact, think that nothing is wrong with it. It is not normal though! Study it and think about it and you may still not find anything that is odd about it, but if you try hard and work at it a bit you may find what it is. Or may not!

For as Piet Hein says;

The Only Solution

We shall have to evolve
problem solvers galore -
since each problem they solve
creates ten problems more.

All of which lead with ease to -

EDUCATION - with a little bit of Employment

A Latin proverb tells us: *'By learning you will teach. By teaching you will learn.'* BB King said; *"The beautiful thing about learning is that nobody can take it away from you."* (Perhaps people didn't suffer from Alzheimer or Dementia in Mr. King's day?).

Education, employment and wealth don't always go hand in hand but to my great pleasure and not a little of his own, in my son's case they did. When Michael won a boarding scholarship to the prestigious Palmer's School for Boys in Grays, Essex, my pleasure at his scholastic achievement was more to do with the fact that having had such peripatetic life as a child and thus an equally fractured education, I wanted his schooling to be consistent and, as I had become addicted to moving house, a boarding school meant that at least his education would be more grounded than my own.

An indication of the high academic levels demanded of its pupils by Palmer's can be seen in many of the items in their end of term magazines. Happily, their curriculum includes not just the prosaic but also the improbable, as highlighted by this clever ode by C. Purdy, that was published in their 1971 Summer edition.

I used to wish I was a fish,
Swimming through the reeds.
No sums to do, nor spelling too;
Or history to read.

But then I found -
While swimming round,
These silly little fools,
Don't just play, or laze all day.
They spend their time in schools.

Impossible People

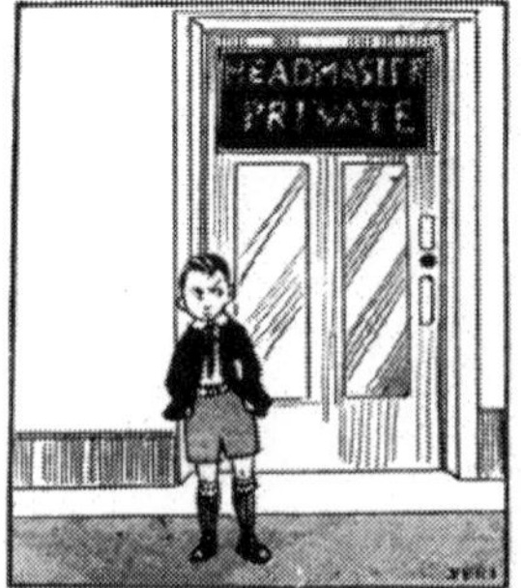

The boy who said "Closed" when asked how he liked school.

Unusually for that time, I was a full time working mother and, as my work involved a great deal of overseas travel, I was not always able to visit Michael at his school as often as I should, or would, have wished. Absences that led him to believe I had little interest in his schooling.

Schooling, that, without my overseas work, would have been unaffordable and that, eventually, enabled him to afford to educate both of his daughters at Private school. However I was very interested in his career and believed his determination to join the Stock Exchange rather than try for university would 'Lock him into The City'.

Having worked within this mad maelstrom of humanity for many years, I thought he would dislike it as much as I had. But his desire overcame my doubt and he joined as a 'Blue Button', which led to a supremely successful career within the complicated ramifications of the business of 'Stocks and Shares'.

So, in later life, I was much gratified by his off the cuff remark; "Sending me to Palmer's was one of the best things you did for me, Mother." Nevertheless, despite my pride and pleasure in my son's first class education and subsequent, successful career, I have no accord with the universal reverence, nor the need, for qualifications, as most of the highly successful people known to me have become so with little schooling or, in a few cases, none.

All of whom maintain that they would not have achieved what they did had they had a formal education as, more profitably, they learnt by the 'seat of their pants.' A view that endorses the assertion of the poet and monk, Thomas Merton that; *'The least of learning is done in the classroom.'*

Confirmed by Piet Hein in his next Grook -

Who Is Learned?

One who, consuming midnight oil,
in studies diligent and slow,
teaches himself, with painful toil,
the things that other people know.

Despite not going to university, two of my dearest friends, Jenny and Hoodie, have been highly successful. Jenny via her brilliant business acumen and Hoodie via an equally brilliant marriage.

Both of which, as JERI's next cartoon indicates, have to be worked equally hard for because; 'A really clever man is one who can earn more than his wife can spend and a really clever woman is one who can find such a man.'

Impossible People

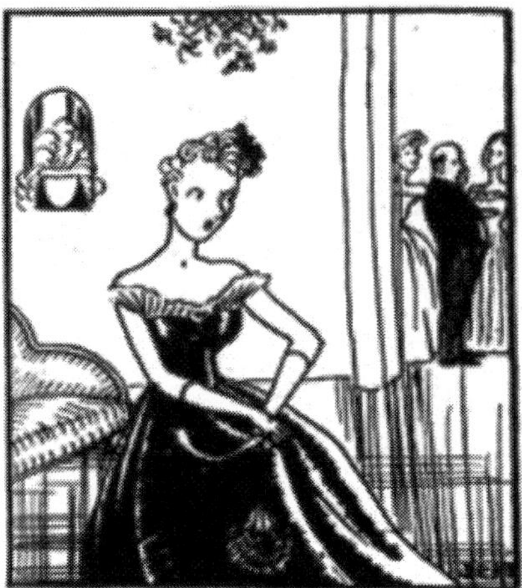

The girl who said one had to work too hard to try to get a rich husband and much harder if one didn't.

A quote that ties in nicely with this next joke, from my Encyclopaedia of Jewish Humour. It is so perfectly perfect for an Impossible People caption, I'm confident Mama, had she known of it, would have used it. 'The girl who said she couldn't marry Marvin, as she would prefer to marry a man who made things - like that nice Mr. Rochmis who makes a million a year.'

But while many believe that money equates to success and happiness, there are few truer sayings than; 'Money doesn't make you happy'.

Although some might say; "If you have money at least you can be miserable in comfort." Thus many highly educated and able people choose to do less well paid work as they love their work more than they love money.

Nevertheless, it is 'love of money' that makes those things for which we pay for directly, such as clothes and cars, of seemingly greater value than those for which we pay indirectly, such as education and healthcare, when, apart from happiness, there is nothing of greater value than knowledge and good health – both of which lead to happiness.

Prior to the Fisher and Balfour Acts, (the first enacted in 1902 and a second in 1918), a good education was much desired, valued and envied. Now, despite the ever increasing numbers of students chasing ever diminishing university qualifications, there are now many young people who neither value nor, in some cases, want it.

In part, no doubt, due to the burgeoning culture of; 'it's not cool to be clever.' and a desire for 'street cred', when even bright children don't always want to be seen by their peers as able. A desire, it would a seem, that is not a new one -

Impossible People

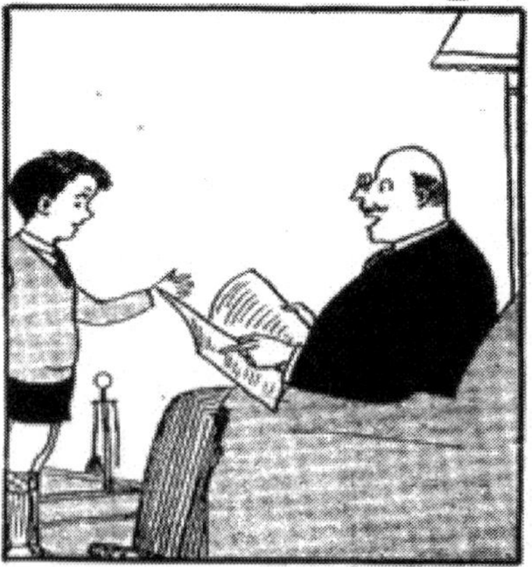

The boy who said it did not matter that he was at the bottom of his class as they taught the same both ends.

And one that is most certainly still with us -

EMPLOYMENT - with a little bit of education

There are now many people - whose numbers increase on a daily basis - who believe it is of greater 'value' to learn how to live off the state than to be self-sufficient.

A fact exposed in this marvelous poem by Martin Newell who, in a few well chosen, well crafted words, describes the 'lack of freedom' of the able unemployed when they choose to work in -

The Job Of Unemployment

It's heavy daytime telly
Or shuffle round the block
While clumsy seconds clatter
Through the hands upon the clock.

The days stubbed out like dog-ends
The minutes poured like tea,
In the job of unemployment.
For a job it seems to me.

And the workers who must do it,
Have their work cut out for sure,
In leaden skips of hours,
Trundled daily through the door.

For those with time to burn.
While days merge into lifetimes,
The seasons drift and turn,
And stokers man the furnaces

With a packet to collect.
Who never knew a Friday,
Or how the notes and coins,
Give a thrill of self respect,

When entering a pub, a shop,
To gesture at a shelf.
For items which you pay for,
In money earned yourself.

Now, some say work is slavery
and never makes you free.
Bur the job of unemployment
seems the hardest one to me.

Although it would seem that whoever composed the next ode, would prefer to work in 'The Job of Unemployment.'

Nothing to do but work,
Nothing, alas alack!
Nowhere to go but out,
Nowhere to come but back!

When discussing this phenomena with a teacher, she told me that it is now well documented within the education establishment that swathes of people, including whole families, from grandparents to teenagers, spend their 'working day' working out the most profitable way to exploit the benefits system.

Exploitation that may, one day, put an end to a system originally designed to help only those in real need.

When living in Tasburgh Hall we held many functions for many different causes at which Richard Bacon, who was then, and, as I write, still is the MP for South Norfolk, was a frequent guest.

In conversation with him at one of these, he said to me; *"You know Karina, if a country doesn't have sufficient private sector workers to sustain a welfare system that increasingly encourages people not to work, with its attendant need for ever more public sector workers, that country will eventually implode."*

Or, as Abraham Lincoln said many years earlier, *"You cannot make the weak strong by making the strong weak!"*

Or, as Margaret Thatcher more succinctly put it: *"The trouble with Socialism is that you eventually run out of other people's money."*

A view, that Dr. Adrian Rogers most strongly agreed with when, in 1931 while discussing the benefits, or otherwise, of a universal benefits system he used the following simple analogy:

An economics professor said he had never failed a single student but had once failed an entire class because, when discussing socialism, all of his pupils had insisted that it worked and that no one need be poor and no one should be rich, and all could be equal.

To which the professor said; *"O.K. We will have an experiment on socialism. All grades will be averaged and everyone will receive the same grade, so no one will fail and no one will receive an A."*

After the first test, the grades were averaged and everyone got a B. A result that upset those students who had studied hard but those who had not, were happy. At the second test, the students who had studied little, studied even less and those who had worked hard decided they also wanted a free ride so they too also studied less.

Thus, after the second test the average was universally lower at D, and, after the third test, had dropped to F. Now no one was happy.

The scores then continued to fall in direct proportion to the hard-feeling, bickering and blame among the students and, as no one was prepared to study to the benefit of anyone else, they all failed the final exam.

The professor then said to them that however much they believed in the 'high ideals of socialism', it was a theory that would also ultimately fail because when the reward is great, the effort to succeed is also great, but when government takes the need for success away no one will try, or even want, to succeed.

"Thus", Dr. Rogers, expounded; *"You cannot legislate the poor into freedom by legislating the wealthy out of freedom as what one person receives without working for, another person must work for without receiving, as the government cannot give to anybody anything that has not first been taken from somebody else.*

"So when half of the people get the idea that they do not have to work because the other half is going to take care of them, and the other half get the idea that it does no good to work because somebody else is going to get what they work for, that is the end of any nation - for you cannot multiply wealth by dividing it."

To which my brother, Stefan would add; *"Adversity promotes the desire to achieve which creates inspiration which can lead to success. But the desire to succeed, when not innate, is usually born of hunger for a better life and without that there is little to strive for."*

Stefan, as did Dr. Rogers, also maintained that 'living off others' is the surest way to bring about the collapse of a society as without ambition, aspiration and motivation, life becomes tawdry and meaningless. A truth emphatically confirmed in the articles of many excellent journalists and commentators such as Melanie Phillips and Max Hastings – and poets such as Martin Newell!

Shortly after winning a considerable sum of money on the lottery, Ron Ullah, of of Ipswich in Essex, started a cake making business. He said; *"The joy of having something to do that I really like and having to get up each morning to do it, far outweighs the pleasure of the Rolls Royce and yacht that wealth has brought me."*

Although many of us might feel that having a Roller to drive or a yacht to play on after a hard day's work would make the work more than worthwhile. Particularly as, unlike those with little money and thus little choice, the rich can choose to work in fields they enjoy.

"Being conscious that you do not know something is the first step to knowledge." is an axiom that George Bush would have been wise to heed when he said, *"The French don't have a word for entrepreneur."*

Impossible People

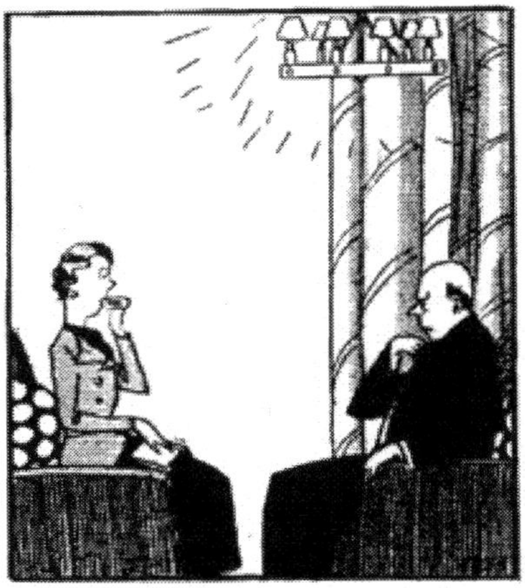

The business man who complained to his wife that his typist did not understand him.

Stefan, who had no formal education apart from one term at the famous Blue Coat School in London when he was five, became supremely successful with a business empire that encompassed many countries – including France.

As I include in an earlier section, his first employment as a negotiator with an Estate Agent 'taught' him that there was a great deal more money to be made from building houses than selling them because, due to the ravages of the war, many new homes needed to be built.

As one of the first builders to install tiles floors and fitted bathrooms and kitchens, he soon became one of the most successful entrepreneurs in our area, and despite his lack of education, won a number of architectural awards that led to him becoming Chairman of the London branch of the CBI. A post that eventually led to him becoming a member of one of Margaret Thatcher's Advisory Panels.

If, as is often presumed, success is based on monetary gain, much less successful was my second husband, Chris, who would often say – and perhaps still does; *"I never read a book I haven't read already."* Presumably on the premise, *"Don't let education get in the way of your learning."*

Having won a scholarship to the excellent Independent Brentwood School in Essex, at his 'End of First Year Assessment', Chris was told by the Headmaster that the selection criteria for those pupils chosen to continue their education at this, much sought after, Public School was based on three things; Their academic excellence; their athletic ability or to add local colour. *"You, Jessiman"*, said his Headmaster, *"Fall into the third category."*

Despite being adept only at 'local colour', Chris did gain a few qualifications, but, although charismatic, charming, witty, a genius with all things mechanical - and a superb raconteur (as was my father), he was (as was my father) incapable of 'holding down a job' -

Impossible People

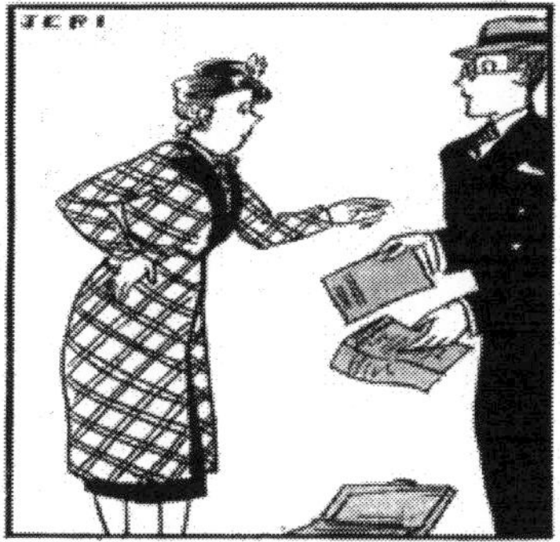

The woman who wanted to take out a fire insurance for her husband because he had been fired six times in the last four weeks.

or of maintaining a relationship -

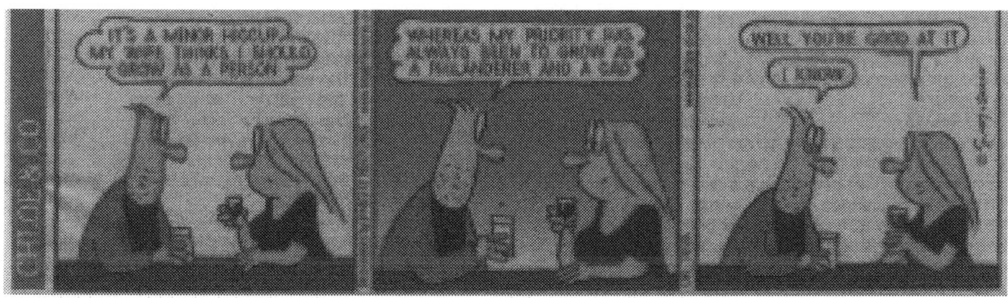

- or of a earning a living, - even when selling his qualifications. During one of my brother's expansive supper parties, on overhearing one of his guests ask another of his guests how, without an education, their host had reached such exalted heights, Stefan turned to Chris and said; *"These gentlemen believe it is not possible to succeed in business without scholastic qualifications. As you've got some you're not doing anything with, would you care to sell me a few?"*

Chris, who believed in *"Give and take good advice and sell everything else."* said Stefan could have them all for a tenner. To which Stefan replied, *"It's a shame money can't be bought as cheaply or so readily"*. Amid much laughter, it was agreed that qualifications are relatively inexpensive but wealth is costly business.

But now that wealth can be bought for just a few pounds on the National Lottery this no longer applies and is an indication of how muddled our values have become when a large win doesn't always change the winner's life for the better.

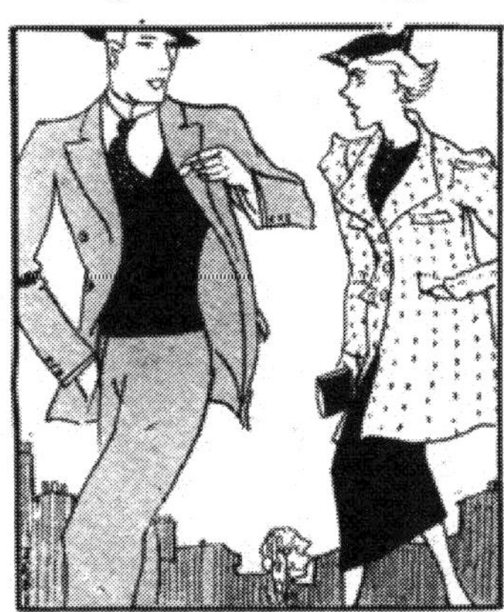

The young man who said the only way he could raise money was to change it from his trouser pocket to his breast pocket.

Whether through the sudden gain, or loss, of riches, having to subscribe to a new, unfamiliar way of life can, (as confirmed by the lottery winner Ron Ullah), be difficult – or even disastrous.

As was the 'Rakes Progress' of the young Norfolk man, Michael Carroll, who, hell bent on hell-raising, speedily squandered a lottery win of nearly ten million pounds on fast motor bikes, fast cars and vast parties. Expenditure that, even more speedily, returned him, after a short spell in prison, back to a life on benefits. Benefits he, no doubt, spends on lottery tickets.

Although at least his win was of benefit to his local Off Licence and car and motor bike dealerships.

But is losing (or squandering), a lottery win after having collected it as painful as not being able to collect a win despite having won it? Just days before the final date for claiming, Martyn Tott, who always used the same numbers, realised his ticket, had won several million pounds. But, search as he might, he could not find the ticket.

Camelot, despite having irrefutable proof of Mr. Tott's purchase of the correct ticket with the correct numbers for the correct day, would not agree to pay him without 'sight' of the ticket.

After many years of trying to find a way to persuade Camelot to agree to pay him his winnings, a road that nearly ruined his life, and lost him his wife, he eventually came to terms with his loss - and found a new wife.

In his book, published in 2009, 'Six Magic Numbers' he writes that in so doing he regained his self-respect because, he maintains; *'Life is not about wealth, but the riches to be found in a love of life and the love of a good wife.'* Which, many would say, is worth more than millions. He also writes that he no longer mourns the loss of his win, nor the loss of his ex-wife.

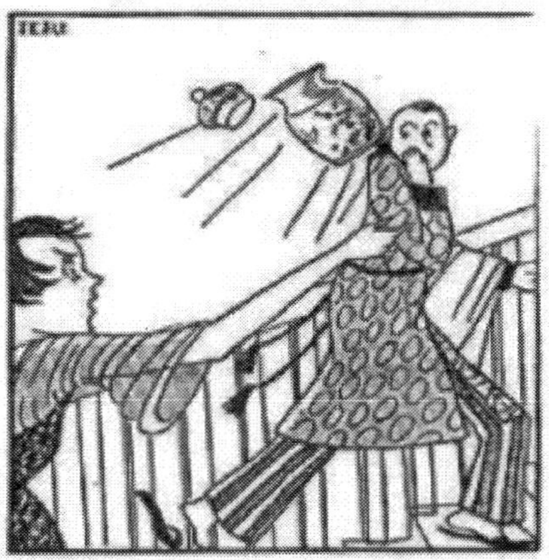

The wife who said she never missed her husband.

And presumably his ex-wife doesn't miss him!

There are probably many people, who, following a very large lottery win, find life a lot easier in terms of paying the bills, but a lot more difficult in terms of how they will spendwhat they don't need for paying the bills. As the euphoria of knowing you are really, really REALLY rich is soon overtaken by the realisation that you have to adjust to a completely new life and lifestyle.

As most people live within certain parameters, to be catapulted out of these with sudden vast wealth can bring with it as many worries as penury with one exception – not having to worry about penury!

Many years ago, on a flight from New York to London, I sat next to the Chairman of Holiday Inns. A gentleman who, considering the business he was in, was as likely to have had his First Class ticket paid for by BOAC for the same reason they had 'gifted' mine to me.

This extremely wealthy man told me that even he had no idea how the really rich live as they all have private planes, homes and holiday homes in the same costly areas, and rarely socialised with people not on their own level of income.

Nevertheless, however the rich enjoy or save their wealth, a lottery win is still more difficult to come by than wealth that is striven for. For as that master of the one-liner, Linda Smith, said, *"I don't do the lottery, which means I'm only marginally less likely to win than someone who does."*

But proof, if proof is needed, that wealth can be obtained merely by application, perseverance and guile is the next item that was sent to me by my son-in-law, MichaelPeter.

From an item in the Bristol Evening Post of June 2009:

Outside Bristol Zoo is a car park, with spaces for 150 cars and 8 coaches.
The charges are £1.00 per car and £5.00 per coach.
It has been manned six days a week for 23 years by the same helpful and polite car park attendant with a ticket machine.
On Monday 1 June 2009, he did not turn up for work.
Bristol Zoo management phoned Bristol City Council and asked them to send a replacement parking attendant.
The Council said; *"That car park is your responsibility."*
The Zoo said; *"The attendant was employed by the City Council - wasn't he?"*
The Council said; *"What attendant?"*
Missing from his home is a man who, for 23 years, had been collecting daily car parking fees of approximately £400 per day!

One hundred and twenty five thousand pounds a year for twenty three years, NO TAXED! *"Genius or what?"* says MichaelPeter.

When we were young there was no lottery, or Welfare State as we know it today. Nor any safes with money in them (revolving or otherwise). Or none that we knew of.

Nor were there any opportunities to nick car parking fees as there were few cars and even fewer car parks as those who owned the few that did exist, whether public or private, had not realised the great wealth that could be made from them until, as I write about on page 208, Donald Gosling started his hugely profitable National Car Parking Company by utilising as car parks, the many vacant areas that had once housed homes, offices and shops.

Impossible People

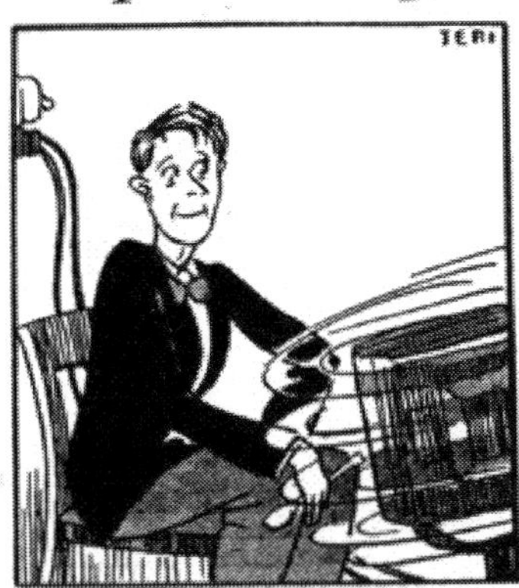

The inventor who made a revolving safe to make his money go round.

Entrepreneurial Activities lead to -

SURVIVAL

Perhaps Mr. Gosling's inspired method of making money was due to having seen JERI's next Impossible Girl?

Impossible People

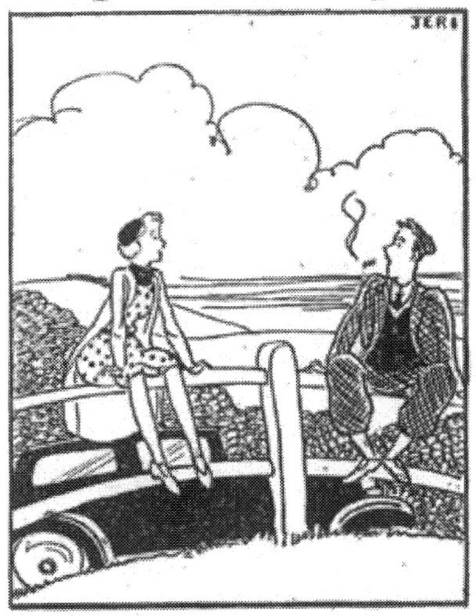

The girl who said surely they could find somewhere else to put cars when told that beauty spots were being turned into national parks.

Its caption is not only clever, amusing and apt, it is possibly more relevant today than when my mother composed it.

It also fits neatly with our father's assumption that; *"Finding parking places and black market petrol is easy peasy, it's penury that's the problem."* Penury that led to our costly private schooling coming to an abrupt end.

Although it was not lack of education but Hitler who was responsible for four of my siblings finding it difficult to learn to read. Born between 1934 and 1941 of a profligate father and working mother, we spent our early years being cared for by a succession of young Eastern European girls fleeing almost certain death by war or genocide - or both.

Known euphemistically as 'Nannies', they could hardly speak English let alone read it. So when, in 1942, our mother's contract with The Daily Sketch came to end she could no longer afford the cost of feeding these 'board and lodge' young ladies. Thus, with a lot of beds to be made and even more washing up to be done and no other help apart from our 'daily' Lizzie, my siblings would do my share of the chores as a reward for reading to them.

It is possible that it was not my sporadic education, but indolence caused by all this sitting and reading, that was the reason why I was not as successful as my elders predicted I would be.

Impossible People

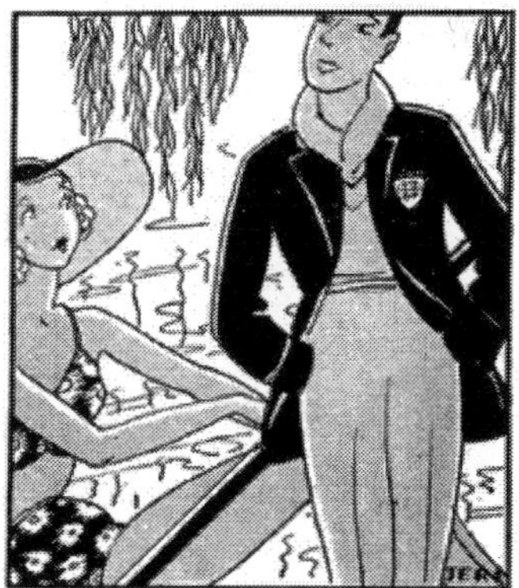

The undergraduate who said he did not get his degree, but he was almost at the top of those who failed.

What could not have been predicted was our extremely fragmented, intermittent schooling resulting from our parents' peripatetic life which, in turn, was a direct result of Hitler's activities - another good reason for being unable to 'Forget or Forgive'.

Thus any form of long-term schooling, private or otherwise, was a luxury denied us, and the number of schools we four sisters and our brother, Boris, eventually attended far outnumbered the months, or sometimes just weeks, we spent at each of them. While, again as I write earlier, Stefan had none apart from his one term at the Blue Coat School in London.

Paradoxically, although we all, eventually, climbed ladders of great height, (or in my case a reasonable one), those with the least education climbed the highest. Not hidebound by being taught how things should be done, they developed the valuable tools, acumen and, as did this next little girl, logic:

A little girl, sent to the greengrocer for some fruit, asked for a pound of apples. On being told by the Greengrocer that as we are now in the common market, we have to say kilos, she said; "O.K. Can I have a pound of kilos please!"

We now have numbers of educators who believe our present obsession with 'Higher Education For All' is self-defeating. They maintain that until it is recognised that those with creative or dexterous agility require a very different educational route from those blessed with academic abilities, we will continue to let down many young people who would otherwise accomplish much in their lives.

What I say, but with forlorn hope, is; *"All grist to their Mill."*

It is also a sentiment born out by a conversation I once had when lunching in the House of Commons with the late Conservative Member of Parliament, and Father of The House, Sir Bernard Braine.

As are many people, he was fascinated by the 'Twin Thing', and on telling him that while Sonya is brilliant at design, my gifts tended towards the more prosaic, he said; *"We are born different in our brains, Karina, not in our pockets. We are not all the same and our differences have different needs. But until we have a government that is brave enough to debate this we will never have parity in education, nor in our lives."*

Proof of which is the ultimate success achieved by my hairdresser, Sarah, and my twin, both of whom, being severely dyslexic, were frequently accused, loudly and unkindly, by their teachers – who obviously had less - with having; "No brain".

Teachers not worthy of the title as they refused to recognise the potential of pupils who found it difficult to read or write, yet who went on to be highly successful in their chosen fields. Fields in which their eventual earnings were far in excess of those of their teachers.

Nevertheless, in the early years of the 21st century the reality of this problem finally filtered through to our legislators who, despite much media hype to the contrary, accepted that dyslexia is real and needs real measures to assist those children afflicted with it. Such as one-to-one teaching by teachers 'schooled' in how to differentiate between those pupils who wish to read and write but can't, as opposed to those who can but won't.

Sadly, as have many similar costly Government projects, it was doomed to fail due to the bizarre idea that teachers should merely be facilitators while their students learn merely by osmosis. A view that many consider insane, one of whom is Peter Hitchens who wrote; *"Ever since Harold Wilson's huge expansion of teacher training in the sixties, the liberal faddists have been gaining control of classrooms in the belief that self-esteem and self-discovery are of greater importance than hard knowledge."*

None of which, say I, will pay the rent as, regardless of how much 'self esteem' a person has, they are unlikely to 'discover' anything unless they are an Einstein a David Attenborough or a Stephen Hawking.

It is now suggested that children should be in charge of what they choose to learn - or don't. Whoever came up with this idea had obviously never read the Latin proverb; 'By learning you will teach. By teaching you will learn.' Which, in just ten words, covers the essence of education and learning. Or would if I had not come across this revelation from Professor Steven Gorad that the high level of education previously required of prospective teachers is gradually being eroded.

He writes: *'Nowadays only one percent of teachers fail to qualify at the end of their training. A warning of even greater catastrophe, for if the teachers themselves are not allowed to fail, their pupils will not be allowed to fail either. Which will, inexorably, lead to the day when nobody fails and there will no longer be any assurance that any real, hard knowledge is taught at all, or that standards are being maintained. The consequence of which would be that all students of whatever level, will gain equal qualifications.'*

Which returns us to hairdressing. Apparently a student studying this subject will, on graduating, be given a qualification equivalent to ten GCSE's. But as Health and Safety legislation now prohibits the use of scissors in schools, how good at styling hair can these students get? The even bigger question is; Why are these young 'trainee' hairdressers not out in the workplace being taught by professionals how to use scissors while earning money and paying taxes – and thus having no student loan to repay?

A letter from Lauren Rogers of Leek In Staffordshire that was published in the 'Out of the Mouth of Babes' section of the Peterborough Column of the Daily Mail in February, 2011, confirmed that not all teachers are a 'fount of knowledge'.

She wrote; 'My five-year-old son James asked me what the date would be tomorrow. On telling him he said; *"Can you write it down for me Mummy?"* Having done so, I asked him why he needed it. His answer was priceless; *"I want to give it to my teacher because she never seems to know and always asks the class."*

But, as this next cartoon of JERI's confirms, teachers who forget things are not a new phenomena.

This amusing anecdote and cartoon aside, it comes as no surprise to learn that a third of all British children now leave school with little ability to read or write.

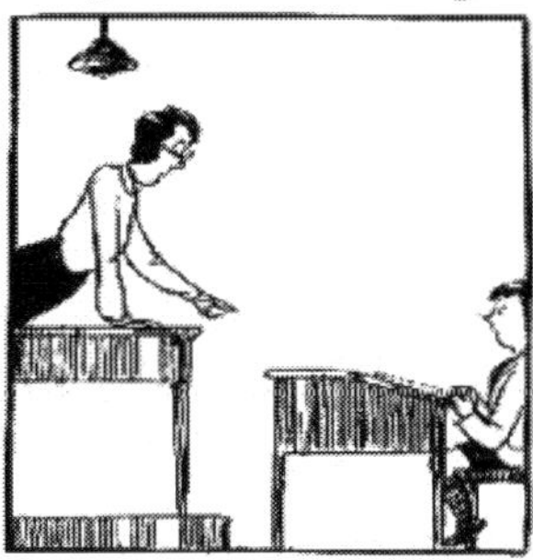

The boy who said surely she had not forgotten already when his teacher asked what it was she had told him in the last lesson about British imports.

Nor, it would seem, are able to do addition?

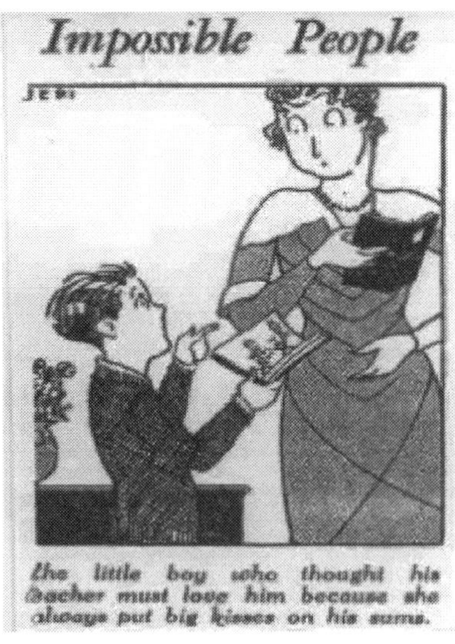

The little boy who thought his teacher must love him because she always put big kisses on his sums.

So, regardless of the grades todays children gain, paradoxically, unless they are all dyslexic, they have failed. So to Alexander Pope's maxim; *"A little learning is a dangerous thing."* could be added; *"Too little learning is even more dangerous."* As is JERI's next typist.

Impossible People

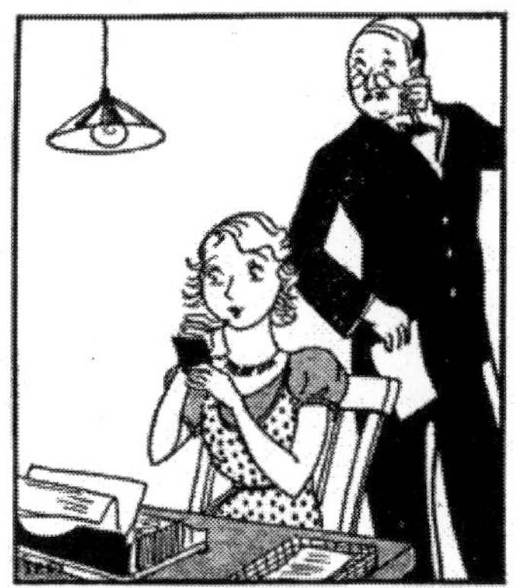

The man who said his typist was called "Little Learning," because she was a dangerous thing.

A retired army General, Derek Boorman, a relative of John, the film director (with whom, as mentioned in my section on The War, I was also once acquainted), told me a most interesting anomaly regarding education and success.

He said; *"Successful businessmen who have had no formal learning of their subject will, in their early careers, rely solely on their wits and instinct until they become chairmen of large corporations, when they have to adhere to the strict regulations that govern such organisations.*

"Conversely, highly educated army officers who have to adhere to strict military regimes, on becoming senior army personnel often have to rely on their wits and instincts when faced with life or death decisions."

Logical as this is, it still does not alter my view that when employing new staff - with the exception of professionals and, with my knuckles now soundly rapped, the armed forces, experience should, in many cases, be favoured over qualifications.

But as qualifications are now always favoured over experience, many young people, not able to live up to these, will not obtain or, more importantly, not be able to maintain positions where life skills are of greater importance and value than academic achievements.Which will inevitably lead to ever more antisocial behavior by frustrated youngsters.

A truly sad end to our envied heritage of British courtesy, pithily described by one of our greatest authors, the socialist, George Orwell when he wrote: *'The gentleness of English civilisation is its most marked characteristic.'*

Anthony Daniels wrote the following superb lines that abrogate the more moral among us from feeling guilty merely because we don't agree with the present-day leniency that is given to the behaviour of those young who drunkenly rampage in our town centres. *'An obligation to behave according to a certain standard would not be an obligation if it did not result sometimes in frustration and unhappiness. The fact that you would be happier if your abusive and noisy neighbours were dead does not release you from the obligation to refrain from killing them.'*

Which naturally applies also to education. The frustration of attempting to teach children who are ineducable does not release you from the obligation of attempting to do so. Nor of creating suitable employment for them despite their lack of qualifications.

Especially employment that requires little learning, but great public relation skills such as hairdressing – or massages and manicures –

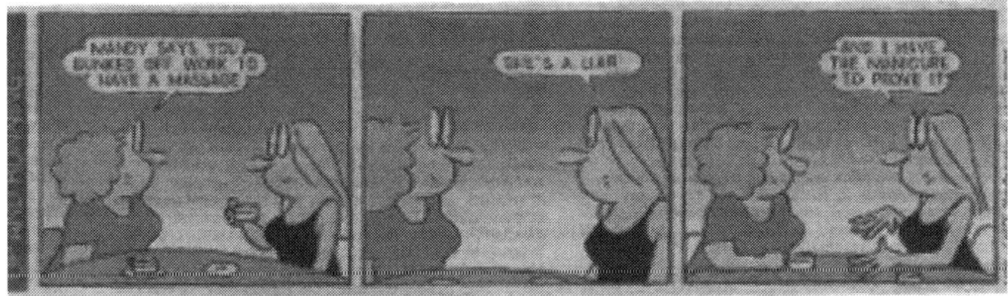

I include this Up & Running' cartoon of Grey's, not just because it fits neatly with the subject of 'employment' - but because it also, neatly compliments JERI's next Impossible People cartoon that sits so neatly with 'education' -

Impossible People

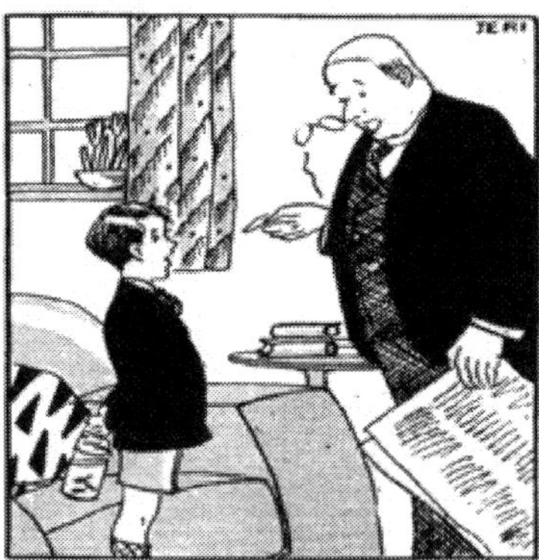

The boy who said he had a jar of minnows to prove he had not played football instead of going to school.

And both are yet further affirmation of my views and those of Maurice Silver on original thought. As would JERI's next two cartoons had they not been composed by the same person.

Impossible People

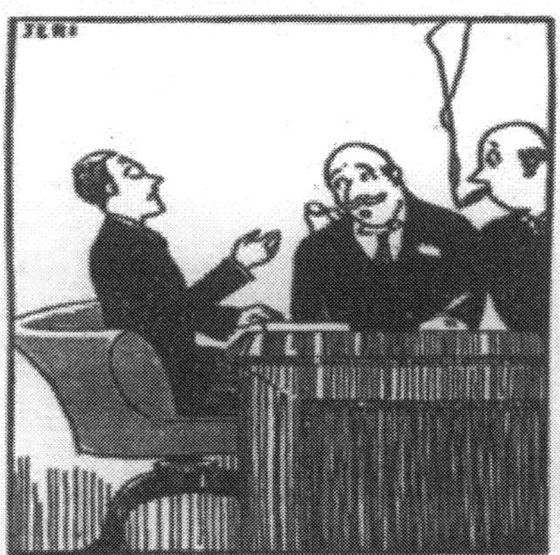

The young man who refused to become president of a company as then there would be no chance of advancement.

Impossible People

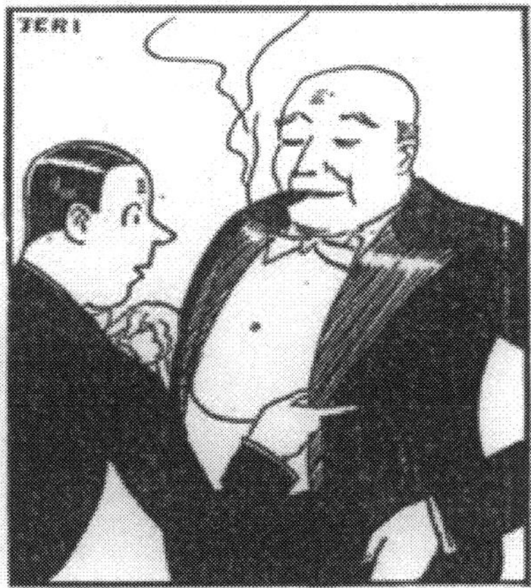

The man who said the only way to climb the ladder of success was to have your grandfather starting at the bottom.

Both of which lead to –

THE GREAT DIVIDE

There has always been a vast gap between the 'have's' and 'have-nots', an iniquity not likely to change for, as Ghandhi famously observed; *"There is enough in this world for everyone's need but not enough for everyone's greed."* And as Leo McKinstry wrote: *'Statistics concerning the riches of the global elite are staggering.'*

According to Rothkopf, the top one per cent of the world's most prosperous people own forty percent of the planet's global wealth. Furthermore, the combined net worth of the thousand richest people in the world is twice that of the poorest three billion.

This iniquity of the unfairness of the distribution of wealth is mainly due to the staggering fact that at least a third of the world's entire wealth, estimated at twenty five trillion pounds, is produced by just 250 companies.

Although would it create true justice, or equality, if the world's entire, estimated, wealth was shared equally among the worlds total population? Which in 1996, was estimated at five billion, a figure that, by 2004, had increased to seven and half billion. Which leads to the very scary prospect that if the worlds population continues to increase at a similar rate, there will, very soon, be 'no standing room' left on our planet.

But regardless of whether people can only stand, education will never improve and poverty will never be eradicated if those at whom expenditure is thrown have neither the will nor the ability to use it well. A view borne out by the broadcaster, Bob Edwards, when he said; *"They say a little learning is a dangerous thing, but a lot of ignorance is just as bad."*

Thus, despite the old saw: 'Those that can, do and those that can't teach.' as far as 'the art of learning' is concerned:
'Some can and do, some can't and don't, but there are many more who can but won't.'

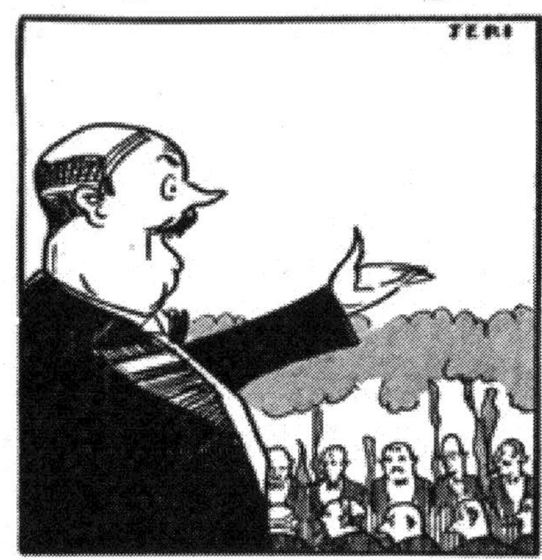

The after-dinner speaker who said opportunity is waiting round the corner of every long lane that has no turning.

Which leads to the paradox that:
those who don't learn to love learning will never learn how to learn and consequently - unless they win the lottery - will never learn how to earn their fair share of all these trillions. So perhaps ignorance, definitely, is bliss, especially if you can't find any long lanes with no turnings.

Which wends its way to –

THE WORKPLACE

Before computers enabled staff to spend their days composing witty, (if not wise), words, most of us spent our days working and, sometimes, being put upon - as in: *'We, the willing, led by the unknowing, are doing the impossible for the ungrateful. We have now done so much for so little for so long, we are qualified to do anything and everything for nothing.'*

An axiom that I nicked from the notice board of an old-style family store in Norwich that, until sold to a developer in 2010, was managed magnificently and energetically by Elizabeth and her brother, Richard, the grandchildren of William Norkett, who established his business in 1930.

Even as late as the late twentieth century, these family-run stores could be found on most street corners of most residential areas. However, with the 'Big Boys' moving in most of them have gone to the great retail graveyard in the sky. Thus the likes of Norkett's will not be seen again.

Except in this cartoon of JERI's.

Impossible People

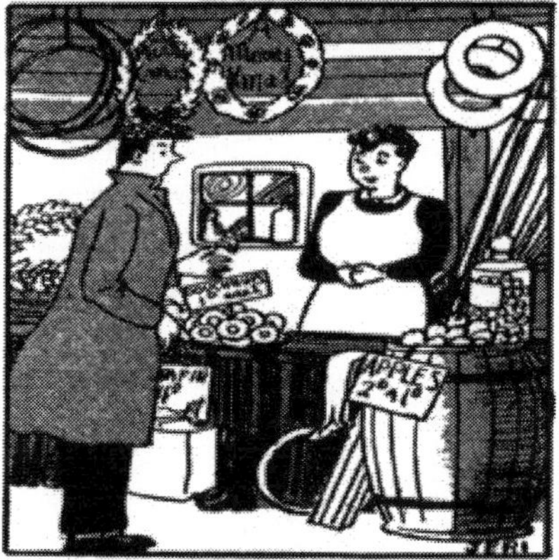

The village shopkeeper who said she had wreaths, lifebelts, children's hoops and doughnuts when asked if she had anything in the shape of a bicycle tyre.

Norkett's was a similar Aladdin's cave of electrical fittings and their allied needs, together with second-hand furniture, bric-a-brac, pictures and jewellery. All of which was presided over by their even tempered mother, Joan, and her bad tempered West Highland White.

You could buy a kettle or a clock, get an old lamp mended, copying done, or a key cut, all at half the price of Tesco's. (Who, in case you hadn't noticed, don't cut keys or mend old lamps - or allow West Highland Whites in their stores – whether bad tempered or not.)

Although we can be confident Tesco's don't turn their price tickets upside down.

Impossible People

The woman who said she was going to report her grocer for profiteering as he was always turning his sixpenny tickets upside down.

Which sends us to something seriously silly that my sister Sasha's seriously sensible sister-in-law, Doreen, sent me.

Anybody, Everybody, Somebody and Nobody.

There was an important job to be done and Everybody was asked if they would do it. Everybody was sure Somebody would do it as Anybody could have done it, but Nobody did as it was Everybody's job. So Everybody thought Anybody could do it and that Somebody would, but Nobody realised that Everybody wouldn't do it. So when Nobody did what Anybody could have done, Everybody blamed Somebody for not doing it.

Which fits well with the poet, Robert Frost's view that: *"The person responsible is the last person who could have done something about it."* Which fits equally well with these astute words from Indira Gahndhi; *'There are two kinds of people; Those who do the work and those who take the credit.'*

Two admonishments that should be displayed in the offices of all those involved in the new religion' of 'Health & Safety'. Put in place to protect employees and the public from harm, these strictures are often more harmful than the harm they profess to prevent or the health they profess to protect.

But are they a smoke-screen for those unwilling to work? For, in a similar vein to those of of Ghandi's; Mr. Frost said; *"The world is full of willing people; some willing to work, the rest willing to let them."* It is also full of people who are not willing to stop -

SMOKING - whether they work

Impossible People

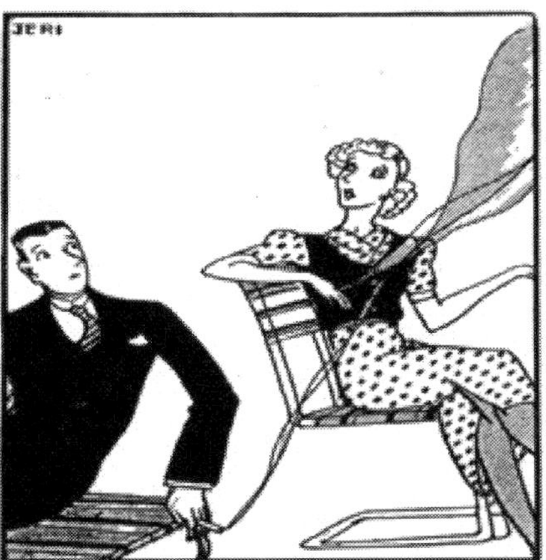

The girl who said she preferred cigarettes when asked if she was a chain smoker.

Or not -

Impossible People

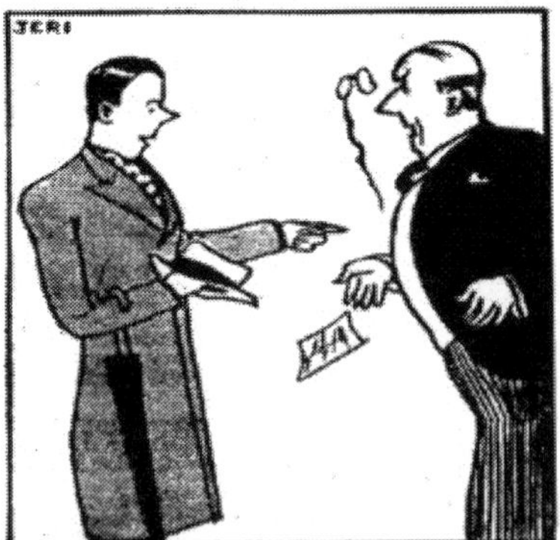

The applicant for a job who said there were several companies after him, including the gas, water and electricity.

Work and smoking while diverse subjects, are inextricably linked, as it is often the stress of work that creates the desire for nicotine. Which gives me an excuse to write about that taboo word 'cigarettes'.

Charles Schulz said, *"Work is the crab grass in the lawn of life."* So if, for many people, work is a necessary evil, it is equally certain that, for an equal number of people, smoking is an evil necessity.

When our mother was composing her cartoons the dangers associated with smoking, although known, were not publicised. There were also no tipped cigarettes. These were devised many years later by an industry that, despite knowing they were of little benefit in reducing the risk of cancer, hoped they would, at least, reduce 'the fear of cancer'. A fear that most smokers seemed untroubled by, especially, according to JERI, the young –

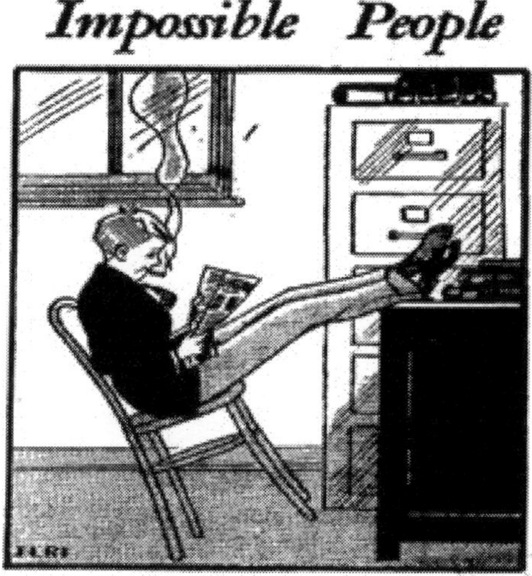

The office boy who was called "Theory" because he hardly ever worked.

Although both World Wars carried equal guilt, it was most certainly the first that was the catalyst for so many people to take up this dangerous habit, for with their dangers then unknown, cigarettes were of great assistance in calming the nerves of those who faced the known dangers of war.

Thus smoking became the panacea to a populace living with the fear of imminent death and the Government exhorted people to smoke their cigarettes down to the 'last puff'. A practice that ensured the early demise of many who had manfully managed to outlive 'Death by War'.

Even as late as 1956, when the British Government first knew of its dangers, our then Prime Minister, Harold Macmillan, worried about loss of tax revenue, argued against giving this information to the public. Now our Leaders have forbidden any publicity of the weed and, if they could, would extend this to all previous allusions to, or depictions of, cigarettes.

However, while they may alter the future with their machinations, they cannot change history. To 'pretend' people didn't smoke is as asinine as denying the Holocaust. Which takes us to Germany where, in the Nazi era, doctors identified the connection between smoking and lung cancer. A discovery that led to a costly anti-tobacco movement.

It also takes us to the scary thought that cigarettes may eventually kill as many as died in Hitler's efforts to rid the world of Jews, Gypsies and the mentally and physically afflicted. But at least 'death by weed' is self-inflicted and by choice.

Even as late as the seventies, depictions of people smoking, both in advertising and films, were thought of as stylish and romantic. And as JERI's previous and next two cartoons show, many of her Impossible People, of both sexes and nearly all ages, smoked.

Had the film 'Titanic' been made before our 'non-smoking revolution', everyone from the musicians to the main characters would have been depicted puffing their hearts out, much in the same way that, in 1912, her crew and not a few of her passengers would have done.

Paradoxically, our present publicity warning of its dangers seems to lead to ever more young people taking to it. Possibly because the young like to live dangerously and the only dangers left to those who can't afford to climb Everest or abseil down it, are alcohol, cigarettes, drugs and the occasional mugging.

The nineteen sixties 'no smoking inside' edict resulted in public areas becoming awash with cigarette stubs with people wading through them as they do leaves in Autumn. This unpleasant tsunami of dog ends is now much less - but is this because most of those who once smoked now work in munitions factories?

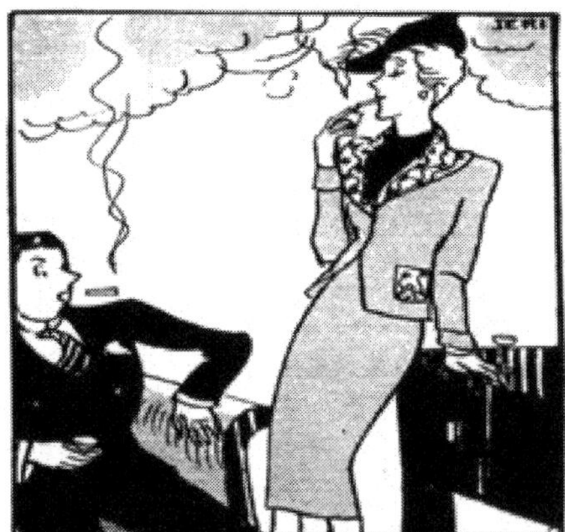

The girl who said she had taken a job in a munitions factory to make herself give up smoking.

Mama was a 'twenty a day' lady until the day prior to her death, when, no doubt, she was seriously miffed at the Grim Reaper for denying her daily quota.
Our youngest sister, Sasha, took to the weed but, on deciding the money saved by not smoking was of greater benefit, soon stopped.

Sadly Sonya's husband, Ray died of cancer caused by his many years of smoking. A costly, unpleasant addiction that, once started, can only be overcome after many tries and much trials.

Tries and trials not unknown to Mark Twain who said, *"Giving up smoking is the easiest thing in the world, I know because I've done it thousands of times."*

Boris's third wife, Kim, also tried to stop - if not a thousand times, certainly several. On finding it difficult to do so without gaining weight, I wrote this for her.

A lovely lady from Southend called Kim
Wants to lay off the weed and stay slim
She has given up butter
And with her heart all a flutter
Is wooing the divine Nosmo King

Having succeeded in her efforts to both stop smoking and stay slim, Kim earned a 'good performance' evaluation, dozens of which, arrive regularly in my inbox. One, tailor made for my son Michael was; *'My goal is to be a meteorologist, but since I possess no training in meteorology, I thought I'd try stock brokerage.'*

On starting his working life as a Blue Button on the London Stock Exchange, his stepfather, Chris, composed this 'advice' for him;

If you keep your ear to the ground, your nose to the grindstone, your chin up, your shoulder to the wheel and your best foot forward with a stiff upper lip and a heavy hand, with any luck you may be sent home on medical grounds.

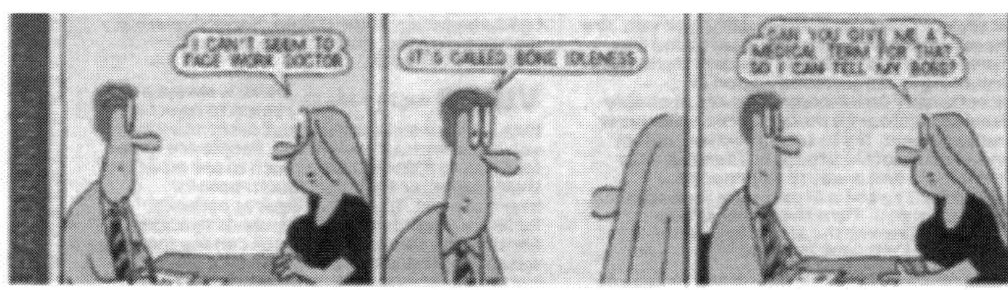

As confirmed by JERI's next Impossible farmer who highlights another strange paradox, as the London Stock Exchange exchanges 'shares' not 'stock.'

Some four decades after this advice to my son, it would now seem that many people are taking it far more seriously than intended. Extraordinarily, even those who are employed to find employment for those wishing to become employed!

Impossible People

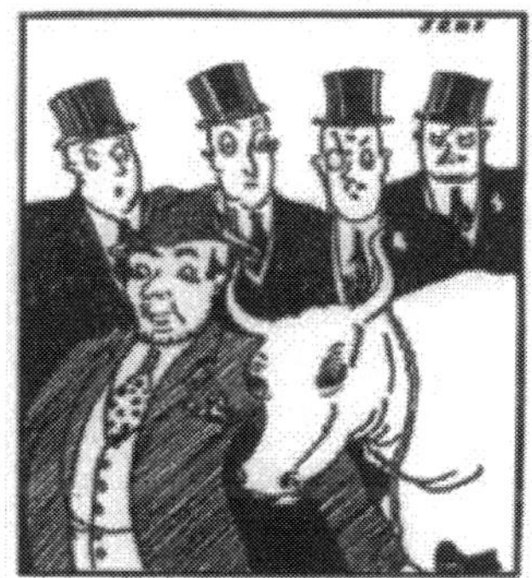

The farmer who tried to sell his cow at the Stock Exchange.

A supposition substantiated by a media item about a genuine job applicant who, despite a slight, temporary foot injury, was eager to find work only to find the staff at his local Job Centre were even more eager for him to apply for incapacity benefit.

So, once again borrowing Richard Littlejohn's catch phrase; 'I only ask the question', my question is: Are Job Centre staff told to do this because people on benefits are more likely to vote for a Party whose largesse in this direction is likely to be more liberal? (Which gives me another, rather more obscure, pun).

It also suggests that the policies of our more recent governments have been designed to increase not just burgeoning numbers of benefits dependents, but also Quangos. Quangos, such as Health & Safety, that, in an attempt to justify their existence,manfully manufacture numerous overweening directives with which to afflict employers who can't breathe from trying to adhere to all those they are already drowning in.

Much as my reader may find it difficult to breathe after reading that sentence. Although, as JERI's next caption confirms, officious diktats are ongoing irritations that have always been with us -

Impossible People

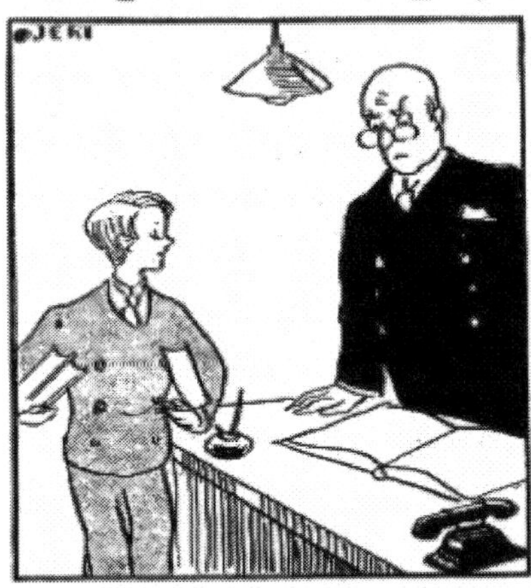

The office boy who said he did not take any notice of the new office efficiency system as someone had to get the work done.

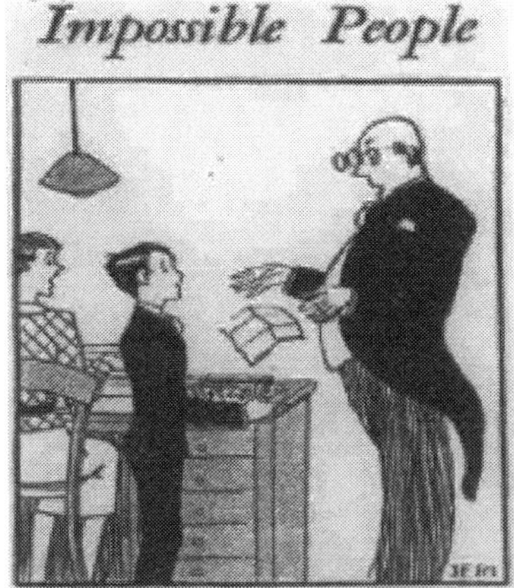

The boy who, when offered the post of office-boy with the chance of working his way up, said he would rather start as managing-director with the chance of becoming office-boy.

As was the 'office boy' – a once much needed, much valued member of staff that appears to no longer exist now that so many young people expect to go straight into 'upper management'.

Much as they apparently did when my mother created her next cartoon –

Which allows me to include this amusing list that, again, has been sent to me many times by many people who, no doubt, also received it on many occasions from many other people. Many of whom were, possibly, also those who also sent it to me?

(My reader should be in no doubt that the previous sentence was as 'uncomfortable' to compose as it is to read.)

Now, with so many employees spending their days circulating such trivia instead of doing any real work, it should come as no surprise to learn their 'evaluations' leave a little to be desired.

Evaluations of Employees:
- He brings a lot of joy whenever he leaves the room
- He would be out of his depth in a parking lot puddle.
- If you gave him a penny for his thoughts, you'd get change.
- This employee is depriving a village somewhere of an idiot.
- Some drink from the fountain of knowledge; he only gargles.
- This employee should go far, and the sooner he starts the better.
- A gross ignoramus - 144 times worse than an ordinary ignoramus.
- His men would follow him anywhere but only out of morbid curiosity.
- He sets low personal standards and then consistently fails to achieve them.
- Since my last report this employee has reached rock bottom and has started to dig.
- This employee is really not so much of a has-been, but more of a definite won't be.
- When she opens her mouth it seems this is only to change whichever foot is presently in it.

and

- This young lady has delusions of adequacy.

Which is tailor made for me – and those who hope to enter the enticing field of

ENTERTAINMENT AND CURRENT AFFAIRS

As I note in 'JERI's Real Impossible People', in her early years, many of her friends were of the famous kind, a number of whom (unlike the twinkly wallpaper that replaced her murals in the Regent's Street Cinema) had names that still twinkle today. Two of whom were Hermonie Gingold and Cecily Courtnedge.

Due to her very striking looks, our mother was persuaded by Cecily Courtnedge to try her hand at a walk-on part in a stage production of Romeo and Juliet. Mama told us that on the first night she became so enthralled with the play in progress that, having 'walked on', she forgot to walk off, thus putting an early end to any possibility of a colourful career in the theatre - or films, which at that time, were only black and white.

However, our mother was very popular with all her contemporaries, theatrical or otherwise, as booking office staff, on hearing her name and taking her to be a relative of the impresario, Sir Charles Cochrane – or as he was better known,

C. B. Cochran – would offer her free seats. So while she was not destined to become a thespian, in her teens and early twenties, she entertained - and was entertained - by many of them. Which, perhaps, gave her the inspiration for many of her cartoons.

In the seventies, Nicola and her son Stefan, lived with our Mother in a house that was within a short walk from the homes of Sonya, Sasha and myself. But, as Mama was getting to an age where she was beginning to need more care and we all wanted to be the one to give it to her, we decided she should move in with all of us.

Sadly, due to Ray's work commitments, he and Sonya could not be part of this venture, or, more correctly, 'adventure.' So Nicola, Sasha and I went in search of a house that would comfortably accommodate seven adults, four children and a few assorted cats and dogs.

Having decided on an area where property, although much less abundant than Essex was much less costly, we purchased Broome Place, a Victorian house in Norfolk.

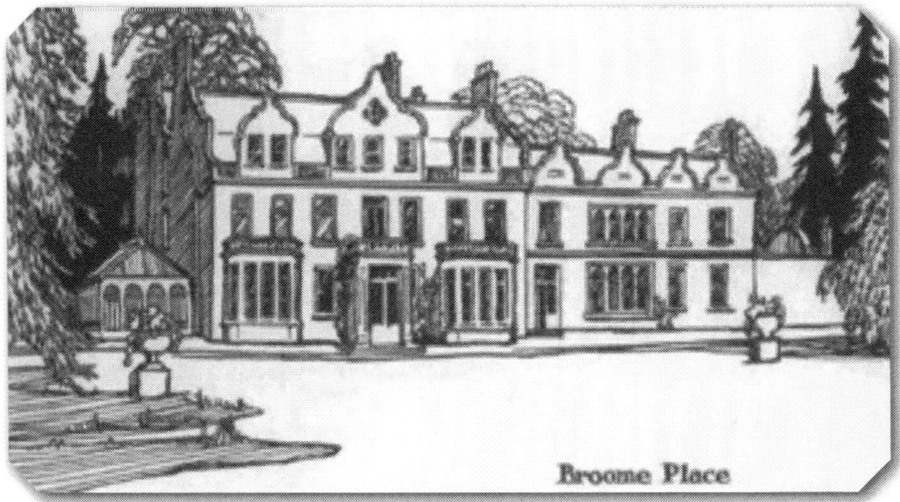

This drawing by our mother shows the present rear of the house, which had once been the front of a smaller property built in the period of Queen Anne. When, in the innovative Victorian era, it was redesigned and much enlarged, for ease of horse and carriage access, the front became the rear of the house and the rear became the front.

Had we not moved to Norfolk or bought Broome Place, my mother would not have done this attractive drawing or written the next poem, and I would no be able to relate the next anecdotes.

Broome Place - 1976

Thick as the dust that films the glass,
Grey as the tarnish that dulls the brass,
Deep as the moss that kills the grass,
Is the sound of silence that muffles the house.

Where women once danced and men carouse,
Now quiet weaves the spider, soft goes the mouse.
And no rustle of silk, no snap of a fan,
Gives a lingering sigh at the last pavane.

No whistle of grooms, no clank of a can,
Heralds the waking of sounds long ago.
So quiet and hush, let us go on tiptoe,
For silence is timid and may very well go.

Yes! Open the doors and let noise come in,
With mowers and washers let it begin,
With the revving of engines to add to the din.
Transistors shall blare, pop singers shall bawl,

And children go racing around the great hall,
With a clatter of feet, and a shout and a call.
Dogs shall bark louder, and cats they will purr.
While carpenters hammer and vacuums will wurr,

To add to the noise that is already there
Doors will be slammed and dishes will clatter,
Men will go shooting, and women will chatter
And none will notice, to none will it matter,

That silence so golden, in utter dismay,
With hands to both ears, has gone right away.
But time runs full circle as night follows day,
And all things that happen will happen again.
So do not crow, you great scatterbrain,
For silence is patient and will come back again.

The house stands in magnificent grounds, and has an equally magnificent staircase that was made, as are all of its doors, wall panels and library, from oak trees that had been felled in order for the house to be built and, later, enlarged.

One of its finest features is a thirty foot stained glass window over the front door which has, within its large roundel centrepiece, these splendid words:

My loyalty to my Sovereign,
My life to my country,
My heart to my family,
My honour to myself.

The window sits above a very large mezzanine landing between the ground and first floors. A landing that acted as the perfect 'stage' for the plays that Chris would write for our children to perform at Christmas and for us, with our friends and neighbours, to enjoy.

Aside from these mini-theatricals, and our grandmother's fairly short, unsung career as a light opera singer (which gives me yet another neat oxymoron), apart from Sonya's American granddaughter Chelsea, none of Mama's offspring or their children showed any desire to become involved in this 'art'.

Nor did any of her children's spouses, apart from my second husband, Chris. A man whose theatrical abilities far outweighed any other field to which he attempted to lay claim, and which I only mention in order to introduce a theatre where once he enjoyed huge acclaim as a thespian and where I enjoyed none as a wardrobe assistant.

During his period as an affiliate actor, Chris played many parts from the comedic to the tragic and was the regular Master of Ceremonies of the Christmas Vaudeville shows.

The Maddermarket Theatre, Norwich, Norfolk.

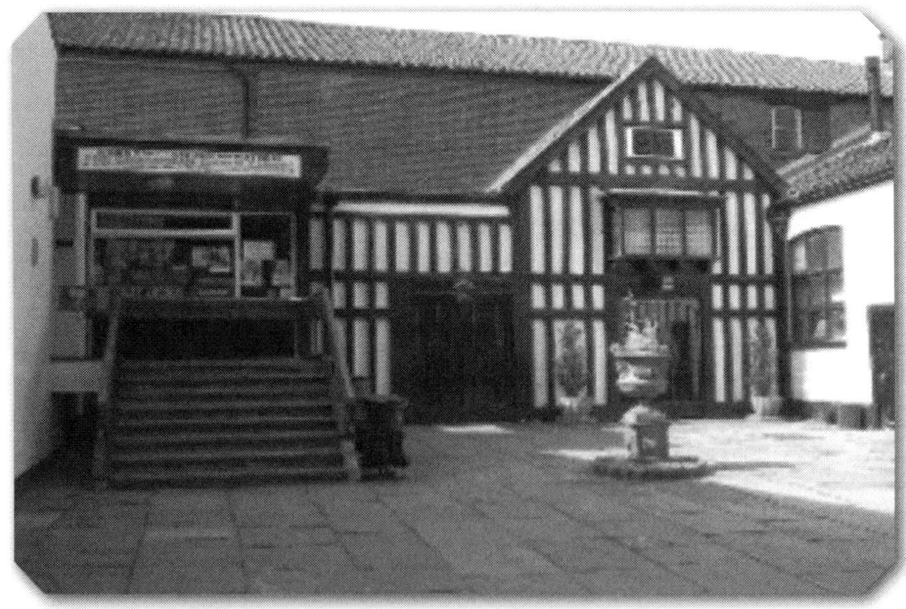

Opened in 1921, it was the first permanent re-creation of an Elizabethan theatre. Many years earlier the building had been a Catholic Chapel sited where, even more years earlier, madder dye had been marketed. Hence the name.

The theatre's founder, Nugent Monck, had worked with William Poel, an actor, dramatist and theatrical manager who was the first to restore Shakespeare's plays with their full text in the original Elizabethan style without elaborate scenery. Thus creating a similar atmosphere to that enjoyed by The Bard's first audiences.

An atmosphere that can still be felt by audiences of the Maddermarket Theatre productions, as access is via a paved pedestrian way that runs beside a church, beside which, hidden from view, sits the theatre. A theatre that is unique in that the only paid personnel are the Director, Producer, Set Director and Wardrobe Mistress, with all other functions carried out by 'Friends of the Theatre' volunteers.

In the mid-seventies, when I was assisting in the wardrobe department, the Wardrobe Mistress told me that George Bernard Shaw had once visited the Theatre to see a production of Pygmalion. Hearsay has it that on this, his first (and possibly last), visit to the theatre, he was displeased to learn, for what he said was one of the play's finer performances, that the audience were not permitted to applaud and the cast were not permitted to take a curtain call.

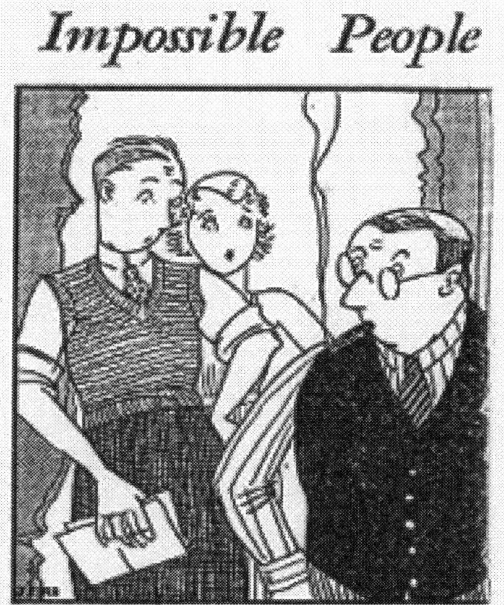

The theatrical manager who, when told that they were trying to revive Shakespeare, said he didn't know the man had been ill.

Whether this tradition still applies at The Maddermarket I do not know, but it was certainly so when I was involved with the theatre. Which makes one wonder how the most famous playwright in the world might have reacted at not having his work applauded.

Or the state of his health fully understood as, according to JERI's next cartoon, there are some people who think, (or, it would seem, did so in when my mother was creating her cartoons), that Shakespeare is still alive. Which, of course, to his trillions of fans, he still is - whether in good health - or not -

In, yet another, letter to the Daily Mail, Audrey Cooper of Walsall wrote that among some old papers of her grandfathers' she had found a 'play on words' that referred to all of the Bards plays.

On reading it I realised its compiler had omitted to include such worthies as Titus Andronicus, Pericles, A Midsummer-Night's Dream and Macbeth. So, with one or two amendments, of which I am confident both Audrey, her grandfather - and Shakespeare - would approve, my revision includes all 34 titles, with each of the King's as a single entity.

Timon of Athens overheard Julius Caesar telling Anthony and Cleopatra that, on the Twelfth Night after The Tempest he had A Midsummer-Night's Dream in which both Coriolanus and Cymbeline told him that Troilus and Cressida were the authors of Shakespeare's plays.

"Take it As You Like It," said Hamlet, Prince of Denmark, "but I don't believe it for I heard Othello, The Moor of Venice, discussing with Romeo and Juliet how they could find Love's Labours Lost after The Two Gentlemen of Verona tried to sell The Comedy of Errors to the Merchant of Venice for a cup of sack and a sack of gold."

Pericles, after drinking Measure for Measure with The Merry Wives of Windsor, became a party to this deal and suggested to Titus Andronicus that they run this past Macbeth, a competent critic, who dismissed it out of hand saying, "Bacon couldn't even write a Winter's Tale." So all the Kings apart from King Lear and King John, who were, at the time, occupied with The Taming Of The Shrew, discussed whether it could be true.

Then after the five kings, Henry IV, Henry V, Henry VI, Richard II and Richard III could not find any evidence to suggest otherwise, Henry VIII asked, " Why are we making so Much Ado About Nothing? If we leave well alone we will ensure that All's Well That Ends Well."

It was once suggested that to make them more interesting to students Shakespeare's plays should be 'dumbed down'. Shakespeare was a literary genius, but appreciation of such genius, as with champagne, is not generally gifted to the young. Thus they are unlikely to enjoy his work whether dumped down or not. Although, if not force-fed Shakespeare when young many, when older, as did I, would learn to admire his work and appreciate its wonders.

Much in the same way they may, one day, learn to love champagne.

Mercilessly teased at the two Grammar schools I attended in Devon and Somerset for my 'posh' accent, following our move to Essex, where my manner of speech received even greater scorn, in order that I would have my siblings to protect me, our Mother arranged for me to join my brother and three sisters at their Secondary Modern school in Shoeburyness. So, when we moved to Benfleet, my final school was a second, Secondary Modern - King John's in Thundersley - where I had the good fortune to be taught by an inspirational English teacher, Mr. Ellis.

Years of experience had taught him the futility of force feeding Shakespeare to disinterested pupils, thus he told us only those things about this playwright and his plays and sonnets that would ignite interest.

He said that English without Shakespeare would be like living on a diet of dry bread, and stirred our grey cells by asking us to search his works for the many quotations that are now used in everyday speech, such as 'a pound of flesh' and 'all's well that ends well'. Also the titles of novels and plays that have been taken from his works such as Blithe Spirit and Salad Days.

As a child I did not understand why Shakespeare was thought of as so consummately superior to any other writer, but with much assistance from Mr. Ellis, and even more from my Mother, I learnt to appreciate and admire his wit and understand the genius of his words.

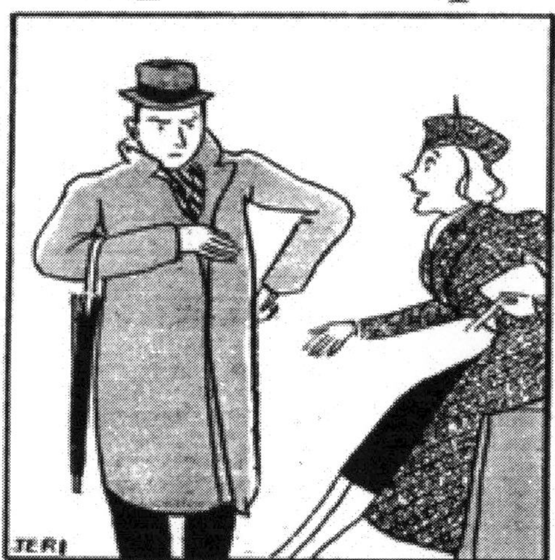

The girl who asked "Who won?" when told that the local dramatic society had just played "Hamlet."

At the start of my last term at King John's, the exceptionally bright and exceedingly pleasant son of immigrant parents joined our class, and the staff ran 'a book' on which of us would end the year with the highest marks. It would be easy, at this distance, to claim this was me, but with our very different skills, the 'contest' ended in a virtual draw. Although we never learnt to which teacher's benefit.

What is of benefit is Sir Bernard Braine's belief that; *'The immutable truth is that people are different.'* Thus many of those who have a passion for football may never learn to love The Bard, nor, perhaps, even champagne, as there are many millions of people all over the world who happily live lives that would be unthinkable to others and who will never know of Shakespeare or champagne, nor - much to the bewilderment of the many millions who are mad about it - football!

Proof of which, if proof is needed, is that in the first decade of this century a tribe of natives were discovered in the rain forests of Brazil who, it was suggested, having had no contact with the civilized world, should be left, as Mama would say - and maybe even Shakespeare; *"To dree their own weird."* A wonderful Scottish expression that means, despite the dire things that may befall us, we should be left to get on with our lives, in all their ramifications, in whichever way we choose.

Should later generations of these natives ever discover the 'real world', one wonders whether they will pursue, through the courts, damages for not being given the opportunity to find out earlier about iPads, Pop music and alcopops. The answer to which we will probably never know, especially if the whole tribe die of a dreadful disease such as the dreaded Ebola. Or from eating stuff that is bad for them, much in the same way many of us, who should know better, die of stuff we can't resist.

Impossible People

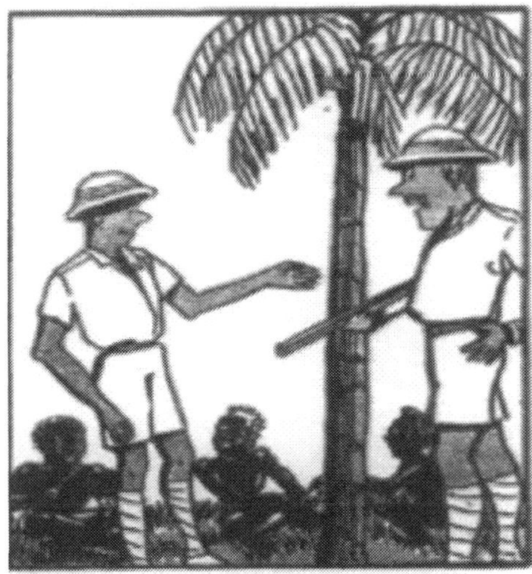

The missionary who said he had not quite got the natives to give up cannibalism, but he had persuaded them to use a knife and fork.

Which begs the question, are their lives better or worse for not being force fed Shakespeare, enticed to drink champagnc. nor taught how to play football. Or how to use cutlery?

Another of my mother's cartoons that the zealous among us would say should not, in these enlightened times, see the light of day. (Another neat oxymoron). To which, yet again, I would say; While geography can, and frequently does, change, history is fixed in stone and is composed of a myriad of both pleasing and unpleasant happenings and doings.

One of the most unpleasant being cannibalism. An activity not just carried out by early Africans, but also by those of other nations, who, on finding themselves in a situation where their only means of staying alive was to eat their brethren - ate them.

As did Dr. Roberto Canessa and his fellow survivors of an Alpine plane crash that I write of on page 181. Although we can be can be confident Piet Hein was not referring to the 'eating of people' when he wrote:

The First Principle of Gastronomy

There's a rule for proper doses in the dinner eater's lore,
One should stop the filling process while one still has room for more.
And if someone at the table had reminded me before -
Hallelujah! I'd be able to absorb a little more.

I once came across, and kemptly kept, this 'Out of the Mouths of Babes' anecdote that was published in the Peterborough Column of the Daily Mail in September, 2011.

Mrs. Jose Hampson of Heath Charnock in Lancashire wrote: "My thirteen year old granddaughter went, with her class, to see Romeo And Juliet. When asked if she had enjoyed it, she said; "Well, they wore modern clothes, but still spoke in Shakespeare."

But was it English Shakespeare or American Shakespeare? Chelsea, Sonya's grand-daughter, who is making headway in her efforts to make a 'name' in this elusive field, also makes and takes time 'to absorb' the works of The Bard. At thirteen she played Mrs. Ford in a production of The Merry Wives of Windsor. A performance that won her that years coveted first prize for drama. A leather-bound volume of 'The Complete Works of Shakespeare'.

When I asked her if it was strange to hear Shakespeare's words spoken with an American accent, she said, with the supreme logic of the young; *"I don't know, Grandma Karina, I've never heard them said in English."* Although having, in 2010, spent two weeks at the Royal Academy of Dramatic Art in London, Chelsea will, undoubtedly have discerned the difference. As did JERI's next Impossible Girl -

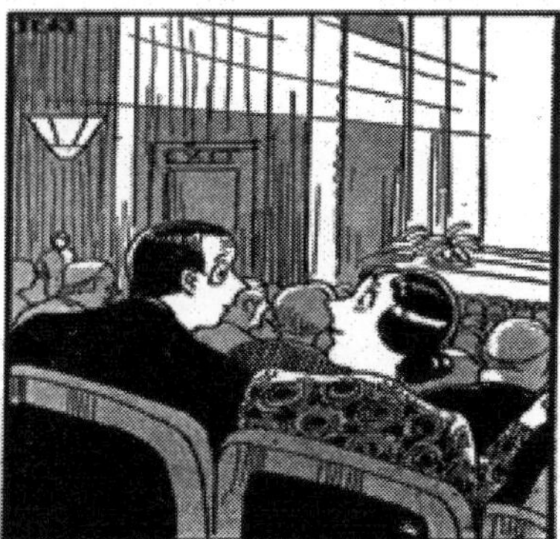

The girl at the pictures who said it was absurd for Cleopatra to speak with an American accent when she should have an English one.

Which takes us to some -

HOME GROWN ENTERTAINMENT

My own peripheral involvements in the business of show business were few and far between, two of which occurred many years earlier than my attempts at plying performers with their various changes of costume at the Maddermarket Theatre.

The first was during our sojourn in the windowless cellar in Weston-Super-Mare, where Sonya and I were chosen (due, yet again, to the twin and long blonde curly hair thing) as junior dancers for that year's annual, professional Christmas pantomime playing at the town's Pier Theatre.

We remember little of this - our first and last sortie into the field of stardom - apart from frequently losing part of our costumes, and forgetting, as did our mother, to leave the stage. Misdemeanors that carried a fine of sixpence each time they were committed, which left very little 'salt' from our two shillings and sixpence a week 'salary'.

On Sundays we were invited to 'take tea' with the leading lady, who, as so many did, had taken a shine to our alikeness and who asked us, as did so many others, many questions about what it was like to be a twin. As we believed we were not remotely similar to each other in thought, word or deed, not only could we not answer their questions, we couldn't understand their fascination with us.

That is until we joined the St Thomas' Twin Research programme when we found that questioning twins about their likeness was of great assistance to medical research. It is also much more interesting than just being looked at just for looking alike and sharing the same birthday.

Having to stay with the Pier Theatre show until its close also resulted in our having to stay in Weston after our siblings had, yet again, been shunted to the other side of the country. It also meant we were, yet again, forced to take several long train journeys with, yet again, little labels attached to our coats. (We had a lot of 'yet agains' when we were little – and even more in our later years.)

My next assault on show business occurred in the 1960's, when I met the 'Two Linda's. Linda number one, (the Linda who named her daughter, Leah, after me) was the sister of a young man called Ronnie who had opened a hairdressing salon near our home in South Benfleet, and Linda number two was Ronnie's first wife.

At that time a hairdresser on your doorstep was a rare luxury, so Sonya and I made much of them, so much so that very soon they became part of our circle of close friends.

Ever in thrall to long legs and a pretty face, Chris persuaded the two Linda's and their friend, Lisa, to form a song and dance group with, as their managers, mentors and comedic sidekicks, he and his friend Bob Stallard. The same Bob Stallard who later became the Manager of my London public house.

They were one of the earliest groups to perform at charitable events, day centres for the elderly and retirement homes. Called 'The Boardwalkers' these five intrepid, performers entertained many audiences whose appreciation was only matched by the significant sums of money they raised for several charities.

As a 'Thank You' for my unstinting, behind-the-scenes, management, at the end of their final show, they presented me with a beautiful gold broach on which had been etched on the back: From The Boardwalkers to Karina with our love. A piece of jewellery I still wear with pride.

Public houses are natural places of entertainment, and even more so if, as did ours, they have a function room. Ours not only served as an excellent wedding reception venue but also acted as a small theatre. (Yet another neat oxymoron.) One or our regulars, Tom Owen, needing a venue for a play he had written, asked if he may use our function room for its Premier. Pleased to agree, we were equally pleased to entertain his father, Bill Owen, of Compo fame in one of television's finest and funniest comedy series, 'The Last of The Summer Wine.' A man whose demeanor was distinctly different from that of his media persona.

We also held regular jazz evenings and asked our French friend, Rene, whether he and his band, 'The Jazzpots', would come to England and perform at our pub, and at several others that held jazz evening.

One of these was at the Bull at Barnes where our friends, Dan and Liz Flemming, (the Dan and Liz who had once been the licensees of the 'Old Caledonia' on the Thames), held regular, extremely popular, jazz evenings.

Most landlords who hosted jazz evenings were pleased to invite a 'new' jazz band to play for them as, with so few jazz bands, aficionados will follow them to all of the public houses at which they are booked to play. Confirmed by the fact that when we accompanied the Jazzpots to their many bookings, many of those in the audience were people we had seen at previous venues.

When we asked about this we were told that, as there are so few really good jazz bands, all true lovers of jazz, on learning there would be a 'new band in town', would wish to hear them play live as often as possible. However loud!

I am always mystified as to why those people who arrange private functions will put up with, and pay for, uncomfortably loud music. Our function room was above our bars, so I would tell our performing bands and groups that if the noise of the bass was louder than a level acceptable to myself and my bar customers, they would not be paid.

A policy that earned me many compliments from both my function room 'guests' and my regular customers. It also, occasionally, saved me a lot of money.

Having left both the pub and my husband, Chris, but not necessarily in that order, with great good fortune I then met and married Simon. A marriage not just made in Heaven but also in France. Where the Consular General of the Mayenne District, Roland Houdiar (father of one of my dearest friends, Valerie and her sisters, Caroline and Veronique), officiated at our wedding.

Roland, who some years earlier had also made a proposal of marriage to me, had, in the ensuing years, realised that my tactful refusal was a blessing much greater than had I agreed to marry him and was, therefore, delighted and, he said, flattered, to be asked to marry me to someone else.

A marriage that a few years later, allowed us to enjoy some of the best years of our lives when together with Sonya and Ray, Nicola and George and Sasha and John, we bought a large property in the tiny village of Tasburgh in Norfolk.

Tasburgh Hall, Tasburgh, Norfolk

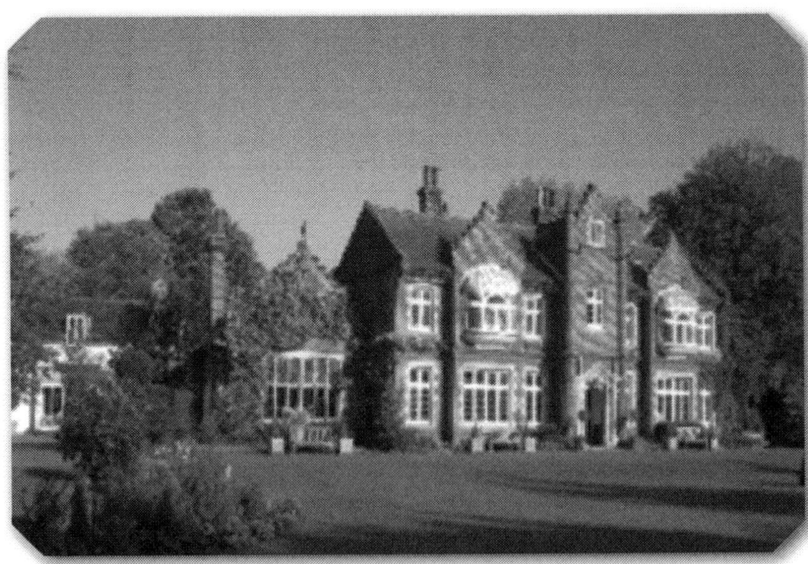

During our tenure of the Hall we were fortunate to have as a close neighbour, a gentleman who lived in one of the Hall's original 'Gate' cottages, and who was the vocalist of a popular jazz band.

Graham and his fellow cohorts kindly agreed to provide their services free of charge at the many, enjoyable and successful charitable events we held. Events that raised even more money when, on learning of them, Rene and his cohorts, offered a similar, free of charge service, from The Jazzpots.

Fortunately the Hall could comfortably accommodate all six musicians and their wives, which allowed us to arrange a number of further venues where they were rewarded for their performances by appreciative audiences. Which ensured their Norfolk popularity was similar to that which they had enjoyed in London so many years earlier.

One of the best being our Tasburgh Hall event that, with both English and French jazz bands, was particularly popular, with the result that we were able to present our charity with a particularly large cheque. By great good fortune, that also increased our charities revenue, the 'main attraction' at this event was Peggy Oliver who, as can be seen in the next photograph of her singing in front of the front door of Tasburgh Hall, is one of London's 'Pearly Queens.'

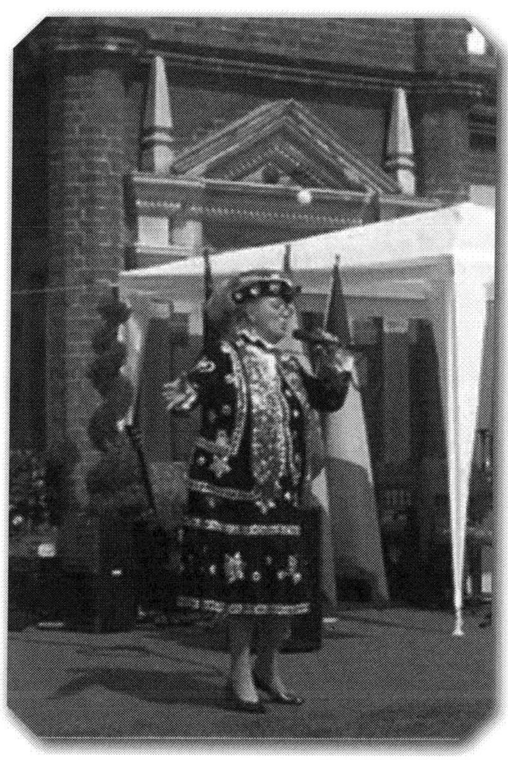

Sonya and I had met Peggy through our Norfolk friends, Jenny and Ken, (he of the new heart), and she was as delighted to be asked to perform at Tasburgh as we were to have the good fortune of being able to ask her.

A few weeks after first meeting Peggy, Sonya and I were parked outside Buckingham Palace waiting to pick up our brother, Stefan, who had been a guest at one of Her Majesty's garden parties, we saw her walking towards us in full regalia – not Her Majesty, Peggy.

During our consequent conversation we were amused and delighted to learn that when she visits the Palace for such events, as she is a 'Queen', she is addressed as Ma'am by Her Majesty's flunkies and footmen and, for the same reason, she gains entry to the Royal gardens via a special route reserved for such dignitaries. Which also allows for speedy egress.

A meeting that leads to real Royalty and four anecdotes about these unapproachable people who, when you do meet them are, in most cases, extremely kind and exceptionally courteous.

My first two 'Royals' were the Queen Mother and Princess Margaret, whom Sonya and I met during the Canvey Island Floods of 1973. A meeting I write about on page 321 in my anecdote on this a disaster. My third encounter was with Her Majesty, The Queen.

The International Confederation of Midwives has a close association not only with the Royal College of Midwives, but also The Central Midwives Board, which has, as their headquarters, the house that was once the home of W. S. Gilbert of Gilbert and Sullivan fame. (A coincidence I could include in my section on these odd happenings due to my Grandmother's association with this light opera company.)

The CMB use as their boardroom what was once the dining room that, carved into the wooden lintel above the large double doors, has the words; 'Abandon Hope All Ye Who Enter Here.' It is also the room where the joint meetings of the CMB, the RCM, and the ICM were held at the time I worked with the ICM - and, as far as I know still are.

As Patron of the CMB, Her Majesty would attend the preliminary sessions of these meetings. On one occasion I noticed that, as she was about to enter the room, she looked up at this inscription and, although I could be reasonably certain she was not unaware of this, it was difficult to forebear from telling Her Majesty that this scary abjuration did not apply to her.

I have wondered since how often she has been deprived of similar witticisms due to the golden rule of; 'Not speaking until spoken to'.

Many years after my meeting with Her Majesty, Sonya's son, Nicholas, more by accident than design, also met the Queen. When working as camera director with a film crew in Piccadilly Circus, he was wondering why it was even more crowded than usual when the Royal car arrived and glided to a stop at the side of the pavement just where he was standing.

As Her Majesty stepped down from the vehicle, to their great delight she spoke to a few of those who had gathered to see her, the first of whom was Nicholas. He was somewhat bemused at this unexpected show of royal 'cordiality' as, having arrived from Los Angeles just a day earlier, he had no idea for whom the gathered throngs were waiting to greet – or, in his case, were to be greeted by.

My own fourth interaction with a Royal, was an unexpected, accidental meeting with one of our more highly thought of and most sorely missed royals, Princess Diana.

With an anticipated visit to London by our cousin Vivien and her daughters, Julie and Jennifer, (whose three children were, years later, caught up in the huge media excitement at the birth of Prince George), I booked seats for a Torvill and Dean ice skating show.

When the tickets arrived with them was a letter asking us to be in our seats half an hour early as Princess Diana was attending that particular performance. When Jennifer and Julie learnt of this, they squealed with delight and asked if they would see her. I told them that Wembley being huge and the Princess being tiny, this would be highly unlikely. But I was wrong.

In the interval we were making our way to a cloakroom when we found our route cordoned off by ropes. We were about to turn away when we saw Princess Diana and her retinue approaching. The two girls became very excited and, being American, despite such close proximity to a Royal, had no inhibitions in showing this.

On seeing - and hearing them - the Princess graciously stopped to exchange a few words with us. A kindness my nieces remember with great pleasure to this day.

My fifth interaction with a Royal was an expected, but somewhat less pleasing meeting with Princess Anne. As Patron of The International League for the Protection of Horses, she had agreed to be the ‘star turn’ at a fund raising event that Simon, as their Publicity Agent, had arranged for the ILPH at the National Gallery.

She was not as warm as the other four Royals I have had the pleasure of engaging in conversation with. However, her terse dismissal of me when we were introduced was well made up for by the large sum that was raised for the ILPH merely due to her presence.

As do most people, I enjoy most forms of artistic talent in most of its variations but, despite my short involvement with the Maddermarket Theatre, unlike many, I have never had any desire to be a part of that world or to mix with those that are. Although, by both accident and design, I have met more than my fair share of public figures and celebrities.

As many of these meetings are of anecdotal interest, it occurred to me they would make an amusing book on their own, which I could call, 'Famous Faces'. Although not being one myself, I could be fairly confident that no one would buy it.

However as my very dear, friends, Alan, a journalist and Tina, a Nanny to children of the famous, have met more celebrities in their working life than most people would meet in ten, I may persuade them to write a book about the many 'Famous Faces' they have met.

Although as they could write only about their own encounters this persuaded me to include a few of mine in my 'Impossible People' - which, some might say, celebrities often are! So here are four of the more interesting anecdotes or, in the case of the first, amusing.

Arriving at the home of our sister-in-law, Barbara, who then lived just off Victoria Street in London, Sonya and I could get no response from our repeated ringing of her bell. Thinking she had forgotten we were coming and had gone out, we were about to leave when Michael Portillo joined us on the landing and asked if we were looking for 'Sobah'.

As, at that time, Barbara's car sported the number 50 BAH, we were highly amused by his 'gift' of this sine-qua-non that proved to be well earned when, during our chat with Mr. Portillo, Barbara emerged from her front door a little unsteady of voice, unsure on her feet and in no condition to drive.

Shortly after her divorce from Simon McQuorkadale I met Fiona Fullerton who, in need of something to cheer her up, bought a mink coat from a furrier friend of mine. She then gave me her old mink from which my furrier friend made me a smart mink gilet. A garment I still wear with pride, both for its heritage and the many compliments it earns.

Due to her name and fame, Fiona's 'Memoir', published in 2012, will reach sales much greater than any that my 'Famous Faces' might have done. Especially as, in 2013, she laid even greater claim to fame by appearing on the hugely popular programme, Strictly Come Dancing. A show that also featured another 'famous face' Vanessa Feltz.

Vanessa and I met in Norwich at the filming of a television show in which we were both to appear. With the recording finished, she engaged me in light hearted conversation in the hope of relieving me of the smart yellow jacket I was wearing. Our differences in height and width made this not possible so I told her where she could buy one.

Some years earlier, during a recording for a television programme about

'Sisters' for which I and my three sisters had been 'persuaded' to feature, we met the Beverley Sisters, who, when filming had finished, were also eager to engage us in conversation. Several months later I met them in the London shopping centre, Brent Cross, where, much to my surprise and not a little pleasure, they recognised me and asked me to pass on their best wishes to my sisters.

'Sisters' neatly take me back to family. A celebrity we knew well was Brian Taylor, the brother of Sonya's husband Ray. A jockey who not only rode for the Queen but who, in 1974, won the Derby on Snow Knight.

We spent many happy hours with Brian - a lot of them dancing, at which, as did Ray, he excelled. Had Brian not been tragically killed when his horse fell during a race in Hong Kong, he could well have been a contender as a 'Strictly Come Dancing' celebrity, but only with a dancer as diminutive as the delightful Flavia Cacace.

Then there is our own budding thespian, Sonya's granddaughter, Chelsea, whose talents, (as I write earlier), may one day make her a 'Famous Face'. Which she certainly was on one of her many visits to Norfolk. For some years Simon attended monthly meetings of a businessman's breakfast club at a hotel in Norwich. One of these meetings coincided with the anniversary of America's Day of Independence and club members were asked to prepare a two-minute presentation on this subject. As fortune would have it, it also coincided with one of Chelsea's visits.

On Simon's turn to speak, he apologised for not being able to make a presentation as it was based on an item he had arranged to have Fed-Exed from America that had not arrived. As he went to sit down, I drew back the curtains behind which Chelsea and I were concealed and, with the insouciance of a born star, she bounced into the room bedecked from top to toe in Stars and Stripes regalia, while joyously singing, with a strong American accent, The Star Spangled Banner.

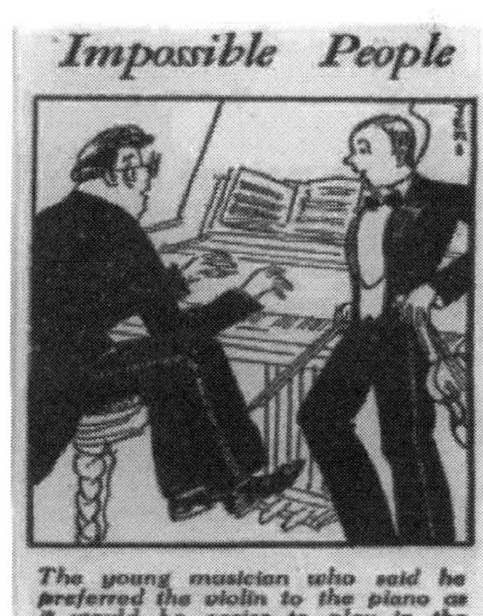
Impossible People

The young musician who said he preferred the violin to the piano as it would be easier to play in the street if he wasn't a success.

A splendid performance that won Simon that month's fiscal award that allowed us to enjoy a pleasing English lunch in an equally pleasing English restaurant. At the time of writing, my grandson, Michael, and great niece, Freya, were learning to play the piano but it will be some time before we know whether they will be virtuosos of this instrument - or will eventually 'prefer the violin'.

Which is a natural lead into the field of –

FAUX ENTERTAINMENT

Despite its difficulties, aiming for fame is now the overriding ambition of many of today's young. The desire to become noteworthy in some facet of this voracious industry is, in most cases, as fruitless as the fatuous belief that the rewards of being 'In The Public Eye' will eclipse any other career.

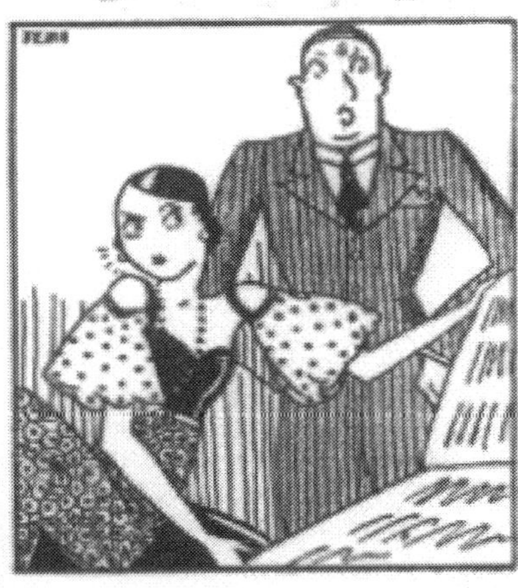

The actress who married secretly and was annoyed because no one heard about it.

Attempting to climb the ladder of fame is, in most cases, the most unrewarding thing the young can do, as the media's frivolous pandering to the public's desire for new, usually fleeting, fodder leads, for many of those who chase it, to little reward – and, according to JERI's next Impossible Person, much disappointment.

It is even worse for those with genuine talent, for if they do not havc a talc of misery to tell, they are thought of as 'being of no value' by those who offer this poisoned chalice.

A fate that may await Chelsea and, sadly, did await Lucy, the daughter of our close friends, Debbie and Roger. With an exquisite singing voice and a face and figure to match, Lucy auditioned twice for these talent shows, but her serene and perfect life with serene and perfect parents and three upstanding brothers made her of little interest to producers looking for 'talent tied to a tale of woe'.

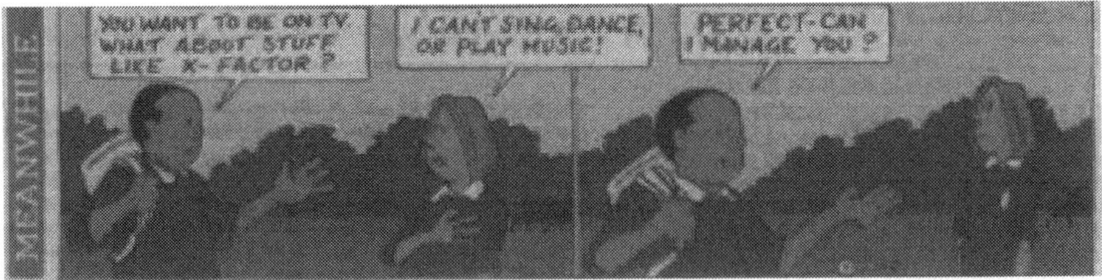

Not dissimilar to many of those who aspire to enter the field of -

PARLIAMENT, POLITICS, PREMIERS AND PRESIDENTS

God grant me the ability to change the things I can. To accept those I can't and the wisdom to know the difference. A fitting axiom for those who choose to climb the precarious precipice of politics by standing for a seat? (A neat alliteration and even neater oxymoron in one short sentence.

Impossible People

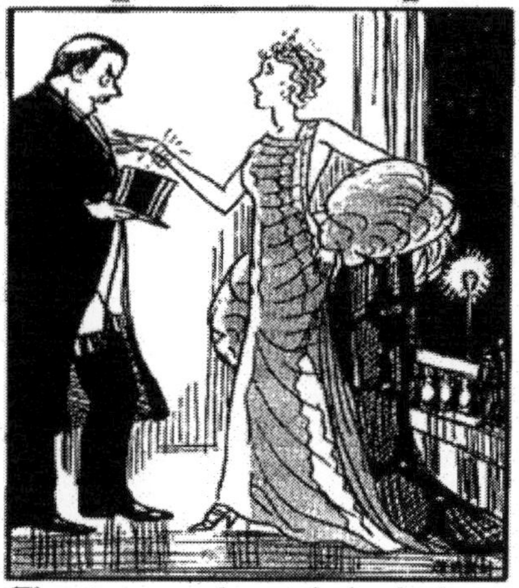

The woman who said she had not stood for any constituency because nowadays there were so few men who would give up their seats to a lady.

Not a lot of change there then!

Was this perhaps why, in 2013, Nadine Dorries, 'gave-up her seat' for a fling in Oz with I'm a Celebrity. Although aspiring for celebrity status may have been why she entered politics in the first place and, on finding it fruitless, took another route in order to achieve this.

A view that fits well with these two oft quoted maxims by my Mama; *"People vote for names without considering whether they have brains."* And; *"The problem with politicians is that they are so fixe` in their ideas."*

The latter being a view propounded by Charles Darwin in his renowned work The Theory of Evolution, in which he wrote these, oft-misquoted, words: *'It is not the strongest of the species who survive, nor the most intelligent, but those who are the most responsive to change.'*

Which sits well with George Bernard Shaw's opinion that; *"Progress is impossible without change, and those who cannot change their minds cannot change anything."* All of which are summed up a little more succinctly by the Labour politician, George Wigg, when he opined; *"If you don't accept change, you end up like the dinosaur – stuffed."*

Although Margaret Thatcher, ‘A lady not for turning,’ when asked during a meeting of new Tory MPs what she would have done differently could she have her time over again, said; “I think I did all right the first time around actually!” A view much the same as the gentleman(?) in this next Chloe cartoon.

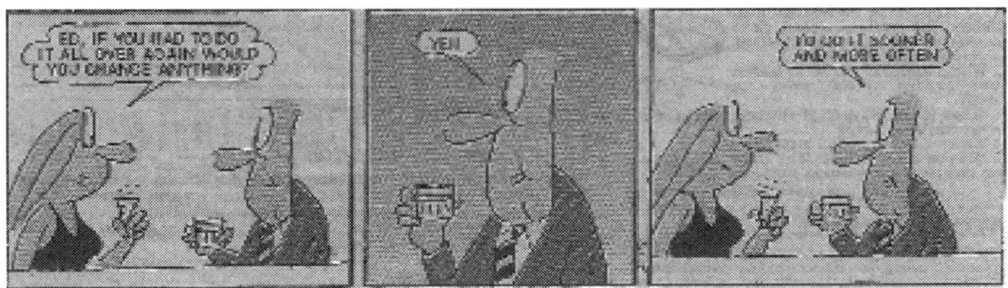

But regardless of ‘how much sooner or more often they would do it’, most people would agree with Lord Salisbury’s view that, *“Politics is the last refuge of a scoundrel.”*

One of whom, apparently, was this Impossible Man in JERI’s next cartoon.

Impossible People

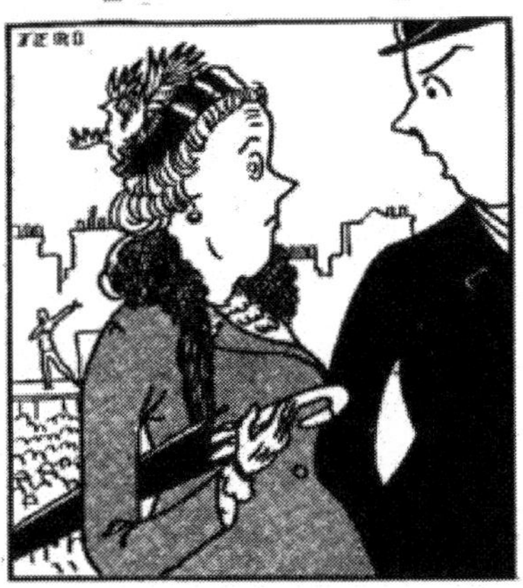

The woman who was surprised that a man with so many convictions should be allowed to stand for Parliament.

An observation that could now be directed at a few of our latter day parliamentarians whose ‘convictions‘ have forced them to ‘stand down’.

One being Michael Portillo, about whom Mandy Rice-Davies said, in one of media’s now most frequently quoted quotes, *“Well he would say that, wouldn’t he?”*

Which might also be directed at my forebear, Lord Admiral Sir Thomas Cochrane, Baron and 10th Earl of Dundonald (who, for good reason, features a lot in my book), and who, despite being much admired for his seagoing adventures and many inventions, was much pilloried for his venture into politics, which was decidedly less noteworthy.

Aside from this unfortunate period, he was a celebrated man of great distinction, whose exploits were the inspiration for authors of fictional hero’s modelled on the activities of the 10th Earl. Such as C.S. Forester’s Horatio Hornblower, the Aubrey-Maturin series of novels by Patrick O’Brian and those written by Captain Frederick Marryat who served aboard Lord Cochrane’s HMS Imperious when, during the Napoleonic Wars, they attacked French and Spanish interests in the Western Mediterranean.

Also G.A. Henty's: 'With Cochrane the Dauntless' which, if a first edition were to be found, would sell for several hundred pounds.

Written in conjunction with G.B. Earp and published in the eighteen fifties, the 10th Earl's autobiography has been followed by a number of biographies. One of the more recent being: 'Cochrane – The Life and Exploits of a Fighting Captain' by Robert Harvey, from which this anecdote about the tenth Earls political shenanigans is taken;

'Between his many and varied seagoing adventures, in one of which he fought with Nelson at the Battle of Trafalgar, he decided to enter Parliament. His reason for doing so were of the highest order for, determined to improve the frightful conditions in which seamen lived and worked, he planned to expose Admiralty corruption.

He was persuaded by his radical friend, William Cobbett, to stand against the Ministerial candidate, Cavendish Bradshaw, in a by-election in Honiton, Devon, which, at that time, was one of the most corrupt boroughs in the country. A reputation borne out by this remark from one voter, "I always vote for Mr. Most."

On losing resoundingly, Cochrane took the unusual step of paying his own electors 'for their honesty' ten guineas each - double the amount that, prior to the election, Bradshaw had paid to his. So when, at the next election, he stood for the same constituency, on the expectation of a similar crock of gold, everyone eligible to vote, voted for him. When asked what was to be expected by those who had supported him in such numbers he said, *"Not one farthing!"*

"But my Lord you gave ten guineas a head to the minority at the last election and the majority have been calculating on something handsome on the present occasion." To which Cochrane replied, *"No doubt! The former gift was for their disinterested conduct in not taking the bribe of five pounds from the agents of my opponent. For me now to pay them would be a violation of my own previously expressed principles."*

But having obtained a seat in parliament via such a corrupt borough and indulging in the necessity of appearing to buy votes, it was many years before he could cleanse himself of the subsequent dirt.

An embroilment that, as I write in JERI's Real Impossible People, earned him opprobrium in many quarters. Despite which, as an Impossible Person on many different levels, he was, possibly above all others, not just adventurous and brave but clever, daring, entrepreneurial, famous, gifted, heroic and intelligent.

From all of the other sixteen letters of the alphabet, apart, perhaps, from J, X and Y, I could find an apt word for this, in his time, world renowned warrior and zealously valiant Admiral, but the time required for this research is not on my side – nor, I can be confident, that of my reader.

Despite losing both his 'seats' - that of his constituency and, if only temporarily, that in The Lady Chapel - it would be pleasing to think our present day admirals and politicians would, or could, be written about in future years with equal respect and admiration.

However, the more recent shenanigans of both our British and American politicians makes this a hollow hope. Neatly confirmed by this American 'history lesson' that requires us to 'hang on to our seats' - whether carved, constitutional or merely cosy!

Attractive and intelligent, prior to her present aspiration to find fame in the film business, Sonya's granddaughter Chelsea once espoused the impressive ambition to be the First Woman President of America. She sent this to me with;

"Have a history teacher explain this - if they can!"

AMERICAN HISTORY LESSON

Abraham Lincoln was elected to Congress in 1846.
John F. Kennedy was elected to Congress in 1946.

Abraham Lincoln was elected President in 1860.
John F. Kennedy was elected President in 1960.

Both were particularly concerned with civil rights.
Both wives lost their children while living in the White House.

Both Presidents were shot on a Friday.
Both Presidents were shot in the head.

Now it gets really weird.

Lincoln 's secretary was named Kennedy.
Kennedy's Secretary was named Lincoln.

Both were assassinated by Southerners.
Both were succeeded by Southerners named Johnson.

Andrew Johnson, who succeeded Lincoln, was born in 1808.
Lyndon Johnson, who succeeded Kennedy, was born in 1908.

John Wilkes Booth, who assassinated Lincoln, was born in 1839.
Lee Harvey Oswald, who assassinated Kennedy, was born in 1939.

Both assassins were known by their three names.
Both names are composed of fifteen letters.

Now hang on to your seat.

Lincoln was shot at a theatre named 'Ford.'
Kennedy was shot in a car called ' Lincoln' made by 'Ford.'

Lincoln was shot in a theatre and his assassin ran and hid in a warehouse.
Kennedy was shot from a warehouse and his assassin ran and hid in a theatre.

Booth and Oswald were assassinated before their trials.

And here's the kicker...

A week before Lincoln was shot, he was in Monroe, Maryland.
A week before Kennedy was shot, he was with Marilyn Monroe.

A History lesson that leads to one on Geography -

THE EUROPEAN UNION AND THE PRICE OF CABBAGES AND DUCK EGGS

This next list lists the number of words in seven of the most famous writings in the English language. An Address; A Constitution; The Commandments; A Declaration; A Prayer; A Principle' A Theorem - together with an eighth, the somewhat less well known; The Price of Cabbages.

A list that, with no attribution, has arrived in my inbox in many differenet formats, many times over many months from many different people from many parts of the globe.

Duncan Mountford of Leatherhead in Surrey sent it to the Daily Mail where, in October 2011, it was published in their Peterborough column. Peterborough attribute it to Mr. Mountford, and for all we - or they - know, he may be its originator, but I must take the compilers of Peterborough to task for classifying it as a joke when it is a truly scary indication of how batty our bureaucrats in both Britain and Brussels have become.

It is to be admired as much for its dedication as its information as whoever compiled it must have burnt much midnight oil in order to get their facts – and word counts – accurate.

Pythagorean theorem - 24
The Lord's Prayer - 66
Archimedes' Principle - 67
The Ten Commandments - 179
The Gettysburg Address - 286
The United States Declaration of Independence - 1,300
The United States Constitution (including all 27 amendments) 7,818
The ECC's common standards for cabbages, sprouts,
celery and spinach - 5,371
The British Industry Protocal's instructions on growing, harvesting, storing and the pricing of cabbages and duck eggs and the import of caramel . The 1987 book of aphorisms, 'Pearls of Wisdom' tells us that the number of words in the Regulations on the import of caramel and the pricing of duck eggs is **26,911**.

Then in November 2017 in Charles Legges 'Answers to Correspondents' column Jim Gallier of Manchester wrote that the 1987 book 'Pearls of Wisdom a Book of Aphorisms' the EEC edict, for the Common Standard for cabbages, sprouts, celery, spinach and plums runs to 5,371 words and their directive on the import of caramel is 26,911 words long.

If true, it tells us that the European Union spends vast sums employing vast numbers of people who spend vast numbers of hours compiling vast edicts that, due to their length, no one will ever read.

An assumption predicated on the premise that probably very few Americans have read all of the 7,818 words of the United States Constitution that, with its 27 amendments, is nineteen thousand and ninety three words less than the European Union's instructions on how, where, when, why and for how much, cabbages may or may not be sold, may or may not be bought or, it follows, may or may not be eaten.

As a lover of the written word - however tedious - I have to admire anyone who can compose this number of words on something as mundane as a cabbage. But if they continue to churn out similar reports of similar length on similar items, will this leave time for them to dine at the many, excellent, mouth – and eye – watering restaurants of Brussels and Strasbourg?

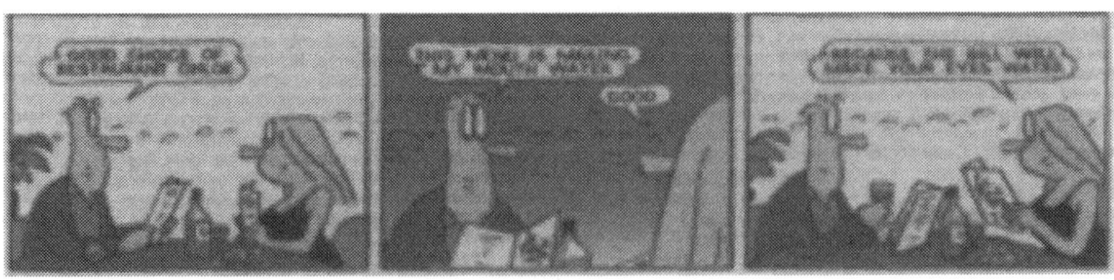

Restaurants that certainly won't have cabbage on their menus as it is a vegetable that, despite the number of words written about it, is now rarely seen and even more rarely eaten. Possibly because the bureaucrats of Brussels would prefer us to eat sprouts?

Such lavish waste of resources - and words - should allow for the Government's of all the other EU member countries to request a refund. Although it is certain that signing up to the European Union does not come with a 'money back guarantee'. So should, due to such a fatuous waste of money, the UK ask Brussels for a rebate we can bet our bottom dollar that they would ask; *"What has the UK's contribution to the EU got to do with the price of cabbages?"*

A paragraph that includes two, frequently used, adages that allow me, with his kind permission, to include this extremely clever poem by Mick Ellis, that, in March 2015, was published in the Peterbrorough Column of the Daily Mail.

It not only 'fills a hole' but also 'fits the bill' – as it does for those who are 'The Bill!

Best Food Forward

I put my best foot forward and my shoulder to the wheel,
My nose was to the grindstone, and soon began to peel.
I needed power to my elbow and I had to shake my leg,
I thought to put my back into it, but pulled my weight instead.

I had a chip on my shoulder, and a flea in my right ear,
I had some bats in the belfry, no wonder I felt queer!
I was looking down my nose at the frog that's in my throat,
A cat had got my tongue and something had got my goat.

I took the bull by both horns, I let the cat out of the bag,
I put the cat among the pigeons, which was really rather sad.
I was eating humble pie because I thought my goose was cooked,
I shall be in a pretty pickle if I'm ever brought to book.

I guess the fat is in the fire, which is not my cup of tea,
So I tried to turn a blind eye, but both worked perfectly.
I was blowing my own trumpet, and paddling my own canoe,
What should have been a piece of cake, was more than I could chew.
But if no one spills the beans, I'll keep the whole thing under wraps.
Once it's swept under the carpet, that'll be the end of that.

From the artist Holbein to the magazine Private Eye and programmes such as; 'Yes Minister' and 'Have I Got News For You', politicians have always been the butt of good-natured jokes.

There are also legions of excellent quotes on the subject in an equal number of books from which it is easy to define which of our leaders were brilliant or brainless. The following are excellent examples of all shades of the spectrum. By, arguably, the greatest, Sir Winston Churchill, who was instrumental in bringing a victorious end to the worst war in history; *"Politics are almost as exciting as war and quite as dangerous. In war, you can only be killed once."*

By, arguably, one of the most controversial, Lady Thatcher. A woman with the strength of mind to stay true to her convictions; *"The greater the trust, the greater the duty upon us to be worthy of that trust."*

By a man better, perhaps, at words than he was at politics, Jeremy Thorpe, who, during the infamous 'Night of the long knives' said; *"Greater love has no man than he lay down his friends for his life."*

From another, rather less worthy, who was responsible for colluding in policies that, with the help of his UK cohort, resulted in both a recession and a couple of wars; *"Yo, Blair."* Who may now wish he had responded with: *"On yer bike Bush!"*

It is a sobering thought that many of our latter day leaders will not be remembered for their orations and sound policies but only for the jokes made against them. Such as Messrs. Blair and Bush for whom 'the stopping of traffic' and 'the starting of wars' may be the only things for which they will be remembered.

It may not be politically correct to make fun of our politicians, whether American, British or European, but when all is said and done (a lot of the first and very little of the second by a lot of them), if they can't take a joke, they shouldn't be in the kitchen - or The House.

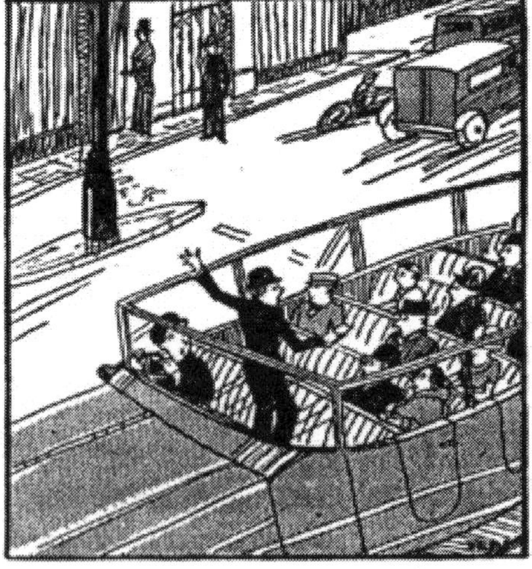

The guide who said the House of Lords was where they played cricket when it was raining.

But the big question is: Why have they stopped playing by the rules of cricket? Despite research, I cannot find anything of quality or note that John Prescott has said or done, but I have read and heard numerous extremely naughty jokes about him. All too rude to include and none that reach heights low enough (a neat oxymoron), to do his antics justice.

Although we can be confident that my mother could have devised an apt caption for him as Prescott, is certainly an Impossible Person – even if only due to his two monickers of Two Jags and Prezza. Although what she would have said had she known of him was; 'Did it do justice to our once great nation to elevate to such heights a man whose nicknames are his main claim to fame?' Or, say I, to appoint as our European Union High Representative - at an annual salary of three hundred and thirty eight thousand pounds - a Baroness about whom a leading MEP said: *"Last year she was unknown in Britain. Today she is she is unknown all over Europe."*

Although, say I, you can bet her bank manager knows her.

The words of this MEP brings to mind the time Sonya and I, when working for a client in the West Country, went in search of some wooden corbels. Directed to the workshop of a local carpenter, we found his atelier full of superb artifacts. From stair rails to statues, his genius had no end.

Having placed our order, we asked if he had ever considered showing his work in London, and were much more than a little amused when he said; *"Nar, never! Up Lunnon I'd be a someone wot no one know, darn 'ere I'm a no one wot everyone know."* A point of view some of our more extravagant Premiers and Presidents who have ambitions to 'turn heads in every major city of the world', might do well to bear in mind.

Ronald Reagan – for all the wrong reasons – being one of the most noteworthy. In one of Des MacHale's excellent books of 'Wit' he records Reagan as having said; *"I never drink coffee at lunch - I find it keeps me awake in the afternoon."*

The chance of Reagan ever having met my mother is about as likely as me ever meeting Reagan, and it is even less likely that he would have seen her next cartoon?

A cartoon that does not feature in the Hutchinson book of her cartoons, many of which were taken to Canada by the many hundreds of people fleeing 'Death by War'. We only know this as many of those we have bought via Amazon have hailed from there.

Impossible People

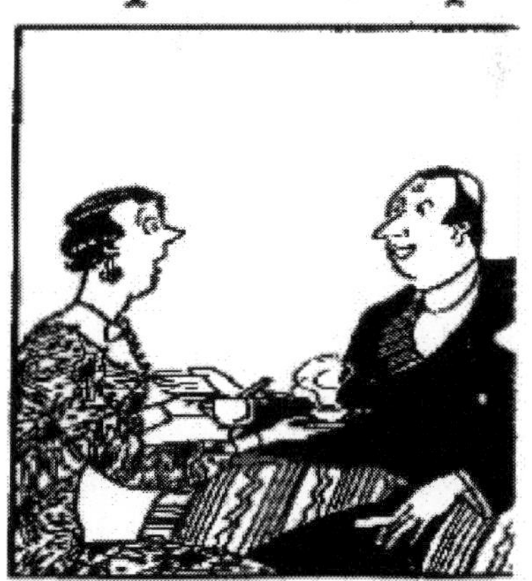

The Member of Parliament who refused coffee after lunch as it kept him awake during the afternoon.

Had it included this particular cartoon it could well have been the likely source for the quote that Des MacHale attributes to Reagan, but as it does not, perhaps, if he ever reads this, Mr. MacHale, from wherever he hales, will be kind enough to let me know why, or from where, he came across this quote or, more correctly, 'caption'?

Having concluded it was merely affirmation of Mr. Silver's views on our thought processes, some years later, when reading Mitchell Simmons Daily Mail column, I saw that he also, had attributed the quote to Reagan.
On asking Mr. Simmons from whence he had come across it, he told me he had taken it from one of Des MacHale's books. He then said; *"On reflection I thought it was too clever for Reagan."*

But not too clever for A.P. Herbert who, after the 1950 election, advised the winner, the Labour Leader, Clement Attlee:

'You wear a party coat, but every day recall,
Whichever way we vote, you represent us all'

So it would behove all of those who hope to win the honour of becoming a member of the Green Bench Club, to have engraved on their hallowed seats Shakespeare's words from Hamlet when Polonius says to his son, Laertes:

This above all; to thine own self be true.
And it must follow, as the night the day,
Though canst not then be false to any man.

Words that are also a natural lead into a 'true' story.

When acting as Senior Assistant to our surrogate aunt, Marjorie Bayes, when she was Executive Secretary of the International Confederation of Midwives, one of my most successful and notable achievements was the seamless organisation of the 1972 Fifth World Congress of Midwifery that was held in Washington.

Two other ICM Congresses my sister Sasha and I worked on with equal success were those held in Rome and Lausanne but with far fewer delegates than that which I worked on in Washington, where we hosted over three thousand midwives and many professional speakers from around the world.

Marjorie, (who had delivered me and my twin. I do not, more correctly, write my twin and I as, more correctly, I arrived first), decided to include a lay-speaker, a first at one of these Congresses, and chose my twin for this awesome task. A 'task' that won her a loud and long standing ovation for her talk on the benefits of 'Legal Terminations'. A law, that, in yet another wondrous coincidence, was enacted by the British Government on the same day, that, given the time difference, allowed her to announce this at the end of her talk.

What she didn't 'announce' were the headlines in our local paper, the Southend Echo. Two days prior to our departure the editor asked if we would talk to one of their reporters about our involvement in the Congress. To our horror and not a little disgust, their next day's front page headline was: *"Twins Go To Washington To Talk About Their Sex Lives."*

In direct contrast, my exemplary efforts earned me an 'Official Invitation' to the White House, an abiding memory of which was reading the words on a small engraved sign sitting on the Oval Office desk. Words that are a constant reminder to those elevated to sit there, of the limits of their influence:

'Lord, your sea is so great and my boat is so small.'

Twelve modest words that should be on the desk of every politician in the world who may get too big for their boots! Not to mention Generals! Admirals don't need it as they already know the difference between the size of their 'boats' and the sea.

Which takes us to another of Piet Hein's Grooks. Composed for those who enjoy parlour games, it applies equally well to those who go out in boats.

Those who've been making the week go by trying to work
out exactly who, with what reservations, and how, and why,
they would (or wouldn't) remain in the room with,
ought to consider, anent their doom, a further point
they can play the goat with, viz; to discover exactly
who might (or mightn't) they be in the same boat with.

There are few politicians of any creed, colour or credentials who can be given credit for their altruism - or their cricket. Although this may be more to do with the persuasions they follow than the positions they hold, as set out in the next 'play on politics' that, in many different forms, has popped into my inbox more times than I care to count.

A TALE OF TWO COWS (The notes in brackets are mine.)

Nazism:
You have two cows. The government takes both of them and shoots you.
(They also kill everyone who doesn't eat pork.)

Fascism:
You have two cows. The government takes both of them, shoots one of them, milks the other one and keeps the milk. (But don't know what to do with it.)

Bolshevism:
You have two cows. The government takes both of them and sells you the milk. (But no tea or coffee to go with it. Nor much else.)

Communism:
You have two cows. The government takes both of them and gives them to a communal farm. (You are also given to a communal farm where you are worked to death.)

Socialism:
You have two cows. The government lets you keep both of them but takes the milk to give it to those in need. (You then become one of 'those in need')

Democracy:
You have two cows. The government lets you to keep both of them and all the milk. (You sell the milk. Your taxes rise in direct proportion to politicians' expenses. You can't afford to keep the cows. You go bankrupt. The Receivers sell the cows to the government. The government makes them into beef burgers for those on benefits. One of whom is you.)

European Union:
You have a two cows. No agreement can be reached about what you are allowed to do with them. (You sell the cows and open a general store that sells milk.)

Capitalism:
You have two cows. You sell one of them and buy a bull. (You sell the resulting calves. You get rich. You sell the cow and the bull and with the money you stand for parliament. You win your seat. You become Prime Minister. Your party is defeated. You then give talks in many countries on the benefits of keeping cows and a bull. You become extremely rich.)

Proof that words can be far more profitable than farming, industry or politics! It also does no one any favours, least of all the cows and the bull. Nor, unless it really was 'original thought', does this next anecdote do any favours for the late M.P. Sir Hector Monro.

Following Margaret Thatcher's third election as Prime Minister, (the first Prime Minister of either sex to win a third term since the introduction of universal adult suffrage), an article in the Sunday Express of June 21st 1987, included these 'very last words.'

'The very last words on the election belong to the Tory MP for Dumfries. During the campaign a constituent said to him; *"You know, I've half a mind to go into politics myself."*

Without a moments hesitation, Sir Hector replied; *"Well that's just about all you need."'*

We shall now never know whether it was Sir Hector's own inspiration or - having at some time seen the next Impossible People caption - a very good memory?

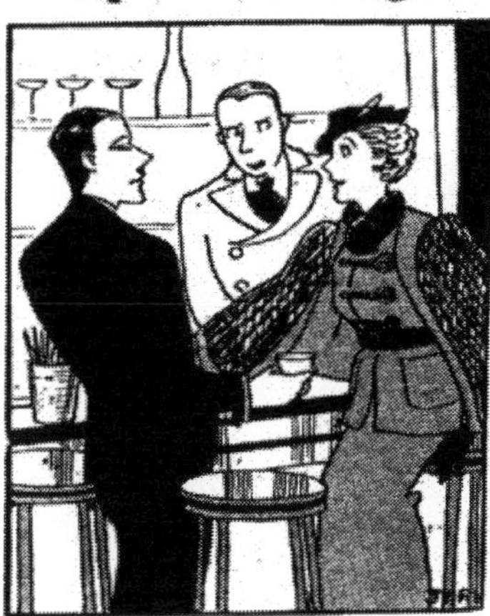

Impossible People

The girl who said that was all that was necessary when her friend said he had half a mind to enter Parliament.

If it wasn't original thought, being a Scot, he should have known better than to nick stuff from another Scot. Although it is much more likely that, as Mr. Silver avers, when it comes to captions, comedy and witticisms, original thought is about as unlikely as Mr. Silver - or myself - becoming Prime Minister.

However, with my considerable number of house moves I might be thought of as a floating voter, as was my mother's next Impossible Person; *"The floating voter who told the canvasser that she didn't know whether she was one of the don't knows or not."*

Although there is not a cartoon with this caption among the hundreds of my mother's cartoons in my possession, it could, possibly, be among the many hundreds that are not. However, as she never lost her ability to compose 'captions', which she would often quote, while I cannot be sure that she used it, I can be sure that she composed it.

The last words on Premiers, Presidents or politicians has to be: 'Never doubt the arrogance of the truly powerful or the really rich.' Nor, say I, their isolation from the real world.

Which, justly, leads to -

JUSTICE - and - less justly - the tax man;

Impossible People

JERI

The income-tax collector who said he always found defaulters out.

Perhaps, having put all their zillions into tax havens well before the tax man cometh, they are, as I write, sunning themselves in some tropical paradise.

Or have gone shopping?

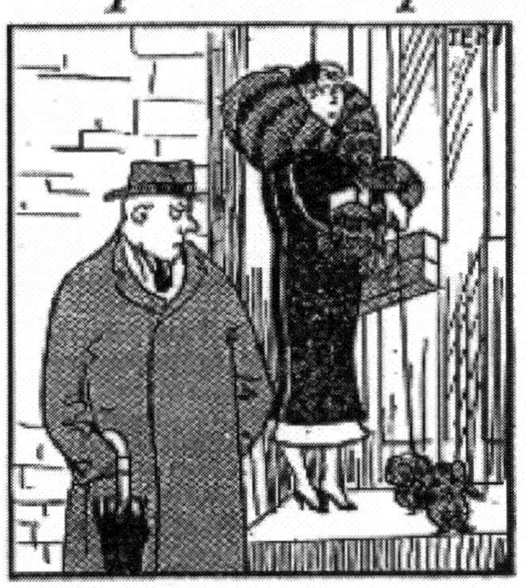

The man who was thankful he had not to pay income-tax on the income his wife lived up to.

Bridging Materials

Is there a mote in your neighbour's eye?
Bridge builder leave it alone!
Humanity's bridges can only be built,
Of the beams in your own.

A Piet Hein Grook that is a neat lead to this quote from the Talmud: *"We do not see things as they are, we see them as we are."* Brilliantly illustrated by the next anecdote.

Having retired, a man moved to a small country town. Within a few days of settling into his new home he asked the local postman what the people in the village were like. The postman asked him what his previous neighbours had been like. The man said they had been *"pleasant, friendly and sociable and were always ready to give you a helping hand."* To which the postman said; *"You will find the people here are much the same."*

On being asked the same question by another newcomer to the village, the postman, again, asked what his previous neighbours had been like. The man said; *"They were really unfriendly and antisocial and you could never ask them for help."* To which the postman said; *"You will find the people here are much the same."*

Our mother once employed a plumber who, a little more succinctly, said to her; *"There's only two types of people in the world, Missus. Thems thats whats like radiators and thems thats whats like drains."* While my brother Stefan maintained that; *"There are only three types of people in the world; Those who make things happen, those to whom things happen, and those to whom nothing ever happens."*

Three 'boxes' that possibly 'house' an equal number of politicians, for while the majority can safely put their hands on their hearts for the purity of their motives, there are a few who can't, as I have heard it said and have also read that, in the opinion of many, politics has always been a magnet for chancers and charlatans.

Which, perhaps, is why some of them never give any thought to the 'unconsidered consequences' of their actions. One of which is their blind belief in targets that are now used in every area of public service life and have created a social unfairness not seen since Hogarth's day.

An unfairness that led one journalist to suggest that the police, whose remit is to prevent crime and protect victims, now, due to the fear of being thought of as politically incorrect, partisan or racist, merely strive to fill their 'quotas' of detected crime.

A consequence foreseen by the brilliant 18th century conservative, Edmund Burke when he warned; *"Very plausible schemes with very pleasing commencements can often have shameful and lamentable consequences."*
A prescient truth borne out by the lack of justice to the taxpayer in spending many millions of their 'hard earned' on a new 'House of Justice' while introducing Human Rights laws that are now used, and abused, on such a grand scale they have begun to belittle the basic rights of all law-abiding residents of the most lawful country in the world. A country where, due to their 'umanrights', murderers, thieves, rapists and terrorists and now freely walk among us.

But 'fairness' is an unattainable Utopia. Confirmed by the Rodean headmistress who, following a complaint from a pupil about 'unfairness' said; *"Fair! Fair! There is no justice in the world and there is certainly going to be none at this school."*

A sentiment most, if not all, educational establishments should adopt and much akin to Sir Alan Sugar's; "Fair! The only fair you're likely to get is your bleedin' bus fare!" A natural lead to a cartoon that, had she known of him, our mother would definitely have 'dedicated' to Sir Alan.

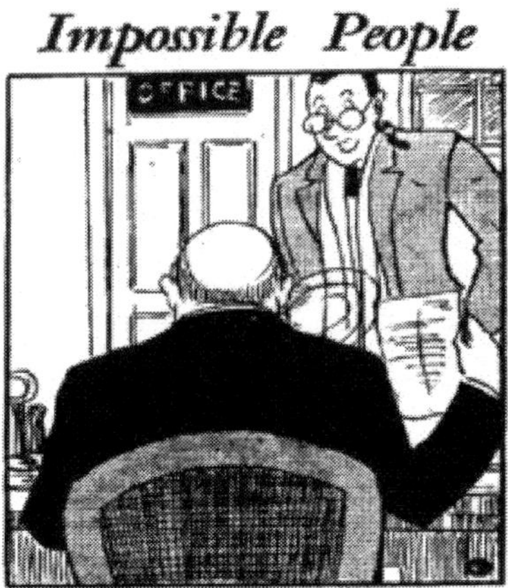

The managing director who, when asked if he had an opening for a well-educated young man, said, "Yes, but don't slam it as you go out."

And for everyone, including Sir Alan, here are some great words from a great man, Edward Wallis Hoch, member of the State Legislator of America from 1889 to 1891 and Speaker from 1893 to 1895 and twice Governor of Kansas, who said; *"There is so much good in the worst of us, and so much bad in the best of us that it hardly becomes any of us to criticise the rest of us."*

So, with my knuckles, yet again, soundly rapped, I take back the unkind things I wrote about Prezza.

For while Peers do not always appear to be better than their peers, it would appear he has now become peerless enough to become one. Although it is probably a good idea not to peer too closely into the reason why. His peerage may also lead many to think this next homily should be 'carved into the back of his seat' - or, more effectively, written on a large sign in large red letters above it.

If you would your good name keep,
Five things observe with care.
To whom you speak,
Of whom you speak,
And how and when and where.

Which applies to Peers and Politicians alike as it is said of the Liberal Democrats;

The Lib Dems are searching the land for
The breakthrough they've long hoped and planned for,
But what gets in their way,

Is that not even they,
Have the slightest idea what they stand for.

While there are those who have an equally dyspeptic view of the Tories;

There's an old Irish word that means 'thief',
With four letters quite pithy and brief.
I tell you no lie,
It is spelt T-O-R-Y
Now doesn't that beggar belief.

Patently, America has had some truly great men in the Senate! But then we once had some truly great men - and women - in our House of Commons. It is just such a shame that there are only two sorts, good and bad and, like buses, the latter all come at once.

Which, no doubt is why Hillaire Belloc wrote:

The accursed power that stands on Privilege
(That goes with Women, and champagne and Bridge)
Broke – And Democracy then resumed her reign:
(Which goes with Bridge, and Women and Champagne.)

The next cartoon looms large in my life (and on this page), as not only is it one of my favourites it is uncannily close to my view on loans; *"If someone only lends you half the amount of money you ask to borrow this leaves them in debt to you."* As in -

Impossible People

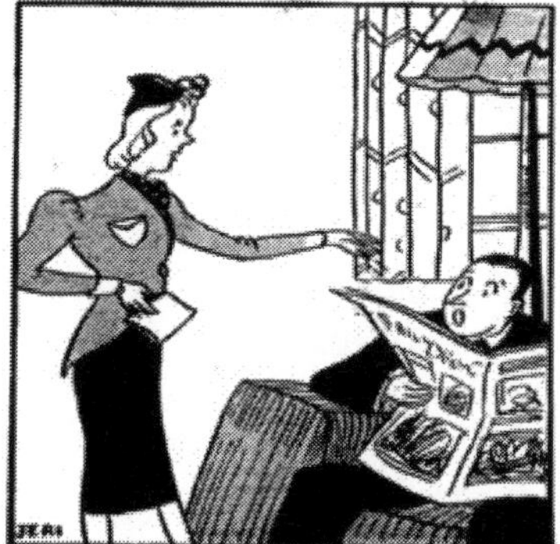

The woman who asked her husband to lend her ten pounds and give her five of them, then he would owe her five, and she would owe him five, so they would be straight.

While most men would believe this Impossible lady's point of view to be 'unjust', true justice - and possibly a need for greater tax revenue, eventually led to -

VOTES FOR WOMEN

And for good measure and not a little pleasure some music as the news that they had won the right to vote must have been music to the ears of most women.

As I write earlier, my twin, Sonya, and brother-in-law, George, are both incredibly lucky. They never have to cross their fingers or worry about passing people on the stairs, nor concern themselves about broken mirrors or walking under ladders, they are just lucky.

The same could not be said of our Mother, for while she always maintained she was lucky to have her children, it is interesting to wonder how much luckier she would have been had she not had two whizz-kid sons, four wilful daughters, a wayward husband and two world wars to contend with.

For it is almost certain that, with her splendid gifts, she would have become - as did many of her peers – a highly renowned artist and writer. Or would she? When in her late teens she had a picture accepted for the Summer Show of the Royal Academy, a well known art dealer showed great interest in it, but, on learning of her gender, said; *"Miss Cochrane is a fine artist but she would not be a good investment as it is rare for the work of a female artist, however fine, to win high renown."*

It was also a great sadness that Mama was not listening to the tune 'Greensleeves' at the time this dealer was viewing her work as, many years later, she told us that should she inadvertently hear this piece of music something lucky would happen. But as music did not surround people's lives then in the way it does now, her chances of hearing it - whether inadvertently or not -were small.

About as small as the chance of the dealer buying her art, as, prior to Emmeline and Sylvia Pankhurst and Women's Suffrage, however wonderful her skills or gifts, a woman's work or achievements were rarely thought of as being equal to that of her male counterpart - unless, as did our grandmother, she sang well.

This Art Dealer's loss was another's gain, but his assumption was correct as, at that time, women were still thought of as 'having little value' and it was not until 1928, after a long fight, the Suffragette Movement won for all women over 21, 'The Right to Vote'. A prize that took them seven years to win.

Fascinatingly, on the 30th January 2017 The Daily Mail included an article by Tom Payne entitled: 'First Woman Voter' in which he writes that, in a recently discovered, 1911 newspaper was an article that maintained that Frances Connelly had made history when she became the first women to: 'have her vote counted'.

As, at that time, Frances was a name gifted only to male offspring, this lady was thought to be a man and had been sent a voting card. So when, in 1911, she arrived at the Yoevil polling station to cast her vote in that years South Somerset by-election, officials were aghast and dithered over whether to allow her to vote.

On consulting the presiding officer, W.W. Henley, he eventually said they had no choice under the rules as her name was on the electoral register, she had a register card and she had not yet voted. So – on the same day that Suffragist campaigners were marching through Yoevil in their fight to win women the vote - Mrs. Connelly was casting hers for the Conservative candidate, Mr. Aubrey Herbert, who, narrowly, beat Sir Edward Strachey.

Whether, on learning of this, the Yoevil Suffragettes broke into song we will never know. What we do know is that Sonya has no musical talent but, although my voice would never have reached the heights of my maternal grandmother, as a child I was able to hold a melody so was always chosen to sing in the choirs of the many schools we attended.

As our alikeness and long, blond, curly hair stood us apart, we would be placed side by side in the front row of the choir with the instruction; *"Karina you sing, Sonya you just mouth the words."*

What an uproar that would cause if said today! But children's psyches are much stronger than people now believe them to be. Sonya knew she couldn't sing and I knew I couldn't draw, and neither of us were remotely concerned if these differences were brought to the notice of our peers.

Even now, I occasionally wonder how good my voice might have become had it been tutored, but our frequent moves and lack of funds did now allow for such luxuries, thus the possibility never arose. Making it yet another notch in my hatred of Hitler.

But there are many more fine men than bad, one being Gandhi, whose statue was erected in Parliament Square in March 2015.

When, in 1947, he won independence from Britain he chose for India's flag orange for courage and sacrifice, green for fertility and white for peace, truth and unity.

Colours similar to those chosen by the Suffragettes to signify their desire to be seen as equally, equal to men, both in Parliament and the workplace, Green for Hope, Purple for Dignity and White for Purity

Which fitted well with my own as with no 'hope' that my voice might become as 'pure' as that of my grandmothers, I bore my loss with 'dignity'. A word that takes us to the extremely dignified radio programme, Roy Plombley's 'Desert Island Discs'.

A programme that was born in 1942, and is still going strong. A few years ago the BBC published a list of the most requested music chosen by those chosen to grace this gracious, much listened to, much loved programme.

The list included only classical pieces with Beethoven way ahead of the field and Elgar as a close contender. But the list did not include Liszt. (A somewhat puny pun).

1, Beethoven Symphony No 9 in D minor - Choral.
2. Rachmaninoff Piano Concerto No 2 in C minor
3. Schubert String Quartet in C major
4. Beethoven Symphony No. 6 in F major - Pastoral
=5. Elgar Pomp and Circumstance March No. 1 in D Major (Land of Hope and Glory)
=5. Beethoven Piano Concerto No. 5 in E flat major. Emperor
6. Elgar Enigma Variations, Nimrod
7. Beethoven Symphony No 7 in A major

There must be many people who have a secret desire to be invited on this programme. A desire that can only be met if you have either fame or distinction - or, perhaps, merely wish to be marooned on an uninhabited island ?

Despite which, even with no chance of being invited as a participant, it is still pleasing to select those pieces of music you would choose should you ever be a cast away on a Desert Island – or have the good fortune to be cast as a celebrity on the programme.

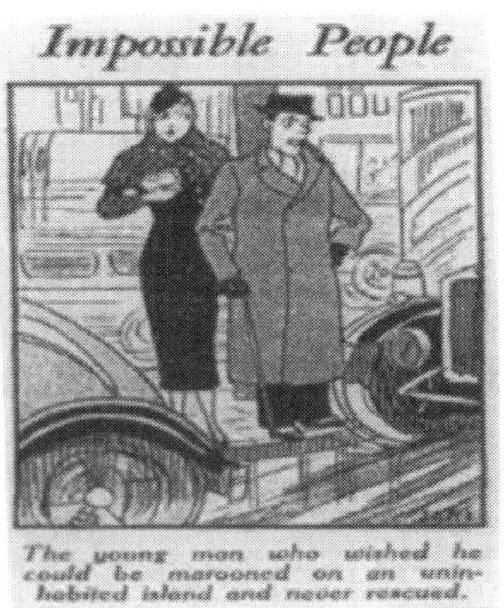

The young man who wished he could be marooned on an uninhabited island and never rescued.

As an avid collector of disparate styles of music, I have always thought that, as there are so many millions of pieces from which to choose, it must be quite difficult for those chosen to choose them, to whittle these down to a mere eight. My choices would be selected, not just because they have all been of significance in my life, but because, should I ever be marooned, I would not mind were I not rescued.

Alexander Pope's Where'er You Walk.
Elgar's Nimrod from his Enigma Variations.
Janice Ian's Light A Light.
Pete Atkin's Have You Got A Biro I Can Borrow
Samantha Storm's Mr. Love'
Scott Joplin's The Entertainer.
Kirsty McColl's England 2 Columbia 0.'
Noel Harrison's The Windmills of Your Mind.

Then, in a coincidence as odd as any I have already included, on Tuesday 22nd of October 2013, I had just typed this list when Jeremy Vine announced on the radio that Noel Harrison had died. He said; *"Noel so disliked the fame the success of this song had brought him, him, he chose to retire from the limelight."*

A much less well known musician with whom I was once acquainted, Pete Atkin, deserved a great deal more 'limelight' than he won. Of those songs he composed, two of his best are the song I include in my list and Touch Has A Memory.' He also recorded an equally pleasing compilation of songs with Clive James.

As all of Pete's magical lyrics are set to magical music, I will sneak the whole CD into my castaway bag. Also, for reasons of nostalgia rather than noteworthiness, these -

Sting's Rise and Fall;
Ronan Keating's I Hope You Dance;
Martine McCutcheon's On The Radio;
Cilla Black's I Would Bring You Flowers;
Gordon Haskell's How Wonderful You Are;
The Olsen Brothers Fly On The Wings Of Love;
Charles Aznavour's Yesterday When I Was Young;
Lyndsay de Paul's Won't Somebody Dance With Me?
Eimear Quin's The Voice;
Ennio Morricone's Theme from the Mission;
Samuel Barber's Adagio for Strings
and Beethoven's 'Fur Elys',

Also a version of 'Greensleeves' because, if Mama was right, and I inadvertently heard it – even if I were not rescued at least I would be lucky.

Another would be Andy Pearson's 'Falling For You.' I knew Andy well and, in an Abbey Road studio, did the 'mix' for this song that, in 1978, was a top seller in Greece.

Although, as Michael Caine is so fond of saying; *"Not a lot of people know that."* In his book of the same name Michael tells us; *"There are more musicians in the Monaco State Symphony Orchestra than soldiers in their army."* Which comes as no surprise.

My book would be 'Impossible People'. No surprise there either! While my luxury item would be 'A Man Of All Trades'. Even less surprising!

As 'laughter is the best medicine', I would also sneak in a book of quotations with witticisms such as, *"To be is to do,"* Aristotle; *"To do is to be."* Jean Paul Sartre; *"Do be do be do."* Frank Sinatra. A singer whose songs are magic to dance to.

It is also is a neat lead to dance enthusiasts, many of whom, so I once read, rushed to see the film 'Last Tango in Paris'. The same media article stated that an elderly lady had invited her rather staid Indian friend to see 'Oh Calcutta'. Whether they remained friends we were not told. But if, as is so often said, music really is the food of love, cartoons must be the food of inspiration for -

QUAINT (OR QUIRKY) QUOTES

For more years than I care to count, a pen holder had been sitting on my desk that has, written on its base; *"Just about the time you think you can make ends meet, somebody moves the ends."*

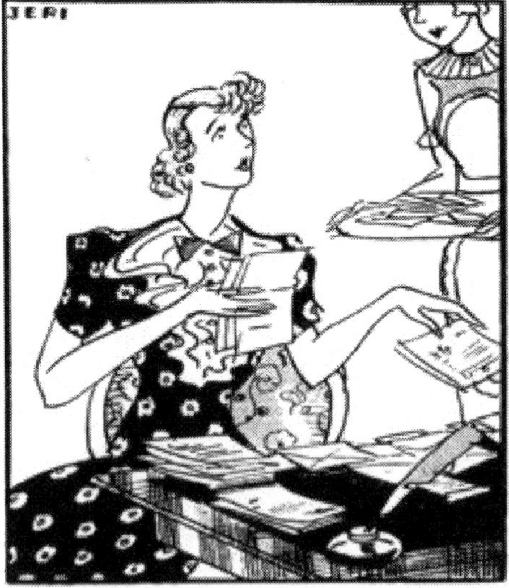

The woman who said just when she could not meet her expenses she kept meeting them everywhere.

As we can be confident that my mother composed this caption many years prior to its 'twin' gracing my pen holder – or any other trinket it may now adorn – yet again, her next cartoon confirms Maurice Silver's assumption regarding 'original thought'.

My OED tells me that the word trinket means 'of little value' although it is safe to say that many millions of pounds will have been made from the sale of the many millions of these ‘little value’ trinkets adorned with similar homilies, such as –

Of all the things I’ve lost, I miss my mind the most.
Today is the tomorrow you worried about yesterday.
I finally got it all together but I forgot where I put it.
Admit your mistakes but always under an assumed name.
If at first you don’t succeed, you have plenty of company.
I would get organised but it would only confuse everyone.
If today is the first day of the rest of my life, I’m in deep trouble.
Never put off until tomorrow what you can avoid doing altogether.
Life is what happens to you while you’re busy making other plans.
Anyone who still thinks the sky is the limit is short on imagination.
Just when you get good at something you don’t have to do it anymore.
Every fourth person is unstable. Look at three friends - if they seem OK - you’re the one.

And: *“Have seen it all, done it all, have forgotten most of it.”*

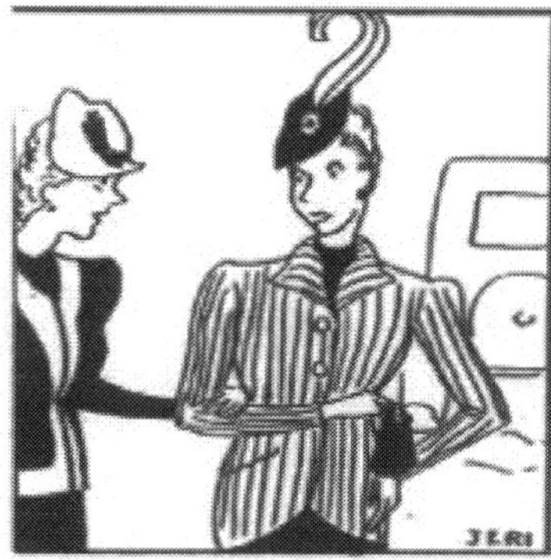

The girl who said there were three things she couldn't remember. She couldn't remember faces, she couldn't remember names and she couldn't remember what the other thing was

And: *“If you think you have someone eating out of your hand, it’s a good idea to count your fingers.”*

Which aims us at -

THE WILDER SIDE OF WILDLIFE

I have put animals before God as I am sure He would do the same. The British also do the same as I have been told, on good authority, that more money is donated to animal charities than to any other.

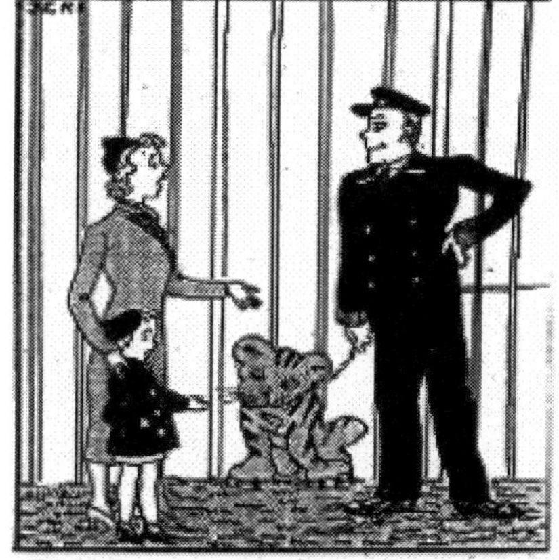

The Zoo keeper who said the tiger cub was so tame that it would eat off your hand.

But as there are more animal charities than any other, this should come as no surprise.

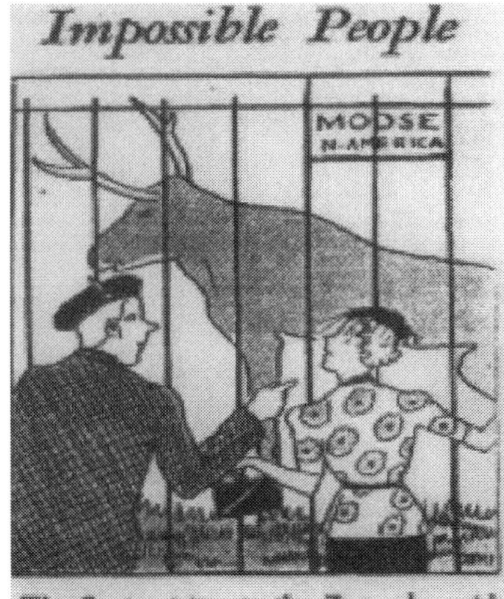

The same 'good authority', Simon, also told me that the single charity that benefits most from the public's largesse is Children in Need. The second is the RNLI with the RNIB and RSPCA as close contenders. It is of equal interest that, being so well known, these last three charities are universally, and deservedly, known by their initials.

I have not checked the accuracy of these 'good authority' facts. Nor of these:

Fact No 1: There are more pigs than people in Denmark.
Fact No 2: There are more cats in London than there are people in Norway.
But apparently nobody owns them –

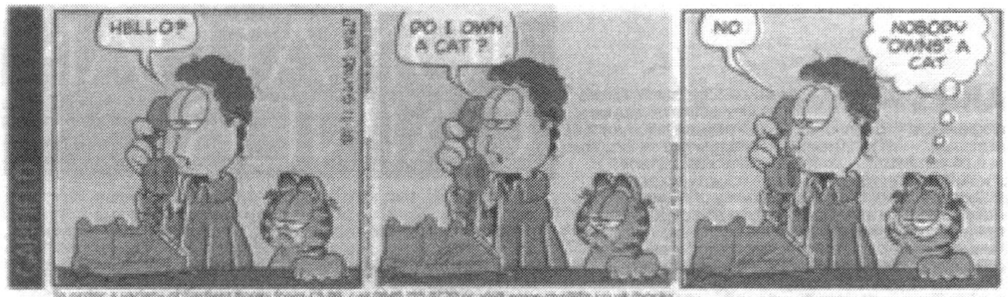

As my grandson, Michael, is fascinated by the world's weird and wonderful wildlife I surfed Wikipedia for generic names of groups of bats, bees, beasts, birds - and werewolves - so that should zoology, zoopharmacology or just bird watching (of the ornithological kind), continue to be of interest, he can begin his research here.

Research that is decidedly quicker via the Internet but not nearly as amusing. From Albatross (rookery) to Zebra (crossing, cohorts, herd, zeal), the generics of all creatures, including humans, can be found at the click of a keyboard.

Many have just one while others have several. Those with the most are Birds, Cats and Ducks, the latter having thirteen which includes the wonderful 'Waddling'. There are no prizes for 'remembering' that Elephants are a Memory, Camels are a Caravan and Peacocks are a Pride. But one could be won for knowing that Bullfinches are a Bellow, the ghastly Cockroaches are an Intrusion and Kittens, intriguingly, are an Intrigue.

Cats when wild are a Destruction and, when not wild, are the wonderful Glorying and also a Clowder, Clutter, Doubt, Glaring, Kindle, Parliament and wondrously, Seraglio.A word, my OED tells me, that means: *'Women's apartments in a Muslim palace, or harem.'* What it doesn't tell me is that 'rookeries' of Seals are also a Harem. How suitable!

Pigs, even more suitably, are Sounders, while Goats are a Tribe or a Trip. Sheep are a Down, Drift, Drove, Flock, Fold, Hirsel, Hurtle, Pack, Parcel, Mob and Trip. Although when in a 'flock' might also be a 'gathering', 'shearing' or 'fleece'. They are also an excellent 'lead' into wool.

In the 1950s the London branch of The International Wool Secretariat, now known as The Woolmark Company, invited members of the public to submit poems that recorded historical events. Their one proviso was that the final line of each poem had to end with the words: *'There is no substitute for wool'*.

Flocks of people responded magnificently and many English teachers set it as a project for their senior pupils. Allied to illustrations by cartoonists such as Bruce Petty, William Hewison and the Daily Mail favourite, Kenneth Mahpod, some of these amusing, informative and often risqué historical vignettes were used by the IWS in an advertising campaign that gave much entertainment to the many thousands of commuters who travel on the London Underground.

They then selected several for publication in an anthology, but despite mine (with a little help from my Mother who suggested I write about writers), winning the school award, sadly it was not one of those chosen by the IWS. Although many may consider it to be of merit equal to any of those that were?

Austen wrote of ladies in satin, silks and muslin,
And men on steeds on darin' deeds a rushin'.
Dickens' women wore clogs and petticoats,
His men, high hats and much-caped coats.

But Austen and Dickens kept their readers warm,
By recommending woollen capes if caught out in a storm.
For both authors knew - they were nobody's fool -
There is no substitute for wool.

When surfing the Woolmark Company website, I came across this Scottish version 'written' with a Scottish accent that makes it a natural for inclusion in 'Impossible People'.

Who, in the opinion of some, the Scots wlll become if ever they devolve from the U.K.

Yon canny Highland crofters keep
A flock of crease-resistant sheep.
They weave wee woollen shirts and slacks,
And flog 'em to the Sassenachs.

Wool keeps its shape, is bound to please,
(Ye nae seen sheep wi' baggy knees)
At birth bairns learn the Golden Rule,
There's nae substitute for wool!

Penguins, that could, or should, be a Crowd, are a Rookery, while Rooks that 'live' in rookeries are a Building, Clamour or Parliament. Mama told us; "It is easy to tell the difference between a crow and a rook as a rook on its own is a crow but a lot of crows together are rooks."

Flock is also the only generic for Ostriches, Hens, Cockerels and Turkeys – which, perhaps, are also Twisler?. Flocks of songbirds are a Dissimulation, flights of lovely larks are an Exultation and the spectacular swirling swallows are a Murmuration.

The charming word Charm is the generic for Finches and Hummingbirds. Perhaps because they are so charming to listen to? As are Nightingales, which should be a Melody but, strangely, are a Watch.

Eagles and Hawks are a Convocation and Kettle. While Jays are a Party, but with no kettle! Doves, sadly, are a Piteousness, while Woodpeckers are a Descent, although tapper or rapper might be more apt. Crows are a Muster or Murder. Magpies are also a Murder but should, perhaps also be Thief.

While the fantastic Flamingos are not only a Flamboyance but, presumably due to their habit of gathering and standing together in such vast numbers, are a Gather or Stand. Snakes and Snipes are a Nest, Pit or Bed. Oysters are also a bed and, when dead, go well with champagne.

Creatures no one would want to go to bed with, even with champagne, are the horrid Rats which are a Horde or a Mischief. Or Prairie Dogs, which are a Coterie and, despite there being few houses on a prairie, Town.
Spiders are a cluster, or a clutter. Even Black Widows that tend to spend their lives in solitary seclusion.

Foxes that rarely, if ever, get together are, if they do, a Skulk or a Leash. But if they find themselves 'shoulder high in deep trouble while skulking about in the wrong crowd, they know it's best to say nothing - let alone admitting to be a Leash.

Packs of Foxhounds, even with a fox in their midst, are a Cry, Mut or Cackle but, perhaps more appropriately, could be a Chase.

Should there ever be enough Hedgehogs to 'get together', they would be an Array, or perhaps could, more appropriately, be an Hooray! Hares are Warrens, Husks and Downs. Downs that are full of Warrens full of Crowds of rabbits, which are also a Colony, Drove, Leash, Nest and Trace - as they come in such numbers it is no wonder they have such numbers of names.

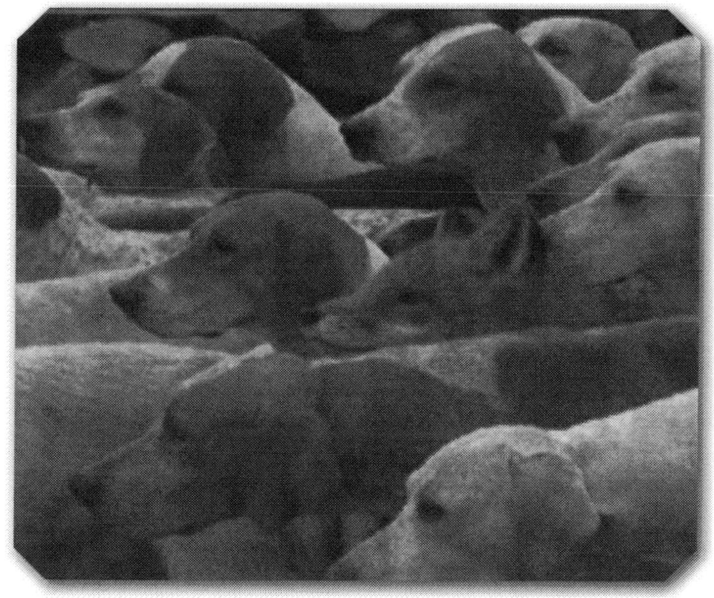

Packs of Foxhounds, even with a fox in their midst, are a Cry, Mut or Cackle but, perhaps more appropriately, could be a Chase.

It is the unfortunate habit
Of the rabbit to breed like a rabbit.
One can say without question,
This leads to congestion
In the burrows that rabbits inhabit.
Horses, as they do when racing, have numbers of names - Stable, Harras, Herd, Team, String and naturally, Field.
While Fields have the generics Pasture, Playing and Level

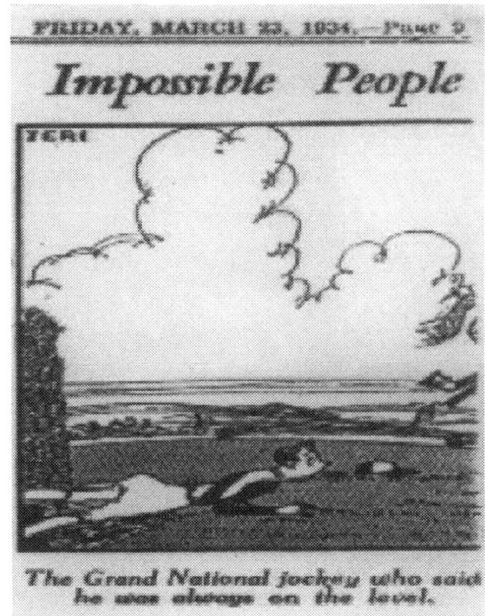

The Grand National jockey who said he was always on the level.

Hyenas have the generic, 'Laughing'. As does the Laughing Kookaburra and the Laughing Dove. Which may look much the same as the little Brown Dove. But not the Long-billed Cockatoo and Long-billed Corella which have the marvelous generic – Cacatua Tenuirostris.

Then there are lizards which can be Blue Tongued, Collared, Desert Spiny, Frilled, Giant Girdled, Goanna or Mexican Beaded. Lions, the King of them all that, deservedly, are known as a 'Pride' have a further ten generics. The first three, and most well known, are African, Asian and Mountain.

The other six, for an animal that wouldn't know a sea if it saw one, are seas; Australian, Californian, Galapagos, South American, Southern and Stellar.

The letter L takes us to the Scaly Beasted Lorikeet which has the truly extraordinary generic - Trichoglossus Haematodus Moluccanus. Which doesn't sound like something you would want to come across even in a bright light, let alone a dark night.

The meek Mole is a Labour, probably because they work so tirelessly at digging their tunnels. Tunnels in which to hide from cats?

The Cat Goes Out A Moleing

The cat goes out a moleing.
Eyes laser-like, limbs fleet.
He views the ravaged lawn,
And pads with padded feet,

To tread the mounds of earth,
To trace his quarry's last retreat.
He plans his battle strategy,
Each movement elegant and neat,

Each change of course considered,
Each dance of war discreet.

He will trail and taunt his captive,
Until his conquest is complete.
He faces hours of waiting,
But will not face defeat.

The cat went out a moleing
To find a morsel he might eat.
The patient hours reward him,
And now he sits - replete.

One of my many prize-winning poems that have found homes in anthologies that house 'prides' of assorted poems on many subjects. But not squirrels or zebras. Squirrels, when en masse, are a Dray, Scurry or Ecureuil – the last being the French word for squirrel whether alone or en-masse.

My French friends find my attempts to pronounce the word 'ecureuil' hilarious until I ask them to say the word squirrel - but they have no difficulty pronouncing the word 'Zebra' which they spell as 'Zebre'. An animal that, according to JERI, is *"lively, has a kick in it and some broad lines."*

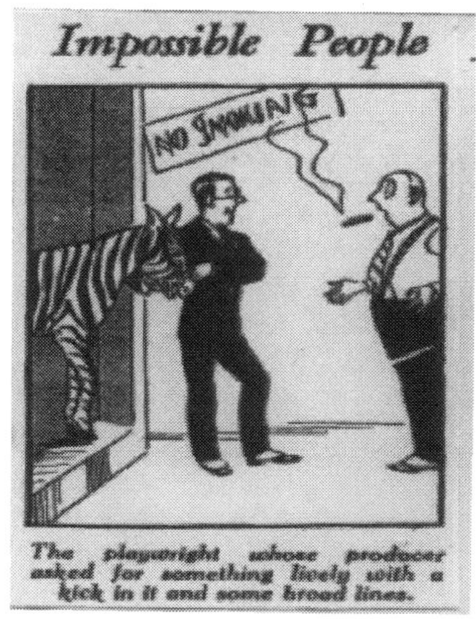

The playwright whose producer asked for something lively with a kick in it and some broad lines.

Tigers, that also have 'broad lines' and are 'lively' are, aptly, an Ambush or Streak. They are also an animal you would most definitely not want to 'stay in with' whether 'out on strike' or not.

Leopards, less deservedly, are a Leap or a Prowl, (perhaps they should also be a 'spot'), while Cheetahs are a Coalition'. (What else could they possibly be?) Ermines and Stoats are a Pack. Stoats are also, as is the sneaky Weasel, a Gang. Which begs the question, *"Are Weasels and Stoats weasely distinguishable because they are stoately different?"*

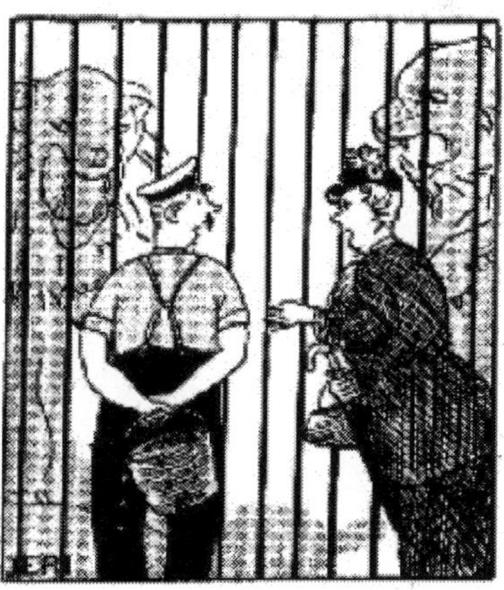

The Zoo attendant whose wife advised him to start a stay-in strike.

Which is definitely the case with Giraffes and Camels, that are so stoately different they are always weasily distinguishable.

Along with 'Caravan' Camels are a Flock and are thus more likely to be 'garaged' in a church, although JERI's next cartoon (that may get me a Fatwa), suggests they might be better off housed in mosques.

Impossible People

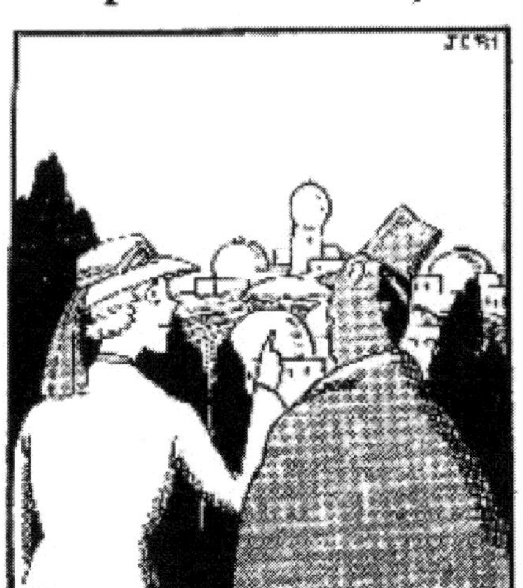

The visitor to the East who asked if all those domed buildings were camel garages.

As our mother composed it with no intention other than to amuse it would need, regardless of present sensitivities, someone severely lacking a sense of humour to attach any other interpretation to it.

No doubt there will be a few who do, to whom I would say that my mother could as easily have suggested that a visitor from the East might ask whether our English churches were giraffe garages as Giraffes, en masse, apart from being a Group or a Corps, are also, as in church, a Tower.

As are Flocks of birds that are also known as a Congregation – and are, by strange irony and a perfect paradox, frequently seen in churches, chapels, temples, tabernacles, synagogues and, of course, mosques.

As British streets don't 'teem' with giraffes my reader might accuse me of using an unfair comparison, but having worked in a few Far Easter countries I can assure them that streets in the East don't teem with camels either as I saw as few camels there as I have seen Giraffes here.

Though in fairness, our giraffes are in zoos while their camels are mostly free-range taxi's and carrier carts. Nevertheless, rather like the mink in the Grey& Shack cartoon, those camels I did meet with were 'nasty, vicious things'. Which, apparently, giraffes are not -

You'd require an extremely long scarf
If you happened to be a giraffe.
They get very hoarse
In the winter of course -
And a sore throat is no cause to laugh.

We could be forgiven for thinking that when nature made the camel and the giraffe she was 'Having a laugh'. Which, of course, was JERI's intention when she composed her cartoons.

Possibly even more evil-smelling and definitely no laughing matter are Rhinoceros that, when in heaps, have the fitting onomatopoeic word 'Crash'. Less evil-smelling are Jellyfish which have the equally fitting onomatopoeic word 'Smack'. Having frequently swum among shoals of them – Jellyfish not Rhinos – I know how apt that generic is.

Skunks, en masse, are a Surfeit - most would think that just one would be a surfeit. The Racoon is a Nursery or Gaze, while Kangaroos are Mobs or Troops, which are also monikers for a multitude of Monkeys - along with 'cartloads of'?

Despite the miles and miles of the Nile being full of Crocodiles, Bask and Float are the only generics for these scary creatures. Although 'splurge' might be a good word to use when they gather together to eat Gnus. Although maybe the risk of offending them is a risk too far.

You will find on the banks of the Nile
The haunts of the great crocodile,
He will welcome you in
With an innocent grin-
Which gives way to a satisfied smile.

But there's no risk with a Bloat of Hippopotamuses, as they 'live half asleep'. Consider the poor hippopotamus;

His life is unduly monotonous.
He lives half asleep,
At the edge of the deep -
And his face is as big as his bottom is.

Koalas are a Cling, Opossums are a Grin and Platypus are a Puddle. Probably due to there now being so few of them, Pandas have none, although Bamboo might be suitable.

Apes are a Shrewdness. (How shrewd is that?) Bears are a Sleuth or a Sloth. (How fitting!) Cranes are, oddly, a Herd, and, less oddly, Sedge and Siege Robins, being territorial, rarely 'collect' together so, despite being our national bird, have no collective name but when, in the bitter winter of 2010, five were sighted on one feeding tray, a journalist was spurred to ask for suggestions.

Mine were: Blaze, Regal, Romance, Royal, Ruby, Round, Retinue or, as they so rarely flock together, Rarity. While, due to their recent cullings, Badgers, along with Cete and Set, may also soon be a Rarity.

As will Bees, which are a Hive, Bije, Drift, Grist and, most well known, Swarm. The vast loss in recent years of these essential plant pollinators will eventually also make humans a rarity. Which, as the she eats the he after sex, should be Spiders, which nonetheless have two, Clutter and Cluster. Although in my experience they rarely, if ever, cluster.

Bee generics are also those for Locusts, Gnats and, strangely, Eels and, naturally Flies. Flyers that, en masse, are also Business and Cloud.

My own overall favourite is the wonderful Owl, which, as do many other birds, have the perfect generic, Parliament. If only a few of our human Parliamentarians were as wise!

There once were three owls in a wood,
Who always sang hymns when they could.
What the words were about,
One could never make out,
But one felt it was doing them good.

Now for an animal so rare they don't have a group name, not because there are so few of them but because it was only discovered, in Papua, New Guinea, at the end of 2011. At just 7.7 millimetres, it is not only the smallest frog, but the smallest of the world's sixty thousand vertebrates - creatures with a backbone. The largest, at twenty six metres, is the Blue Whale.

Large frogs are an Army or a Knot and their tadpoles are Froglets or Polliwogs, and we can be confident that they are not remotely concerned at being thought of as worthy oriental gentlemen. Toads are also a Knot, but not Toad of Toad Hall who is a 'Gentleman'.

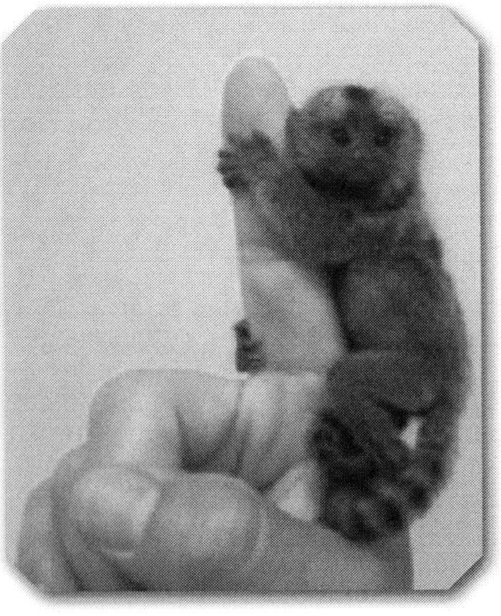

Then there are Buzzle Finger Monkeys. Dinky creatures with the generics; Pocket Monkeys or Tiny Lions. Native to the rain forests of Colombia, Bolivia, Brazil, Ecuador and Peru these minute mammals, the smallest in the world, are Pygmy Marmosets.

The following could be of assistance to my reader when choosing their next pet, as Zoologists rate animals in order of their intelligence as; Chimpanzee, Orang-Utan, Elephant, Gorilla, Dog, Beaver, Horse, Sea Lion, Bear, Cat.

As Cats know more than they let on they are probably intelligent enough to be at number one, but cannily prefer to stay at number ten rather than reveal what they don't want us to know what they do know. Although this low rating did give one cat suicidal thoughts:

A cat in despondency sighed,
And resolved to commit suicide.
She passed under the wheels
Of eight automobiles,
And after the ninth one she died.

As do dogs, cats have such a special place in the hearts and homes of those who love them they tend to rule both our homes and our hearts. They also, apparently, rule the world.

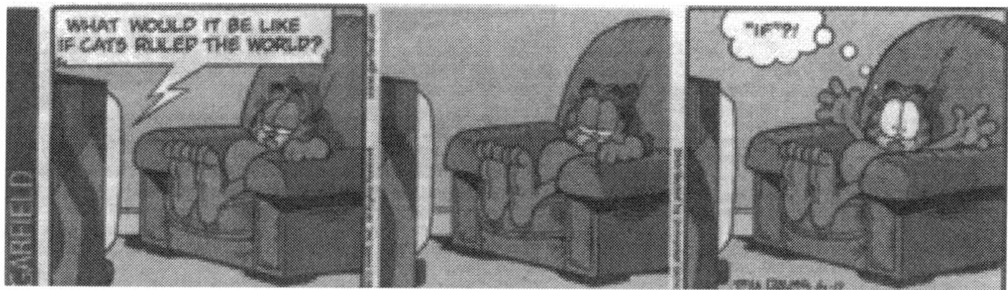

And sleep a lot while doing it -

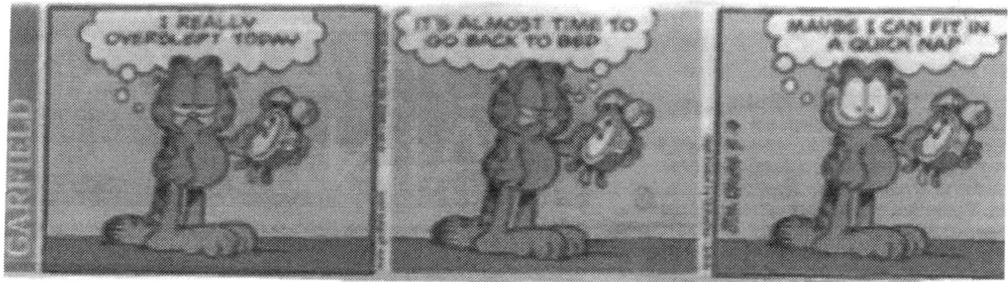

-as confirmed by both Garfield and my next poem

Sleep

In youth,
when the days
are never too long,
and the hours don't
slip away too soon.
When a week seems forever,
and Sundays start at noon,
To submit to sleep
seems sublime.

In mid age,
with so much work to be done,
between the rising
and the setting of the sun.
When thirty hours a day
would be a welcome boon.
To submit to sleep
seems a crime.

In old age,
when the hours
go ever more slow,
and there's little to do,
and nowhere to go.
While we wait for The Reaper,
who will come quite soon.
To submit to sleep seems divine

But cats who have
obviously been here before,
get it absolutely right.
They take time to eat,
to groom, to play
Then, not only do they sleep
through most of the night,
they sleep through most of the day.

Dogs, due to their bravery, intelligence and loyalty were chosen by humans to be their house companions. Cats, cleverly and craftily, chose to be the other natural house companion of humans and as such have become the muse of poets throughout the ages. A truth confirmed by the number of poems about felines that I include in Impossible People.

As with Marmite, people are rarely ambivalent about these very special animals and either adore or dislike them.

Or are slightly 'afeared' of them, as was W.H. Davies (1870 - 1940), who wrote the next poem which, in just eight lines, evocatively, describes the occasionally scary character of these, equally often, comical creatures called Cats.

Within the porch, across the way,
I see two eyes this night;
Two eyes that neither shut nor blink,
Searching my face with a green light.

But cats to me are strange, so strange,
I cannot sleep if one is near;
And though I'm sure I see those eyes,
I'm not sure a body's there.

Everyone in my family has a passion for cats and, as many have done, I could write a book about the foibles and antics of these clever creatures. Animals that, without harming their instinct to hunt, have 'contracted' to live with humans in preference to having to fend for themselves while retaining their independence.

As in; "Dogs come when they are called, cats send a message saying they will get back to you". A truth more succinctly expressed in this anonymous poem that was sent to the Daily Mail by Maureen Ellis of Scarborough, North Yorkshire and was published in their Peterborough column in October, 2011.

I wish I knew your trick of thought,
The perfect balance of your ways.
They seem an inspiration caught
From other laws in older days.

But there are cats and then there are CATS. The pricelessly funny book, 'The Holy Moly Rules of Modern Life', published by The Friday Project, tells us; *"Arriving anywhere with a pride of lions is guaranteed to draw attention to yourself. Unless you're in Africa."*

A country where we are likely to find that even rarer and much valued specimen, David Attenborough, a man who is in a class of his own when it comes to knowing all about wildlife and life in the wild.

Which wafts us to humans who, by heredity, nationality, profession and artistry, have an A to Z of generics far too long to list here so I will confine myself to just a few of the most important. The butcher, the baker, the candlestick maker and - of most value - artists, authors, cartoonists, playwrights, poets and My

Mama. Among the more torturous titles for weeks set aside for such things is: The Animal Protection Trust Awareness Week. Which, if he had known of it, would definitely have won the approval of President Abraham Lincoln as he said; *"I care not for a man's religion whose dog or cat are not the better for it."*

Mama was passionate about animals and was never without a cat or dog. They were also passionate about her, a passion that definitely led her to agree with the French novelist, Collette, who said; *"Our perfect friends never have fewer than four feet".*

Nor do they have bicycles; "The police called and told me my dog was chasing a man on a bike. I told them it couldn't be my dog because he doesn't have a bike."

Although, according to Irene MacLoad, he may be a bit wild.

I'm a lean dog, a keen dog, a wild dog, and lone;
I'm a rough dog, a tough dog, hunting on my own;
I'm a bad dog, a mad dog, teasing silly sheep;
I love to sit and bay the moon to keep fat souls from sleep.

While Mama would most certainly agree with W. Dayton Wedgefarth (now there's a name to conjure with), who wrote: *"If my dog is barred by the heavenly guard, we'll both brave the heat!"*

Due to both their intelligence and good looks, Alsatians, whether able to ride a bike or not, were Mama's preferred canine breed and I can never remember a time when she was not owned by one, whether they:

Had a low growl,
or a loud bark.
Were little or lean,
pale or dark.
Or dirty or clean.

She also believed in this anonymous couplet:

My sunshine doesn't come from the skies,
It comes from the love in my dog's eyes.

Which perhaps is why Douglas Mallock wrote and Mama believed:

Thorns may hurt you,
Men desert you,
Sunlight turn to fog,

But you are never,
Ever friendless,
If you have a dog.

Her first, Brunwolf, is with Mama in this sepia photograph taken in the twenties.

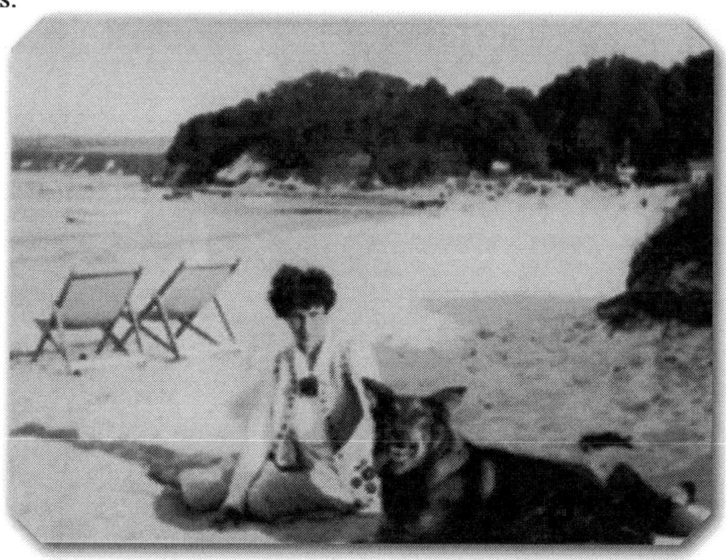

Of equal interest, it would seem that, in the close to a hundred years since this photograph was taken, deck chairs, unlike most things, have not changed their look in one iota, nor, it would seem, their usefulness.

An indication of how important Brunwolf was in our mother's life is that of the fifteen copper etched plates she made from her various artworks in a variety of mediums, fourteen depict towns or rural scenes in England and France while the fifteenth is of her precious dog.

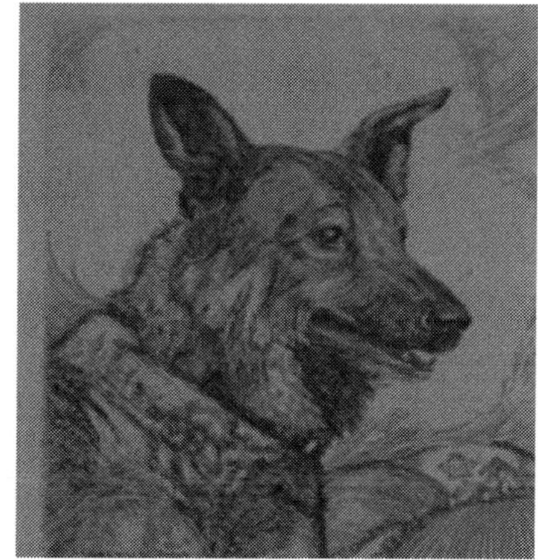

Another of her dogs was a beautiful, clever, calm Golden Retriever that was the only dog she ever owned that was not an Alsation, But as wonderful as Brunwolf, Krussa, and all of the other German Shepherds that, in later years and having gone our separate ways, owned and took care of us, none came close to the character and intelligence of Maximillian.

A superb Alsatian we called 'Dusky'.

Possibly due to his Diligence, Usefulness, Skills, Kindness and Youthful looks. To which must be added; Unswerving Loyalty.

Dusky lived with us, loved us and, above all, cared for us during our childhood and early teens. Years that, again, require a minor detour.

While both the 1920 and 1937 Firearms legislation restricted general ownership of guns, during the war this was largely ignored, as prior to the 1968, much stricter, Firearms Act, when the owning of guns became more heavily regulated, many homes housed a gun or pistol - or both. Thus, at that time, owning a firearm was considered no different from how people now feel about their mobile phones. They didn't feel secure without one - and we were no exception.

Dusky, a most gentle and even-tempered dog, had, we were told by our parents, been bred for military or police work but, due to his refusal to fight or catch criminals, he was, to our great good fortune, considered unsuitable for this pastime.

However, while he had balked at the duties required of him for police work, he had been well trained and if anyone, adult or child, picked up a gun, whether real or toy, he would immediately jump up and wrest it from their hand.

There was also no need for him to wear a collar. Not just due to his intelligence and obedience but because most people are so scared, or at the very least, wary, of Alsations, they won't go near them, whether they are collarless or not.

On our move to Sidmouth, a small seaside town wedged between two enormous hills known as Salcombe Hill and Pier Hill, we children would spend our days in separate groups of our different friends in different places. Within days, Dusky became well known by the local tradespeople, populace and police, as he would spend his days padding between the High Street, the two hills, The Ham and the promenade in order to ensure that none of us had been run over, swept out to sea, or fallen off a cliff.

Of the many poems our mother wrote about her various animals, I consider this, unquestionably, to be her best. Being sufficiently erudite to be able to compose such a magnificent, arrhythmic poem is, for me, unimaginable.

For Maximillian - Known as Dusky.

With Chaucer's Prioress let us 'weep full sore',
For vanished faith and trust, and virtues many more.
Argos, who died of joy at Odysseus' returning,
Herrick's Troy, who deserved 'a million tears',

Cowper's Beau, who 'killed birds not time',
Lupa, who in battle never left the Douglas' side.
Burn's Luath, 'a gash and faithful tyke'
Named for the mighty hound of legendary Cuchullan.

Bran of the hero Finn, who wept but twice only, and once for him.
Gerlet who from the wolf, Llewellyn's son did save.
Mary Stewart's broken-hearted pet who defied her executioners.
Liz Browning's kind and gentle Flush.

Ruskin's Dash, 'alert and always gay',
Robert Southey's Phyllis, who was 'of infinite goodness',
Byron's Boatswain, with all the virtues of mankind without the vices.
Geist, Matthew Arnold's 'dearest friend'.

World famous Rin-Tin-Tin, born in a trench and buried with his toys.
Douvalle's Satan, who, though wounded, saved the Verdun day.
The actress Lassie, whom all children loved.
And many millions more whose names you will recall.

But I remember one who lived and died lang syne,
Worthy to lead this list, Maximillian mine,
Maximillian mine who was 'nonesuch' of them all.

Having such a deep love of dogs, Mama could often be heard to say; *"If there is no heaven for dogs, then I want to go where they go when I die."* Anna Hempstead Branch felt the same as she wrote; *"If there is no God for thee, then there is no God for me."* Which of course 'Only God knows' or 'God only knows'. A song by the Beach Boys, but perhaps more apt had it been sung by The Pet Shop Boys.

As would the next, superb, anonymous quatrain:

I explained it to St. Peter, I'd rather stay here, outside the pearly gate.
I won't be a nuisance, I won't even bark, I'll be very patient and wait,
I'll be here, chewing on a celestial bone, no matter how long you may be.
I'd miss you so much if I went in alone, as it wouldn't be heaven for me.

Thus I would like think that my mother is now walking in Dog Heaven with all of the dogs she loved and who loved her; Brunwolf, Dusky, Dutch, Prince, Satan, Hecate and her last Alsatian, Echo, together with all the heroic dogs she included in her Maximillian poem.

So in my belief that He, (whose name is a neat anagram of dog), loves dogs almost as much as my mother did.

GOD

You mayn't believe in God - so strange yet true – but there's no doubt he believes in you.

Having allied God with animals, I am as perplexed as the poet U.A. Fanthorpe who in her, thought provoking, poem, for which she gave me permission to include here, asks why cats were not mentioned as being among the array of animals in the stable at the birth of Jesus.

Although it has been suggested, and is possibly true, that a kitten crawled under the shawl in which he was wrapped. But possibly not true, as cats who live in stables are usually feral and won't go near anyone, however sacred.

Cat In The Manger

In the story, I'm not there.
Ox and ass, arranged at prayer;
But me? Nowhere.

Anti-cat evangelists,
How could you have missed
Such an obvious and able
Occupant of any stable?

Matthew, Mark,
Luke and John,
Who got it wrong?
Who left out the cat?

Who excluded mouse and rat?
The harmless necessary cat.
Who snuggled in with the holy pair?
Me, and my purr.

Remember that
Wherever He went
In this great affair,
I was there.

Despite a 2016 media debate about whether cats should be kept at home or let out to roam about, Miss Fanthorpe's poem highlights a glaring omission for, as my next poem confirms, cats ARE everywhere - even more so, and more of them, in stables. So if we really are 'All Gods Children' He must have had a an excellent sense of humour or He wouldn't have given us cats - or ducks - or the ability to laugh at jokes. Such as this from Chuck Welch of Houston, Texas, that was published in the Daily Mail's Peterborough column:

A pastor said to his congregation, *"Next Sunday I will be preaching on the subject of lying and, in preparation I would like you all to read chapter seventeen of the Gospel of Mark."* The following Sunday the vicar asked his congregation how many of them had read chapter seventeen of Mark, and many hands went up. *"Ah,"* said the vicar; *"You are the those to whom I will direct my sermon, as Mark has only sixteen chapters."*

Had he wished to endear himself to his flock, rather than antagonise them he may have been wise to ask, as Arthur Wellesley suggests; What they would like his sermon to be about, to which the answer would probably be: *'About ten minutes.'* Because, as H.S. Taylor avers, *"Like a woman's dress, a sermon ought to be long enough to cover the subject but sufficiently short to arouse attention."*

Time, (whether allied to God, Satan or sermons), is, paradoxically, both infinite and finite. Although most mothers would consider putting only 24 hours in a day is a joke, as in; *"Please God grant me the serenity to accept the things I cannot change. The courage to change the things I can, and twenty eight hours a day in which to do it."*

Mama, (who needed 48 hours), rarely put religion, and never God, in her cartoons. Nor did she mention Mohammed or Allah, or any other deity for that matter, perhaps because she could not think of them as Impossible People. But, as confirmed by my next poem, cats are Impossible Animals.

Cats Are Everywhere

Capricious and crazy,
contented and lazy,
cats are everywhere.
They will catch you on a stair;
or anywhere, you least expect,
with little thought, less care.

Having no interest in it,
they will always choose to sit
exactly on the bit of news you reading.
Or will make a nest in your best hat,
Leaving it quite flat and fit
only for the bin.

Will purr in places where they aren't,
and can't, be reached.
Take pride to hide in your favourite chair,
where they clean and preen themselves,
or merely gloat, leaving their hair
to cling to your coat.

Unaware of any danger darkness
might bring, their seeing sight
can let them nimbly spring
without the use of wing,
or other means of flight,
to the highest height.

Their lithe limbs, carelessly
and casually tangled in play,
or tidily tucked away,
deep, deep in sleep by day,
unwind to glide and slide,
taught and hawser tight by night

They hunt with skill their pray to kill.
Mice and mole, shrew and vole.
Then in the dawns first light,
will bring to your unmade bed,
their tiny, shiny silken dead,
in homage for the food they're fed.

While Mama adored animals, she was not a follower of any particular religion, but, as do most people, she greatly admired the myriad of glorious abbeys, cathedrals, chapels and churches that are available, world-wide, to worshippers and non-believers of all nationalities and sects, who take great pleasure in visiting these hallowed halls of history.

Hallowed halls of such magnificence and beauty it is impossible to imagine how they were conceived by their architects - or built.

It is also almost impossible to make a distinction between them for splendour. Some of the most magnificent are London's St Paul's Cathedral and Westminster Abbey. Rome's St Peters, Madrid's Almunda, the Notre Dame and Sacre Coeur in Paris while the one with the most glorious exterior is the Basilica di San Marco in Venice.

Two others that, for me, are of equal splendour are the Norfolk Cathedrals of Ely and Norwich and, as an artist, the one our mother most admired was the Sistine Chapel of the Vatican with its incredible painted ceiling that took Michelangelo four years to complete.

Almost as incredible is a painting in the tiny English Martyrs Catholic church in Goring, West Sussex, where - often working at night by candlelight – Gary Bevans, a sign writer, spent five and half years copying the ceiling of the Sistine Chapel.

Although thirty feet nearer the ground and 1,500 square feet smaller, it is the only full copy in the world, which has led to this tiny English church being one of the most visited.

There are so many clever witticisms about religion, one of the most amusing being Ronnie Shakes; *"I fear one day I will meet God and he will sneeze and I won't know what to say to him."* Another is; *'In God we trust. All others must pay cash.'* Which perhaps was why Woody Allen said; *"If only God would give me some clear sign! Like making a large deposit in my name in a Swiss bank."*

Strangely I did once have a deposit in a Swiss bank which did make me, if not a lot of money, certainly a little more than it should have done. During the two years I worked in Geneva my salary was paid, each month, from America, but on having to relocate to Paris, I went to my bank to clear my account. The young cashier, who had taken a shine to me, told me that my monthly credit had not arrived but as it always had, I could have it in advance.

On my arrival in Paris a few weeks later I found that it had been paid into my account there, thus giving me twice my usual monthly salary. While I took pleasure from this bonus I was a little concerned for the Swiss teller who had given me the money when it was not there to give.

Now, at a distance in both time and space, I now rarely worry about what befell my teller and look back on it as the best banking coup I will ever enjoy and which, if not 'music to my ears' was certainly music to my eyes.

Some of the best music we will ever enjoy is that heard in cathedrals and churches that have choirs that, we can be reasonably confident, also have trebles -

Impossible People

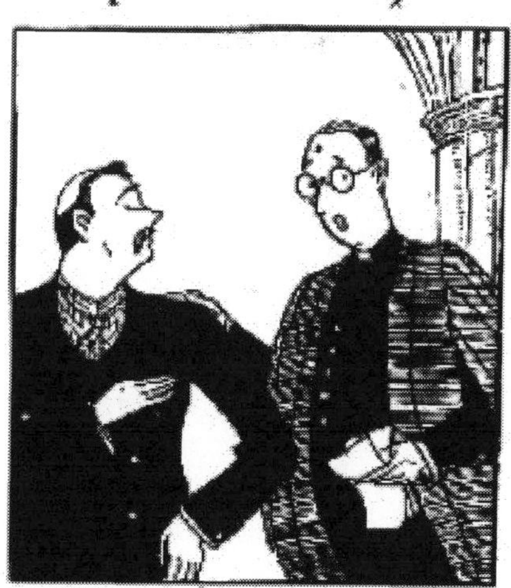

The verger who said he never studied the racing news when the choir-master asked him if he knew of a good treble.

I wrote the next poem following my first visit to Chartres. It is on a vast subject into which I would not normally stray but, on reading it, Simon persuaded me to enter it for a competition where it won first prize. A prize that, while not as large as the subject, was a sizable sum of money.

Chartres Cathedral

Every aspect of you
is beyond imagination,
beyond configuration
of mortal hand or eye.

You are monumental
and magnificent,
from your portalled,
powerful, battlements,
to your rising spires
and pinnacles, soaring
high into the sky.

Myriad and marvelous
is your brilliant fenestration,
a cornucopia of colour,
that lifts the heart,
and makes the spirit fly.

Wonderfully and widely
your walls, that
surround us so securely,
seem yet more wondrous
in their immensity.

In silent contemplation,
in contemplative awe,
your faithful congregation,
follow in the footsteps,
of those who've gone before.

In granite and in marble,
parapet and pilaster
are fashioned to perfection,
that is rarely ever,
elsewhere to be seen.

They walk your pathways,
tread your pavings,
those solid firm foundations,
made more solid
by their strength,
and density.

There is not a
centimeter of you
that is not remotely perfect,
or would the work
of genius demean.

A strength that lends
a new dimension,
gives each private prayer
new meaning,
brings to each a new,
divine, intensity.

In architecture glorious,
and inspiration Gothic
you are man's sublime memorial
to an unimagined dream.

And as you tower above us,
on your plateau placed before us,
mighty and majestic,
stately and stupendous,
and silently serene.

We know that time
will pass you and timelessly
you will stand there,
to ever reign supreme.

One of the most pleasing Americans I have had the good fortune to know and whose company I enjoyed hugely was Ivis, the mother of my friend Leonore. In 2014 Ivis went, happily, to meet her Maker. I write 'happily' because, although we will never know how true until we join them, Leonore and I are both convinced Ivis had a special deal going on with The Man Upstairs.

While we may be right about the deal it is possible we are not about the gender. A supposition confirmed by my next anecdote. My public house in West London was in an area with a large Irish population. This meant that we were no strangers to slightly merry customers who were always politely asked to leave if they were deemed to be beyond their 'serve by' time.

One day a gentleman came into the pub who had obviously imbibed more than his brain - or legs - could cope with, making the word 'gentleman' somewhat of a misnomer. He was not a regular and my manager, Bob, in his impeccable Public School manner, told the drunk that he was not welcome, at which the man shouted – in the time worn phrase of all drunks (and a frequently used oxymoron); *"Ooh tha 'ell d'ja think u are, God?" "No"*. said Bob, *"She's down at the hairdressers and you would be wise to leave before she gets back."*

Confirmed by: *'When God made man she was only joking.'*

So maybe God really does like women better than men. Or is it that women like God better than men? (My reader may take that whichever way they prefer.) Perhaps this is due to the fact that women really are 'all seeing' as in: 'God sees all but the neighbours miss nothing.' and: 'A Scotswoman was told by her neighbour; *"Hoots, Janet, ye'd think there wis naebody good enough for heaven but yersel' and the meenister!"* To which Janet said, *"Ay, and sometimes ah haev verra grave doots aboot the meenister."*

So Janet would have no doubts about which of these next two groups are unfit for heaven: *'What is the difference between people who pray in church and those who pray in casinos? The ones in casinos are serious.'*

To which my Catholic friend Jenny would say; *"Going to church doesn't make you a Christian any more than going to a garage makes you a mechanic."* Probably in the same way that people who frequently frequent casinos are not all good at poker, and the constant cleaning of a house doesn't get rid of the dust.

Which, as JERI's next cartoon affirms, is what all men and women will, in time, become.

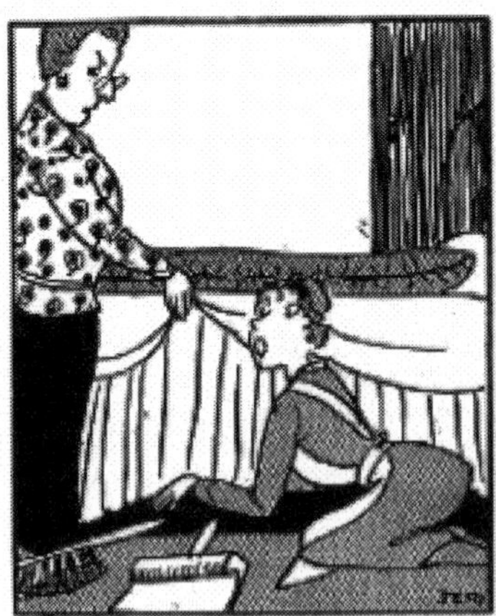

The woman who said if man was made of dust there would soon be one under the spare bed.

An assumption that, as we no longer have maids at our beck and call, could now apply to many, if not most, spare beds - and more than a few that are in constant use.

In a letter published in the Daily Mail, Jim Price from Luton in Bedfordshire asks; *"What gives atheists the right to be sanctimonious?"* While the author and politician, John Buchan, said; *"An atheist is a man who has no invisible means of support."* From which we must presume that all women do whether they are a believer or non believer.

All of which ties in nicely with *"For those who believe, no explanation is necessary. For those who don't, no explanation will suffice."*

But as Piet Hein so succinctly wrote.

Nothing is Indispensable

The Universe may
be as great as they say,
But if didn't exist
it wouldn't be missed.

Born into a veritable maelstrom of religious beliefs; Baptist, Church of England, Methodist, Jewish, Protestant. And disbeliefs; Agnostic, Atheism and, no doubt if we go back far enough, cannibalism, paganism and witchcraft, my siblings and I belong to the religion the majority of English people now appear to adhere to. That of Non-Secular, Non-Denominational Believer.

Thus we have an enviable tolerance of all other religions. A tolerance that only wavers on learning that a Jehovah Witness would prefer to die than have a blood transfusion.

My friend Tina told me that another of her friends, Jill, had a grandmother with the wonderful name, Hannah Rose Winter, who, following a doorstep conversation with a Jehovah's Witness said; *"These Jovial Witnesses always seem so miserable, so finding Jesus obviously hasn't made them happy. They need to laugh a little and lighten up their lives."*

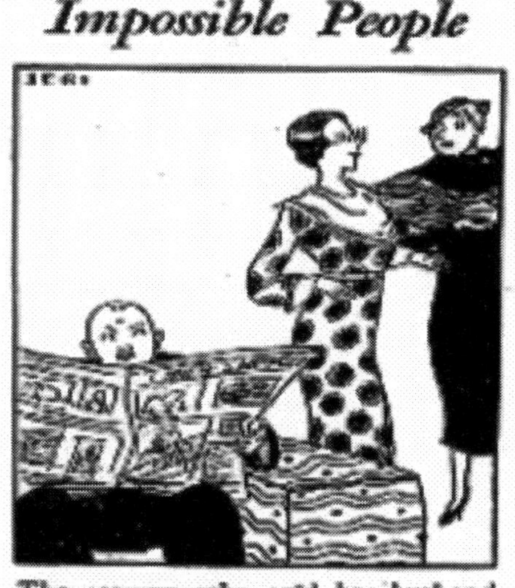

The woman who said her husband was the light of her life and she did not allow him to go out.

But what is difficult to understand is the inability of all the adherents of these many different religions to understand each other, and why they so rarely bring any amusement into their musings. marvelously illustrated by the next true tale that sits so well with JERI's previous cartoon.

One of our father's brother's, Nathaniel, whose religion was knavery, had a very religious wife, Ruth - a devoutly committed Catholic, devoutly committed to birth control. With the substantial way of life that knavery often brings, she had ambitions to place an illuminated cross above the imposing front door of their large, rambling Victorian house. A plan that, to the great relief of our uncle, was thwarted by the local planning office.

A refusal that possibly had something to do with the fact that their house, with an irony totally lost on our aunt and uncle, had once been an Anglican vicarage. An anecdote that might have led Piet Hein to compose this next Grook:

A Diplomatic Compromise

A fellow I know can get mountains to move,
and all opposition appeases;
He preaches what God cannot help but approve,
and does what the devil he pleases.

G. K. Chesterton said; *"When people stop believing in God they don't believe in nothing they believe in anything."* John Letts, in his delightful, 'Little Treasury of Limericks, Fair and Foul', includes, under the heading, 'A Convocation of Curates', many neat, thought-provoking odes. Odes our Mother would often quote, one of which was prefaced with: 'In ideology it is always thought correct to start at the top.'

So starting at the top, I came across this widely quoted verse by Ronald Knox on the philosophical theory that things only exist when seen – or observed?

There once was a man who said, God
Must find it exceedingly odd,
If he finds that this tree
Continues to be
When there's no one about in the Quad.

Which, writes Mr. Letts, produced this anonymous, inspired reply.

Dear Sir, Your astonishment's odd,
I am always about in the Quad;
And that's why this tree
Will continue to be.
Since observed by, Yours faithfully, God.

Despite various media discussions concerning its possible demise due to lack of use, another thing we must hope 'will continue to be' is the large book, The Bible.

Another is the tiny book, 'Children's Letters to God', compiled by Stuart Hample and Eric Marshall, with illustrations by Tom Bloom, that includes these gems:

Dear God,
Are you really invisible or is that just a trick? Lucy

How come you did all those miracles in the old days and don't do any now? Seymour

I like the Lord's prayer best of all. Did you have to write it a lot or did you get it right first time? I have to write everything I ever write over again. Lois.

And,

I love you because you give us what we need to live. But I wish you would tell me why you made it so we have to die. Daniel

So, before I do, I include a few more Dear God letters that are -

Pragmatic:	I am English. What are you? Robert.
Curious:	How did you know you were God? Charlene
Practical:	Its great you always get the stars in the right places. Jeff
Inquisitive:	What does begat mean? Nobody will tell me. Love Alison.
Complimentary:	I think the stapler is one of your greatest inventions. Ruth M
Realistic:	I read your book and I like it. Where did you get your ideas? John
Amusing:	Did you mean giraffes to look like that or was it an accident? Norma
Perspicacious:	Why is Sunday School on Sunday. I thought it was your day of rest. Tom
Critical:	Why don't you keep the sun out at night when we need it the most. Barbara
Challenging:	Did you really mean do unto others as they do unto you, because if you did then I'm going to fix my brother. Darla

All of which are so much better when read from the book as they are reproduced as these children have written them. Children who take my reader to another Impossible Child -

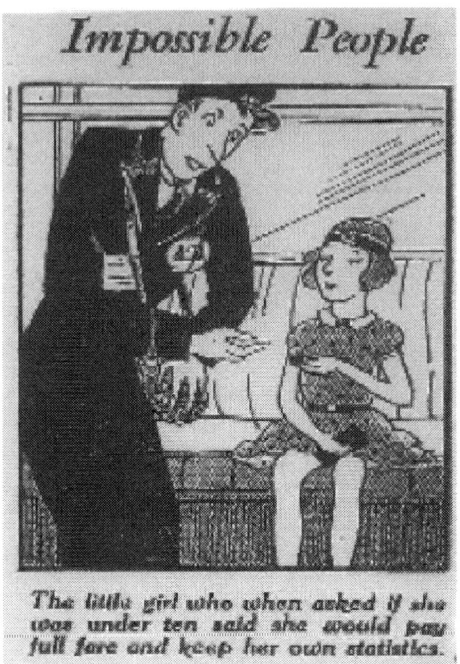

The little girl who when asked if she was under ten said she would pay full fare and keep her own statistics.

Which takes us from one clever small girl to a not so clever small boy:

I am a little boy who has but a little wit,
And the longer I shall live, no more shall I get;
Nor shall I do so until the day that I shall die,
For as I grow older, the greater the fool am I.

IT TAKES ALL SORTS

THE POOR

The respected economist, Peter Bauer, once said: "Aid is an excellent method of transferring money from poor people in rich countries to rich people in poor countries."

What he didn't say is that, while aid from poor people in rich countries doesn't make them poorer, it rarely makes the poor in poor countries richer, but often makes, not only the rich in poor countries richer, but also the rich in rich countries richer.

The old saw; 'Rags to riches in three generations' is undoubtedly an abbreviated version of this anonymous, 18th century homily: Rags make paper,

paper makes money, money makes banks, banks make loans, loans make beggars, beggars make rags.

Which may lead beggars to ask, *"God grant me the serenity to accept the things I cannot change, the courage to accept the things I can, and the money to not really care either way."* Which, no doubt, led to the original: *'Early to bed, early to rise makes a man healthy, wealthy and wise. Which has now morphed into: Early to bed, early to rise, until you make enough money to do otherwise.'*

John Kingsley said; *"Whether you are rich or poor, it's nice to have money."* What I say is; *"if you are rich you not only have to worry about how to use it, but also how you might lose it. If you are poor you only have to worry about how to get it."*

A dilemma neatly highlighted by this next Impossible Young Man's view of how he hopes to manage his own lack of money -

For, as Finley Peter Dunne so presciently said; "One of the strangest things about life is that the poor, who need money the most, are the very ones that never have it."

So, on a lighter note (which some may think a little too light), I include this next Yiddish homily: 'If the rich could pay the poor to die for them, the poor could make a wonderful living.'

Which also applies to the -

Impossible People

The young man who was paid on Thursday and "broke" on Saturday, and advertised to exchange small loans with a man who was paid on Saturday and "broke" on Thursday.

THE PROFLIGATE

Despite having put 'The Poor' before 'The Profligate', profligacy usually precedes penury, as those who are impecunious don't have much chance - or small change - to be profligate.

Cicero wrote in his Philippic: *'Male parta, male dilabuntur,'* Which, in English, is the much wordier; *'That which is dishonourably obtained is dishonourably squandered.'*

Impossible People

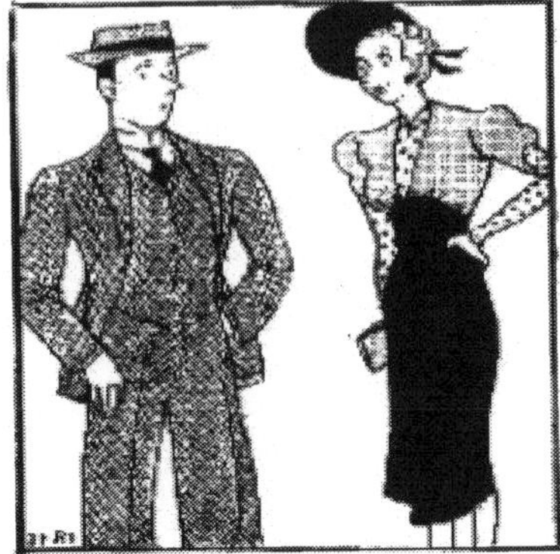

The young man who said it was not his fault he got into debt; it was all owing to other people.

Which, perhaps, could be directed at politicians and bankers who, not having learned the lessons of previous recessions, continue their headlong disastrous

and dangerous dives into deep and deadly depressions, (much as this writer does into alliterations), but then they are not using their own money.

Or, perhaps, they keep a copy of this Piet Hein Grook in their top pockets?

Budgeting : The First Law

If you want to know
where your money went,
you must spend it quickly,
before it's spent.

Which allows for inclusion of my plagiarism of another anonymous rhyme -

There are several reasons for spending your money,
And one has just entered my head,
If you don't spend your money when you are living,
How can you spend it when you are dead.

Which applies to everyone, including the -

THE MEEK

While Sonya and Nicola inherited the essential good luck of both our maternal and paternal grandmothers, Sasha and I (the youngest and the eldest), have always been a little short of this benefit.

Thus, she and I are occasionally prone to wonder, *"If the meek and - by inference - the weak will truly inherit the earth, we would like to know which*

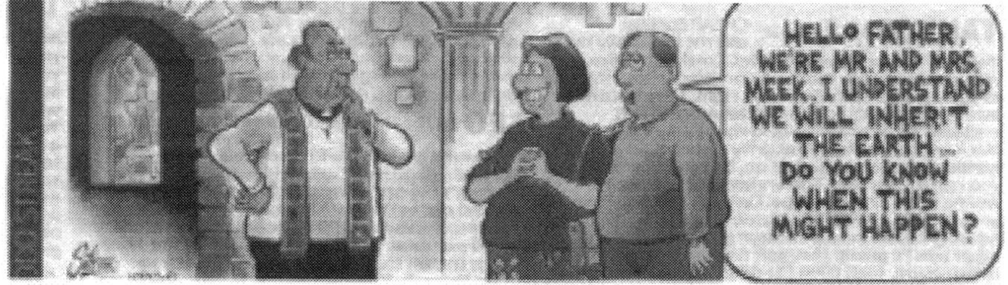

week this might be? For, having been quite patient - as the meek tend to be – we are now running out of time!"
Or, as Piet Hein suggests, are we all:

Out of Time

My old clock used to tell the time
and subdivide diurnity,
but now it's lost both hands and chime
and only tells eternity.

Which applies a great deal more to -

THE OLD

As with all things there are innumerable sayings and quips about this eventual, inevitable and often painful, happening. One of the best is from Shel Siverstien, but as he is Jewish it would be wouldn't it! He averred that; *"Many unpleasant things in life are preventable but old age is not one of them – unless you stop it in its tracks by dying young."*

The Little Boy and the Old Man

Said the little boy, *"Sometimes I drop my spoon."* Said the old man, *"I do that too."* Said the little boy, *"I often cry."* The old man nodded, *"So do I."* The little boy whispered, *"I wet my pants." "I do that too,"* laughed the little old man. *"But worst of all,"* said the boy, *"it seems Grown-ups don't pay attention to me."* He then felt the warmth of a wrinkled hand. *"Nor do they pay any attention to me,"* said the little old man.

One of the most quoted is Jules Renard's; *"It's not how old you are, it's how you are old."* But the best is from 'Children's Letters to God'.

Dear God, Instead of letting people die and having to make new ones why don't you just keep the old ones you've got now? Jane.

To which God may have replied; *"Because I have to try and make the money go round."*

To which, many might say, why then does He keep giving it to The Rich Perhaps because, as my friend Tina can often be heard to say; *"To those that have shall be given even more."*

It is also said that: *"Ignorance is degrading only when found in the company of riches."*

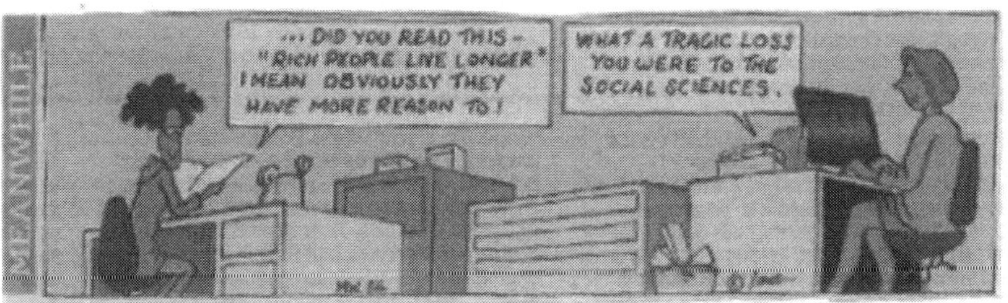

Which fits well with the assumption that; *"Money is not everything. Someone with nine million pounds can be just as happy as someone with ten million pounds."*

While, born free, now I'm expensive, fits well with Alan Alda's, *"It isn't necessary to be rich and famous to be happy it's only necessary to be rich."*

And all three fit well with this next anecdote: While shopping in Harrods a woman said to her friend, *"My dear, you do seem to spend a great deal of money!"* To which she replied, *"That, my dear, is because I have never found any other useful purpose for it."*

Perhaps she hoped to become one of those to whom John Paul Getty alluded in his assumption that: *"If you owe the bank a hundred pounds, that's your problem. If you owe the bank a hundred million pounds, that's the bank's problem."*

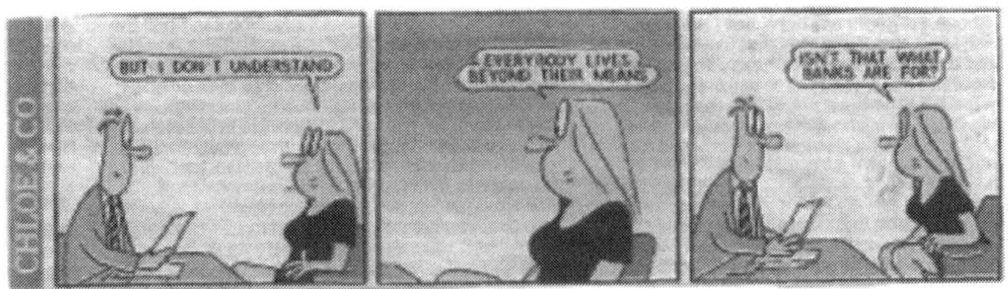

Although if, as E.W. Howe maintains: *"No man's credit is as good as his money."* few will ever be in that enviable position.

Except, of course The Rich for as F. Scott Fitzgerald writes in the Great Gatsby: *'The rich are different from you and me.'* It is also said, *"The rich are different because they never have to turn right when boarding an aeroplane."* (Unless of course they own their own when they can turn any way they wish.)

However, despite this assertion made by Fitzgerald's friend, Ernest Hemingway; *"That's because they have more money"*, what I say is; *"The Rich are different not because they never have to turn right on a plane, but because they have made all the right moves."*

It is also a 'difference' illustrated more subtly by a marvelous sentence in a 19th century book on gardening that my sister, Nicola, has in her library. With the artless insouciance only available to the exceptionally wealthy, the writer advises her readers; *"However small your garden, you should always leave at least an acre for trees."*

But the finest words on universal wealth came from one of the finest brains, that of Gandhi when he said; *"There is enough in this world for everyone's need, but not enough for everyone's greed."*

"I know you believe you understood what you think I said, but I'm not sure you realise that what you thought I said was not what I meant." is a quotation that is attributed to both Prince Phillip and U.S. State Department Spokesman, Robert McCloskey. It is possible that both gentlemen like to quote quotes and, having read it, said it.

But, did Prince Phillip nick it from Mr. McCloskey or did McCloskey nick it from Prince Phillip. Or were both statements, as Mr. Silver suggests, 'Original Thought'?

Yet again, as does Richard Littlejohn, *"I only ask the question."* For as Hanlon says; *"Never attribute to malice what can be attributed to stupidity"*.

But knowing neither His Highness nor Mr. McCloskey personally, it would be - malicious and stupid of me to attribute malice or stupidity to either of them.

Impossible People

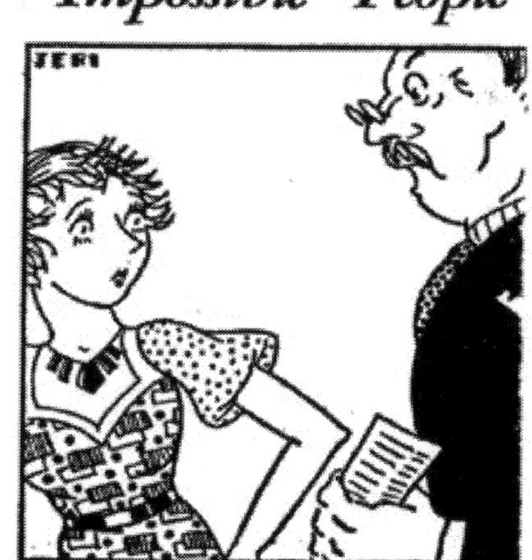

The girl who thought untold wealth was the money father didn't put on his income-tax return.

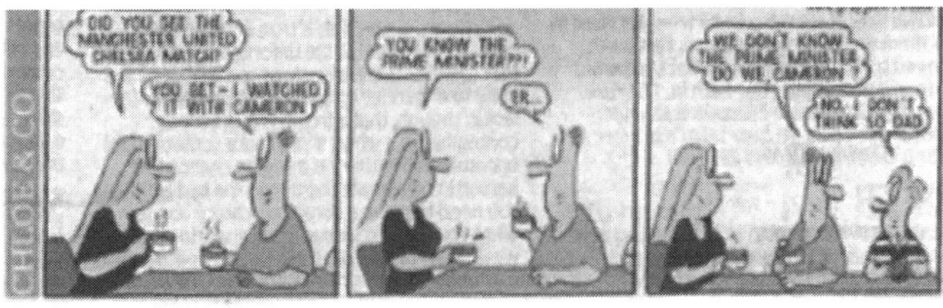

Which takes us to –

THE FOOLISH AND THE WISE AND THE WISE AND THE FOOLISH

Undoubtedly 'stupidity' was the foundation for this, oft used saw: *"A fool and his money are soon parted"*. Which begs the question; *"How did he get it in the first place?"*

Being a female, it is very pleasing that there is no equivocation about the sex of those who are soon parted from their money. Or (in another apt oxymoron), is that because, at the time this homily was first coined, women rarely enjoyed money of their own? Or were deemed to have much common sense -

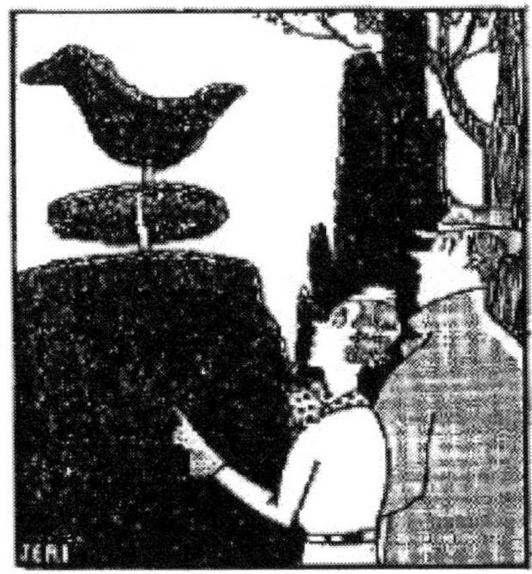

The girl who exclaimed, "Isn't nature wonderful!"

An assumption that apparently applies not only to topiary but also to elephants as confirmed by JERI's next cartoon. It is also a cartoon that fits well with this next very sensible, frequently quoted quote; *"It is better to keep your mouth shut and be thought a fool than to open it and remove all doubt."*

As in; During a lecture on ecology the speaker told his audience that every year over 5,500 camels are used to make paintbrushes. To which a woman in the audience said; "Isn't it wonderful what they can teach animals to do nowadays?"

A fascinating fact is that although elephants are the largest and thus the heaviest mammals on earth, their bio-mass weight is three million tons as opposed to the biomass weight of ants which is thirty three million tons. What is equally fascinating is how they work this stuff out - or even think of doing it.

A programme about Elephants tells us that, in order to prevent ivory hunters

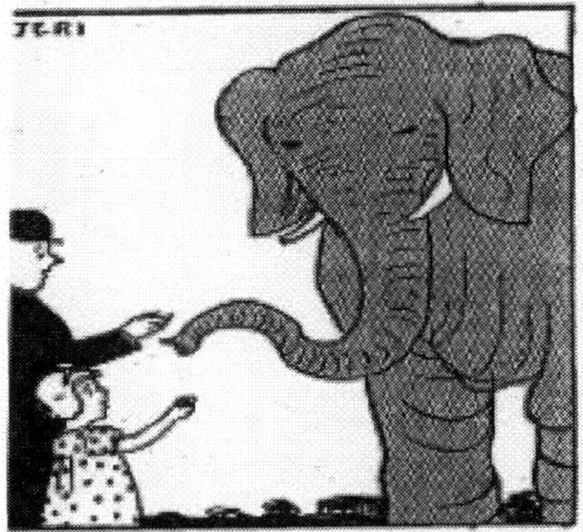

from digging up their graves, dead elephants are not buried with their tusks. While it is fascinating to learn that when they die these wonderful animals now have 'proper' burials, we are not told what is done with their tusks when they do.

The innocent and marvelous assumption of JERI's next Impossible Little Girl is not only endearing, it is excellent confirmation that elephants are greatly, in both senses of the word, more wonderful than anything that can be made from their tusks. Particularly billiard balls -

It has been suggested that, as ivory is one of nature's finest materials and dead elephants no longer need them, there is no good reason not to make, under strict licence, beautiful and useful objects from the tusks of elephants that die from old age or natural causes.

However, (if we believe everything we see on television), the world-wide ban on the production and sale of ivory artifacts, unless they have a verifiable provenance prior to the ban, has led to little reduction in the killing of these truly glorious animals.

So it may be a good idea to allow safari wardens to be permitted to impale all ivory poachers on the tusks of the elephants they kill - because -

The elephant never forgets:
Neither messages, shopping or debts,
He can take in his trunk
A whole load of junk -
And the small ones make fabulous pets.

It has been suggested that man's more despicable activities and practices should be erased from History, but to deny the atrocities of ivory traders would be as dangerous as to deny the Holocaust, the Slave Trade or to ban all early depictions of people smoking.

If all bad practice is wiped from history's slate, it will, eventually, be forgotten and, with no memory of its vileness, will recur. For while it is said that a little knowledge is a dangerous thing, no knowledge is even more dangerous because, as Piet Hein writes:

Wisdom is the booby prize,
Given when you've been unwise.

INVENTIONS AND FAME

In today's media fest and fascination with the merely mediocre and blatantly banal, there is nothing more true than this anonymous saying: *"Some people obtain fame and others deserve it."*

My second husband's father, Ron Jessiman, was a true 'Gentleman'. A man of much patience and even greater courtesy, he was often heard to say, *"If all the worries in the world were placed in a great big pile, most of us would be content to take our own."*

A homily that would fit well in my section on 'The Worried' but is in 'Inventions' as Ron, who worked within the pharmaceutical industry, to his great credit and the even greater benefit of many, was one of the chemists instrumental in the development of Cold Dialysis that enabled those waiting for renal transplants to have Dialysis in their own homes.

Unlike JERI's next Impossible 'couple', I didn't 'intend' to marry three times - but mention of my second father-in-law's claim to fame made me realise that my three husbands have all had relations who have made significant contributions to humanity.

Impossible People

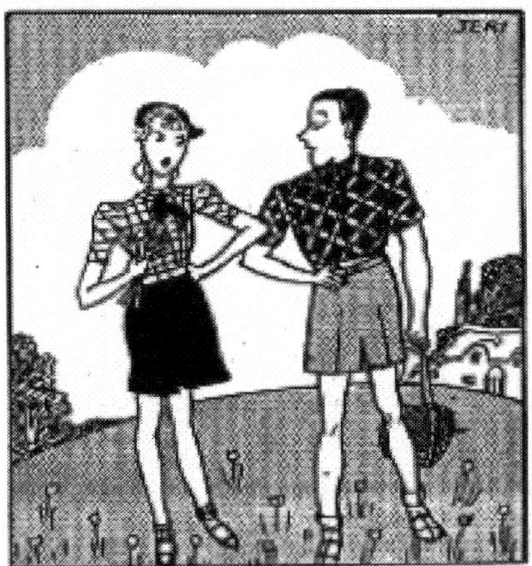

The girl who asked how many times he intended to marry when her friend said that a great many women would be unhappy when he married.

Or, in the case of my first husband Terry, entertainment, as his mother was related to the acclaimed Chipperfield Circus family.

Most magnanimous was David Robinson, a cousin of Muriel, my much loved third mother-in-law.

Having made a considerable fortune from his Robinson Rentals Company, not only did he endow the last of the Cambridge University colleges, Robinson College, he also, in memory of his much loved wife, Rosie, endowed the famous Rosie Maternity Unit of the renowned Cambridge

hospital, Addenbrooks. Would these three associations connected to me merely by marriage, be considered merely accidental?
Or merely coincidental -

COINCIDENCES

Most people will think that what I am about to write on this subject is ridiculous and, as I tend to view life prosaically, I would agree. Or perhaps, not!

Frequently unable to find an apt adjunct to a piece of text or cartoon within days or even hours, and often from the most unlikely source, a suitable item would be brought to my attention. It reached the point where I would no longer 'look' for the right thing as I could be confident it would 'arrive'. Or was I being guided to them by my mother? Which perhaps is why most of them involve my family. As does this next anecdote.

Prior to completion of our purchase of Tasburgh Hall in Norfolk where, with Mama,we four sisters and our husbands planned to live together, albeit in separate areas, as a temporary measure we popped Mama into a care home. Fortunately this was well before the present, absurdly stringent, draconian regulations that now govern care home accommodation. Regulations that, due to reams of red tape, fear of litigation and subsequent loss of revenue, resulted in the closure of most of these small, well run, 'home from home' comfortable care homes.

Much to our own and Mama's pleasure Susan and David Winter, the very caring owners of this care home, said she may have her own pictures. They also, to her even greater pleasure, owned a 'free range' cat and dog, both of which immediately 'adopted' our mother.

During one of our daily visits, another 'guest' of the Winter's invited us into his room to see a picture that, he told us, he had bought from a studio in Elm Hill in Norwich, and was the only thing he always brought with him on his regular stays at the home when his live-in carer took her holidays.

On seeing it we were delighted to tell him that, not only did we know the artist but he also knew her as they often dined together. His pleasure on learning our mother was the artist equalled her own when she learned how much he admired and valued her work.

My next coincidence involves Sonya's brother-in-law, the jockey, Brian Taylor, a 'clear winner' in his flat racing career of over a thousand races, including the Derby, which he won in 1974. Tragically killed when thrown from his horse during a race in HongKong, he left three children, Brian, Kate and Jane.
Some years after her father's death, Jane, was attending an ante-natal clinic at

the Newmarket General Hospital, when, in conversation with her doctor, Roy Newman, the hospitals Senior House Officer in Obstetrics and Gynaecology, they found they were related via their grandparents.

Several years later Roy became a General Practitioner and joined a Norfolk practice at which our family were registered. Following which Jane learned that Roy was the doctor of her Uncle Ray which led to Ray and Roy learning they were cousins.

Roy and his partner, Peter, live in a splendid property near Norwich where they hold splendid Open Garden Days, and where we enjoyed a number of equally splendid meals. An excellent doctor, Roy made regular visits to our home during the final illness of our brother, Stefan. His exceptional care when easing Stefan's last days was exemplary and, in being so, greatly eased our sorrow.

At about the same time that we learned of Ray's 'family ties' with Roy, Sonya and I, on behalf of clients, were regular customers of a small privately run fabric shop in the market town of Diss that was run by a young lady called Louise, and her mother, Berenice. After working for several weeks overseas, Sonya and I, on returning to Norfolk, were more than a little disappointed to find this store closed with no trace of its proprietors.

A few months later, on a visit to Earsham Hall in Bungay, where the owner, John, runs a magnificent furniture outlet (an outlet where we frequently shopped for clients and, equally frequently lunched in their excellent restaurant), we learned, to our great delight, that the reason we had 'lost' Louise was because she had been 'found' by John.

Pleased to resurrect our friendship we asked after her mother. Louise told us that Berenice had moved to Spain and had joined an art class where she had met an English lady whose mother, aunts and uncle all lived near Norwich. When Louise told me the name of the lady her mother had met, I said to her; *"Your mother is attending art classes in Spain with my daughter."* A fact that AlisonJane confirmed when next we spoke.

A coincidence that takes me to yet another 'long distance' tale, that involves another Alison who, following a failed relationship, took a cruise where she started a romance with one of the crew, a Chef who lived in Paris. But their relationship did not last the distance, as his work on liners and hers in London, made it a 'distance too far'.

Some years later Alison, with her new beau, John, bought a house in the South of France close to our own holiday home. We became acquainted when we met in our local bar. A bar that is never short of customers reading English newspapers.

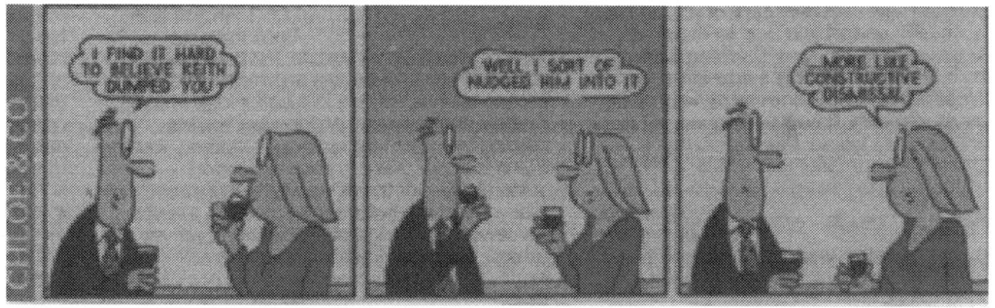

Alison said, in much the same way, in the same bar, she met a lady who was always on her own reading the Daily Mail. Over the next few days they met for coffee and Alison learned that her new acquaintance was living in Paris with a man she had met on a cruise who, it transpired, was Alison's own ex - 'The Chef'.

She told Alison she had fled to Cabris to put some distance between herself and a relationship that was going nowhere, as her new amour was always going somewhere.

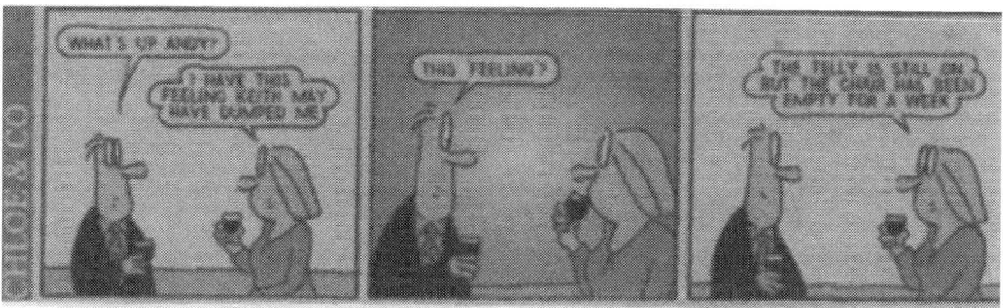

Alison kindly forbore from suggesting that his emotional distance from her may be due to a new, closer affair, in some far-flung place. Staying with cruises and far flung places, Nicola, and George, wanting to book a holiday for a particular cruise, found the liner had just two available First Class cabins so hastily booked one of these.

She then e-mailed our New York cousin telling her of their proposed holiday. Vivien e-mailed back to say that she had, that day booked, for she and her husband, Richard, the last First Class cabin available on the same liner for the same dates and destination. An extraordinary coincidence that gave them the pleasure of enjoying a magical and very pleasurable holiday together.

Equally far fetched, (in time rather than distance), is the next coincidence. A client wished to read an article about Sonya and I that been published in The Independent. Much to our surprise and not a little of hers, the lead page of the paper showed the interview in full. Which would not have been odd had our online search, in October 2008 not been over three years after its inclusion in the paper on the 9th August 2005.

In yet another unusual coincidence, particularly as we have little passion for politics or politicians, Sonya met John Major the day following his election as Prime Minister and I met Margaret Thatcher the day following her election as Prime Minister. A meeting I relate in my item on the Earls Court Russian Exhibition.

Sonya and her husband Ray met John Major and his wife Mary through the good auspices of a friend of the family, Jean Temple, who was also the Major's Bank Manager.

Jean had arranged a supper party in Huntingdon, but having, that day, become Prime Minister, Mr. Major was unable to attend, but not wanting to disappoint Jean and her guests, he invited them to join him for breakfast the following day, which, Sonya said, was a lot more fun. Possibly because our new Prime Minister had, the previous day, routed his opponents?

However, the most extraordinary coincidence, that eclipses all those I have so far related, relates to numbers not names. Having requested new PIN codes for cards issued by different banks, they arrived on the same day. On opening the strips I idly wondered what the odds were against these PINS being the same and whatever zillions to one against them being so, they were.

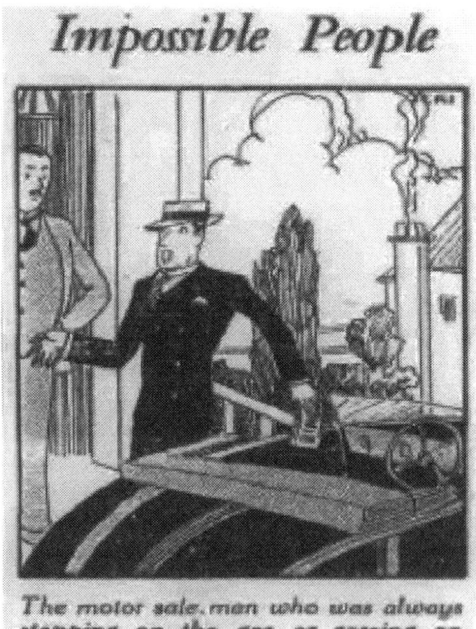

The motor salesman who was always stepping on the gas or gassing on the step.

A much less odd coincidence is that, at some time in their careers, all three of my husbands, in one capacity or another, were involved in 'selling'.

A coincidence I include merely to allow for the inclusion of the next cartoon, the caption of which, had it not been composed so many years earlier, could well refer to my wayward second husband, Chris. A man whose love of cars and 'gift of the gab' would have made him a brilliant salesman, had he not had such similar tendencies to that of JERI's Impossible Salesman.

An Impossible Person that,

yet again, requires a short detour, as one frequently makes when driving - whether in a sports car or a car that sports a cherished number. Particularly as ‘cherished’ as Sonya’s, which closely replicates her surname; TAY7OR.

In a similar way that English students were once taught French via the phrase; ‘Le plume de ma tante’, French students learnt English via the phrase, ‘My tailor is rich.’ Thus Sonya’s number plate allowed us to park freely, and free, in prominent areas in front of any and all of the grander hotels in Cannes, Nice and Monaco.

Impossible People

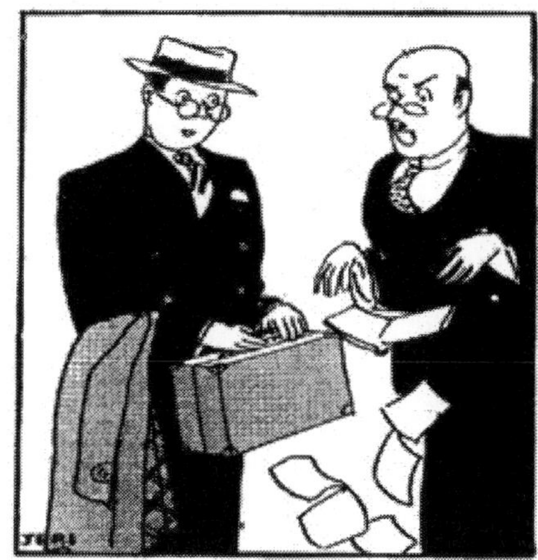

The commercial traveller who said he had taken only two orders — one to get out and one to stay out.

Which, much as I have no desire to do so, takes me back to Chris who was never going to be rich, whether as a tailor, or anything else, as he treated his many sojourns as a car salesman as stop gaps between the many and myriad activities he tried his hand at. At all of which he was gifted and at all of which, due to lack of staying power, he failed miserably - including a short stint as a travelling salesman -

Chris’s attitude to work mirrored his attitude to life. There were always bigger and better pastures to move onto without a backward glance - or forward thinking!

Thus he was more frequently out of work than in it and, for all his brilliance, ended what could have been an illustrious career in almost any field as a school caretaker, which entailed the taking care of ‘playing fields’ which was very apt considering his penchant for ‘playing away’ in both his business and domestic activities.

It is also, perhaps, was why he was such a cheerful man who appeared to have ‘not a care in the world.’ Which, of course he didn’t, for, as was my father,

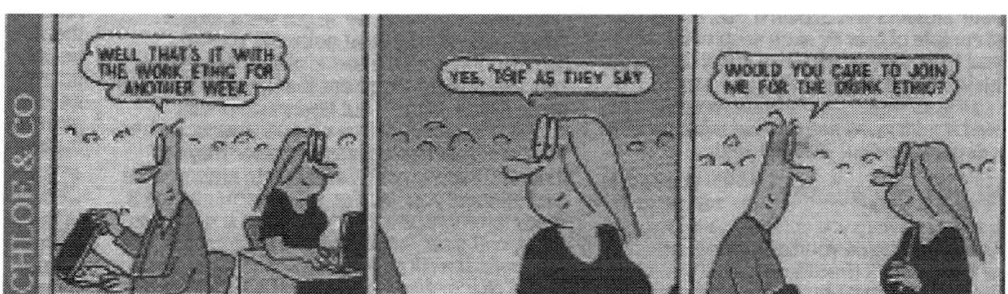

Chris was so amusing, courteous, charming and interesting that most people were - and perhaps still are - more than happy, in the same way they were for my father, to put their hands in their pockets for him.

Which leads, or should, to happiness. The next coincidence regarding happiness popped up unexpectedly, (as coincidences by their very nature are wont to do), just as I was putting these oddities to bed. Preparing to leave the house I put on a coat I had not worn for at about a year and found, in one of its pockets, a ten pound note.

This would have had no significance, nor would I have remembered the day or the date, 29th October, 2011, if, while waiting for Simon and with the note still in my hand, I had not been glancing through the Daily Mail, where I came across an item headlined: ‘Why it Really is the Simple Things that make us happy.’ Number one of the thirty ‘Simple Things’ listed was: ‘Finding a ten pound note in an old pair of jeans.’ Finding my ten pounds did not exactly make me ecstatic, but it did please me that I had just stumbled on yet another odd, unlikely coincidence – even though my ten pounds was in an old jacket not an old pair of jeans.

Coincidentally, when telling people I was including a section on ‘coincidences’, I was given enough factual stories of these odd occurrences to fill a ‘loo book’. An enticing project – but would it sell? Which neatly takes us back to ‘sales’. Simon worked in the field of advertising (an occupation that is definitely aligned with selling), in which he ‘stayed and played’, with great success, throughout his working life, much of which involved the promotion of charities. Organisations that don’t have to sell things in order to make money.

He suggested I include the next two quotations from one of the most successful ‘salesmen’ in history, Henry Ford: *“To stop advertising in order to save money is much the same as stopping the clock in order to save time.” “I know that half of my eight million budget spent on advertising is wasted. The trouble is I don’t know which half.”* Had the gentleman in this next cartoon of Gray’s also invested in advertising?

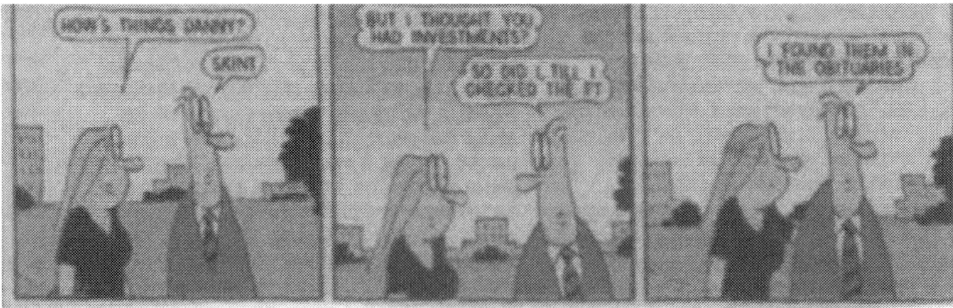

Obituaries that wing us to -

DEAD TREES

In the garden of our holiday home in France were a number of small trees in boxes which, despite our excellent sprinkler system, had, during our absence, become yellow. Presuming they were dead we replaced them, at huge cost, with similar trees from a market garden in Grasse. But as the dead trees still looked pretty, Sonya said we should spray paint them green and dot them about in the nether regions of the garden.

While we were diligently doing this our gardener arrived. On telling him what we were doing, he said; *"Those trees are not dead, they're just resting." "Well they're dead now!"* said Sonya.

A rejoinder that led Simon to mutter under his breath; *"It's no wonder the French think the English are mad."*

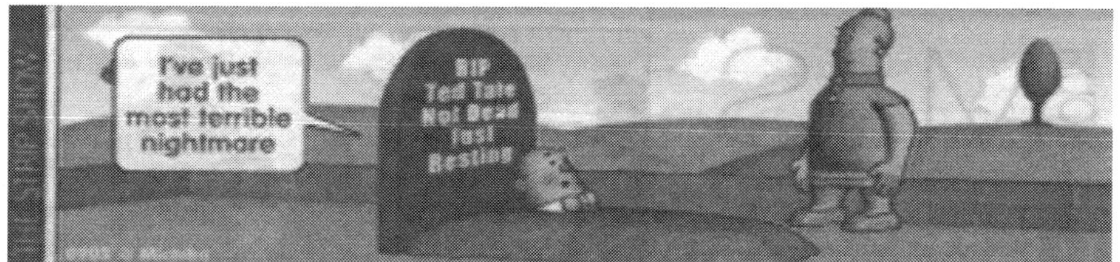

Mad or not, Sonya was right on all counts as, dead or not, the painted trees did look pretty dotted about the garden and on his next visit Sebastion said, if it were not so drastic, he'd do the same for patio plants which are difficult to maintain, with or without water, through the hot French summers.

Although what his French clients would make of this mad idea is another matter and, unless JERI's next Impossible Artist was mad, she would definitely not have used olive oil, as their liberalism does not stretch to messing about with their olive trees that are as sacred to the French as cows are to Indians.

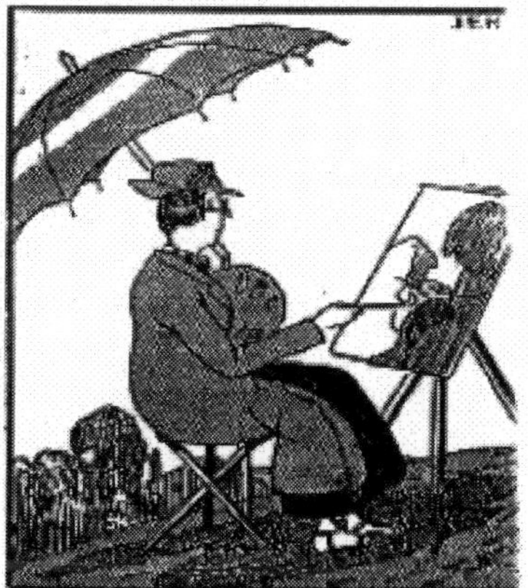

The water colourist who painted in oils during the drought.

Despite our mother being a truly gifted gardener, oddly few of her cartoons refer to the subject, although I'm confident they would have done had she known of Michael Caine's view's on the benefits of this pastime when he said: *"If, instead of visiting a psychiatrist, people spent their time and money on their gardens, they wouldn't need a psychiatrist – and they'd have a lovely garden."* A garden similar to that of the gardener in this next Gray Jolliffe cartoon?

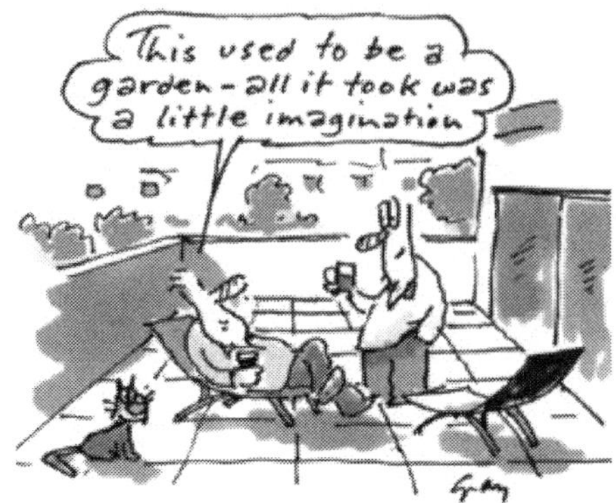

In the same way, perhaps, that someone used their imagination to create this next delightful, anonymous, poem:

Kind hearts are the garden,
Kind thoughts are the roots,
Kind words are the blossoms,
Kind deeds are the fruits.

So maybe it would pay all of 'the worried' to concentrate on their gardens or, if they don't have one, to go and play in someone else's. As noted in my introduction, my three sisters are all great gardeners - great as in good, not large. Over many years they have all owned many, extremely beautiful, gardens of considerable acreage. Gardens they maintained superbly and I enjoyed enormously.

Even now, with their somewhat smaller gardens, they all still spend an enormous number of hours tending them, while I still spend a similar number of hours enjoying them.

When Nicola and George left Norfolk to move back to Essex, they bought one of the most admired houses in Southend, a beautiful Victorian property facing a park and a promenade.

Thus its tiny front garden that Nicola worked her magic on attracted many admirers. So much so that this miniscule, well tended garden won, in 2010, the Silver Award in the annual Front Garden Contest run by their local borough. But while the vast majority of people (even those French who mess about with their olive trees), do not spend too much time worrying about whether their garden might win a prize, they do spend an inordinate amount of time worrying about -

'Whether it will or whether it won't' when it comes to -

THE WEATHER

A subject I have not yet touched on because it is so enormous and my book is so small. Its enormity means we are all 'with it' twenty four hours of every day through all of our lives. We listen to it, watch it, discuss it, experience it, bear with it, enjoy it and, equally frequently, defend ourselves from it. It is a subject that could fill many books and has often done so.

One of which is 'The Great British Obsession' by the BBC TV weatherman, Francis Wilson, in which he writes of a freak tornado that, on Thursday the 14th of December, 1989, devastated the small village of Long Stratton in Norfolk. On page 65 is a photograph of the main street that shows the extent of the damage to many of the shops and houses, one of which is The Guild House, in which my husband, Simon and I lived at the time.

Fortunately we were out when the tornado, which lasted only minutes, hit our home. Had we not, we may have been badly injured or even killed because when the police finally agreed it was safe for us to go inside we found splintered shafts of wood, slate and glass embedded in many of the interior walls and doors.

And although it took some hours before we were 'allowed' to go in, it took only minutes for an insurance assessor to arrive. Nevertheless, our insurers were very fair about this 'Act of God', and the consequent, necessary repairs did not turn us into debtors.

So, unlike JERI's next Impossible Person, we could still 'afford' to go out in all weathers - although not always 'in'.

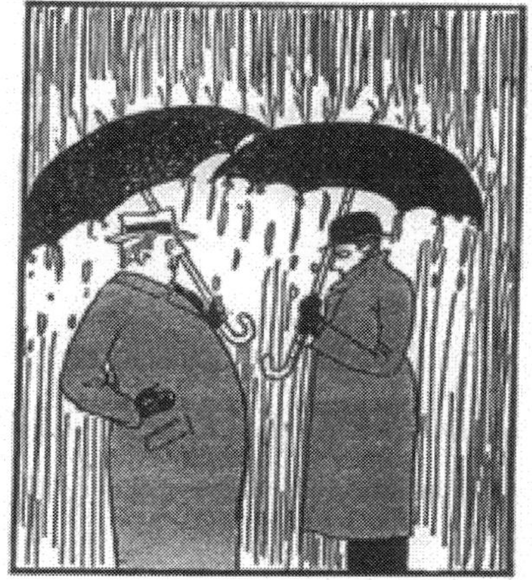

The debtor who went out only in unsettled weather.

Forecasters make assumptions about future weather and possible climate change by making comparisons between our present and previous weather cycles, when what would give them a much clearer picture would be to consider what people were wearing during those times.

It is only necessary to look at fashion during the Tudor years or when Jane Austen was writing her books, to get a clear indication of how cold it must have been during the reign of Queen Elizabeth the First and how hot it must have been during the 'reign' of the 'Queen of Romantic Fiction'.

My reader may note that I only use female fashion when making these comparisons that are also highlighted by the Victorian and Edwardian eras when it must have been bitterly cold in the former and much warmer in the latter.

Impossible People

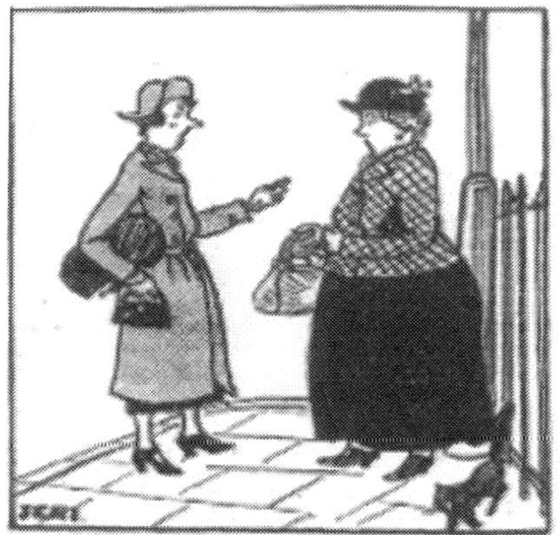

The woman who said this weather was very trying—one day so hot and the next so cold, one never knew what to pawn.

Impossible People

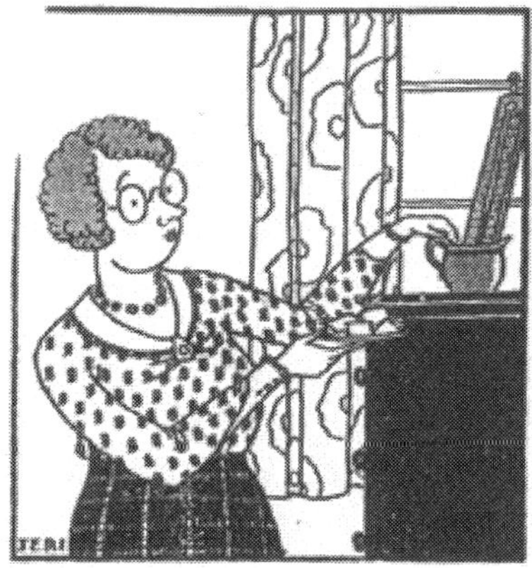

The woman who put ice round the thermometer to keep the temperature of the room down.

The universal assumption that 'most people have a book inside them' may not be true, but what is certain is that everyone has a story about the weather. Mine is -

THE GREAT STORM

Canvey Island, Essex - January 31 1953.

There was nothing between our Benfleet home and Canvey Island except the Creek and the railway line. In the 1970's a new road bridge was built, but, in 1953, everyone had to wait for the level crossing to be opened - and, nearly as often for the bridge over the causeway to be closed - before they could either enter or leave the Island.

Although cars were on the increase, at that time most people still travelled by public transport and Mama's 1950's water colour depiction of the level crossing shows the constant pedestrian activity. It also shows a man looking out of the window of the signal box who, when we 'visited' him, would allow us, with his governance, to work the levers that adjusted the signals and the gates.

Yet another example of the vast sea change in the way we conduct our lives as if our present day elf'n'safety zealots had been around then, despite this being an enjoyable and interesting experience for us and a harmless one for both the passenger and pedestrians, the signalman would have lost his job, our mother would have been fined and we would have been put in homes to keep us out of harms way.

By courtesy of the paintings present owner, Ted Cook

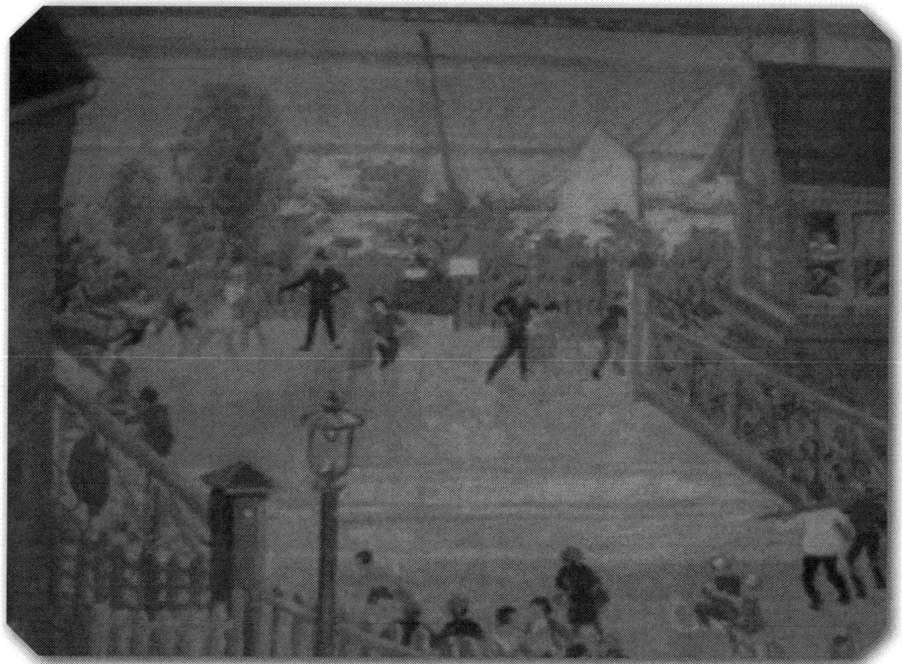

The distinctive sound of the steam trains that clattered back and forth from London to Shoeburyness and the traffic that clattered over the level crossing were a constant in our daily lives to which we had become inured.

So on the night of January 30th, as teenagers have done through the ages, we slept the sleep of the dead. We knew when we went to bed that it was windy and wet, but just how windy and wet we were not to learn until the early dawn when we woke to an eerie silence.

No morning traffic, no trains, not a sound. It was, literally, deathly quiet. What there was, was a smooth sheet of water as far as the eye could see, it was as if Canvey Island and its causeway had disappeared. We then saw groups of bewildered, extremely bedraggled people, reminiscent of the grimy newsreel pictures shown towards the end of the war, of refugees trudging along the roads of France.

As one we threw on our clothes and rushed out to give whatever help we could. At first it was just a case of helping people to reach dry land. All of whom were soaked to the skin and wore the same look of disbelief and despair of the homeless following an air raid.

Those that could, swam, and those that couldn't, having somehow managed to get as far as the creek, just stood waiting to be rescued. As in the manner of Dunkirk, there were several small dinghies already in action, making as many journeys as possible, packed with as many people as possible.

To begin with there was no sign of any of the authorities, many of whom did not arrive until mid morning and, in their usual way, falling over themselves trying to decide what to do and how to do it when much of it had already been done – and far too late to save the 307 people who had already died. A huge number for a place that, at that time, was so sparsely populated.

Billeting the homeless was a first priority. Our local school, ten minutes away by bus, was opened and the dazed, dispossessed Islanders were taken there to be dried out, fed, clothed and bedded. Sonya and I were sent to a local doctor's house which had been set up to provide round-the-clock food for the rescuers.

Nicola and Sasha cared for a few of the Islands rescued pets, while our brothers went by boat further onto the Island to help with the rescue of those too old or infirm to make it to sanctuary. After evacuation of all the survivors, including livestock, our brothers joined the taskforce making temporary repairs to the sea walls, and Sonya and I were then sent to the school to assist with feeding the evacuees.

A highlight of this was having to make tea for Her Majesty, The Queen Mother and Princess Margaret, who had made an an unscheduled visit to the school. Unable to find the key to the cupboard that housed the bone china we resorted to using the pottery cups and saucers.

On making our apologies to these two very regal ladies we fell in love with them forever when they kindly said they didn't mind at all and nobly drank their tea from their 'common' cups. (Which gives me another neat pun.) Their visit was a great moral boost for all these homeless people who, one might suppose, would have wished to look a little smarter for, possibly, their first, (and probably only), meeting with a Royal - or two.

A needless concern, for having visited the East End during the Blitz our much valued Queen Mother was well versed in how to feel compassion when meeting and speaking to the dispossessed and poorly dressed.

Equally dispossessed were the pets of the Island's refugees. Many of the dogs that didn't drown were able to swim to safety, but cats just clambered as high as they could into trees. Therefore the men who were working on shoring up the sea defenses nailed tins of cat food to the trees.

One lucky cat called 'Lucky' had escaped with his family. They couldn't keep him at the school so we agreed to adopt him until they could return to their home. He lived with us for several months and we found that when he wanted a drink, he would ignore his bowl of water and sit in the sink looking up at the tap, asking for it to be turned on.

He would then catch the falling droplets with his paw from where he would lick the water. Perhaps, following his experience in the flood, he had decided that water en-masse, even in a cat bowl, was a dangerous thing. We were sorry to have to return him to his family, but were very pleased that we could!

Shortly after our efforts we children were awarded with a small badge to mark, so we were told, our 'Courage and Fortitude'. Courage and Fortitude that seemed to us more like 'Adventure and Excitement'.

Four things to which Sir Winston Churchill was no stranger –

OUT IN ALL WEATHERS

Sir Winston is purported to have said; *"England is the only country in the world where everyone, regardless of where they are, can always go out in any weather."* Many may think this is not so, but he was not wrong as, during the night of these terrible floods in 1953, regardless of the appalling conditions, everyone who lived on Canvey Island had to go out in the weather, whether they wanted to or not.

So, although not sure about the rest of the world, what I do know is most it certainly applies to France. While summers in the South are always hot, the winters can be variable and much the same as England. Even the southern area of the Alps Maritime region can have up to eight or ten inches of snow. Which makes Cold Calling definitely not the business to be in -

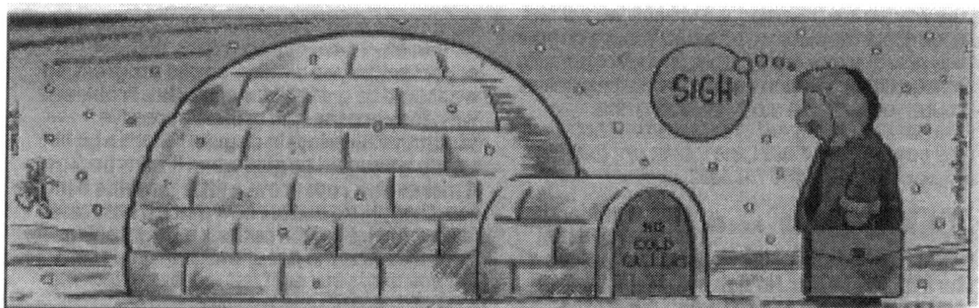

Another cartoon the young would not find humorous now that 'cold-calling' is an occupation centered on call centres and no longer requires 'uncalled for' visits to our homes - whether the weather is cold or not. Or it's raining?

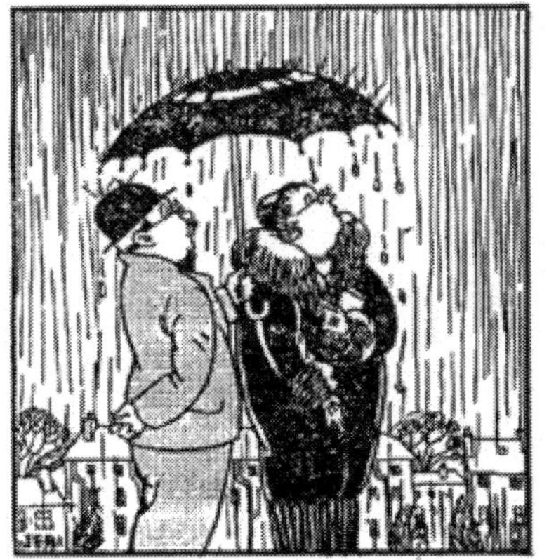

The woman who thought all this rain would be more appreciated if it came in a drought.

While the rain in Spain falls mainly on the plain, the rain in France falls everywhere, and Spike Milligan once famously said;

"There are holes in the sky where the rain gets in. The holes are very small, that's why rain is thin."

But the holes in France must be very big as their rain is very wide. Although, as Dolly Parton succinctly said; *"The way I see it, if you want a rainbow, sometimes you gotta put up with the rain."*

When we first bought our French house we were told there would be days when we wouldn't be able to go out because of the 'rain'. Being British we said; *"Why ever would you not be able to go out in the rain?"* But they were right.

Occasionally the rain is so fierce it is impossible to see through it, let alone walk in it. And you most certainly couldn't picnic in it.

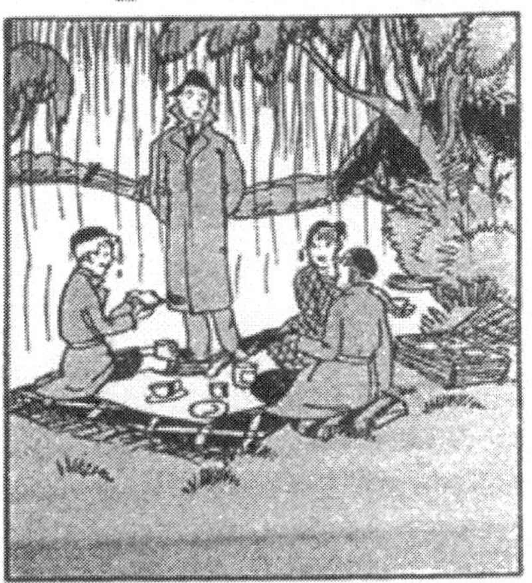

The family who always chose a wet day for a picnic because there were no wasps to get into the jam.

Which is interesting when one considers that 'picnic' is a French word purloined by us British. As are many others such as 'cafe', 'ennui' and, says Simon, 'camouflage', which compliments another we nicked 'maquillage' meaning to 'hide or cover-up' – which is why it is now used by the French for 'make-up'.

The face sort not the 'getting together again' sort. A strange anomaly considering how many more English words there are than in any other language – even, apparently, Chinese. Although we probably have so many because we have nicked so many from other languages.

I am not a lover of picnics but I love rain, whenever and wherever it falls, as in my youth, when rain 'stopped play', this rescued me from the purgatory of the dreaded 'field sports'. On one such occasion and with little else to do we were set to write an 'essay' on 'The Weather'. My 'essay' was the next poem.

Rain

Shower, shower, shower,
Shining, shimmering purity,
Dancing down on doorways,
More from joy than duty,
Flooding down on floorways,
Transparent forms of beauty,
Shower, shower, shower.

Rain, rain, rain,
Dirt and dust will scatter,
Relentless, ceaseless raindrops,
Spatter, clatter, spatter,
Cascading down on rooftops,
In endless noisy chatter,
Rain, rain, rain.

Pour, pour, pour,
Pounding peoples shutters,
Spreading out in sheets,
Drowning thunderous mutters,
Spreading out in streets,
Rivers in the gutters,
Pour, pour, pour.

Drip, drip, drip,
From sparkling, spangled branches,
They drop and are gone,
Brighter than jewels entrances,
They drop and are gone,
Like shy girls glances.
Drip, drip, drip.

During the war rain, snow, sleet or sun didn't stop anyone in Britain from 'going out' despite England having, at that time, some bitterly cold winters and extremely hot summers.

Summers that were so hot you could fry an egg on a pavement. That's if you could find one - egg that is, not pavement. Although, after the Blitz pavements were also often hard to find. But while eggs - and pavements - were in short supply, American soldiers were not, and one of them gave me a tiny, egg-shaped, plastic pop-up bean with a face on it.

No matter how it was pushed, dropped or thrown around it would always pop-up again into the standing position. I kept it for years and would come across it occasionally in a box or drawer where such knick-knacks are kept.

It always reminded me that humans nearly always 'pop-up' again from the dire things that befall them - even really dire weather. Unless they are worried, which led me to compose this -

Rain may pour down on your windowpane,
Thunder may rage, and lightening may leap,
Hail may beat against your window frame,
But its worry that keeps you from sleep

But - why DO we worry when worrying is so futile?

A WORD (OR TWO) ON WORRY

J. H Beattie asked:

The Question

Yes, Yes, I grant the sons of earth,
Are doomed to trouble from their birth.
We all of sorrow have our share;
But, say I, is yours without compare?

Whether comparable or not, apart from the various trials of war and the tribulations that arise from death, divorce and moving house, not to mention the multitudes of murders, muggings and mayhem, it is my view that few people remember the minor or mundane things they we were fretting about six months ago? (Which gives me, and my reader, another neat alliteration.)

So, if trivial vexations are so fleeting, why do we concern ourselves with them at all? For as Piet Hein so wisely said in his next Grook:

On Problems;

Our choicest plans have fallen through,
Our airiest castles tumbled over,
Because of plans we neatly drew,
And later, neatly stumbled over.

And as JERI said in her next cartoon - one of her best -

Impossible People

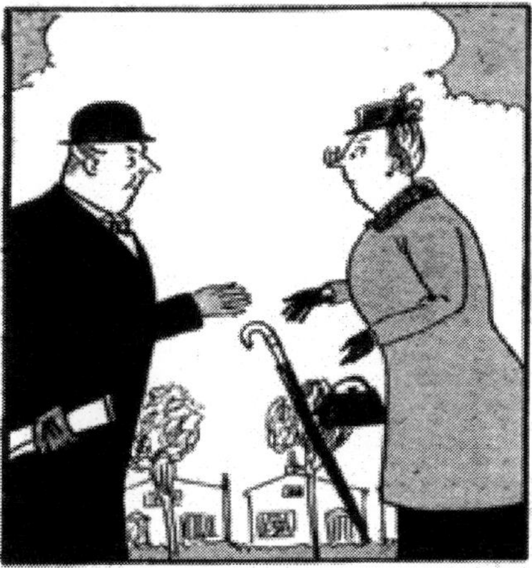

The man who said " An acquittal " when asked what was our greatest comfort in times of trial.

With which most would agree, especially me - and those who suffer -

CATASTROPHES. MISFORTUNES AND TRAGEDIES

Hugh Wheeler said: *"It is a misfortune to lose a lover, husband or wife, but it is a catastrophe to lose your teeth!"* Many might consider that losing your teeth is not just a catastrophe and misfortune but also a tragedy, as nowadays new dental implants can be more costly than a divorce.

It has also been said; *"Be sad for the many who know how it feels and glad for the many who don't."* Or, in the case of published and unpublished writers: *"Be glad for the many who know how it feels and sad for the many who don't."* And all are views that lead neatly to the next two jokes.

The first from my Encyclopaedia of Jewish Humour:

Goebbels had written a propaganda speech for Hitler, but they began to argue over the proper use of the words 'catastrophe' and 'misfortune'. Goebbels maintained that there was a difference in degree between the two, while Hitler insisted that it was purely a matter of semantics and that the words were synonymous.

To settle this difference of opinion they agreed to ask the first intelligent-looking person they met, and that his decision would be final.

They stepped outside the Reichstag and stopped a man whose appearance marked him out as, not only an intellectual but also as Jewish. After they had explained the problem to him the man said:

"Well, as one who appreciates the nuances of language, I can assure you that there is a subtle difference between these two words. For if today allied tanks were to demolish the Reichstag and kill everyone in it, including yourselves, that could be considered a catastrophe but it would not be considered a misfortune."

The second, sent to me by Michael Peter, is a sad reflection on Tony Blair's public image, both as Prime Minister and his, then, exalted post as The Quartet Representative to the Middle East.

Tony Blair, when Prime Minister, was visiting a school and was asked by a teacher if he would like to join the class discussion on what constituted a 'tragedy'. On agreeing to do so, he asked if any pupil could give him an example. A boy stood up and said;, *"If my best friend, who lives on a farm, is playing in a field and a tractor runs into him and kills him, that would be a tragedy." "No,"* said Blair; *"That would be an accident".*

A girl raised her hand: *"If a school bus carrying fifty children drove over a cliff killing all the children and the driver, wouldn't that be a tragedy?" "No it wouldn't"* said Mr. Blair; *"That is what we would call a great loss."* The room went silent as no other child volunteered an answer. So Blair, searching the room, asked; "Isn't there anyone who can give me an example of a tragedy?"

Finally, a boy at the back, raised his hand and in a quiet voice said: *"If an aircraft with you on board, Mr. Blair, was struck by a friendly-fire missile and was blown to bits, that would be a tragedy." "Absolutely!"* exclaimed Blair; *"And can you tell me why that would be a tragedy?"*

"Well!" said the boy; *"It has to be a tragedy, because it probably wouldn't be an accident, and it certainly wouldn't be a great loss."*

A Prime Minister in the making, perhaps?

Accidents take us to

THE CAR

It has been said that: *'Cars only hit trees in self-defense.'* They are also, as this next anecdote illustrates, sometimes 'sold in self-defense':

My brother-in-law, George, has a passion for interesting vintage cars allied to a number of equally interesting, vintage friends.

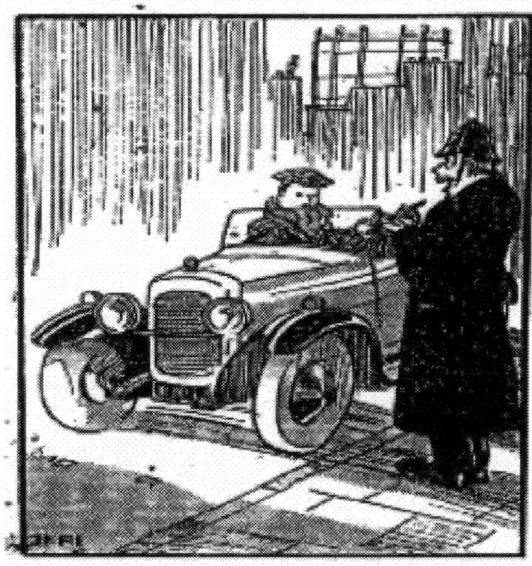

The motorist who asked if he could be summoned for driving at 60 miles an hour instead of 30 because he wanted to sell the car.

One of these, who had a very young wife, had a Bentley George hoped to buy.

Following several rejected offers George regretfully accepted that the car was not for sale. So when, some months later, George's friend called and asked him if he was still interested in buying the Bentley, George, on assuring him he was, said; *"What brought about your change of mind?"* *"I'm selling it,"* said his friend, *"because my wife is having an affair and it's bad enough having to tolerate the young man in my bed without having to tolerate him in my car as well."*

Some years after the event George regaled us with this story at a dinner party at which his friend who had sold him the Bentley was also a guest. Having left his young wife for pastures new, he was delighted to be reminded of it. As was I to be told of it as it steers us to -

DRIVING

On the 17th August 1896, Bridget Driscoll, when walking in the area of the Crystal Palace in London, was the first person to be killed by a car. (She should not be confused with Bridget O'Driscoll, who survived the sinking of the Titanic and who died in 1976 aged 91.)

It is recorded that Bridget stood transfixed as though hypnotised by the lights of the oncoming vehicle and, although the car was travelling at only four miles per hour, the impact killed her. The most interesting thing about this nugget of information is that a car travelling at only four miles an hour could kill someone.

When, in 1916, our Grandfather's chauffeur taught our mother to drive he told her that when the motor car was first invented a member of the House of Lord's said; *"Driving will never catch on as the lower classes will never be able to master its intricacies."* If only he were alive today!

Notwithstanding the Earl's disdain of the 'lower classes', soon after the first car, then known as a 'petroleum motor carriage', was driven in Britain in 1895, the public took to driving in much in the same way that the proverbial ducks take to water. So, early in the 1930's, horse-drawn vehicles had virtually disappeared from our streets and, presumably, our country lanes and, by 1934, there were nearly two and a half million vehicles being driven by all classes - and most ages.

Most of whom were undoubtedly men. Or learners? Although at the time of writing it is not yet obligatory, drivers who have just passed their driving tests can now display a P for Provisional Driver in their rear window. Which makes one wonder whether it will soon be popular for novice drivers to display a GB sign, because –

Impossible People

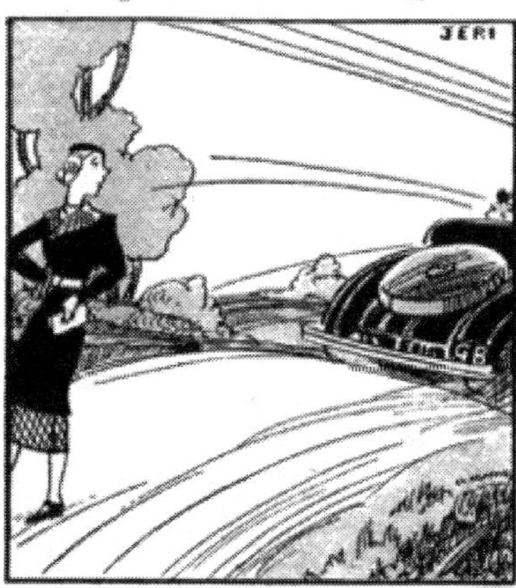

The girl who thought that if "L" meant "learner" "G.B." must mean "getting better."

It was presumed that those who had been driving prior to the introduction of the 1934 official driving test were sufficiently experienced and were, therefore, not required to take a test – practical or written.

Which, perhaps, was just as well for, as the late Eddie Cantor said; *"When my wife, Ida, took her driver's test she got three tickets and that was just in the written part."*

Apart from the advice, that I found on Wikapedia, that new drivers should display a 'P' sign in their rear window, all the other facts I include about driving were gleaned from an informative book by Juliet Gardiner that was published in 2010 by Harper Press called 'The Thirties. An Intimate History of Britain'.

Juliet, the critically acclaimed author of the best selling book: 'Wartime' is a highly respected commentator on British Social History from the Victorian times to the 1950's and is the editor of the magazine, History Today.

She doesn't tell us when the twenty miles per hour speed limit was first made law, but she does tell us that it was rescinded in 1930 because, *'It was universally flouted and an unmanageable backlog of court cases had built up, which made it unenforceable.'*

She also doesn't mention when our present day speed limits first became law, or when the limit of twenty miles an hour in 'built up' areas was reintroduced. But she does tell us that the 1930 Act not only introduced the Highway Code, it also made Third Party Insurance a legal requirement. Due, Juliet claims; *"To the endless claims and counter claims made on behalf of their clients by the Royal Automobile Club (RAC) and the Automobile Association (AA) bristling in defense of their members."*

I'm confident my mother could have devised a suitably saucy cartoon from those last few words. As she did from these; *"After you've heard two eyewitness accounts of a car accident, you begin to wonder about history."*

Impossible People

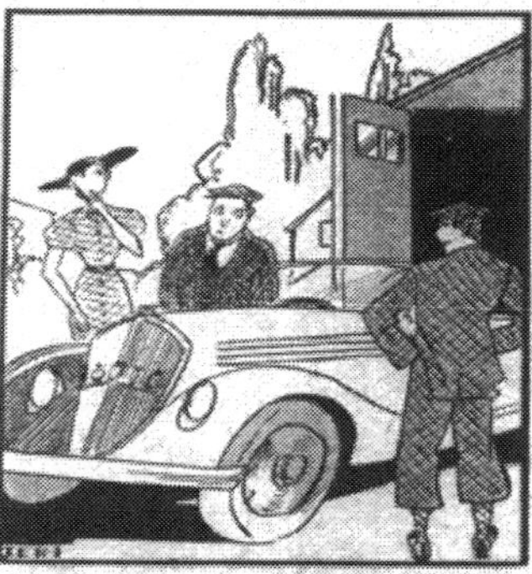

The young man who said he had his car painted red on one side and blue on the other because it was such fun listening to the witnesses contradicting each other.

Juliet also tells us that prior to 1934 it was legal for a 17 year old to drive anything, anywhere, regardless of whether they had passed a test or not. A test that, patently, this next Impossible Person had not taken - or was JERI referring to herself - or one of her friends?

Impossible People

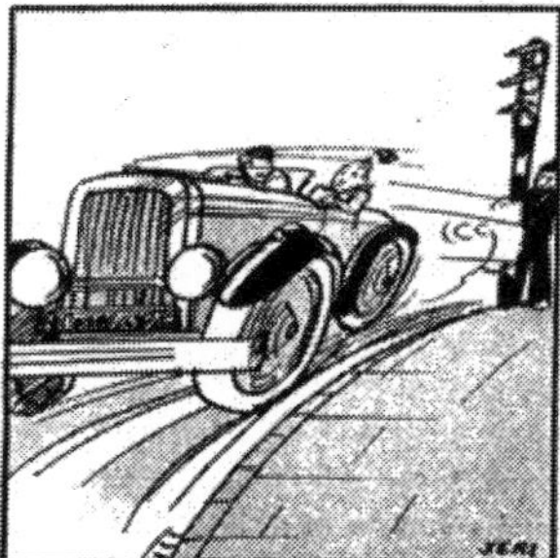

The girl who said it was all right as she had no licence when her friend said she would get her licence endorsed.

These next two once again confirm that there is no such thing as 'original thought'. A 1930's Impossible Person.

Impossible People

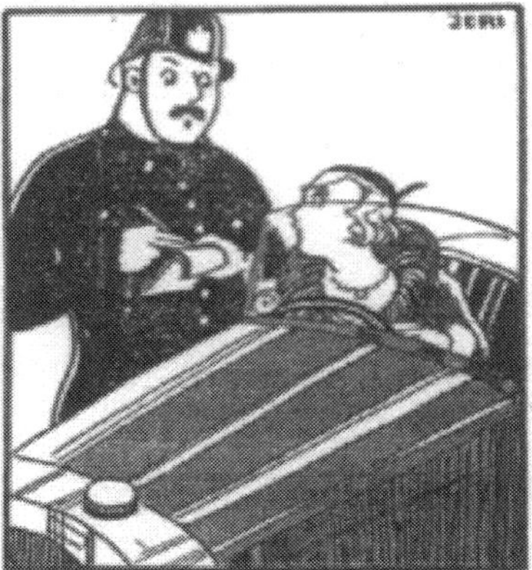

The girl who said she couldn't have been doing 60 miles an hour as she had been out only ten minutes.

A 2009 Chloe & Co

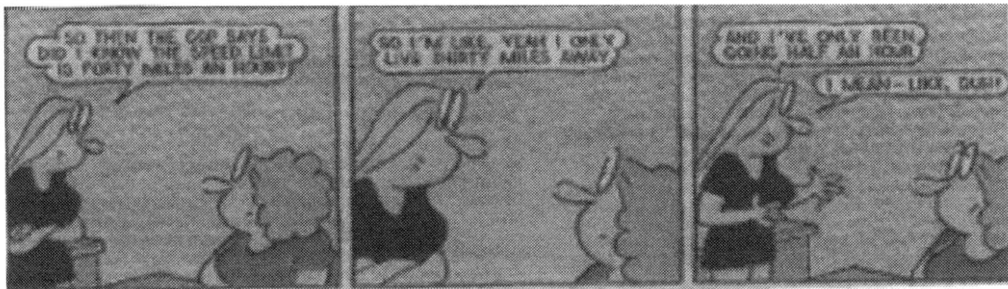

In her book Juliet cites the AA before the RAC, possibly because of their higher membership numbers (or their standing in the alphabet), but, as the RAC was inaugurated in 1897, prior to the 1905 inauguration of the AA and they are of equal excellence, the RAC should be notated first.

It is an organisation that Mama joined in its infancy, and nearly that of her own for even in her teens she would occasionally drive her father's car from London to Scotland. She said that there were so few garages if you were doing a long journey it was necessary to carry full cans of petrol on the running boards. A practice that would give our present day Health and Safety zealots apoplexy!.

It would be fascinating to know if many, or any, people were killed or injured as a result of all these cans of petrol being driven about in such a carelessly casual fashion, but I have never heard, nor read, of any such incidents and, according to my mother, neither had she, but she did suggest that there were people who had no idea how petrol was found -

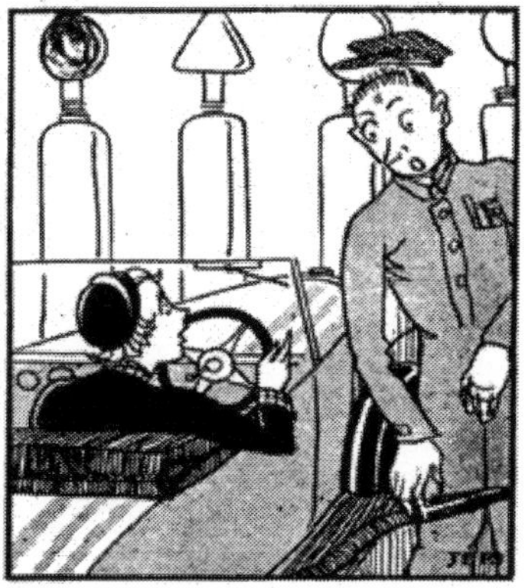

The girl who asked if they employed a petrol-diviner to find out where to sink the pumps.

A year into the First World War, Mama enlisted as an auxiliary ambulance driver with the First Aid Nursing Yeomanry, or FANYS. (So that's where that word came from!).

Of interest to few people apart from myself, the American word 'fanny' refers to the French 'derriere' or English 'bottom' or 'behind' and not the part of the lower frontal female anatomy for which the English use the word. Which is as low as I intend to go.

So, a little more safely – or, perhaps, not - I take my reader to some, higher anatomy. The Crossley lorries Mama drove had to be cranked to start. She broke her arm while doing this, which brought about the discovery of her age and the end of her army career - but not an end to her driving career.

At eighteen, she won an 'Off Road' driving event in Essex. (An event she was preparing for in the photograph I include on page 10), and for which she won a set of six silver teaspoons emblazoned with the Essex motif of little sabres.

Many years later she gave these to my daughter, Alison, who, in her youth, had started to collect interesting or unusual examples of these tiny pieces of cutlery. Which takes me to a short 'off road' detour. As a point of interest (yet again to few people apart from myself), other than being able to compose a reasonable poem, the only other talent I inherited from my mother was her ability to drive well.

Having passed my Driving Test at my first attempt, (rare in those days for a woman), I earned the title Novice Driver of the year for Essex, and then Lady Driver of the Year the next and, two years later, was Driver of the Year. I then became a member of the Institute of Advanced Motorists and, over the next few years, won several further, varied driving events in various counties.

A few years later I won an almost hundred percent mark in a Driving Instructors course. Marks that might have been higher had I not, with no desire to 'instruct', opted out of the 'teaching'bit. Many years later I won, together with my friend Hoodie, first prize in a raffle she had organised for one of her charitable events for which she had bought a Police Driving Course. A hugely enjoyable experience – especially the skidding about on the skid pan and lunch with some tasty police drivers!

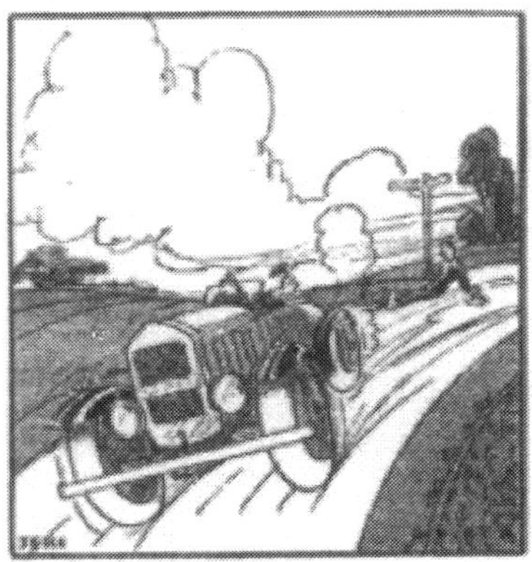

The girl who said when it came to motoring she could leave any man standing.

Nevertheless, despite a driving prowess that has allowed me to leave many men standing, these achievements do not necessarily make me a 'good' driver, merely a very experienced one, and none, however accomplished, in both the 'good' and the 'got' sense, have allowed for a reduction in my insurance premiums.

Although it is likely that vehicle insurance may, sometime in the far future, also be a thing of past as a recently released prediction suggests that, by the year 2040, three quarters of all cars will be autonomous. A word that Google tells us is: 'Navigated and maneuvered by a computer, without a need for human control or intervention under normal road conditions.'

In the same year as her Essex driving conquest, Mama won her Lord Mayor of London Award for her Regent Street Cinema murals. Achievements for which her father rewarded her with the Maxwell, in which she and her friends would drive through France on their painting trips.

Journey's that took them from Mont St Michelle to La Rochelle. Our American friend, Leonore, (who did a lot of driving as a trouble shooter for hospitals), could often be heard to say; *"A truly happy person is one who can enjoy the scenery on a diversion."*

'Diversions' our mother would never have experienced had her father not given her the Maxwell that took her so often to France where she did some of her finest work.

One being a superb water colour of the La Rochelle marina. A painting from which she then made both an etching and this pastel which Mama gifted to me as a wedding present for my first marriage.

With no mount it sits straight onto the glass in an ancient oak frame and, in the same way she was concerned about her cars method of transport when being hoisted aboard a ferry, I am equally concerned that, should the glass break, this treasured picture may be damaged beyond repair. Thus during my many house moves, I have always ensured it is extremely well wrapped.

Mama gave the water colour 'twin' of the same scene to my brother, Boris. But the greater value of both these pictures is that they are the only examples still

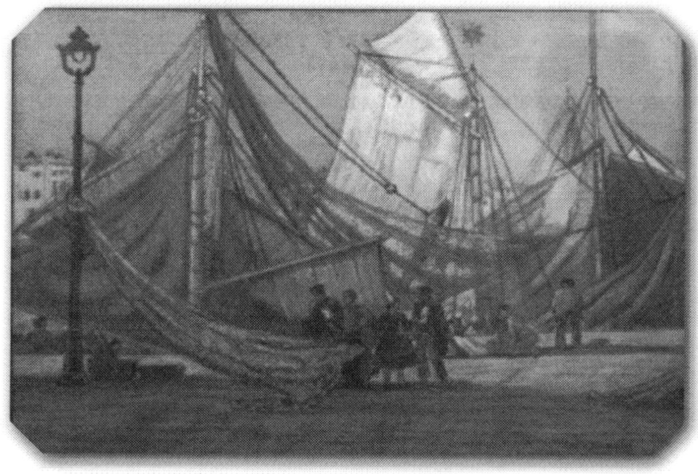

held by the family of both a water colour and a pastel from which our mother made her fourteen etchings.

We can only hope that, apart from those still in the family, all the other pieces of art she gifted or sold, are still admired and appreciated, if not for their heritage, their excellence. Which neatly takes us to

JERI'S ART AND ETCHINGS

One of our mother's travelling companions was one of her North London Collegiate school friends, Dolly Freeman, whose brother, Ralph, while Mama and Dolly were busily painting, was busily designing both the Sydney Harbour Bridge and the Victoria Falls Bridge.

His son, also a Ralph, also became a designer of bridges, his most notable being the Humber Suspensions Bridge. As a matter of interest, possibly to no one apart from myself and my twin, the first names of Dolly and her twin sister, Dot, (who became a doctor - a rare achievement for a women at that time), were Marion and Dorothea. Names that Mama gifted to myself and Sonya as our third Christian names.

Thus mine is the neat Leah Karina Marion while my twin has the more untidy, but prettier, Sonya Rosalia Dorothea. Rosalia being the name of our father's sister, Rose, who was of great assistance to our mother when she was pregnant with us. So while we know from whence our other names came, we have never known from where the names Karina and Sonya came.

Names that, when asked to spell them, we always have to say; *"Karina without a 'T' and Sonya with a 'Y"*.

Two letters that are a BIG T.Y. to our Mother for having us as, with four children under the age of five and having to compose cartoons for the Sketch, this must have left her with little time for her art.

Art that, from those she was pleased with, she would make, pastel copies and, from those she was particularly pleased with, copper plate engravings. One of which is this depiction of a hotel in La Rochelle.

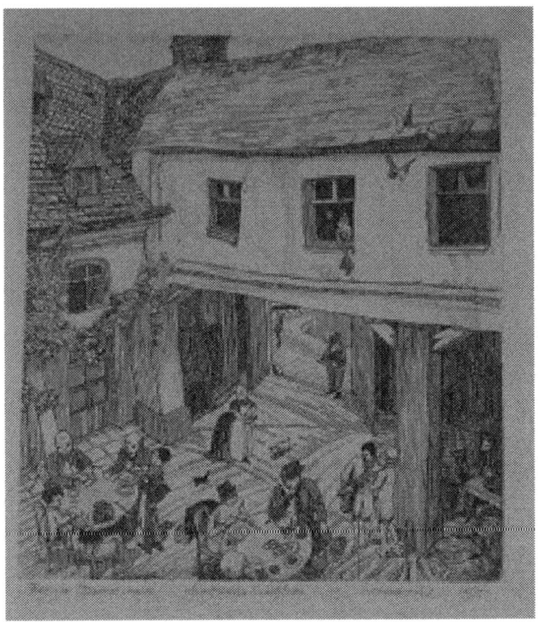

A hotel where, many, many years later, our sister, Sasha, and her husband, John, with our, now long standing, friends, Diana and Jack, once stayed when on holiday in France.

As I include in an earlier section of the book, during the war we moved a number of times to a number of different and distant locations. Moves that, on one occasion, entailed our household goods being left on a train that had been left overnight on a siding which, that night, suffered an air raid. An air raid in which the box with our mother's copper plates was badly damaged.

Thinking them to now be unusable, our mother was going to throw them away but could not bring herself to do so. Many years, and nearly as many house moves, later I found them languishing in a box in the same parlous condition that had been inflicted on them during their fling with Hitler.

Having researched the possibility of having prints taken from them but finding this fruitless, I gave up. Nevertheless, despite a few further house moves and different husbands, not being able to bring myself to dispose of them (the plates not the husbands who were not difficult to dispose of), I kept them.

On the pleasing programme, 'Flog It', the presenter, Paul Martin, visits many people and places of interest to his viewers. In particular mine as, in early 2006, he made a visit to a photographure company in Berkshire, where he discussed with the proprietor, a charming gentleman with an equally charming name, Lyndsay Nutbrown, the process of taking prints from copper etched plates

Lindsay said that his company, Thomas Ross, were the last to use the old method of printing these and viewers, (one of whom, fortunately, was myself), were then shown footage of an employee demonstrating this process which entailed the use of two ancient presses.

Thinking I may at last have found the end of my rainbow, (and possible pot of gold), I got in touch with Lindsay who said he was confident that Mama's plates could still have prints taken from them. So Sonya and I took some to Berkshire to see whether he could work his magic on them.

Having made several similar trips to similar printers, I thought this visit would prove fruitless. Sonya was equally convinced it would not. Fortunately, as she is about most things apart from spelling, she was right. On seeing the plates Lindsay said that prints could definitely be taken from them and within an hour of our arrival, his colleague, Raymond, produced perfect prints from two of the plates.

As with many of the various sorties Sonya and I venture on, several interesting things resulted from this visit. On taking the rest of them to Berkshire, Raymond and his assistant made clear prints from all fifteen plates.

Lindsay then said that as only a few etchings could be made from a copper plate, and as we could not know how many prints had previously been taken from them, he would recommend they were steel plated. A process that, apparently, was not available at the time they were made but when done, would allow for many numbers of prints to be taken from them.

Having also taken a few examples of Mama's art and cartoons, Lindsay then said we should meet his brother, Simon, the proprietor of the greetings card company, Cornflower.

Simon, much taken with our mother's work, asked if he could use twelve of her water colours and twenty four of her cartoons as greetings cards. Lindsay, equally impressed with our mother's work asked if he might reproduce four as hand water colour etchings for the Thomas Ross catalogue.

Two requests I was more than just pleased to agree with and am equally pleased to include here, as my reader may like these Thomas Ross prints enough to buy one – or even two.

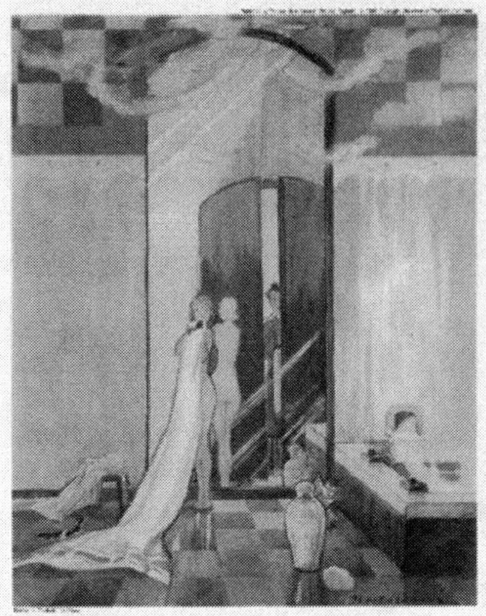

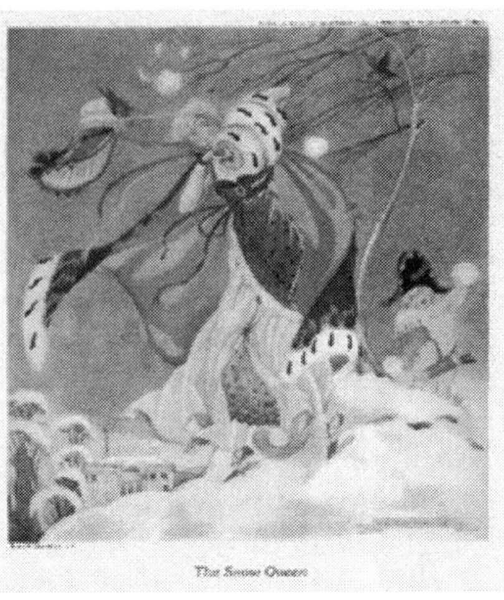

The Snow Queen

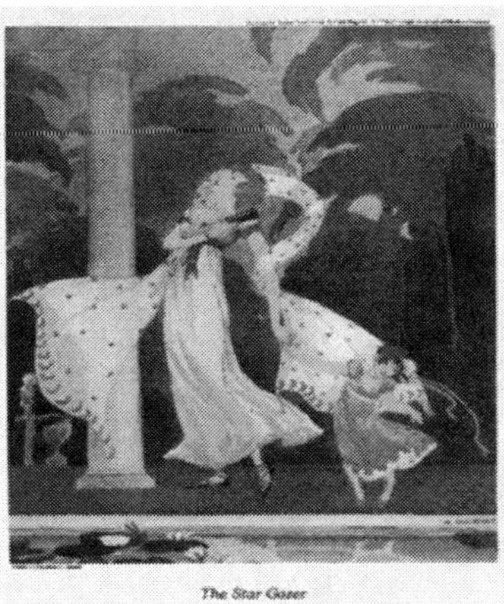

The Star Gazer

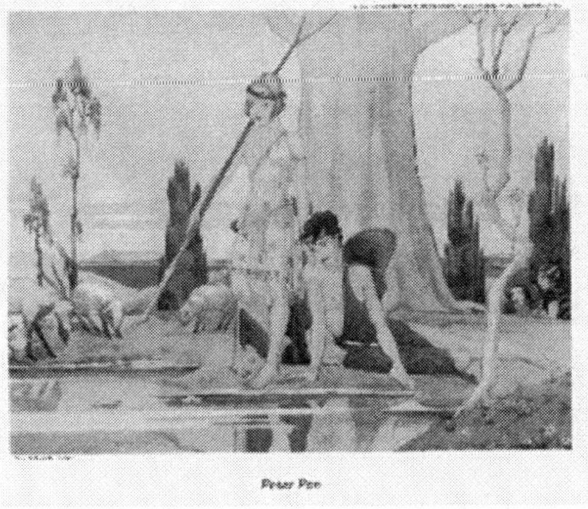

Peter Pan

As were our sisters and brothers, who were definitely much more than just pleased to have them. We also gifted to all of our children full sets of the etchings and the four water colour prints.

We learned from Lindsay that Thomas Ross are the largest producers of fine art prints in the country. Fine art prints in many different styles that now enhance the walls of the homes and offices of the many people who enjoy and appreciate quality art. An extremely interesting 'find' on this first visit was that while waiting to see the results of Raymond's magic, we were admiring the artworks in the showroom, one of which was an enormous print of four different groups of eminent people at eminent, high level, meetings that had been held at different times in history. (A perfect print for the boardrooms of businesses - whether high level or not.)

The four scenes were of the Admiralty, the Army, the Church and the Government. Seated at the head of the first of these groups of 'high-flyers', was Lord Admiral Sir Thomas Cochrane, 10th Earl of Dundonald. Naturally, despite not having boardrooms, both Sonya and I bought copies.

It has been a long held ambition of myself and my sisters to bring our mother's work to a wider audience. An ambition that, with the help of Chris Martin, 'Flog It' and Lyndsay Nutbrown, together with all those cartoonists who have agreed I may include their work and, last but by no means least, my exceptionally erudite, equally humerous and extremely patient husband, Simon, I may now achieve.

The four hand-painted water colour prints, together with the fifteen etchings can be found on - www.thomasross.co.uk

Attractive paintings of Mama's take us to the attractive work of -

ERTE - with a bit of Travel and a little Interior Design

When working with clients, Sonya and I always bore in mind these very sensible words said by William Morris, *"Have nothing in your house that you do not believe to be either beautiful or useful."*

The useful being much less difficult to obtain than the beautiful, we were always pleased when our research, however far afield, turned up an item that we knew a client would be pleased to own.

Despite the numbers of clients that passed under the umbrella of our many years in the business of interior design, it was rare for any of them to meet, but, when working in tandem with Jenny and Hoodie, for both of whom we did several projects, we arranged for them to meet and they became firm friends. So much so that my reader has already been 'introduced' to them in the previous pages of 'Impossible People'.

They are still two of our dearest friends and Jenny, as I also mention earlier, is the 'other' Grandma of my grandson, Michael. (Who was tiny when I started this book but is now, as I finish it, over six feet tall.)

Over many years we have enjoyed many social events, lunches, outings, high-days and holidays with one or other of them and, equally frequently, with both of them. Which is why I won my Police Driving Course and was in Tenerife with Jenny and Hoodie when we found our German lady who had "Only 'ats und 'andbags".

Having decorated a hairdressing salon for Jenny themed on the artist Erte using framed prints decorating the walls, Hoodie fell in love with this artist – or, more correctly, his work. So Sonya and I were delighted when, just a few months later while holidaying in Hawaii with Jenny, we found an original Erte.

A 'find' that came about because the two weeks we were there coincided with the anniversary of a major hurricane that, some years earlier, had devastated the Island. A film of which was being shown in a hotel close to where we were staying.Having watched the film we visited the hotel's small but smart art shop where, while twirling a small statue of a figurine on a stand, I said to Sonya; *"This is reminiscent of an Erte."* On hearing this, the proprietor said he had an original Erte and would we like to see it.

Delighted to have come across such an item in such an unlikely setting, we made an offer for it. As an hotel in Hawaii is unlikely to have too many visitors interested in an Erte, whether original or not, thus the eventual, mutually agreed, sum was much more than just acceptable.

The next stage of our trip was to California where, in order to verify its authenticity, we took the picture to a dealer in Los Angeles who, much to our delight, told us that the signature was worth as much as we had paid for the picture.

We then called Hoodie's husband, Robin, who said he would be very pleased to buy her a gift that, due to the 'history' behind its purchase, would be more fabulous than many of the presents he usually gave her - however fabulous. So, on our return to England, we had the Erte framed and wrapped in readiness for him to give to Hoodie at Christmas.

In yet another extraordinary coincidence, just days later, Simon, while browsing in a bookstore in Holborn, came across a book of Erte designs that had, on its cover, the picture we had bought in Hawaii. Naturally he bought me a copy. I then ordered two more, one for Sonya and another to give to Hoodie as a Christmas gift. Hoodie was as delighted with the stories of how they were found as she was thrilled with her gifts.

We still have the books and the original Erte is still the centre piece of Hoodie and Robin's master bedroom.

From a glamorous women by Erte to a few more

WOMEN

'How do women get minks? The same way minks get minks.'
"Woman was God's second mistake." and; *"Ah! Women. They make the highs*

higher and the lows more frequent." Two quotes from Friedrich Nietzsche that pre-suppose he was not a great lover of women, or, perhaps, just not a great lover, or, more likely, he just didn't understand them.

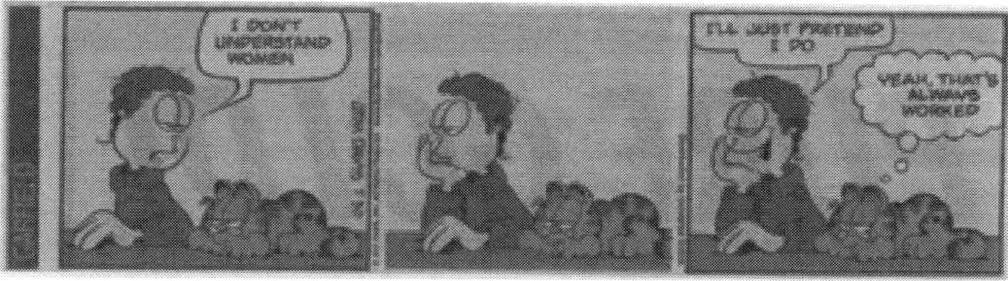

As I verify in 'my' Impossible People, women, even if you don't understand them, can also be good artists, cartoonists and poets, one of whom, inarguably was my Mother, whose exceptional skills in these fields were matched by her equally excellent skills in both horticulture and cuisine.

Impossible People

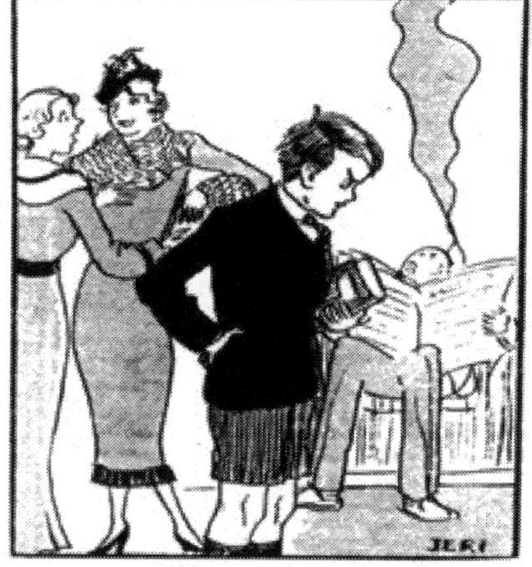

The boy who asked if a woman always got the last word what happened when she argued with another woman.

The last two being fields where women are usually thought of as being as equally skilled, or better, than men, as opposed to those in which they are not, such as driving. An art at which, when skilled, woman can often be better than men.

A fact few of my female readers would argue with.

Or would they?

Although few would argue with Nancy Reagan when she said; *"Women are like a tea bag, you don't know how strong she is until you put her in hot water."*

Nor with James M. Barrie when he said; *"It is not true that women was made from man's rib. She was really made from his funny bone."* Male and female interpretations of Barrie's view will be quite different, but we can be confident he did not mean that women make superior comedians – or cartoonists.

We can be equally confident that, were he still with us, he would be pleased to 'eat his words' as our modern methods of bringing entertainment into people's lives has given us many women possessed of comic genius. Some of the best being Mae West, Dawn French, Jennifer Saunders, Anne Landers, Joan Rivers, Julie Walters, Phyllis Diller, Sue Perkins, Miranda Hart, Ruby Wax, Rita

Rudner, Victoria Wood, and Elizabeth JERI Hayklan. all of whom have (or did have) the ability make us laugh as equally as do their male counterparts.

Any of the women listed above might have said this, but it most certainly wasn't Nietszche! *"Would you like to speak to the man in charge, or the woman who knows what's happening?"* A remark that could well lead to a domestic crisis which women have three ways to settle: A good cry; a divorce; or rearranging the furniture. From personal experience the last two are a great deal more efficacious than the first.

It is also said, *"One of the deepest mysteries of life is knowing what women want."* My sister Nicola says; *"What all women want is a roof over their heads."* What I say is; *"Roofs lead to houses and houses lead to housework, and although it is said that housework doesn't kill you, why take the risk?"*

Impossible People

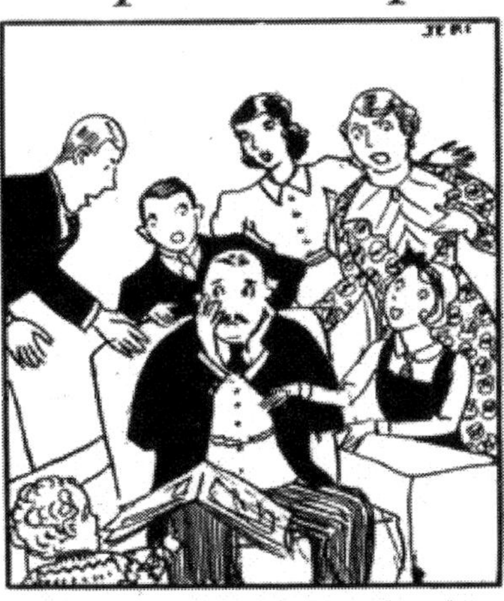

The man who said that when his family began arguing Dad became Mum.

It is also said: *"Women are the nearest thing to an insoluble enigma that God ever made."* But, if the enigma of women can't be solved by men then men are just dumb or, now that some men act as 'househusbands', many are now, in the nicest possible way, Mum!

MEN

Who allow for the inclusion of these oft quoted, quotes: *"The more I know about men the more I like dogs." "If they can put a man on the moon, why can't they put all of them on on it?"* And, from the humorist Helen Rowland; *"A man never quite gets over the idea that he is a thing of beauty and a boy forever."*

Impossible People

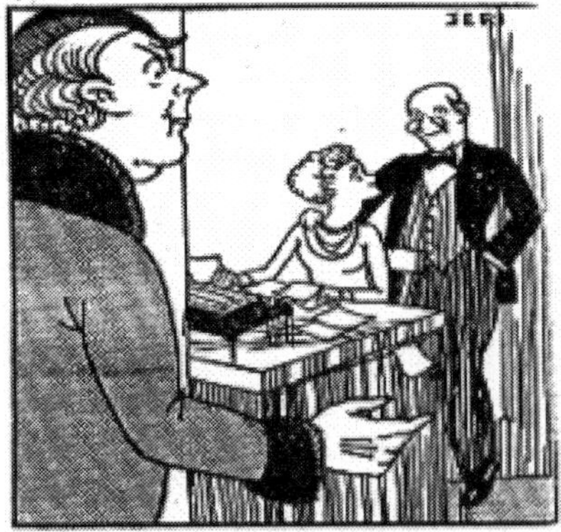

The woman who said her husband was in, but she found him out.

A cartoon that confirms that the only thing that can safely be said about men is that 'none of them are safe.' And another that confirms that women talk a lot – 'talk' that is often about how 'unsafe' men are. Although according to JERI, this is not a new phenomena - Or did he?

Impossible People

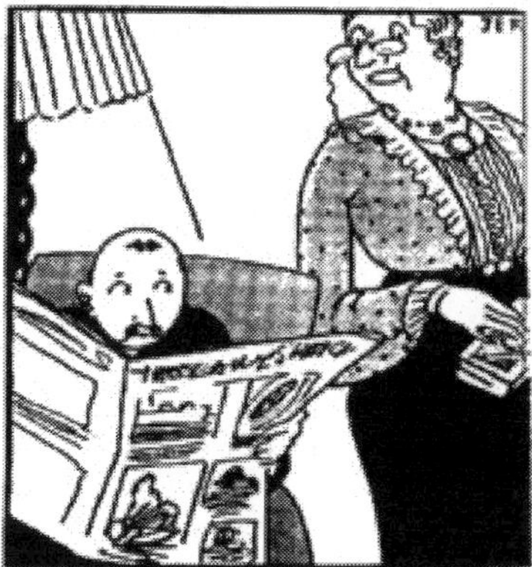

The man who wondered why his wife had a double chin, because he had been told that exercise removed fat.

Three further quotes for which JERI could have created Impossible People are:

'Never engage in idle gossip, only important, meaningful gossip.' 'The man who said his wife had a keen sense of rumour.' And, from Amanda Lear: *"I hate to spread rumours, but what else can you do with them?"*

But she did create this;

Impossible People

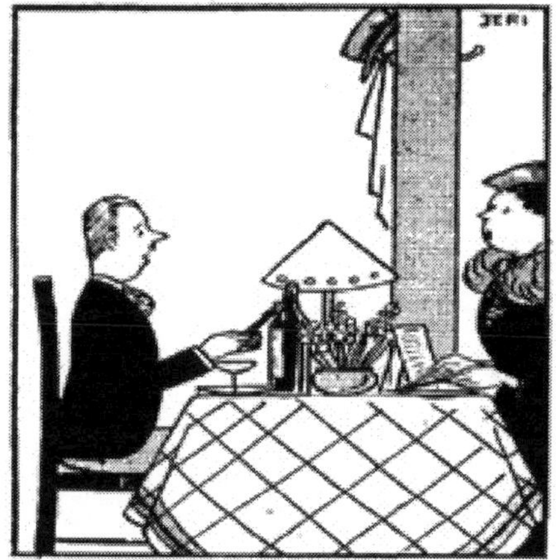

The man who said he did not believe in clubs for women unless kindness failed.

And this, on clubs of the more effective kind;

Impossible People

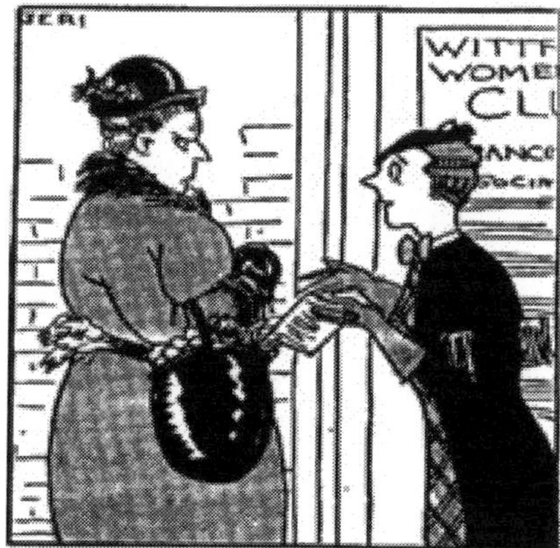

The woman who said she did not believe in clubs for women, as the old-fashioned rolling-pin was good enough for her.

But at least my Mama played fair in the gender stakes.

As did, Jane Austin. A.A. Milne wrote, "A garden is not a garden without a blackbird in it." Similarly, a book of this nature is not a book without a quote, (or two), from the wise, witty and wonderous writings of Jane Austen.

Particularly as 'it is a truth universally acknowledged' that the first sentence of her most popular book; Pride and Prejudice, is, with good reason, one of the best known, most frequently quoted quotes from literature. Which is an excellent reason to include it here; *"It is a truth universally acknowledged that a single man in possession of a good fortune must be in want of a wife."*

From the same novel, her second most quoted is this injunction from Mr. Bennet to his daughter; *"An unhappy alternative is before you Elizabeth. From this day you must be a stranger to one of your parents. Your mother will never see you again if you do not marry Mr. Collins, and I will never see you again if you do."*

Anne Elliot maintains in Persuasion that; *"Man is more robust than woman, but he is not longer to live; which exactly explains my view of the nature of their attachments."* While Mary Musgrove opined; *"If there is anything disagreeable going on, men are sure to get out of it."* (By going to their clubs' perhaps?)

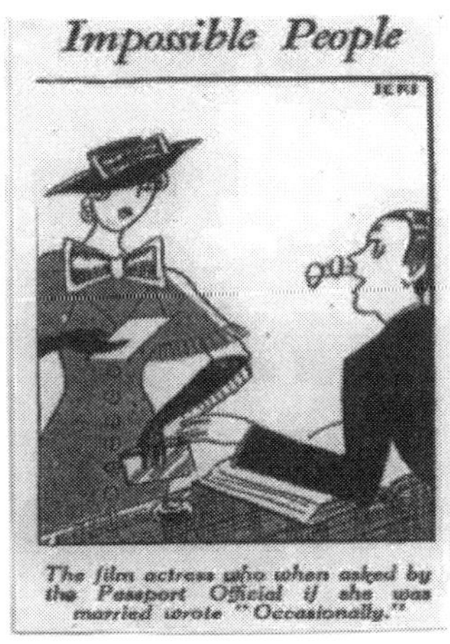

Which presupposes that, despite being a spinster, Jane Austen knew a great deal more about men than most women do - even those women, such as myself, who married frequently - or just 'occasionally' -
It is also said that behind every unsuccessful man is a woman beavering away to make him think he is. And; A man's got to do what a man's got to do - a women does what he can't. Although not, perhaps, when it comes to the law –

SOLICITORS

It is said: A man who acts as his own solicitor has a fool for a client. During a grand dinner we once attended, Sonya was seated between a solicitor and a vicar. Much to their amusement, and not a little to some of the other guests, she said; *"Such close proximity to a representative of both God and the Devil gives me the opportunity to tell a joke that I was once regaled with at a similar dinner party."*

"God and the Devil were having trouble sorting out who was responsible for repairs to the boundaries of their two kingdoms. Finally they had a meeting and, following much obfuscation from the Devil, God said, "Well if we can't reach a suitable agreement then perhaps we should consult our lawyers. To which Satan said, "That's fine by me, but where are you going to find a solicitor?"

This next Impossible Person of JERI's tells us that many might be found in the Bahamas or Switzerland.

A caption that, nearly a century after its creation, will be understood by all – even the young among us - and a few of those who shouldn't be among us!

Max Hastings, in a splendid article about the political mire caused by uncontrolled immigration, wrote: 'The Human Rights industry, vastly profitable to a legion of shameless British lawyers, will continue to frustrate deportations of many foreign criminals.'

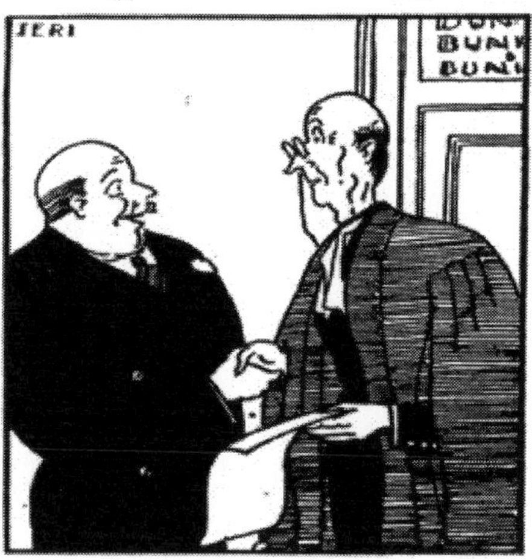

The man who left all his money to his lawyers to save everyone a lot of time and expense.

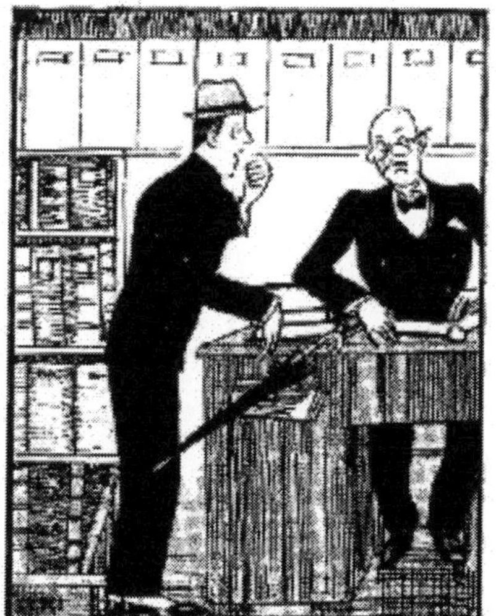

The clerk who said; "Yes, but no one could prove it." when asked if his boss was a criminal lawyer.

So it would seem that JERI's next caption could be considered as topical now as when she composed it.

Many years ago, when staying in Philadelphia with my cousin Vivien and her husband, Richard, he regaled me with the next joke. As, at that time, he was Vice President of the Medical College of the University of Pennsylvania, I doubt anyone will sue him for telling a joke. Or will they?

"Four American surgeons were discussing the merits of operating

on professional people. The first said he preferred Academics as their organs are coded by letter. The second said he preferred Accountants as their internal organs are all numbered. The third said he preferred Electricians as their organs are colour coded. The fourth said that by far the best were lawyers as they were gutless, heartless and spineless, and their brains were in their backsides."

I have, in the intervening years, had this joke sent to me on many occasions, with many variations. Some of which replace solicitors with politicians, and most of which are too rude or crude to include here!

Nor have any of them been quite as apt as Richard's, who, as a surgeon, must know better than most, regardless of any anatomical differences, on which of these four different professionals it is easiest to perform surgery. And, despite my probable need to solicit the services of a solicitor quite soon, the next anecdote does little to redress the balance.

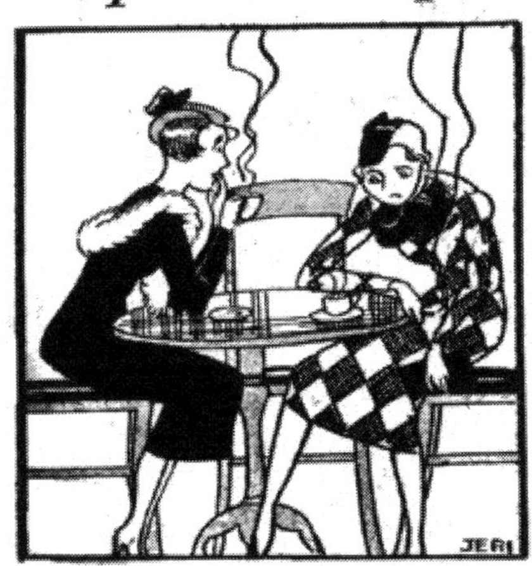

The girl who said she had lost her job at the solicitor's because she always mistook the will for the deed.

A doctor who, during a function, had been solicited by a number of the guests regarding their ailments, asked a fellow guest, a solicitor, if he had a similar problem when meeting people socially and, if so, what he did about it. *"Well"* said the solicitor, *"I answer as best I can, and in the morning I send them a bill." "Excellent advice."* said the doctor. Two days later he received an invoice from the solicitor for 'Advice'.

Perhaps JERI's next Impossible girl should have 'sought advice' before taking a job with a solicitor.

Or should have followed the advice in this Peit Hein Grook:

A Reproof

In view of your manner of spending your days,
I hope you may learn before ending them,
That the effort you spend on defending your ways,
Could better be spent on amending them.

So perhaps JERI's Impossible Girl would have been equally inept whoever she worked for - or went out with -

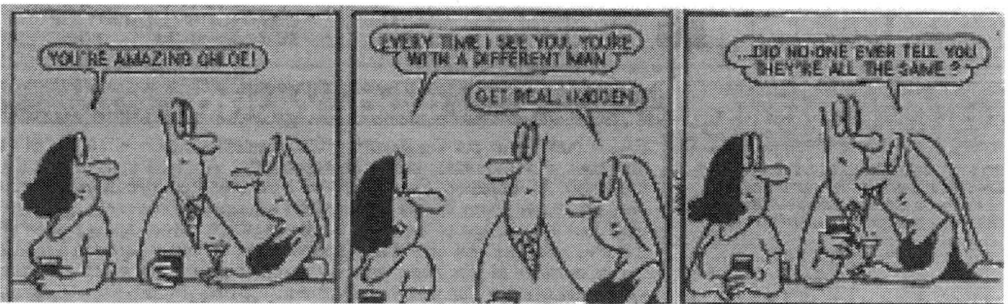

Including -

ARCHITECTS

Properties, both in interest and numbers, have been a major feature in the lives of myself and my siblings. We have designed them, built them, redesigned and renovated them.

Have decorated, fitted-out and furnished them. We have bought and sold them in enormous numbers in many areas both in England and overseas for our clients, our families and friends. As I write in my introduction, Stefan, with no education or qualifications, became a brilliant designer of properties of all sizes, styles and prices, which not only won him numerous architectural awards but allowed him to become a highly thought of Surveyor.

While Boris was an equally successful property developer both in England and overseas. Sonya's husband, Ray, ran a highly profitable property construction company and Sasha's husband John, was a highly esteemed Structural Engineer and, for over thirty years, Sonya and I ran an exceptionally successful Interior Design Company.

Nicola and George with their son, Stefan, still have, as I write, a company that continues to flourish in the construction, re-design, sale and rental of both residential and commercial premises. All of which allowed all of us to become, if not, as did Stefan, extremely wealthy, most certainly well heeled. But despite our long years in, and wide knowledge of, property, none of us knew that Stonehenge came flat-packed -

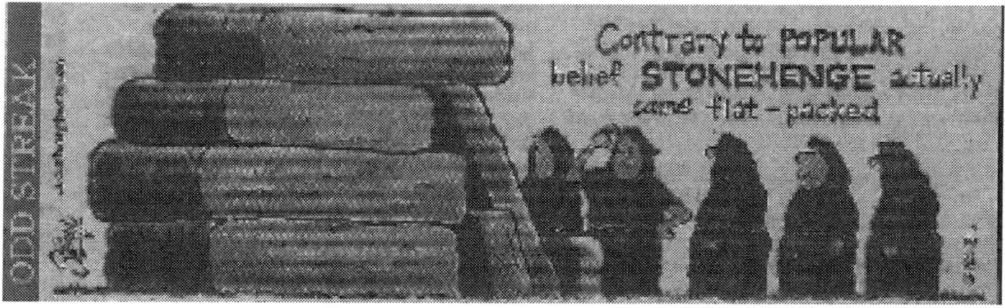

But was this for reasons of ease or scale?

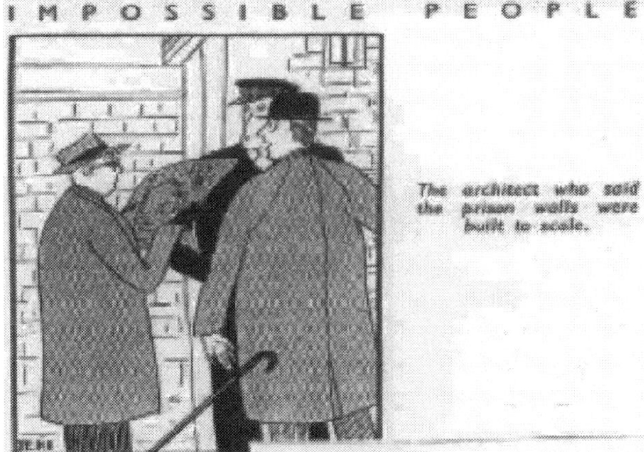

Or economy?

ECONOMISTS

Knowing nothing about economists and even less about 'economy', I cannot make any comment on them, but someone did: *"An Economist is someone who tells you what to do with your money after you have done something else with it."*

As, occasionally, do husbands whose wives, generally, take as little notice of these strictures as governments do of economists. For as Robert Fuoss said, *"An economist is someone who lectures on capital and labour - and the baffling thing is that most of them qualified for this career by having no capital and having done no labour."*

And George Meany believed: *"It is the one profession where you can gain great eminence without ever being right."* To which John Papworth said; *"Economists are quite unique in their failure to solve a single one of the problems of their profession."*

Assumptions confirmed by Herbert Prochnow's assertion that; *"An economist is someone who talks about something they don't understand and makes you feel ignorant."*

Although George Bernard Shaw's view that; *"If all economists were laid end to end they would not reach a conclusion."* should make those who do feel ignorant, to feel a little less so.

While the words of JERI's next caption compliment, not only my own belief but that of many women, her illustration also gives me another neat coincidence.

When living in Norfolk my sister's and I patronised a high fashion outlet called JANE, where purchases were packaged in identical fashion to that depicted in our mother's next cartoon that she devised many years prior to the birth of our Norwich JANE.

Impossible People

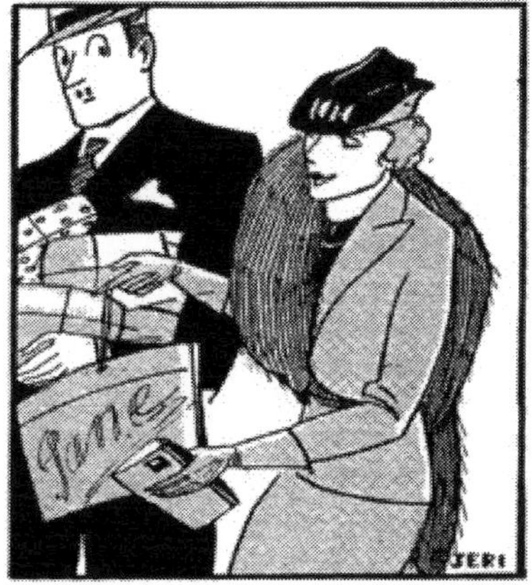

The woman who thought economy was a way of spending your money without getting any enjoyment out of it

Much as many may think when spending money on -

ACCOUNTANTS - Numbers

A number will find
fulfillment enough
in knowing its mind
and doing its stuff.

Apart from how the word is spelt I know little or nothing about 'numbers' and, where possible, have always avoided any 'relationship' with people who add-up things as, aside from our excellent accountant, Phillip Needham, they have invariably cost me more than they have saved me.

Impossible People

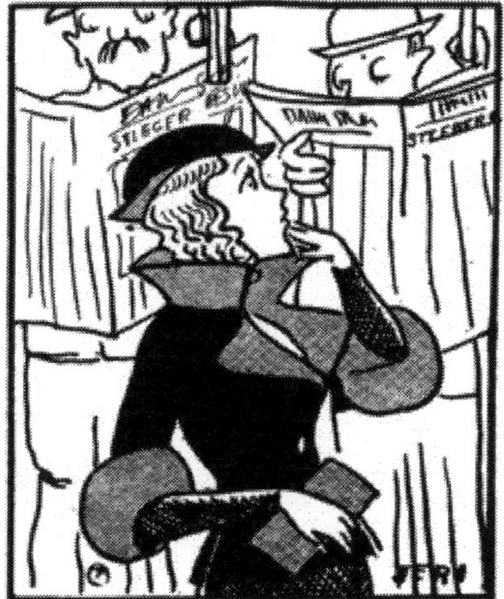

The typist who thought St. Leger was the patron saint of bookkeepers.

If you want to know
where your money went
You must spend it quickly
before it's spent.

When very young I thought bookkeepers, (one of only 49 English words spelt with a double 'k'), were people who worked in lending libraries which led me to think it would be a pleasing career until I learnt it had little to do with books and a lot to do with ledgers.

But not Horse racing - or Patron Saints.

Nor my father's career in the highly charged, costly field, that involved -

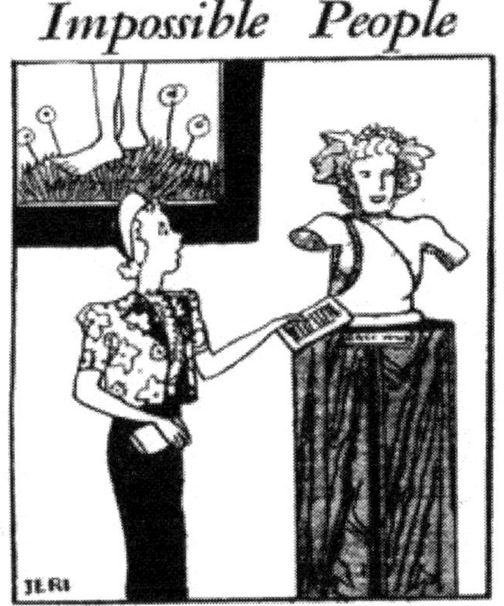

The girl who thought Bacchus was the god of bookmakers.

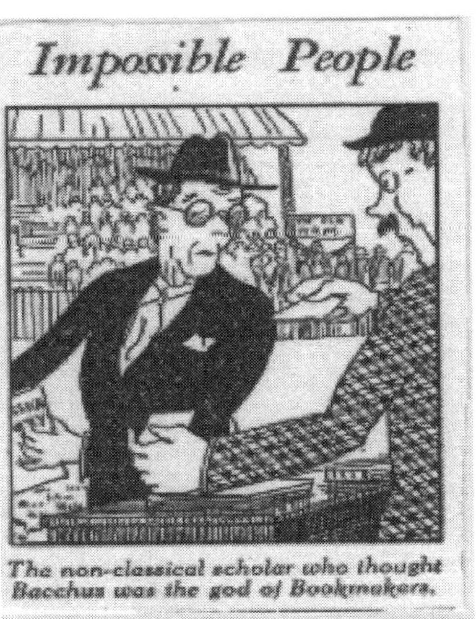

The non-classical scholar who thought Bacchus was the god of Bookmakers.

GAMBLERS

It is clear that our mother would often gain inspiration for her captions from our father's love of gambling. She would, as I mention earlier, also get inspiration by revisiting her own captions - as in

As also mentioned previously, our brother, Boris, once owned the Lillybrook Hotel situated just a few miles outside Cheltenham. A hotel where we spent many 'happy hours' enjoying many glamorous functions and where, when unattached, I spent an equal number of hours hiding from unsuitable suitors.

But not from my female friends, whom I would invite to join me at such delights as Gold Cup Day. One of whom, Janet, was patently not a fan of this sport as, shortly after our arrival, she looked up at the crowds of excitable race goers in the viewing stands and then down at the frenetic activity at the edge of the course and said, *"You know, Karina, I have just realised why I have*

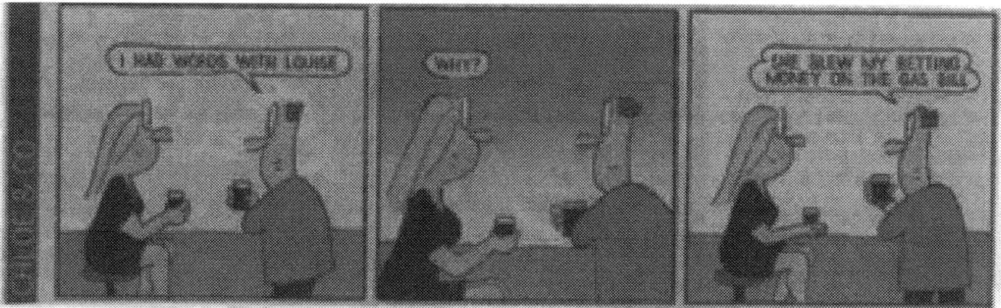

never been to the races before and have just remembered why I'm never going again."

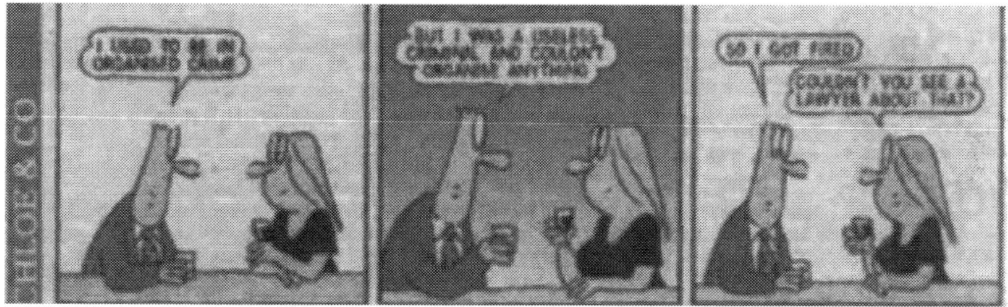

It is very sad that Mama would never see this Grey and Schapp Chloe & Co cartoon, particularly as our father's 'gambling money' was provided by our mother's ability to be so humorous about his penchant for this activity.

Or this one, as she was equally amusing about our father's propensity to dabble in (dis)organized crime, at which he was equally inept - even if he saw a lawyer

Media articles frequently propound the theory that people are either lucky or unlucky. This is true. They also suggest that those who think they are going to win do, and those who think they won't, don't. This is not true. I always thought I would win and didn't. So now I don't try as I know I won't.

Conversely, Sonya, who never even bothers to think about whether she will or she won't, always wins - everything. She and our brother-in-law, George, are both inherently lucky. George even won his Vintage Bentley in the end.

Sonya is the only person I know who never loses money in Vegas. She nags me to go and says I will love it. I won't!

Impossible People

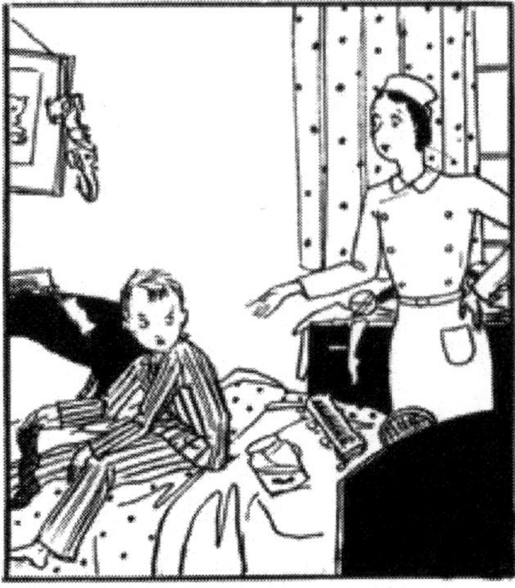

The boy who said not for the horses his daddy backed when told there was a place for everything.

I have fallen in love with men who have lost me money and have no intention of falling in love with a place that has an even greater propensity to do the same. Men very similar to my father who, having majored in gambling, gained a degree in 'Hedging-Your-Bets'. Although, as is often the case with qualifications, it was of little benefit to him.

Was this because he always put too much faith in 'St Leger'? Which, somewhat philosophically, takes us to -

PHILOSOPHERS

Many of whom, if they knew of them, might have this Piet Hein Grook hung large on their walls;

Wanting To Be Able To

Impossibilities' are good
not to attach that label to;
since, correctly understood,
if we wanted to,
we would be able to.

But not these: The First Law of Philosophy: For every philosopher there exists an equal and opposite philosopher. The Second Law of Philosophy: They're both wrong.

And from Louis Pasteur; *"A bottle of wine contains more philosophy than all the books in the world."* A belief that many people, even the Impossible ones, would agree with. But whether we imbibe wine or not, the questions is: 'Do philosophers gamble with our beliefs?' One of which is that 'Laughter Is The Best Medicine' –

HUMOUR - and a Few Funny Facts

Writers who make us laugh are one of our most precious commodities, because you can go back to them again and again if you need a fix.

My thirty-ninth year was one of the lowest of my life, but these are not the pages to go into the woes that beset me at that time. However, I was saved, not from attempts at suicide - I'm too much of a scaredy-cat for that - but from thoughts of how it might be done without making a mess on the carpet or frightening the cat, by a book, a very funny book.

My saviour was 'My Uncle Oswald' by Roald Dahl. I laughed so much I thought I would die – which, of course, was not the point of the exercise. So die I did not and now, if I get low, I get high again by reading something equally hilarious such as Guy Browning's. 'Never Hit A Jellyfish With A Spade', a much appreciated gift from my equally beloved, late, cousin, Elaine. Or my husband's; 'Dear Mr. Archimedes - The First Health and Safety Loo Book.' A book as funny when read outside a 'loo' as in one.

I am not alone. Quentin Letts, a writer with a wit sharper than a stiletto, wrote: *'A girlfriend of mine once dabbled with going to a shrink. I managed to steer her on to the novels of P.G Wodehouse instead. She soon cheered up and it saved us a great deal of money.'*

It is also the best means of defusing any situation heading towards acrimony - in all walks of life - including sport which, for something seemingly so enjoyable, seems to lead to a great deal of ire.

Impossible People

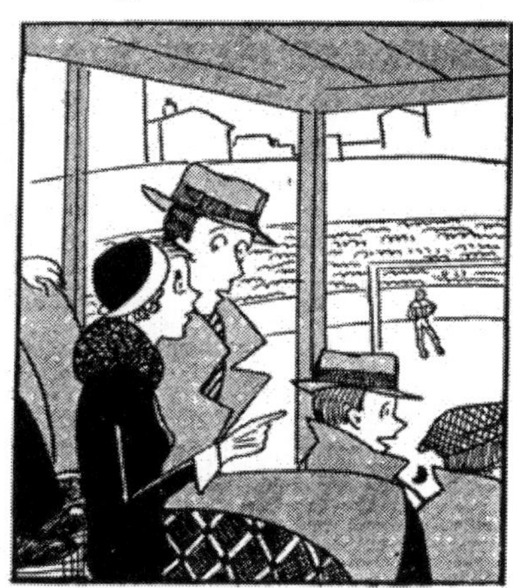

The girl who asked if the fouls in football were the same as the ducks in cricket.

Perhaps that was Hitler's problem - too many fouls, not enough ducks and no sense of humour. He was going to bump off my mother because she made the odd joke about him.

"A country that has a name that starts with the word 'Germ' has to be a little suspect!" was one of her more frequent offerings. A very 'Non PC' remark in today's world, but as my mother lived through, or, more correctly, suffered, both of Germany's attempts at annihilating the rest of us, she could be forgiven for making the odd joke against The Enemy.

She was not alone as, in 1966, when England and Germany were about to 'battle it out' in the World Cup final Vincent Mulchrone quipped; *"If today Germany beats us at our national game, we will have the consolation of knowing that we have beaten them twice at theirs."*

It has also been said of the Germans: *"Their sense of humour is no laughing matter."* Which most certainly does not apply to the three nations deserving awards for their citizens' ability to laugh at themselves - England, Ireland and Israel. As I have the inner and outer workings of two of these, my ability to laugh at myself is possibly greater than that of most.

The English make jokes about the Irish and the Irish make jokes about the Kerry people. The same applies to France. The French joke about the Belgians, the Belgians about the Flemish. It is all harmless, good, clean fun. But about whom do the Flemish and the Kerry people make jokes?

My dearly beloved, but sadly late, friend, Ivis, who lived in Newport Beach, told me about a wealthy Californian who, on being diagnosed with an apparently incurable illness, took a hotel suite, employed a team of nursing staff and, by viewing nothing but comedies, laughed himself well. Which, if true, confirms that laughter really IS the best medicine.

Unlike cartoons, jokes rely on the ability of their raconteur for impact. Many Irish and Jewish jokes told without their respective accents can 'fall flat'. However English jokes told in virtually any accent, are universally amusing. Unless told to Americans, of whom it has been said: *"It is impossible to underestimate their bad taste"*.

Nor do they understand English humour, but they do deserve merit for their 'good humour' when being laughed at!

I am not the only person with this opinion. Bill Bryson, one of the most amusing writers on the planet whose English home is adjacent to that of our Norfolk doctor friends, (Sonya's cousin-in-law, Roy and his partner, Peter), writes in his highly hilarious book; 'Notes From A Big Country', anecdotal evidence of why he believes Americans don't have a Funny Bone.

Substantiated by the occasion when, following a flight from Denver, a friend asked Bill; *"Who did you fly with?"* and then looks at him with an expression of near panic when Bill said; *"I don't know, they were all strangers."*
He writes; *'The easy conclusion to draw from this evidence, and one to which even the most astute outside observers are all too often tempted, is that Americans are inherently incapable of getting a joke.'*

He continues; *'Howard Jacobson, a man of great intelligence and discernment, notes in his work: 'In The Land of Oz.' that Americans don't have a sense of humour.' And; 'It would be but a day's work to find thirty or forty comments in a similar vein in modern works.'*

He then contradicts this view by listing many Americans who have an equal ability to be as hilarious in both their writing and speech as the brilliant Mr. Bryson.

Nevertheless, as he points out: *"Wit is not venerated as a quality (in America), as it is in Britain."* And then quotes John Cleese who said; *"An Englishman would rather be told he was a bad lover than that he has no sense of humour."* Bill then says; *"However, when you do meet an American with humour it is similar to two Masons recognising each other."*

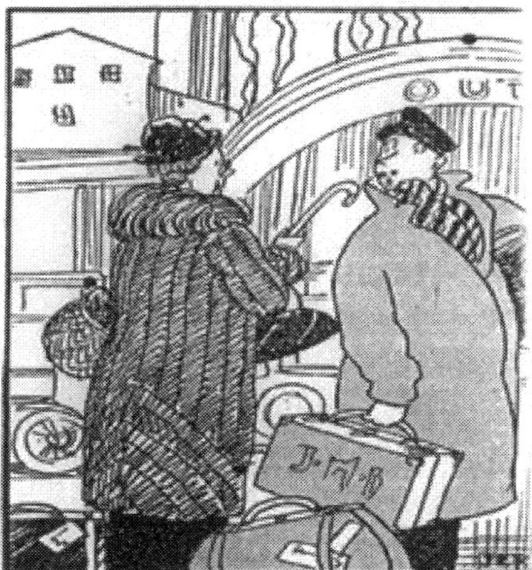

The old lady who, when the taxi-driver told her he was engaged, said she wished him every happiness, but he must not let love interfere with business.

Recognition superbly illustrated by an exchange Bill once had with an airport cabbie. On being asked if he was free, the cabbie looked at Bill with an expression he recognised as that of someone who knows a good line when it's handed to him, confirmed by his straight faced response of; *"No I charge just like everyone else."*

Most cabbies, especially those in London and New York, do have a highly defined sense of humour. Although this may be due to the fact that many of them are new immigrants.

I write this with some confidence as my own experience of New York cabbies is that they hale from every corner of the globe. Thus it is possible that the heritage of Mr. Bryson's cabbie was possibly nearer to Europe than Bill's. Even, perhaps, England, the home of the humorous riposte that are said daily by our own cabbies and taxi drivers. Or by their Fares?

And while many British people, and even the odd, in both senses of the word, American - Bill Bryson for one – believe Americans don't have a sense of humour, is this because they don't always find it easy to understand ours because they don't always know what it means?

Confirmed by Prince Phillip's suggestion (and that of Robert McCloskey) that; *"Understanding of what is said isn't always an understanding of what is meant."* But, despite the supposition that Americans do not understand English humour, the British most certainly understand and love American humour that wafts over to us like a health giving tonic from the other side of The Pond.

Impossible People

The girl who said it was absurd to say that women had no sense of humour, because the more they were humoured the better they liked it.

The magnificent comical genius of American authors, cartoonists, writers - and their citizens in general - give us enjoyment beyond pearls. While their supremely clever comedians can take us to heights of laughter rarely reached.

Many of the best, say I, being women.

Also, much to their credit, Americans go in for a great deal of razzmatazz and razzle-dazzle, which is very jolly, cheers everyone up and gives me four more double zz's.

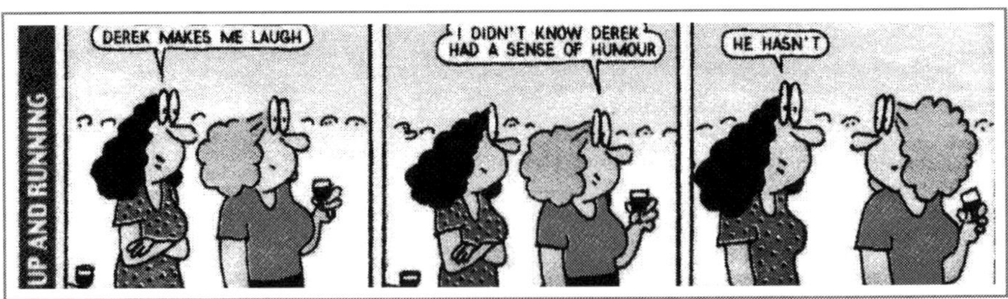

It is also another good reason to be ever thankful to them for using, if not in the same way, the same language. My second husband, Christopher, was a gifted mimic of accents. This gave him the ability to tell a joke better than anyone I've ever known - as in 'known to me personally.'

Although, on hearing me tell someone what a great sense of humour he had, Chris said: *"It's Karina who has the sense of humour, I just tell the jokes, she laughs at them."*
To my 'enjoyment' I have married two men with a finely tuned sense of humour, for while Chris was (and possibly still is), a master raconteur, Simon is a genius of the witty riposte.

A gift much easier to live with because when 'holding the floor' while telling a joke, Chris, required an attentive audience, while Simon's is more relaxed, as his witty, amusing and clever repartee in conversation merely requires an 'attentive ear' –

As in -

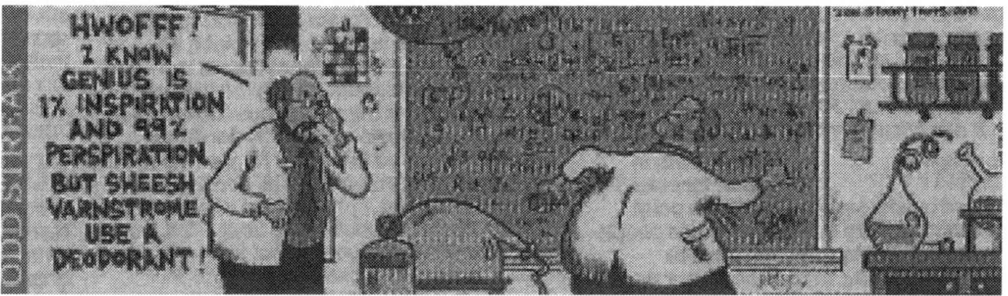

On asking him whether it was Edison or Einstein who said, *"Genius is one percent inspiration and ninety nine percent perspiration,"* He said; *"Edison."* To which I said; *"Yes, I suppose it must have been as Edison invented things while Einstein only thought of things."*

To which Simon said; *"I think you have slightly underestimated Einstein's contribution to humanity."*

An exchange that allows for inclusion of this next Odd Steak cartoon.
And this next neat exchange.

Professor Higgins: "Good morning, sir. How are you"?
Professor Einstein: "Relative to what"?

Impossible People

The woman who said "Whisky the night before" when her husband asked her what to take for a head-ache.

Simon, among his many other attributes, is a great connoisseur of Malt whisky – that is not to say he drinks it greatly, he just enjoys it greatly - so his mother-in-law's next cartoon could have been composed especially for him.

Her next cartoon, on the same topic, might as easily have been composed for Sonya's husband, Ray, who has now joined those drinkers at the great cocktail bar in the sky.

The man with a passion for tidiness who would only have his whisky neat.

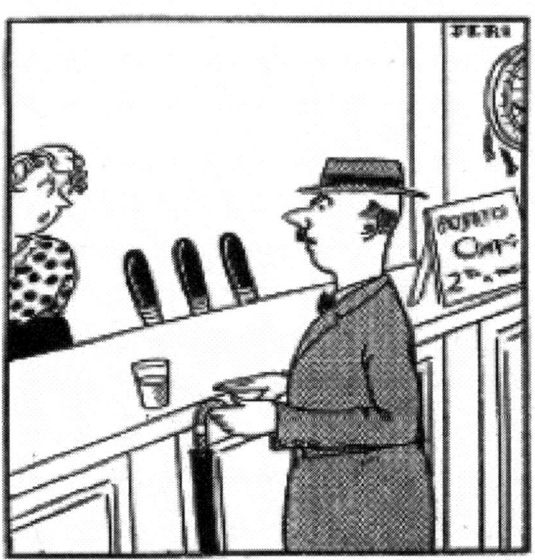

So perhaps he and Mama, with our brother Stefan, Sasha's husband John , his sister Doreen, our cousin, Elaine, and my two darling grandsons, Laurence and Ralph, are, as I write, enjoying a tipple together?

Ray was not a great lover of whiskey – his preferred drink being a G&T - but he was a very tidy man in every sense of the word and, had he drunk it, would have taken it 'neat'.

Ray died in February 2009, two weeks after the anniversary of an exceptionally happy, fifty year marriage to Sonya. Knowing him for the same length of time, I knew him to be a man deserving of a memorial in my book - even if it is just a cartoon. (Although it is unjust to describe JERI's cartoons as just 'just'!)

Despite attempts to hang on to our sense of humour, a new, nasty, disease: 'The Presumption of Offence' is now intent on killing all forms of this life enhancing gift. An example is the Jihad, imposed in 2007, on the Danish cartoonist who 'dared to insult' Mohammed. A cartoon, we can be confident, Mohammed himself would have found amusing as one of the most notable things about the truly good and the truly great is their ability to laugh at themselves.

Much as God must have done when he made ducks quack. For, as F.W. Harvey maintains in the final part of his wonderful poem; 'Ducks';

When God had finished the stars and whirl of coloured suns,
He turned His mind from big things to fashion little ones.
Beautiful tiny things (like daisies) He made, and then,
He made the comical ones in case the minds of men
Should stiffen and become
Dull, humourless and glum:
And so forgetful of their Maker be
As to take even themselves - quite seriously.

Caterpillars and cats are lively excellent puns;
All God's jokes are good - even the practical ones!
And as for the duck, I think God must have smiled a bit,
Seeing those bright eyes blink on the day He fashioned it.

And He's probably laughing still
At the sound that came out of its bill.

The first two parts of this lengthy poem can be found (if you're lucky enough to find a copy), in a book compiled and Illustrated by Fougasse, entitled 'Animal Anthology'. In 1955 I gave a copy to my mother as a birthday gift and, as I am now 'the keeper' of her large collection of anthologies, this delightful book is still in my possession.

While I know a great deal about Mama and poetry, I know little about Mohammed, but can, again, be reasonably confident he would be pleased to be associated with some of Mother Nature's more amusing foibles. Much as I am equally confident both he and God would very unhappy if they knew how 'dull, humourless and glum' some of their respective Flocks have now become.

A glumness caused, perhaps, because the greater the number of people within a country from different ethnic and religious backgrounds, the greater the diminution in their ability 'to take a joke'. Or, of even greater importance, 'to make a joke'.

Confirmed by media reportage about a popular and well liked Editor of a British provincial journal, Mr. Lusby, who was forced to resign by his local council after they received 'a complaint' about his Irish jokes! The Daily Mail then bravely published some of these jokes and I then, bravely, saved them.

However, the worst aspect of this 'witch hunt' is that Mr. Lusby is IRISH! If an Irishman can't make jokes about the Irish, who can? 'Negative' coming before

'Positive' in the dictionary seems to determine its order of priority in the brain. Which may be the reason for the human failing of always thinking the worst.

However authors - and editorial journalists such as Mr. Lusby – never mean, or wish, to be unkind, they just want to inform, entertain and amuse their reader. A truth that applies world-wide.

As does this Irish Prayer:

May you live a long life full of gladness and health,
With a pocket full of gold as the least of your wealth.
May the dreams you hold dearest be those that come true,
And the kindness you spread keep returning to you.
May the friendships you make be those that endure,
And may all of your grey clouds be small ones for sure.
And as through your life you travel each day,
May a song fill your heart each step of the way.

A prayer obviously unknown to the 'Politically Correct Brigade' and the 'Thought Police,' who now deem it illegal to tell any joke anywhere at any time in case it might cause offence to someone - or anyone.

Which, perhaps, is why comedy writers now take cover under a hail of expletives. A tactic that may, eventually, lead to all comedy being an endless string of rude words. A supposition exquisitely criticized in Talirand's abjuration: *"Swearing is the means by which the inarticulate give themselves the impression of eloquence."*

Which gives me yet another, if somewhat obscure, pun and once again allows me, (if not quite in its true sense), to use the wonderful word 'abjure'.
A word, my OED tells me, that is from the Latin word: abjurare' as in 'ab' – 'away' aligned to the word 'jurare' - 'swear'. Which the Irish rarely have need to do when being whacky and witty or hilariously funny.

Impossible People

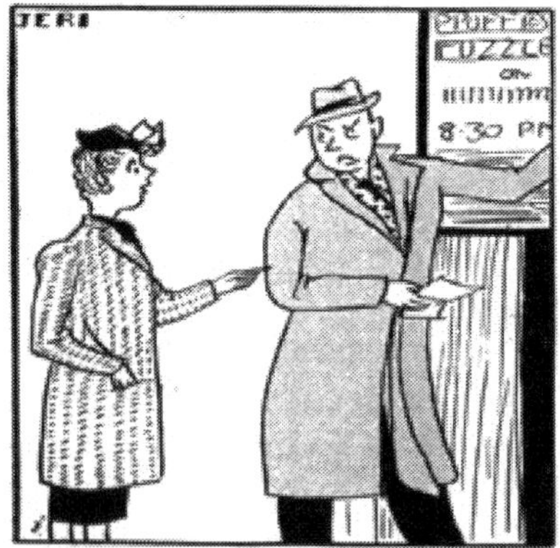

The man who said he was going to a lecture with an unprejudiced, unbiased, open mind to listen to something he was convinced was absolute rubbish.

As confirmed in –

LAUGH AWHILE IRISH STYLE

The Irish, helped enormously by their delightful accent and mode of speech, have always had a magical ability to be hilarious in their everyday interaction with their nearest and dearest – and many not so near - which allows them, always, to keep an open mind -

A cartoon that would have appealed greatly to the brilliant Irish comedian, Dave Allen. A comedian whose relaxed, insouciant manner made him one of our finest and funniest.

With the universal fame of such people as Mr. Allen, via a little help from the internet and television, (with their attendant benefits and not a few ills), Ireland has now caught up with the rest of the world, but when I worked there in the 1960's it was like stepping back in time.

As are most people when they first arrive, I was enchanted and enraptured by this beautiful island and its wonderful people and, as most people do following a stay there, I came away from my numerous visits with numerous, hilarious anecdotes. A few of which I now share with my reader.

As had Mama when driving her Maxwell in France, I loved driving my Sunbeam Tiger on roads that had little traffic on them. Roads which, at that time, sported equally few road signs.

On asking why this was so, I was told quite seriously (but almost certainly with tongue in cheek), that during the Second War, in order to confuse the Germans should they find their way to Ireland, all the road signs had been taken down and had not been replaced because, by the end of the war, everyone had learnt how to find their way without them.

But not me! When having stopped to ask a farm worker how far it was to Killarney, he looked at me admiringly, even more admiringly and much longer, at my car and said; *"It's twenty mile but in that you'll do it in ten!"* An anecdote that leads to an Irish joke that also sports a sports car and Irish farmers.

Two Irish farmers on a tractor are pulling out of a field onto a narrow lane where, racing towards them, is a sports car travelling at a trillion miles an hour. The driver, on seeing the road blocked by the tractor, brakes so hard his car skids full circle, somersaults over a hedge into the field and bursts into flames. Turning to his companion the tractor driver said, *"Thanks be to God, Patrick, didn't we just get out of that field in time?"*

As Patrick is such a pleasing name when said with an Irish accent, is this why so many Patricks feature in so many Irish jokes? My next anecdote may also feature more than a few Patrick's as it involves many Irish men.

One bright sunny morning I was walking through Bantry Bay market wearing an orange mini dress when an elderly lady, dressed from tip to toe in black, on seeing me from the other side of the square, turned to her similarly garbed companion and in an extremely loud and very shrill voice, said; *"Sweet Jaesus, will you look at herr skirrt!"*

Thus ensuring me a warm welcome by all of the, mainly male, stall holders and their, mainly male, customers. Of equal warmth to the Irish was my financial standing. During one of the many bank strikes that occurred in Ireland at that time, I was staying in the tiny village of Scull where the Landlady of the pub in which, again, I spent many 'Happy Hours' was the mother of the impersonator, Mike Yarwood.

Mike told me he was 'resting' at his mother's in order to, 'Get over the drink!' I did wonder whether a bar was the best place in which to accomplish this, although despite his 'problem' I found him to be as entertaining in person as he was on television. Which made many of my 'Happy Hours' extremely amusing, as alcohol did not seem to impinge on his ability to be funny.

Which is often not the case with celebrities, but maybe it was the Guinness that made him so garrulous and, certainly to me, so gentlemanlike.

As credit and debit cards were then a 'thing of the future', with the banks closed, purchases of any kind, even a glass of Guiness, could only be made by cheque. Apparently mine, being English, had greater fiscal security than those of the Irish variety as, on my return to England, all those I'd written in Ireland were covered in dozens of other peoples signatures. Signatures that allowed for purchases of dozens of different things by dozens of people in dozens of shops, garages and not a few bars.

My very young reader (if I am lucky to have one), may not know that prior to our present almost blanket use of 'plastic' and internet banking, cash, cheques or a Standing Order, were the only methods of payment for anything and everything and a cheque, once issued, could continue to be used for payment by the recipient for something else if they signed the back of it. Then these re-issued cheques, when eventually paid into their account by one of these recipients, would be returned, with their statements, to the owner.

As it is now the intention that all transactions of any kind will eventually be made by card or via computer (thus saving a lot of time and paper but probably not fraud), the BIG question is: Will this be the death of all 'walking-about money' and thus all 'walk-in-banks'?

As Mama was often wont to say, "As things get better so they get worse." But not everything. Many years after my sojourn working in Ireland, Simon and I spent a delightful holiday in Killarney with our friends, Jenny and Mike,

Jenny's daughter, Jacqui, (who later gifted me with my grandson, Michael), and her daughter, Jessica.

One evening, as often happens in Ireland, we joined in light-hearted banter with several other diners of several other nationalities with all of whom we, later, joined in the piano bar for a riotous singalong. On apologising to one of the staff for our noisy exuberance, I asked if she and her colleagues would like us to leave.

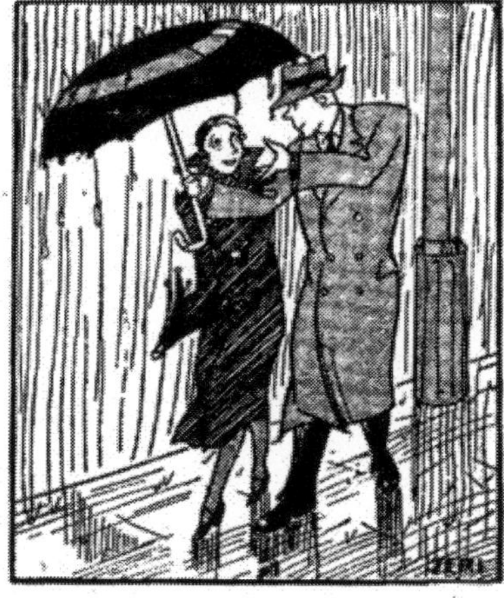

The Irishman who said one hour of this rain would do more good in two minutes than a month of it would do at any other time.

To which she said; *"Why in the name of St Patrick would we be askin' you to leave? It's such a great time we're havin' we've locked the doors so you cann'a."*

Which was just as well as, being Ireland, it was pouring with rain –

Possibly because the Irish accent is one of the most pleasing in the world, most of our more amusing jokes are about, or from, or on, the Irish.

As in;

Atheist parents, extremely concerned about their son's low school grades due to his lack of concentration and zero initiative to do his homework, decided, after much soul searching, to send him to an Irish Catholic school.

Within weeks they noticed an improvement in his school performance, especially
in maths, as every day he would come home from school and promptly head to his room to study his numbers.

Delighted with this transformation, his parents asked him why he was now so motivated. *"Is it that the Nuns are strict?"* they asked. *"No,"* said the boy. *"Is it that their subjects are more challenging?" "No,"* he said. *"Well,"* they queried, *"what is it that makes you so eager to study at this new school?"*

"Well," said the boy, *"On my first day, I was sitting in class looking around and saw, high up on the end wall, this naked guy nailed to a plus sign and figured these people really mean business!"*

And -

Having finished school, a bright young girl named Lena shook the dust of Ireland off her shoes and went to New York where she became successful in show business.

On a visit back to her home town, she went to confession in the church she had attended as a child where the priest, Father O'Sullivan, pleased to see her, asked about her new life. She told him she was now an accomplished acrobatic dancer and that she would be happy to show him what this was. So stepping out of the confessional but still within sight of the priest, she did several cartwheels, splits, backflips and handsprings.

Sitting near the confessional, waiting their turn, were two middle-aged ladies. One of whom turned to her friend and said; *"Will you just look at the penance Father O'Sullivan is givin' out this night, and me with no bloomers on!"*

My ex-sister-in-law, Leslie, as good a raconteur of jokes as her brother Chris, would say; *"Before I tell this joke is anyone here Irish?"* If anyone said yes, she would say, *"In that case I will tell it very slowly."*

My own experience of the Irish is that they don't need other people's jokes, whether told slowly or not, as they are some of the funniest and finest people on earth, even if some of them do get a bit too merry at times. Or occasionally sit on bits of land that don't belong to them.

One of my many business trips to Ireland was a mission to regain a tract of building land that had been legally purchased by Stefan and then immediately and illegally, claimed back by the vendor. There must be many, including myself, who wish they had the courage to do the same, but my courage at the time did win this building land back for Stefan.

Many years later when, as a London Landlady, I had occasion to refuse service to one of my Irish regulars, I said; *"Charlie, you're unwashed, unshaven and have already had too much to drink!"* About an hour later I had a message that he was outside and, although insisting he needed to talk with me, wouldn't come into the bar. On going outside I saw that he was washed, shaven and, if not smelling of roses, was at least close to it.

He said; *"I know you won't serve me today Missus but if I comes back termorrer, all shaven and with no drink inside me, will you so?"* How could I refuse?

An anecdote that reminded me of a similar story told to us by our mother who, in her twenties, witnessed the following amusing exchange between a haughty, up-market lady and a down-at-heel man who were both drinking tea in the Buffet at Victoria Station. Or, in the case of the woman, attempting to.

Endeavouring to drink her very hot cup of tea before her train left without her, she was manfully sipping the hot beverage when the concerned 'gentleman' at the next table leaned towards her and said; *"'Ere Missus, 'ave mine, it's all sugared, saucered and blowed."*

Thus the wonderful phrase, *"Sugared, saucered and blowed,"* became, in times of trouble or frustration, a regular saying of our mother and all of her offspring. As is –

Murphy's Law

If anything can go wrong it will;
Nothing is ever as simple as it seems;
Everything takes longer than you think;
If everything seems to be going well you have obviously overlooked something.

O'Toole's opinion of Murphy's Law: *"Murphy was an optimist."* But I'm not sure the same law could be applied to the Scots.

LAUGH AWHILE SCOTTISH STYLE

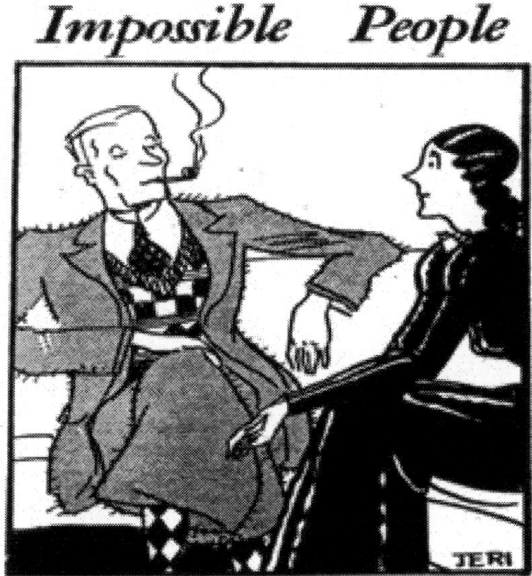

The Scotsman who said he came south as it was easier to make money where the population was more dense.

Are the English 'kilt' if they call a kilt a skirt? Yet again, as does Richard Littlejohn; 'I only ask the question'.

My mother's frequently expressed view, and nearly as often expressed by me in my Impossible People, that; *"All the brightest people come from Scotland and the brighter they are the quicker they come."* was possibly the inspiration for her next Impossible Scotsman.

Many years after the birth of this cartoon, our brother, Boris, when in Scotland on business was, by unfortunate circumstance, caught up in a fracas in Glasgow with the result that he spent a number of uncomfortable hours in an uncomfortable cell with some even more uncomfortable cell mates. (Definitely no laughing matter.)

The police, having established he was a man of probity and some standing, made a profuse apology to Boris for taking him for one of the miscreants. Instead of suing the police, as most people now would, he said; *"I just happened to be in the wrong place at the wrong time, and you were only doing your job."*

It is a great pity more people don't have his sense of 'justice'. But it does 'justly' allow for a neat pun and this next similar, joke.

A pharmacist in Ballater is visited by the local policeman. The two men had known each other all their lives, so it was with some regret that the policeman has to tell his friend that he has been instructed to arrest him on suspicion of making illegal whisky from the still in his pharmacy.

"Ye ken, I have never used the pharmacy still to make liquor," said the Chemist. *"Och aye, I ken that"*, said the Policeman, *'"But I haeve to be takin' ye in because ye haeve the equipment." "Wheil in that case,"* said the Chemist *"Ye'll need to arrest me on several counts of indecent exposure and rape." "I canna do that."* said his friend, *"Yu're no that kinda man."*

"That's as maybe," said the Chemist, *"but I haeve the equipment."*

An eighteenth century English visitor to Scotland is recorded as saying; *"A Scottish funeral is indeed merrier than an English holiday."* Has this anything to do with bagpipes, I ask?

I purchased some bagpipes last week,
And practiced their droning and squeak.
My neighbour next door who hails from Jaipur,
Said the noise of the pipes made him Sikh.

As I write in JERI's Real People, her father and forebears hailed from North of the Border, most of whom were very bright - hence their many awards and titles –

A student who hailed from Dumfries,
Weighed down by B.A.'s and Litt D.s,
Collapsed from the strain,
Alas, it was plain
She was killing herself by Degrees.

Impossible People

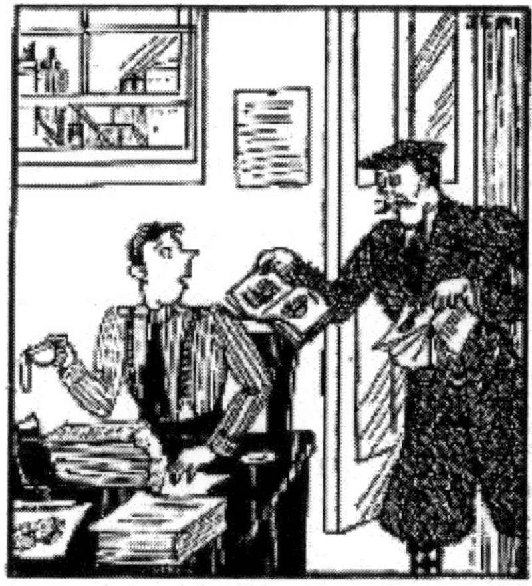

The Aberdonian who told the editor that if he published any more jokes about Scotsmen he would stop borrowing his paper.

Which, perhaps, is why so many of them made their way south? Although according to JERI's next caption, due perhaps to all the jokes made by the English about the Scots, a few do stay North of the Border.

Some, it would seem, in Aberdeen - A city that was one of our mother's favourite places and having visited Aberdeen with our friends Jenny and her Scottish husband, Mike, I now know why.

An Aberdonian, Sandy MacGregor, attended an international convention in New York. On his return to Scotland a friend asked him what he thought of the American people.

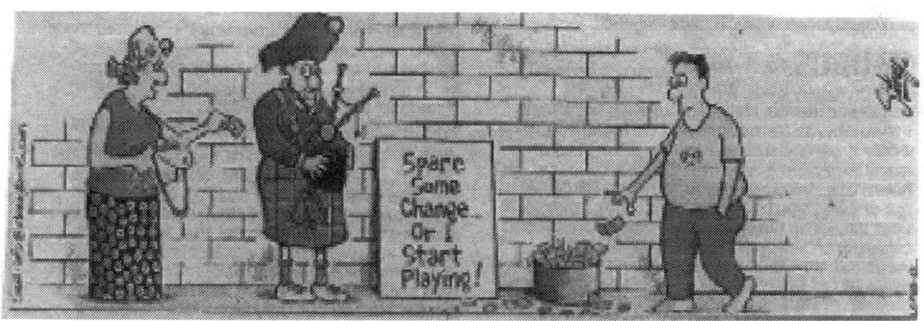

"Och! They were fine," said Sandy, *"but they had'na the sense to go to sleep at nicht." 'What do ya mean?"* asked his friend. *"Weel,"* said Sandy; *"all thru the nicht they kept poundin' on my hotel room door."*

His friend asked him; *"Did you no' go to see what all the to-do was about?" "Naw."* said Sandy, *"I just kept playin' ma bagpipes."*

A joke and Stoneytoons cartoon that confirm Sir Thomas Beacham's assertion that; *"Bagpipes sound exactly the same when you start learning them as when you finish."* Is this because, as Alfred Hitchcock said; *"I believe the inventor of bagpipes was inspired when he saw a man carrying an indignant, asthmatic pig under his arm. Unfortunately, the man-made object never equalled the purity of the sound achieved by the pig."*

You tell us, the pipes you abhor;
You're just one amongst many more;
Who believe in the past
That bagpipes were classed,
As an inhumane weapon of war.

It is said that bagpipers walk when they play to get away from the noise. Which, no doubt, is why the Scottish definition of a gentleman is: *'Someone who knows how to play the bagpipes but doesn't.'*

Nevertheless, regardless of the many unkind things that are thought or said about these musical instruments they do sound magnificent when played in the marvelous arenas of Edinburgh Castle and Fort George for both the Royal and Military Tattoos.

There is little, if any, historical information about bagpipes - instruments that are made almost entirely of organic materials, making them, generally, not durable.

Also, until recent modern alterations and improvements were made to their design and construction, they were thought of as 'the instrument of the common people' or those of low social status, such as shepherds, farmers and gypsies, and were thus used mainly, and understandably, outdoors.

For this reason not much seems have been written about them apart from their frequent use in jokes and cartoons, but they are now revered in Scotland in the same way the English revere stoicism, the Irish revere laughter, the Italians revere l'amour, the French revere gastronomy and the Germans once, or twice, revered Kreig.

The Scottish, in their own way, also revere love as they have their own distinct description of it: "A yeukieness o' the heart that the hand canna claw." But while there may be only one Scottish definition of love -

There must be many hundreds of French ones.

LAUGH AWHILE, a little more that a little while, **FRENCH STYLE**

It is said that: *"England is a country that has many religions and only one sauce while France is a country that has many sauces and only one religion."*

Impossible People

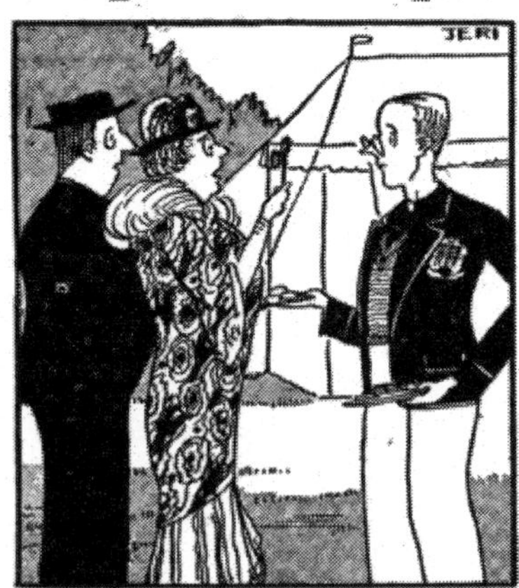

The young curate who said his ambition was to become Bishop of the B.B.See.

And according to JERI's next cartoon, England keeps adding ever more religions:

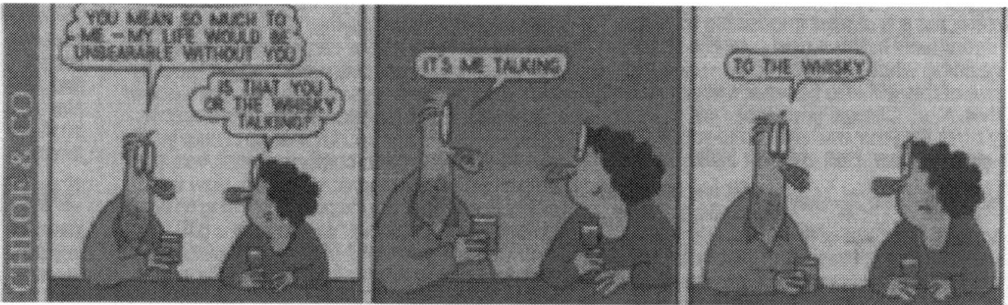

As I speak French well enough to tell a joke in that language, no mean feat, and can, mostly, understand those told to me, even more difficult, I can also vouch for the humour of the French – who prefer wine to whiskey -

As with most 'Impossible People,' the French enjoy jokes on all subjects, even those directed at themselves - or their loved ones - such as this next one told to us by our friend, Rene, who delights in telling bad French jokes in equally awful English.

"Jacqueline, while looking in the mirror, was bewailing the lines on her face, her lank hair and the bags under her eyes and asked me to say something nice about her, so I told her; At least your eyesight's O.K."

As I love Jacqueline, and my many other French friends, in both the North and the South, in equal measure, I know they will forgive me for including this observation by a Belgian acquaintance: *"If God could choose to live in any country in the world he would choose France. It is just such a pity that he gave it to the French."*

Above all, I love my gifted, unofficially adopted, daughter, Aurelie, who, when in her teens, told me she planned to study law and asked what the English word for Notare was. After several, unsuccessful attempts to pronounce the word lawyer she said she might prefer to be a writer instead. I said; *"In that case, Aurelie, you will be an author."*

After several agonising attempts at this word, she said, *"I think I will be a loyrer as orthrer is too difficult to pronounce."* Then, on learning that the English word for an arc-en-ciel is rainbow, she said; *"I think I will be an orthrer after all and write a Franglais book and call it Arc-en-Bow."*

Having gained her Baccalaureate at the Sorbonne and then a First in

International Law at King's College in London, she then graduated, two years later, with a First in the same subject from Madrid University.

Having become fluent in French, English, German and Spanish, she obtained work within the labyrinthine European Union. Her 'internment' as a Brussels internee was a great loss to her French family, her English friends and, by marriage, her German family.

In July 2013, Sonya, Simon and I were guests at her wondrous wedding in Brussels when she married her exceptionally bright, extremely pleasing, handsome German fiancé, Bodo Franz-Wilhelm Zebedaus Lehman. An extraordinary name that made the Acrostic poem I wrote for their wedding, the most difficult I have composed and impossible to translate into French – or German.

Nonetheless, as English is now widely spoken and, of more importance, understood, it was rewarded with much appreciative applause and 'Bravos'. Which I echoed when, a year later, Aurelie and Bodo 'rewarded' Simon and I with a surrogate grandson, Felix.

We first met Aurelie and her parents, Katrine and George when they made one of their regular visits to Katrine's parents, Jeanette and Alex. A charming couple who were the only near neighbour's of Sonya and Ray when they had a holiday home near Laval in the Pays de la Loire region of France, that was in a tiny village with the extremely large name of; Ruillé Froid Fonds,

However, despite her frequent visits to France Sonya found it impossible to learn French. She was also unable to overcome her intolerance to the preservative used in wheat but as the French don't put preservative in the flour from which they make their baguettes, she can enjoy their pain with no resulting pain!

A painless Franglaise pun that takes us to another amusing anecdote.

When dining in a restaurant in Laval with Rene and Jacqueline, her sister, Danielle and her husband, Guy, Sonya was telling them she had a severe intolerance to English bread due to the preservative in it. A disclosure that not only caused our companions, but also a few other diners to sit up and take notice.

Amid much hilarity, I told Sonya that the French for preservative is conservateur, (*"Isn't that a school?"* she asked), and that their word for contraceptive is preservatif.

A misunderstanding that turned our conversation, with somewhat less levity, to the pros and cons of immigration and the increasing size of these incomers families. Particularly in Laval which, at that time, appeared to be the worlds capital for enceinte African women. (Enciente being the rather more delicate French word for pregnant.)

Hoping to lighten the conversation, I said the French could save themselves this pain if they put preservatif in their pain? Amid much laughter, it was agreed that multiculturalism, while excellent in principle, is devilish in the detail. The subject of birth control makes me wonder how long it will be before the word 'condom' becomes as archaic as 'telephone box' and 'wireless'.

Although it will not be lost completely as, on my many journey's between England and Geneva, it always amused me to see the sign to 'Condom'. A town in the Gers region of the Midi-Pyrenees.

Even those English who don't speak French know that condoms are known as French Letters and that a hat or cap is a 'chapeau'. What they may not know is that the French word for cape is 'capote', (pronounced capo). Which is why the French call condoms: 'Les Capote Anglais'. So I think it's safe to include this next, amusing French joke. (Or even anecdote?)

When, on a visit to Paris, the wife of an English couple died, her distraught widower, wishing to buy a black hat, visits a gentleman's outfitters. On asking for a 'capeau noir' and being told they didn't stock them, he was about to leave the store when the salesman, a little puzzled, asked him why he wanted one.

When told by the man that his wife had just died, the assistant, without a hint of irony, said; *"Quelle finesse, Monsieur!"*

Misunderstandings of similar mispronunciations can be the cornerstone of amusing anecdotes, many of which I have already included together with a few more that I intend to bore my reader with. As may this tale on the same subject but a little closer to home.

Many moons ago, when working as P.A. to my mother's close friend, Marjorie Bayes, she was notified that, in recognition of her tireless and successful endeavours to improve maternity care throughout the world, she was to receive the French award of the *'Distinction de Legion d'Honneur'*.

At a grand gathering she was relating this exciting news to a small group of people when, due to a lull in the conversation, all of the guests heard her say, in tones redolent of Lady Bracknell; *"And I have the French letter in my handbag."* A superb oxymoron that dramatically changed the solemnity of the evening.

It also takes me, and my reader, to the time when we were investigating and, where possible, introducing family planning to those countries where, at that time, it was little used.

We were amused, but not surprised, to find a number of African countries (many of which have French as their first language), where white condoms were a 'turnoff' but all other colours, including black, were a definite 'turn-on'.

On reading this anecdote I hope my reader will consider that my phraseology refers to a period over half a century ago - a span of years during which untold changes now govern the way we talk, write or even think.

Much as, throughout the centuries, similar spans of time have created similar changes in the way we speak, write and think. But not necessarily how we behave?

The French footballer with the marvelous name of Zinedine Zidane (or Zizou or ZZ'), may not be a scholar but he is certainly a gentleman who could have saved the 2006 World Cup for France, (and himself from the opprobrium of his fellow citizens), had he,when responding to a barracking from an excitable Italian, kept his cool and answered with the classic put-down only possible in his own language; *"Monsieur, veuillez donner mes salutation distangué à Mademoiselle, votre Mere!"*

A phrase impossible to translate, with any delicacy, into English, which is why we use the more explicit, *"You bastard!"* An insult that, regardless of our parentage and our present, and correct, respect for the offspring of unmarried, single parents, still packs a punch.

Which takes us to yet another conundrum to which we will, almost certainly, never know the answer: Why, until relatively recently, were children who were born out of wedlock so badly thought of and equally badly treated, when their births were no fault of their own?

But, while it is certain that nothing is certain, nothing is more certain than that, language is certain to change –
even French –

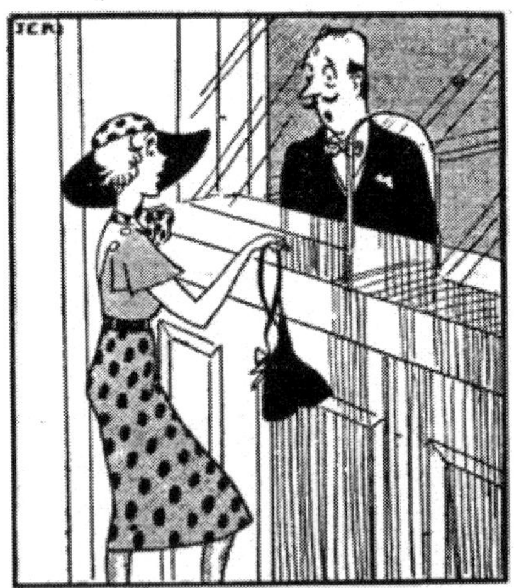

The visitor to a French coast resort who wanted to put on her bathing costume in the Bureau de Change.

Although she may have been better off leaving all the men in thrall by not changing at all.

There was a young lady from France
Who had an aversion to pants.
She said, "It sounds daft,
It's cold in a draft,
But I hope it will lead to romance."

As a frequent traveller to France, my mother would have known of these small, convenient Bureaus de Change that, even then, proliferated in that country.

Although when she composed her cartoon and its caption, few people, apart from those in the armed forces, government personnel, the adventurous or the very rich, and those who catered for them, would have had need to use these money-changing outlets that were, then, fairly foreign to most other countries. (Which gives me another neat pun.)

Now, nearly a century later, with levels of income and advances in methods of travel that allow vast numbers of people to visit vast numbers of foreign countries (for business or pleasure), there are few English speakers of any nationality, status, inclination or age who would not find my mother's cartoon amusing.

Apart, perhaps, from any young lady who thinks it might be a suitable place in which to change into her bathing costume, as, among the many millions of visitors who now invade France each year, there may still be a few who think a Bureau de Change is 'a changing room'.

Also what many may not know is that rabbit is an extremely popular food of the French. So much so that a young chef, Jean Luc, thought he would raise a few in Paris and sell them to the finer restaurants. Unable to find a suitable place to house them he was about to abort his plan when an elderly priest, Father Pierre, said he could house his pens in a small area behind the old rectory of the Cathedral. Having successfully bred a number, he went about Paris selling them.

When asked by his customers from where he got such fresh rabbit meat, he would say; *"I breed them near the cathedral where I have a hutch back of Notre Dame."*

The Eiffel Tower, (another famous icon of Paris that we can be confident, doesn't have a hutch back of it), was designed by Alexandre Gustave Eiffel for the 1889 World Fair, and, as the authorities wouldn't fund it, Eiffel agreed to finance and build the tower in return for all visitor entry fees for the next twenty years. A deal that, at that time, made him one of the richest entrepreneurs in France, and, to this day, one of the most famous.

Whether its numerous visitors are mainly foreign or French we are not told, but since it opened to the public, four hundred people have attempted to commit suicide by jumping from the top of it. Of these only two survived, one of whom was a lady who fell on a car and, later, married the owner of the car that saved her life. (*"Was this because it was a soft-top?"* asks Simon).

Staying with 'great heights', The Statue of Liberty, a gift from France to the United States of America was built, in 1886, by the French sculptor, Andre Bartoldi, and was then sent to America in 350 parts. (*"So it started life as a jigsaw!"* says Simon.)

If Napoleon had not sold French Louisiana to the United States in 1803, the States of Louisiana, Arkansas, Oklahoma, Kansas, Missouri, Colorado, Iowa, Nebraska, Wyoming, Montana, Minnesota, South and North Dakota would, today, be partly or completely French.

There are those who maintain that the Limerick was born in France during the Middle Ages, and then crossed the English Channel. As did this medieval lady;

A medieval lady from France,
Was daring enough to wear pants.
A knight named Sir Faust
Said, "I'd ask you to joust,
But I see that you don't have a lance."

There are many others, among whom was once myself, who believed, due to their name, that these, often naughty, fiver liners were first conceived in Limerick in Ireland.

However there more likely place of birth was Italy, confirmed by the Latin limerick I include on page 115 by St Thomas of Aquinas, Or even Greece, as Aristotle was also thought to have composed these odd odes – although I can find no proof of how or why.

What I did find was the name of a small French town in the Somme Department that is renowned for having the shortest name in the world; Y. The female inhabitants of Y are known by the, unpronounceable, Ypsiloniennes and its menfolk by the even more difficult, Ypsiloniens.

Y is twinned with a town on the Isle of Anglesey with a name that has 58 letters. It is recorded in the Guinness Book of Records as having the longest place name in Britain – or, say I, anywhere else?

Llanfairpwllgwyngyllgogerychwyrndrobwllllantysiliogogogoch

A word that, when translated into English, becomes: 'Saint Mary's church in the hollow of the white hazel near to the fierce whirlpool and the church of Saint Tysilio of the red cave.' A name conceived in the 1860s by a local tailor who wanted to make his village famous for having a railway station with the longest name.

Which takes us, with some amusement, to –

LAUGH AWHILE - just a little while – **ENGLISH STYLE**

When, as Senior Assistant to my unofficial 'aunt', Marjorie Bayes, I learned that, although she was very highly thought of and excellent at her job, she was amusingly naïve.

When driving her to a meeting in my Hillman Imp, she told me she had once refused a proposal of marriage from a man who had offered to give her a gift of a Humber Hawk, and then asked me; *"Why would you marry a man who wanted to give you a bird?"*

She may, many years earlier, have told our mother the same tale, which, in turn, may have led to the creation of this next Impossible girl –

Impossible People

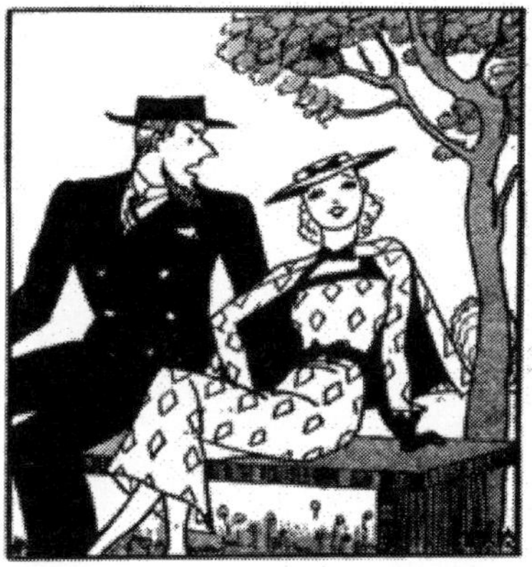

The girl who asked what horse-power it was when her friend told her he had just bought a Rembrandt.

A young lady who makes me think that, although I can find no trace of it, at that time there must have been a car called a Rembrandt.

The 'creation and standardisation' of horsepower almost certainly made its Scottish inventor, the engineer, James Watt, wealthy enough to buy several Rembrandts.

When working out the most efficient use of steam engines he decided that, as horses were used to 'generate shaft power', the horse was the logical unit on which to base engine power. His final, 'rounded up' calculations resulted in 33,000 foot-pounds per minute. Which, usefully, was a multiple of 60 minutes.

A 'calculation' a little above my understanding – and, no doubt that of Marjorie's, who, on being told that a 'moggie' would rid her of the mice that were plaguing her ancient apartment in Prince of Wales Drive, Battersea,

visited a hardware store in search of this 'apparatus'.
At one ICM luncheon at which the VIP speakers were Sir John Peel, who, at the time, was the Queen's gynaecologist, and Sir Keith Joseph, our then, Minister of Health, Marjorie, announced, in her usual stentorian tones; *"The prenuptial drinks are about to be served in the next room".*

On hearing this marvelous malapropism, the look on the faces of these two men suggested they may have preferred to make a swift move to the nearest exit. Despite her many hilarious faux-pas, Marjorie was dynamic and industrious in her 'avowed intent' to improve midwifery throughout the world.

Towards the end of her career, she persuaded the World Health Organization, in conjunction with our own Health Ministry, to run a five year research and analysis of world midwifery. The findings, published in 1969 as 'Maternity Care in the World', radically changed for the better the lives of millions of women - and not a few babies.

Marjorie was a 'Yorkshire Lass', a county that is one of our most hilly, while Norfolk is one of our flattest. Which led to the belief that jokes told in Norfolk often 'fall flat'. An assumption I believe is a joke, as I have been entertained by as many Norfolk folk telling as many very funny jokes as I have been by anyone from any other county - whether hilly or not.

As is this one from our friend, Ken Dewing, a man who, despite having a heart that once lived in another county, still speaks with a full-on Norfolk accent.

A couple walked into a garage and found exactly the make, model and colour of the car they were looking for. When the salesman told them the price, the man said; *"At the garage down the road, they said it would be a thousand pounds less." "Then best you go and buy it from them,"* said the salesman. *"But they haven't got one,"* said the punter. *"Well Bor,"* said the salesman, *"When we haven't got one ours are a thousand pounds less."*

I once overheard one of my London public house customers describe his ex-wife as; *"Flat and uninteresting, similar to Norfolk, the county where she was born."* It took only a nanosecond to disabuse him of this notion, as Norfolk's Cathedrals are all tall, extremely

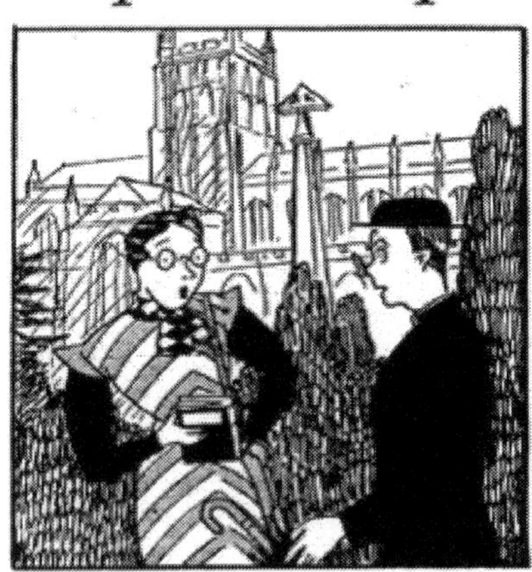

The American visitor who said there were so many cathedrals it was no wonder these countries were called the British Aisles.

interesting and, according to JERI, are full of Aisles. Which is a natural lead to:

LAUGH AWHILE - a very little while - **AMERICAN STYLE**

The owner of a golf course in Texas was confused about paying an invoice, so he decided to ask his secretary for some mathematical help. He called her into his office and said; *"You graduated in math, if I were to give you $20,000, minus 14%, how much would you take off?"* The secretary thought for a moment, then said, *"Everything but my earrings."*

Did she once work for Bill Clinton, one wonders?
There are many leaders world-wide who, having said little of any import and done less, sink into oblivion once their term of office is over. Nevertheless much amusement can be gained from politicians of all persuasions and nationalities - whether they are 'movers and shakers' or are just 'marking time'.

Some of the latter, despite there having been comparatively so few of them, being American. With the numerous colourful and hilarious anecdotes and innuendos made about America's Presidents, it is surprising that no one has yet written a book about their mad antics, proclivities, and (occasionally asinine), activities. Perhaps Bill Bryson may like to lend his pen to this?

Impossible People

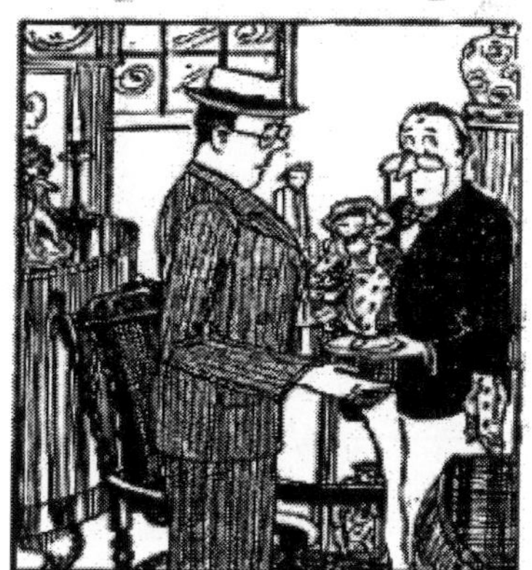

The American who said Queen Anne must have had an enormous dining room, as this was the tenth sideboard of hers he had seen this week.

For while the British have a good grounding and understanding of American history, this is not reciprocated by the Americans when it comes to English politics or history or, it would seem, antiquity.

A cartoon that also illustrates how our mother's incredible artistry allowed her to interpret how an American gentleman might look in the twenties and thirties as opposed to an English gentleman of the same period.

As she could have done for many nationalities – even, perhaps, Israel.

LAUGH AWHILE - a little longer - **JEWISH STYLE**

My own background being a smidgeon Jewish, I find their humour some of the best in the world. As are the Irish, Jews are genetically wired to be amusing.

Even when cranky they are funny, and when they are trying to be funny they are hilarious. Also, as with the Irish, their immediately recognisable accent makes their mode of speech a delight to listen to. Perhaps due to their wondrous words: 'shikse' (which could possibly apply to me), schnook' (which definitely applies to me), 'schmaltz', 'schlemiel', 'schnorrer' and, most marvelous of all, 'schnozz'.

With the integration of Jewish immigrants into Britain, their humour, over many years, has filtered into our own and many of our greatest comedians and writers of comedy are, or have been, Jewish.

Among my many books is a 'An Encyclopedia of Jewish Humour' a gift from my brother, Stefan. Compiled by Henry D. Spalding, it is a hefty tome of riotous and ribald digs about Jews on Jews by Jews and includes this version of the many different versions of this verse, devised from the quatrain that, so Wikipedia tells me, was first composed in 1590 by Sir Edmund Spense,

Roses are reddish,
Violets are bluish,
If it weren't for Christmas,
We would all be Jewish.

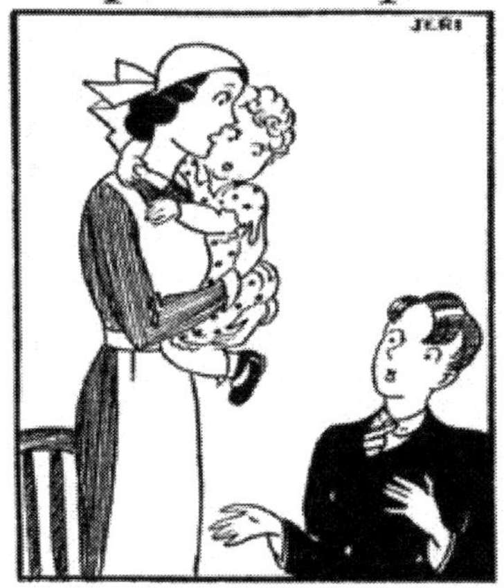

The boy who said he had made his hands so dirty washing his face.

It also includes a joke that is identical to the wording of the caption that my mother composed for this next Impossible Child. A child whose Nanny patently doesn't view her charges dirty hands as remotely amusing.

As the previous cartoon was published over forty years prior to the 1969 publication of Mr. Spalding's Encyclopedia, perhaps he had seen my mother's cartoon prior to compiling his book.

Although as the caption and the joke were created years apart, we can be confident that, with no knowledge by the creators of their 'twin', they were, as both I and Mr. Silver suggest: 'Original Thought'.

Jewish jokes are legion, so it is difficult to choose which to include, particularly as there are so few Impossible People cartoons with which to complement them. But these, next two, if not the funniest, typify superbly the reason why Jewish jokes are not only very clever, but are instantly recognisable as being Judaic, even when told with an English accent.

A young girl on a plane is admiring the extremely large diamond ring of the lady sitting in the adjoining first class seat. *"Oh my!"* said the girl, *"what a fantastic diamond! I would just love to have one like that." "No you wouldn't,"* said her neighbour, *"This is the Finklefeffer diamond, no woman in her right mind would want it." "Why is that?"* asked the girl. *"Because it has a dreadful curse on it."* replied the woman. *"Goodness!"* said the girl, *"What is this dreadful curse?" "It's my husband, Mr. Finklefeffer,"*

And:

A Rabbi and a Priest were alone together on a train and got into conversation. After a while the Priest said to the Rabbi, *"As no one can hear us, tell me, Rabbi, have you ever eaten pork?" "Yes, Father,"* said the Rabbi, *"I have to admit that I have, just once."*

The Rabbi then asked the Priest; *"Now I've admitted this sin, tell me Father, in the strictest confidence between two men of the cloth, have you ever been with a woman?"*

"Yes, Rabbi." said the Priest, *"I have to admit, I have, just once."* To which the Rabbi said; *"It's better than pork, isn't it."*

And two of Sonya's favourites:

Nat and Rafael were having a drink together when Nat said to Rafael, *"At last I've done a deal on that small menswear shop situated between Austin Reed and Burtons." "Why would you want to buy that store?"* said Rafael, *"The last three tailors who opened there went bust. What makes you think you will do any better?" "Because."* said Nat, *"I'm going to call it 'Main Entrance'."*

Some years later these two friends met at their regular watering hole and Rafael told Nat he had just been paid the insurance for a fire at his store. *"That's a coincidence."* said Nat; *"I've just been paid out the insurance for the flood I had in my store."* Admiringly Rafael asked; *"How did you arrange a flood?"*

Much of Jewish humour is based on business. One of which is the proudly displayed name of a restaurant in Philadelphia: 'The Kosher Noshstra.' Another is the sign on the Crown Car Wash in Los Angeles: 'Drive in and give us the Latest Dirt.'

Walter Winchell wrote that he had seen this on a West 56th Street coal and kerosene dealer's sign: 'Fuel's Paradise.' On the wall of Grasnoff's grocery store in Milwaukee:

'I'm sure your check (sic) is good, I just don't trust your bank.' How prophetic! And on a bulletin board outside a synagogue in Miami is: 'Come Early and Get a Back seat'.

As with their highly-charged sense of humour, their sense of the ridiculous is second to none. An excellent, extremely amusing, example is the sign in the window of Alpertson's Antique Store in Chicago: 'Best prices paid for old furniture and Junk - Genuine Antiques sold here!'

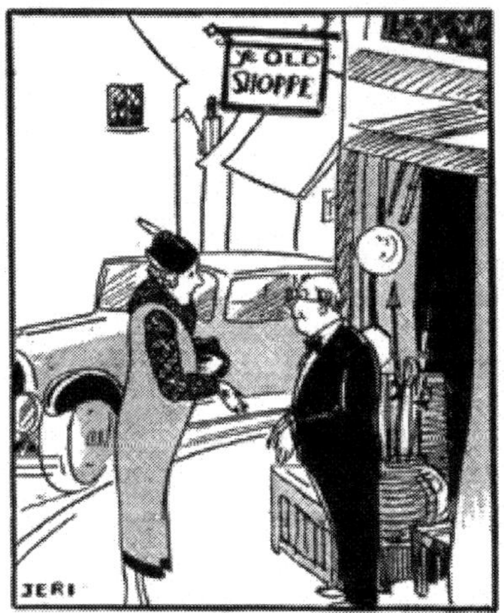

The dealer who said he had the very newest thing in antiques.

A cartoon that takes us back to Norfolk and a time when, wishing to buy a gift for my sister, Nicola, her husband, George, visited one of his 'colourful friends', a wheeler-dealer with the marvelous name of, Evan La Duce.

On seeing a grandfather clock George thought she would like, Evan said that as he was down to his last half dozen, if George made a quick decision he could have one at half price; *"Your last half dozen?"* queried George incredulously. *"How many did you buy?" "Six."* said Evan.

Another is an old joke about 'antique' food. Which, when tiny, I thought was true as I had overheard my father tell someone about a consignment of tinned sardines that his brother Harry, another wheeler-dealer who majored in villainy, had sold.

My father then said that some days later Harry was contacted by the purchaser who told him the sardines hadn't tasted very nice. To which Harry said; *"You ATE them! You shouldn't have done that, those sardines were for selling not for eating."*

As, presumably, were these –

A certain young gourmet from Crediton
Opened a tin of sardines with no date on.
He spread them on dried biscuit,
And then murmured; 'I'll risk it.'
His tomb bears the date that he said it on.

Nevertheless, it did not take me long to learn that sardines are not always 'just for selling as, if not out of date, they are very tasty - especially on toast with a cup of tea - which is not easy when you -

LAUGH AWHILE – just a little - WELSH STYLE

I was extremely fond of my Welsh brother-in-law, John; I loved his mother Nancy and was equally fond of his sister Doreen with whose daughter, Debbie, and her family we have enjoyed many happy hours.

Apart from this I know little about Wales, other than that it is one of the most beautiful bits of our Sceptered Isles. That it once gave us a lot of coal and, best of all, that it continues to give us some of the most glorious vocalists in the world. So much so, that I can be confident I am not alone in my belief that listening to a Welsh choir is one of the most uplifting and profound pleasures available to us.

A pleasure we had not experienced when, at eight, Sonya and I, unaccompanied, and with little brown parcel labels attached to our coats, were sent to Llanelli to stay with our Aunts Rose and Anne, who had not seen us since we were babes in arms.

Our Aunt Rose's daughter, Vivien, and our Aunt Anne's son, Barry, were both babies at the time and after we were sent back to our mother, (with new parcel labels attached to our coats), we saw neither of our cousins again for many years, because not long after Sonya and I left Wales, they left, with their parents, for Los Angeles.

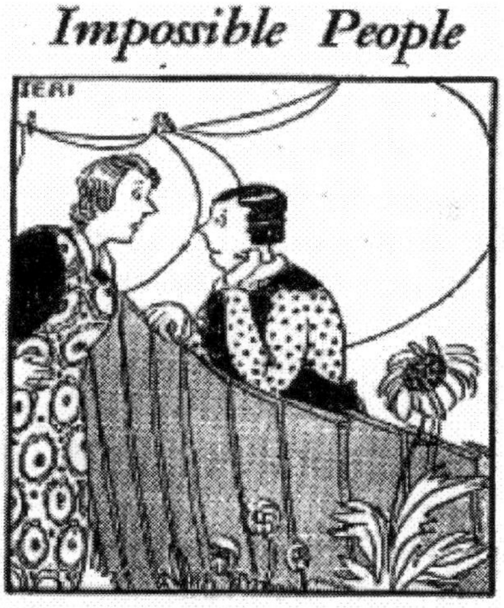

Along with my limited knowledge of Wales, apart from learning that Llanelli is the 'th' word with no 'th' in it, I have little memory of our brief sojourn there and can only recall three things.

The first was attending a school where we could not understand a word that was said. The second was our young Welsh nanny telling us that she cleaned her teeth with salt. The third, and most strange, was being taken to the cinema - A LOT.

Impossible People

The woman who said she did not enjoy her day by the sea because all the cinemas were full and she had to wander about the beach all day.

Sometimes twice in one day -

Now we rarely go to the cinema but still have a close relationship with our cousin, Vivian, her second husband, Richard and her two delightful daughters, Jenny and Julie.

All of whom we take pleasure in knowing well, as we frequently visited them in Los Angeles and, now, in Philadelphia. A move they made owing to Richards's elevation as Head of the Philadelphia Medical College, where, later, he was awarded a Medical Research Bursary.

When Richard retired they all moved to New York where Jenny (one of the best people on the planet), met her future husband, Greg (one of the nicest men on the planet), and where, as I write earlier, we attended their magnificent wedding in Central Park.

A venue that is one of the most difficult to obtain due to the limited number of such celebrations that are permitted to be held there each year.

An event for which I composed this Acrostic:

Jennifer, a beautiful girl, has an equally beautiful nature, with no ire, no guile.
Everyone is enveloped in her warmth, her hospitality, her wonderful smile.
Nothing phases her, no mountain is too hard to climb, nor is too much of a trial.
No one she meets does not wish to be her friend, does not wish to stay with her awhile.
You are always welcome in her home, whatever the time or the state of the weather.

AND

Greg knew when he met her, that Jennifer would make him the perfect wife,
Realised that Jenny was everything he had ever hoped for in married life.
Each year their love will grow stronger, will overcome any trouble or strife,
Giving them much joy, and love, and laughter through all the years they are together.

They now have three wonderful children, to whom my reader was introduced, in 'Jubilant Jubilees and Royal Events'.

In December 2013, us four 'ancient great aunties' attended the wedding of their Aunt Julie (one of the loveliest people on the planet), who married her fiance, Jonathan, (one of the finest men on the planet), in the palatial settings of the New York History Museum.

A magnificent, joyful celebration for which I wrote this Acrostic;

Julie, who has a nature as strong as a lion and as gentle as a kitten,
Usually takes life in her stride, is always considerate, is rarely blue.
Luckily she was living her life as free as a bird on the wing, when
In meeting Jonathan, she was bowled over, was immediately smitten,
Equally quickly he fell for her and became her new love, her new beau.

AND

Jonathan, a man whose steadfastness Julie now knows to be true,
Offered her his love, his loyalty, his life and, in marriage, his hand.
Now, with their lives tied together with a gold wedding band,
And a future that may give them their hoped for son or daughter,
There is not one among us who would not wish for them this joy,
Health and happiness, good luck, few tears, much love and more laughter,
All through the years they will enjoy, the years their lives may span,
Now that Jonathan has found Julie and Julie has found her Gentle Man.

Their 'hoped for baby boy' Benjamin, was born in October 2015 and, as I write this, they are awaiting the birth of their 'hoped for' baby girl.

Half of me hailing from there have to include a Laugh Awhile Russian style – or, more correctly -

THE RUSSIAN EXHIBITION, Earls Court, London, 1979.

Russians, despite their various trials and tribulations have a very finely tuned sense of humour. A view confirmed by my experience as the Senior Organising Secretary of the first Russian Exhibition hosted in London at Earls Court in 1979, when Perestroika was just a dream.

My time working with the Russians taught me some important lessons. The first was: 'Never doubt the arrogance of the truly powerful, nor the insularity of the really rich.'

A truth that made the incidents and events of my sojourn working with the Russian Secretariat and their construction personnel both myriad and marvelous.

After years of experience as an Organising Secretary for conferences and congresses, I knew how essential it was to make myself known to the most important people, such as the cleaners and post-boys, and, having introduced myself to the gentleman who manned the main lift, we would occasionally take a coffee break together.

During one of these he said to me, *"When a member of the Royal Family, Head of State, dignitary or celebrity visits Earls Court, I have to wear white gloves. As I have never before been treated like a real person by a member of any organising personnel, let alone be invited to take a coffee break with them, this puts you up there with all of those for whom I have to wear white gloves."*

Without doubt the finest compliment I would ever receive.

The proprietor of the company granted the contract to set up the exhibition, was a much 'larger than life' gentleman who had a white Rolls Royce. A car in which we would drive the more senior Russian personnel around London.

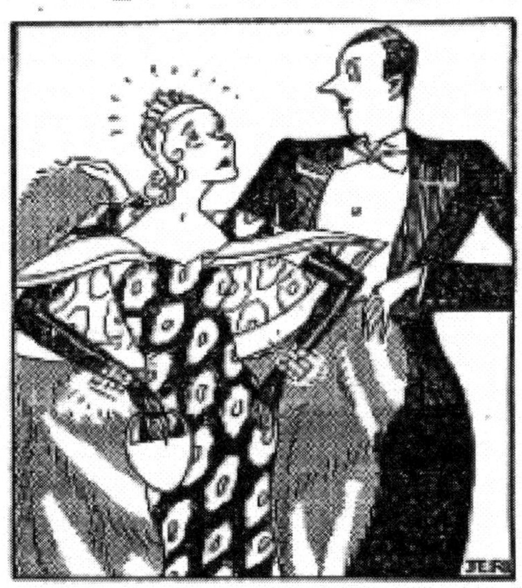

The film star who said times were so bad she didn't know where her next husband was coming from.

One of whom, an ebullient lady called Kira, would show her pleasure at this means of transport by graciously waving in regal manner at passing pedestrians while saying; *"I now know what it feels like to be your Queen or a film star."*

We thought it unkind to tell her that few film stars behave in the seemliness fashion of that of our much loved and much admired, extremely seemly, Queen.

The day after Margaret Thatcher became Prime Minister she visited the Exhibition. I was with her when she entered the lift, when, not only did she shake the hand of the lift operator, she also exchanged a few words with him. She was equally inestimably polite to everyone she met, including myself.

Her meticulous courtesy to, and interest in, both the British and Russian workforces and their secretariats endeared her to all.

The next day the lift operator said to me; *"I've been working this lift for over twenty five years and have met more famous people than most people will meet in ten lifetimes. Some ignore you, some merely nod, and then there are people like Mrs. Thatcher, who treat you like a proper person even though you're 'only a lift man' who they may never meet again."*

During the early stages of the setting-up of the exhibition, entertaining members of the Senior Russian personnel became my personal responsibility and, having exhausted the sites of London, I asked permission to take 'my Russians' to Southend-on-Sea, where a music festival was due to be held that weekend.

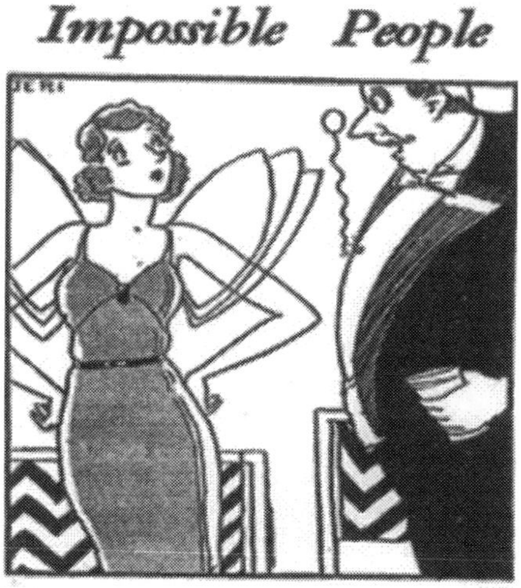

Impossible People

The girl who said she wasn't going all the way to the seaside just to hear one of those Promenade Concerts.

After a riotous lunch in Leigh Old Town, I drove them, via Chalkwell, along the sea front through Westcliff and Southend to Thorpe Bay so that they could enjoy the music being played at the various sites along the promenade and enjoy, even more, a few Rossi's ice cream cornets.

While I lodged in London for the duration of the Exhibition, I still had my Benfleet town house, so, after a long day of sight-seeing, I took them there for a 'fish and chip' supper where nothing could have prepared me for their 'shock and awe' on learning that I had a three bedroom property that, not only did I own without a loan, but occupied on my own.

When I told them that many of the houses we had driven past that day, even the very large ones, possibly had just one or two people living in them, they could not, and would not, believe me.

Later, when I said it was a pity they had not made arrangements to stay overnight, their shock and awe turned to fear and I was told in no uncertain terms that staying away from their hotel overnight was forbidden. By whom and for why I was never to discover.

Towards the end of the Exhibition we held a cocktail party for the Russian secretariat after, which Kira asked if they may return the compliment. As they wished to do it entirely on on their own I found them a suitable room and left them to their own devices.

On the due date and time all the members of British Secretariat arrived at the party to be met with a large central table adorned with dozens of tiny plates of caviar, dozens of tiny glasses twinned with bottles of vodka, and an equal number of platters piled high with an abundance of whole fresh fruit.

When I said, *"Why the fruit, Kira?"* she said; *"As your markets have so much of it you must love it, and as it is such a rare luxury in Russia, we couldn't resist it."* I forbore from telling her that mountains of fruit was not a suitable adjunct to an over abundance of caviar and vodka.

The 'over abundance' of everything in our shops was also irresistible to a few of their personnel and construction workers who became a little 'light fingered'. The police politely explained to them that, although our stores freely displayed many numbers of goodies, this did not mean they were free or, if nicked, would not be missed and a mutual understanding was reached whereby the 'nicked' stuff would be returned and none of the 'shop-lifters' would be 'nicked'.

On my daily rounds of the Exhibition Floor, in order to be easily seen by any of the workforce who might need assistance, I wore a bright yellow jacket with a badge with my photograph and my name in both English and Russian.

Within days the workers started to pin small decorative pins to the front of my jacket. When adorned with many numbers of these it was suggested by my immediate superior that, as the Senior Organizing Secretary, it might be inappropriate for me to continue to wear them.

To which I replied; *"It would be inappropriate for me not to wear them as this could, and almost certainly would, cause offence to those workers who had gifted them to me!"*

Thus I continued to accept them and by the end of the Exhibition close to a fifty of these tiny gestures of 'Good Will' adorned my jacket and are still treasured possessions. As is my name badge and porcelain Russian Bear, the Exhibition symbol.

Another 'symbol' of the Exhibition was the inordinate number of 'minders', one of whom (as, possibly, are most Russian minders), was called Boris, who would sit with me in my office when any of his 'charges' were in discussion with the Senior Management.

One day this very large, very gentle gentleman taught me a valuable lesson regarding the fluorescent lights of Roneo copiers. He asked me to stand with my arm outstretched and try to keep it horizontal while he pushed down on it. Despite his size and strength I was able to withstand the pressure of his hands on my arms for several seconds.

He then asked me to do the same with my arm over the lights of the open copier and no matter how hard I tried I could not withstand the pressure of his hands for even a nanosecond. He then told me it was well known in Russia that fluorescent lights were injurious to the muscles of the heart.

Injurious or not, the introduction of Roneo copiers was manna from heaven to typists as, even more injurious to their sanity was the tedium and time consuming activity that was, at that time, required to make copies of typed work. A torture that will never be known by those who have only worked with our present day computers and their independent instant printers that are injurious neither to life nor limb, only to the time they consume.

Which gives me an opportunity to compose another plagiarism of an anonymous ode I have previously plagiarised.

Before we had copiers, making copies was time wasting, tedious, and a pain,
But now we have them it is easy to make copies over and over, again and again.
Which is not just pleasing to life and limb but greatly more pleasing to the brain.
But, apparently, not pleasing to the heart, a worry that could drive us insane.

Limbs - and Life - lead to -

THE FACTS OF LIFE

Nicola has a wall plaque in her conservatory that reads: 'The three essentials for life - Someone to love, something to do, and something to look forward to'.

While my own kitchen walls are adorned with similar plaques that have been gifted to me over the years, all of which confirm my hatred of kitchens and catering:

I only have a kitchen because it came with the house.
If you are what you eat then I'm fast, easy and cheap,
Dinner will be ready when the smoke alarm goes off.
Todays menu – Take it or leave it.

Millions of homes are similarly adorned with similar plaques with similar homilies, such as -

It takes less time to do a thing right than to explain why you did it wrong
The sound of a kiss is not as loud as that of a cannon but its echoes last longer.
There are bad people who would be less dangerous if they had no good in them.

Another oft-used quote written on many mugs and an equal number of wall plaques is; Don't meet trouble halfway, it is quite capable of making the entire journey on its own.

As possibly it did for JERI's next Impossible Person –

Impossible People

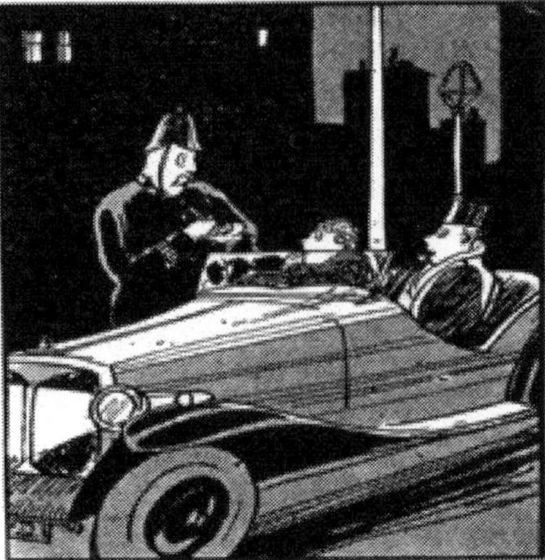

The girl who said she had no third-party insurance because she never went to more than two parties in one evening.

Which is similar to the homily with which I would often admonish my own children; *"Don't trouble trouble until it troubles you."* To which they would say; *"The trouble with trouble is that it always troubles you when you're trying not to trouble it."*

An amusing lead into a few more quotes-

THE POSITIVE SIDE OF LIFE

The next quotes were sent to me by two of the finest people I know, Clare and Bill, who live in the Pacific Palisades in California and whose daughter, Kate, is a close friend of Sonya's granddaughter, Chelsea.

Bill, who, having staunchly overcome throat cancer and now lives on a liquid diet, and talks through a speaking tube, can often be heard to say; *"It doesn't matter what you can or cannot eat as long as you can still have a life with a wonderful wife."*

His positivity is an inspiration to everyone who knows him. As are these:

A helping hand is no further than your sleeve.
Anger improves nothing except the arch of a cat's back.
Birthdays are good for you; the more you have, the longer you live.
Happiness comes through doors you didn't even know you'd left open.
People who are late are often much jollier than those who have to wait for them.
Living on Earth is expensive, but it does include a free trip around the sun every year.

We could learn a lot from crayons: some are sharp, some are pretty, some are dull, some have weird names - and all are different colours but exist very nicely in the same box.
It takes a minute to find a special person, an hour to appreciate them, just a day to love them, but an entire life to forget them.

All of which fit nicely with Dean Martin's prophetic, *"Dream as if you will live forever. Live as if you will die tomorrow."*

And what I say is, *"Live a lot, laugh a lot, but above all read a lot."* Because it has been said that; *"Most of us go to our graves not just regretting what we didn't do - but what we don't know."*

As in -

Impossible People

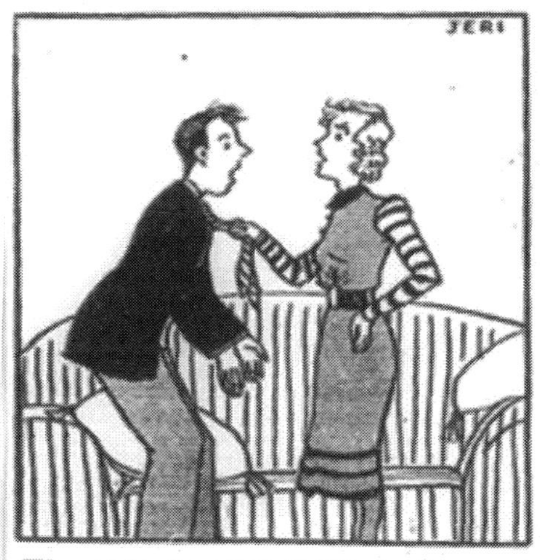

The girl who said " Who's Pearl?" when her young man said she had teeth just like pearls

THE IMPROBABLE SIDE OF LIFE

Another caption that the young of today are unlikely to understand - even if they have been to college and their parents had to 'pinch and save' to send them there. It also leads to the earning, (or in the case of the next Impossible husband), not earning, money -

Impossible People

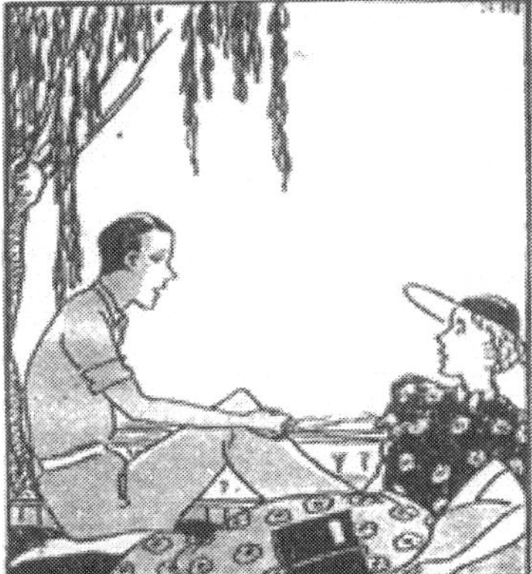

The girl who, when told that her friend's parents had had to pinch to send him to college, was surprised that they were never caught.

Which marries into -

RELATIONSHIPS

There are zillions of happy, untroubled, tidy relationships that, however exciting to their owners are of little interest to others. While those relationships that are perpetually tormented are of perpetual interest to others.

My own passage of right though the messy maelstrom of love, dating, engagements, marriage, affairs and divorce would fill a book twice the size of 'Impossible People'.

Which, if I were famous, might be worth the effort of writing, but as Impossible People is about love and laughter, not torment and tears, its few readers will be happier ones. As does thc weather, many relationships include a great deal of 'whether she will, or whether she won't.' I use the female gender as most men usually will and rarely won't.

Unless, that is, they are about to commit to a long-term relationship or marriage when they, more often than not, also don't know whether they should or they shouldn't. So while I cannot keep this topic short, I will attempt to keep it amusing.

While many of Mama's Impossible People smoke, few wear glasses. Perhaps this is because, as that masterly poet Ogden Nash said in his battle of verbal rhetoric with Dorothy Parker; *"Men seldom make passes at girls who wear glasses."* Which perhaps is why the German Philosopher, Friedrich Nietzsche said, *"A pair of powerful spectacles has sometimes sufficed to cure a person in love."* Which may have led Ogden Nash to write; *"A girl who is bespectacled, she may not get her nectacled, but safety pins and bassinets awaits the girl who fascinates."*

Three clever quotes that allow for the inclusion of these few words on unrequited love from Nicholas Monserrat's, 'The Master Mariner; that follow on from his description of the woes that befell the ill-fated ship, the 'Albermarle', that left Nelson and his crew stranded in Quebec.

'Mary Simpson, the daughter of Saunders Simpson, Provost Marshal of the Quebec garrison, was 'fair of face and of much wit' and the fairest sixteen year old to be met on a summers day. A captivating beauty, tall and dark with a strange blend of tenderness and aloofness, which could entice a man to the most foolish of hopes or the most morbid despair.

As the Belle of the Ball, Mary was much admired by all the officers during their long and enforced stay in Quebec; Christened Diana by the Quebec Gazette common gossip knew her as Diana, Goddess of the Moon.

It was soon noticed that their commander, Nelson, had been sorely smitten by this paragon of all the virtues and all the lures known to man. But, common gossip averred that Nelson's passion was not returned as: 'Only sixteen she had other ideas beyond a young Post Captain of twenty three, without fortune, without looks, without a manly frame or a manly height, who had been pale before he met her and was now a positive death mask of thwarted love.'

For there were endless years ahead in which to enjoy such vain attention before Prince Charming, or perhaps Lord Charming or even Monsieur le Comte de Charme, would come sailing into Quebec to sweep her off her entrancingly pretty feet.'

A glorious and gracious description of unrequited love that, despite Nelson's passion, would never lead to mutual love. For as, Bill Russell, one of America's finest basketball players, is reputed to have said ; *"To love is nothing. To be loved is something. But to love and be loved, that is everything."*.

Rather more cynical is Albert Einstein's view that; *"Women marry men hoping they will change. Men marry women hoping they will not. So each is inevitably disappointed."*

Which, perhaps, is why Somerset Maugham said; *"Love is only a dirty trick played on us to achieve continuation of the species"* But the best is Oprah Winfrey's; *"Lots of people want to ride with you in the limo, but what you want is someone who will take the bus with you when the limo breaks down."*

Which may lead to mutual -

LOVE

The Romantic - Four wonderful lines from Jay Asher for all who truly love -

If my love were an ocean, there would be no more land,
If my love were a desert, you would see only sand,

If my love were a star - late at night - only light,
And if my love could grow wings, I'd be soaring in flight.

The Opportunistic -

Impossible People

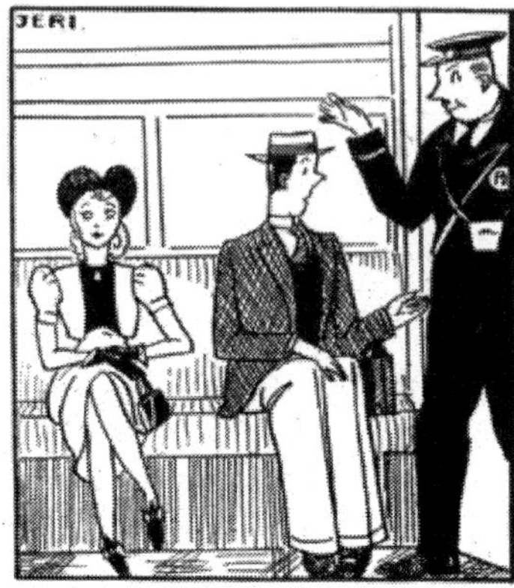

The conductor who said, "Now is your chance" when the young man said he wanted to get off.

The Unrequited -

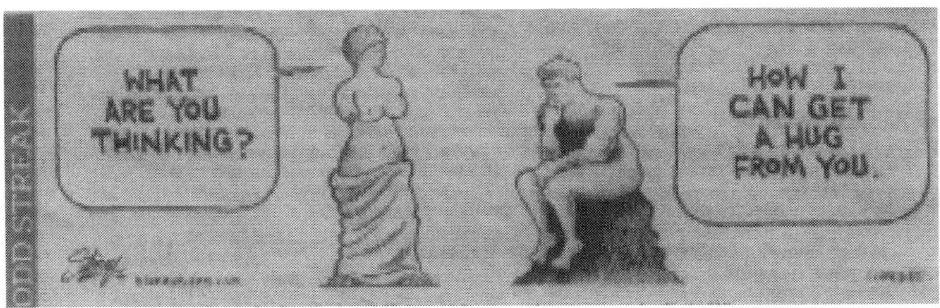

The Disappointed – As was JERI's next girl.

DAY, FEBRUARY 27, 1934.—Page 8

Impossible People

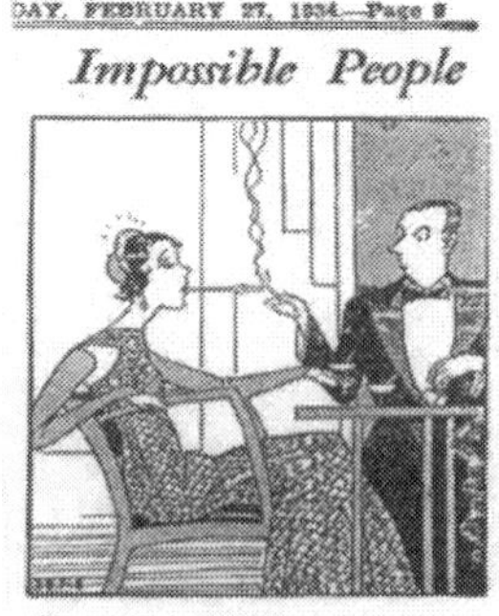

The girl who said love in a cottage had become a little flat.

The Philosophic –
As is my next poem.

It Seems to Matter Now

It seems not to matter now,
That the love we thought would last,
Was transient as the passing day,
Was just another lie.

It seems not to matter now,
That when we ran, we ran so fast,
The dreams we chased were chased away,
And left to die.

It seems to matter now,
Now the pain is long since past,
We couldn't find a better way,
To say Goodbye.

Which, perhaps, was why I never engaged in any -

ENGAGEMENTS

The Unexpected -

Impossible People

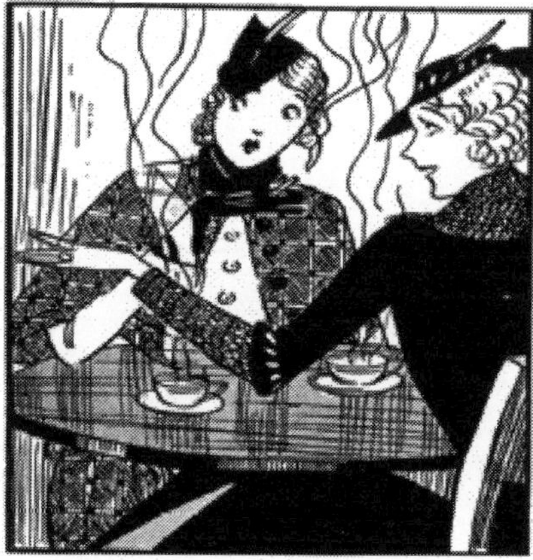

The girl who said her employer had talked business with her when they went out, and to prove it she could show the ring.

The Secret -

Impossible People

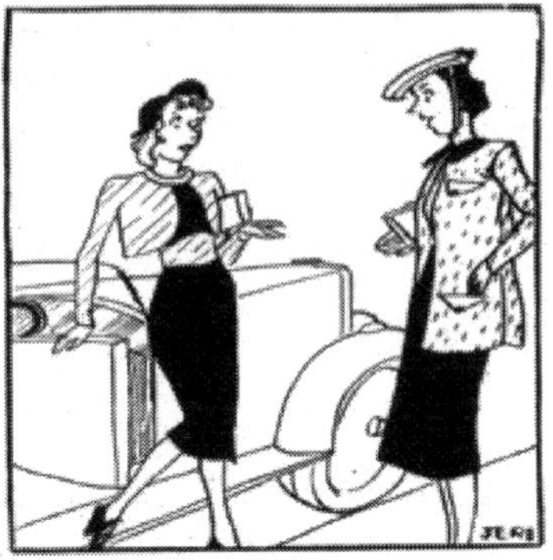

The girl who said she was telling everyone she was keeping her engagement a secret.

The Plentiful -

Impossible People

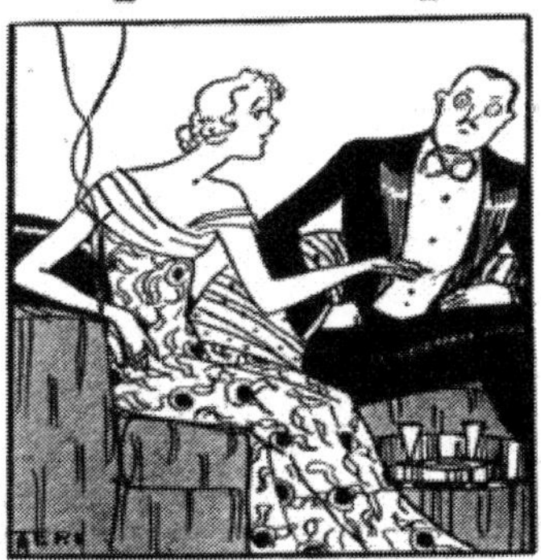

The girl who said she had enjoyed the winter sports; in fact she had become engaged to three of them before she left Switzerland.

The Impossible -

Impossible People

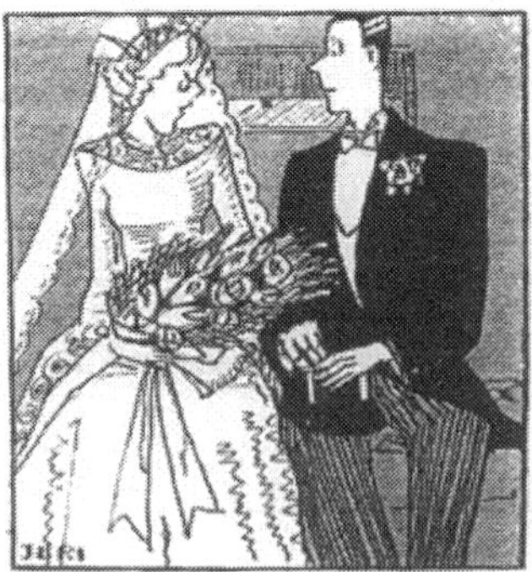

The bride who said she wanted to be taken for better when she was at her worst.

All of which can lead to -

MARRIAGE

Roses are red, violets are blue,
I'm married to someone else,
But would prefer to be married to you.

I wrote this many years prior to reading this homily from Dr. James Dobson, an American Psychologist, who was born two years before me in 1936. *"Don't marry the person you think you can live with; marry the person you think you can't live without."*

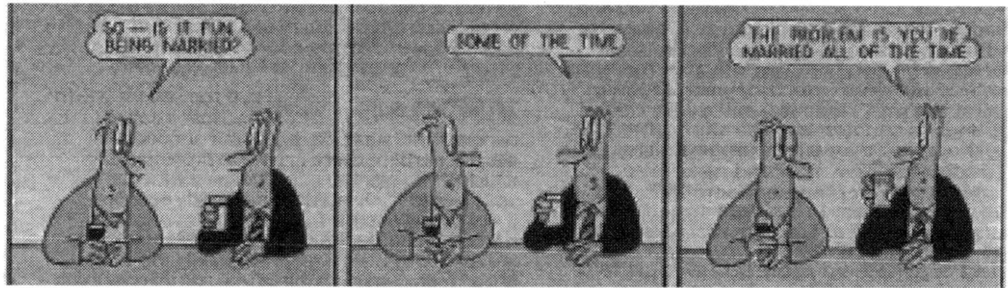

Even more years ago - and I now can't remember for which of my many marriages – an American colleague, Lucille, sent me these sobering words about this tried and tested, but now frequently failed, institution:

Living as a couple never means that each gets half. You have to take turns at giving more than getting and sometimes the turns aren't equal. This may seem unfair but gets easier to understand as we get older.

In a young partnership, the man lives on his side of the marriage and the woman on hers. They are gracious opponents in competition over career, social and economic status, frequency and intensity of applause. They meet at table or in bed, each exhausted from the solitary race.

In later marriage, even if they work at different things, they still work as a team, remembering that being together is why they are together, and why they got married in the first place.

Even if they can't remember they are?

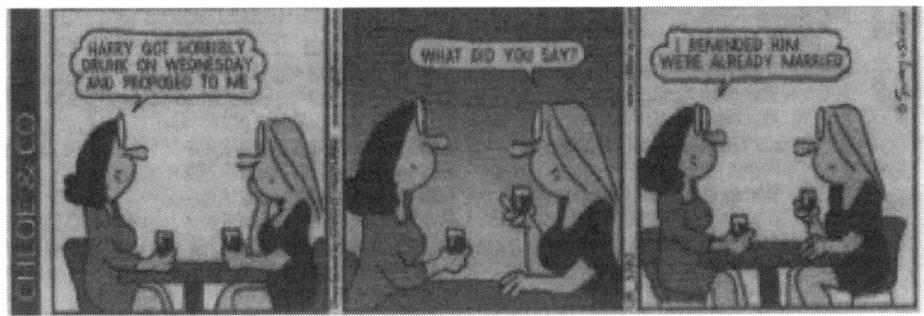

Or would like to put a stop to them?

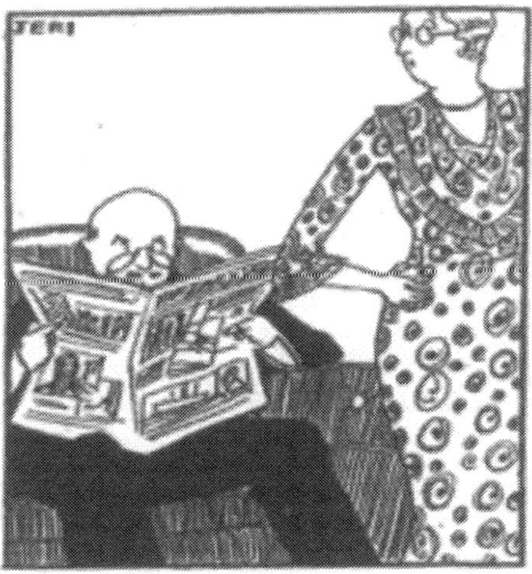

The man who said if the government were going to do away with lotteries the first one they ought to stop is marriage.

A view that may have led a Roedean Headmistress to say; *"There is no justice in the world and there is most certainly none in marriage."* While Rupert Everett opined; *"Bigamy is having one wife too many, monogamy is the same."*

As Mr. Everett was born in 1959 we can be confident that JERI did not steal his quip for her next caption - yet again, confirming Mr. Silver's views on original thought.

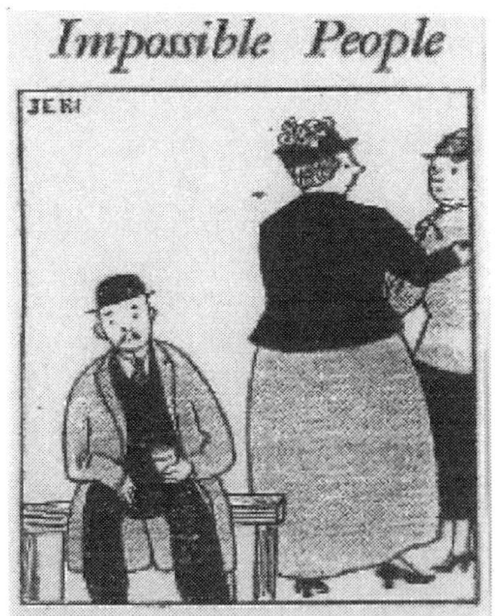

The man who said his wife was so big that his marriage was practically bigamy.

A cartoon that is also a neat lead into Oscar Wilde's famous opinion of multiple marriages: 'The triumph of hope over experience.' Parodied by the socialite, Celia Walden, who, on her engagement to Piers Morgan, said; *"It would be pleasant to think of marriage as a rare case of individual optimism triumphing over mass, institutionalised cynicism."* Or, a little more succinctly: *'The triumph of experience over hope.'*

Which may be the reason why so many indulge in so many marriages, most of which invariably run true to Einstein's view of governments; *"Insanity is doing the same thing over and over again and expecting different results."*
Or as Piet Hein says in his next Grook:

Vita Brevis

A lifetime is more than sufficiently long
for people to get what there is of it wrong.

The caption of JERI's next cartoon compliments a conversation I had with a London taxi driver, Andy May, with whom I 'enjoyed' one of my more amusing journeys. Much as are many that are taken with our famous London Cabbies who, in my many conversations with many of them, I have found to be some of the most amusing, and, equally often, helpful people on the planet.

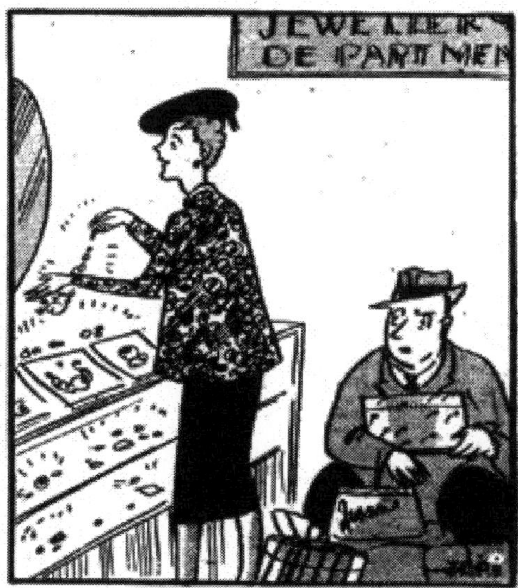

The man who said his wife was a little dear, but at Christmas she became really expensive.

Andy told me he works as a Cabbie while his wife Claire, who, he said, is a 'little dear', works at shopping. Employment that, at the time of my conversation with her husband in December 2014, she was diligently working at in New York.

The next joke, taken from my Encyclopedia of Jewish Humour, is so perfectly perfect for an Impossible Person I'm confident my mother, had she known of it, would have used it as a caption; *"The girl who said she couldn't marry Marvin as she would prefer to marry a man who make things - like that nice Mr. Rochmis who makes a million a year."*

Again as I write earlier, we will never know whether any of JERI's caption's were composed from the musings of other people - voiced or written - or whether they were all 'original thought', but what we do know is that her next Impossible housewife definitely did not marry a man who makes a million a year -

Prior to the emancipation of women in the 1920's there were many things far worse to complain about than lack of money - particularly if she lived between 1095 and 1291 during the Crusades.

A Crusader put a chastity belt on his wife and, in case he should die while away, gave the key to his best friend for safekeeping. He had ridden only a few miles when his friend, riding hard, caught up with him and said; *"You gave me the wrong key!"*

Which fits well with Oscar Wilde's view that: *"Marriage has many pains but celibacy has no pleasures".*

And would most definitely not lead to –

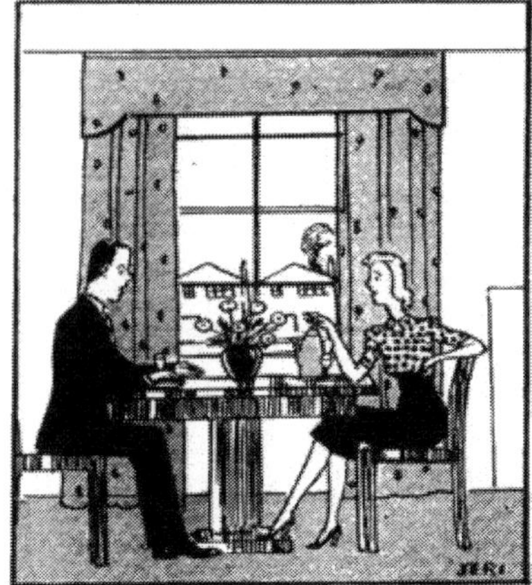

The housewife who said she could live on a small income if she did not have to spend so much keeping it a secret.

CONNUBIAL BLISS

The French have a wonderful saying for the four 'ages' of connubial bliss which are known as Le M.M.S.

Young couples make love at matin, midi et soir.
Middle-aged couples make love on Mardi, Mercredi et Samedi.
Older couples make love in Mars, Mai et Septembre.
And the elderly have, "Mon Meilleur Souvenir."

I will not insult my reader by presuming they do not know the French for times of the day, days of the week or months of the year – although there may be a few who do not know that 'Mon meilleur souvenir' means *"My best memory."*

My friend, Berenice told me that; *"Cosmopolitan tells you how to have an orgasm. She Magazine tells you how to fake one and Woman's Own tells you how to knit one." She says; "The knitted ones are the best as not only do you enjoy the activity, you feel a sense of achievement when you have finished."*

Allison Pearson writes in the Daily Mail; *"Women used to fake orgasms and make mince pies. Now we can all do the orgasm, but we fake the mince pies."* But as that master of the quotable quote, Friedrich Nietzsche, said; *"It is not lack of love but lack of friendship that makes unhappy marriages."* Which, say I; *" Leads to cheating."*

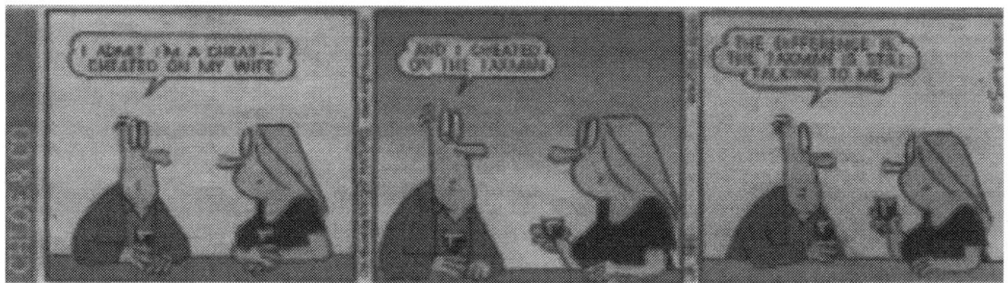

I also say; *"Never persuade your lover to leave his wife because if he cheats on his wife with you, he will cheat on you with someone else when you are his wife."*

For, as a renowned philanderer more famously said; *"If a man marries his mistress he creates a vacancy."* Although it is not always infidelity that leads to a women's lack of libido - or her tears - sometimes it is a hatred of housework but, more often, it is a hatred of husbands.

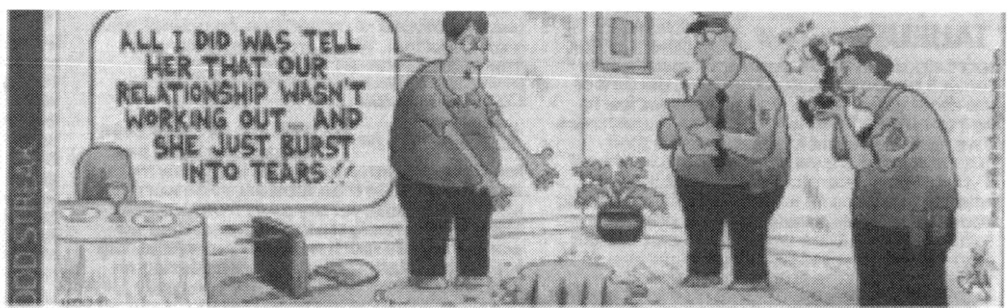

Which generally leads to -

ARGUMENTS

Malcolm Bradbury said; *"Marriage is the most advanced form of warfare in the modern world."*

The Young Couple: During a heated argument he shouts at her, *"I cannot think how God made you so beautiful and so stupid at the same time."* To which she said, *"He made me beautiful so that you would be attracted to me and stupid so that I would be attracted to you."*

The Newly Married Couple: A husband bought his wife a mood ring as a gift. It turns mauve when he's happy, blue when she's sad, green when she's in a good mood, and when she's in a bad mood it leaves a big red mark where she has hit him.

The Middle-Aged Couple: A doctor and his wife are arguing and as he slams out of the door he hurls a final insult at her, *"And what's more, you're no good in bed!"* Later he calls his wife to apologise. Slightly peeved by the time it takes for her to answer, he asks, somewhat curtly; *"Why did it take you so long to answer, where were you?" "In bed,"* she said. Even more disgruntled he asked; *"What were you doing in bed at this time of day?"* To which his wife said; *"I was getting a second opinion."*

The Elderly Couple: Towards the end of a bitter row a husband shouts at his wife; *"When you die I'm going to have a headstone made for you with the inscription 'Silent At Last'."* Equally cross, his wife shouts back, *"And when you die I'm going to have a headstone made for you with the inscription 'Stiff At Last'."*

The Heading for A Divorce Couple:

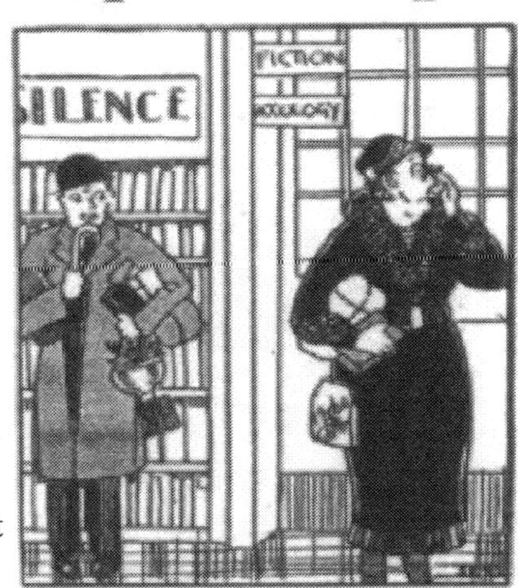

The husband who took refuge under the "Silence" notice in the library.

But now that councils are completely silencing them with closure, very soon our precious public libraries will no longer exist, thus leaving nowhere for JERI's Impossible husband to take refuge.

Nevertheless - apart, in the case of women, new makeup and new underwear and, in the case of men, a new car and new deodorant - 'silences' are the clearest indicator of a relationship taking place outside the confines of an existing one.

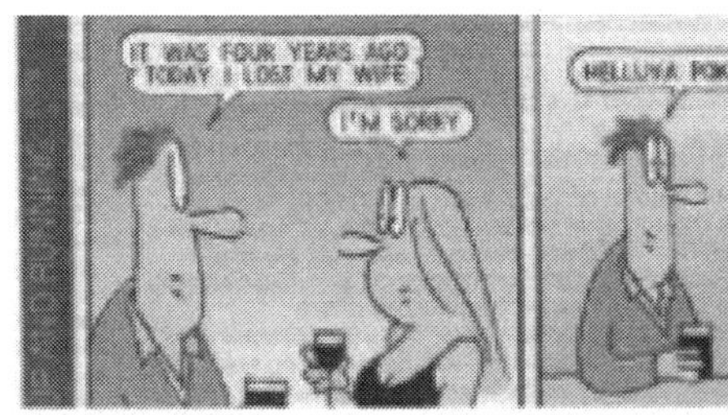

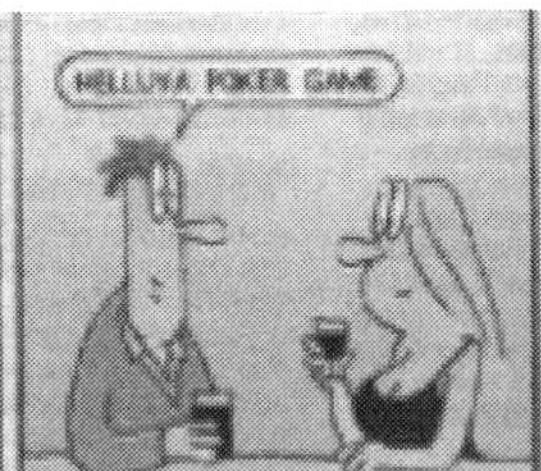

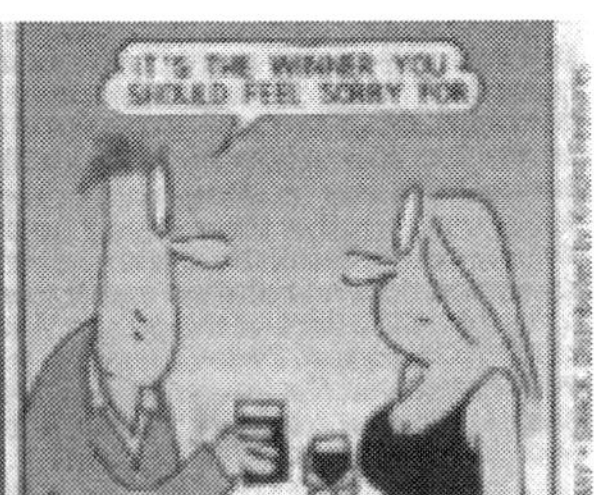

The Confused:

As also many might be, after reading this 'thought' from Friedrich Nietzsche: *"You have your way. I have my way. As for the right way, the correct way, and*

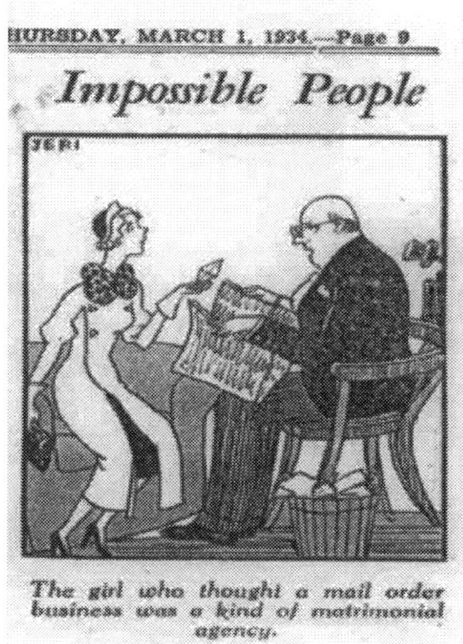

The girl who thought a mail order business was a kind of matrimonial agency.

the only way, it does not exist."

It certainly didn't for the woman who, on being told to expect the worst when her husband was in hospital following a serious accident, said; *"Oh Doctor, don't tell me he is going to pull through."*

The Abused

An Impossible Woman who had obviously never read the following advice from Ogden Nash;

To keep your marriage brimming,
With love in a loving cup,
Whenever you're wrong admit it;
Whenever you're right, shut up.

Impossible People

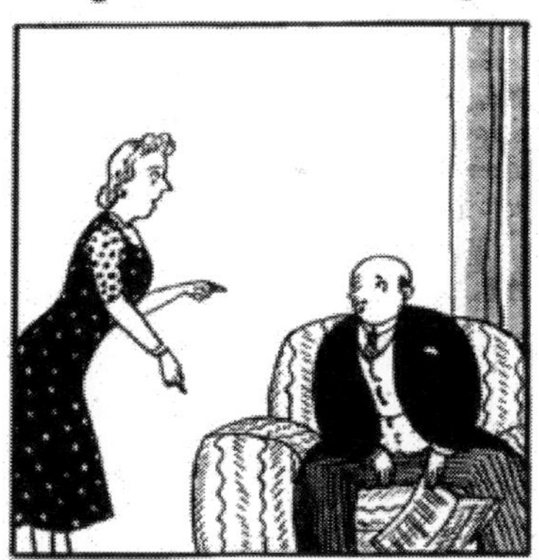
The woman who said he was listening in a very unpleasant manner when her husband said he had never spoken a word.

A doctor, when addressing a large audience in Oxford on the subject of diet, said; *"Much of the food and additives we now put into our stomachs are so lethal it is surprising that most of us here today are not already dead.*

"Chinese food is loaded with MSG. High trans-fat diets can be disastrous. Red meat is full of steroids and dye. Salt clogs our arteries. Soft drinks corrode the stomach lining and none of us realise that the germs in our drinking water can

be even more harmful. Although there is one thing even more dangerous and it is something that most of us will eat at some time during our lives. So, can anyone here tell me what food can cause the most suffering and grief for years after we eat it?"

After a few seconds with no response from the audience, the doctor repeated the question, and asked; *"Can no one tell me what this food is?"* At which an elderly man in the front row raised his hand and said; *"Wedding Cake?"*

Wedding cake or not, it would appear that faithfulness is now a 'faith' that few are able to adhere to faithfully. As in: *'What happens to a boy when he reaches puberty? He says goodbye to his boyhood and looks forward to his adultery.'*

Which, more often than not, leads to –

AFFAIRS

This next 'advice' is from the book 'Vicious Circles and Infinity' -

If you don't know you don't know, you think you know.
If you don't know you know, you think you don't know.

A more convoluted way of saying; *"The more you think you know, the less you do know."* Less convoluted is this homily from J.H. Froggatt that was published in the Daily Mail's Peterborough column:

When you're 21 you know you know.
When you're 31 you think you know.
When you are 41 you know you don't always know.

A philosophy similar to my own regarding my second husband's infidelity, as at 30 I thought it didn't matter, at 40 I pretended it didn't matter, at 50 I knew it did matter. A 'coup de foudre' that allowed me to extricate myself from a relationship that, whilst full of fun, was also full of frequent extramarital couplings, coupled with equally frequent patches of penury.

And all are apt descriptions of the tortured vacillations people experience when they suspect their 'other half' of having an affair. An unendurable sorrow perfectly defined by these emotive words from Rupert Brooke.

And I shall find some girl perhaps,
And a better one than you,
With eyes as wise but kindlier,
And lips as soft, but true.
And I daresay she will do.

Tragically, infidelity can also lead to people taking their own lives. So for those who might be considering this route out of their travails, they may, before they do, like to heed these wise words of Piet Hein in his next Grook;

Here is a fact that should help you to
fight a bit longer.
Things that don't actually kill you outright
make you stronger.

Having spent many years with a serial philanderer I am now a walking encyclopedia on 'affairs' and 'affairs of the heart' - two very different things. So, while my poems are on many different subjects, many of them, helped by heartache, are of this genre. Thus, after much persuasion from my present, wonderful husband, Simon, the first I submitted to a Poetry Society competition was on a romantic theme that, much to my surprise and delight, and not a little of his, won first prize.

After several years of similar success, an adjudicator of a poetry society said they received so many requests for copies of my romantic poems, I should consider putting them together in an anthology. Thus 'Shades of Love' was published in 1993. It has been reprinted three times as, has 'Reflection'. An anthology of my mother's poems that was also first published in the same year.

The most liked poems in 'Shades of Love' are 'Bed' and 'Fat & Thin', that, in the year I wrote it, won first prize for both the best humorous poem and the overall contest. It is a factual Tale of Two Cities that relates to one of the many periods of my life when, figuratively speaking, I was 'between husbands'.

Whether 'tis better to be FAT or THIN that is the question?

I once had an affair with a man
Who seemed just right for things like that,
As he drove a posh car and rented a Barbican flat.
We would dine discreetly in restaurants
Where the tables were dressed in pink,
Where we would dance and drink Champagne.
Once, he had a car waiting on the runway,
When we got off his plane in France.
And once he bought me a mink.

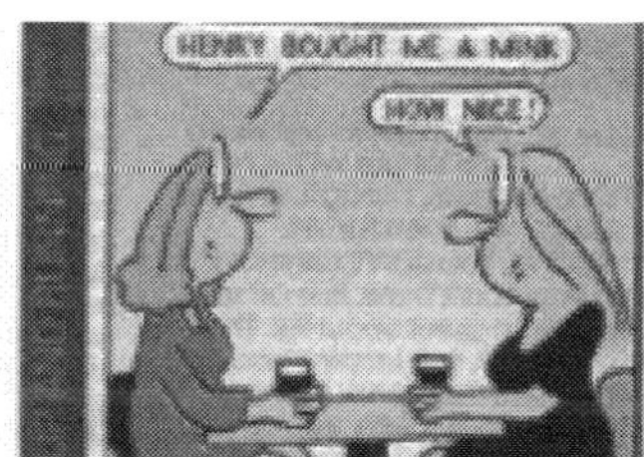

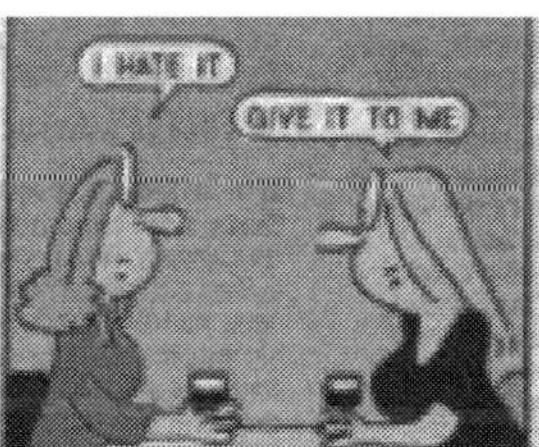

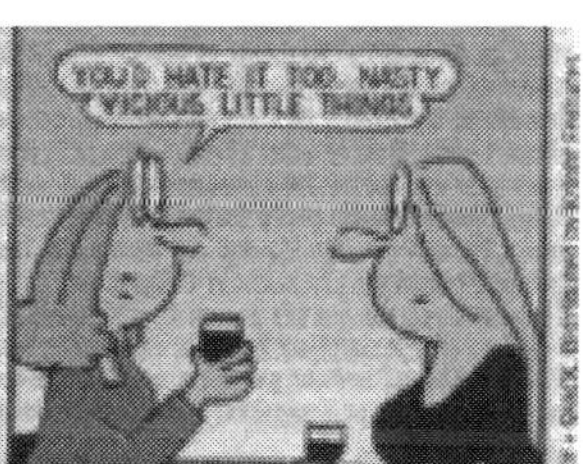

He would phone to say Hi!
And that without me he'd die.
But 'though he was well mannered
And spoken and read,
His conversation was somewhat dead.
He hadn't a spark of humour,
Nor much of interest inside his head,
Not to mention being useless in bed.

So I knew I couldn't stand him for life.
So I sent him back to his wife.
Who liked him because he was slim,
It was his only joke this bloke,
As he'd say he had famine with me
(I was decidedly thin),
Or with her he had feast
(She was rather round to say the least.)

Meanwhile his wife,
Who was much jollier than him,
Had got herself slim
And run away with my brother.
Who, she said, had a wit like a knife,
Laughed a great deal
And had plenty of bread.
Not to mention being brilliant in bed.

But he was decidedly fat!
What do you think of that?

But there will never come a time in the affairs of men and women when they no longer have affairs because so many;

Make a mistake -

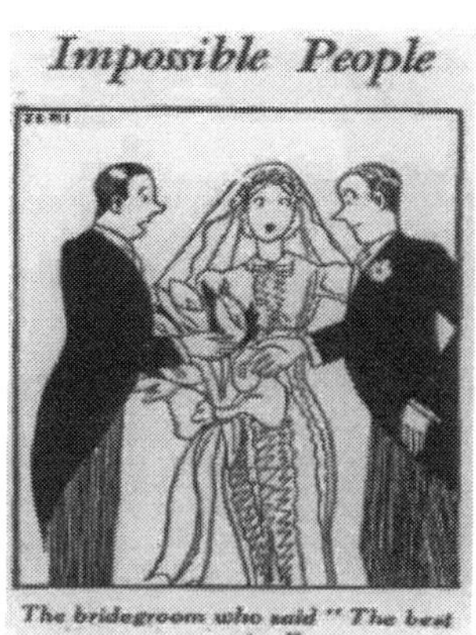

Are indifferent –

Impossible People

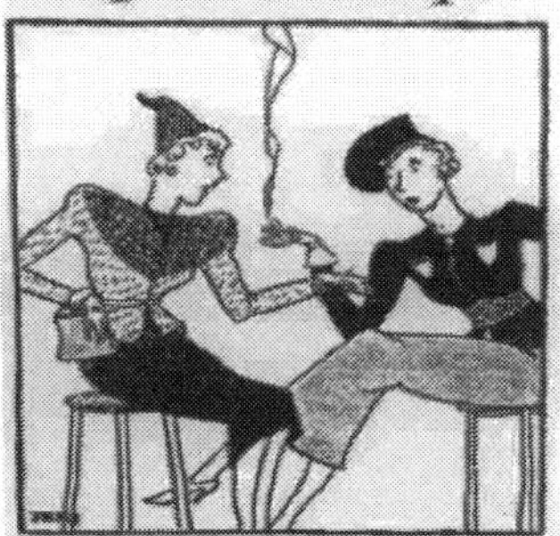

The woman who said she had often wondered where her husband spent his evenings until she came home early one night, and there he was.

Are close to separating -

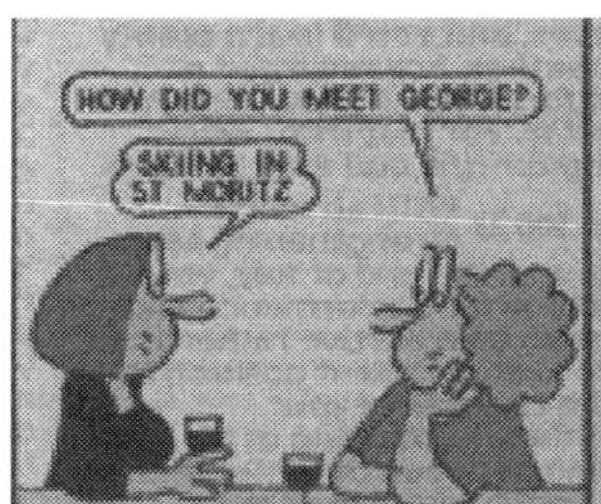

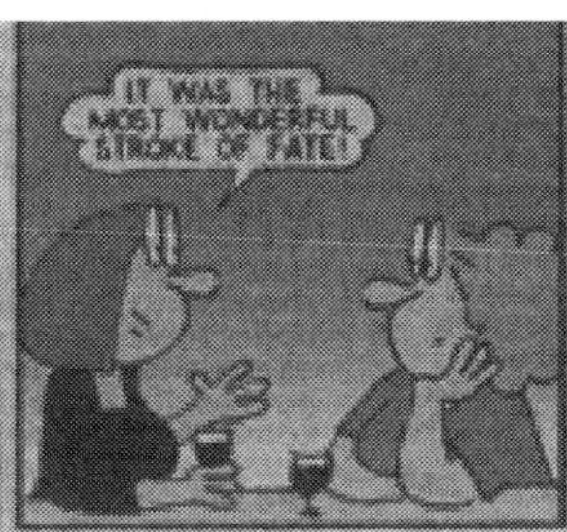

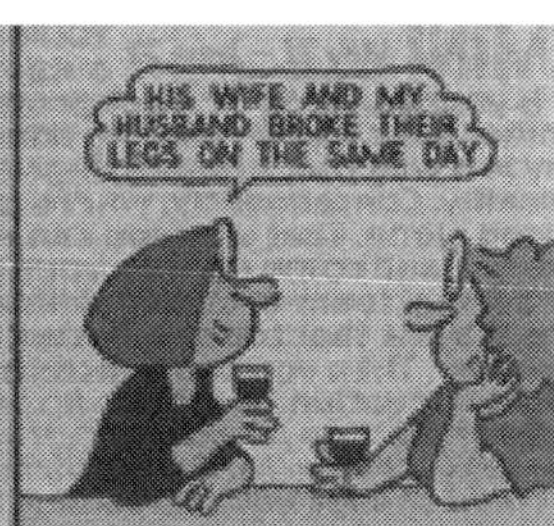

Are too laid back to be bothered -

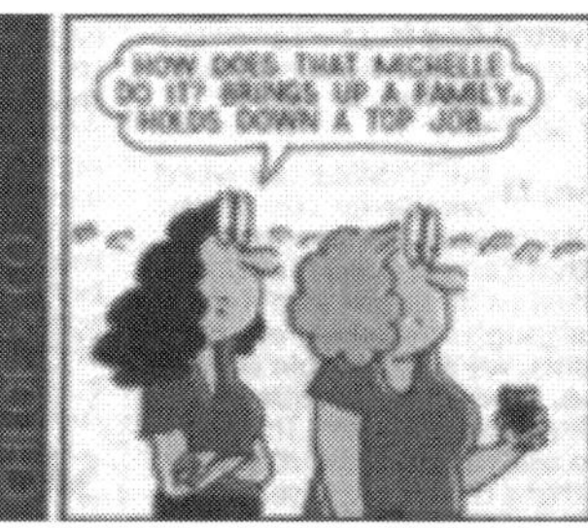

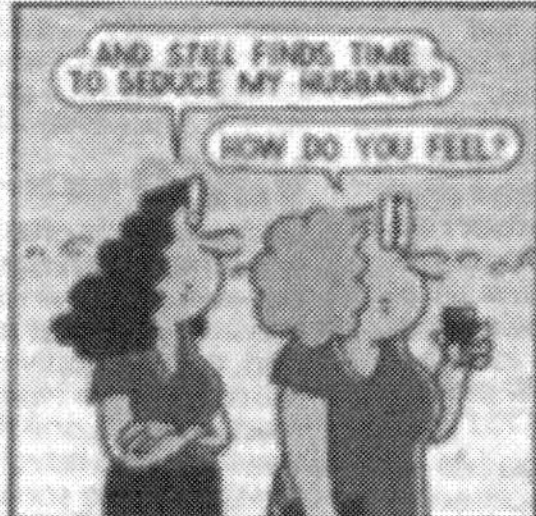

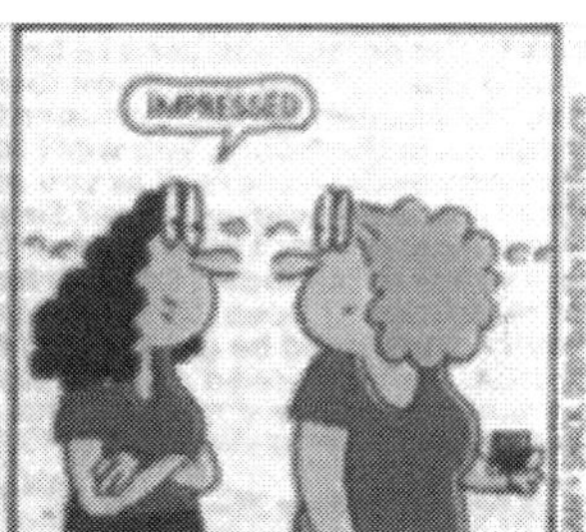

Don't care either way:
Which would definitely lead to -

DIVORCE

Impossible People

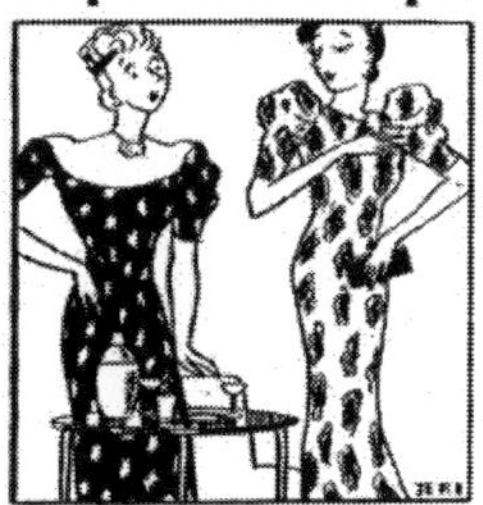

The woman who said she had never tried when asked if her husband was difficult to please.

David Lichfield, when Publisher of Ritz Magazine, presciently and prophetically, said; *"While Paul McCartney may claim that Heather Mills didn't marry him for his money, she will no doubt divorce him for it."*

Money and infidelity are neck and neck in the race to be the main reason for divorce. Together with religion, for, as the recently divorced man said to a friend; *"My wife divorced me for religious reasons. She worshipped money and I didn't have any."*

Another good reason is ill health, as in; *"My wife divorced me due to illness. She got sick of me."* As did Chloe in this next cartoon by Gray Jolliffe that he composed as a gift for his close friend, Jeremy Levison, a divorce Lawyer. Patently an excellent one –

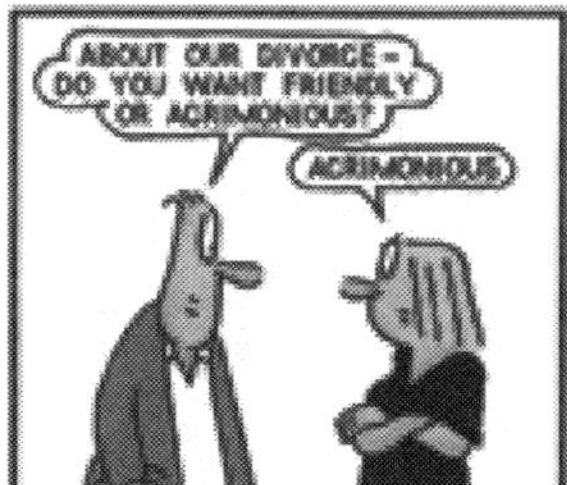

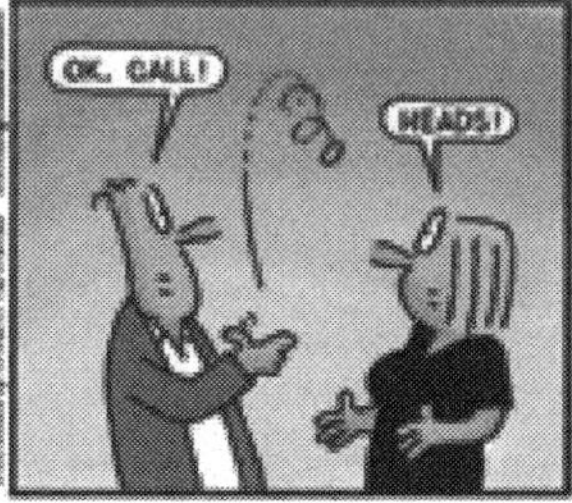

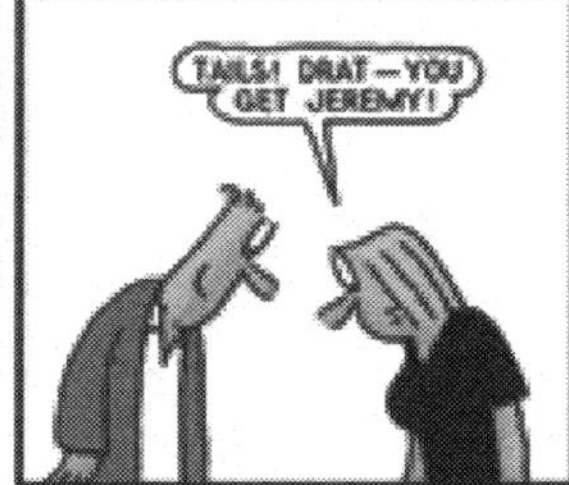

As Chloe's 'drat you get Jeremy', would not be found amusing by any reader of the Daily Mail who does not know Gray, Jeremy or myself, it is not a cartoon that is likely to see the light of day in any paper or periodical. So I was much more than just delighted when, in conversation with Gray, he said he would send it to me for inclusion in Impossible People.

One of whom, most definitely, is not Gray, although Chloe could be a strong candidate. As is this next Impossible actress.

Impossible People

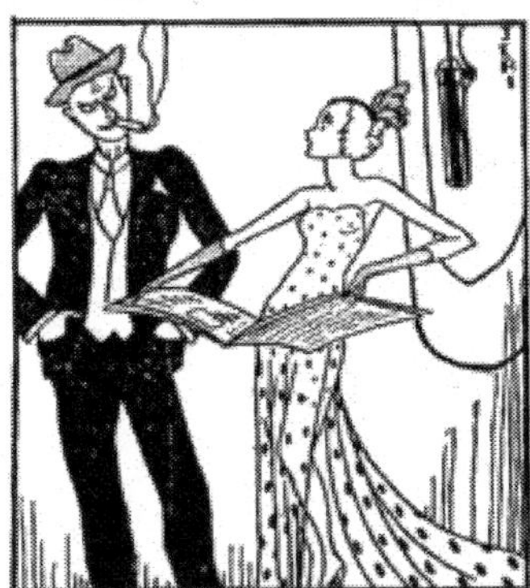

The film actress who discovered that she had been divorced more times than she had been married.

Which takes us to those who can now marry - and divorce – as they please

HOMOSEXUALS, TRANSVESTITES AND PROSTITUTES

Kinky Friedman said, *"I support homosexual marriage - why shouldn't they be as unhappy as the rest of us?"*

Already in danger of receiving death threats from the Thought Police, I shall be in equal danger of a similar fate from the Equality Evangelists if I don't I include homosexuals, transvestites and prostitutes.

As they are all a foreign country to me, I have not much to say on the subject except that I am very fond of Lesbians and Gays as my friendships with them have always been most 'satisfactory'. As I have never had a friend who is a transvestite or prostitute - or none that I know of - I do not know if I would be equally fond of them.

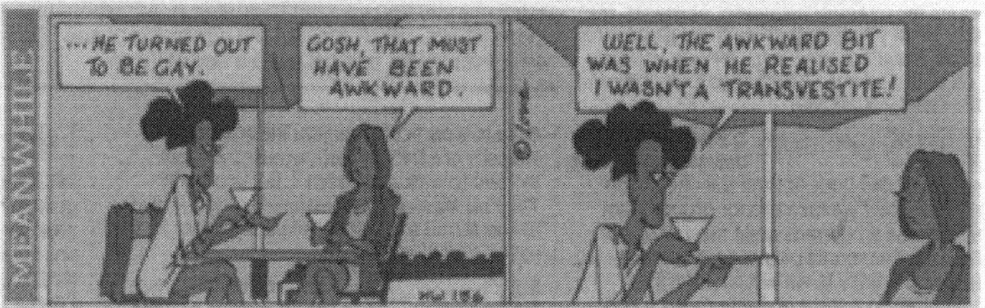

So, apart from a sneaky desire in my youth to be a 'Madam' because I thought it might make me a lot of money, other than two cute stories, I know nothing at all about these 'Ladies of the Night'.

When my sister Nicola and brother-in-law, George first moved to Norwich, George thought it a most genteel place and could not imagine anything as seedy as 'Love for Sale' taking place in such an august city. So when, one winter evening, they were driving along Bere Street, (then the Red Light district of Norwich and perhaps still is), Nicola was very amused when George said; *"These girls should wear warmer clothes or they will catch their death of cold."* Nicola forbore from telling him that they might catch their death of something, but it probably would not be the cold.

Some years later I arranged a rendezvous in a public house in the same street with a prospective client prior to inspecting a nearby vacant property. A house he hoped to buy and that Sonya and I hoped to renovate for him if he did. On leaving the house, cold, tired and hungry, I found a note on my windscreen: 'When you've finished here, come back to the pub, I'll be waiting.' My client was incandescent, but, not knowing whether to be horrified or flattered, I did wonder, for just a nanosecond, if joining the only trade in the world where: 'You've got it, you sell it, and you've still got it' might not be more profitable than the one in which I was already prostituting myself.

But having inherited the 'neat gene' from both my grandmothers, I'm not sure I could cope with the disorder of a 'Disorderly House'. A House that my Roget tells me is a 'brothel' where, purportedly and presumably, prostitutes live.

As will be seen from JERI's next cartoon that I have cleverly contrived to include, my mother did not stray into the realms of the various proclivities of those ladies who like other ladies or those gentlemen who like other gentlemen as when she was composed her cartoons, homosexuality being illegal, they would have discomposed too many people.

Now that it is legal my 'neat gene' enables me to much admire the almost universal ability of gay men to entertain brilliantly and beautifully - and keep an immaculate home - whether in dry weather or whether it's raining.

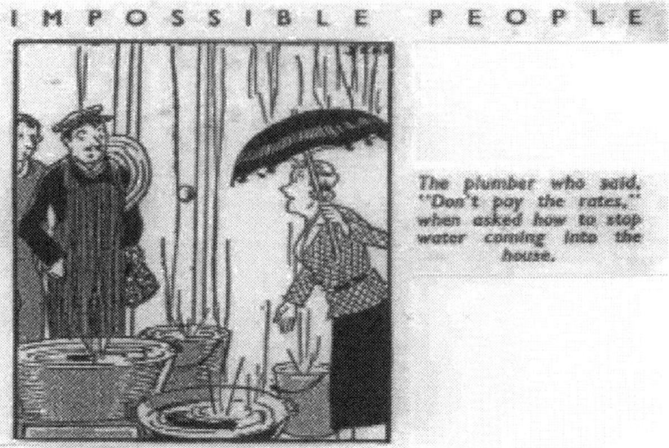

They also adore shopping, can be hilariously funny are kind to animals and, best of all, never make a pass at you. Which for those women for whom this is an ever-present 'threat' (a discomfort not unknown to myself), the pleasure of a pleasant evening in good company with no other expectation - or complication – is a true joy.

One of Mama's artist friends, Basil Nubell, was disowned by his father due to his two desires, to play with paint and play with men. Before he met his soul mate, a charming Spaniard, Jose, his paintings, although good, were moody and gloomy. After he and Jose became partners his work became greatly more colourful and greatly more sought after.

Two of our gay friends, Alexander and Patrick, whom Sonya and I had met through our mutual work as interior designers, arrived late for supper one night in a fit of the giggles as, hoping to redesign themselves, they had spent too long in a tanning chamber. To our amusement, and equally to their own, having become a beautiful shade of amber, they continued to darken at the same rate as the evening did.

The only other thing I know about homosexuals, or rather the word itself, is that it is often pronounced incorrectly. My dictionary tells me the word homo, as in 'homo sapiens' 'describes people of both sexes' - while the word for 'those who prefer to bed others of the same sex' is also 'homo' but is pronounced as 'hom-mo' not 'home -o.'

Pedantry at its best, or merely an attempt at accuracy?
When it comes to transvestites, having never knowingly known one, I don't know whether they cross-dress to hide their gender, or merely to be seen in clothes of the opposite sex.

Those I have seen have been on television, and if, as it would appear, broadcasters welcome them as a diversion from the norm, perhaps, with the present desire of all and sundry to be seen via this medium, we may now see a great deal more of them - in numbers not in the flesh!

Conversely, while IVF has now brought about the possibility for same sex couples to have children, relationships between gays and lesbians can, naturally, never naturally, lead to offspring.

Which naturally leads to -

THE BIRDS AND THE BEES

Conception: It is said that, *"The best a child can hope for from his father is that he is there at the conception."* And Steven Pearl said to his son; *"I cannot believe that out of a hundred thousand sperm, you were the quickest."*

Birth: A little boy asked his father about the birds and the bees. *"As you will have to learn sooner or later, I may as well tell you now,"* said his father. *"Your mother and I first met in a Yahoo chat room. We set up a date via e-mail and met at a cyber-cafe. Your mother agreed to download my hard-drive, so we sneaked into a back room. But just as I was about to upload we realised neither of us had a firewall. It was too late to hit the delete button and nine months later a little pop-up appeared and said; 'You've got male'."*

Children: Cloris Leachman said, *"Husbands and wives should always live in separate houses and if there's enough money the children should live in a third."*

Growing Older: A man, on seeing the son of his neighbour filling in a hole in their back garden, asked him what he was doing. *"My goldfish died and I'm burying him,"* said the boy.

The man, while watching the child pat down the last bit of earth, asked, *"Why did you need such a large hole for a goldfish?" "Because,"* said the boy, *"It was inside your cat."*

AND

When asked by his gangster father why he had failed his exams, his son said; "They questioned me for hours but I never told them anything."

AND

The boy who prayed for a bike but realising that God didn't work that way, decided to steal one and then pray for forgiveness.

Which presents us with -

SANTA CLAUS

For those who don't believe –

Impossible People

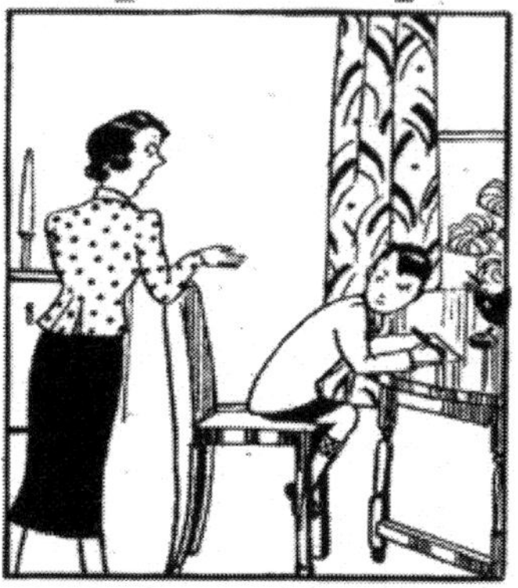

The boy who said he was just writing a final demand note to Father Christmas.

For those who do –

Impossible People

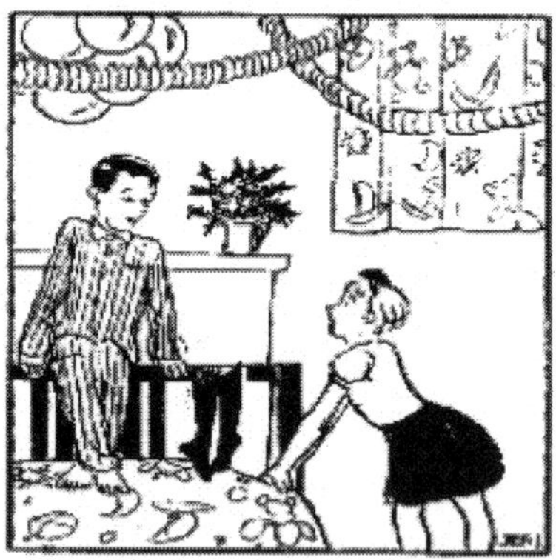

The boy who said he was going to keep up the Santa Claus idea for a year or two so as not to disillusion his parents.

One Christmas Eve Simon's five year old, half-sister, Sue, became over excited, so her father said to her, *"As it is not quite dark yet, if you stand by the window*

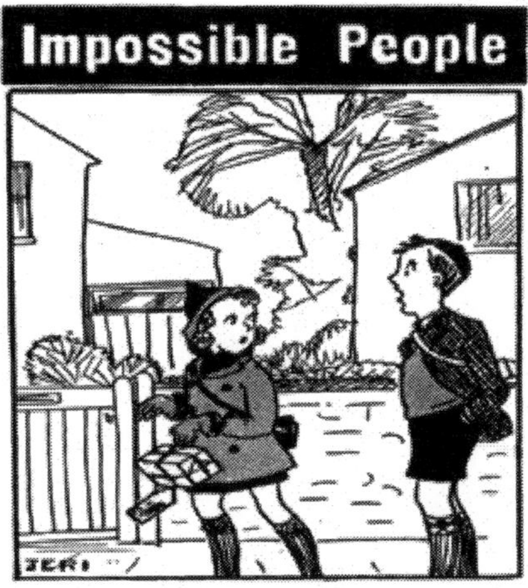

The little girl who said she was just going to post a gas mask to Father Christmas.

you might catch a glimpse of Santa on his sleigh. But you have to be very still and very quiet because if he sees you he will be gone in a flash."

Sue rushed to the window and became much calmer but, with her attention beginning to wane her father pointed to the sky and said, *"Quick, quick, Sue, look! There he is! Oh, you just missed him, he's just disappeared behind the moon."*

To his great delight Sue said; *"No I didn't Daddy, I saw him, and all the reindeers and the sacks of presents as well."* Many years later, with adult children of her own, Sue had to pretend Santa Claus doesn't exist but now that her beautiful daughter, Annabelle, and her handsome son-in-law, Alexander, have given her two equally beautiful and handsome grandchildren Sue is, once again, 'free to believe'.

Although there are still many children who don't -
During the war parents found it difficult to keep up the Santa Claus belief because, as with everything else, toys and games were in short supply.

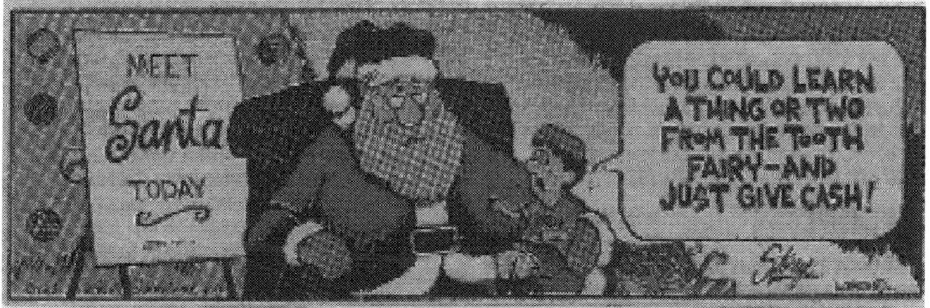

Nevertheless, the over abundance of 'all year round goodies' now available to children will never match the delight and wonder of waking on Christmas morning to a sock full of fruit and a tree laden with gifts of books, scarves and socks.

Now our present consumer society continues to promulgate this indulgence to the extent that most children know what they are getting, and will often have demanded it, at a cost to their parents (or in many cases - a parent), of a sum of money that would keep a Third World country in socks and scarves for years.

That 'first world country' America, that is one of the biggest perpetrators of this unseemly indulgence, has one redeeming feature at this wonderful time of year. When Sonya's granddaughter, Chelsea, was a toddler, her father found that the NASA Space Station charts, online, throughout the night, Santa's worldwide journey on his sleigh with his 'flying' reindeers.

An enchanting and enthralling experience for small children that is done with such gravitas and style that even adults who know it is a myth, wish to believe. America also, to its great credit, is a country that believes in the benefits of nurturing its young. Confirmed by these fine words from Henry Ford about the care we should take in rearing our children;

"A hundred years from now it will not matter what my bank account was, the sort of house I lived in or the kind of car I drove - but the world may be different because I was important in the life of a child."

Because children ARE more important than Father Christmas – although I would not want him to know that I think that.

OUT OF THE MOUTHS OF BABES

When I found Mama's cartoons in my Grandmother's biscuit tin, with them was this letter from The Sketch's 'Letters From the Man in the Street.' It has no date but must have been written sometime during the twenty years between 1922 to 1942, when our mothers cartoons were a daily feature of The Sketch.

This letter from Mr. Best also confirms that these 'Out of the Mouths of Babes' gems have always been of interest to compilers of journals and newspapers.

From the many that are sent to them, Peterborough publish about 250 a year, which indicates that there must be many thousands of these amusing, succinct, innocent 'pearls of wisdom' being said by small children every day, in many different languages, all over the world

Pearls of Wisdom that also make up many, equally small, amusing books of

Impossible People

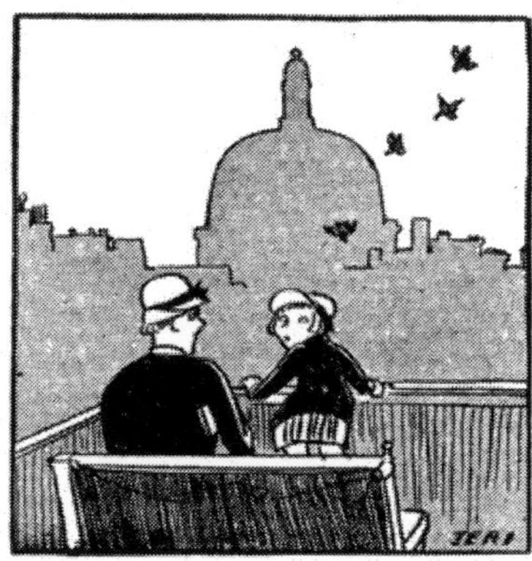

The little girl who thought St. Paul's Cathedral was built by Christopher Robin.

WREN—ROBIN—THRUSH

My son John (aged eight), who reads a lot of the *Daily Sketch*, asked his mother what was meant by the "Impossible People" feature: "The little girl who thought St. Paul's Cathedral was built by Christopher Robin."

Later he wished to impart his newly acquired knowledge to me.

"Daddy, did you see the 'Impossible People' joke?"

"No, John. What was it?"

"A little girl who thought St. Paul's Cathedral was built by Christopher Robin."

"That's a funny one. Who did build St. Paul's, John?"

"Why, Christopher Thrush."—W. A. Best. S.W.2.

these gems from which I have, earlier, nicked a few - and now nick a few more.

A mother, in the hope that the motion of the car would lull her small daughter to sleep, would, each day, take a different and longer route home from the child's school, until one day the little girl said, *"Mummy why do you keep forgetting where we live?"*

And: A little girl who, while watching her grandfather digging up potatoes, asked him why he had buried them.

And: A small child at a family christening asked her brother's new girlfriend if she was a Catholic or a Prostitute.

But the best was said by the little girl who, during a power cut, was holding a torch for a doctor as he delivered her brother. When the doctor slapped the baby into life his sister said; *"You should slap him again, he shouldn't have crawled up there in the first place."*

Impossible People

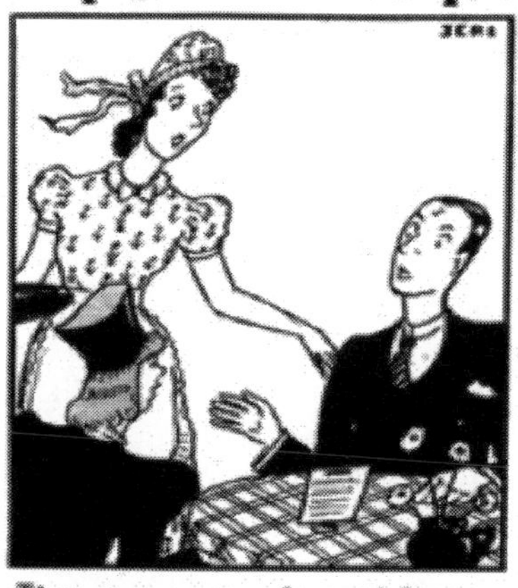

The young man who said he preferred China or Indian when asked if he wanted a Devonshire tea.

And few a little nearer to home - In the good old days of children being put to bed at a sensible time, as a special treat my, then six year old, son Michael, was allowed to stay up for a celebration supper party. Endeavouring to show how grown-up he was, he behaved impeccably. So when, at the end of the meal, the guest were asked if they would like white or black coffee, he said; *"May I have a brown one please?"*

At a similar meal Michael and his cousin Nicholas, were vying to outdo each with their numeric ability. On being asked how old his sister Sasha was, Nicholas said; *"She's free"*. Following a short lesson on the TH sound he was eventually able to say the word three correctly. A little later, much to our delight and even greater amusement, he asked; *"Please may I have some thruit?"* A word that has remained a constant in our lives.

At that time, Sonya and I lived in detached, adjacent, houses. One day, one of Nicholas's feet became entangled in his bed-end and he screamed for his mother who calmed him down, freed his foot and, as precursor in self-reliance, asked him what he would have done if she had not been there. To which he said; *"I would have gone and fetched Auntie Karina."*

Stefan and Barbara (who, at that time, also lived just doors from us), installed a sun-bed in a spare bedroom. Their eight year old son Guyon, was fascinated by this contraption and would tell visitors that his Mummy was lying under her; *"Ultra Violent X-ray machine"*.

When, on a visit to the home of a colleague, Peggy, the front door bell rang, her seven year old daughter, Judy, ran to open it. On seeing two Nuns in full habit she turned to her mother and, with a startled look on her face, said; *"Mummy there are two Dooms at the door"*. After a reasonable donation to their cause, the two 'Dooms' forgave her.

Sonya and I are known by our grandchildren (and everyone else's), as Grandma Karina and Grandma Sonya. When Sonya's granddaughter, Hannah, was five, her teacher, endeavouring to instill in her pupils the importance of reading, asked Hannah what she would do if she wanted find out about something. Hannah said, *"I'd ask my Mummy." "What if Mummy doesn't know?"* asked her teacher. *"I'd ask my Grandma."* said Hannah.

"But what if Grandma doesn't know?" said the now somewhat exasperated teacher, to which Hannah said; *"I would ask my Grandma Karina, because she knows everything."*

Hannah now lives in Paris and reads well in both English and French and knows I don't know everything. But there may, somewhere, be a retired teacher who still believes I'm the fount of all knowledge.

I lost touch with Peggy many years ago so know nothing of her daughter Judy. My nephews now have adult children of their own, as does my son, Michael who has two very beautiful, talented daughters, Charlotte and Sophia, and my much loved, exceptionally bright, grandson, Michael.

When young, Michael was told by his father that if he wanted to interrupt an adult conversation he must say, *"Excuse me please."* At a boisterous lunch party, he started to shout, *"Scuse me please, scuse me please!"* When asked what he wanted to say, he said; *"I don't want to say anything, I just can't hear myself listen."*

Just days later he told me the ducks on his other Grannie's pond had had ducklings. I told him the swans that visit our pond each year had just had cygnets and asked him if he knew what colour they were. He said, *"Yellow?"* I said, *"No not baby ducks, baby swans. You know what they look like!"* To which he said; *"They're like giraffes but are white and don't have legs!"*

All of which admirably illustrate that most original thought does come from 'Out of The Mouths Of Babes'. Or from Piet Hein -

Originality

Original thought is a straightforward process
It's easy enough when you know what to do.
You simply combine, in appropriate doses,
The blatantly false and the patently true.

(i.e. - Swans are like Giraffes!)

Which takes us to

THE TEENS - Are kids quick thinkers or thick tinkers?

Sent to me by my much loved, surrogate son, Hugh, these school howlers taken from test papers and essays, are by both English and American students of all ages. Apart from 'twinning' well with my 'Out of the Mouths of Babes' anecdotes, I thought they would make good 'loo book', but was beaten to it by Norman McGreavy, whose: 'Must Try Harder', (a worthy addition to any 'loo library'), was published by Constable in 2007.

As one teacher noted, *"It is truly astonishing what weird stuff our young scholars can create under the pressures of time and grades."* So whoever said; *"Just when you discover your parents were right, your children start telling you are wrong."* got it very wrong.

Ailments:
For asphyxiation apply artificial respiration until the patient is dead.
When you breathe you inspire, when you do not breathe you expire.
What is a major disease associated with cigarettes? Premature death.
For a head cold use an agonizer, spray the nose until it drops in your throat.

Geography:
The sun never set on the British Empire because the British Empire's in the East and the sun sets in the West.

History:
Queen Victoria was the longest queen. She sat on a thorn for 63 years
Where was the Declaration of Independence signed? At the bottom of the page.
Magna Carta provided that no man should be hanged twice for the same offence.
The Greeks were a highly sculptured people. Without them we wouldn't have any history.

Music:
Beethoven expired in 1827 and later died of this.
Beethoven was deaf. He was so deaf he wrote loud music.
Handel was half German half Italian and half English. He was very large.

Places:
The Caesarean Section is a district in Rome.
Houses in France are made of plaster of Paris.
The inhabitants of Moscow are called Mosquitoes.
A vacuum is the large empty space where the Pope lives.

Science:
Gravity was invented by Isaac Walton. It is chiefly noticeable in the Autumn when the apples are falling off the trees.

Better:
In which battle did Napoleon die? His last.
What is the main reason for divorce? Marriage.
Name the four seasons: Salt, pepper, mustard and vinegar.
What is the main reason for failure? Exams.

Best:
A census taker is a man who goes from house to house increasing the population.
The Greeks also had myths. A myth is a female moth. (So Sonya is right!)

And the treatment for fainting – which my reader may be inclined to do on reaching the end of this list.

Rub the person's chest or, if a lady, rub her arm and put her head between the knees of the nearest doctor.

An Impossible nurse and some Impossible doctors take us to -

Impossible People

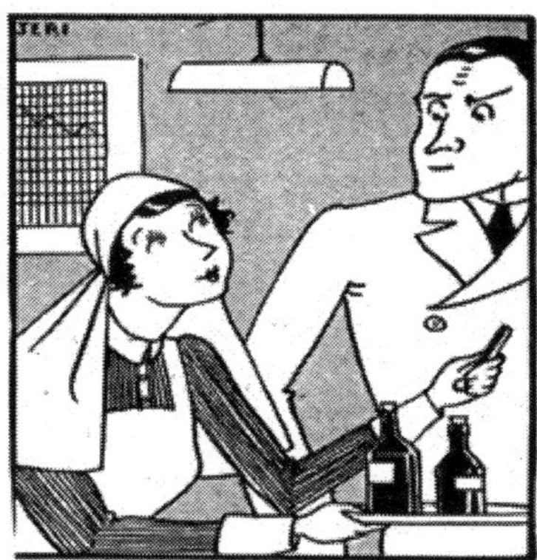

The nurse who was nicknamed "Tonsils" because all the doctors wanted to take her out.

Anatomy:
The parts of speech are lungs and air.
Respiration is composed of two acts, inspiration and expectoration.
Before giving blood find out whether the blood is positive or negative.
Bodies have three parts. The branium contains the brain, the borax contains the heart and lungs, the abominable cavity contains the bowels of which there are five: A, E, I, O and U.
The Spinal column is a long bunch of bones. The head sits on the top, you sit on the bottom.

Ridiculous:
To prevent milk from turning sour, keep it in the cow.
The pistol of a flower is its only protection against insects.
Syntax is all the money collected at the church from sinners.
A super saturated solution is one that holds more than it can hold.
When you smell an odourless gas it is probably carbon monoxide.
To collect fumes of sulphur hold down a deacon over a flame of a test tube.
Mushrooms always grow in damp places that is why they look like umbrellas.

And finally, the one that wins the highest marks:
What is artificial insemination? When the farmer does it to the cow instead of the bull.

Which propels us to the pleasures and perks of

GROWING OLDER

It is said that; *"Getting old is being constantly punished for a crime you haven't committed."* It is also said that; *"Despite nothing being certain, it is certain that the lucky among us will get older."*

Richard Needham, Earl of Kilmorey, avers that this does have a few benefits because; *"As you grow old you lose interest in sex, your friends drift away, and your children ignore you. There are other advantages, of course, but these are the outstanding ones."*

David Croft averred in his marvelous sit-com, 'Waiting For God', *"Old age is in its infancy."* So perhaps Bernard Baruch was wrong when he said; *"There is only one thing wrong with the younger generation - a lot of us don't belong to it anymore."*

And when Robbie Williams sang, *"I want to grow old before I die"* he obviously hadn't heard Groucho Marx's axiom, *"Anyone can get old - all you have to do is live long enough."*

Although it is of greater importance to concern ourselves with how we grow old, rather than how old we grow, because it is also said that;

On reaching sixty, in human years you are antiquated. In car years you are vintage. In dog years you are dead.

While the most comforting is possibly this next anonymous axiom: *"Growing old doesn't stop you laughing, it's not laughing that makes you grow old."*

Impossible People

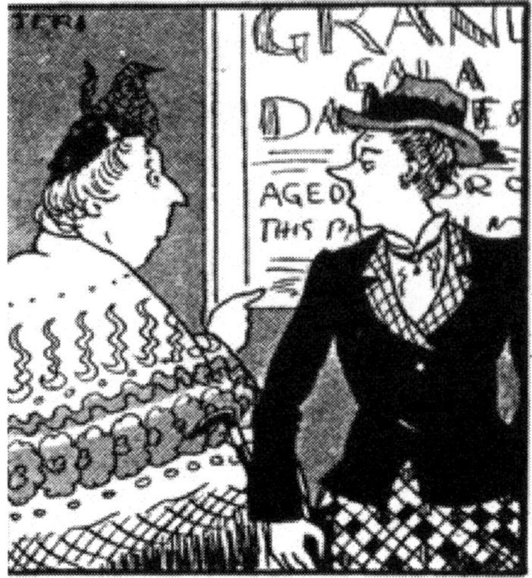

The woman who wondered why they had a dance for the aged poor when a hot supper would do them far more good.

Or Even Older

Cyril had just retired and was having a discussion with his wife, Ethel, on what the future might hold for them *"What will you do if I die before you?"* asked Cyril. After some thought Ethel said; *"As I'm still very active and young for my age I'll probably find two other, younger widowed women to share a house with." "What will you do?"* Ethel asked. *"I'd probably do the same,"* said Cyril.

And Even Older Than Older

A young man in a pub said to a 98 year old regular, *"I'm not sure I want to live to be 98"*. To which the old man said: *"They all say that, but you will when you're 97."*

Which ties in nicely with George Burns' assertion that, *"At our age we are very pleased to be anywhere."* But not, apparently, a synagogue – Arnold, who had reached his 105th birthday, hadn't been seen at the synagogue for some weeks. Worried by his absence, the Rabbi went to see him. He found Arnold in excellent health and asked him why, after so many years, he was no longer attending service.

"Well it's like this, Rabbi." said the old man; *"When I reached 95 I expected*

God to take me any day. Then I got to 100 and he didn't take me and now I'm 105 and he still hasn't taken me. So I think he's forgotten about me and I don't want to remind him I'm still here."

Then there was the pensioner who phoned her doctor in some distress, *"Is it true,"* she asked, *"that the medication you prescribed for me yesterday has to be taken for the rest of my life?" "Yes, I'm afraid so."* the doctor told her. After a few seconds silence she then said; *"Then could I ask you how serious my condition is, because the prescription is marked: No Refills?"*

A Mother Superior's Prayer -

Dear Lord,

Thou knowest better than I know myself that I am growing older and will, some day, be old, but please, Lord, keep me from getting talkative, and particularly from the fatal habit of thinking I must say something on every subject and on every occasion. Keep me free from the recital of endless details and give me wings to get to the point.

Give me grace enough to listen to the tales of other people's pains. Help me to endure them with patience, and release me from the craving to try and straighten out everyone else's affairs.

Please seal my lips on my own aches and pains, they increase as the years go by and my love of regaling other people with news of them becomes an ever greater temptation.

Keep me reasonably sweet; I do not want to be a saint (some of them are so hard to live with), but a sour old woman is one of the crowning works of the devil.

So teach me the glorious lesson that occasionally it is possible that I may be mistaken. Make me thoughtful but not moody, helpful but not bossy and, although I have a vast store of wisdom, protect me from seeming to 'know too much' as Thou knowest, Lord, I crave a few friends at the end.

Perhaps we can all hope, if we are fortunate enough to 'grow old', that we can retain a similar sense of humour, and an equal sense of what to not to say and when not to say it. An ever increasing problem, particularly if you don't adhere to what is considered 'the norm' such as being overweight.

Which few older people are, although they may prefer to be a little overweight if this means it will keep them alive a little longer - if only by two weeks - Totie Fields said, *"I've been on a diet for two weeks and all I've lost is two weeks."*

Unlike JERI's next Impossible Person who diets by running up bills.

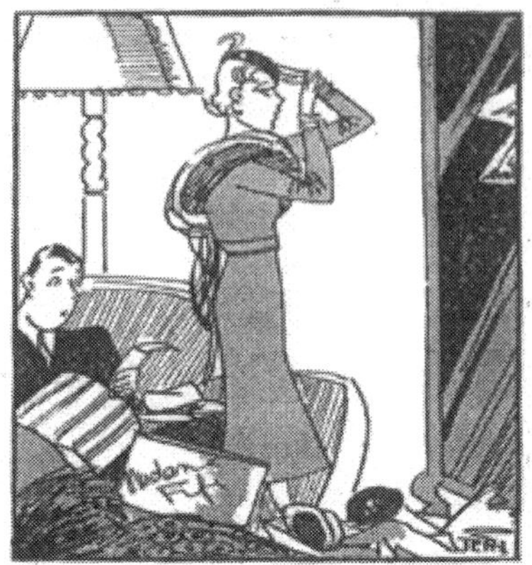

The girl who said she had no need to diet as she got plenty of exercise running up bills.

Woody Allen's opinion that; *"You can live to be a hundred if you give up all the things that make you want to live to be a hundred"*, ties in with my opinion that; *'You can get thin if you stop eating all the food that makes you want to stay alive.'*

Both of which tie in neatly with; 'The older you get the better you get unless you are a banana.'

Nicola's mother-in-law, Amy, in shape, colour or inference, was certainly not a banana. A bright nonagenarian worthy of much admiration, I had the profound pleasure of knowing her for half my life, and, as with the rest of my family, came to love her dearly. To be in her company was always a delight, and there are many anecdotal stories I could relate, but will confine myself to just one.

On returning from a shopping trip she deftly set about unwrapping some vacuum-packed items and, having quickly and efficiently completed the task, she turned to me and, without a hint of irony, said; *"You know, Karina, with everything now packed in this way, I really cannot imagine how old people manage."* She was 86 at the time!

She and I shared many talks and much merriment. We also shared the same size feet. Thus, despite her dress sense being superior to my own, we also, occasionally, shared shoes.

In her youth she was a Court Couturist and well into her nineties, still made some of her own clothes. Amy also paid me one of the biggest compliments of my life when, at the wedding of Nicola and George's son Stefan to his fiancé, Kirsty, she said I looked as if I had just walked off the cover of Vogue. I was pleased to return the compliment because, as always, so did she.

Fortune smiled on us and allowed us another eleven years with Amy who would definitely agree with Abraham Lincoln when he said, *"In the end it's not the years in your life that count but the life in your years."* For as Bette Davies said, a little more succinctly; *"Old age ain't no place for sissies."*

Had Amy known there were going to be over a hundred family and friends' at her funeral, she would not have agreed with Ogden Nash's observation that,

"Middle age ends and senescence begins, the day your descendants outnumber your friends." Slim or rotund!

My assumption that a book of this nature is not a book without a Jane Austen quote, also applies to Pam Ayres, a poet whom Mama much admired.

Pam's poems are always better when recited in her own inimitable way in her wonderful West Country accent, although this is not a good enough reason not to include this next 'offering' for my reader to read and enjoy. Particularly as it also compliments JERI's previous cartoon with its caption's inspired oxymoron.

The Slimming Poem

I'm a slimmer by trade, I'm frequently weighed,
I'm as slim as a reed in a river,
I'm slender and lean, and hungry and mean.
Have some water, it's good for your liver.

Don't give me cheese rolls or profiteroles,
And don't show me that jelly a-shakin',
Don't give me cream crackers, nor snackers
Or a great big ice cream with a flake in.

Don't give me swiss roll or toad-in-the-hole,
Don't show me that Black Forest gateau.
You sit and go mouldy you old Garibaldi,
Your pastry all riddled with fat. Oh!

When fat, I feel weary and tubby and dreary,
The stairs make me struggle and grunt dear.
And yet I'm so happy and punchy and snappy,
With hip bones all stuck out in front dear.

No it's white fish for me, no milk in me tea,
And if we don't like it we lump it,
No figs or sultanas, no mashed up bananas,
No pleasure and no buttered crumpet.

Don't get any bigger, me old pear shaped figure
I can and I will become thinner.
So cheer up, take heart, pass the calorie chart,
Let's see what we're having for dinner.

Dieting often being a necessity whether -

IN SICKNESS OR IN HEALTH

The most thought-provoking quote on this subject comes, yet again, from The Master: Oscar Wilde; *"In whom of our friend's houses would we be choose to be ill?"* Another is Voltaire's, *"The art of medicine consists in amusing the patient while Nature effects a cure."*

Which morphed into this quote by Don Herold, *"Doctors think a lot of patients are cured who have simply just quit in disgust."*

But not this next patient of JERI's:

Diseases that may have been two of these: 'cretin', idiot', 'imbecile' or 'moron'.

All of which, Tom Nuttall tells us in his book, 'In Fact', were once medical diagnoses.

As are two of the most awful, Alzheimers and Parkinsons - of which, says Sonya, most would prefer the latter because; "It's better to spill some of your drink than to forget where you put it."

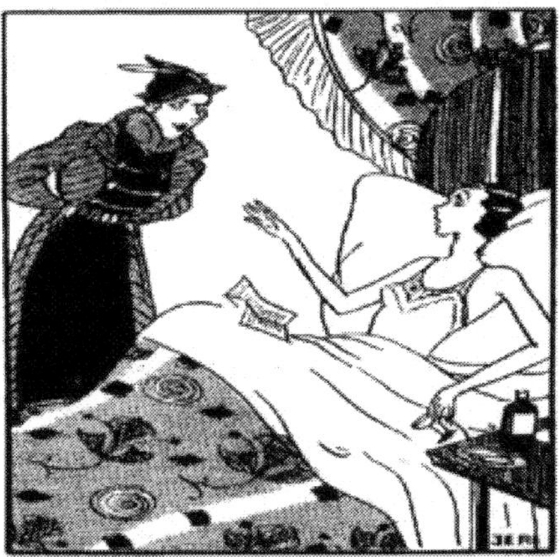

The woman who said the patent medicine had cured her all right, but when she read the folder she found she had two more diseases.

Perhaps one of the 'two more diseases' that JERI's Impossible Person found she had on reading the folder of her patent medicine' was that which most suffer from at some time in their lives.

I will seek you and I will find you
I shall take you to your bed and have my way with you.
I will make you ache, shake and sweat until you moan and groan.
I will make you beg for mercy, beg for me to stop.
And when I am finished, you will be weak for days.
All my love, The Flu

JERI's next impossible child obviously hadn't read P.G. Wodehouse's dictum: *"An apple a day, well aimed, keeps the doctor away."*

A doctor who will, no doubt, prescribe a few pills, for as Piet Hein maintains:

Impossible People

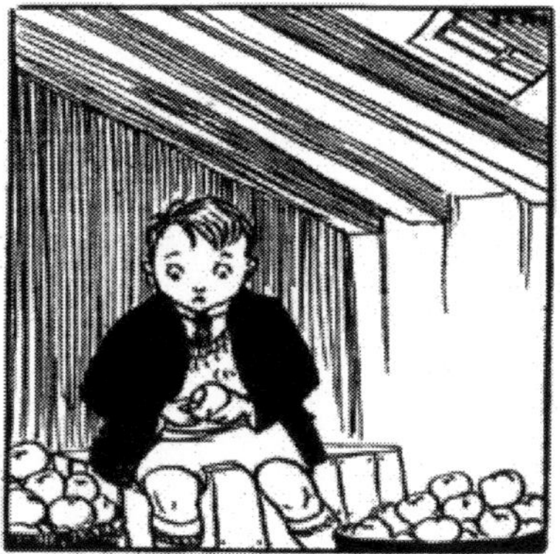

The boy who said he had kept fifteen doctors away this morning, but he was afraid one would have to come this afternoon.

Pills are useful against all ills,
And against too, too many pills.

But not my truly stoic brother-in-law, John, who, having manfully battled Rheumatoid Arthritis for most of his adult life (which necessitated the taking of many thousands of pills), sadly climbed the ladder to Heaven in November 2013.

Despite being a structural engineer, the climbing of ladders was not really his thing after he had two new knees that were replaced in a tandem operation.

With two surgeons working on each knee, his life support began to fail, but with great skill, his surgical team managed to rebalance these and successfully complete the two operations.

Within two days John was sitting up and having work brought to his bed and within three weeks was back in his office. On returning to hospital for his first check-up, his consultant, surrounded by medical students, told them of John's history and how he had come so dangerously close to dying.

He then said; *"Patients who have less complicated operations and suffer none of the problems encountered by Mr. Thomas, will, following similar but less life threatening surgery, often remain in hospital for many weeks. But as you can see he made a quick recovery and has now been back at work for several weeks. What does that tell you about this patient?"* When none of his bemused students could give him a satisfactory answer, he said; *"It tells you he's self-employed."*

Although it is possible he had to get back to work in order to make sufficient money to settle a 'big bill'. As did JERI's next patient.

IMPOSSIBLE PEOPLE

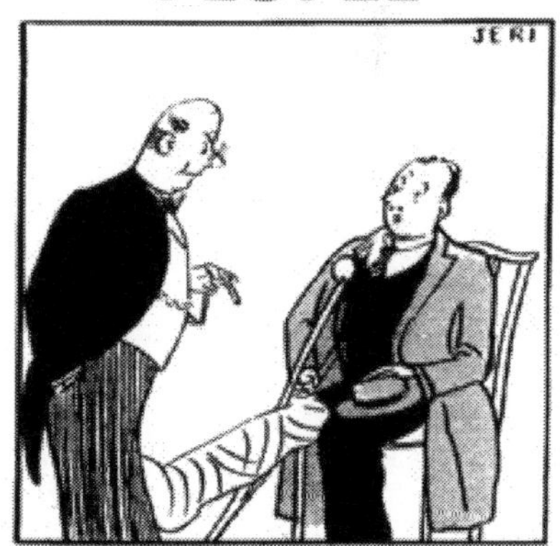

The specialist who said he would have the patient walking in no time —in fact, he would send him such a big bill that he would have to sell his car.

Most are in awe of the things surgeons achieve and, even more so, how they do it. In particular that of neurologists and cardiologists. As this encounter, sent to the Daily Mail by Roger Dembino of

Hertfordshire illustrates, it is even more tricky than we imagine.

A mechanic was removing a cylinder head from the engine of a Harley Davison when a well known cardiologist, while waiting for the service manager to take a look at his car, walked across the garage to watch the mechanic working on the Harley.

After several minutes of much manipulation, the mechanic straightened up, wiped his hands on a rag and said, *"So Doc, you've watched me open the head of this engine and repair the damaged valves, clean them, replace them and fix the casing back in position so the bike will go just like new."*

On starting the engine, the mechanic then said to the cardiologist, *"Mending hearts or engines is all just engineering, Doc, so how come you earn so much more than me for doing, basically, the same thing?"*.

To which the cardiologist said; *"That's because when mending a heart I have to do it with the engine still running"*.

While it is definitely 'no laughing matter', an amusing word, joke - or cartoon - can often help to ameliorate the sorrow of those left bereft by the loss of a loved one. Nevertheless, regardless of the universal pleas that it 'should never happen again', it will 'always happen again', as every living thing , in one way or another, by accident or design - or just time – will, inevitably, die.

As there is nothing more certain than -

DEATH – The funny side

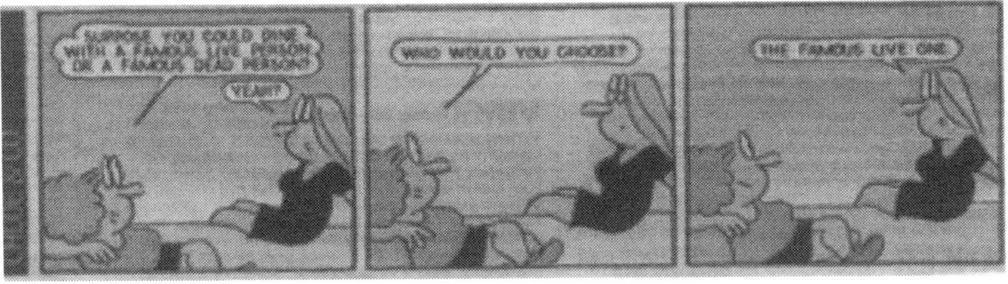

There are millions of quotations on the subject of death, but as millions of people die each and every day this should come as no surprise – which, sadly, death has a habit of doing. Very often when we are eating or drinking;

Many a man both young and old,
Has gone to his sarcophagus,
Through pouring liquids icy cold,
Down his warm oesophagus.

It is said that the richer you are the more likely you are to indulge in things that can bring about your early demise.

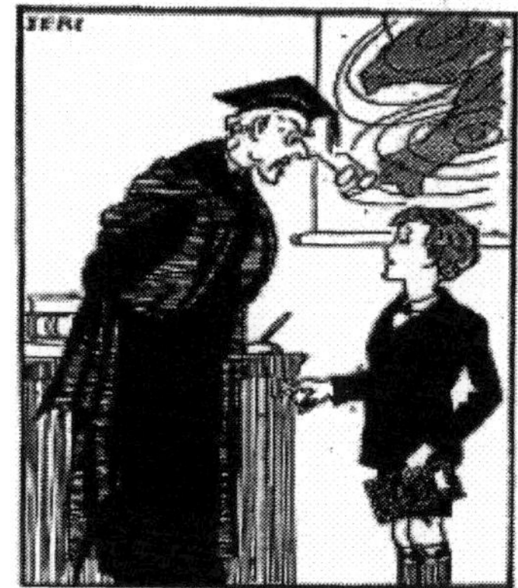

The boy who thought it was Laurel who said "Kiss me, Hardy."

The church in Little Harrowden, near Wellingborough, has a marble effigy of a medieval Knight, Sir Jack Badsaddle (names don't come better than that!), who, very hot after energetically killing a wild boar, drank from an ice cold spring, which brought about his early demise, and certainly no time to say any 'Last Words'. The most famous being Nelson's "Kiss me Hardy". Which, it is now suggested, were actually; "Kismet, Hardy".

Here are another two that are nearly as famous, together with another four that, if enough people read my book, soon will be -

The most amusing:	I told you my feet were killing me.
The most mundane:	Oscar Wilde's; "I hate this wallpaper."
The most righteous:	At least I know where he's sleeping tonight.
The most relieved:	Here Isabel my wife doth lie, She's at peace and so am I
The most heedless:	From Groucho Marx; 'Either he's dead or my watch has stopped."
The most hedonistic:	Here lies the body of Mary Sexton, who pleased many a man but never vexed one.

Ed Furgol said; *"My luck is so bad that if I bought a cemetery people would stop dying."* So I for one hope he does buy one – and quite soon.

Fritz Spiegl's 'A Small Book of Grave Humour' is as gravely funny as it gets. As are these from old newspaper cuttings that Matt Roper may wish he had included in his killingly funny book; '101 Crazy Ways To Die'. A book suitably subtitled by the journalist, Jan Fryer, as, 'Dead Unlucky'. And from Woodton in Norfolk, an inscription that bears out the earlier assumption about fools and their money:

Here lies John Rackett in his wooden jacket.
He kept neither horses nor mules;
He lived like a hog; He died like a dog;
And left all his money to fools.

And their foolhardiness? Thomas Snell's stone says, *"Here lie I, and no wonder I'm dead, for a wagon wheel ran over my head."* Which is similar to the words on a headstone in a cemetery in Union, Pennsylvania that would sit neatly with my piece on 'Cars' but fits just as neatly here: *"Here lies the body of Jonathan Blake, who stepped on the gas instead of the brake."* And from a headstone in a cemetery in Bromsgrove:

Here lies a man that was Knott born and his father was Knott before him.
He lived Knott and did Knott die yet underneath this stone doth lie.
Knott begot, Knott christened, and here he lies and yet was Knott.

Then there are those who beat all the odds; In 1885 Martha Southwell of Romsey workhouse, while being taken to the local cemetery for burial, pushed open her coffin, stepped out of it, took the lid and walked back with it to the institution where, until her death 50 years later, she used it as an ironing board. An attitude to death that mirrors that of Jewish people who are unique in their ability to show their grief with great, or even grave humour. (One of my better puns?) Illustrated by this next joke from my American 'Encyclopedia of Jewish Humor.'

Old Mr. Keppleman's health was declining so his family decided to send him on a two week recuperative holiday to Palm Beach. Towards the end of his holiday the man died and his family had his body flown back to New York. As the mourners surrounded the open casket to pay their respects, a nephew, on seeing how well the dead man looked, said; "Doesn't he look great!" "He sure does." said another family member; "Those two weeks in Palm Beach did him the world of good."

Death is such a difficult subject I thought, on reaching it (the subject not the fact), I would find little of any amusement as, on trawling through my poetry books and the net for poems on the subject, I found them all to be, as Mama would say; 'Dirges'. I then came across this wonderful poem that is so suitable for Impossible People Mr. Emberson might have written it for me – or my Mama.

Danse Macabre
by Ian Emberson

Death came to me in a mini skirt,
As skittish as a kitten,
And said; I am come for your final flirt."
But added; "You don't seem smitten."

Says I: "Well not in my wildest whim
Did I picture you looking like this,
I'd been told that you were a reaper grim
And behold – you're a saucy miss."

"Ah - many a one is like yourself
Surprised by my winning smile,
I have jokes and jests like a playful elf."
And I know the way to beguile.

But please - just pass me by with a nod
I've poems and plays unwritten
There are footpaths I have never trod,
And, as you say, I'm not much smitten

"Oh hush my darling and don't repine",
And she gave a gracious prance.
Then she twined her fingers into mine
And whispered; "Shall we dance?"

Although we can be reasonably certain that when Mama's next Impossible villager did meet his maker, it was by the good offices of the 'Grim Reaper' himself – and not some frolicsome maiden wanting to dance.

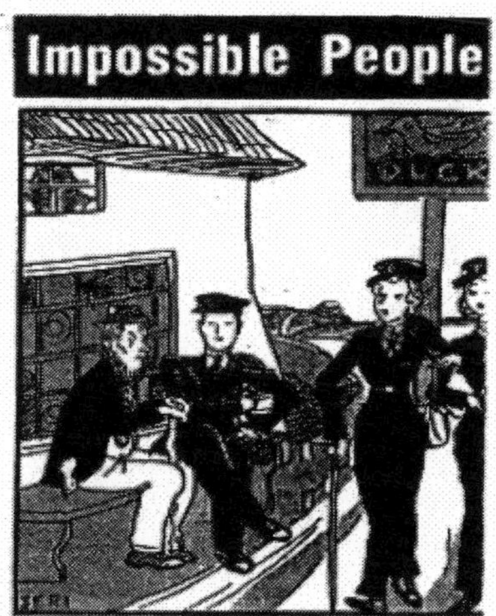

The villager who said not yet, when asked if he had lived here all his life

A caption that takes us to -

DEATH – The serious side – plus a few diversions that most people make or take before they die

A doctor at Mount Sinai hospital said; *"Death is simply nature's way of telling us to slow down."* What he didn't say was how we slow down our ever increasing world population. A need, according to many media discussions, that will soon become an imperative if the world is to continue to maintain its sustainability.

It is recorded that by early 2016 the world's population had increased from its 1999 total of six billion to over seven and a half billion. Which even I, to whom maths is a foreign language, can deduce is an increase of one and a half billion in just over 16 years.

We are not told how long, from the time of creation, each of the previous billions took to arrive, but we can be confident it wasn't remotely as short as sixteen years!

I have read that it will not be long before India is more populated than China, a country that, despite the ghastly and gruesome efforts of Mao Tse Tung and their, later, much kinder, rule of only one child per couple, (that was rescinded in 2015), has, until now, been the most populated in the world. While most of the increase has been in Western Europe, both Africa and Asia, have now, in a neat homonym, joined the race to see how many more people they can add to the human race.

In my items on Wars I ask how many people of merit the world has lost through such conflict, contagious diseases and the many ghastly 'cleansings' humans have suffered. It is also possible that, in her own efforts to stabilise the population, Nature devised the numerous natural events with which we are regularly plagued, such as famine, floods, pestilence and plague's. (If this subject were not so serious I might add 'puns' to these many trials and tribulations.)

Efforts considerably thwarted by our inexorable advances in medicine and technology and now, perhaps, aided by space travel -

Fascinatingly, of the three creatures essential to the wellbeing of our planet and

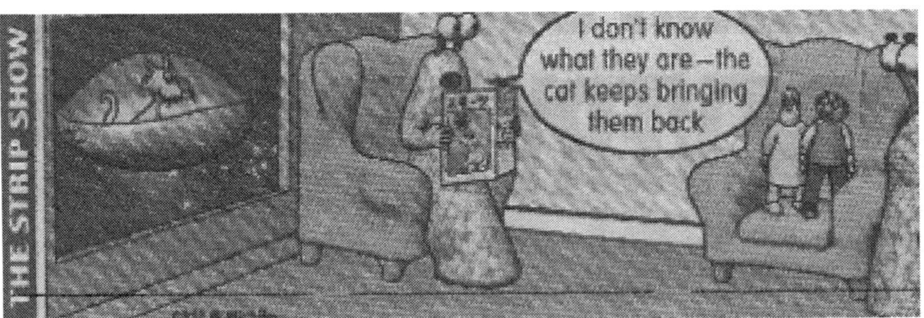

the continuation of humankind - ants, bees and bats - two have the propensity to kill us, while the third puts the Fear of God into most people.

As does death, or the thought of it - but not all of us. Winston Churchill – a man to whom we English should be 'eternally' grateful - famously said; *"I am ready to meet my Maker. Whether my Maker is ready for the ordeal of meeting me is another matter."*

Although, if gambling were my forte I would bet that few people are ever really ready to 'Meet their Maker. Particularly those who have lived lives as meritorious as Sir Winston. Merits that, were possibly assisted by his love of cigars and whiskey. Both of which, no doubt, also went a long way towards steadying his nerves when making the many difficult decisions needed in order to steady the country. Decisions he rarely, if ever, got wrong!
With or without whiskey.

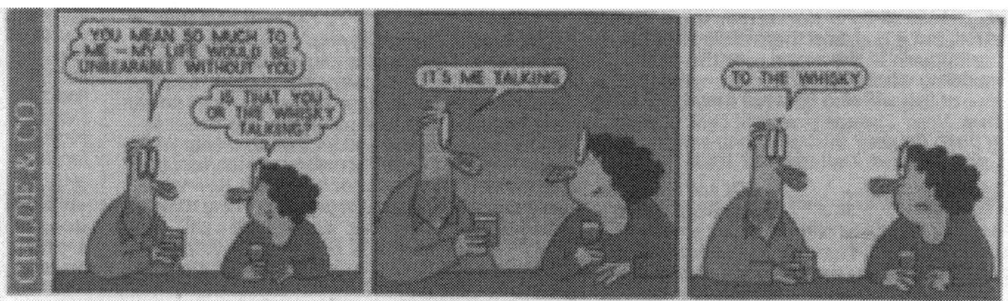

Which might be considered a phobia -

There must be more than a few people who have a 'running out of whisky' phobia, or 'running out of alcohol' in general'. A condition for which, despite much research, I have been unable to find a word.

But I did find the interesting 'Abibliphobia' from which both Nicola and Simon suffer, which is; 'The fear of running out of things to read.' A cure for which both writers and publishers must pray will will never be found.

Although someone may try find a cure for Cynophobia, the fear of signs and symbols, as sufferers are likely to be frightened to death by the many notices outside churches asking their flocks to; 'Prepare to Meet Your Maker'. Which, patently, JERI's next Impossible Person is not prepared to do.

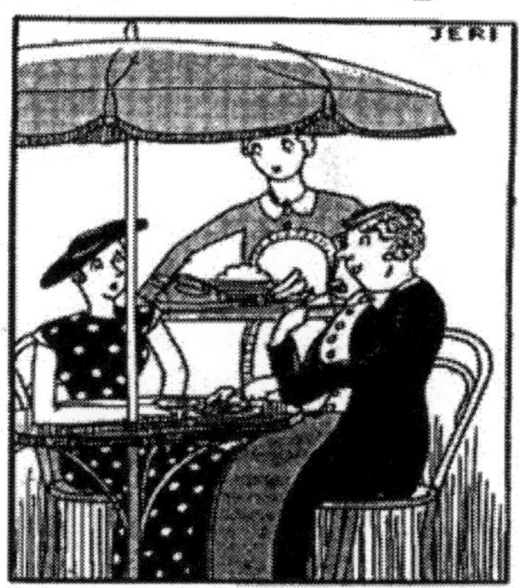

The woman who said she was not going to starve herself to death for the sake of living a few years longer.

It is to be hoped she wasn't eating chocolate at the time, as a Peterborough item titled 'This England' included a letter from Jim Payne, who wrote, "In September 2011, a planned talk to the, predominately elderly congregation of St. Michael's Church, West Hill in Devon, was advertised as; 'Dying Matters. Free coffee or tea with cakes including Death by Chocolate.' Although, as Charles Schulz opined; *"It's said all you need is love, but a little chocolate now and then doesn't hurt."*

Although advertising is necessary, especially that which offers free coffee, tea and chocolate cake, it is little wonder Cynophobia is so prevalent now that our habitat is so lavishly adorned with so many signs. So much so that it is often impossible to differentiate between those telling us where we can't go from those telling us what we can't do.

Mr. Payne hails from Ottery St. Mary in Devon, where I spent three terms at its famous Grammar School. Originally founded in 1335 as a choir school by Bishop John Grandisson, it then, in 1545, became, by order of Henry VIII, a King's Grammar School. Only to lose this proud heritage when relegated, in 1982, to a Comprehensive.

Perhaps these Grammar Schools have been demoted to Comprehensives due to Pediophobia, a fear of children. Or numbers? A common phobia is Triskaideka, a fear of the number 13, to which I may have succumbed when, yet again having to change schools, I was required to take another exam, the very rare Thirteen Plus. Having yet again passed, I went, yet again, to another grammar school.

It is now thought by some that comprehensive schools give an education equal to that provided by Grammar Schools, but as this requires the impossible criteria that all children are equal academically, what they can't do is to give all pupils a pride in their school - or their achievements - whether these are in academia, artistry or athletics.

An assumption admirably illustrated by Dr. Adrian Rogers' 'test', which I include in my section on 'Education and Employment'. Thus the excellent heights of higher academia and the valuable artistic and spatial skills previously reached by many students via selection, will die a slow death.

Two other, more common phobias are Agoraphobia and Arachnophobia, which, for those who suffer from both, must be very scary if, having found a safe enclosed space, they find it is full of spiders.

Another, from which my twin suffers, is Claustrophobia. Then there is a fear of snakes, Ophidiophobia, from which many people suffer - as do those who are killed by them, snakes not phobias. Although a few severe sufferers of phobias have been known to die from them.

Which neatly takes us back to the 'subject' of 'death'. Of which infants are not aware, the young ignore, the middle-aged hope won't happen and the elderly make jokes about. One of whom is my brother-in-law, George, who, on finding he had reached an age where he was attending more funerals then he has friends, said, somewhat indignantly; *"They are cutting down the trees in my forest."*

From a funeral that was not for one of George's friends, although it could have been, are these rather poignant words that were published in the National Press following media coverage of how, nowadays, nursing care of the elderly often falls short of what they expect, hope for, and most certainly deserve.

They will disappear, those elderly parents who are taking so long to make way for you.
The mother whose old age imposes duties on you which you find inconvenient.
The father who has become an old grouch as he can longer walk without a stick.
They will disappear; those careful watchers over your childhood; those lovely protectors of your adolescence.
They will disappear and as soon as they are no longer here, they will strike you in a new light. Because time, which makes older those who are alive, makes them seem younger as soon as death has taken them away.
And when they are gone you will search in vain for better friends.

One wonders how these uncaring carers ever consider how they will feel if, when old, they are treated in a similar, uncaring manner. for as Piet Hein so aptly writes;

Memento Vivere

Love while you've got love to give,
Live while you've got life to live.

During her later years Mama did 'impose duties' on her children, but none that any of us, even for a nanosecond, considered remotely inconvenient. Written in her mid-seventies, I read this poem at her funeral. She wrote it with only three verses, and, wondering why she would exclude that part of her life that was the most exciting, successful and least stressful, I composed the second verse which covers the time when, as a 'Golden Girl of the 'Roaring Twenties', she made many visits to France.

Her later years were spent writing, painting, gardening and enjoying her pets and her ten grandchildren - all of whom adored her.

If I Should Go To Heaven

If I had gone to heaven in my childhood,
I would have packed my case with these:

A bow wave like lace on salt water;
A derrick swinging bananas over a hold;
A peacock's feather;
The smell of wood smoke;
A forest of oak trees.

If I had gone to heaven in my youth,
I would have packed my case with these:

A golden girl I shared a flat with;
A fast car with a tonneau top;
A French landscape in the Pyrenees;
The lights of London late at night;
Dancing 'til dawn in a chemise.

If I had gone to heaven in mid age,
I would have packed my case with these:

A Conte pencil and clean paper;
A box of paints, a sable brush;
A young man who used to love me;
Two small boys with curly hair;
Four little girls with fat knees.

If I should go to heaven now I've aged,
I would pack my case with these:

A dark hound with pricked ears;
A blue-eyed Siamese cat;
A bottle of port, some Stilton cheese;
A new book unread; an old melody;
Ships hooters on foggy seas.

Which takes us from a poem of Mama's (with a little help from me) to one of mine (with a little help from Sonya), both of which we read at her funeral, as they encapsulate our mother's life and character without being, in one of her favourite words; 'Mawkish'.

Mama - 1900 to 1995

Friday the 26th May,
Not a special day;
No birthday to remember;
No Christmas in December.

Just the day you said your last "Goodbye".
Just the day you chose, so quietly, to die.

At ninety four,
You paused for breath,
And death, for once so kind,
Gently closed the door.

All you ever wanted in your life,
Was a paint brush, a clean canvass,
And a palette knife.
A dog, a cat, A cigarette

A little peace a little quiet,
A pen, some paper,
And nothing more.
Except your children to adore

And 'though these things
Seem simple to relate,
Your achievements were too great,
For lesser souls to emulate.

In later life with a brain still so alert
But a body so impaired,
To bring you comfort
We despaired.

You wanted still to cook,
To paint, to write, to draw.
To garden as you'd
Always done before.

You wanted even more,
Your youth, your sight,
Your hearing
Things we could not give.

And you will stay the lynchpin,
And the lodestar of our lives.

And although we gave you all we could,
In thought and deed and word,
We always gave far less
Than you deserved.

And now with your last farewell,
Everyone you ever knew,
Will mourn your worth,
Will not forget.

The rich legacy you leave behind,
Your paintings, your poems,
The wealth of your wisdom,
Your cartoons, your clarity of mind.

Your wit and understanding,
And your innate ability,
To be always thoughtful,
Generous and kind.

Yes, Mama,
We will always remember,
With love and gratitude,
The summers of your life.

The gifts you gave,
The hardships you endured,
That made us all so brave.
And your last long, sad,

September Days'.
And 'though you've died,
In this year of nineteen ninety five,
To us you will always and forever,
Be alive.

After the reading my grandson Michael's other granny, Jenny, said, *"I would die to have something similar read at my funeral."* So it is very sad that none of us will ever know if we do.

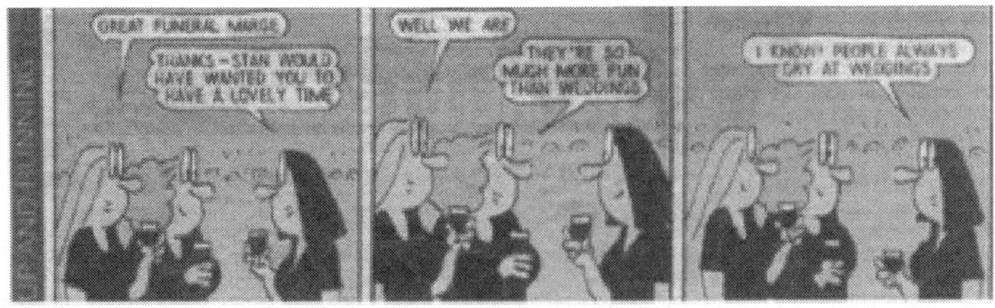

All of the many funerals I have attended have become a celebration of the lives of those mourned and have turned into very 'jolly' affairs while remaining dignified, and there are few better ways to dignify death than by reading a poem. W.H. Auden's 'Stop All The Clocks' must be read at many thousands of funerals.

As will this anonymous, emotive poem, from which Tony Crafter devised this haunting and ingenious anagram for his much loved brother, Paul, who died in February, 2011.

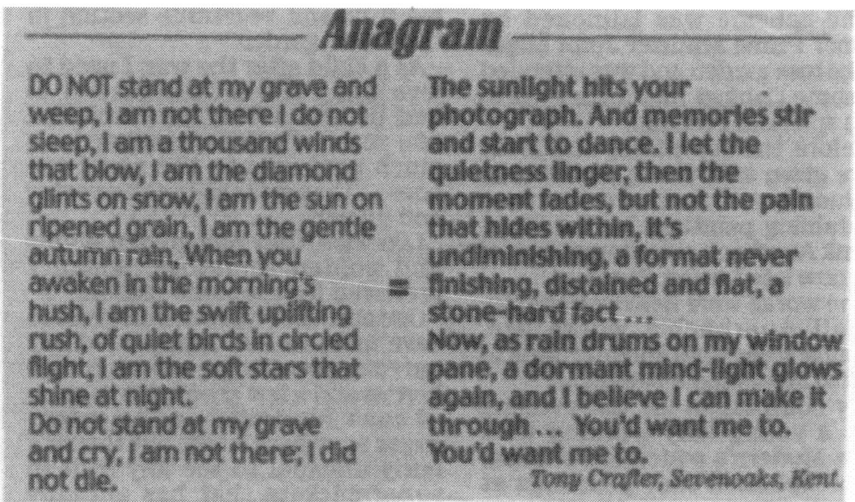

Anagram

DO NOT stand at my grave and weep, I am not there I do not sleep, I am a thousand winds that blow, I am the diamond glints on snow, I am the sun on ripened grain, I am the gentle autumn rain, When you awaken in the morning's hush, I am the swift uplifting rush, of quiet birds in circled flight, I am the soft stars that shine at night.
Do not stand at my grave and cry, I am not there; I did not die.

=

The sunlight hits your photograph. And memories stir and start to dance. I let the quietness linger, then the moment fades, but not the pain that hides within, it's undiminishing, a format never finishing, distained and flat, a stone-hard fact …
Now, as rain drums on my window pane, a dormant mind-light glows again, and I believe I can make it through … You'd want me to. You'd want me to.

Tony Crafter, Sevenoaks, Kent.

The poem 'Do Not Stand At My Grave And Weep', found among the clothing of a soldier killed in Ulster, is variously attributed to various poets. Read by his father at his sons funeral, it was, six years later, included in the BBC programme,'Bookworm,' that was aired for Remembrance Sunday.

Following much demand for copies of the poem it was then published, in 1966, by the aptly named, Souvenir Press as a single poem in a tiny, beautifully illustrated, book, and is now the natural choice of many, if not most, people as the perfect funeral poem.

Mama always knew how much we loved her but there are many who, following the loss of a person who is near or dear – or both - long for a second chance to say all those things they wish they had said when their loved one was still alive.

Dr. Frank Beckles, with whom I worked during our research into Maternity Care in the World and who, at the time, was the world's leading authority on Sickle Cell Anaemia, could frequently be heard to say that most people's biggest regret following the death of someone close to them, is not having told them how much they were valued and loved.

A view expressed a little more succinctly by the American, Garrison Keillor; *"People say such nice things about you at your funeral, it is very sad that you have to miss it by just a few days."*

Which is why Berton Braley (1882-1966) urges us, in his next inspirational poem to do the imperative, because -

He Cannot Read His Tombstone When He's Dead

If with pleasure you are viewing,
Any work a man is doing,
If you like him, or you love him,
Tell him now.
Don't withhold you approbation
'Til the parson makes oration,
And he lies with snowy lilies,
On his brow.

For no matter how you shout it,
He won't really care about it,
He won't know how many teardrops
You have shed.
If you think some praise is due him,
Now's the time to slip it to him,
Let the words of encouragement
Be said.
For he cannot read his tombstone
When he's dead.

More than fame and more than money,
Is the comment kind and sunny,
And the warm approval of a friend.
For it gives to live a savour,
And it makes you stronger, braver.
And it gives you heart and spirit to the end.
If he earns your praise,
Bestow it.
If you like him,
Let him know it.

Do not wait 'til life is over,
And he's underneath the clover.
For he cannot read his tombstone
When he's dead.

Our Mother believed that it behoves all of us to tell those we love, regardless of what they have or do not have - or what they do or do not do - that we love them. Having manfully soldiered through two world wars, several recessions and the odd depression, (of the fiscal kind not the mental), she also believed in the valuable premise that; *"You should respect the dead but save your friendship for the living."* and would often regale us with tales of fortitude and bravery, right from wrong and sense and sensibility.

Another of our dearest friends, Leonore, (the daughter of my equally dear, but now sadly departed friend, Ivis), now lives in Newport Beach, Los Angeles with her husband, Russell. Leonore who has battled cancer for many years, says that one of the highlight of her life was when they gave her boobs back. What Russell says is, boobs or no boobs, he just thanks God every day that she is still alive and still in his life.

Which take us to some life lessons on -

HONOUR AND VALOUR - America

Al Capone's accountant, Easy Eddie, would have earned neither honour nor valour had he not, for the sake of his son, shopped Capone to the police.

The reason for him taking this action that effectively amounted to 'suicide', was to ensure his son, whom he loved above anything, even money, would not be tainted by his long association with Capone, for whom, over many years, he had 'cooked the books'. (Which, my OED tells me, means: 'To change numbers dishonestly in accounts and financial records of an organisation, especially in order to steal money.') After Easy Eddie was assassinated by Capone's Heavies, this poem was found in one of his pockets.

The clock of life is wound but once,
And no man has the power
To tell just when the hands will stop
At late or early hour.

Now is the only time you own,
Live, love, toil with a will.
Place no faith in time.
For the clock may soon be still.

Tragically the clock was 'still' far too early for the highly educated, extremely valiant fighter pilot who, during the Second World War served as a Lieutenant Commander assigned to the aircraft carrier, Lexington, in the South Pacific.

A pilot whose bravery and skill was such that, on February 20th 1942, having, due to lack of fuel, been ordered to leave his formation and return to his carrier, met with a squadron of Japanese pilots on their way to Pearl Harbour and brought down five of them.

Action that led to him becoming, in 1942, America's first Navy's Flying Ace of World War Two, and the first naval aviator to win their Congressional Medal of Honour. Two years before the end of the war, in November 1943, he was killed during one of his many aerial combats, My reader, if they do not already know, will by now have guessed that the son for whom Easy Eddie gave his life so honourably, was the pilot who gave his live so valiantly for his country, Butch O'Hare.

His memorial, adorned with a replica of his Medal of Honour, is situated between Terminals 1 and 2 of Chicago's O'Hare Airport.

VALOUR AND HONOUR - Scotland

A farmer, when working in some woods, heard, from a nearby bog, a cry for help. On rushing to the area he found a struggling, terrified boy mired to his waist in mud. Thanking God he was in the area, the farmer saved the boy from what could have been a slow and terrifying death and then took him back to his home.

The next day the father of the boy the farmer had saved arrived at the farm in a carriage and said he had come to reward the farmer for saving the life of his son. The farmer, who had been joined at the door by his own son, said that he could not accept payment for what was just an act of human kindness.

The Nobleman spoke to the farmer's son for a few minutes and then said to the farmer; *"Your son is a very intelligent boy and if he is anything like you he will grow into a man we can both be proud of, so if you won't let me repay you for saving my son's life, would you allow me to provide your son with the same level of education as that of my own son?"*

On agreeing to this the boy was enrolled at a top class academy and, later, graduated from St Mary's Hospital Medical School in London as a physician and is now, universally, known as the world renowned discoverer of Penicillin, Sir Alexander Fleming. Merits that can often be seen in -

SPORT - with a bit of gambling.

Someone once asked me if I liked ironing and I told them I didn't understand the question. This is even more true of sport, which for me, in any make, shape, or form, is uncharted territory. The only thing I know about it is that it is spelt

S-P-O-R-T and I'm not even sure about that.

Much like Chloe in the next Grey & Shack cartoon.
However, I do know one tiny snippet of information about sport that few people, even water skiers, may not. One of my numerous books of miscellaneous and, mostly useless information, told me the first water skis were invented in 1922 by Ralph Samuelson, an eighteen year old American, who used two planks of wood tied to his feet with scraps of leather.

The book does not record whether his 'invention' made the young Mr. Samuelson any money.

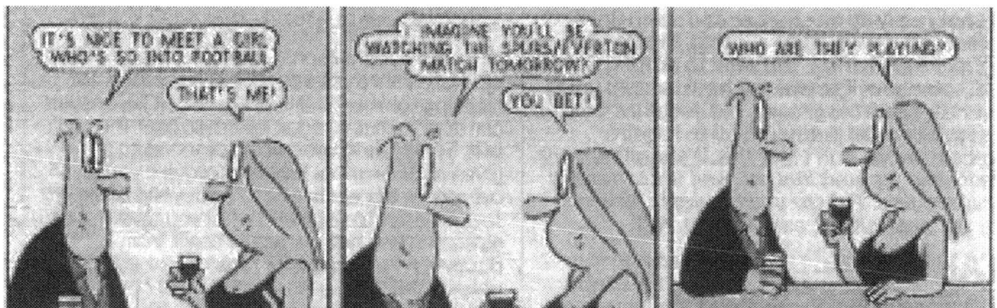

Despite my dislike of sport in all its myriad forms, I have to admit to being fond of football as it keeps the men, and not a few women, off the streets on Saturday afternoons.

I also have to bow to pressure as the vast numbers of people who do enjoy or, more correctly, are mad about sport, can't all be wrong because I have read that: *'They do it because they love the game, and life without sport would not be the same.'*

Mama, for whom sport was low on her list of priorities, composed some very amusing cartoons on the subject. As does Grey Jolliffe. Words similar to those our mother probably had with our father who frequently blew her gas bill money on 'The Horses'.

When we were young gambling was an activity almost exclusively aligned with the Royal sport of horse racing. A sport that was the eventual downfall of our father whose number one passion – and pastime - was 'Laying Bets'.

An activity that undoubtedly led to the creation of more than a few of JERI's racier Impossible People. Two of whom are –

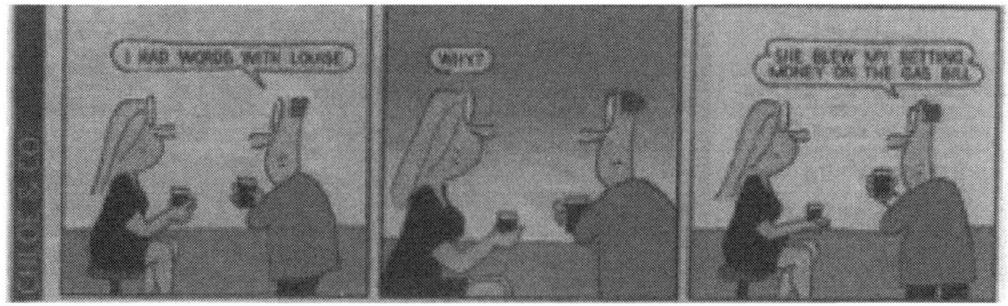

As mentioned earlier, Sonya's brother-in-law, Brian, was a talented jockey and Derby winner, but being a flat racer he had little chance of winning the Grand National, or of being 'given the winner'.

There are some sporting events that are seamlessly British and create, annually, much partisan feeling – often for such trivial reasons as a preference for dark or pale blue.

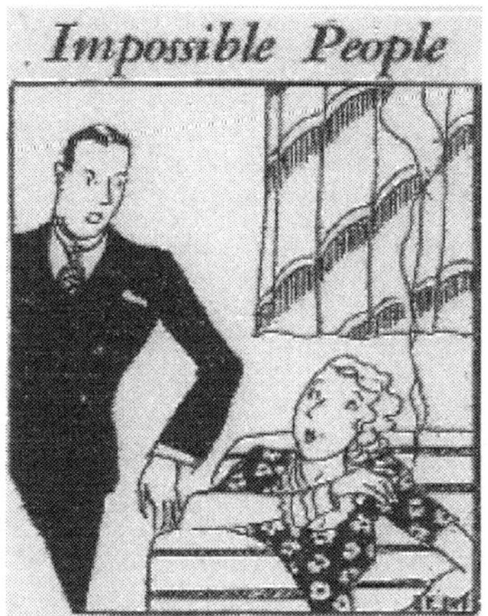

The man who bet his wife twenty shillings to one that he would give up gambling

Even I, who find no joy in getting wet, cold and windswept for the sake of exertion that could otherwise be better spent, have been known to urge on the Oxford crew, who have my support merely because my mother had a degree from that University. While Simon has a preference for pale blue merely because his son, Oliver, gained his degree from Cambridge.

Long-standing friends of the family, Dan and Liz, who have been introduced to my reader in an earlier section of the book, were the licensees of The Old Caledonian paddle steamer on the Thames, and then became, until 2013, the Licensees of The Bull, a public house that fronts the Thames at Barns, where they would invite us to join them on Boat Race Day.

Impossible People

The girl who said she had nowhere to keep a horse when a friend offered to give her the winner of the Grand National.

A race that was first run or, more correctly, rowed in 1856.

Each year we would gather there to watch the race from their first floor balcony. A superb 'viewing platform' from where we would argue a great deal about which crew we wanted to win, which we thought would, and less so about what wine we would drink.

When young, I and my siblings spent many hours in our dinghy, Rory, riding the waves of the English Channel off the Devon coast, and an equal number riding the calmer, but equally cold waters of the Essex estuary coast in a similar dinghy. Now both water and boats are very low on my list of things to enjoy.

Simon's charming friends, Larraine and Michael, have two charming daughters, Alexandra and Victoria, who, in their teens, were avid scull racers to Olympic standard. A pastime that allowed Simon and I to spend a truly delightful day with them at a Thames regatta, where I engaged in conversation with a number of pleasant people, ate some delicious food, drank some excellent wine, and got neither wet nor windblown!

Wet and windblown being the two prerequisites of Angling. A 'sport' the two step-grandfathers of my grandson Michael, enjoy. So, as Simon and Jenny's husband, Michael are so keen on fishing, (yet another deep mystery to me), these next two cartoons of JERI's are for them.

Impossible People

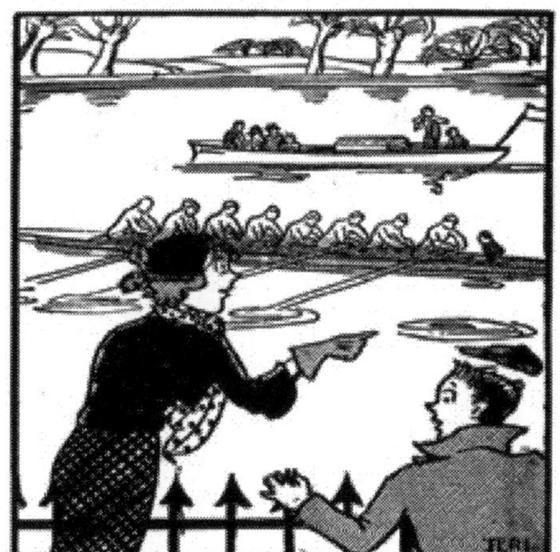

The flapper who wanted to know why they needed eight strong men to row that little boy along.

For Simon who fishes for trout:

Impossible People

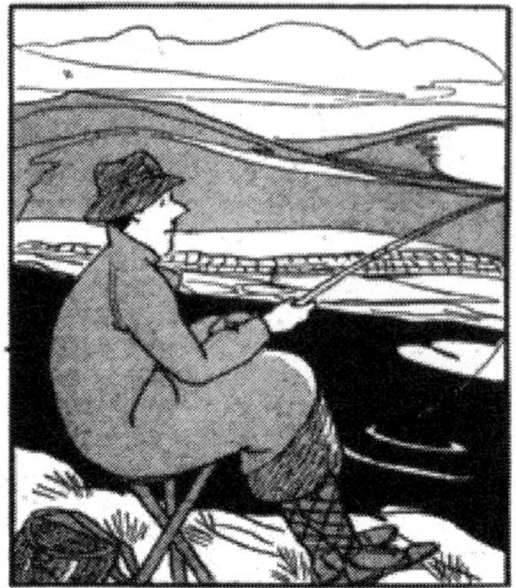

The angler who said he was just going to let two more big ones get away and then go home.

For Michael, who fishes for salmon:

Impossible People

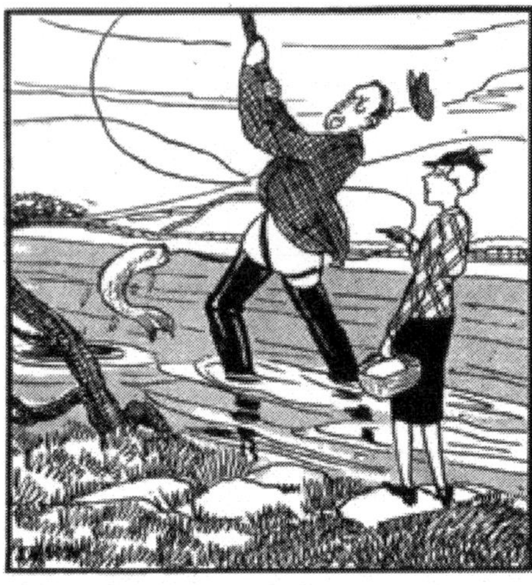

The girl who asked the angler why he did not cut the string and get rid of the brute.

My mother's next two Impossible People are to cheer up all those still smarting from the loss of the 2006 and 2014 World Cups. But did we lose because the players got in each other's way so much? Or didn't know when to pass the ball?

The probablity of 'No spectators' is wildly unlikely as Google tells us that the World Cup is among the worlds most widely viewed sporting event.

Estimates of the number of people who watched the final match of the 2006

Impossible People

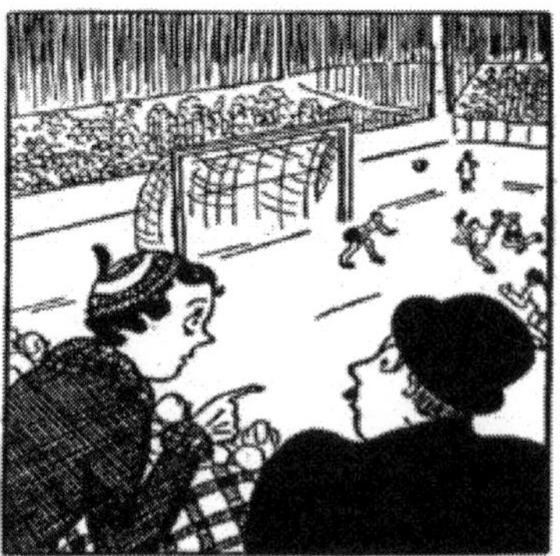

The girl who said the footballers would shoot more goals if they didn't get in each other's way so much.

FIFA World Cup held in Germany range from sixty million to close to a billion. (Yet again I have to ask; How do they get these figures?).

Numbers that, with our ever growing population and their continuing passion for 'footie', will, no doubt, continue to grow. I once came across a cartoon in a national daily with a caption similar to this next cartoon of JERI's that is tailor made for my late brother-in-law, Ray Taylor, (perhaps my most creative pun so far?).

Ray was an avid golfer and, while slender, would sometimes play a round – but not 'around' - with a partner with a similar problem to the gentleman in JERI's next cartoon.

Impossible People

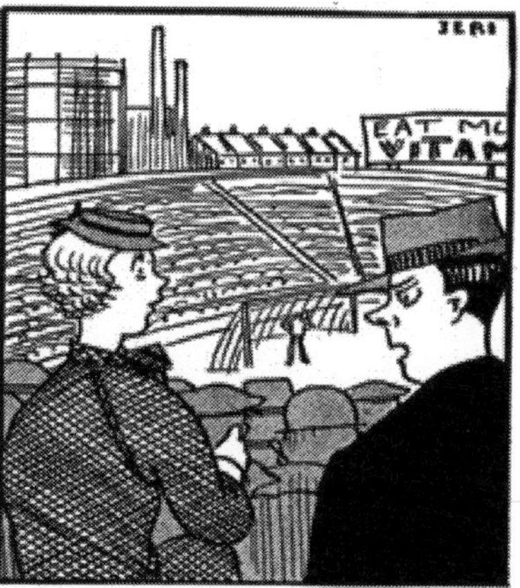

The girl who asked what footballers did when there were no spectators to tell them when to pass the ball.

Impossible People

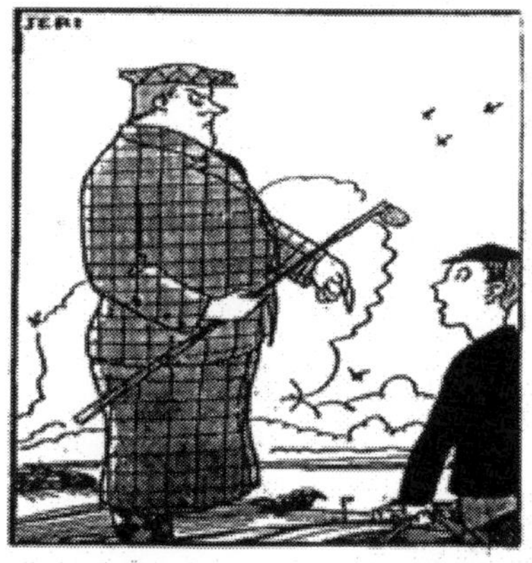

The golfer who said when he put the ball where he could see it he couldn't reach it, and when he put it where he could reach it he couldn't see it.

Mark Twain said, "Golf is a good walk spoiled." Although most keen golfers might consider a walk would not be good without a game of golf to go with it.

One of my many male friends insisted I would love the game and persuaded me to try it, but with a very different game in mind, at the first bit of rough (which he seemingly likened to me), this game of golf changed to an attempt at foreplay, (which allows for a somewhat naughty pun), thus ensuring that - as the passenger said to the pilot - this game of golf was my first and my last!
My very dear friend, Debbie, loves the game of golf and plays it very well. Maybe it is her elegance that deters anyone from taking her for a 'bit of rough' - or from attempting to take her 'into the rough' for any inelegant activity.

Despite my 'knowing nothing about sport', there are three games which, at a pinch, I can be persuaded to watch – cricket, golf and tennis.

I don't know anyone who plays cricket but Debbie's husband, Roger, is reputed to be as good at tennis as his wife is at golf, and we can be confident this is not because he 'plays rough'.

Sonya's great nephew, David Watson, boded well to be a future Wimbledon star. Had his next interest, car racing, not overtaken his first (a better pun?), Henman Hill or Murray Mount as it is now known, may one day, have become Watson Way.

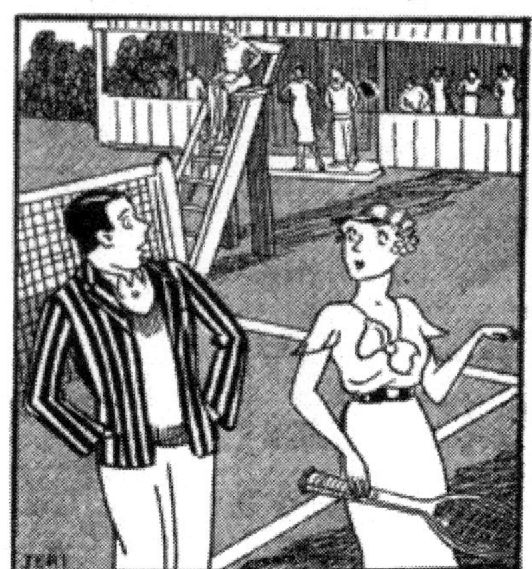

The cricketer who asked why a tennis player did not retire when the umpire shouted " Out."

I overheard my grandson, Michael, telling his other granny, Jenny, that he was going to be in a race at his school sports day, but knew he wasn't 'allowed to win'. Losing may be one of life's most valuable lessons but at six years old nothing beats the euphoria of winning a school race, and then being able to boast about it.

Just days later, when lunching with some friends of Jenny's in Aberdeen, Helena, their bright young daughter who will go far, told us she had won three races at her school's sports day but could claim only one as a win, as apparently; *"Winning is now 'Not The Thing', it is the 'Taking Part' that matters"*. Someone should point out to our educators that winning IS 'The Thing' as that is why we won two World Wars.

We are reaching a point where the ElfnSafety zealots and the Thought Police will forbid, on one pretext or another, all acts of valour or humanitarian goodness, together with everything that people have enjoyed through the ages, such as fetes, street parties, bonfire nights and now, it would seem, cycling.

I read a bizarre report that a village policeman had been forbidden to patrol his patch by bicycle as he had not passed a 'proficiency test' in cycling. On reading this I checked to make sure it was not the April the First.

As I also did on reading that now, when cruising for clients, prostitutes have to wear hi-viz jackets. One would have thought that their abundant make-up and lack of adequate clothing makes them more than adequately hi-viz,

But from where do they come, these killjoys who dream-up all these Nazi, Stalinist nd Stazi regulations that cause a great deal more harm than the harm they profess to protect?

A question that takes us to some -

Quixotical Quangos - The Equal Opportunities Opportunists – The Health and Safety Zealots -The Politically Correct Brigade - The Unthinking Thought Police - and a pinch of -

COMMON SENSE

It is famously said that 'a child knows his own father' but, back in the days of yore, a father could not always be certain that a child was his. Thus to be Jewish a child had to have a Jewish mother. Therefore, as our mother was not Jewish nor were her children.

Even so, when we were young 'Jew Baiting' was a common sport and we were often teased for being; "Them Jew Boys.' On learning of this our father stood us in a row and said; *"You are English first, Russian second and Jewish third and must always remember that you are as good as everyone and better than no one."*

Although 'the 'better than no one' bit did not sit comfortably with our mother who believed that all of her six children were; *"God's Good Gift to the Human Race."*

One of our greatest, most colourful Prime Ministers, Benjamin Disraeli (who would certainly have agreed with our father), may also have thought of himself as English first and Jewish second, as he once famously said of his political opponents; *"To the liberalism they profess, I prefer the liberties we enjoy. To the rights of man, the rights of Englishmen."*

Hitler, as did a few other historical despots, burned both books and people with similar abandon and was thus able to spread his ideologies by oratorical rantings. For, as Mama was wont to say; *"It is easy to manipulate the minds of those who only listen."* Thus we have the paradox that, due to Hitler's evil and inhumane regime, we now suffer the unintended consequences of, (as that excellent journalist, Richard Littlejohn so pithily describes them), 'Yuman Rights laws'.

Laws put in place to prevent a recurrence of such inhumane activities that now allow for an ever increasing litigious society to pursue, via an ever increasing and ever more liberal legislative system, any perceived grievance, whether voiced, physical, written - or for just an overlarge bill -

There are many masters of the written word who are excellent, very readable, newspaper columnists, four of whom are Melanie Phillips, Richard Littlejohn, Kevin Mackenzie and Max Hastings. And all of whom have the courage to denounce this rubbish in print.

Impossible People

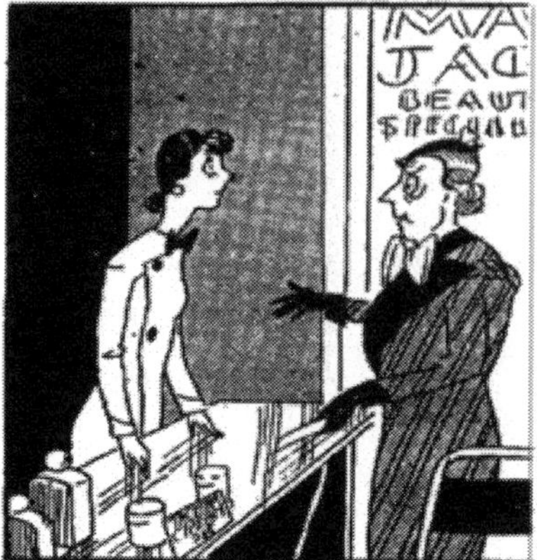

The woman who threatened to sue the beauty specialist who lifted her face because it dropped again when she saw the bill.

The rest of us just pray that their common sense will save the day. But will it?

The Labour MP, Emily Thornberry, denounced Common Sense as; *"A cover for discrimination, narrowness and an inability to face the twenty-first century."*

Apart from making neither sense nor sensibility it would appear that there are now many others who share this opinion and would cast aspersions on my belief that Common Sense is an essential and valuable tool – particularly insofar as politics and politicians are concerned.

Which is almost certainly one of the reasons why the House of Commons is a 'litigation-frce' zone - possibly the finest example of the use of Common Sense. Nothing in Nature is straight. We have a circular world where, if it has occurred before, it can happen again - often via the legislation put in place in order to prevent it.

Thus the policing of what we think or say born of Nazism, is now being perpetuated by our own Thought Police whose raison d'etre for their actions is, ostensibly, to prevent such ideologies coming to the fore again. This has now created the paradox that we are now not just rushing, but hurtling headlong towards a society in which no one will even think let alone speak, for fear of being 'banged up'.

As Stan Rogers was warned he might be for sending an e-mail to his local council in which he included Pastor Neimoeller's 'Statement of Universal Values.' Before prosecuting (and persecuting), Mr. Rogers, these councillors should visit the Washington Holocaust Museum where Pastor Neimoeller's statement is written in letters three feet high.

I include it here in the forlorn hope it will be hung, in three feet high lettering, on the walls of every government and municipal council office in the country, as seeing it each day might persuade them get their priorities right.

A Statement of Universal Values

In Germany the Nazis first came for the Communists and I did not speak up because I was not a Communist.
Then they came for the Jews and I did not speak up because I was not a Jew.
Then they came for the Trade Unionists and I did not speak up because I was not a Trade Unionist.
Then they came for the Catholics and I did not speak up because I was not a Catholic.
Then they came for me but by then there was no one to speak up for anyone.
Pastor Martin Neimoeller

Possibly unknown to Pastor Neimoeller, the Nazis first came for the physically incapacitated and mentally impaired, and there was certainly no one to speak up for them.

The following are some amusing stories from my years as a London landlady that emphatically illustrate, how essential it is to apply common or garden common sense to any and every situation.

Especially if those situations are fraught with interference from the E.O.O. the T.P. the P.C.B. and the HnS Zealots.

All of which figure largely in the incidents I now relate that may, as was threatened might happen to Mr. Rogers, get me 'banged up'. The twelve full and part time employees of my London Public House hailed from as far afield as Australia, Canada, Iran, Ireland, Malta, New Zealand and a South African cat burglar who, having taken refuge in England, had decided booze was better than burglary.

A veritable League of Nations but without the angst, among whom was an extremely quick-witted, industrious Australian called Judy. When singing the praises of one our regulars who had made no secret of the fact he would like to take her out, she said to me, *"Go out wiv 'im, never, if brains was dynamite 'e wouldn't 'ave enough to blow 'is bleedin' nose."*

A response that is now imprinted on my mind, and if Judy had known of JERI's next cartoon she would, no doubt, have had it's caption printed on a t-shirt for this gentleman.

A caption that is a twin to that of the cover cartoon of the 1993 Michael O'Marra book, 'Stupid Men Jokes'. Compiled by Nancy Gray, its cover depicts a couple very similar to JERI's with a caption that asks; *"What do you call a man with half a brain?."* with the woman thinking; *'Gifted'*.

Among my team of exceptionally hardworking and loyal employees were two young men who had been friends since school.

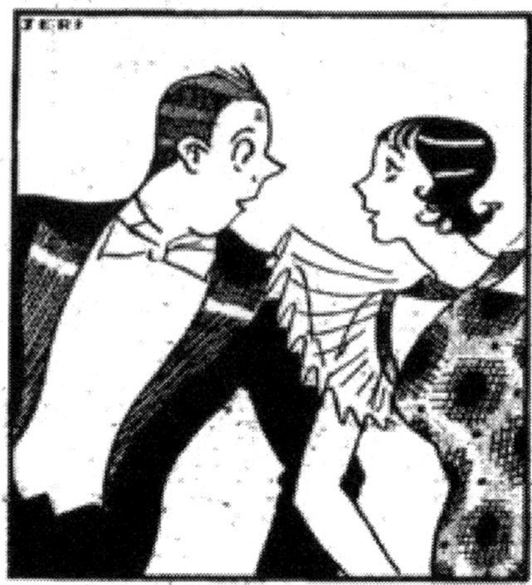

The girl who told her fiancé if only he had a few brains he would be half-witted.

Mannie, an Iranian who, for all his light-fingered tendencies, was worth his weight in gold as he worked at twice the speed and did four times the work of anyone else and his best friend, a lanky lad called Chalkie who, until he joined us, had been unable to find a job.

Not because he was black, but because he was epileptic. When Mannie asked me if I would consider employing Chalkie, I said; *"Of course, but we can't call him Chalkie, what is his name?" "Chalkie's 'iss name, innit?"* said Mannie. *"But what is his real name?"* I asked, *"I dunno,"* said Mannie; *"e's always bin Chalkie."*

Having the same conversation with Chalkie, I bowed to the inevitable! But as the only black member of my staff, he soon began to refer to himself as the Obligatory Nigger. When I remonstrated with him about this he said, *"I don't mind bein' called a Nigger Missus, wot I 'ates is bein' called an 'effin one."*

I have to admit to feeling relieved that I was not the only person with an antipathy for this particular expletive. In yet another coincidence even more odd than those I write of in my item on these quirky happenings, at the same time that Chalkie became one of my employees, Sonya and Ray bought a large house in Colne Engaine in Essex. A house that came with a handyman. Handy mostly because, Essex born and bred, he had lived all his life in this same tiny village as had all of his predecessors – hence his skin was of a similar hue to that of most English people - well certainly all those who live in the wilds of Essex, Suffolk and Norfolk.

When he introduced himself with; *"Mornin' Missus, mornin' Sir, I'm Nigger."* Sonya and Ray had much the same conversation with him that I'd had with Mannie and Chalkie. His response being much the same, *'Nigger'* he remained until the day he died. Nor, as with Chalkie, did they ever learn his real Christian name.

Nor did my delightful Australian barmaid, Judy, ever learn from where Chalkie's family originated: Judy: *"Where d'jer come from Chalk?"* Chalkie:

"Darn Acton, Jude." "Nah, not now, Chalk, whered'jer parents come from?" Chalkie; *"Oh them, Souffall."*

One of Chalkie's favourite tasks was to chalk the daily menu boards. (How'zat for a pun?) He said it fitted with his persona. Our most popular meal was The Ploughman's, thus each day he would write this in large colourful letters to which he would add equally colourful illustrations.

One day we received a letter from the Thought Police in which they wrote that, as it was no longer 'politically correct' to use the word 'Ploughman's', we must, in future, use the more 'politically correct'; 'Ploughpersons'. Amid much merriment, with Chalkie asking how he should illustrate a Ploughperson, perhaps in a bikini over a boiler suit, I composed the following response to the T.P.

'Having noted your instruction to use the word Ploughperson's as opposed to the word Ploughman's, we would like to know if we should, in future, call my stepdaughter, Amanda Jessiman, Apersonda Jessiperson.'

Chalkie continued to draw a yellow and green tractor with the word 'Ploughman's' beside it, and we heard no more from the T.P. Chalkie's good humour and easy-going nature made him a favourite with all the staff, despite having to watch that he didn't fall onto a batch of glasses when having a fit - which, (pun intended), he was prone to do.

He loved working for us, an enjoyment marred only by his fear that the Health and Safety zealots would find out and forbid him to do so. Apart from Mannie, Chalkie seemed to have few friends, so we were really pleased when he became pals with a young lad from Cheltenham, whose parents had asked if we would give him a live-in job.

This young man's desire to come to London was mainly due to his desire to make a fortune which, fortunately, he believed could be done by hard work. E-mails not being part of our lives in those days, as his new activities, friends and a faster pace of life overtook his spare time, less of this was given to replying to his mother's weekly letters. On receiving one of these, he contritely admitted to not having written to her for several weeks.

An omission he obviously did not put right as he then received a 'letter' from his father that had, in the envelope, another envelope addressed to his mother with a stamp on it.

A father who definitely believed in the benefits of common sense, confirmed by the fact that, after this 'reminder', his son never failed to write his weekly letter to his mother. A difficulty now overcome by new technology that, although cheaper, quicker, and much easier, doesn't come close the pleasure of receiving a hand written letter or just a Thank You note.

Although I am more guilty than most for, having, at the age of sixteen learnt to use a computer and having, in my late twenties, severely burnt my right, writing, hand, being able to write with a key-board is Manna from Heaven. As are the legions of pub conversations that would make a book of humour on their own, rarely did a day go by in ours without a customer saying something amusing, curious, odd or ridiculous. Such as when my manager, Bob, asked one of our regulars why he was looking so pensive, to which Charlie said; *"I'm not pensive Bob, I'm just thinkin'."*

It is a great pity our faceless, nameless civil servants don't do a little more 'pensive thinkin'. A fatuous instruction from the Divisional Head of Baber Council in Essex, 'advised' their senior Council Officer that he should no longer refer to his secretary by her real name as it might be considered, by some women, to be offensive. Presumably to all those Sheila's who live many thousands of miles away in Australia.

One wonders if the Council were prepared to fund the fee for a 'Deed Poll Change of Name' and, of more importance, how much they had considered the feelings of an employee who had thus far, happily lived with this name, happily gifted to her by her parents.

On telling this tale to my Australian friend, Wendy, she said, "Any Australian Sheila would reckon that these fellas had lost their marbles." Or were mugs?

A civil service directive demanding all government computer systems had to be programmed to reject anything that has the slightest hint of a non-P.C. word is, as most people would say; "A madness beyond words".

Thus, the truly inspired media headline for an article about Rochdale Council that installed a new computer system that was programmed

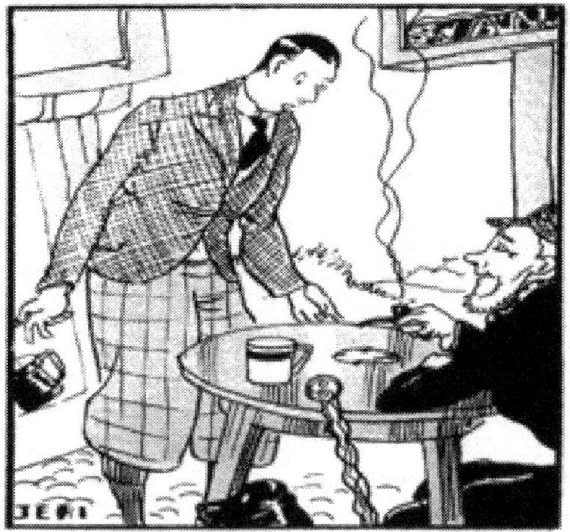

The yokel who said he did not mind who gave it to him when asked if he would take his beer from a mug.

to filter out any mail that included politically incorrect words, was: DAY THE COUNCIL'S PC's WERE TOO PC.

Among many others, their filter included (or more correctly, excluded) the word 'erection'. The business of planning departments is building and buildings need erecting. Thus the words erection and erections are used many times a day not only by architects and builders, but also all of those who work in planning departments.

Some years earlier, following an unresolved, extremely irksome problem, I wrote a letter to the Chief Executive of EON in which I asked whether their staff ran their computers or their computers ran their staff. His Private Assistant's prompt response and equally prompt helpful assistance in sorting the vexing problem that had beset me for many months, proved this was not so.

Nevertheless the day is drawing ever nearer when all companies will be run by computers. And all computer programmes will be designed by overweening addicts of 'Political Correctness'.

Kelvin Mackenzie writes in the Daily Mail that computers are now being 'designed' to reject names that 'might be deemed distasteful' as a reader wrote that, having ordered a gift online from Marks Spencers, he was typing the details for the gift tag, when his name, Nobby, was rejected. A perfectly proper nickname that many Nobby's have been known by.

Kelvin asks whether anyone with the name of Balls, Cockburn, Dick, Ramsbottom, Roger, or Willie will now have to change their names before being accepted as bona fida online purchasers of products. Or, perhaps, for any other online service such as a passport or driving licence?

The idiocy of these piffling (another much used word by my Mama), pronouncements by the P.C.B. is superbly parodied in this limerick by Brian Jones of Bournemouth.

I am furnished with thoughts of despair,
For each chairman will now be a chair,
In the House, what commotions,
Can a chair table motions,
For which cabinet just would not care?

The PC brigade's efforts to ban any word of which they don't approve, including any word with 'man' in it and, perhaps, the word 'man' itself, may impede the OED from maintaining their magical figure of one million words. (See 'All About Words.')

Impossible People

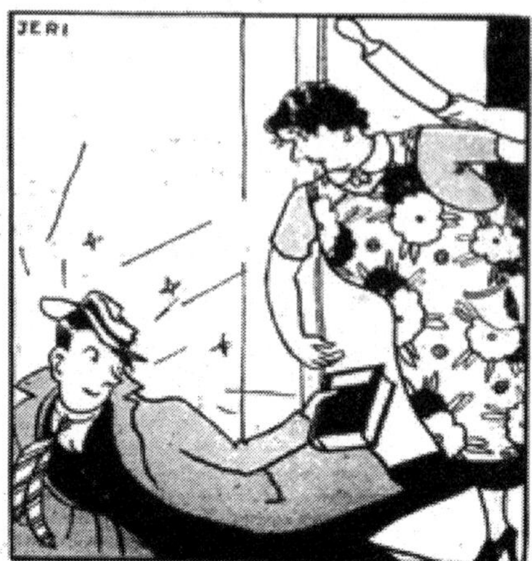

The salesman who said he could see the lady was a woman of few words so could he interest her in a dictionary?

Rather like JERI's salesman, the TP would like all dictionaries to exclude words they regard as being not PC.

People generally feel more comfortable within their own circle and surroundings, but, much as the TP would have us think otherwise, the majority are liberal minded and do not expect nor have a desire for people to change in order to 'fit; with a particular ethos.

Apart, perhaps, from a few Muslims. A sentence that will most definitely get me a Fatwa. Although in my experience, the reason we are more - or less - comfortable with others has a great deal more to do with their behaviour and attitude than their heritage, ethnicity or religion.

As, I'm confident, do most of us, I rate everyone I meet, regardless of creed or colour, whether they are worthy of being invited into my home or, when that applied, of being served in my bar.

When summoned to attend a hearing at the Race Relations Board to whom four West Indians had made a complaint after being refused service, Chalkie and several of our regular African and West Indian customers insisted on accompanying us.

Our barrister began by citing a law that applies only to the licensed trade that allows a Licensee to refuse service to anyone without having to give a reason. He then said, *"But in this instance my clients wish to do so and in their defence have asked me to use an interesting analogy. In a recent discussion about the possibility of whether their cat could ever become Pope they concluded that the fact she was a female, did not speak Italian and was not a Roman Catholic made the fact that she was a cat totally irrelevant.*

Based on the same rationale, the fact that when they entered my clients premises, these four 'gentlemen' were already inebriated, were loud, crude, rude and were dealing in drugs, made the fact they were black totally irrelevant."

A truth that, with corroboration from our staunch supporters, roundly won us not only the day but also our costs.

And ALL of this AGGRAVATION (something I've always thought one should be able to insure against), could, with the 'genius of common sense', be avoided. For even while we laugh at these many hilarious anecdotes, lack of it is beginning to cause untold harm, not just to the fabric, but the very threads of our society.

As that master of the 'put-down', Michael Winner, was wont to say; *"Calm down dears!"* While his admonishment to the T.P. and P.C.B. might be; *"People are different, which is just as well because if everyone liked champagne and oysters there wouldn't be enough to go round."*

An admonishment well illustrated when, as a conference organiser, I was invited by the Bermuda Tourist Association to join a group of representatives who had been asked to assess their hotels as suitable conference venues.

Among the group was a director of Harris Sausages who, on being asked why his company would hold an overseas conference said; *"We wouldn't! What we are going to do is to run a competition for which the first prize is a plate of Harris sausages to be eaten in one of a choice of quality hotels in various countries.*

In order to ensure our winners enjoy their prize, we need to vet hotels in the all of different destinations offered and select three different types of hotel in each of the resorts from which our winners may select their holiday. They can then choose the style of hotel they prefer, which, in Bermuda, might be the bustling Princess or the quieter, privately run Invurerie."

These words were his, not mine. But it should be borne in mind they were said in 1962 when people tended to be much less well travelled and couples were more likely to be married.

They also ensured Harris sausages of another long-term, loyal customer because, I surmised, if they took such care with their prizes they would do the same with their product. It also demonstrated, I write tongue in cheek or even a bit cheekily, that being a Senior Director of a company can sometimes be a very arduous and onerous job.

As, it would seem, is that of Government officials who have decreed that Common Sense should no longer be used in our hallowed halls of justice, where its calming influence has always been one of the laws finest tools.
An ancient Persian proverb tells us that: *'One pound of learning requires ten pounds of common sense to apply it.'* A proverb that, perhaps, should now also include the word 'Law'.

Law and learning take us to the incorporation in junior schools of keeping a record of any use of words by infants that might be considered to be a 'homophobic or ethnic slur', but now that, via technology, our homes are bombarded on a daily basis with such expressions how can we expect our young, most of whom have no understanding of what they mean, not to use them?

Children argue, they throw things and yell expletives at one another. They have always done so and will always do so, and, while their parents or educators rush to court, the combatants in these fleeting fracas are linking arms and rushing, happily to the nearest play area – or McDonalds.

Bullying is exempt from this argument. It is an ongoing nightmare that, tragically, can persuade those children who are victims of this evil, that the only way to put an end to it is to put an end to themselves. As this vile practice is now frequently perpetrated on-line perhaps the young should have lessons on its dangers and how to tackle it, rather than lessons on how to avoid getting pregnant.

As spending time and money on something that may help to prevent one death may be preferable to spending even more time and money on something designed to prevent, but probably won't, a few births.

This skewed and somewhat puzzling attitude applies in abundance to the new Equal Opportunities Laws. The world has always been an unequal place and always will be, but many things that might be thought to create inequality are actually beneficial. One of which is Dyslexia. For, as I write earlier, people with this 'perceived disadvantage' are, very often, gifted with skills that are more beneficial than being able to spell.

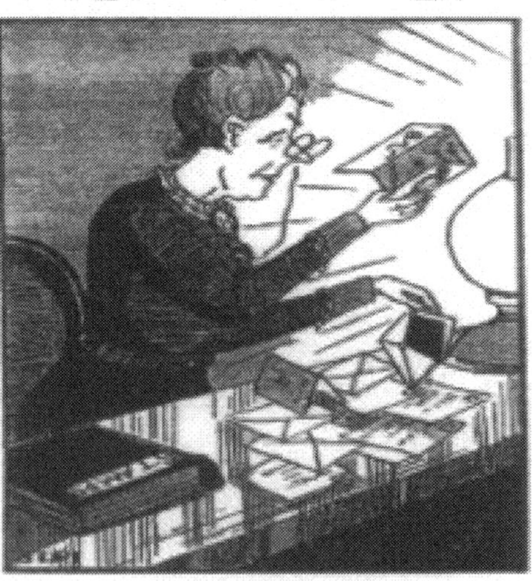

The village postmistress who said she was so busy she hardly had time to put the cards back in their envelopes.

So instead of attempting to teach children who can't spell to spell, they should be encouraged to develop the abundant, and, usually, useful talents given to those who can't. Skills that people are prepared to pay well for, as did my twin's many clients and, no doubt, the clients of other dyslexics who excel in various

artistic fields. Such as designing greetings cards?
However there are some things my twin could never do. To ask Sonya, who is word blind, to be a post-woman would be much the same as offering the job to someone who is actually blind.

Thus, the idiocy of the, unequal, Equal Opportunities law is finely illustrated by the words of a spokeswoman from The Royal Mail, who, when defending the decision to employ a dyslexic who found the work impossible due to his dyslexia, said; *"A person is judged on their skills to do the job, irrelevant of any disability they may have."*

Where, I ask, as would Richard Littlejohn, is the common sense in that? The Head of the Equality and Human Rights Commission, Trevor Phillips, would definitely agree with me as he said; *"You just can't park people in jobs simply because they happen to be female, black or disabled."*

Although maybe there are just not enough females, (either black or disabled or both), to staff our precious Post Offices, which, perhaps, is why they are all closing. Or is this due to the fact, as my mother's next Impossible Boy suggests, that things have not improved in the seventy or so years since she composed her cartoon.

But it would seem that, whether black or female, or both, the Post Office, due to the strictures of the Equal Opportunities Quango, will, regardless of their usefulness, employ a blind person merely because they are local to the area or have great stamina?

'Great stamina', that, according to JERI's next caption, has always been, and still is, needed in Post Offices - but more by their customers than their workforce -

As have dyslexics, the blind have many unusual and valuable skills that make them eminently employable in many capacities. However, regardless of the E.O. policy of total inclusion, delivering mail is not one of them - especially as some dogs are known to bite before they bark!.

Impossible People

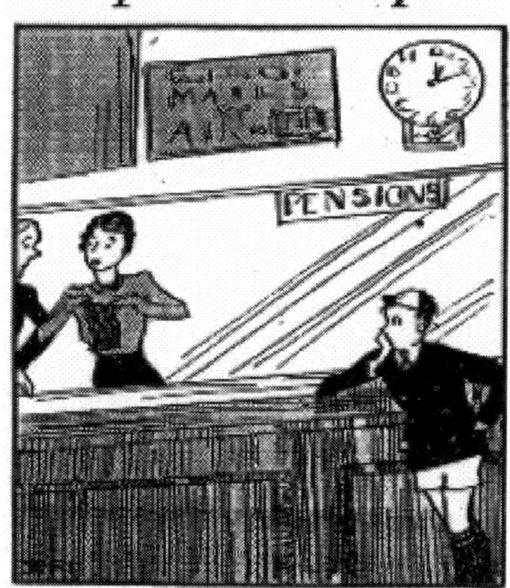

The boy in the post office who said he wanted a stamp but he stood at the old age pensions part of the counter as he expected to be able to draw one before he was served.

As I write earlier, (and in another neat oxymoron) my first 'post', at sixteen, was, with Methuen the publishers, in the long forgotten days of manual 'eyeball' switchboards. Two young blind men manned this equipment and it was fascinating to watch them as they, unerringly, plugged the extension leads into the correct sockets when the eyeballs clicked down - and there were 36 of them! Despite all my efforts I was never able to master their speed or accuracy.

My reader may notice I forbore from claiming another clever pun - an act of blatant cowardice in case I was jumped on from a great height by those who believe the blind can't take a joke. However, over my many years I have known many blind people, all of whom could take a joke and most of whom were extremely adept at what they did.

Thus it came as no surprise to learn Pakistan field a blind cricket team. Or should that be, more correctly, a cricket team of blind players. Seeing them play is a revelation and is of equal enjoyment as watching a 'sighted' team. While watching them play, it occurred to me that there are probably many people who, while watching a match of sighted players in which a fielder misses a catch, will shout at their television screens; *"Are you blind or what?"* Which led me to suppose that the blind Pakistani cricketers, who most certainly won't have this epithet directed at them, must be more skillful players than their sighted brethren.

Much in the same way that my colleagues at Methuen were far more skilled on the switchboard than myself. One of the 'Readers' at Methuen was a very classy lady called Marigold, a name I did not meet with again until I found my mother's next cartoon. Methuen's Marigold was extremely glamorous and somewhat superior and I admired her enormously.

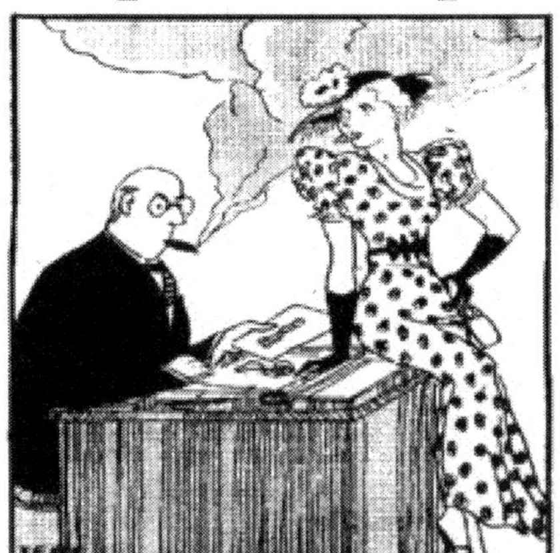

The theatrical agent who said he wanted her name, not her aim in life, when she replied " Marigold."

Her demeanour suggested she had the same 'aim in life' as JERI's Marigold, who in both dress and composure, looks much as Methuen's Marigold did.

My 'aim in life' is for someone to take sufficient offence with something I have written to sue me, for if they do 'Impossible People' may reach the dizzying heights of Dan Brown's, The Da Vinci Code, following media coverage of his dalliance with his detractors.

On the other hand, I have no real wish to be embroiled in such brouhaha. So should my reader find in 'Impossible People' anything they find offensive, I hope they will just use their common sense and bin it or burn it. It is not something I advocate but once or twice in my life I have binned or burnt a book in disgust at its style or dislike of its content.

The 'e-book' will make the 'burning of books' a thing of the past. They may also, due to their portability and the saving of trees, make bookshops and Lending Libraries, things of the past. Much like history? And when there are no books to 'worm' our way through, the word 'bookworm' will also eventually die.

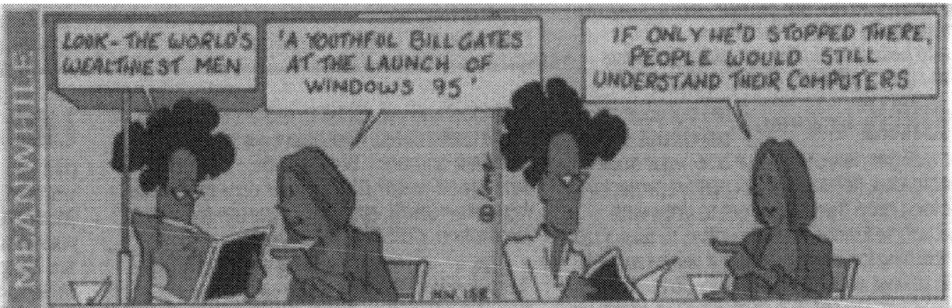

It is sad that the sweeping changes now being brought about by the advances in technology will be as ephemeral as those books that will, in future, be deleted from their owners iPads. But while we are still here to do so, we bibliophiles and bookworms will mourn the passing of the 'real thing', for nothing will ever replace the pleasure of turning the pages of a book. A fact neatly confirmed by this next witty, and pithy, ditty by Jully Henderson-Long.

Page Turner

No!
We must not lose the humble book
No matter what they say.
I do not want to carry
Nasty e-books every day.

I want to properly turn the page,
With finger and with thumb,
Not twiddle button, switch or knob
Once reading has begun.

I do not like the scary thought
Of book shops gone to pot,
Or libraries slamming shut their doors,

And sealing with a lock.
Nothing will replace the smell
Of new unopened tomes.
Nor the thrill of seeing our
Collections in our homes.

We must protect the precious book.
It's history is unique,
It entertains, it educates,
It stimulates, it speaks.

I'm all for progress marching on,
But progress is a crook,
If evolution means we have
To give up on the book.

From a poem packed with common sense to an Obituary with even more

OBITUARY FOR COMMON SENSE

Today we mourn the passing of a beloved old friend, Mr. Common Sense. He had been with us for many years, but it is not known how old he was as his birth records were lost, long ago, in reams of bureaucratic red tape.

Mr. Common Sense lived by simple, sound policies:-

Finance	Don't spend more than you earn.
Law	The victim is more important than the criminal.
Parenting Strategies:	Adults, not children, are in charge.
Children:	It's O.K. for them to be seen and heard, but children do not rule the world.
Food:	If it looks O.K. smells O.K. tastes O.K. (and the cat or dog like it), it's O.K. to eat.
Drugs:	Should be taken to make you well if you are ill, not make you ill when you are well.
Compassion:	All are worthy of respect and courtesy, unless they act in an unworthy manner.

He will be remembered for having cultivated such valuable lessons as knowing when to come in out of the rain, why the early bird gets the worm and that life isn't always fair.

Mr. Common Sense began to lose hope when politicians became tax collectors; banks became charlatans, churches became businesses and the Ten Commandments became contraband.

He lost all hope when bureaucracy became more important than people and well-intentioned but over-bearing regulations created the eleventh deadly sin of: 'Unintended Consequences'.

His despair deepened when the fit unemployed could get lifelong handouts while the old and ailing who had worked all their lives, were neglected.

He despaired when the courts began to use the Human Rights Act to award greater damages to people who suffered minor accidents than those awarded to seriously injured servicemen.

He died when, greedy Lawyers began to sue servicemen for damages to civilians caught up in wars in which these servicemen had, with no allegiance to them, been sent to fight.

He realised the futility of fighting back when parents and teachers were disenfranchised, and lack of discipline gave pupils the power to carry weapons, take drugs, smoke, and watch pornography on their iPads.

Mr. Sense's health declined further when Health and Safety killjoys decreed that anything that is fun or pleasant is unhealthy or unsafe. He became seriously ill when paedophiles, psychotics and schizophrenics could walk among us, while those needing care but not able to afford assistance became prisoners in their homes.

He came closer to death when householders were imprisoned for protecting their families and property, while those who burgled and threatened them received merely a 'caution'.

He lost the will to live on finding that Government Targets in our NHS hospitals became more important than patient care and that those who had never paid into the system were, very often, given better care than those who had.

His mortality was assured when it was decreed that his valuable influence must not, in future, be used, seen or heard in any local council, judicial or government proceedings. Not many attended his funeral because so few realised he was gone. He was preceded in death by his grandparents,, 'Honesty and Honour', his parents, 'Truth and Trust', his wife, 'Discretion', his son, 'Reason' and his daughter, 'Responsibility'.

He is survived by his two wicked stepsisters, Dis Respect and Ima Whiner, and his equally wicked stepbrother, Mi Rights.

As is much in Impossible People, this 'Obituary' was sent to me by many people, all of whom are definitely not 'impossible' and all of whom still use Common Sense. Of which, it is said; *"Common sense is instinct; enough of it is genius."* But what should we call the lack of it? 'Idiocy' perhaps!

However, despite the ever increasing advances in technology that make ever increasing changes to our lives, people don't change fundamentally – neatly illustrated by the next three cartoons that, as I write, JERI composed nearly a hundred years ago.

Impossible People

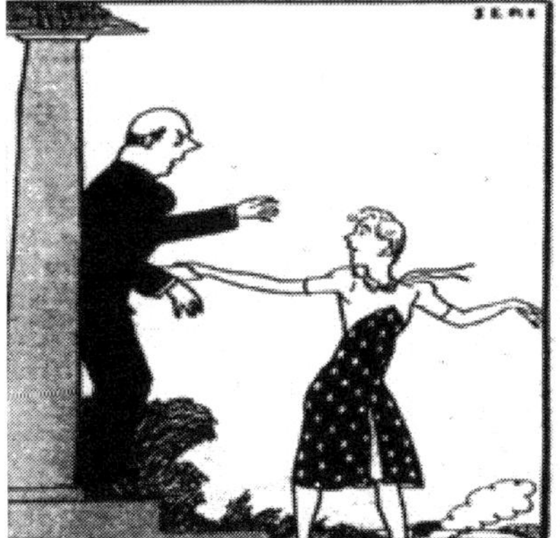

The woman who said she did not notice the appearance of the man who had stolen her husband's car, but she had taken its number.

Impossible People

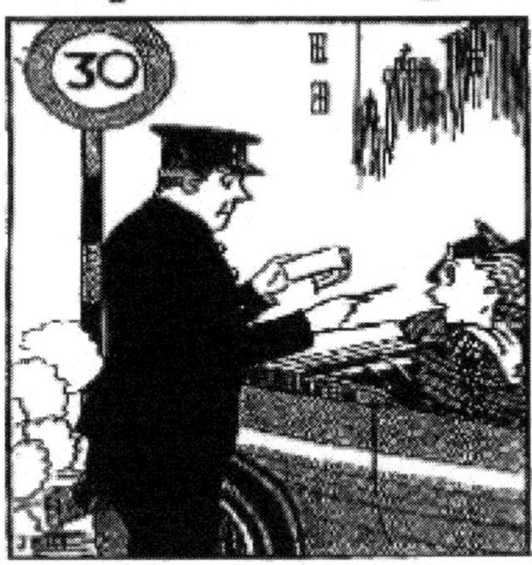

The policeman who stopped a motorist for exceeding the speed limit, and then summoned her for obstructing the traffic because her car refused to start again.

A caption that gives me the opportunity to raise a conundrum, the answer to which has always eluded me. Why do those who report accidents always write that the 'vehicle lost control', when it is the driver who lost control of the vehicle?

Even in her caption, my mother writes; 'her car 'refused' to start which implies the engine has a 'mind of its own'. Which, of course, many people think they do.

It is also a cartoon that proves little changes in the field of overzealous officialdom, as it is the 'twin' of a 2011 media report about a traffic warden who issued a parking ticket for a car that, when correctly parked during a non-chargeable period, had, during the night, fallen into a cavity in the road caused by subsidence.

A situation where common sense was not only severely lacking but non-existent. As JERI's cartoons illustrate with such wit, even when it did exist, this eminently useful 'sixth sense' was often in short supply. So sadly, this seriously sensible solution solver, will never again be considered the valuable tool it was once thought to be, because so many of the things we now see, hear and read must make most of us think, as far as our leaders and legislators go, that the vehicle is still there but the engine is missing - and even if it isn't, it's making all the wrong noises!

Impossible People

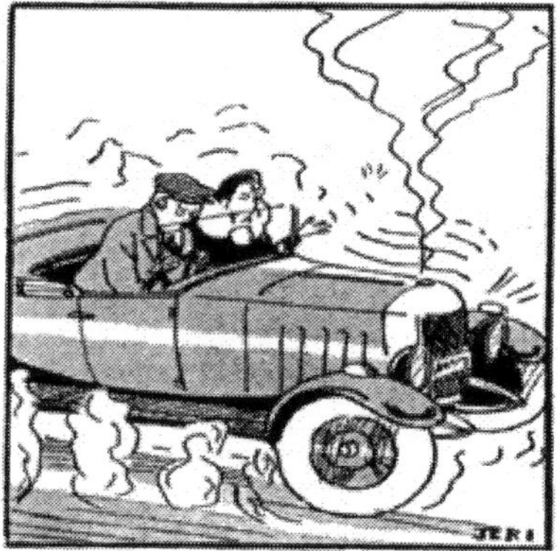

The woman who said it was silly to say the engine was missing when anyone could hear it making that awful noise all the time.

Is this because, as is this cartoon, it is on an incline? Or, more correctly, is facing a decline? Although in our impossible world of Impossible People perhaps everything IS possible because:

While we pessimistic British say; "It's impossible!"

And the laid-back Spanish say; "Impossible or not, we'll do it tomorrow."

And Americans, to their great credit, say; "The impossible we can do today, miracles take a little longer."

The fabulous French will say; "Tout est Possible." Which is why Impossible People became possible.

A TOUT A L'HEURE

Just days prior to finally 'putting Impossible People to bed,' Tony Crafter sent me this acrostic he had composed from Edgar Allen Poe's poem, 'Alone'. Tony told me that when he had finished it he realised it was a perfect Mother's Day ode and kindly agreed that I may include it as a dedication to, not only the memory of my dearly loved much missed, Mama, but for all mothers everywhere, whether alive or mourned.

A LOAN
by Tony Crafter

Our childhood is a short-term loan,
To be repaid when we have grown;
Our children are a moment's gift,
That we may one day set adrift
On life's harsh seas in stormy weather,
With no connective link or tether.
And we, the lighthouse lamp that burns,
For them to find when they return.
The child that left might yet come home,
But not for good, and just on loan.

Their lives flash by, and soon do ours,
And memory dims, like fading flowers;
Fond moments of their childhood fun
Then mark fond moments of our own.
Perhaps, some sunny Mother's Day,
If they've a mind to come my way,
They'll stop a moment, one last time,
To linger, look and find this line
Above my grave, carved in the stone:
'Life is but a short-term loan'.

ALONE
by Edgar Allan Poe

From childhood's hour I have not been
As others were; I have not seen
As others saw; I could not bring
My passions from a common spring.
From the same source I have not taken
My sorrow; I could not awaken;
My heart to joy at the same tone;
And all I loved, I loved alone.
Then - in my childhood, in the dawn
Of a most stormy life - was drawn
From every depth of good or ill,
The mystery which binds me still:

From the torrent, or the fountain,
From the red cliff of the mountain,
From the sun that round me rolled
In its autumn tint of gold.

From the lightning in the sky
As it passed me flying by,
From the thunder and the storm,
And the cloud that took form
(When the rest of Heaven was blue)
Of a demon in my view.

Lewis Carroll presciently wrote: *'What is the use of a book, thought Alice, without pictures or conversation?'* So if the conversations – and cartoons - in Impossible People have made you laugh, or at least smile, please pass it on - not the book, the smile – because -

You are never alone with a family a nice as mine.

My twin Sonya is fond of saying; *"Life may not be the party we had hoped for but while we are here we may as well dance and smile because; "Yesterday is history, tomorrow is a mystery but today is a gift."*

My sister Nicola is of the opinion that; *"A good friend is like a four-leaf clover, very hard to find and lucky to have."* Which is exactly how her friends feel about her.

My sister, Sasha, keeps this next poem in her diary to cheer herself up. I asked her; *"Why do you need to do that, you are always so cheerful?"* She said; *"That's why!"*

Smiling is infectious, you can catch it like the flu.
When someone smiled at me today, I started smiling too.
I passed around the corner and someone saw me grin,
When he smiled, I noticed that I'd passed it on to him.

I thought about that smile, and then realised its worth.
A single smile, just like mine, could travel round the earth.
So if you feel a smile begin, don't leave it undetected,
Let's start an epidemic and get the world infected.

Although easier to find than a four leaf clover we have been much more than just lucky to have in our lives our four husband's. Sonya's reliable and devoted husband, Ray; Nicola's resourceful and astute husband, George, Sasha's charming and stoic husband John; and my wonderful, witty and wise, but now slightly weather worn, husband, Simon.

While my prosperous, successful, sensible son, Michael, who is brilliant at 'sums' looks on life in much the same way as this summation by Graham Lester -

To sum it all up in one word,
Existence is clearly absurd,
A cold world of hot air,
But at least we can share
In the wonder it ever occurred.

To which his partner, the lovely Laura, who is lovely in every way, would say;

In winter snow and summer sunshine,
In Autumn winds and spring sublime,
I'll always give thanks that you are mine.

As do I for my grandson, Michael, the magical mathematician.

And last but by no means least, my darling, delightful daughter, Alison, who is;

Loving and giving. Caring and kind.
Generous of spirit and gentle of mind.

As, was her grandmother - Elizabeth 'JERI' Cochrane

ESCAPE

With the help of this Escape Key, and with eternal gratitude to my courteous,

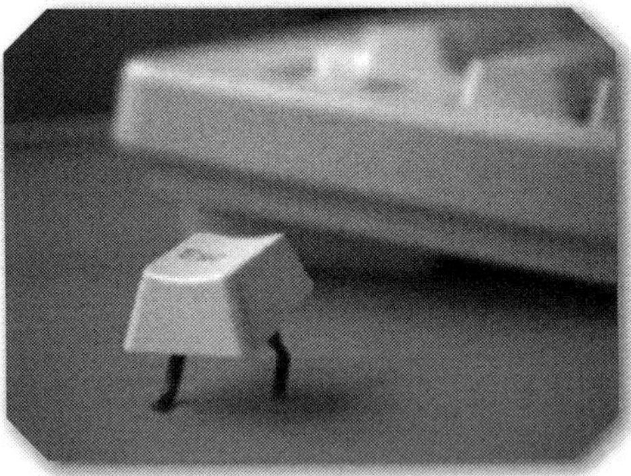

kind, helpful and above all, extremely patient publishing contacts, I can now escape from writing this book and get on with the rest of my life, for as Piet Hein wrote;

A Tip To Members of the Literary Profession,

Those who can write
have a lot to learn
from those bright
enough not to.

This escape key must have escaped from numbers of keyboards as numbers of people have e-mailed it to me. Perhaps in the hope that I will stop writing this book and write a few e-mails?

It also makes me wonder how much more mileage would have been given to my Mother's pen or, more pertinently, her fingers, had our present technology been available to her. Although as, in my view, my Mother's cartoons, paintings and poems are as perfect as she was herself, few are more deserving of the years of toil I have spent in writing this book.

Therefore, as the memory of someone as wonderful and talented as my mother never dies, I will not write:

THE END

but merely

'A TOUT A L'HEURE'

ACKNOWLEDGEMENTS

With much gratitude to:

My husband Simon for his love, constancy, courtesy, patience and forbearance.
My daughter Alison Jane for her gentleness and tranquility.
My son Michael for his strength, support and success.
My daughter-in-law Laura for loving my son and liking me.
My twin Sonya for her encouragement and empathy.
My sister Nicola for her sense and sensibility.
Nicola's husband, George for his benevolence and benignity.
My sister Sasha for her caring and kindness.
Sasha's husband John for his benevolence and bravery.
My brother Boris for his bravura.
His lovely lady Kim for loving him.
My dear friend Jenny Wrightson for her magnanimity.
Jenny's daughter Jacqui for being the mother of my grandson, Michael.

And even more gratitude to my late Mama for her extraordinary talents that were matched only by her.

INDEX

Printed in Poland
by Amazon Fulfillment
Poland Sp. z o.o., Wrocław

54305401R00298